Text/Reference Books on Data Communications and Computer Architecture

(Available from Macmillan Publishing Co.)

DATA AND COMPUTER COMMUNICATIONS, THIRD EDITION

A broad but detailed survey, covering four main areas: (1) data communications, including transmission, media, signal encoding, link control, and multiplexing; (2) communication networks, including circuit- and packet-switched, local, packet radio, and satellite; (3) communications architecture, including the OSI model and related protocols; and (4) ISDN.

LOCAL NETWORKS: AN INTRODUCTION, THIRD EDITION

An in-depth presentation of the technology and architecture of local networks. Covers topology, transmission media, medium access control, standards, internetworking, and interface issues.

COMPUTER ORGANIZATION AND ARCHITECTURE, SECOND EDITION

A unified view of this broad field. Covers fundamentals such as CPU, control unit, microprogramming, instruction set, I/O, and memory. Also covers advanced topics such as RISC and parallel organization.

ISDN: AN INTRODUCTION

An in-depth presentation of the technology and architecture of integrated services digital networks (ISDN). Covers the integrated digital network (IDN), ISDN services, architecture, signaling system no. 7 (SS7) and detailed coverage of the 1988 CCITT standards.

BUSINESS DATA COMMUNICATIONS

A comprehensive presentation of data communications and telecommunications from a business applications perspective. Covers voice, data, image, and video communications and applications technology and includes a number of case studies.

All of these books include a glossary, a list of acronyms, homework problems, and recommendations for further reading. These books are suitable as references, for self-study, and as textbooks.

Data and Computer Communications

WILLIAM STALLINGS, Ph.D.

DATA AND COMPUTER COMMUNICATIONS

THIRD EDITION

Macmillan Publishing Company
New York

Collier Macmillan Canada
Toronto

Maxwell Macmillan International
New York Oxford Singapore Sydney

Editor: *Ed Moura*
Production Supervisor: *John Travis*
Production Manager: *Valerie Sawyer*
Cover designed by *Ken Fredette*
Index prepared by *Jaine Saffir*

This book was set in Times Roman by Waldman Graphics
and printed and bound by Arcata Graphics/Hawkins

Macmillan Publishing Company
866 Third Avenue, New York, New York 10022

Collier Macmillan Canada, Inc.
1200 Eglinton Avenue, E.
Suite 200
Don Mills, Ontario M3C 3N1

Library of Congress Cataloging-in-Publication Data

Stallings, William.
    Data and computer communications / William Stallings.—3rd ed.
      p.   cm.
    Includes bibliographical references and index.
    ISBN 0-02-415454-7
    1. Data transmission systems. 2. Computer networks. I. Title.
TK5105.S73   1991
384.3--dc20   90-37896
                                          CIP

Printing: 1 2 3 4 5 6 7 8   Year: 1 2 3 4 5 6 7 8 9 0

To my loving wife, Tricia

PREFACE

The 1970's and early 1980's saw a merger of the fields of computer science and data communications that profoundly changed the technology, products, and companies of the now combined computer-communications industry. Although the consequences of this revolutionary merger are still being worked out, it is safe to say that the revolution occurred, and any investigation of the field of data communications must be made within this new context.

Objectives

It is the ambitious purpose of this book to provide a unified view of the broad field of data and computer communications. The organization of the book reflects an attempt to break this massive subject into comprehensible parts and to build, piece by piece, a survey of the state of the art. The book emphasizes basic principles and topics of fundamental importance concerning the technology and architecture of data and computer communications.

The book explores the key topics in the field in the following general categories:

- *Principles:* Although the scope of this book is broad, there are a number of basic principles that appear repeatedly as themes which unify this field. Examples are multiplexing, flow control, and error control. The book highlights these principles and contrasts their application in specific areas of technology.
- *Design approaches:* The book examines alternative approaches to meeting specific communication requirements. The discussion is bolstered with examples from existing implementations.

- *Standards:* Standards have come to assume an increasingly important, not to say dominant, role in this field. An understanding of the current status and future direction of the technology is not possible without a comprehensive discussion of the role and nature of the related standards.

The subject, and therefore this book, is highly technical. Nevertheless, an attempt has been made to make the book self-contained. Part I, in particular, draws upon the disciplines of probability and electrical engineering, but the emphasis is on results rather than derivations. In general, a building-block approach is taken. The principles of data communications are carefully and thoroughly explored. These principles are then applied to the complex systems found in communication networks and computer-communications architectures.

Intended Audience

The book is intended for a broad range of readers interested in data and computer communications:

- *Students and professionals in data processing and data communications:* This book is intended as both a textbook for study and a basic reference volume for this exciting and complex field.
- *Designers and implementers:* The book discusses the critical design issues and explores alternative approaches to meeting user requirements.
- *Computer and communication system customers and managers:* The book provides the reader with an understanding of what features and structure are needed in a communications capability, as well as a knowledge of current and evolving standards. This information provides a mean of assessing specific implementations and vendor offerings.

Plan of the Text

The book is organized to clarify the unifying and differentiating concepts underlying the field of data and computer communications. It is divided into four parts:

I *Data communications:* This part is concerned primarily with the exchange of data between two directly-connected devices. Within this restricted environment, the key aspects of transmission, interfacing, link control, and multiplexing are examined.

II *Data communication networking:* This part examines the internal mechanisms by which communication networks provide a data transfer service for attached devices.

III *Computer communications architecture:* This part explores both the architectural principles and the specific mechanisms required for the exchange of data among computers, terminals and other data processing devices.

IV *Integrated Services Digital Networks:* This part introduces the ISDN, which is an emerging worldwide digital telecommunications facility. The ISDN pulls together many of the concepts examined throughout the book.

The organization of the chapters is as follows:

1. *Introduction:* Provides an overview of the book as well as a discussion of the roles of the various standards-making organizations.
2. *Data transmission:* Explores the behavior of signals propagated through a transmission medium.
3. *Data encoding:* Describes the techniques used for encoding analog and digital data as either analog or digital signals.
4. *Digital data communication techniques:* Examines interfacing and synchronization issues.
5. *Data link control:* Describes the techniques used for converting an unreliable transmission link into a reliable communications link.
6. *Multiplexing:* Examines frequency-division multiplexing and both synchronous and statistical time-division multiplexing.
7. *Communication networking techniques:* Serves as an overview to Part II.
8. *Circuit switching:* Discusses circuit-switching mechanisms and network design.
9. *Packet switching:* Examines the mechanisms of packet switched networking, including routing, traffic control, and error control.
10. *Radio and satellite networks:* Explores design and performance issues for antenna-based communication networks.
11. *Local area networks:* Examines alternative approaches in the areas of transmission medium, topology, and medium access control technique.
12. *Protocols and architecture:* Defines communications protocols and motivates the need for a communications architecture.
13. *Network access protocols:* Examines techniques for accessing circuit-switched, packet-switched, and local networks.
14. *Internetworking:* Explores alternative techniques for communicating across multiple networks.
15. *Transport protocols:* Provides a detailed analysis of the most complex and important class of communications protocols.
16. *Session services and protocols:* Examines the services provided for the user to manage a logical communications connection, and looks at the protocol mechanisms to support those services.
17. *Presentation/application protocols:* Provides examples of higher-layer protocols.
18. *Integrated services digital network:* A preview of the network which represents the culmination of the computer-communications revolution.

The four parts of the book have been written to be sufficiently independent so that shorter courses could also be conducted using this book. For example, a course on fundamentals of data communications would cover just Part I. A course on communications networks could cover Parts II and IV. A course on communications architecture and the OSI model could cover Chapters 4, 5, 7, and Part III.

In addition, the book includes an extensive glossary, a list of frequently-used acronyms, and a bibliography. Each chapter includes problems and suggestions for further reading.

The book is suitable for self-study and can be covered in a two-semester course. It covers material in Subject Area 9 (Interfacing and Communication) and Subject Area 25 (Computer Communications Networks) of the 1983 IEEE Computer Society Model Program in Computer Science and Engineering. It also covers the material in CS 24 (Computer Communication Networks and Distributed Processing) of the 1981 ACM Recommendations for Master's Level Programs in Computer Science.

Related Materials

Computer Communications: Architectures, Protocols, and Standards, second edition (IEEE Computer Society Press, 1987) is a companion to this text, covering topics in Chapters 4 and 5 and Part III. It contains reprints of many of the key references used herein. The IEEE Computer Society Press is at P. O. Box 80452, Worldway Postal Center, Los Angeles, CA 90080; telephone (800) 272-6657.

A set of videotape courses specifically designed for use with *Data and Computer Communications* is available from the Association for Media-Based Continuing Education for Engineers, Inc.; 430 Tenth Street, NW; Suite 8-208, Atlanta, GA 30318; telephone (404) 894-3362. A videotape course designed for managers is available from Professional Development Video Programs; The Media Group; Boston University; 565 Commonwealth Avenue; Boston, MA 02215; telephone (617) 353-3227.

The Third Edition

In the three years since the second edition of this book was published, the field has continued to evolve and expand. Noteworthy developments include the rapid increase in the use of local area networks, the increasing reliance on standards, the growing importance of optical fiber, and the emergence of ISDN.

The increasing importance and pervasiveness of data communications and computer networking facilities confirm the need for a book that covers the fundamentals of data and computer communications. The author is gratified by the positive response to the first two editions of this book and has tried to respond to constructive suggestions for improvements, as well as to changes in technology, in this third edition.

The same chapter organization has been retained, but much of the material has been revised and new material has been added. As an indication of this, approximately one-third of the figures (115 out of 345) and one-third of the tables (42 out of 115) in this edition are new. Every chapter has been revised. The most significant changes are the following:

- A more detailed discussion of the concept of communications architecture and the OSI model is included in Chapter 1. This allows the reader to see where the various chapters fit in that model (see Figure 1-11). A discussion of the various standards-related organizations has also been added.
- The discussion of digital signaling encoding formats in Chapter 3 has been expanded to include schemes that are relevant to ISDN.
- The discussion of physical interfaces in Chapter 4 has been completely rewritten. It now includes the important EIA-232-D and EIA-530 standards, plus the ISDN physical connector.
- Chapter 8 (circuit switching) now includes sections on routing and control signaling, especially common channel control signaling.
- In Chapter 9 (packet switching) the discussion of least-cost routing algorithms

has been rewritten to improve clarity, and the discussion of congestion control has been expanded.

- Chapter 11 (local area networks) has been substantially revised to reflect advances in standards and technology. For example, twisted-pair star-wire LANs are now covered.
- A section on the ISDN I.451 common channel signaling protocol has been added to Chapter 13 (network access protocols).
- A major change in this edition is the treatment of internetworking. In recent years, there have been substantial advances in the technology and application of two types of internetworking devices: bridges and routers. Accordingly, Chapter 14 has been completely rewritten to reflect these developments.
- A section has been added to Chapter 15 (transport protocols) to cover the exciting new development of lightweight transport protocols.
- Chapter 17 (presentation/application protocols) now includes a discussion of the ISO virtual terminal service and of the ISO application layer structure. The material on X.400 has been revised to reflect the significant changes between the 1984 and 1988 versions.
- Chapter 18 has been substantially updated to reflect the changes from 1984 and 1988 in ISDN standards. In addition several new topics are covered: frame relay, signaling system number 7, and broadband ISDN, which includes a discussion of asynchronous transfer mode (ATM).
- An appendix on queuing analysis has been added. Queueing concepts arise in many areas of data and computer communications, and the appendix endeavors to provide a practical guide to the use of this tool.

All in all, this third edition constitutes a major revision. I have tried in a balanced manner to provide a comprehensive survey of this fascinating field.

Acknowledgments

I would like to thank the following reviewers: Gokhan Gercek, Penn State University; Matthias Laucht, University of Manitoba; Lee Danner, East Tennessee State University; and Mark Crews, US Air Force Academy.

                                                                        W. S.

CONTENTS

IV ISDN

Data and Computer Communications

CHAPTER 1

Introduction

THE COMPUTER-COMMUNICATIONS REVOLUTION

The 1970s and early 1980s saw a merger of the fields of computer science and data communications that profoundly changed the technology, products, and companies of the now combined computer-communications industry. Although the consequences of this revolutionary merger are still being worked out, it is safe to say that the revolution has occurred, and any investigation of the field of data communications must be made within this new context.

The computer-communications revolution has produced several remarkable facts:

- There is no fundamental difference between data processing (computers) and data communications (transmission and switching equipment).
- There are no fundamental differences among data, voice, and video communications.
- The lines between single-processor computer, multi-processor computer, local network, metropolitan network, and long-haul network have blurred.

The result has been a growing overlap of the computer and communications industries, from component fabrication to system integration. The forthcoming result is the development of integrated systems that transmit and process all types of data and information. Both the technology and the technical standards organizations are driving toward a single public system that integrates all communications and makes virtually all data and information sources around the world easily and uniformly accessible.

It is the ambitious purpose of this book to provide a unified view of the broad field of data and computer communications. The organization of the book reflects an attempt to break this massive subject into comprehensible parts and to build, piece by piece, a survey of the state of the art. This introductory chapter begins with a general model of communications. Then, a brief discussion introduces each of the three major parts of this book. Next, the all-important role of standards is introduced. Finally, a brief outline of the rest of the book is provided.

1-2

A COMMUNICATIONS MODEL

We begin our study with a simple model of communications. A block diagram of this model appears as Figure 1-1.

The fundamental purpose of data communications is to exchange information between two agents. In Figure 1-1, the information to be exchanged is a message labeled m. This information is represented as data g and is generally presented to a transmitter in the form of a time-varying signal, $g(t)$.

The terms data and information are defined in Table 1-1. These definitions seem rather academic, but for our purpose they might be given the following interpretation: data can be identified; data can be described; data do not necessarily represent something physical in terms of the measurable world; but above all data can be and should be used, namely for producing information. They also imply that data to one person may appear as information to another. Information is born when data are interpreted. To exchange information, then, requires access to elements of data and the ability to transmit them.

Returning now to Figure 1-1, the signal $g(t)$ is to be transmitted. Generally, the signal will not be in a form suitable for transmission and must be converted to a signal $s(t)$ that is in some sense matched to the characteristics of the transmission medium. The signal is then transmitted across the medium. On the other end, a signal $r(t)$, which may differ from $s(t)$, is received. This signal is then converted by a receiver into a form suitable for output. The converted signal $\tilde{g}(t)$, or data $\tilde{g}$, is an approximation or estimate of the input. Finally, the output device presents the estimated message, $\tilde{m}$, to the destination agent.

This simple narrative conceals a wealth of technical complexity. To attempt to

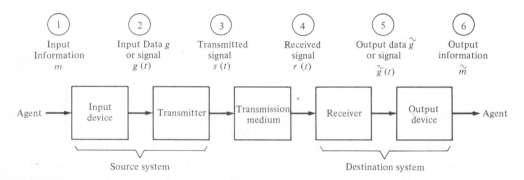

FIGURE 1-1.   Simplified communications block diagram.

TABLE 1-1 Data and Information

Data	A representation of facts, concepts, or instructions in a formalized manner suitable for communication, interpretation, or processing by human beings or by automatic means
Information	The meaning that a human being assigns to data by means of the conventions applied to those data

Source: [ANSC82].

elaborate, we present two examples, one using electronic mail, the other a telephone conversation.

For the case of electronic mail, consider that that input device and transmitter are components of a personal computer. The agent is a user who wishes to send a message to another user, for example, "The meeting scheduled for March 25 is canceled" (m). This string of characters is the information. The user activates the electronic mail package on the personal computer and enters the message via the keyboard (input device). The character string is briefly buffered in main memory. We can view it as a sequence of characters (g) or, more literally, a sequence of bits (g) in memory. The personal computer is connected to some transmission medium, such as a local network or a telephone line, by an I/O device (transmitter), such as a local network transceiver or a modem. The input data are transferred to the transmitter as a sequence of bits [$g(t)$] or, more literally, a sequence of voltage shifts [$g(t)$] on some communications bus or cable. The transmitter is connected directly to the medium and converts the incoming bits [$g(t)$] into a signal [$s(t)$] suitable for transmission; specific alternatives will be described in Chapter 3.

The transmitted signal $s(t)$ presented to the medium is subject to a number of impairments, discussed in Chapter 2, before it reaches the receiver. Thus the received signal $r(t)$ may differ to some degree from $s(t)$. The receiver will attempt to estimate the nature of $s(t)$, based on $r(t)$ and its knowledge of the medium, producing a sequence of bits $\tilde{g}(t)$. These bits are sent to the output personal computer, where they are briefly buffered in memory as a block of bits or characters ($\tilde{g}$). In many cases, the destination system will attempt to determine if an error has occurred and, if so, cooperate with the source system to eventually obtain a complete, error-free block of data. These data are then presented to the user via an output device, such as a printer or screen. The message ($\tilde{m}$) as viewed by the user will usually be an exact copy of the original message (m).

A variation is worth mentioning. The agent at either end may be a computer process rather than a human user. For example, messages might be stored on disk or tape to be automatically sent when a certain condition occurs (e.g., in the evening, when phone rates are lower). Or a message might be received when the user is unavailable and stored on disk or tape for later retrieval.

Now consider a telephone conversation. The agent in this case is the speaker, who generates a message (m) in the form of sound waves. The sound waves are converted by the telephone into electrical signals of the same frequency. These signals are transmitted without modification over the telephone line. Hence the input signal $g(t)$ and the transmitted signal $s(t)$ are identical. The signal $s(t)$ will suffer some distortion over the medium, so that $r(t)$ will not be identical to $s(t)$. Nevertheless, the signal $r(t)$ is converted back into a sound wave with no attempt at correction or improvement of signal quality. Thus $\tilde{m}$ is not an exact replica of m. However, the received sound message is generally comprehensible to the listener.

TABLE 1-2   Communication Tasks

Transmission system utilization
Interfacing
Signal generation
Synchronization
Exchange management
Error detection and correction
Flow control
Addressing
Routing
Recovery
Message formatting
Protection
System management

Again, we mention a variation. In so-called digital telephones, the input signal $g(t)$ is digitized (i.e., converted into a sequence of bits). It is this sequence of bits, in the form of a sequence of voltage shifts, that is transmitted as $s(t)$.

These two examples give some idea of the nature of data communications. Another view is expressed in Table 1-2, which lists key tasks that must be performed in a data communications system. The list is somewhat arbitrary: Elements could be added; items on the list could be merged; and some items represent several tasks that are performed at different "levels" of the system. However, the list as it stands is suggestive of the scope of this book.

The first item, *transmission system utilization*, refers to the need to make efficient use of transmission facilities that are typically shared among a number of communicating devices. Various techniques (referred to as *multiplexing*) are used to allocate the total capacity of a transmission medium among a number of users. Congestion control techniques may be required to assure that the system is not overwhelmed by excessive demand for transmission services.

In order to communicate, a device must *interface* with the transmission system. All the forms of communication discussed in this book depend, at bottom, on the use of electromagnetic signals propagated over a transmission medium. Thus, once an interface is established, *signal generation* is required for communication. The properties of the signal, such as form and intensity, must be such that they are (1) capable of being propagated through the transmission system, and (2) interpretable as data at the receiver.

Not only must the signals be generated to conform to the requirements of the transmission system and receiver, but there must be some form of *synchronization* between transmitter and receiver. The receiver must be able to determine when a signal begins to arrive and when it ends. It must also know the duration of each signal element.

Beyond the basic matter of deciding on the nature and timing of signals, there are a variety of requirements for communication between two parties that might be collected under the term *exchange management*. If data are to be exchanged in both directions over a period of time, the two parties must cooperate. For example, for two parties to engage in a telephone conversation, one party must dial the number of the other, causing signals to be generated that result in the ringing of the called phone. The called party completes a connection by lifting the receiver.

For data processing devices, more will be needed than simply establishing a connection; certain conventions must be decided upon. These conventions may include: whether both devices may transmit simultaneously or must take turns, the amount of data to be sent at one time, the format of the data, and what to do if certain contingencies such as an error arise.

The next two items might have been included under exchange management, but seem important enough to list separately. *Error detection and correction* are required in circumstances where errors cannot be tolerated. This is usually the case with data processing systems. For example, in transferring a file from one computer to another, it is simply not acceptable for the contents of the file to be accidentally altered. *Flow control* is required to assure that the source does not overwhelm the destination by sending data faster than they can be processed and absorbed.

Next, we mention the related but distinct concepts of *addressing* and *routing*. When a transmission facility is shared by more than two devices, a source system must somehow indicate the identity of the intended destination. The transmission system must assure that the destination system, and only that system, receives the data. Further, the transmission system may itself be a network through which various paths may be taken. A specific route through this network must be chosen.

Recovery is a concept distinct from that of error correction. Recovery techniques are needed in situations in which an information exchange, such as a data base transaction or file transfer, is interrupted due to a fault somewhere in the system. The objective is either to be able to resume activity at the point of interruption or at least to restore the state of the systems involved to the condition prior to the beginning of the exchange.

Message formatting has to do with an agreement between two parties as to the form of the data to be exchanged or transmitted. For example, both sides must use the same binary code for characters.

Frequently, it is important to provide some measure of *protection* in a data communications system. The sender of data may wish to be assured that only the intended receiver actually receives the data. And the receiver of data may wish to be assured that the received data have not been altered in transit and that the data actually come from the purported sender.

Finally, a data communications facility is a complex system that cannot create or run itself. *System management* capabilities are needed to configure the system, monitor its status, react to failures and overloads, and plan intelligently for future growth.

Thus we have gone from the simple idea of data communication between source and destination, to a six-stage model (Figure 1-1) of data communications, to a rather formidable list of data communications tasks. In this book, we further elaborate this list of tasks to describe and encompass the entire set of activities that can be classified under data and computer communications.

1-3

DATA COMMUNICATIONS

This book is organized into three parts. The first part deals primarily with the portion of Figure 1-1 between points 2 and 5. For want of a better name, we have given Part I the title Data Communications, although that term arguably encompasses some or even all of the topics of Parts II and III.

Since the purpose of this chapter is merely to preview the remainder of the book, little needs to be added to the discussion of the preceding section to introduce Part I. The topics that will be covered are:

- Data transmission.
- Data encoding.
- Digital data communication techniques.
- Data link control.
- Multiplexing.

Data transmission deals with the portion of Figure 1-1 between points 3 and 4. As was mentioned, the received signal will differ from the transmitted signal due to distortions, or transmission impairments. These distortions are in large part determined by the nature of the transmission medium used. *Data encoding* is the process of transforming input data or signals into signals that can be transmitted. The encoding technique is tailored to the method of data transmission to optimize performance.

The next two topics, *digital data communications techniques* and *data link control*, move the discussion from the simple transmission of data signals to true data communications. Referring again to Figure 1-1, the objective is to transfer data from the input device to the output device, with these two devices cooperating to minimize or eliminate error and to coordinate their actions. We will see that some rather complex techniques are required to achieve these objectives.

Finally, *multiplexing* refers to a variety of techniques used to make more efficient use of a transmission facility. In many cases, the capacity of a transmission facility exceeds the requirements for the transfer of data between two devices. That capacity can be shared among multiple transmitters by multiplexing a number of signals onto the same medium. In this case, the actual transmission path is referred to as a *circuit* or *link*, and the portion of capacity dedicated to each pair of transmitter/ receivers is referred to as a *channel*.

1-4

DATA COMMUNICATION NETWORKING

In its simplest form data communication takes place between two devices that are directly connected by some form of point-to-point transmission medium. Often, however, it is impractical for two devices to be directly, point-to-point connected. This is so for one (or both) of the following contingencies:

- The devices are very far apart. It would be inordinately expensive, for example, to string a dedicated link between two devices thousands of miles apart.
- There is a set of devices, each of which may require a link to many of the others at various times. Examples are all of the telephones in the world and all of the terminals and computers owned by a single organization. Except for the case of a very few devices, it is impractical to provide a dedicated wire between each pair of devices.

The solution to this problem is to attach each device to a *communication network*. Figure 1-2 illustrates this concept in a general way. We have a collection of devices that wish to communicate; we will refer to them generically as *stations*. The stations

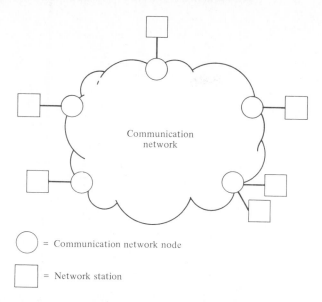

FIGURE 1-2.   Interconnection via a communication network.

may be computers, terminals, telephones, or other communicating devices. Each station attaches to a network *node*. The set of nodes to which stations attach is the boundary of a communication network that is capable of transferring data between pairs of stations.

Communication networks may be categorized based on the architecture and techniques used to transfer data. In this book we will be concerned with the following types of communication networks:

- Switched networks.
  - Circuit-switched networks.
  - Packet-switched networks.
- Broadcast networks.
  - Packet radio networks.
  - Satellite networks.
  - Local networks.

In a *switched communication network* (Figure 1-3), data are transferred from source to destination through a series of intermediate nodes. These nodes (including the boundary nodes) are not concerned with the content of the data; rather, their purpose is to provide a switching facility that will move the data from node to node until they reach their destination.

In a *circuit-switched network*, a dedicated communications path is established between two stations through the nodes of the network. That path is a connected sequence of physical links between nodes. On each link, a logical channel is dedicated to the connection. Data generated by the source station are transmitted along the dedicated path as rapidly as possible. At each node, incoming data are routed or switched to the appropriate outgoing channel without delay. The most common example of circuit switching is the telephone network.

A quite different approach is used in a *packet-switched network*. In this case, it is not necessary to dedicate transmission capacity along a path through the network.

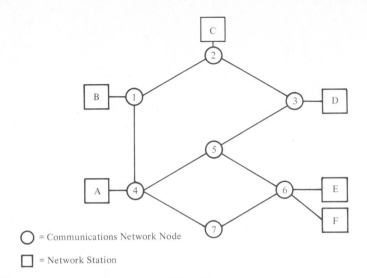

= Communications Network Node

= Network Station

FIGURE 1-3. Generic switching network.

Rather, data are sent out in a sequence of small chunks, called *packets*. Each packet is passed through the network from node to node along some path leading from source to destination. At each node, the entire packet is received, stored briefly, and then transmitted to the next node. Packet-switched networks are commonly used for terminal-to-computer and computer-to-computer communications.

With a *broadcast communication network*, there are no intermediate switching nodes (Figure 1-4). At each station, there is a transmitter/receiver that communicates over a medium shared by other stations. A transmission from any one station is broadcast to and received by all other stations. A simple example of this is a CB radio system, in which all users tuned to the same channel may communicate. We will be more concerned with networks used to link terminals and computers. In the latter case, data are often transmitted in packets. Since the medium is shared, only one station at a time can transmit a packet.

Two similar types of broadcast networks are packet radio networks and satellite networks. In both cases, stations transmit and receive via antenna, and all stations share the same channel or radio frequency. In a *packet radio network*, stations are within transmission range of each other, and broadcast directly to each other. In a *satellite network*, data are not transferred directly from transmitter to receiver but are relayed via satellite: each station transmits to the satellite and receives from the satellite.

Another common instance of broadcasting is the *local network*. A local network is a communication network that is confined to a small area, such as a single building or a small cluster of buildings. The two most common types of local networks are depicted in Figure 1-4c and d. In a *bus local network*, all stations are attached to a common wire or cable. A transmission by any one station propagates the length of the medium in both directions and can be received by all other stations. The *ring local network* consists of a closed loop, with each station attached to a repeating element. A transmission from any station circulates around the ring past all other stations, and can be received by each station as it goes by.

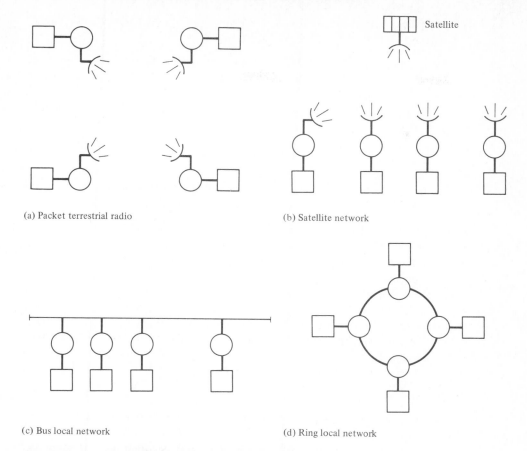

(a) Packet terrestrial radio

(b) Satellite network

(c) Bus local network

(d) Ring local network

FIGURE 1-4. Broadcast communication networks.

Each of these types of communication network, in its own fashion, overcomes the problems cited at the beginning of this section. A detailed discussion of these networks comprises Part II of this book.

1-5

COMPUTER COMMUNICATIONS ARCHITECTURE

As we have mentioned, the term ''data communications'' as used in this book refers primarily to the area between points 2 and 5 of Figure 1-1. That is, it is concerned with the transfer of a signal or set of data between two points, with no regard for the meaning or intent of those data. Similarly, communication networks are concerned primarily with such a data transfer, again with no regard for data content.

However, when computers, terminals, and/or other data processing devices exchange data, the scope of concern is much broader. Consider, for example, the transfer of a file between two computers. There must be a data path between the two computers, either directly (Figure 1-1) or via a communication network (Figure 1-2). But more is needed. Typical tasks to be performed:

1. The source system must either activate the direct data communication path, or inform the communication network of the identity of the desired destination system.
2. The source system must ascertain that the destination system is prepared to receive data.
3. The file transfer application on the source system must ascertain that the file management program on the destination system is prepared to accept and store the file for this particular user.
4. If the file formats used on the two systems are incompatible, one or the other system must perform a format translation function.

It is clear that there must be a high degree of cooperation between the two computer systems. The exchange of information between computers for the purpose of cooperative action is generally referred to as *computer communications*. Similarly, when two or more computers are interconnected via a communication network, the set of computer stations is referred to as a *computer network*. Since a similar level of cooperation is required between a user at a terminal and a computer, these terms are often used when some of the communicating entities are terminals.

In discussing computer communications and computer networks, two concepts are paramount:

- Protocols.
- Computer-communications architecture.

A protocol is used for communication between entities in different systems. The terms "entity" and "system" are used in a very general sense. Examples of entities are user application programs, file transfer packages, data-base management systems, electronic mail facilities, and terminals. Examples of systems are computers, terminals, and remote sensors. Note that in some cases the entity and the system in which it resides are coextensive (e.g., terminals). In general, an *entity* is anything capable of sending or receiving information, and a *system* is a physically distinct object that contains one or more entities. For two entities to communicate successfully, they must "speak the same language." What is communicated, how it is communicated, and when it is communicated must conform to some mutually acceptable conventions between the entities involved. The conventions are referred to as a *protocol*, which may be defined as a set of rules governing the exchange of data between two entities. The key elements of a protocol are:

- *Syntax:* includes such things as data format and signal levels.
- *Semantics:* includes control information for coordination and error handling.
- *Timing:* includes speed matching and sequencing.

Having introduced the concept of a protocol, we can now introduce the concept of a computer-communications architecture. It is clear that there must be a high degree of cooperation between the two computers. Instead of implementing the logic for this as a single module, the task is broken up into subtasks, each of which is implemented separately. As an example, Figure 1-5 suggests the way in which a file transfer facility could be implemented. Three modules are used. Tasks 3 and 4 in the preceding list could be performed by a file transfer module. The two modules on the two systems exchange files and commands. However, rather than

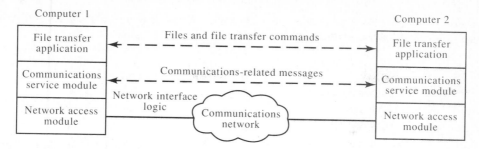

FIGURE 1-5. A simplified architecture for file transfer.

requiring the file transfer module to deal with the details of actually transferring data and commands, the file transfer modules each rely on a communications service module. This module is responsible for making sure that the file transfer commands and data are reliably exchanged between systems. Among other things, this module would perform task 2. Now the nature of the exchange between systems is independent of the nature of the network that interconnects them. Therefore, rather than building details of the network interface into the communications service module, it makes sense to have a third module, a network access module, that performs task 1 by interacting with the network.

Let us try to summarize the motivation for the three modules in Figure 1-5. The file transfer module contains all of the logic that is unique to the file transfer application, such as transmitting passwords, file commands, and file records. There is a need to transmit these files and commands reliably. However, the same sorts of reliability requirements are relevant to a variety of applications (e.g., electronic mail, document transfer). Therefore, these requirements are met by a separate communications service module that can be used by a variety of applications. The communications service module is concerned with assuring that the two computer systems are active and ready for data transfer and for keeping track of the data that are being exchanged to assure delivery. However, these tasks are independent of the type of network that is being used. Therefore, the logic for actually dealing with the network is separated out into a separate network access module. That way, if the network to be used is changed, only the network access module is affected.

Thus, instead of a single module for performing communications, there is a structured set of modules that implements the communications function. That structure is referred to as a **communications architecture.** In the remainder of this section, we generalize the preceding example to present a simplified communications architecture. Following that, we look at more complex, real-world examples.

A Three-layer Model

In very general terms, communications can be said to involve three agents: applications, computers, and networks. One example of an application is a file transfer operation. These applications execute on computers that can often support multiple simultaneous applications. Computers are connected to networks, and the data to be exchanged are transferred by the network from one computer to another. Thus, the transfer of data from one application to another involves first getting the data to the computer in which the application resides and then getting it to the intended application within the computer.

With these concepts in mind, it appears natural to organize the communication task into three relatively independent layers:

- Network access layer.
- Transport layer.
- Application layer.

The *network access layer* is concerned with the exchange of data between a computer and the network to which it is attached. The sending computer must provide the network with the address of the destination computer, so that the network may route the data to the appropriate destination. The sending computer may wish to invoke certain services, such as priority, that might be provided by the network. The specific software used at this layer depends on the type of network to be used; different standards have been developed for circuit-switching, packet-switching, local area networks, and others. Thus it makes sense to separate those functions having to do with network access into a separate layer. By doing this, the remainder of the communications software, above the network access layer, need not be concerned about the specifics of the network to be used. The same higher-layer software should function properly regardless of the particular network to which the computer is attached.

Regardless of the nature of the applications that are exchanging data, there is usually a requirement that data be exchanged reliably. That is, we would like to be assured that all of the data arrive at the destination application and that the data arrive in the same order in which they were sent. As we shall see, the mechanisms for providing reliability are essentially independent of the nature of the applications. Thus, it makes sense to collect those mechanisms in a common layer shared by all applications; this is referred to as the transport layer.

Finally, the application layer contains the logic needed to support the various user applications. For each different type of application, such as file transfer, a separate module is needed that is peculiar to that application.

Figures 1-6 and 1-7 illustrate this simple architecture. Figure 1-6 shows three computers connected to a network. Each computer contains software at the network access and transport layers, and software at the application layer for one or more applications. For successful communication, every entity in the overall system must have a unique address. Actually, two levels of addressing are needed. Each computer on the network must have a unique network address; this allows the network to deliver data to the proper computer. Each application on a computer must have an address that is unique within that computer; this allows the transport layer to deliver data to the proper application. These latter addresses are known as *service access points* (SAPs), connoting the fact that each application is individually accessing the services of the transport layer.

Figure 1-7 indicates the way in which modules at the same level on different computers communicate with each other: by means of a protocol. A protocol is the set of rules or conventions governing the ways in which two entities cooperate to exchange data. A protocol specification details the control functions that may be performed, the formats and control codes used to communicate those functions, and the procedures that the two entities must follow.

Let us trace a simple operation. Suppose that an application, associated with

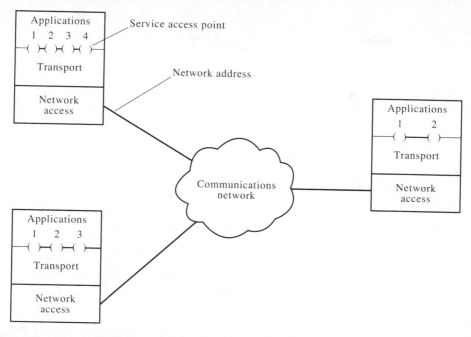

FIGURE 1-6. Communications architectures and networks.

SAP 1 at computer A, wishes to send a message to another application, associated with SAP 2 at computer B. The application at A hands the message over to its transport layer with instructions to send it to SAP 2 on computer B. The transport layer hands the message over to the network access layer, which instructs the network to send the message to computer B. Note that the network need not be told the identity of the destination service access point. All that it needs to know is that the data are intended for computer B.

To control this operation, control information, as well as user data, must be transmitted, as suggested in Figure 1-8. Let us say that the sending application generates a block of data and passes this to the transport layer. The transport layer may break this block into two smaller pieces to make it more manageable. To each of these pieces the transport layer appends a transport header, containing protocol control information. The combination of data from the next higher layer and control information is known as a protocol data unit (PDU); in this case, it is referred to as a transport protocol data unit. The header in each transport PDU contains control

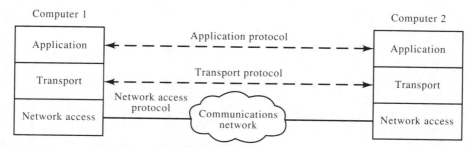

FIGURE 1-7. Protocols in a simplified architecture.

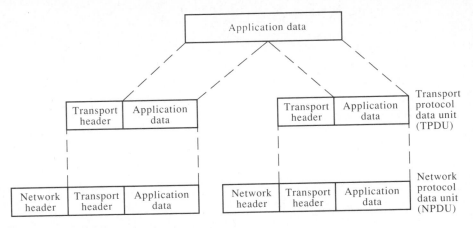

FIGURE 1-8. Protocol data units.

information to be used by the peer transport protocol at computer B. Examples of items that may be stored in this header include:

- *Destination SAP:* When the destination transport layer receives the transport protocol data unit, it must know to whom the data are to be delivered.
- *Sequence number:* Since the transport protocol is sending a sequence of protocol data units, it numbers them sequentially so that if they arrive out of order, the destination transport entity may reorder them.
- *Error-detection code:* The sending transport entity may include a code that is a function of the contents of the remainder of the PDU. The receiving transport protocol performs the same calculation and compares the result with the incoming code. A discrepancy results if there has been some error in transmission. In that case, the receiver can discard the PDU and take corrective action.

The next step is for the transport layer to hand each protocol data unit over to the network layer, with instructions to transmit it to the destination computer. To satisfy this request, the network access protocol must present the data to the network with a request for transmission. As before, this operation requires the use of control information. In this case, the network access protocol appends a network access header to the data it receives from the transport layer, creating a network-access PDU. Examples of the items that may be stored in the header include:

- *Destination computer address:* The network must know to whom (which computer on the network) the data are to be delivered.
- *Facilities requests:* The network access protocol might want the network to make use of certain facilities, such as priority.

Figure 1-9 puts all of these concepts together, showing the interaction between modules to transfer one block of data. Let us say that the file transfer module in computer X is transferring a file one record at a time to computer Y. Each record is handed over to the transport layer module. We can picture this action as being in the form of a command or procedure call, A-SEND (application-send). The arguments of this procedure call include the destination computer address, the destination service access point, and the record. The transport layer appends the destination service access point and other control information to the record to create a transport PDU. This is then handed down to the network access layer in a

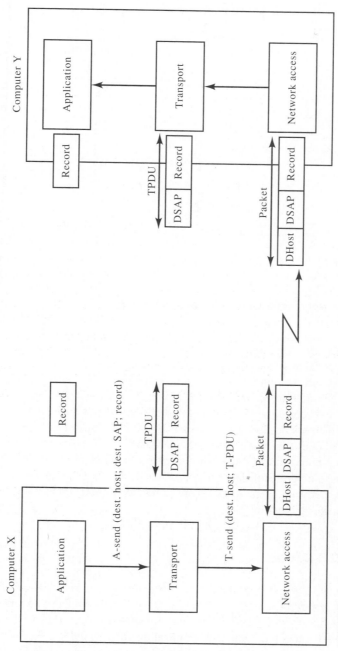

FIGURE 1-9. Operation of a communications architecture.

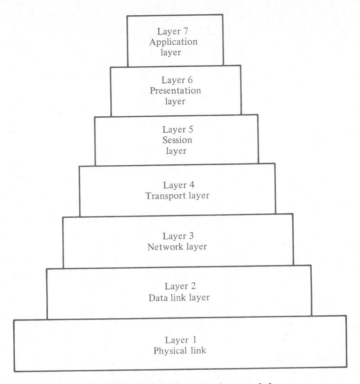

FIGURE 1-10.   Open systems interconnection model.

T-SEND command. In this case, the arguments for the command are the destination computer address and the transport protocol data unit. The network access layer uses this information to construct a network PDU. The transport protocol data unit is the data field of the network PDY, and the network PDU header includes information concerning the source and destination computer addresses.

The network accepts the network PDU from X and delivers it to Y. The network access module in Y receives the PDU, strips off the header, and transfers the enclosed transport PDU to X's transport layer module. The transport layer examines the transport protocol data unit header and, on the basis of the SAP field in the header, delivers the enclosed record to the appropriate application, in this case the file transfer module in Y.

The OSI Model

Figure 1-7 suggests that the various elements of the structured set of protocols are layered, or form a hierarchy. This concept is also evident in Figure 1-10, which depicts the open systems interconnection (OSI) model. The OSI model was developed by the International Organization for Standardization as a model for a computer communications architecture, and as a framework for developing protocol standards. Table 1-3 briefly defines the functions performed at each layer. The intent of the OSI model is that protocols be developed to perform the functions of each layer. Part III of this book will examine protocols in detail, and make use of this model for that purpose.

TABLE 1-3

1. Physical	Concerned with transmission of unstructured bit stream over physical medium; deals with the mechanical, electrical, functional, and procedural characteristics to access the physical medium
2. Data link	Provides for the reliable transfer of information across the physical link; sends blocks of data (frames) with the necessary synchronization, error control, and flow control
3. Network	Provides upper layers with independence from the data transmission and switching technologies used to connect systems; responsible for establishing, maintaining, and terminating connections
4. Transport	Provides reliable, transparent transfer of data between end points; provides end-to-end error recovery and flow control
5. Session	Provides the control structure for communication between applications; establishes, manages, and terminates connections (sessions) between cooperating applications
6. Presentation	Provides independence to the application processes from differences in data representation (syntax)
7. Application	Provides access to the OSI environment for users and also provides distributed information services

1-6

STANDARDS-MAKING ORGANIZATIONS

It has long been accepted in the communications industry that standards are required to govern the physical, electrical, and procedural characteristics of communication equipment. In the past, this view has not been embraced by the computer industry. Whereas communication equipment vendors recognize that their equipment will generally interface to and communicate with other vendors' equipment, computer vendors have traditionally attempted to monopolize their customers. The proliferation of computers and distributed processing has made that an untenable position. Computers from different vendors must communicate with each other and, with the ongoing evolution of protocol standards, customers will no longer accept special-purpose protocol conversion software development. The result is that standards now permeate all of the areas of technology discussed in this book.

Throughout the book, especially in Part III, we will describe the most important standards that are in use or being developed for various aspects of data and computer communications. The Appendix to this chapter looks at the key organizations involved with the development of standards.

There are a number of advantages and disadvantages to the standards-making process. We list here the most striking ones. The principal advantages of standards are:

- A standard assures that there will be a large market for a particular piece of equipment or software. This encourages mass production, and in some cases, the use of large-scale-integration (LSI) or very-large-scale-integration (VLSI) techniques, resulting in lower costs.
- A standard allows products from multiple vendors to communicate, giving the purchaser more flexibility in equipment selection and use.

The principal disadvantages are:

- A standard tends to freeze the technology. By the time a standard is developed, subjected to review and compromise, and promulgated, more efficient techniques are possible.
- There are multiple standards for the same thing. This is not a disadvantage of standards per se, but of the current way things are done. Fortunately, in recent years the various standards-making organizations have begun to cooperate more closely. Nevertheless, there are still areas where multiple conflicting standards exist.

Interesting discussion of this topic can be found in [CERN84] and [CARG89].

1-7

OUTLINE OF THE BOOK

Chapter Summary

This chapter, of course, serves as an introduction to the entire book. A brief synopsis of the remaining chapters follows.

Data Transmission.   The principles of data transmission underlie all of the concepts and techniques presented in this book. To understand the need for encoding, multiplexing, switching, error control, and so on, the reader must understand the behavior of data signals propagated through a transmission medium. Chapter 2 provides an understanding of the distinction between digital and analog data and digital and analog transmission. Concepts of attenuation and noise are introduced, and the various transmission media described.

Data Encoding.   Data come in both analog (continuous) and digital (discrete) form. For transmission, input data (point 2, Figure 1-1) must be encoded as an electrical signal (point 3, Figure 1-1) that is tailored to the characteristics of the transmission medium. Both analog and digital data can be represented by either analog or digital signals; each of the four cases is discussed in Chapter 3.

Digital Data Communication Techniques.   In Chapter 4 the emphasis shifts from data transmission to data communications. For two devices linked by a transmission medium to exchange digital data, a high degree of cooperation is required. Typically, data are transmitted one bit at a time over the medium. The timing (rate, duration, spacing) of these bits must be the same for transmitter and receiver. Two common communication techniques—asynchronous and synchronous—are explored. This chapter also looks at techniques for detecting bit errors. Finally in this chapter, we look at transmission line interfaces. Typically, digital data devices do not attach to and signal across a transmission medium directly. Rather, this process is mediated through a standardized interface.

Data Link Control.   True cooperative exchange of digital data between two devices requires some form of data link control. Chapter 5 examines the fundamental techniques common to all data link control protocols, and then examines the most commonly used protocol, HDLC.

Multiplexing. Transmission facilities are, by and large, expensive. It is often the case that two communication stations will not utilize the full capacity of a data link. For efficiency, it should be possible to share that capacity. The generic term for such sharing is multiplexing.

Chapter 6 concentrates on the three most common types of multiplexing techniques. The first, frequency-division multiplexing (FDM), is the most widespread and is familiar to anyone who has ever used a radio or television set. The second is a particular case of time-division multiplexing (TDM) often known as synchronous TDM. This is commonly used for multiplexing digitized voice streams. The third type is another form of TDM that is more complex but potentially more efficient than synchronous TDM; it is referred to as statistical or asynchronous TDM.

Communication Networking Techniques. Chapter 7 serves as an overview of Part II. The two switched communication network techniques mentioned earlier, circuit switching and packet switching, as well as the less well known message switching, are introduced and compared. The discussion gives insight into the relative performance of these techniques. Broadcast networks are also introduced, and relevant access techniques are discussed.

Circuit Switching. Any treatment of the technology and architecture of circuit-switched networks must of necessity focus on the internal operation of a single switch. This is in contrast to packet-switched networks, which are best explained by the collective behavior of the set of switches that make up a network. Thus Chapter 8 begins by examining digital switching concepts, including space- and time-division switching. This leads to a discussion of the devices most commonly used to build circuit-switched local networks (although these are rarely thought of as "true" local networks): digital data switches. We are then ready to look at the digital private branch exchange, which supports both digital data devices and telephones. Finally, the concepts of a multinode circuit-switched network are discussed; the topics of routing and control signaling are covered.

Packet Switching. There are three main technical problems associated with a packet-switched network, and each is examined in Chapter 9:

- *Routing:* Since the source and destination station are not directly connected, the network must route each packet, from node to node, through the network.
- *Traffic control:* The amount of traffic entering and transiting the network must be regulated for efficient, stable, and fair performance.
- *Error control:* Inevitably, packets will be lost in the network. Some networks ignore this contingency; most take measures to at least partially alleviate the suffering of the attached stations.

The key features in each of the foregoing areas are presented, and the discussion is supported by examples from specific systems currently in operation.

Radio and Satellite Networks. Chapter 10 begins the discussion of broadcast networks by looking at the related technologies of packet-radio and satellite networks. In each case, the overall architecture is examined, followed by a detailed discussion of the techniques by which the common transmission capacity is shared.

Local Area Networks.   The nature of a local area network is determined primarily by three factors: transmission medium, topology, and the technique used to share access to the transmission medium. The bulk of Chapter 11 is devoted to these topics, together with a look at local area network performance. Throughout, reference is made to standards developed for local area networks. These are described briefly at the end of the chapter.

Protocols and Architectures.   Chapter 12 introduces the subject of computer-communications architecture and motivates the need for a layered architecture with protocols defined at each layer. Protocols are defined and the important constituent elements discussed. The Open Systems Interconnection (OSI) model is introduced and justified.

Although the OSI model is almost universally accepted as the framework for discourse in this area, there is another point of view which grows out of the extensive research and practical experience of ARPANET. This viewpoint, which is characterized by a hierarchy of protocols, is also presented.

Both of the foregoing viewpoints describe the communications function in terms of an architecture, which specifies protocols and their interrelationships. To lend concreteness to the discussion, a commercial architecture is presented: IBM's SNA.

Network Access Protocols.   When two stations communicate across a network, a network access protocol between station and network is needed. The requirements for such a protocol differ significantly for circuit-switched, packet-switched, and broadcast networks. After a review of general principles, each of these three cases is examined in Chapter 13 using a specific protocol standard.

Internetworking.   Packet-switched and packet broadcasting networks grew out of a need to allow the computer user to have access to resources beyond that available in a single system. In a similar fashion, the resources of a single network are often inadequate to meet users' needs. Because the networks that might be of interest exhibit so many differences, it is impractical to consider merging them into a single network. Rather, what is needed is the ability to interconnect various networks so that any two stations on any of the constituent networks can communicate. This ability is referred to as internetworking, and protocols have been developed for this purpose. Chapter 14 includes an examination of the requirements for an internetworking capability and the various approaches that can be taken to satisfy those requirements. Then several standardized protocols are examined.

Transport Protocols.   The transport protocol (OSI layer 4) is the keystone of the whole concept of a computer communications architecture. It can also be one of the most complex of protocols. Chapter 15 examines the mechanisms of transport protocols and the services they provide. The two major standardization efforts for transport protocols are also described.

Session Services and Protocols.   A session protocol is used to control the dialogue between two applications. Chapter 16 focuses on the ISO standards in this area, which define a range of services to be provided and specify session protocol mechanisms to support those services. The corresponding protocol in IBM's System Network Architecture (SNA) is presented for comparison.

Process/Application Protocols. The higher layers of a communications architecture are those most visible to the ultimate user. They must support a wide variety of process and application requirements. This is a broad subject, and only a representative sample of techniques are examined in Chapter 17.

Integrated Services Digital Network. The *integrated services digital network* (ISDN) is a projected worldwide public telecommunications network that will service a wide variety of user needs. The ISDN will be defined by the standardization of user interfaces, and will be implemented as a set of digital switches and paths supporting a broad range of traffic types and employing many of the concepts discussed in this book.

Because the ISDN does not yet exist and is defined only by an evolving set of standards (being developed on a truly massive scale, both in terms of content and participants), Chapter 18 can only suggest the likely characteristics of the future ISDN.

Relationship of Chapter Organization to the OSI Model

Roughly speaking, this book is organized along the lines of the OSI architecture, going from the bottom (physical) to the top (application) layer. However, for the sake of clarity of presentation, a strict mapping of chapters to successive layers has not been followed.

Figure 1-11 indicates the relationship. Most of Part I deals with the fundamentals of data communications, and corresponds to OSI layer 1. The exception is Chapter 5, on data link control, which covers functions assigned to OSI layer 2. This material is introduced before multiplexing in Chapter 6, which is a layer 1 concern, because of the implications for multiplexing with respect to data link control frame structure.

Part II deals with communications networks. Thus, much of the material in this part is concerned with functions assigned to OSI layer 3. However, the design and functioning of a network involves consideration of layer 1 and 2 issues as well. Thus, it is fair to say that Part II covers OSI layers 1 through 3.

Part III begins with an overview of protocols and communications architectures in Chapter 12, covering the entire 7-layer architecture. Then, Chapter 13 deals with network access protocols, such as X.25. Although such protocols are often thought of as residing at layer 3, in fact they encompass layers 1 and 2 as well. To fully explain these protocols, it is necessary to look at all three layers at the same time. Chapter 14 is devoted to a specific layer 3 function referred to as internetworking. Chapters 15 (transport protocols) and 16 (session services and protocols) cover layers 4 and 5, respectively. Chapter 17 deals with applications with associated presentation-level issues, thus covering layers 6 and 7. Again, to fully explain the design issues involved, the two layers need to be examined together.

Finally, Part IV covers ISDN. Since ISDN is a communication network, it too maps into layers 1 through 3.

OSI Layer	Chapters					
Physical	2–Data transmission 3–Data encoding 4–Digital data communication techniques	6–Multiplexing	7–Networking techniques 8–Circuit switching 9–Packet switching 10–Radio and satellite networks 11–Local area networks	12–Protocols and architecture	13–Network access protocols	18–ISDN
Data link	5–Data link control					
Network					14–Inter-networking	
Transport					15–Transport protocols	
Session					16–Session services and protocols	
Presentation					17–Presentation/application protocols	
Application						

FIGURE 1-11. Relationship of chapters to the OSI model.

APPENDIX 1A

STANDARDS ORGANIZATIONS

Throughout this book, especially in Parts III and IV, we describe the most important standards in use or being developed for various aspects of data and computer communications. Various organizations have been involved in the development or promotion of these standards. This appendix provides a brief description of the most important (in the current context) of these organizations.

1A-1   Standards-Making Organizations

International Organization for Standardization (ISO).   ISO is an international agency for the development of standards on a wide range of subjects. It is a voluntary, nontreaty organization whose members are designated standards bodies of participating nations, plus nonvoting observer organizations. Although ISO is not a governmental body, more than 70 percent of ISO member bodies are governmental standards institutions or organizations incorporated by public law. Most of the remainder have close links with the public administrations in their own countries. The United States member body is the American National Standards Institute (ANSI), described later in this section.

ISO was founded in 1946 and has issued more than 5000 standards on a broad range of areas. Its purpose is to promote the development of standardization and related activities to facilitate international exchange of goods and services and to develop cooperation in the sphere of intellectual, scientific, technological, and economic activity. Standards have been issued to cover everything from screw threads to solar energy. One important area of standardization deals with the open systems interconnection (OSI) communications architecture and the standards at each layer of the OSI architecture.

In the areas of interest in this book, ISO standards are actually developed in a joint effort with another standards body, the International Electrotechnical Commission (IEC). IEC is primarily concerned with electrical and electronic engineering standards. In the area of information technology, the interests of the two groups overlap, with IEC emphasizing hardware and ISO focusing on software. In 1987, the two groups formed the Joint Technical Committee 1 (JTC 1). This committee has the responsibility of developing the documents that ultimately become ISO (and IEC) standards in the area of information technology.

The development of an ISO standard from first proposal to actual publication of the standard follows a seven-step process. The objective is to ensure that the final result is acceptable to as many countries as possible. The steps are briefly described here (time limits are the minimum time in which voting could be accomplished, and amendments require extended time):

1. A new work item is assigned to the appropriate technical committee, and within that technical committee, to the appropriate working group. The working group prepares the technical specifications for the proposed standard and publishes these as a **draft proposal** (DP). The DP is circulated among interested members for balloting and technical comment. At least three months are allowed, and there may be iterations. When there is substantial agreement,

the DP is sent to the administrative arm of ISO, known as the Central Secretariat.

2. The DP is registered at the Central Secretariat within two months of its final approval by the technical committee.

3. The Central Secretariat edits the document to ensure conformity with ISO practices; no technical changes are made. The edited document is then issued as a **draft international standard** (DIS).

4. The DIS is circulated for a six-month balloting period. For approval, the DIS must receive a majority approval by the technical committee members and 75 percent approval of all voting members. Revisions may occur to resolve any negative vote. If more than two negative votes remain, it is unlikely that the DIS will be published as a final standard.

5. The approved, possibly revised, DIS is returned within three months to the Central Secretariat for submission to the ISO Council, which acts as the board of directors of ISO.

7. The DIS is accepted by the Council as an **international standard** (IS).

8. The IS is published by ISO.

As can be seen, the process of issuing a standard is a slow one. Certainly, it would be desirable to issue standards as quickly as the technical details can be worked out, but ISO must ensure that the standard will receive widespread support.

International Telegraph and Telephone Consultative Committee (CCITT). CCITT is a committee of the International Telecommunications Union (ITU), which is itself a United Nations treaty organization. Hence the members of CCITT are governments. The U.S. representation is housed in the Department of State. The charter of CCITT is "to study and issue recommendations on technical, operating, and tariff questions relating to telegraphy and telephony." Its primary objective is to standardize, to the extent necessary, techniques and operations in telecommunications to achieve end-to-end compatibility of international telecommunication connections, regardless of the countries of origin and destination.

CCITT is organized into 15 study groups that prepare standards, called Recommendations by CCITT. There are three areas of activity concerned with ISDN matters (see Part IV): data communications, telematic services, and integrated services digital networks (ISDN). Telematic services are user-oriented services that involve information transfer, query, and update.

Work within CCITT is conducted in four-year cycles. Every four years, a Plenary Assembly is held. The work program for the next four years is established at the assembly in the form of questions submitted by the various study groups, based on requests made to the study groups by their members. The assembly assesses the questions, reviews the scope of the study groups, creates new or abolishes existing study groups, and allocates questions to them.

Based on these questions, each study group prepares draft recommendations to be submitted to the next assembly, four years hence. After approval by the assembly, these are published as CCITT Recommendations. If a certain draft recommendation is very urgent, a study group may employ a balloting procedure to gain approval before the end of the four years. In general, however, the process of standardization within CCITT is a slow one.

Within the fields of data communications and information processing, there has traditionally been a split between the interests of CCITT and ISO. CCITT has

primarily been concerned with data transmission and communication network issues. Roughly, these occupy the lower three levels of the OSI architecture. ISO
has traditionally been concerned with computer communications and distributed
processing issues, which correspond roughly to layers 4 through 7. The increasing
merger of the fields of data processing and data communications, however, has
resulted in considerable overlap in the areas of concern of these two organizations.
Fortunately, the growth of the overlap has been accompanied by a growth in
cooperation, so that competing standards are not being used.

The American National Standards Institute (ANSI).   ANSI is a nonprofit,
nongovernment federation of standards-making and standards-using organizations.
Its members include professional societies, trade associations, governmental and
regulatory bodies, industrial companies, and consumer groups. ANSI is the national
clearinghouse for voluntary standards in the United States and is also the
United States-designated voting member of the ISO.

ANSI publishes national standards but does not develop them. Rather, standards
are developed by other groups that are accredited to develop standards for ANSI
consideration. Much of this work is done directly by ANSI member organizations,
such as the Institute of Electrical and Electronics Engineers (IEEE), which developed the IEEE 802 local area network standards. Additionally, an important group
of standards is developed by quasi-independent committees, known as Accredited
Standards Committees, which are administered by ANSI member organizations.
In either case, once a consensus is reached on the content of a standard within a
committee, it is published by ANSI for open public review and comment. If and
when ANSI determines that there is a consensus, the proposal is adopted as an
American National Standard. The federal government frequently uses ANSI
standards in its procurement specifications.

Other Standards-making Organizations.   Other groups are also involved in
the publication of standards for telecommunications and computer communications.
Among the most important:

- *National Institute of Standards and Technology:* Part of the Department of
  Commerce, it was until 1988 called the National Bureau of Standards. It issues
  Federal Information Processing Standards (FIPS) for equipment sold to the
  federal government. The concerns of NIST are broad, encompassing the areas
  of interest of both CCITT and ISO. NIST is attempting to satisfy federal
  government requirements with standards that, as far as possible, are compatible
  with international standards.
- *Defense Communications Agency:* Promulgates communications-related military standards (MIL-STD). DOD feels that its requirements in some areas are
  unique, and this is reflected in standards that are unlike those used elsewhere.
  However, the agency works closely with NIST to attempt to have military
  requirements satisfied by broader-based standards.
- *Electronics Industries Association (EIA):* Trade association of electronics firms
  and a member of ANSI. It is concerned primarily with standards that fit into
  OSI layer 1 (physical)
- *Institute of Electrical and Electronics Engineers (IEEE):* Professional society
  and also a member of ANSI. Their concerns have primarily been with the
  lowest two layers of the OSI model (physical and data link).

1A-2 Standards-related Organizations

The success of standards related to OSI depends not only on the development of timely, technically appropriate standards, but on their acceptance by the vendors who supply and the customers who buy equipment that conforms to the standards. One of the most promising developments in recent years is the creation of a number of organizations whose goal is to ensure that acceptance. In this subsection, we briefly mention three of these organizations.

MAP/TOP Users' Group.   The Manufacturing Automation Protocol (MAP) is an effort begun by General Motors in 1982; it since has been taken over by the MAP/TOP Users' Group, administered by the Society of Manufacturing Engineers. The objective of MAP is to define a local area network and associated protocols for terminals, computing resources, programmable devices, and robots within a plant or a factory. It sets standards for procurement and provides a specification for use by vendors who want to build networking products for factory use that are acceptable to MAP participants. The strategy has three parts:

1. For cases in which international standards exist, select those alternatives and options that best suit the needs of the MAP participants.
2. For standards currently under development, participate in the standards-making process to represent the requirements of the MAP participants.
3. In those cases where no appropriate standard exists, devise interim MAP standards until the international standards are developed.

Thus, MAP is intended to specify those standards and options within standards appropriate for the factory environment. Because of the widespread support for MAP among manufacturing companies, this guarantees a large market for products that conform to those standards.

A similar effort, called Technical and Office Protocols (TOP), addresses the needs of the office and engineering environments. Like MAP, TOP specifies standards and options within standards and has received widespread support. TOP was begun by Boeing and is now, together with MAP, part of the MAP/TOP Users' Group.

Corporation for Open Systems.   An equally important development is the creation, in 1986, of the Corporation for Open Systems (COS). COS is a nonprofit joint venture of more than 100 of the major suppliers of data processing and data communications equipment. Its purpose is:

> to provide a vehicle for acceleration of the introduction of interoperable, multi-vendor products and services operating under agreed-to OSI, ISDN, and related international standards to assure widespread customer acceptance of an open network architecture in world markets.

COS is involved in a number of standards-related activities. Its most important activity is the development of a single consistent set of test methods, test facilities, and certification procedures. This will allow vendors to certify that their products do in fact meet the international standards and will work with certified equipment from other vendors.

U.S. Government OSI Users' Committee.   A final significant development worth noting is the creation in 1986 of the U.S. Government OSI Users' Committee. The U.S. government is the world's largest user of computers and thus has a profound impact on the product plans of many of the vendors. The objectives of the committee are to:

- Develop implementable OSI specifications.
- Coordinate cooperative efforts between government agencies and industry to introduce products that meet government needs and are compliant with international standards.
- Define unique agency requirements and work for OSI incorporation.

The most important outcome of this committee's efforts has been the government open systems profile (GOSIP). Like MAP and TOP, GOSIP specifies standards and options within standards that are suitable for government use. Furthermore, GOSIP provides detailed implementation guidelines that should help assure that products from different vendors do in fact work together. GOSIP is now a federal information-processing standard (FIPS) and is mandatory for use on government procurements. This, together with the MAP/TOP and COS efforts, guarantees the widespread availability of products that conform to international OSI-related standards.

DATA COMMUNICATIONS

This first part of the book deals with the transfer of data between two devices that are directly connected; that is, the two devices are linked by a single transmission path rather than a network.

Chapter 2 looks at the key aspects of data transmission. A distinction is drawn between the concepts of analog and digital, in the context of data, signaling, and transmission. The effect of impairments and choice of medium on transmission are also examined. Chapter 3 then reviews the various means of encoding data for transmission.

With Chapter 4, the text moves from the simple transmission of data to the additional processing required to achieve true data communications. This chapter introduces some of the basic data communication processing techniques. Chapter 5 examines data link control procedures, which are designed to turn an unreliable transmission medium into a reliable data link. Chapter 6 examines various methods of multiplexing data signals to achieve more efficient utilization of the transmission medium.

Data Transmission

The successful transmission of data depends principally on two factors: the quality of the signal being transmitted and the characteristics of the transmission medium. The objective of this chapter is to provide the reader with an intuitive feeling for the nature of these two factors.

The first section presents some concepts and terms from the field of electrical engineering. This should provide sufficient background to deal with the remainder of the chapter. Section 2-2 clarifies the use of the terms "analog" and "digital." Either analog or digital data may be transmitted using either analog or digital signals. Furthermore, it is common for intermediate processing to be performed between source and destination, and this processing has either an analog or digital character.

Section 2-3 looks at the various impairments that may introduce errors into the data during transmission. The chief impairments are attenuation, delay distortion, and the various forms of noise.

Finally, Section 2-4 looks at the most common types of transmission media, and the behavior of signals on those media.

2-1

CONCEPTS AND TERMINOLOGY

In this section we introduce some concepts and terms that will be referred to throughout the rest of the chapter and, indeed, throughout Part I.

Transmission Terminology

Data transmission occurs between transmitter and receiver over some *transmission medium*. Transmission media may be classified as guided or unguided. In both cases, communication is in the form of electromagnetic waves. With *guided media,* the waves are guided along a physical path; examples of guided media are twisted pair, coaxial cable, and optical fiber. *Unguided media* provide a means for transmitting electromagnetic waves but do not guide them; examples are propagation through air, vacuum, and seawater.

The term *direct link* is used to refer to the transmission path between two devices in which signals propagate directly from transmitter to receiver with no intermediate devices, other than amplifiers or repeaters used to increase signal strength. Both parts of Figure 2-1 depict a direct link. Note that this term can apply to both guided and unguided media.

A guided transmission medium is *point-to-point* if it provides a direct link between two devices and those are the only two devices sharing the medium (Figure 2-1a). In a *multipoint* guided configuration, more than two devices share the same medium (Figure 2-1b).

A transmission may be simplex, half-duplex, or full duplex. In *simplex* transmission, signals are transmitted in only one direction; one station is transmitter and the other is receiver. In *half-duplex* operation, both stations may transmit, but only one at a time. In *full-duplex* operation, both stations may transmit simultaneously. In the latter case, the medium is carrying signals in both directions at the same time. How this can be is explained in due course.

We should note that the definitions just given are the ones in common use in the United States (ANSI definitions). In Europe (CCITT definitions), the term "simplex" is used to correspond to half-duplex as defined above, and "duplex" is used to correspond to full-duplex as defined above.

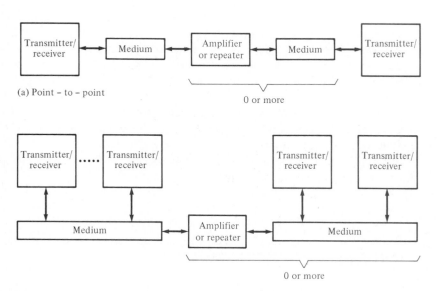

(a) Point – to – point

0 or more

(b) Multipoint

FIGURE 2-1.   Guided transmission configurations.

Frequency, Spectrum, and Bandwidth

At point 3 in Figure 1-1, a signal is generated by the transmitter and transmitted over a medium. The signal is a function of time, but it can also be expressed as a function of frequency; that is, the signal consists of components of different frequencies. It turns out that the "frequency-domain" view of a signal is far more important to an understanding of data transmission than a "time domain" view. Both views are introduced below.

Time-Domain Concepts. We begin by looking at a signal as a function of time. A signal $s(t)$ is *continuous* if

$$\lim_{t \to a} s(t) = s(a)$$

for all a. In words, there are no breaks or discontinuities in the signal. A signal is *discrete* if it takes on only a finite number of values. Figure 2-2 shows examples of both kinds of signals. The continuous signal might represent speech, and the discrete signal might represent binary 1's and 0's.

A signal $s(t)$ is *periodic* if and only if

$$s(t + T) = s(t) \quad -\infty < t < +\infty$$

where the constant T is the *period* of the signal (T must be the smallest value that satisfies the equation). Otherwise, a signal is aperiodic.

Amplitude (volts)

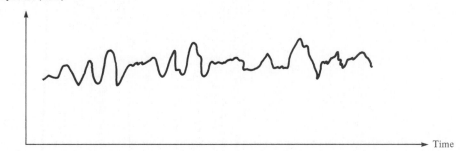

Time

(a) Continuous

amplitude

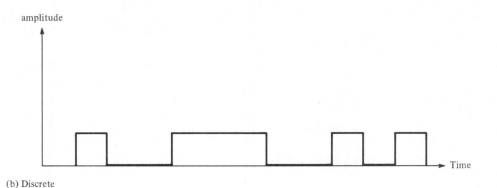

Time

(b) Discrete

FIGURE 2-2. Continuous and discrete signals.

Figure 2-3 displays portions of two periodic signals, the sine wave and the square wave. Three important characteristics of a periodic signal are amplitude, frequency, and phase. The *amplitude* is the instantaneous value of a signal at any time. Since the signals discussed in this book are all electrical or electromagnetic waves, amplitude is measured in volts. The *frequency* is the inverse of the period ($1/T$), or the number of repetitions of the period per second; it is expressed in cycles per second, or hertz (Hz). *Phase* is a measure of the relative position in time within a single period of a signal. As an example, Figure 2-4 shows two signals that are out of phase by $\pi/2$ radians (2π radians $= 360° = 1$ period).

Thus we can express a sinusoid as

$$s(t) = A \sin(2\pi\, ft + \theta)$$

where A is the maximum amplitude, f is the frequency, and θ is the phase. Note that the sine wave in Figure 2-3 can be expressed as either

$$s(t) = A \sin(2\pi ft)$$

or

$$s(t) = A \cos(2\pi ft - \pi/2)$$

Frequency Domain Concepts.   So far, we have viewed a signal as a function of time. But any signal can also be viewed as a function of frequency. For example, the signal

$$s(t) = \sin 2\pi\, ft + 1/3\sin 3(2\pi f)t + 1/5\sin 5(2\pi f)t$$

Amplitude

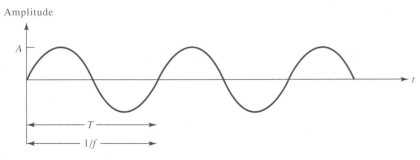

(a) Sine wave

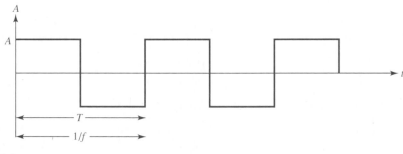

(b) Square wave

FIGURE 2-3.   Example of periodic signals.

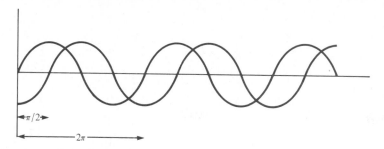

FIGURE 2-4. **Example of a phase difference.**

is shown in Figure 2-5. The components of this signal are just sine waves of frequencies f, $3f$, and $5f$. Indeed, it can be shown, using a discipline known as Fourier analysis, that any signal is made up of components at various frequencies, where each component is a sinusoid. For the interested reader, this subject is pursued in Appendix 2A at the end of this chapter.

So, we can say that for each signal there is a time-domain function $s(t)$ that specifies the amplitude of the signal at each instant of time. Similarly, there is a frequency-domain function $S(f)$ that specifies the constituent frequencies of the signal. Figure 2-6a shows the frequency-domain function for the signal of Figure 2-5. Note that, in this case, $S(f)$ is discrete. Figure 2-6b shows the frequency domain function for a single square pulse that has value 1 between $-T/2$ and $T/2$, and 0 elsewhere. Note that $S(f)$ is continuous, and that it has nonzero values indefinitely, although the magnitude of the frequency components becomes smaller for larger f. This is not uncommon for real signals.

The *spectrum* of a signal is the range of frequencies that it contains. For the signal of Figure 2-5, the spectrum extends from f_1 to $5f_1$. The *absolute bandwidth* of a signal is the width of the spectrum. In the case above, the bandwidth is $4f_1$. Many signals, such as that of Figure 2-6b, have an infinite bandwidth. However, most of the energy in the signal is contained in a relatively narrow band of frequencies. This band is referred to as the *effective bandwidth*, or just *bandwidth*.

One final term to define is *dc component*. If a signal includes a component of zero frequency, that component is a direct current (dc) or constant component. For example, Figure 2-7 shows the result of adding a dc component to the signal of Figure 2-6. With no dc component, a signal has an average amplitude of zero, as seen in the time domain. With a dc component, it has a frequency term at $f = 0$ and a nonzero average amplitude.

Relationship Between Data Rate and Bandwidth.   The concept of effective bandwidth is a somewhat fuzzy one. We have said that it is the band within which most of the signal energy is confined. The term "most" in this context is somewhat arbitrary. The important issue here is that, although a given waveform may contain frequencies over a very broad range, as a practical matter any transmission medium that is used will be able to accommodate only a limited band of frequencies. This in turn limits the data rate that can be carried on the transmission medium.

To try to explain these relationships, consider the square wave of Figure 2-3b. Suppose that we let a positive pulse represent binary 1 and a negative pulse represent binary 0. Then, the waveform represents the binary stream 1010 . . . The duration of each pulse is $1/2f$, thus the data rate is $2f$ bits per second (bps). It can

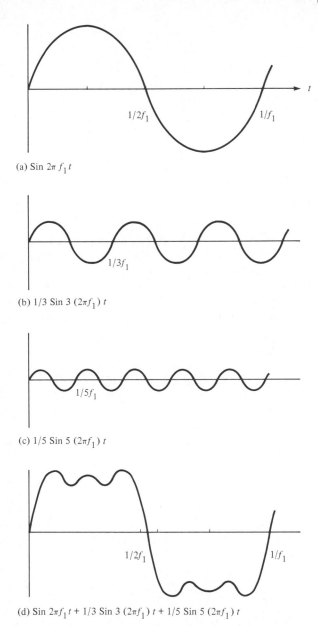

(a) Sin $2\pi f_1 t$

(b) $1/3$ Sin 3 $(2\pi f_1)$ t

(c) $1/5$ Sin 5 $(2\pi f_1)$ t

(d) Sin $2\pi f_1 t$ + $1/3$ Sin 3 $(2\pi f_1)$ t + $1/5$ Sin 5 $(2\pi f_1)$ t

FIGURE 2-5.   Signal with three frequency components.

be shown that the frequency-domain representation of this waveform is:

$$s(t) = \sum_{k=1}^{\infty} \frac{1}{k} \sin (2\pi kft)$$

Thus, this waveform has an infinite number of frequency components and hence an infinite bandwidth. However, the amplitude of the kth frequency component, kf, is only $1/k$, so most of the energy in this waveform is in the first few frequency components. What happens if we limit the bandwidth to just the first three frequency components? We have already seen the answer, in Figure 2-5. As we can

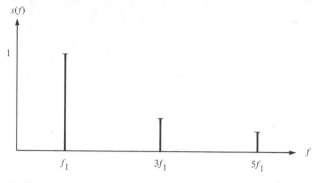

(a) $s(t) = \mathrm{Sin}\ 2\pi f_1 t + 1/3\ \mathrm{Sin}\ 3\ (2\pi f_1)\ t + 1/5\ \mathrm{Sin}\ 5\ (2\pi f_1)\ t$

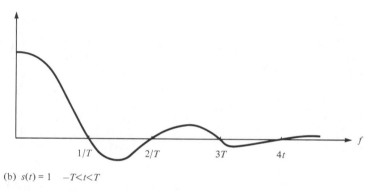

(b) $s(t) = 1\quad -T < t < T$

FIGURE 2-6.   Frequency-domain representations.

see, the shape of the resulting waveform is reasonably close to that of the original square wave.

The importance of these matters is this: In general, any digital waveform will have infinite bandwidth. If we attempt to transmit this waveform as a signal over any medium, the nature of the medium will limit the bandwidth that can be transmitted. Furthermore, for any given medium, the greater the bandwidth transmitted, the greater the cost. Thus, on the one hand, economic and practical reasons dictate that digital information be approximated by a signal of limited bandwidth. On the other hand, limiting the bandwidth creates distortions, which makes the task of interpreting the received signal more difficult. The more limited the bandwidth, the greater the distortion, and the greater the potential for error by the receiver.

One more illustration should serve to reinforce these concepts. Figure 2-8 shows a digital bit stream with a data rate of 2000 bits per second. With a bandwidth of 1700 to 2500 Hz, the representation is quite good. With a bandwidth of 4000 Hz, the representation is very good. Furthermore, we can generalize these results. If the data rate of the digital signal is W bps, then a very good representation can be achieved with a bandwidth of 2W Hz.

Thus, there is a direct relationship between data rate and bandwidth: the higher the data rate of a signal, the greater is its effective bandwidth. Looked at the other way, the greater the bandwidth of a transmission system, the higher the data rate that can be transmitted over that system.

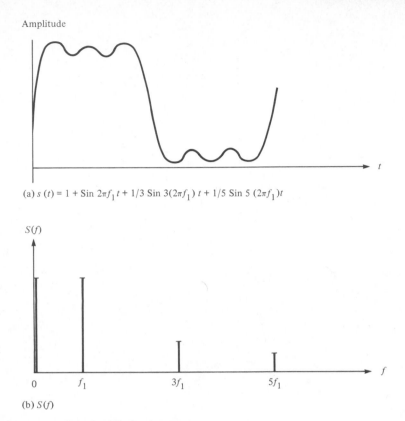

(a) $s(t) = 1 + \text{Sin } 2\pi f_1 t + 1/3 \text{ Sin } 3(2\pi f_1) t + 1/5 \text{ Sin } 5 (2\pi f_1)t$

(b) $S(f)$

FIGURE 2-7. Signal with dc component.

Another observation worth making is this: If we think of the bandwidth of a signal as being centered about some frequency, referred to as the *center frequency,* then the higher the center frequency, the higher the potential bandwidth and therefore the higher the potential data rate. Consider that if a signal is centered at 2000 Hz, its maximum bandwidth is 4000 Hz. As the center frequency increases, so does the potential bandwidth, and hence the potential data rate.

We will return to a discussion of the relationship between bandwidth and data rate later in this chapter, after a consideration of transmission impairments.

Signal Strength

An important parameter in any transmission system is the strength of the signal being transmitted. As a signal propagates along a transmission medium, there will be a loss, or *attenuation*, of signal strength. To compensate, amplifiers may be inserted at various points to impart a gain in signal strength.

It is customary to express gains, losses, and relative levels in decibels because:

- Signal strength often falls off logarithmically, so loss is easily expressed in terms of the decibel, which is a logarithmic unit.
- Gains and losses in a cascaded transmission path can be calculated with simple addition and subtraction.

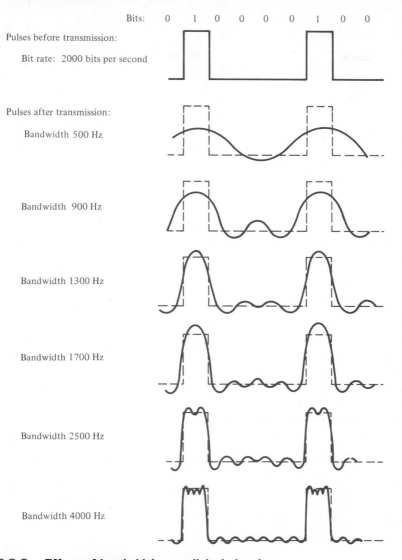

Bits: 0 1 0 0 0 0 1 0 0

Pulses before transmission:

Bit rate: 2000 bits per second

Pulses after transmission:

Bandwidth 500 Hz

Bandwidth 900 Hz

Bandwidth 1300 Hz

Bandwidth 1700 Hz

Bandwidth 2500 Hz

Bandwidth 4000 Hz

FIGURE 2-8. Effect of bandwidth on a digital signal.

The decibel is a measure of the difference in two power levels:

$$N_{dB} = 10\log_{10} \frac{P_1}{P_2}$$

where

N_{dB} = number of decibels
$P_{1,2}$ = power values
$\log_{10}$ = logarithm to the base 10 (from now on, we will simply use log to mean $\log_{10}$)

For example, if a signal with a power of 10 mw is inserted onto a transmission line and the measured power some distance away is 5 mw, the loss can be expressed as

$$\text{LOSS} = 10\log(5/10) = 10(-0.3) = -3 \text{ dB}$$

Note that the decibel is a measure of relative, not absolute, difference. A loss from 1000 w to 500 w is also a -3dB loss. Thus, a loss of 3 dB halves the magnitude; similarly, a gain of 3 dB doubles the magnitude.

The decibel is also used to measure the difference in voltage, taking into account that power is proportional to the square of the voltage:

$$P = \frac{V^2}{R}$$

where

P = power dissipated across resistance R
V = voltage across resistance R

Thus

$$N_{\text{dB}} = 10 \log \frac{P_1}{P_2} = 10 \log \frac{V_1^2/R}{V_2^2/R} = 20 \log \frac{V_1}{V_2}$$

Decibel values refer to relative magnitudes or changes in magnitude, not to an absolute level. It is convenient to be able to refer to an absolute level of power or voltage in decibels so that gain and losses may be easily calculated. Thus several derived units are in common use.

The dBW (decibel-watt) is used extensively in microwave applications. The value of 1 w is selected as reference and defined to be 0 dBW. The absolute decibel level of power in dBW is defined as:

$$\text{Power(dBW)} = 10 \log \frac{\text{Power(W)}}{1\text{W}}$$

For example, a power of 1000 w is 30 dBW. A power of 1 mw is -30 dBW.

The dBmV (decibel-millivolt) is used in video applications and is an absolute decibel unit with 0 dBmV equivalent to 1 mV. Thus

$$\text{Voltage(dBmV)} = 20 \log_{10} \frac{\text{Voltage(mV)}}{1 \text{ mV}}$$

The voltage levels are assumed to be across a 75-ohm resistance.

The decibel is convenient for determining overall gain or loss in a system. For example, consider a point-to-point link that consists of a transmission line with a single amplifier partway along. If the loss on the first portion of line is 13 dB, the gain of the amplifier is 30 dB, and the loss on the second portion of line is 40 dB, then the overall gain (loss) is $-13 + 30 - 40 = -23$ dB. If the original signal strength is -30 dBW, the received signal strength is -53 dBW.

2-2

ANALOG AND DIGITAL DATA TRANSMISSION

In transmitting data from a source to a destination, one must be concerned with the nature of the data, the actual physical means used to propagate the data, and what processing or adjustments may be required along the way to assure that the received data are intelligible. For all of these considerations, the crucial point is whether we are dealing with analog or digital entities.

The terms *analog* and *digital* correspond, roughly, to continuous and discrete, respectively. These two terms are used frequently in data communications in at least three contexts:

- Data.
- Signaling.
- Transmission.

We discussed data, as distinct from information, in Chapter 1. For present purposes, we define *data* as entities that convey meaning. *Signals* are electric or electromagnetic encoding of data. *Signaling* is the act of propagating the signal along a suitable medium. Finally, *transmission* is the communication of data by the propagation and processing of signals. In what follows, we try to make these abstract concepts clear, by discussing the terms ''analog'' and ''digital'' in these three contexts.

Data

The concepts of analog and digital data are simple enough. *Analog data* take on continuous values on some interval. For example, voice and video are continuously varying patterns of intensity. Most data collected by sensors, such as temperature and pressure, are continuous-valued. *Digital data* take on discrete values; examples are text and integers.

The most familiar example of analog data is audio or acoustic data, which, in the form of sound waves, can be perceived directly by human beings. Figure 2-10 gives some examples. Figure 2-9 shows the acoustic spectrum for human speech. Frequency components of speech may be found between 20 Hz and 20 kHz. Although much of the energy in speech is concentrated at the lower frequencies, tests have shown that frequencies up to 600 to 700 Hz add very little to the intelligibility

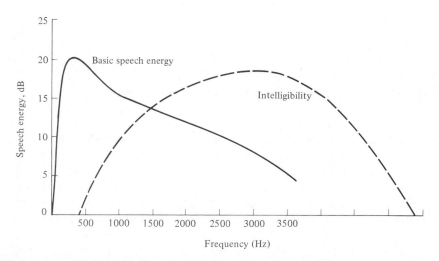

FIGURE 2-9. Acoustic spectrum for speech. Source: [FREE89]

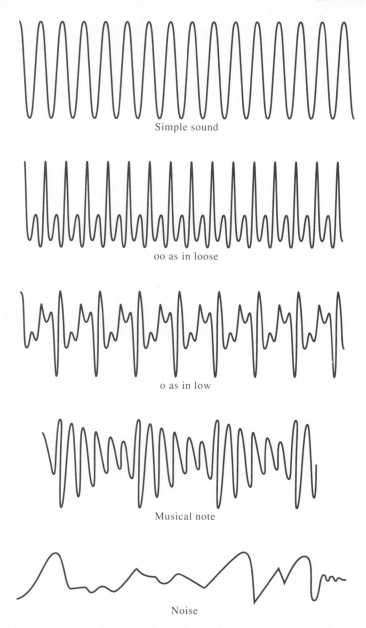

Simple sound

oo as in loose

o as in low

Musical note

Noise

FIGURE 2-10.   Wave patterns of some sounds. Source: [ATT61]

of speech to the human ear. The dashed line more accurately reflects the intelligibility or emotional content of speech.

Another common example of analog data is video. Here it is easier to characterize the data in terms of the viewer (destination) of the TV screen rather than the original scene (source) that is recorded by the TV camera. To produce a picture on the screen, an electron beam scans across the surface of the screen from left to right and top to bottom. For black-and-white television, the amount of illumination produced (on a scale from black to white) at any point is proportional to the intensity of the beam as it passes that point. Thus at any instant in time the beam takes on an analog value of intensity to produce the desired brightness at that point on the screen. Further, as the beam scans, the analog value changes. Thus the video image can be viewed as a time-varying analog signal.

Figure 2-11a depicts the scanning process. At the end of each scan line, the beam is swept rapidly back to the left (horizontal retrace). When the beam reaches

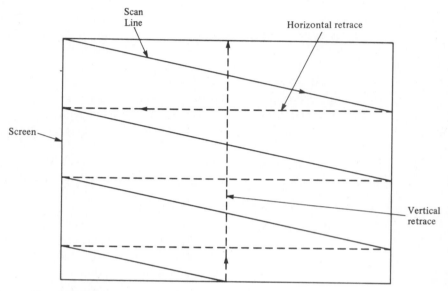

(a) Composition of a TV field

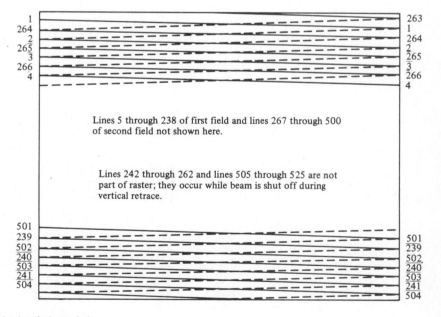

Lines 5 through 238 of first field and lines 267 through 500 of second field not shown here.

Lines 242 through 262 and lines 505 through 525 are not part of raster; they occur while beam is shut off during vertical retrace.

(b) Video interlacing technique

FIGURE 2-11. TV picture production.

the bottom, it is swept rapidly back to the top (vertical retrace). The beam is turned off (blanked out) during the retrace intervals.

To achieve adequate resolution, the beam produces a total of 483 horizontal lines at a rate of 30 complete scans of the screen per second. Tests have shown that this rate will produce a sensation of flicker rather than smooth motion. However, the flicker is eliminated by a process of interlacing, as depicted in Figure 2-11b. The electron beam scans across the screen starting at the far left, very near the top. The beam reaches the bottom at the middle after 241 $\frac{1}{2}$ lines. At this point, the beam is quickly repositioned at the top of the screen and, beginning in the middle, produces an additional 241 $\frac{1}{2}$ lines interlaced with the original set. Thus the screen is refreshed 60 times per second rather than 30, and flicker is avoided. Note that the total count of lines is 525. Of these, 42 are blanked out during the vertical retrace interval, leaving 483 actually visible on the screen.

A familiar example of digital data is text or character strings. While textual data are most convenient for human beings, they cannot, in character form, be easily stored or transmitted by data processing and communications systems. Such systems are designed for binary data. Thus a number of codes have been devised by which characters are represented by a sequence of bits. Perhaps the earliest common example of this is the Morse code. Today, the most commonly used code in the United States is the ASCII (American Standard Code for Information Interchange) code (Table 2-1) promulgated by ANSI. ASCII is also widely used outside the United States. Each character in this code is represented by a unique 7-bit pattern; thus 128 different characters can be represented. This is a larger number than is necessary, and some of the patterns represent ''control'' characters. Some of these control characters have to do with controlling the printing of characters on a page. Others are concerned with communications procedures and will be discussed later. ASCII-encoded characters are almost always stored and transmitted using 8 bits per character (a block of 8 bits is referred to as an *octet* or a *byte*). The eighth bit is a parity bit used for error detection. This bit is set such that the total number of binary 1's in each octet is always odd (odd parity) or always even (even parity). Thus a transmission error which changes a single bit can be detected.

Signals

In a communications system, data are propagated from one point to another by means of electric signals. An *analog signal* is a continuously varying electromagnetic wave that may be propagated over a variety of media, depending on spectrum; examples are wire media, such as twisted pair and coaxial cable, fiber optic cable, and atmosphere or space propagation. A *digital signal* is a sequence of voltage pulses that may be transmitted over a wire medium; for example, a constant positive voltage level may represent binary 1 and a constant negative voltage level may represent binary 0.

In what follows, we first look at some specific examples of signal types, and then discuss the relationship between data and signals.

Examples. Let us return to our three examples of the preceding subsection. For each example, we will describe the signal and estimate its bandwidth.

In the case of acoustic data (voice), the data can be represented directly by an electromagnetic signal occupying the same spectrum. However, there is a need to compromise between the fidelity of the sound as transmitted electrically and the cost of transmission, which increases with increasing bandwidth. Although, as mentioned, the spectrum of speech is approximately 20 Hz to 20 kHz, a much narrower bandwidth will produce acceptable voice reproduction. The standard spectrum for a voice signal is 300 to 3400 Hz. This is adequate for voice reproduction, minimizes required transmission capacity, and allows the use of rather inexpensive telephone sets. Thus the telephone transmitter converts the incoming acoustic voice signal into an electromagnetic signal over the range 300 to 3400 Hz. This signal is then transmitted through the telephone system to a receiver, which reproduces an acoustic signal from the incoming electromagnetic signal.

Now, let us look at the video signal which, interestingly, consists of both analog and digital components. To produce a video signal, a TV camera, which performs similar functions to the TV receiver, is used. One component of the camera is a photosensitive plate, upon which a scene is optically focused. An electron beam sweeps across the plate from left to right and top to bottom, in the same fashion as depicted in Figure 2-11 for the receiver. As the beam sweeps, an analog electric signal is developed proportional to the brightness of the scene at a particular spot.

Now we are in a position to describe the video signal. Figure 2-12a shows three lines of a video signal; in this diagram, white is represented by a small positive voltage and black by a much larger positive voltage. So, for example, line 3 is at

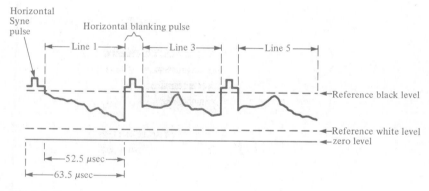

(a) Horizontal lines of video

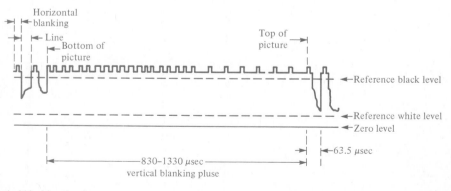

(b) Vertical blanking signal

FIGURE 2-12. Video signal (different scales for a and b).

TABLE 2-1   The U.S. ASCII Code

Bit positions 5, 6, 7:

Bit positions 1, 2, 3 4:		000	100	010	110	001	101	011	111
		0	1	2	3	4	5	6	7
0000	0	NUL	DLE	SP	0	@	P	'	p
1000	1	SOH	DC1	!	1	A	Q	a	q
0100	2	STX	DC2	"	2	B	R	b	r
1100	3	ETX	DC3	#	3	C	S	c	s
0010	4	EOT	DC4	$	4	D	T	d	t
1010	5	ENQ	NAK	%	5	E	U	e	u
0110	6	ACK	SYN	&	6	F	V	f	v
1110	7	BEL	ETB	'	7	G	W	g	w
0001	8	BS	CAN	(	8	H	X	h	x
1001	9	HT	EM	)	9	I	Y	i	y
0101	10	LF	SUB	*	:	J	Z	j	z
1101	11	VT	ESC	+	;	K	[	k	{
0011	12	FF	FS	,	<	L	\	l	¦
1011	13	CR	GS	–	=	M	]	m	}
0111	14	SO	RS	.	>	N	^	n	~
1111	15	SI	US	/	?	O	–	o	DEL

This is the U.S. national version of CCITT alphabet number 5. The control characters are explained opposite.

TABLE 2-1 **(continued)**

FORMAT CONTROL

BS (Backspace): Indicates movement of the printing mechanism or display cursor backwards in one position.

HT (Horizontal Tab): Indicates movement of the printing mechanism or display cursor forward to the next preassigned "tab" or stopping position.

LF (Line Feed): Indicates movement of the printing mechanism or display cursor to the start of the next line.

VT (Vertical Tab): Indicates movement of the printing mechanism or display cursor to the next of a series of preassigned printing lines.

FF (Form Feed): Indicates movement of the printing mechanism or display cursor to the starting position of the next page, form, or screen.

CR (Carriage Return): Indicates movement of the printing mechanism or display cursor to the starting position of the same line.

TRANSMISSION CONTROL

SOH (Start of Heading): Used to indicate the start of a heading which may contain address or routing information.

STX (Start of Text): Used to indicate the start of the text and so also indicates the end of the heading.

ETX (End of Text): Used to terminate the text which was started with STX.

EOT (End of Transmission): Indicates the end of a transmission which may have included one or more "texts" with their headings.

ENQ (Enquiry): A request for a response from a remote station. It may be used as a "WHO ARE YOU?" request for a station to identify itself.

ACK (Acknowledge): A character transmitted by a receiving device as an affirmation response to a sender. It is used as a positive response to polling messages.

NAK (Negative Acknowledgment): A character transmitted by a receiving device as a negative response to a sender. It is used as a negative response to polling messages.

SYN (Synchronous/Idle): Used by a synchronous transmission system to achieve synchronization. When no data is being sent a synchronous transmission system may send SYN characters continuously.

ETB (End of Transmission Block): Indicates the end of a block of data for communication purposes. It is used for blocking data where the block structure is not necessarily related to the processing format.

INFORMATION SEPARATOR

FS (File Separator): Information separators
GS (Group Separator): to be used in an optional
RS (Record Separator): manner except that their
US (United Separator): hierarchy shall be FS (the most inclusive) to US (the least inclusive).

MISCELLANEOUS

NUL (Null): No character. Used for filling in time or filling space on tape when there is no data.

BEL (Bell): Used when there is need to call human attention. It may control alarm or attention devices.

SO (Shift Out): Indicates that the code combinations which follow shall be interpreted as *outside* of the standard character set until a SHIFT IN character is reached.

SI (Shift In): Indicates that the code combinations which follow shall be interpreted according to the standard character set.

DEL (Delete): Used to obliterate unwanted characters (for example, on paper tape by punching a hole in *every* bit position).

SP (Space): A nonprinting character used to separate words, or to move the printing mechanism or display cursor forward by one position.

DLE (Data Link Escape): A character which shall change the meaning of one or more contiguously following characters. It can provide supplementary controls, or permits the sending of data characters having any bit combination.

DC1, DC2, DC3 and DC4 (Device Controls): Characters for the control of ancillary devices or special terminal features.

CAN (Cancel): Indicates that the data which precedes it in a message or block should be disregarded (usually because an error has been detected).

EM (End of Medium): Indicates the physical end of a card, tape or other medium, or the end of the required or used portion of the medium.

SUB (Substitute): Substituted for a character that is found to be erroneous or invalid.

ESC (Escape): A character intended to provide code extension in that it gives a specified number of contiguously following characters an alternate meaning.

a medium gray level most of the way across with a blacker portion in the middle. Once the beam has completed a scan from left to right, it must retrace to the left edge to scan the next line. During this period, the picture should be blanked out (on both camera and receiver). This is done with a digital "horizontal blanking pulse." Also, to maintain transmitter-receiver synchronization, a synchronization (sync) pulse is sent between every line of video signal. This horizontal sync pulse rides on top of the blanking pulse, creating a staircase-shaped digital signal between adjacent analog video signals. Finally, when the beam reaches the bottom of the screen, it must return to the top, with a somewhat longer blanking interval required. This is shown in Figure 2-12b. The vertical blanking pulse is actually a series of synchronization and blanking pulses, whose details need not concern us here.

Next, consider the timing of the system. We mentioned that a total of 483 lines are scanned at a rate of 30 complete scans per second. This is an approximate number taking into account the time lost during the vertical retrace interval. The actual U.S. standard is 525 lines, but of these about 42 are lost during vertical retrace. Thus the horizontal scanning frequency is 525 lines $\div \frac{1}{30}$ s/scan = 15,750 lines per second, or 63.5 μs/line. Of this 63.5 μs, about 11 μs are allowed for horizontal retrace, leaving a total of 52.5 μs per video line.

Finally, we are in a position to estimate the bandwidth required for the video signal. To do this we must estimate the upper (maximum) and lower (minimum) frequency of the band. We use the following reasoning to arrive at the maximum frequency: The maximum frequency would occur during the horizontal scan if the scene were alternating between black and white as rapidly as possible. We can estimate this maximum value by considering the resolution of the video image. In the vertical dimension, there are 483 lines, so the maximum vertical resolution would be 483. Experiments have shown [CUNN80] that the actual subjective resolution is about 70% of that number, or about 338 lines. In the interest of a balanced picture, the horizontal and vertical resolutions should be about the same. Since the ratio of width to height of a TV screen is 4:3, the horizontal resolution should be about $\frac{4}{3} \times$ 338 = 450 lines. As a worst case, a scanning line would be made up of 450 elements alternating black and white. The scan would result in a wave with each cycle of the wave consisting of one higher (black) and one lower (white) voltage level. Thus there would be 450/2 = 225 cycles of the wave in 52.5 μs, for a maximum frequency of about 4 MHz. This rough reasoning, in fact, is fairly accurate. Thus the maximum frequency is 4 MHz. The lower limit will be a dc or zero frequency, where the dc component corresponds to the average illumination of the scene (the average value by which the signal exceeds the reference white level). Thus the bandwidth of the video signal is approximately 4 MHz − 0 = 4 MHz.

The foregoing discussion did not consider color or audio components of the signal. It turns out that, with these included, the bandwidth remains about 4 MHz.

Finally, the third example described above is the general case of binary digital data. A commonly used signal for such data uses two constant (dc) voltage levels, one level for binary 1 and one level for binary 0. (In Chapter 3, we shall see that this is but one alternative, referred to as NRZ.) Again, we are interested in the bandwidth of such a signal. This will depend, in any specific case, on the exact shape of the waveform, and the sequence of 1's and 0's. We can obtain some understanding by considering Figure 2-8 (compare Figure 2-5). As can be seen, the greater the bandwidth of the signal, the more faithfully it approximates a digital pulse stream.

Data and Signals.   In the foregoing discussion, we have looked at analog signals used to represent analog data and digital signals used to represent digital data. Generally, analog data are a function of time and occupy a limited frequency spectrum; such data can be represented by an electromagnetic signal occupying the same spectrum. Digital data can be represented by digital signals, with a different voltage level for each of the two binary digits.

As Figure 2-13 illustrates, these are not the only possibilities. Digital data can also be represented by analog signals by use of a *modem* (modulator/demodulator). The modem converts a series of binary (two-valued) voltage pulses into an analog signal by encoding the digital data onto a *carrier frequency*. The resulting signal occupies a certain spectrum of frequency centered about the carrier and may be propagated across a medium suitable for that carrier. The most common modems represent digital data in the voice spectrum and hence allow those data to be propagated over ordinary voice-grade telephone lines. At the other end of the line, the modem demodulates the signal to recover the original data.

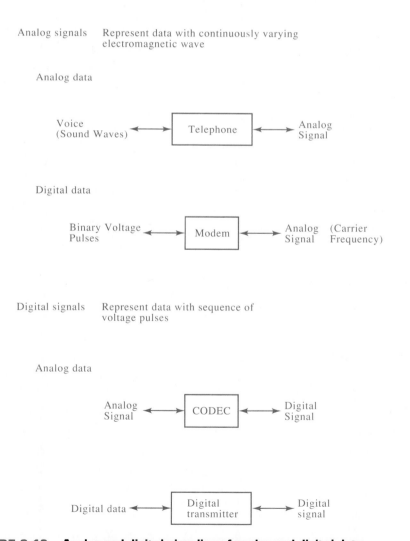

FIGURE 2-13.   Analog and digital signaling of analog and digital data.

In an operation very similar to that performed by a modem, analog data can be represented by digital signals. The device that performs this function for voice data is a *codec* (coder-decoder). In essence, the codec takes an analog signal that directly represents the voice data and approximates that signal by a bit stream. At the receiving end, the bit stream is used to reconstruct the analog data.

Thus Figure 2-13 suggests that data may be encoded into signals in a variety of ways. We will return to this topic in Chapter 3.

Transmission

A final distinction remains to be made. Both analog and digital signals may be transmitted on suitable transmission media. The way these signals are treated is a function of the transmission system. Table 2-2 summarizes the methods of data transmission. *Analog transmission* is a means of transmitting analog signals without regard to their content; the signals may represent analog data (e.g., voice) or digital data (e.g., binary data that pass through a modem). In either case, the analog signal will become weaker (attenuate) after a certain distance. To achieve longer distances, the analog transmission system includes amplifiers that boost the energy in the signal. Unfortunately, the amplifier also boosts the noise components. With amplifiers cascaded to achieve long distances, the signal becomes more and more distorted. For analog data, such as voice, quite a bit of distortion can be tolerated and the data remain intelligible. However, for digital data, cascaded amplifiers will introduce errors.

Digital transmission, in contrast, is concerned with the content of the signal. A digital signal can be transmitted only a limited distance before attenuation endangers the integrity of the data. To achieve greater distances, repeaters are used. A repeater receives the digital signal, recovers the pattern of 1's and 0's, and retransmits a new signal. Thus the attenuation is overcome.

The same technique may be used with an analog signal if it is assumed that the signal carries digital data. At appropriately spaced points, the transmission system

TABLE 2-2 Analog and Digital Transmission

	Analog Transmission	Digital Transmission
a. Treatment of Signals		
Analog signal	Is propagated through amplifiers; same treatment for both analog and digital data	Assumes digital data; at propagation points, data in signal are recovered, new analog signal is generated
Digital signal	Not used	Repeaters retransmit new signal; same treatment for both analog and digital data
b. Possible Combinations		
Analog data	Analog signal	Digital signal
Digital data	Analog signal	Digital signal Analog signal

has repeaters rather than amplifiers. The repeater recovers the digital data from the analog signal and generates a new, clean analog signal. Thus noise is not cumulative.

The question naturally arises as to which is the preferred method of transmission. The answer being supplied by the telecommunications industry and its customers is digital, this despite an enormous investment in analog communications facilities. Both long-haul telecommunications facilities and intrabuilding services are gradually being converted to digital transmission and, where possible, digital signaling techniques. The most important reasons:

- *Digital technology:* The advent of large-scale integration (LSI) and very large-scale integration (VLSI) technology has caused a continuing drop in the cost and size of digital circuitry. Analog equipment has not shown a similar drop.
- *Data integrity:* With the use of repeaters rather than amplifiers, the effects of noise and other signal impairments are not cumulative. Thus it is possible to transmit data longer distances and over lesser quality lines by digital means while maintaining the integrity of the data. This is explored in Section 2-3.
- *Capacity utilization:* It has become economical to build transmission links of very high bandwidth, including satellite channels and optical fiber. A high degree of multiplexing is needed to effectively utilize such capacity, and this is more easily and cheaply achieved with digital (time-division) rather than analog (frequency-division) techniques. This is explored in Chapter 6.
- *Security and privacy:* Encryption techniques can be readily applied to digital data and to analog data that have been digitized.
- *Integration:* By treating both analog and digital data digitally, all signals have the same form and can be treated similarly. Thus economies of scale and convenience can be achieved by integrating voice, video, and digital data.

2-3

TRANSMISSION IMPAIRMENTS

With any communications system, it must be recognized that the signal that is received will differ from the signal that is transmitted due to various transmission impairments. For analog signals, these impairments introduce various random modifications that degrade the signal quality. For digital signals, bit errors are introduced: A binary 1 is transformed into a binary 0 and vice versa. In this section, we examine the various impairments and comment on their effect on the information-carrying capacity of a communication link; the next chapter looks at measures that can be taken to compensate for these impairments.

The most significant impairments are:

- Attenuation and attenuation distortion.
- Delay distortion.
- Noise.

Attenuation

The strength of a signal falls off with distance over any transmission medium. For guided media, this reduction in strength, or attenuation, is generally logarithmic and thus is typically expressed as a constant number of decibels per unit distance. For unguided media, attenuation is a more complex function of distance and the makeup of the atmosphere. Attenuation introduces three considerations for the transmission engineer. First, a received signal must have sufficient strength so that the electronic circuitry in the receiver can detect and interpret the signal. Second, the signal must maintain a level sufficiently higher than noise to be received without error. Third, attenuation is an increasing function of frequency.

The first and second problems are dealt with by attention to signal strength and the use of amplifiers or repeaters. For a point-to-point link, the signal strength of the transmitter must be strong enough to be received intelligibly, but not so strong as to overload the circuitry of the transmitter, which would cause a distorted signal to be generated. Beyond a certain distance, the attenuation is unacceptably great, and repeaters or amplifiers are used to boost the signal from time to time. These problems are more complex for multipoint lines where the distance from transmitter to receiver is variable.

The third problem is particularly noticeable for analog signals. Because the attenuation varies as a function of frequency, the received signal is distorted, reducing intelligibility. To overcome this problem, techniques are available for equalizing attenuation across a band of frequencies. This is commonly done for voice-grade telephone lines by using loading coils that change the electrical properties of the line; the result is to smooth out attenuation effects. Another approach is to use amplifiers that amplify high frequencies more than lower frequencies.

An example is shown in Figure 2-14a which shows attenuation as a function of frequency for a typical leased line. In the figure, attenuation is measured relative to the attenuation at 1000 Hz. Positive values on the y axis represent attenuation greater than that at 1000 Hz. A 1000-Hz tone of a given power level is applied to the input, and the power, P_{1000}, is measured at the output. For any other frequency f, the procedure is repeated and the relative attenuation in decibels is

$$N_f = -10 \log_{10} \frac{P_f}{P_{1000}}$$

The solid line in Figure 2-14a shows attenuation without equalization. As can be seen, frequency components at the upper end of the voice band are attenuated much more than those at lower frequencies. It should be clear that this will result in a distortion of the received speech signal. The dashed line shows the effect of equalization. The flattened response curve improves the quality of voice signals. It also allows higher data rates to be used for digital data that are passed through a modem.

Attenuation distortion is much less of a problem with digital signals. As we have seen, the strength of a digital signal falls off rapidly with frequency (Figure 2-6b); most of the content is concentrated near the fundamental frequency or bit rate of the signal.

Delay Distortion

Delay distortion is a phenomenon peculiar to guided transmission media. The distortion is caused by the fact that the velocity of propagation of a signal through a guided medium varies with frequency. For a bandlimited signal, the velocity tends to be highest near the center frequency, and fall off toward the two edges of

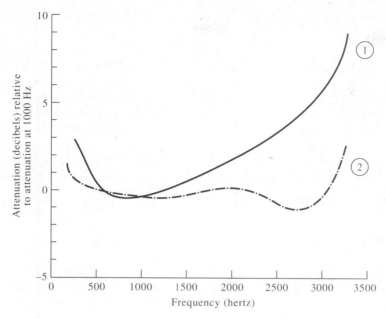

(a) Attenuation

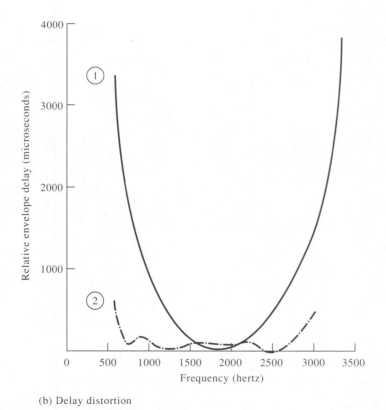

(b) Delay distortion

FIGURE 2-14.   Attenuation and delay distortion curves for a voice channel.

the band. Thus various frequency components of a signal will arrive at the receiver at different times.

This effect is referred to as delay distortion, since the received signal is distorted due to variable delay in its components. Delay distortion is particularly critical for digital data. Consider that a sequence of bits is being transmitted, using either analog or digital signals. Because of delay distortion, some of the signal components of one bit position will spill over into other bit positions, causing *intersymbol interference,* which is a major limitation to maximum bit rate over a transmission control.

Equalizing techniques can also be used for delay distortion. Again using a leased telephone line as an example, Figure 2-14b shows the effect of equalization on delay as a function of frequency.

Noise

For any data transmission event, the received signal will consist of the transmitted signal, modified by the various distortions imposed by the transmission system, plus additional unwanted signals that are inserted somewhere between transmission and reception. The latter, undesired signals are referred to as noise. It is noise that is the major limiting factor in communications system performance.

Noise may be divided into four categories [FREE81]:

- Thermal noise.
- Intermodulation noise.
- Crosstalk.
- Impulse noise.

Thermal noise is due to thermal agitation of electrons in a conductor. It is present in all electronic devices and transmission media and is a function of temperature. Thermal noise is uniformly distributed across the frequency spectrum and hence is often referred to as white noise. Thermal noise cannot be eliminated and therefore places an upper bound on communications system performance. The amount of thermal noise to be found in a bandwidth of 1 Hz in any device or conductor is

$$N_0 = kT$$

where

N_0 = noise power density, watts/hertz
k = Boltzmann's constant = 1.3803×10^{-23} J/°K
T = temperature, degrees Kelvin

The noise is assumed to be independent of frequency. Thus the thermal noise in watts present in a bandwidth of W hertz can be expressed as

$$N = kTW$$

or, in decibel-watts:

$$N = 10 \log k + 10 \log T + 10 \log W$$
$$N = -228.6 \text{ dbW} + 10 \log T + 10 \log W$$

When signals at different frequencies share the same transmission medium, the result may be *intermodulation noise.* The effect of intermodulation noise is to produce signals at a frequency which is the sum or difference of the two original frequencies or multiples of those frequencies. For example, the mixing of signals at frequencies f_1 and f_2 might produce energy at the frequency $f_1 + f_2$. This derived signal could interfere with an intended signal at the frequency $f_1 + f_2$.

Intermodulation noise is produced when there is some *nonlinearity* in the transmitter, receiver, or intervening transmission system. Normally, these components behave as linear systems; that is, the output is equal to the input times a constant. In a nonlinear system, the output is a more complex function of the input. Such nonlinearity can be caused by component malfunction or the use of excessive signal strength. It is under these circumstances that the sum and difference terms occur.

Crosstalk has been experienced by anyone who, while using the telephone, has been able to hear another conversation; it is an unwanted coupling between signal paths. It can occur by electrical coupling between nearby twisted pair or, rarely, coax cable lines carrying multiple signals. Crosstalk can also occur when unwanted signals are picked up by microwave antennas; although highly directional, microwave energy does spread during propagation. Typically, crosstalk is of the same order of magnitude as, or less than, thermal noise.

All of the types of noise discussed so far have reasonably predictable and reasonably constant magnitudes. Thus it is possible to engineer a transmission system to cope with them. *Impulse noise,* however, is noncontinuous, consisting of irregular pulses or noise spikes of short duration and of relatively high amplitude. It is generated from a variety of causes, including external electromagnetic disturbances, such as lightning, and faults and flaws in the communications system.

Impulse noise is generally only a minor annoyance for analog data. For example, voice transmission may be corrupted by short clicks and crackles with no loss of intelligibility. However, impulse noise is the primary source of error in digital data communication. For example, a sharp spike of energy of 0.01 s duration would not destroy any voice data, but would wash out about 50 bits of data being transmitted at 4800 bps. Figure 2-15 is an example of the effect on a digital signal. Here the noise consists of a relatively modest level of thermal noise plus occasional spikes of impulse noise. The digital data are recovered from the signal by sampling the received waveform once per bit time. As can be seen, the noise is occasionally sufficient to change a 1 to a 0 or a 0 to a 1.

Channel Capacity

We have seen that there are a variety of impairments that distort or corrupt a signal. For digital data, the question that then arises is to what extent these impairments limit the data rate that can be achieved. The rate at which data can be transmitted over a given communication path, or channel, under given conditions, is referred to as the *channel capacity*.

There are four concepts here that we are trying to relate to one another.

- *Data rate:* This is the rate, in bits per second (bps), at which data can be communicated.
- *Bandwidth:* This is the bandwidth of the transmitted signal as constrained by the transmitter and the nature of the transmission medium, expressed in cycles per second, or Hertz.
- *Noise:* The average level of noise over the communications path.
- *Error rate:* The rate at which errors occur, where an error is the reception of a 1 when a 0 was transmitted or the reception of a 0 when a 1 was transmitted.

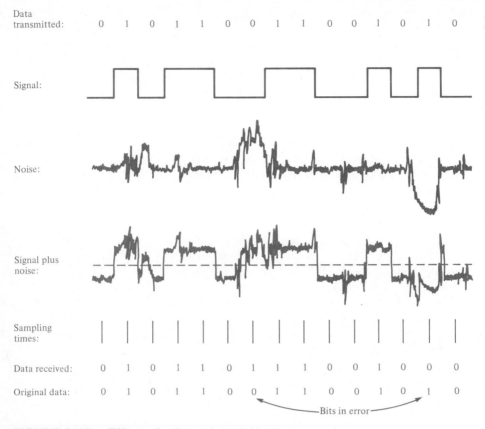

FIGURE 2-15.   Effect of noise on a digital signal.

The problem we are addressing is this: Communications facilities are expensive and, in general, the greater the bandwidth of a facility, the greater the cost. Furthermore, all transmission channels of any practical interest are of limited bandwidth. The limitations arise from the physical properties of the transmission medium or from deliberate limitations at the transmitter on the bandwidth to prevent interference from other sources. Accordingly, we would like to make as efficient use as possible of a given bandwidth. For digital data, this means that we would like to get as high a data rate as possible at a particular limit of error rate for a given bandwidth. The main constraint on achieving this efficiency is noise.

To begin, let us consider the case of a channel that is noise-free. In this environment, the limitation on data rate is simply the bandwidth of the signal. A formulation of this limitation, due to Nyquist, states that if the rate of signal transmission is 2W, then a signal with frequencies no greater than W is sufficient to carry the data rate. The converse is also true: Given a bandwidth of W, the highest signal rate that can be carried is 2W. This limitation is due to the effect of intersymbol interference [FREE80], such as is produced by delay distortion. The result is useful in the development of digital-to-analog encoding schemes and is derived in Appendix 3A.

Note that in the last paragraph, we referred to signal rate. If the signals to be transmitted are binary (two voltage levels), then the data rate that can be supported by W Hz is $2W$ bps. As an example, consider a voice channel being used, via modem, to transmit digital data. Assume a bandwidth of 3100 Hz. Then the capacity, C, of the channel is $2W = 6200$ bps. However, as we shall see in Chapter 3, signals with more than two levels can be used; that is, each signal element can represent more than one bit. For example, if four possible voltage levels are used as signals, then each signal element can represent two bits. With multilevel signaling, the Nyquist formulation becomes

$$C = 2W \log_2 M$$

where M is the number of discrete signal or voltage levels. Thus, for $M = 8$, a value used with some modems, C becomes 18,600 bps.

So, for a given bandwidth, the data rate can be increased by increasing the number of different signals. However, this places an increased burden on the receiver: Instead of distinguishing one of two possible signals during each signal time, it must distinguish one of M possible signals. Noise and other impairments on the transmission line will limit the practical value of M.

Thus, all other things being equal, doubling the bandwidth doubles the data rate. Now consider the relationship between data rate, noise, and error rate. This can be explained intuitively by again considering Figure 2-15. The presence of noise can corrupt one or more bits. If the data rate is increased, then the bits become ''shorter'' so that more bits are affected by a given pattern of noise. Thus, at a given noise level, the higher the data rate, the higher the error rate.

All of these concepts can be tied together neatly in a formula developed by the mathematician Claude Shannon. As we have just illustrated, the higher the data rate, the more damage that unwanted noise can do. For a given level of noise, we would expect that a greater signal strength would improve the ability to correctly receive data in the presence of noise. The key parameter involved in this reasoning is the signal-to-noise ratio (S/N), which is the ratio of the power in a signal to the power contained in the noise that is present at a particular point in the transmission. Typically, this ratio is measured at a receiver, since it is at this point that an attempt is made to process the signal and eliminate the unwanted noise. For convenience, this ratio is often reported in decibels:

$$(S/N)_{dB} = 10 \log \frac{\text{signal power}}{\text{noise power}}$$

This expresses the amount, in decibels, that the intended signal exceeds the noise level. A high S/N will mean a high-quality signal and a low number of required intermediate repeaters.

The signal-to-noise ratio is important in the transmission of digital data because it sets the upper bound on the achievable data rate. Shannon's result is that the maximum channel capacity, in bits per second, obeys the equation:

$$C = W \log_2 \left(1 + \frac{S}{N} \right)$$

where C is the capacity of the channel in bits per second and W is the bandwidth of the channel in Hertz. As an example, consider a voice channel being used, via modem, to transmit digital data. Assume a bandwidth of 3100 Hz. A typical value of S/N for a voice-grade line is 30 dB, or a ratio of 1000:1. Thus

$$C = 3100 \log_2(1 + 1000)$$
$$= 30,894 \text{ bps}$$

This represents the theoretical maximum that can be achieved. In practice, however, only much lower rates are achieved. One reason for this is that the formula assumes white noise (thermal noise). Impulse noise is not accounted for, nor are attenuation or delay distortion.

The capacity indicated in the preceding equation is referred to as the error-free capacity. Shannon proved that if the actual information rate on a channel is less than the error-free capacity, then it is theoretically possible to use a suitable signal code to achieve error-free transmission through the channel. Shannon's theorem unfortunately does not suggest a means for finding such codes, but it does provide a yardstick by which the performance of practical communication schemes may be measured.

The measure of efficiency of a digital transmission is the ratio of C/W, which is the bps per Hertz that is achieved. Figure 2-16 illustrates the theoretical efficiency of a transmission. It also shows the actual results obtained on a typical voice-grade line.

Several other observations concerning the above equation may be instructive. For a given level of noise, it would appear that the data rate could be increased by increasing either signal strength or bandwidth. However, as the signal strength increases, so do nonlinearities in the system, leading to an increase in intermodulation noise. Note also, that since noise is assumed to be white, the wider the bandwidth, the more noise is admitted to the system. Thus, as W increases, S/N decreases.

Finally, we mention a parameter related to S/N that is more convenient for determining digital data rates and error rates. The parameter is the ratio of signal energy per bit to noise power density per hertz, E_b/N_0. Consider a signal, digital or analog, that contains binary digital data transmitted at a certain bit rate R. Recalling that $1 \text{ w} = 1 \text{ J/s}$, the energy per bit in a signal is given by $E_b = ST_b$, where S is the signal power and T_b is the time required to send one bit. The data rate R is just $R = 1/T_b$. Thus

$$\frac{E_b}{N_0} = \frac{S/R}{N_0} = \frac{S}{kTR}$$

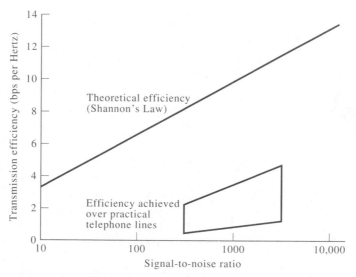

FIGURE 2-16.   Theoretical and actual transmission efficiency.

or, in decibel notation

$$\frac{E_b}{N_0} = S - 10 \log R + 228.6 \text{ dbW} - 10 \log T$$

The ratio E_b/N_0 is important because the bit error rate for digital data is a (decreasing) function of this ratio. Given a value of E_b/N_0 needed to achieve a desired error rate, the parameters in the formula above may be selected. Note that as the bit rate R increases, the transmitted signal power, relative to noise, must increase to maintain the required E_b/N_0.

Let us try to grasp this result intuitively by considering again Figure 2-15. The signal here is digital, but the reasoning would be the same for an analog signal. In several instances, the noise is sufficient to alter the value of a bit. Now, if the data rate were doubled, the bits would be more tightly packed together, and the same passage of noise might destroy two bits. Thus, for constant signal and noise strength, an increase in data rate increases the error rate.

EXAMPLE. For binary phase-shift keying (defined in Chapter 3), $E_b/N_0 = 8.4$ dB is required for a bit error rate of 10^{-4} (probability of error $= 10^{-4}$). If the effective noise temperature is 290°K (room temperature) and the data rate is 2400 bps, what received signal level is required?

We have

$$8.4 = S(\text{dbW}) - 10 \log 2400 + 228.6 \text{ dBW} - 10 \log 290$$

$$= S(\text{dBW}) - (10)(3.38) + 228.6 - (10)(2.46)$$

$$S = -161.8 \text{ dBW} \qquad \blacksquare$$

2-4

TRANSMISSION MEDIA

The transmission medium is the physical path between transmitter and receiver in a data transmission system. The characteristics and quality of data transmission are determined both by the nature of the signal and the nature of the medium. In the case of guided media, the medium itself is more important in determining the limitations of transmission. Table 2-3 contains typical characteristics for guided media, including the total data rate that the medium can support, the bandwidth the medium can transmit, and the required repeater spacing for digital transmission.

For unguided media, the spectrum or frequency band of the signal produced by the transmitting antenna is more important than the medium in determining trans-

TABLE 2-3 Point-to-Point Transmission Characteristics of Guided Media

Transmission Medium	Total Data Rate	Bandwidth	Repeater Spacing
Twisted pair	4 Mbps	250 kHz	2–10 km
Coaxial cable	500 Mbps	350 MHz	1–10 km
Optical fiber	2 Gbps	2 GHz	10–100 km

mission characteristics. As we have already mentioned, the higher the center frequency of a signal, the greater the potential bandwidth and hence data rate. Another property of signals transmitted by antenna is *directionality*. In general, at lower frequencies signals are omnidirectional; that is, the signal propagates in all directions from the antenna. At higher frequencies, it is possible to focus the signal into a directional beam.

Two general ranges of frequencies are of interest in this discussion. Microwave frequencies cover a range of about 2 to 40 GHz. At these frequencies, highly directional beams are possible, and microwave is quite suitable for point-to-point transmission. We will refer to signals in the range 30 MHz to 1 GHz as radio waves. Omnidirectional transmission is used and signals at these frequencies are suitable for broadcast applications.

The reader should also be aware of a finer subdivision of the electromagnetic spectrum defined by the International Telecommunications Union, and shown in Table 2-4. The table also summarizes key characteristics of each band. Microwave covers part of the UHF and all of the SHF bands, and radio covers the VHF and part of the UHF band. Note that this is a restricted use of the term ''radio'' that is appropriate for the concerns of this book.

Figure 2-17 depicts the electromagnetic spectrum and indicates the frequencies at which various guided media and unguided transmission techniques operate. In the remainder of this section we examine the three most important guided media—twisted pair, coaxial cable, and optical fiber—as well as the three most important unguided transmission techniques—terrestrial and satellite microwave, and radio. In all cases, we describe the systems physically, then briefly discuss applications, and finally look at transmission characteristics.

Twisted Pair

Physical Description.   A twisted pair consists of two insulated copper wires arranged in a regular spiral pattern. A wire pair acts as a single communication link. Typically, a number of these pairs are bundled together into a cable by wrapping them in a tough protective sheath. Over longer distances, cables may contain hundreds of pairs. The twisting of the individual pairs minimizes electromagnetic interference between the pairs. The wires in a pair have thicknesses of from 0.016 to 0.036 in.

Uses.   By far the most common transmission medium for both analog and digital data is twisted pair. It is the backbone of the telephone system as well as the workhorse for intrabuilding communications.

In the telephone system, individual telephone sets are connected to the local telephone exchange or ''end office'' by twisted-pair wire. These are referred to as ''local loops.'' Within an office building, telephone service is often provided by means of a private branch exchange (PBX). The PBX will be discussed in detail in Chapter 8. Essentially, it is an on-premise telephone exchange system that services a number of telephones within a building. It provides for intrabuilding calls via extension numbers and outside calls by trunk connection to the local end office. Within the building, the telephones are connected to the PBX via twisted pair. For both of the systems just described, twisted pair has primarily been a medium for voice traffic between subscribers and their local telephone exchange

TABLE 2-4 Characteristics of Unguided Communications Bands

Frequency Band	Name	Analog Data		Digital Data		Principal Applications
		Modulation	Bandwidth	Modulation	Data Rate	
30–300 kHz	LF (low frequency)	Generally not practical		ASK, FSK, MSK	0.1–100 bps	Navigation
300–3000 kHz	MF (medium frequency)	AM	To 4 kHz	ASK, FSK, MSK	10–1000 bps	Commercial AM radio
3–30 MHz	HF (high frequency)	AM, SSB	To 4 kHz	ASK, FSK, MSK	10–3000 bps	Shortwave radio CB radio
30–300 MHz	VHF (very high frequency)	AM, SSB; FM	5 kHz to 5 MHz	FSK, PSK	To 100 kbps	VHF television FM radio
300–3000 MHz	UHF (ultra high frequency)	FM, SSB	To 20 MHz	PSK	To 10 Mbps	UHF Television Terrestrial Microwave
3–30 GHz	SHF (super high frequency)	FM	To 500 MHz	PSK	To 100 Mbps	Terrestrial microwave Satellite microwave
30–300 GHz	EHF (extremely high frequency)	FM	To 1 GHz	PSK	To 750 Mbps	Experimental short point-to-point

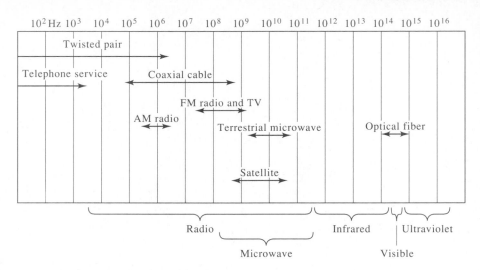

FIGURE 2-17. The electromagnetic spectrum.

office. Digital data traffic can also be carried over moderate distances. For modern digital PBX systems, data rates of about 64 kbps are achievable using digital signaling. Local loop connections typically require a modem, with a maximum data rate of 9600 bps. However, twisted pair is used for long-distance trunking applications and data rates of 4 Mbps or more may be achieved.

Twisted pair is also the medium of choice for a low-cost microcomputer local network within a building. This application is discussed in Chapter 11.

Transmission Characteristics.   Wire pairs may be used to transmit both analog and digital signals. For analog signals, amplifiers are required about every 5 to 6 km. For digital signals, repeaters are used every 2 or 3 km.

Compared to other transmission media, twisted pair is limited in distance, bandwidth, and data rate. Figure 2-18 shows that the attenuation for twisted pair is a very strong function of frequency [FREE85a]. Other impairments are also severe for twisted pair. The medium is quite susceptible to interference and noise because of its easy coupling with electromagnetic fields. For example, a wire run parallel to an ac power line will pick up 60-Hz energy. Impulse noise also easily intrudes into twisted pair.

Several measures are taken to reduce impairments [PICK83c]. Shielding the wire with metallic braid or sheathing reduces interference. The twisting of the wire reduces low-frequency interference, and the use of different twist lengths in adjacent pairs reduces crosstalk. Another technique is the use of a balanced transmission line. With an unbalanced line, one wire is at ground potential; with balanced transmission, both wires are above ground potential, carrying signals with equal amplitude but opposite phase.

For point-to-point analog signaling, a bandwidth of up to about 250 kHz is possible. For voice transmission, such as the local loop, the attenuation is about 1 dB/km over the voice frequency range. A common standard for telephone lines is a maximum loss of 6 dB; hence a 6 km section of line represents an upper limit on the distance that can be covered. For digital point-to-point lines, data rates of up to a few Mbps are possible. Figure 2-19 shows the achievable data rate versus

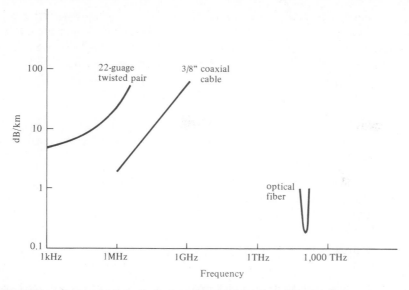

FIGURE 2-18.   Attenuation of typical guided transmission media.

distance for a common balanced electrical signaling technique, the EIA standard RS-422.

Coaxial Cable

Physical Description.   Coaxial cable, like twisted pair, consists of two conductors, but it is constructed differently to permit it to operate over a wider range

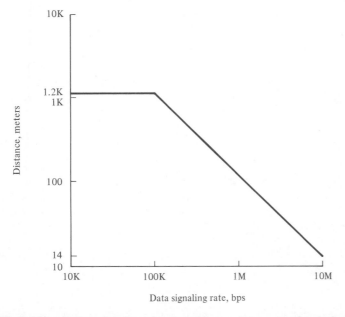

FIGURE 2-19.   Twisted-pair cable length vs. data rate for balanced transmission (RS-422).

of frequencies (Figure 2-20). It consists of a hollow outer cylindrical conductor which surrounds a single inner wire conductor. The inner conductor can be either solid or stranded; the outer conductor can be either solid or braided. The inner conductor is held in place by either regularly spaced insulating rings or a solid dialectric material. The outer conductor is covered with a jacket or shield. A single coaxial cable has a diameter of from 0.4 to about 1 in.

Uses.   Coaxial cable has been perhaps the most versatile transmission medium and is enjoying increasing utilization in a wide variety of applications. The most important of these are:

- Long-distance telephone and television transmission.
- Television distribution.
- Local area networks.
- Short-run system links.

Coaxial cable has been an important part of the long-distance telephone network, although it is being rapidly supplanted by optical fiber, microwave, and satellite. Using frequency-division multiplexing (FDM, see Chapter 6), a coaxial cable can carry over 10,000 voice channels simultaneously. Cable is also used for long-distance television transmission.

Coaxial cable is also spreading rapidly as a means of distributing TV signals to individual homes—cable TV. From its modest beginnings as Community Antenna Television (CATV), designed to provide service to remote areas, cable TV will eventually reach almost as many homes as the telephone. A CATV system can carry dozens of TV channels at ranges up to a few tens of miles.

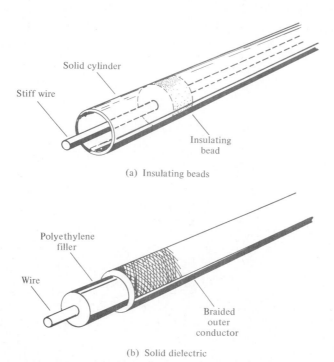

(a) Insulating beads

(b) Solid dielectric

FIGURE 2-20.   Coaxial cable construction.

An equally explosive growth area for coaxial cable is local area networks (Chapter 11). It is the medium of choice for many local network systems. Coaxial cable can support a large number of devices with a variety of data and traffic types, over distances that encompass a single building or a complex of buildings.

Finally, coaxial cable is commonly used for short-range connections between devices. Using analog signaling, coaxial cable is used to transmit radio or TV signals. With digital signaling, coaxial cable can be used to provide high-speed I/O channels on computer systems.

Transmission Characteristics. Coaxial cable is used to transmit both analog and digital signals. Long-distance systems may be either analog or digital. CATV is analog, and both analog and digital techniques have been used for local networks.

As can be seen from Figure 2-18, coaxial cable has superior frequency characteristics to twisted pair, and can hence be used effectively at higher frequencies and data rates. Because of its shielded, concentric construction, coaxial cable is much less susceptible to interference and crosstalk than twisted pair. The principal constraints on performance are attenuation, thermal noise, and intermodulation noise. The latter is present only when several channels (FDM) or frequency bandwidths are in use on the cable.

Figure 2-21 is an instructive look at the engineering constraints faced in transmission systems. To achieve proper signal quality, a certain signal-to-noise (S/N) ratio must be maintained on the cable. The engineer has two variables to play with: signal power and amplifier spacing. The S/N can be raised by spacing amplifiers closely to boost the signal frequently. However, it is desirable to maximize amplifier spacing to reduce cost and because amplifiers introduce nonlinearities. S/N can be increased, of course, by boosting S. This will work, however, only in a region of operation where the dominant noise source is thermal noise, which is relatively constant independent of the signal. When a number of signals in adjacent bandwidths are being carried on the cable, intermodulation noise increases as signal power increases. This phenomenon is seen clearly in Figure 2-21. Figure 2-21b is derived from 2-21a, and shows that, as the spacing between amplifiers increases, the maximum attainable S/N declines and, further, that increasing signal power is required to achieve the maximum.

For long-distance transmission of analog signals, amplifiers are needed every few kilometers, with closer spacing required if higher frequencies are used. The usable spectrum for analog signaling extends to about 400 MHz. For digital signaling, repeaters are needed every kilometer or so, with closer spacing needed for higher data rates. On experimental systems, data rates as high as 800 Mbps have been achieved with a repeater spacing of 1.6 km [KASA83].

Optical Fiber

Physical Description. An optical fiber is a thin (2 to 125 μm), flexible medium capable of conducting an optical ray. Various glasses and plastics can be used to make optical fibers [JORD85]. The lowest losses have been obtained using fibers of ultrapure fused silica. Ultrapure fiber is difficult to manufacture; higher-loss multicomponent glass fibers are more economical and still provide good performance. Plastic fiber is even less costly and can be used for short-haul links, for which moderately high losses are acceptable.

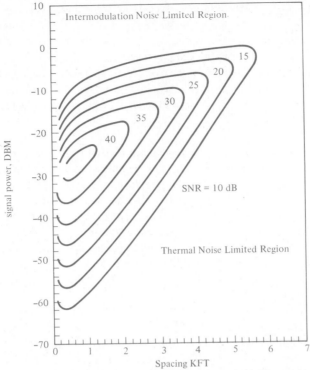

(a) Dependence of T1 SNR on signal power and amplifier spacing
for systems using 0.375–in cables. The bandwidth occupied by each
channel is 1.5 MHz. System length is 20 mi.

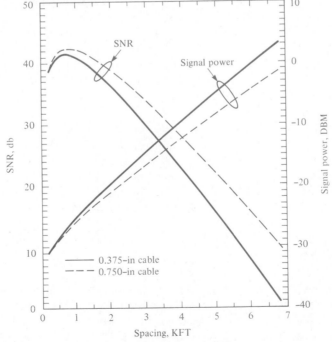

(b) Maximum attainable SNR and the corresponding signal power.
as a function of spacing. The bandwidth for each channel is 1.5 MHz.

FIGURE 2-21.   **Dependence of S/N on signal power and amplifier spacing for
coaxial cable.**

An optical fiber cable has a cylindrical shape and consists of three concentric sections: the core, the cladding, and the jacket. The *core* is the innermost section, and consists of one or more very thin strands, or fibers, made of glass or plastic. Each fiber is surrounded by its own *cladding,* a glass or plastic coating that has optical properties different from those of the core. The outermost layer, surrounding one or a bundle of cladded fibers, is the *jacket*. The jacket is composed of plastic and other materials layered to protect against moisture, abrasion, crushing, and other environmental dangers.

Uses. One of the most significant technological breakthroughs in data transmission has been the development of practical fiber optic communications systems. The following characteristics distinguish optical fiber from twisted pair and coaxial cable.

- *Greater bandwidth:* The potential bandwidth, and hence data rate, of a medium increases with frequency. At the immense frequencies of optical fiber, data rates of 2 Gbps over tens of kilometers have been demonstrated. Compare this to the practical maximum of hundreds of Mbps over about 1 km for coaxial cable and just a few Mbps over 1 km for twisted pair.
- *Smaller size and lighter weight:* Optical fibers are considerably thinner than coaxial cable or bundled twisted-pair cable—at least an order of magnitude thinner for comparable information transmission capacity. For cramped conduits in buildings and underground along public rights-of-way, the advantage of small size is considerable. The corresponding reduction in weight reduces structural support requirements.
- *Lower attenuation:* Attenuation is significantly lower for optical fiber than for coaxial cable or twisted pair (Figure 2-18), and is constant over a wide range.
- *Electromagnetic isolation:* Optical fiber systems are not affected by external electromagnetic fields. Thus the system is not vulnerable to interference, impulse noise, or crosstalk. By the same token, fibers do not radiate energy, causing little interference with other equipment and providing a high degree of security from eavesdropping. In addition, fiber is inherently difficult to tap.
- *Greater repeater spacing:* Fewer repeaters means lower cost and fewer sources of error. The performance of optical fiber systems from this point of view has been steadily improving. For example, Standard Elektrik Lorenz AG in Germany has developed a fiber transmission system that achieves a data rate of 5 Gbps over a distance of 111 km [ANON88] without repeaters. Coaxial and twisted-pair systems generally have repeaters every few kilometers.

Five basic categories of application have become important for optical fiber:

- Long-haul trunks.
- Metropolitan trunks.
- Rural exchange trunks.
- Local loops.
- Local area networks.

Long-haul fiber transmission is becoming increasingly common in the telephone network. Long-haul routes average about 900 miles in length and offer high capacity (typically 20,000 to 60,000 voice channels). These systems compete economically with microwave and have so underpriced coaxial cable in many developed countries that coaxial cable is rapidly being phased out of the telephone network in such countries. US Sprint, one of the major long-distance telephone communications providers, was the first to use optical fiber for 100 percent of its traffic, and the percentage of traffic carried by fiber is increasing steadily for all other U.S carriers.

Metropolitan trunking circuits have an average length of 7.8 miles and may have as many as 100,000 voice channels in a trunk group. Most facilities are installed in underground conduits and are repeaterless, joining telephone exchanges in a metropolitan or city area. Included in this category are routes that link long-haul microwave facilities that terminate at a city perimeter to the main telephone exchange building downtown.

Rural exchange trunks have circuit lengths ranging from 25 to 100 miles and link towns and villages. In the United States, they often connect the exchanges of different telephone companies. Most of these systems have fewer than 5000 voice channels. The technology used in these applications competes with microwave facilities.

Local loop circuits are fibers that run directly from the central exchange to a subscriber. These facilities are beginning to displace twisted pair and coaxial cable links as the telephone networks evolve into full-service networks capable of handling not only voice and data, but also image and video. The initial penetration of optical fiber in this application is for the business subscriber, but fiber transmission into the home will soon begin to appear [SHUM89].

A final important application of optical fiber is for local area networks. Recently, standards have been developed and products introduced for optical fiber networks that have a total capacity of 100 Mbps and can support hundreds or even thousands of stations in a large office building or a complex of buildings [MIER89].

The advantages of optical fiber over twisted pair and coaxial cable become more compelling as the demand for all types of information (voice, data, image, video) increases. By the end of the century, fiber will be the dominant medium for virtually all fixed-location applications [COCH88].

Transmission Characteristics.   Optical fiber transmits a signal-encoded beam of light by means of total internal reflection. Total internal reflection can occur in any transparent medium that has a higher index of refraction than the surrounding medium. In effect, the optical fiber acts as a waveguide for frequencies in the range 10^{14} to 10^{15} Hz, which covers the visible spectrum and part of the infrared spectrum.

Figure 2-22a shows the principle of optical fiber transmission. Light from a source enters the cylindrical glass or plastic core. Rays at shallow angles are reflected and propagated along the fiber; other rays are absorbed by the surrounding material. This form of propagation is called multimode, referring to the variety of angles that will reflect. When a fiber core radius is reduced, fewer angles will reflect. By reducing the radius of the core to the order of a wavelength, only a single angle or mode can pass: the axial ray. This single-mode propagation provides superior performance for the following reason. With multimode transmission, multiple propagation paths exist, each with a different path length and hence time to traverse the fiber. This causes signal elements to spread out in time and limits the rate at which data can be accurately received. Since there is a single transmission path with single-mode transmission, such distortion cannot occur. Finally, by varying the index of refraction of the core, a third type of transmission, known as multimode graded index, is possible. This type is intermediate between the other

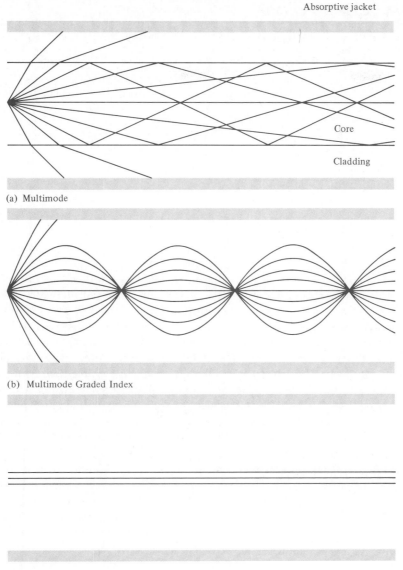

(a) Multimode

(b) Multimode Graded Index

(c) Single mode

FIGURE 2-22. Optical fiber transmission modes.

two in characteristics. The variable refraction has the effect of focusing the rays more efficiently than ordinary multimode, also known as multimode step index. Table 2-5 compares the three fiber transmission modes.

Two different types of light source are used in fiber optic systems: the *light-emitting diode* (LED) and the *injection laser diode* (ILD) [WERN86]. Both are semiconductor devices that emit a beam of light when a voltage is applied. The LED is less costly, operates over a greater temperature range, and has a longer operational life. The ILD is more efficient and can sustain greater data rates.

The detector used at the receiving end to convert the light into electrical energy is a *photodiode* [FORR86]. Two solid-state devices have been used: the PIN de-

TABLE 2-5   Comparison of Three Types of Optical Fiber

Light Source	LED or laser	LED or laser	Laser
Bandwidth	20 MHz/km	>1 GHz/km	up to 1000 GHz/km
Splicing	Difficult	Difficult	Difficult
Typical Application	Computer data links, local area networks	Moderate-length telephone lines	Long-distance telecommunication lines
Cost	Least expensive	More expensive	Most expensive
Core Diameter (μm)	>80 μm	50–60 μm	1.5–5 μm
Cladding Diameter (μm)	>160 μm	100–120 μm	15–50 μm
Attenuation (dB/km)	0.5–2.0	0.5–2.0	0.15

Source: [BASC87]

tector and the APD detector. The PIN photodiode has a segment of intrinsic (I) silicon between the P and N layers of a diode. The APD, avalanche photodiode, is similar in appearance but uses a stronger electric field. Both devices are basically photon counters. The PIN is less expensive and less sensitive than the APD.

There is a relationship among the wavelength employed, the type of transmission, and the achievable data rate [MIER86]. Both single mode and multimode can support several different wavelengths of light and can employ laser or LED light sources. In optical fiber, light propagates best in three distinct wavelength "windows," centered on 850, 1300, and 1500 nanometers (nm). These are all in the infrared portion of the frequency spectrum, below the visible-light portion, which is 400 to 700 nm. Most local applications today use 850-nm LED light sources. Although this combination is relatively inexpensive, it is generally limited to data rates under 100 Mbps and distances of a few kilometers. To achieve higher data rates and longer distances, a 1300-nm LED or laser source is needed. The highest data rates and longest distances require 1500-nm laser sources.

The amplitude-shift keying technique is commonly used to transmit digital data over optical fiber; in this context, it is known as *intensity modulation*. For LED transmitters, binary one is represented by a short pulse of light and binary zero by the absence of light. Laser transmitters normally have a fixed "bias" current that causes the device to emit a low light level. This low level represents binary zero, while a higher-amplitude lightwave represents binary one.

Terrestrial Microwave

Physical Description.   The most common type of microwave antenna is the parabolic "dish." A typical size is about 10 ft in diameter. The antenna is fixed rigidly and focuses a narrow beam to achieve line-of-sight transmission to the receiving antenna. Microwave antennas are usually located at substantial heights above ground level in order to extend the range between antennas and to be able to transmit over intervening obstacles. With no intervening obstacles, the maximum distance between antennas conforms to

$$d = 7.14 \sqrt{Kh} \qquad (2\text{-}1)$$

where d is the distance between antennas in kilometers, h is the antenna height in meters, and K is an adjustment factor to account for the fact that microwaves are bent or refracted with the curvature of the earth and will hence propagate farther than the optical line of sight. A good rule of thumb is $K = \frac{4}{3}$ [FREE80]. So, for example, two microwave antennas at a height of 100 m may be as far as $7.14 \times \sqrt{133} = 82$ km apart. To achieve long-distance transmission, a series of microwave relay towers is used, and point-to-point microwave links are strung together over the desired distance.

Uses. The primary use for terrestrial microwave systems is in long-haul telecommunications service, as an alternative to coaxial cable for transmitting television and voice. Like coaxial cable, microwave can support high data rates over long distances. The microwave facility requires far fewer amplifiers or repeaters than coaxial cable for the same distance, but requires line-of-sight transmission. Microwave is commonly used for both voice and television transmission.

Another increasingly common use of microwave is for short point-to-point links between buildings [RUSH82]. This can be used for closed-circuit TV or as a data link between local networks.

Finally, a potential use for terrestrial microwave is for providing digital data transmission in small regions (radius <10 km). This concept has been termed ''local data distribution'' and would provide an alternative to phone lines for digital networking [ROCH79].

Transmission Characteristics. As Table 2-4 indicates, microwave transmission covers a substantial portion of the spectrum. Common frequencies used for transmission are in the range 2 to 40 GHz. The higher the frequency used, the higher the potential bandwidth and therefore the higher the potential data rate. Table 2-6 indicates bandwidth and data rate for some typical systems.

As with any transmission system, a main source of loss for microwave is attenuation. For microwave (and radio frequency), the loss can be expressed as

$$L = 10 \log \left(\frac{4\pi d}{\lambda}\right)^2 \text{ dB} \qquad (2\text{-}2)$$

where d is the distance and λ is the wavelength, in the same units. Thus loss varies as the square of the distance. This is in contrast to twisted pair and coaxial cable where the loss varies logarithmically with distance (linear in decibels). Thus repeaters or amplifiers may be placed farther apart for microwave systems—10 to 100 km is typical. Attenuation is increased with rainfall. The effects become noticeable above 10 GHz.

Another source of impairment for microwave is interference. With the growing popularity of microwave, transmission areas overlap and interference is always a danger. Thus the assignment of frequency bands is strictly regulated.

TABLE 2-6 Typical Digital Microwave Performance

Band (GHz)	Bandwidth (MHz)	Data Rate (Mbps)
2	7	12
6	30	90
11	40	90
18	220	274

Source: [PICK83a].

Table 2-7 shows the authorized microwave frequency bands as regulated by the FCC. The most common bands for common carrier long-haul communications are the 4-GHz and 6-GHz bands. With increasing congestion at these frequencies, the 11-GHz band is now coming into use. The 12-GHz band is used as a component of the cable TV system [CUNN80]. Microwave links are used to provide TV signals to local CATV installations; the signals are then distributed to individual subscribers via coaxial cable. The FCC has reserved the 10-GHz band for local data distribution, called the Digital Termination Service. Finally, we mention that higher-frequency microwave is being used for short point-to-point links between buildings [RUSH82]. Typically, the 22-GHz band is used. The higher microwave frequencies are less useful for longer distance because of increased attenuation, but are quite adequate for shorter distances. In addition, at the higher frequencies, antennas are smaller and cheaper.

Satellite Microwave

Physical Description.   A communication satellite is, in effect, a microwave relay station. It is used to link two or more ground-based microwave transmitter/

TABLE 2-7   Principal Microwave Bands Authorized for Fixed Telecommunications in the United States (1979)

Band Name	Range (GHz)	Maximum Channel Bandwidth (MHz)	Necessary Spectral Efficiency (bits/Hz)	Type of Service
2 GHz	1.71 – 1.85	—		Federal government
2 GHz	1.85 – 1.99	8		Private; local government
2 GHz	2.11 – 2.13	3.5	2	Common carrier (shared)
2 GHz	2.13 – 2.15	0.8/1.6		Private; local government
2 GHz	2.15 – 2.16	10		Private; multipoint
2 GHz	2.16 – 2.18	3.5	2	Common carrier
2 GHz	2.18 – 2.20	0.8/1.6		Private; local government
2 GHz	2.20 – 2.29	—		Federal government
2 GHz	2.45 – 2.50	0.8		Private; local government (shared)
4 GHz	3.70 – 4.20	20	4.5	Common carrier; satellite
6 GHz	5.925– 6.425	30	3	Common carrier; satellite
6 GHz	6.525– 6.875	5/10		Private; shared
7–8 GHz	7.125– 8.40	—		Federal government
10 GHz	10.550–10.680	25		Private
11 GHz	10.7 –11.7	50	2.25	Common carrier
12 GHz	12.2 –12.7	10/20		Private; local government
13 GHz	13.2 –13.25	25		Common carrier; private
14 GHz	14.4 –15.25	—		Federal government
18 GHz	17.7 –19.7	220		Common carrier; shared
18 GHz	18.36 –19.04	50/100		Private; local government
22 GHz	21.2 –23.6	50/100		Private; common carrier
31 GHz	31.0 –31.2	50/100		Private; common carrier
38 GHz	36.0 –38.6	—		Federal government
40 GHz	38.6 –40.0	50		Private; common carrier
	Above 40.0	—		Developmental

receivers, known as earth stations or ground stations. The satellite receives transmissions on one frequency band (uplink), amplifies (analog transmission) or repeats (digital transmission) the signal, and transmits it on another frequency (downlink). A single orbiting satellite will operate on a number of frequency bands, called *transponder channels*, or simply *transponders*.

Figure 2-23 depicts in a general way two common uses of communications satellites. In the first, the satellite is being used to provide a point-to-point link between two distant ground-based antennas. In the second, the satellite provides communication between one ground-based transmitter and a number of ground-based receivers. In fact, these depictions are only suggestive of the ways in which satellites are used, a subject that we explore in Chapter 10.

For a communication satellite to function effectively, it is generally required that it remain stationary with respect to its position over the earth. Otherwise, it would

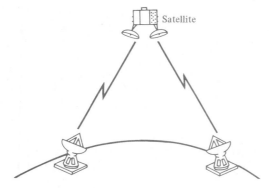

(a) Point–to–point link via satellite microwave

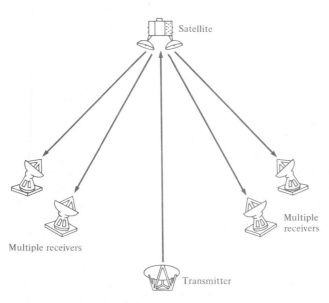

(b) Broadcast link via satellite microwave

FIGURE 2-23. Satellite communications configurations.

not be within the line of sight of its earth stations at all times. To remain stationary, the satellite must have a period of rotation equal to the earth's period of rotation. This match occurs at a height of 35,784 km.

Two satellites using the same frequency band, if close enough together, will interfere with each other. To avoid this, current standards require a 4° spacing (angular displacement as measured from the earth) in the 4/6-GHz band, and a 3° spacing at 12/14 GHz. Thus, the number of possible satellites is quite limited.

Uses.   The communication satellite is a technological revolution as important as fiber optics [PRIT84, CROC89]. Among the most important applications for satellites are:

- Television distribution.
- Long-distance telephone transmission.
- Private business networks.

Because of their broadcast nature, satellites are well suited to television distribution and are being used extensively in the United States and throughout the world for this purpose. In its traditional use, a network provides programming from a central location. Programs are transmitted to the satellite and then broadcast down to a number of stations, which then distribute the programs to individual viewers. One network, the Public Broadcasting Service (PBS), distributes its television programming almost exclusively by the use of satellite channels. Other commercial networks also make substantial use of satellite, and cable television systems are receiving an ever-increasing proportion of their programming from satellites. The most recent application of satellite technology to television distribution is direct broadcast satellite (DBS), in which satellite video signals are transmitted directly to the home user. The dropping cost and size of receiving antennas have made DBS economically feasible, and a number of channels are either already in service or in the planning stage.

Satellite transmission is also used for point-to-point trunks between telephone exchange offices in public telephone networks. It is the optimum medium for high-usage international trunks and is competitive with terrestrial systems for many long-distance international links.

Finally, there are a number of business data applications for satellite. The satellite provider can divide the total capacity into a number of channels and lease these channels to individual business users. A user equipped with the antennas at a number of sites can use a satellite channel for a private network. Traditionally, such applications have been quite expensive and limited to larger organizations with high-volume requirements. A recent development is the very small aperture terminal (VSAT) system, which provides a low-cost alternative [FINN89, SHAR89]. Figure 2-24 depicts a typical VSAT configuration. A number of subscriber stations are equipped with low-cost VSAT antennas (about $400 per month per VSAT). Using some discipline, these stations share a satellite transmission capacity for transmission to a hub station. The hub station can exchange messages with each of the subscribers and can relay messages between subscribers.

Transmission Characteristics.   The optimum frequency range for satellite transmission is in the range 1 to 10 GHz [SHAR87]. Below 1 GHz, there is significant noise from natural sources, including galactic, solar, and atmospheric

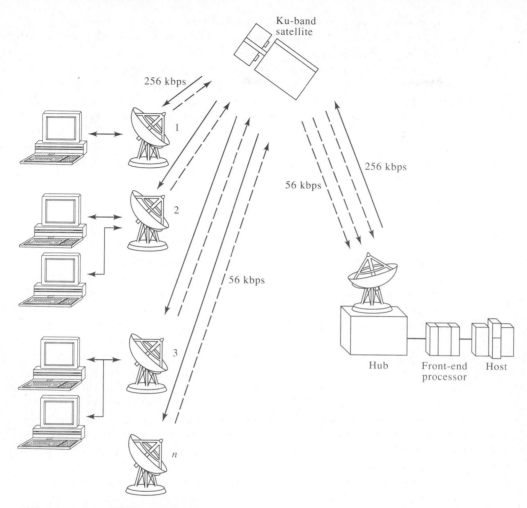

FIGURE 2-24. VSAT configuration.

noise, and human-made interference from various electronic devices. Above 10 GHz, the signal is severely attenuated by atmospheric absorption and precipitation.

Most satellites providing point-to-point service today use a frequency bandwidth in the range 5.925 to 6.425 GHz for transmission from earth to satellite (uplink) and a bandwidth in the range 3.7 to 4.2 GHz for transmission from satellite to earth (downlink). This combination is referred to as the 4/6 GHz band, or C band. Note that the uplink and downlink frequencies differ. For continuous operation without interference, a satellite cannot transmit and receive on the same frequency. Thus signals received from a ground station on one frequency must be transmitted back on another.

The C band is within the optimum zone of 1 to 10 GHz but has become saturated. Other frequencies in that range are unavailable because of sources of interference operating at those frequencies, usually terrestrial microwave. Therefore, the 12/14 GHz band, or Ku band, has been developed (uplink: 14 to 14.5 GHz; downlink: 11.7 to 12.2 GHz). At this frequency band, attenuation problems must be overcome. Thus, relative to C band, the Ku band systems require higher uplink and downlink radiated power and greater transponder receiver sensitivity. However, smaller and cheaper earth-station receivers can be used. Ku band is particularly well-suited for VSAT applications, although C band is also used for this purpose.

A new development is the use of the satellite for mobile communications. For this purpose, small, low-cost transmitter/receiver devices are used, and transmission is full-duplex directly between the users and the satellite. The service offered is similar to cellular radio, except that the coverage is nationwide. To enable this service, the Federal Communications has recently allocated a portion of the microwave frequency band, known as the L band, for mobile satellite service [CAST88]. The frequencies involved are 1.6465 GHz to 1.66 GHz uplink and 1.545 GHz to 1.5585 GHz downlink.

Several peculiar properties of satellite communications should be noted. First, because of the long distance involved, there is a propagation delay of about 240 to 300 ms from transmission from one earth station to reception by another earth station. This delay is noticeable in ordinary telephone conversations. It also introduces problems in the areas of error control and flow control, which we discuss in later chapters. Second, satellite microwave is inherently a broadcast medium. Many stations can transmit to the satellite, and a transmission from a satellite can be received by many stations.

Radio

Physical Description.   The principal difference between radio and microwave is that radio is omnidirectional and microwave is focused. Thus radio does not require dish-shaped antennas, and the antennas need not be rigidly mounted to a precise alignment.

Uses.   Radio is a general term sometimes used to encompass all the frequency bands of Table 2-4. We use it in a more restricted sense to cover the VHF and part of the UHF band: 30 MHz to 1 GHz. This range covers FM radio and UHF and VHF television. In addition to these traditional uses, new applications have grown up in this band, and we mention several of these briefly.

A well-known use of radio for digital data communications is packet radio, which is discussed in Chapter 10. A packet radio system uses ground-based antennas to link multiple sites in a data transmission network.

Transmission Characteristics.   The range 30 MHz to 1 GHz is a very effective one for broadcast communications. Unlike the case for lower-frequency electromagnetic waves, the ionosphere is transparent to radio waves above 30 MHz. Thus transmission is limited to the line of sight and distant transmitters will not interfere with each other due to reflection from the atmosphere. Unlike the higher frequencies of the microwave region, radio waves are less sensitive to attenuation from rainfall. For digital data communications, the primary drawback of this frequency range is that lower data rates are achievable: in the kilobit rather than the megabit range.

As a line-of-sight propagation technique, radio obeys Equation (2-1); that is, the maximum distance between transmitter and receiver is slightly more than the optical line of sight, or $7.14\sqrt{Kh}$. As with microwave, the amount of attenuation due simply to distance obeys Equation (2-2), namely $10 \log \left(\dfrac{4\pi d}{\lambda}\right)^2$ dB. Because of the longer wavelength, radio waves suffer relatively less attenuation.

A prime source of impairment for radio waves is multipath interference. Reflection from land, water, and natural or human-made objects can create multiple paths between antennas. This effect is frequently evident when TV reception displays multiple images as a plane passes by.

The transmission characteristics of radio used for broadcast communications are straightforward. The first such system was the ALOHA system in Hawaii [ABRA70]. Two frequency bands were used, one at 407.35 MHz for transmitting from users' terminals to a central controller and one at 413.475 MHz for transmission in the opposite direction; the bandwidth on both channels was 100kHz, with the data rate of 9600 bps. Transmission is in the form of short bursts of data called packets. The point-to-point range is about 30 km; repeaters were used to extend the system to a radius of about 500 km. A similar system is in operation in Montreal [ROUL81] using frequencies in the 220-MHz range. A system with mobile stations has been developed by the Printer Terminal Corp. [FORB81] using frequencies between 450 and 510 MHz.

2-5

RECOMMENDED READING

There are a large number of books on data transmission for the reader to choose from. [FREE89] provides readable and thorough coverage of all the topics in this chapter. [BELL82a] is a more difficult treatment, recommended for those with an electrical engineering background. Descriptive coverage can be found in [CHOU88] and [MART88]. A mathematical treatment of signal transmission is provided in [COUC87]. A detailed study of Fourier analysis can be found in [ZIEM83].

2-6

PROBLEMS

2-1 a. For the multipoint configuration of Figure 2-1, only one device at a time can transmit. Why?

b. There are two methods of enforcing the rule that only one device can transmit. In the centralized method, one station is in control and can either transmit or allow a specified other station to transmit. In the decentralized method, the stations jointly cooperate in taking turns. What do you see as the advantages and disadvantages of the two methods?

2-2 Figure 2-6b shows the frequency domain function for a single square pulse. The single pulse could represent a digital 1 in a communication system. Note that an infinite number of higher frequencies of decreasing magnitudes are needed to represent the single pulse. What implication does that have for a real digital transmission system?

2-3   Suppose that data are stored on 800 kbyte floppy diskettes that weigh 1 oz each. Suppose that a Boeing 747 carries 10 tons of these floppies at a speed of 7600 mph over a distance of 3000 miles. What is the data transmission rate in bits per second of this system?

2-4   ASCII is a 7-bit code that allows 128 characters to be defined. In the 1970s, many newspapers received stories from the wire services in a 6-bit code called TTS. This code carried upper and lower case characters as well as many special characters and formatting commands. The typical TTS character set allowed over 100 characters to be defined. How do you think this could be accomplished?

2-5   Figure 2-12 indicates that the vertical blanking pulse has a duration of 830 to 1330 μs. What is the total number of visible lines for each of these two figures?

2-6   For a video signal, what increase in horizontal resolution is possible if a bandwidth of 5 MHz is used? What increase in vertical resolution is possible? Treat the two questions separately; that is, the increased bandwidth is to be used to increase either horizontal or vertical resolution, but not both.

2-7   a. Suppose that a digitized TV picture is to be transmitted from a source that uses a matrix of 480×500 picture elements (pixels), where each pixel can take on one of 32 intensity values. Assume that 30 pictures are sent per second. (This digital source is roughly equivalent to broadcast TV standards that have been adopted.) Find the source rate R (bps).
        b. Assume that the TV picture is to be transmitted over a channel with 4.5-MHz bandwidth and a 35-dB signal-to-noise ratio. Find the capacity of the channel (bps).
        c. Discuss how the parameters given in part (a) could be modified to allow transmission of color TV signals without increasing the required value for R.

2-8   Figure 2-5 shows the effect of eliminating higher-harmonic components of a square wave and retaining only a few lower harmonic components. What would the signal look like in the opposite case; that is, retaining all higher harmonics and eliminating a few lower harmonics?

2-9   What is the channel capacity for a teleprinter channel with a 300-Hz bandwidth and a signal-to-noise ratio of 3 dB?

2-10   A digital signaling system is required to operate at 9600 bps.
        a. If a signal element encodes a 4-bit word, what is the minimum required bandwidth of the channel?
        b. Repeat part (a) for the case of 8-bit words.

2-11   What is the thermal noise level of a channel with a bandwidth of 10 kHz carrying 1000 watts of power operating at 50° C?

2-12   Study the works of Shannon and Nyquist on channel capacity. Each places an upper limit on the bit rate of a channel based on two different approaches. How are the two related?

2-13   Given a channel with an intended capacity of 20 Mbps. The bandwidth of the channel is 3 MHz. What signal to noise ratio is required in order to achieve this capacity?

2-14   Explain the logical flaw in the following argument.
According to Table 2-3, a twisted pair can carry a digital data rate of 4 Mbps. Home computers can use a modem with the telephone network to communicate with other computers. The telephone outlet is connected to the central exchange by a local loop, which is a twisted pair. It is very difficult to establish communication by this method at a data rate higher than 9600 bps. This is much lower than 4 Mbps. Therefore a mistake must have been made in Table 2-4.

2-15   Given a 100-watt power source, what is the maximum allowable length for the following transmission media if a signal of 1 watt is to be received?
a. 22-gauge twisted pair operating a 1 kHz
b. 22-gauge twisted pair operating a 1 MHz
c. $\frac{3}{8}''$ coaxial cable operating a 1 MHz
d. $\frac{3}{8}''$ coaxial cable operating a 1 GHz
e. optical fiber operating at its optimal frequency

2-16   Coaxial cable is a two-wire transmission system. What is the advantage in connecting the outer conductor to ground?

2-17   The relationship between frequency f and wavelength λ is $\lambda f = c$, where c is the speed of light (3×10^8 m/s). Determine the wavelength ranges for the frequency bands of Table 2-4.

2-18   If an amplifier has a 30-dB gain, what voltage ratio does the gain represent?

2-19   An amplifier has an output of 20 W. What is its output in dBW?

2-20   A periodic bandlimited signal has only three frequency components: dc, 100 Hz, and 200 Hz. In sine-cosine form:

$$x(t) = 12 + 15\cos200\pi t + 20\sin200\pi t$$
$$- 5\cos400\pi t - 12\sin400\pi t$$

Express the signal in amplitude/phase form.

APPENDIX 2A

FOURIER ANALYSIS

2A-1   Fourier Series Representation of Periodic Signals

With the aid of a good table of integrals, it is a remarkably simple task to determine the frequency-domain nature of many signals. We begin with periodic signals. Any periodic signal can be represented as a sum of sinusoids, known as a Fourier series:

$$x(t) = \sum_{n=0}^{\infty} a_n \cos(2\pi n f_0 t) + \sum_{n=1}^{\infty} b_n \sin(2\pi n f_0 t)$$

where f_0 is the inverse of the period of the signal ($f_0 = 1/T$). The frequency of f_0 is referred to as the *fundamental frequency*; multiples of f_0 are referred to as *harmonics*. Thus a periodic signal with period T consists of the fundamental frequency $f_0 = 1/T$ plus harmonics of that frequency. If $a_0 \neq 0$, then $x(t)$ has an additional *dc component*.

The values of the coefficients are calculated as follows:

$$a_0 = \frac{1}{T} \int_0^T x(t) dt$$

$$a_n = \frac{2}{T} \int_0^T x(t) \cos(2\pi n f_0 t) \, dt$$

$$b_n = \frac{2}{T} \int_0^T x(t) \sin(2\pi n f_0 t) \, dt$$

This form of representation, known as the *sine-cosine representation*, is the easiest form to compute, but suffers from the fact that there are two components at each frequency. A more meaningful representation, the *amplitude-phase representation*, takes the form

$$x(t) = c_0 + \sum_{n=1}^{\infty} c_n \cos(2\pi n f_0 t + \theta_n)$$

This relates to the earlier representation as follows:

$$c_0 = a_0$$

$$c_n = \sqrt{a_n^2 + b_n^2}$$

$$\theta_n = -\tan^{-1}\left(\frac{b_n}{a_n}\right)$$

Examples of the Fourier series for periodic signals are shown in Figure 2-25.

2A-2   Fourier Transform Representation of Aperiodic Signals

For a periodic signal, we have seen that its spectrum consists of discrete frequency components, at the fundamental frequency and its harmonics. For an aperiodic signal, the spectrum consists of a continuum of frequencies. This spectrum can be defined by the Fourier transform. For a signal $x(t)$ with a spectrum $X(f)$, the following relationships hold:

$$x(t) = \int_{-\infty}^{\infty} X(f) e^{j2\pi ft} df$$

$$X(f) = \int_{-\infty}^{\infty} x(t) e^{-j2\pi ft} dt$$

Figure 2-26 presents some examples of Fourier transform pairs.

Fourier series

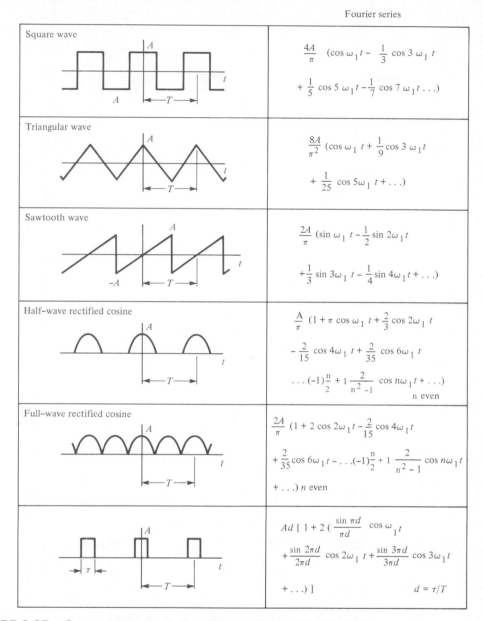

Square wave	$\frac{4A}{\pi} (\cos \omega_1 t - \frac{1}{3} \cos 3\omega_1 t$ $+ \frac{1}{5} \cos 5\omega_1 t - \frac{1}{7} \cos 7\omega_1 t \ldots)$
Triangular wave	$\frac{8A}{\pi^2} (\cos \omega_1 t + \frac{1}{9} \cos 3\omega_1 t$ $+ \frac{1}{25} \cos 5\omega_1 t + \ldots)$
Sawtooth wave	$\frac{2A}{\pi} (\sin \omega_1 t - \frac{1}{2} \sin 2\omega_1 t$ $+ \frac{1}{3} \sin 3\omega_1 t - \frac{1}{4} \sin 4\omega_1 t + \ldots)$
Half–wave rectified cosine	$\frac{A}{\pi} (1 + \pi \cos \omega_1 t + \frac{2}{3} \cos 2\omega_1 t$ $- \frac{2}{15} \cos 4\omega_1 t + \frac{2}{35} \cos 6\omega_1 t$ $\ldots (-1)^{\frac{n}{2}+1} \frac{2}{n^2-1} \cos n\omega_1 t + \ldots)$ n even
Full–wave rectified cosine	$\frac{2A}{\pi} (1 + 2 \cos 2\omega_1 t - \frac{2}{15} \cos 4\omega_1 t$ $+ \frac{2}{35} \cos 6\omega_1 t - \ldots (-1)^{\frac{n}{2}+1} \frac{2}{n^2-1} \cos n\omega_1 t$ $+ \ldots) n$ even
	$Ad [1 + 2 (\frac{\sin \pi d}{\pi d} \cos \omega_1 t$ $+ \frac{\sin 2\pi d}{2\pi d} \cos 2\omega_1 t + \frac{\sin 3\pi d}{3\pi d} \cos 3\omega_1 t$ $+ \ldots)]$ $d = \tau/T$

FIGURE 2-25.   Some common periodic signals and their Fourier series.

2A-3   Power Spectral Density and Bandwidth

The absolute bandwidth of any time-limited signal is infinite. In practical terms, however, most of the power in a signal will be concentrated in some finite band, and the effective bandwidth will consist of that portion of the spectrum that contains most of the power. To make this concept precise, we need to define the power spectral density.

First, we observe the power in the time domain. A function $x(t)$ usually specifies a signal in terms of either voltage or current. In either case, the instantaneous

Signal $x\,(t)$ Spectrum $\overline{X}\,(f)$

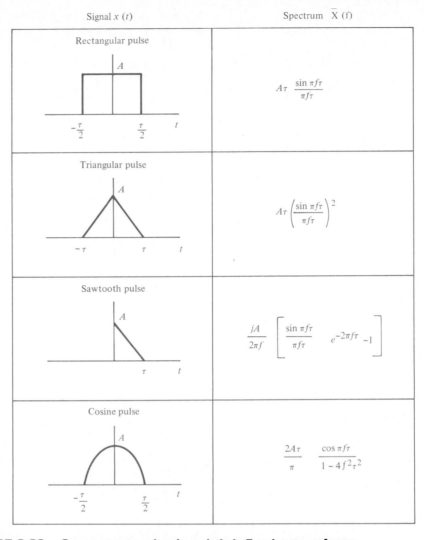

FIGURE 2-26. Some common signals and their Fourier transforms.

power in the signal is proportional to $|x(t)|^2$. We define the average power of a time-limited signal as

$$P = \frac{1}{t_2 - t_1} \int_{t_1}^{t_2} |x(t)|^2 \, dt$$

For a periodic signal the average power in one period is

$$P = \frac{1}{T} \int_0^T |x(t)|^2 \, dt$$

We would like to know the distribution of power as a function of frequency. For periodic signals, this is easily expressed in terms of the coefficients of the exponential Fourier series. The power spectral density $S(f)$ obeys

$$S(f) = \sum_{n=-\infty}^{\infty} |X_n|^2 \, \delta \, (f - nf_0)$$

The power spectral density $S(f)$ for aperiodic functions is more difficult to define. In essence, it is obtained by defining a "period" T_0 and allowing T_0 to increase without limit.

For a continuous valued function $S(f)$, the power contained in a band of frequencies, $f_1 < f < f_2$, is

$$P = 2 \int_{f_2}^{f_1} S(f) \, df$$

For a periodic waveform, the power through the first j harmonics is

$$P = \tfrac{1}{2} \sum_{n=0}^{2} |C_n|^2$$

With these concepts, we can now define the half-power bandwidth, which is perhaps the most common bandwidth definition. The half-power bandwidth is the interval between frequencies at which $S(f)$ has dropped to half of its maximum value of power, or 3 dB below the peak value.

CHAPTER 3

Data Encoding

In Chapter 2 a distinction was made between analog and digital *data* and analog and digital *signals*. Figure 2-12 suggested that either form of data could be encoded into either form of signal.

Figure 3-1 is another depiction that emphasizes the process involved. For digital signaling, a data source $g(t)$, which may be either digital or analog, is encoded into a digital signal $x(t)$. The actual form of $x(t)$ depends on the encoding technique, and is chosen to optimize use of the transmission medium. For example, the encoding may be chosen to conserve bandwidth or to minimize errors.

The basis for analog signaling is a continuous constant-frequency signal known as the carrier signal. The frequency of the carrier signal is chosen to be compatible with the transmission medium being used. Data may be transmitted using a carrier signal by *modulation*. Modulation is the process of encoding source data onto a *carrier signal* with frequency f_c. All modulation techniques involve operation on one or more of the three fundamental frequency-domain parameters:

- Amplitude.
- Frequency.
- Phase.

The input signal $m(t)$ may be analog or digital and is called the *modulating signal* or *baseband signal*. The result of modulating the carrier signal is called the *modulated signal $s(t)$*. As Figure 3-1b indicates, $s(t)$ is a bandlimited (bandpass) signal. The location of the bandwidth on the spectrum is related to f_c and is often centered on f_c. Again, the actual form of the encoding is chosen to optimize some characteristic of the transmission.

Each of the four possible combinations depicted in Figure 3-1 is in widespread

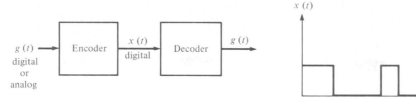

(a) Encoding onto a digital signal

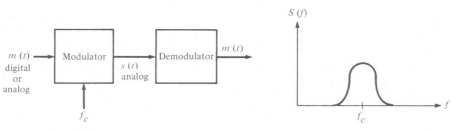

(b) Modulation onto an analog signal

FIGURE 3-1. Encoding and modulation techniques.

use. The reasons for choosing a particular combination for any given communication task vary. We list here some representative reasons:

- *Digital data, digital signal:* In general, the equipment for encoding digital data into a digital signal is less complex and less expensive than digital-to-analog modulation equipment.
- *Analog data, digital signal:* Conversion of analog data to digital form permits the use of modern digital transmission and switching equipment. The advantages of the digital approach were outlined in Section 2-2.
- *Digital data, analog signal:* Some transmission media, such as optical fiber and the unguided media, will only propagate analog signals.
- *Analog data, analog signal:* Analog data in electrical form can be transmitted as baseband signals easily and cheaply. This is done with voice transmission over voice-grade lines. One common use of modulation is to shift the bandwidth of a baseband signal to another portion of the spectrum. In this way multiple signals, each at a different position on the spectrum, can share the same transmission medium. This is known as frequency-division multiplexing.

We now examine the techniques involved in each of these four combinations.

3-1

DIGITAL DATA, DIGITAL SIGNALS

A digital signal is a sequence of discrete, discontinuous voltage pulses. Each pulse is a *signal element*. Binary data are transmitted by encoding each data bit into signal elements. In the simplest case, there is a one-to-one correspondence between bits and signal elements. An example is shown in Figure 2-14, in which binary 0 is represented by a lower voltage level and binary 1 by a higher voltage level. As we shall see in this section, a variety of other encoding schemes are also used.

First, we define some terms. If the signal elements all have the same algebraic sign, that is, all positive or negative, then the signal is *unipolar*. In *polar* signaling, one logic state is represented by a positive voltage level, and the other by a negative voltage level. The *data signaling rate*, or just *data rate*, of a signal is the rate, in bits per second, that data are transmitted. The *duration* or length of a bit is the amount of time it takes for the transmitter to emit the bit; for a data rate R, the bit duration is $1/R$. The *modulation rate*, in contrast, is the rate at which signal level is changed. This will depend on the nature of the digital encoding, as explained below. The modulation rate is expressed in *bauds*, which means signal elements per second. Finally, the terms *mark* and *space*, for historical reasons, refer to the binary digits 1 and 0, respectively.

The tasks involved in interpreting digital signals at the receiver can be summarized by again referring to Figure 2-14. First, the receiver must know the timing of each bit. That is, the receiver must know with some accuracy when a bit begins and ends. Second, the receiver must determine whether the signal level for each bit position is high (1) or low (0). In Figure 2-14, these tasks are performed by sampling each bit position in the middle of the interval and comparing the value to a threshold. Because of noise and other impairments, there will be errors, as shown.

What factors determine how successful the receiver will be in interpreting the incoming signal? We saw in Chapter 2 that three factors are important: the signal-to-noise ratio (or, better, E_b/N_o), the data rate, and the bandwidth. With other factors held constant, the following statements are true:

- An increase in data rate increases bit error rate (the probability that a bit is received in error).
- An increase in S/N decreases bit error rate.
- An increase in bandwidth allows an increase in data rate.

There is another factor that can be used to improve performance, and that is the encoding scheme. The encoding scheme is simply the mapping from data bits to signal elements. A variety of approaches have been tried. In what follows, we describe some of the more common ones; they are defined in Table 3-1 and depicted in Figure 3-2.

Before describing these techniques, let us consider the ways of evaluating or comparing the various techniques. [LIND73] lists five evaluation factors:

- *Signal spectrum:* Several aspects of the signal spectrum are important. A lack of high-frequency components means that less bandwidth is required for transmission. In addition, lack of a direct-current (dc) component is also desirable. With a dc component to the signal, there must be direct physical attachment of transmission components; with no dc component, ac-coupling via transformer is possible. This provides excellent electrical isolation, reducing interference. Finally, the magnitude of the effects of signal distortion and interference depend on the spectral properties of the transmitted signal. In practice, it usually happens that the transfer function of a channel is worse near the band edges. Therefore, a good signal design should concentrate the transmitted

TABLE 3-1 Definition of Digital Signal Encoding Formats

Nonreturn-to-Zero-Level (NRZ-L)
  0 = high level
  1 = low level
Nonreturn to Zero Inverted (NRZI)
  0 = no transition at beginning of interval (one bit time)
  1 = transition at beginning of interval
Bipolar-AMI
  0 = no line signal
  1 = positive or negative level, alternating for successive ones
Pseudoternary
  0 = positive or negative level, alternating for successive zeros
  1 = no line signal
Manchester
  0 = transition from high to low in middle of interval
  1 = transition from low to high in middle of interval
Differential Manchester
  Always a transition in middle of interval
  0 = no transition at beginning of interval
  1 = transition at beginning of interval
B8ZS
  Same as bipolar AMI, except that any string of eight zeros is replaced by a string with two code violations
HDB3
  Same as bipolar AMI, except that any string of four zeros is replaced by a string with one code violation

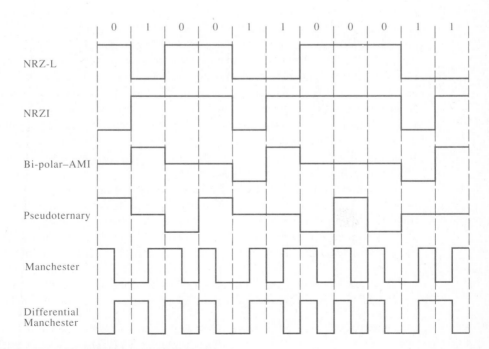

FIGURE 3-2. Digital signal encoding formats.

power in the middle of the transmission bandwidth. In such a case, a smaller distortion should be present in the received signal. To meet this objective, codes can be designed with the aim of shaping the spectrum of the transmitted signal.

- *Clocking:* We mentioned the need to determine the beginning and end of each bit position. This is no easy task. One rather expensive approach is to provide a separate clock lead to synchronize the transmitter and receiver. The alternative is to provide some synchronization mechanism that is based on the transmitted signal. This can be achieved with suitable encoding.

- *Error detection:* We will discuss various error-detection techniques in Chapter 4, and show in Chapter 5 that these are the responsibility of a layer of logic above the signaling level that is known as data link control. However, it is useful to have some error detection capability built into the physical signaling encoding scheme. This permits errors to be detected more quickly.

- *Signal interference and noise immunity:* Certain codes exhibit superior performance in the presence of noise. This is usually expressed in terms of a bit error rate.

- *Cost and complexity:* Although digital logic continues to drop in price, this factor should not be ignored. In particular, the higher the signaling rate to achieve a given data rate, the greater the cost. We will see that some codes require a signaling rate that is in fact greater than the actual data rate.

We now turn to a discussion of various techniques.

Nonreturn to Zero (NRZ)

The most common, and easiest, way to transmit digital signals is to use two different voltage levels for the two binary digits. Codes that follow this strategy share the property that the voltage level is constant during a bit interval; there is no transition (no return to a zero voltage level). For example, the absence of voltage can be used to represent binary 0, with a constant positive voltage used to represent binary 1. More commonly, a negative voltage is used to represent one binary value and a positive voltage is used to represent the other. This latter code, known as **Nonreturn-to-Zero-Level** (NRZ-L), is illustrated[1] in Figure 3-2. NRZ-L is generally the code used to generate or interpret digital data by terminals and other devices. If a different code is to be used for transmission, it is typically generated from an NRZ-L signal by the transmission system (in terms of Figure 1-1, NRZ-L is $g(t)$ and the encoded signal is $s(t)$).

A variation of NRZ is known as **NRZI** (Nonreturn to Zero, invert on ones). As with NRZ-L, NRZI maintains a constant voltage pulse for the duration of a bit time. The data itself is encoded as the presence or absence of a signal transition at the beginning of the bit time. A transition (low-to-high or high-to-low) at the beginning of a bit time denotes a binary 1 for that bit time; no transition indicates a binary 0.

NRZI is an example of **differential encoding.** In differential encoding, the signal is decoded by comparing the polarity of adjacent signal elements rather than de-

---

[1]In this figure, a negative voltage is equated with binary 1 and a positive voltage with binary 0. This is the opposite of the definition used in virtually all other textbooks. However, there is no "standard" definition of NRZ-L, and the definition here conforms to the use of NRZ-L in data communications interfaces and the standards that govern those interfaces.

termining the absolute value of a signal element. One benefit of this scheme is that it may be more reliable to detect a transition in the presence of noise than to compare a value to a threshold. Another benefit is that with a complex transmission layout, it is easy to lose the sense of the polarity of the signal. For example, on a multidrop twisted-pair line, if the leads from an attached device to the twisted pair are accidentally inverted, all 1's and 0's for NRZ-L will be inverted. This cannot happen with differential encoding.

The NRZ codes are the easiest to engineer and, in addition, make efficient use of bandwidth. This latter property is illustrated in Figure 3-3, which compares the spectral density of various encoding schemes. In the figure, frequency is normalized to the data rate. As can be seen, most of the energy in NRZ and NRZI signals is between dc and half the bit rate. For example, if an NRZ code is used to generate a signal with data rate of 9600 bps, most of the energy in the signal is concentrated between dc and 4800 Hz.

The main limitations of NRZ signals are the presence of a dc component and the lack of synchronization capability. To picture the latter problem, consider that with a long string of 1's or 0's for NRZ-L or a long string of 0's for NRZI, the output is a constant voltage over a long period of time. Under these circumstances, any drift between the timing of transmitter and receiver will result in loss of synchronization between the two.

Because of their simplicity and relatively low frequency response characteristics, NRZ codes are commonly used for digital magnetic recording. However, their limitations make these codes unattractive for signal transmission applications.

Multilevel Binary

A category of encoding techniques known as multilevel binary address some of the deficiencies of the NRZ codes. These codes use more than two signal levels. Two examples of this scheme are illustrated in Figure 3-2, bipolar-AMI (alternate mark inversion) and pseudoternary.[2]

In the case of the **bipolar-AMI** scheme, a binary 0 is represented by no line signal, and a binary 1 is represented by a positive or negative pulse. The binary 1 pulses must alternate in polarity. There are several advantages to this approach. First, there will be no loss of synchronization if a long string of 1's occurs. Each 1 introduces a transition, and the receiver can re-synchronize on that transition. A long string of 0's would still be a problem. Second, since the 1 signals alternate in voltage from positive to negative, there is no net dc component. Also, the bandwidth of the resulting signal is considerably less than the bandwidth for NRZ (Figure 3-3). Finally, the pulse alternation property provides a simple means of error detection. Any isolated error, whether it deletes a pulse or adds a pulse, causes a violation of this property.

The comments of the previous paragraph also apply to **pseudoternary.** In this case, it is the binary 1 that is represented by the absence of a line signal, and the binary 0 by alternating positive and negative pulses. There is no particular advantage of one technique versus the other, and each is the basis of some applications.

---

[2]These terms are not consistently used in the literature. In some books, these two terms are used for different encoding schemes than those defined here, and a variety of terms have been used for the two schemes illustrated in Figure 3-2. The nomenclature used here corresponds to the usage in various CCITT standards documents.

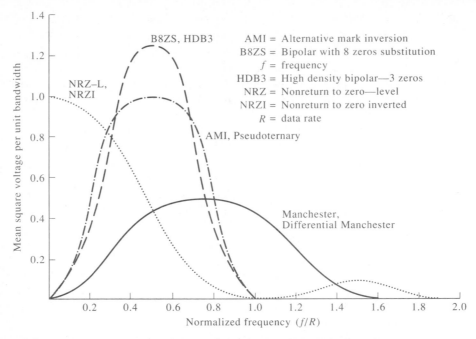

FIGURE 3-3. **Spectral density of various signal encoding schemes.**

Although a degree of synchronization is provided with these codes, a long string of 0's in the case of AMI or 1's in the case of pseudoternary still presents a problem. Several techniques have been used to address this deficiency. One approach is to insert additional bits that force transitions. We will see that this technique is used in ISDN for relatively low data rate transmission. Of course, at a high data rate, this scheme is expensive, since it results in an increase in an already high signal transmission rate. To deal with this problem at high data rates, a technique that involves scrambling the data is used. We examine two examples of this technique later in this section.

Thus, with suitable modification, multilevel binary schemes overcome the problems of NRZ codes. Of course, as with any engineering design decision, there is a tradeoff. With multilevel binary coding, the line signal may take on one of three levels, but each signal element, which could represent $\log_2 3 = 1.58$ bits of information, bears only one bit of information. Thus multilevel binary is not as efficient as NRZ coding. Another way to state this is that the receiver of multilevel binary signals has to distinguish between three levels ($+A$, $-A$, 0) instead of just two levels in the other signaling formats previously discussed. Because of this, the multilevel binary signal requires approximately 3 db more signal power than a two-valued signal for the same probability of bit error. This is illustrated in Figure 3-4. Put another way, the bit error rate for NRZ codes, at a given signal-to-noise ratio, is significantly less than that for multilevel binary.

Biphase

There is another set of alternative coding techniques, grouped under the term *biphase,* which overcomes the limitations of NRZ codes. Two of these techniques, Manchester and Differential Manchester, are in common use.

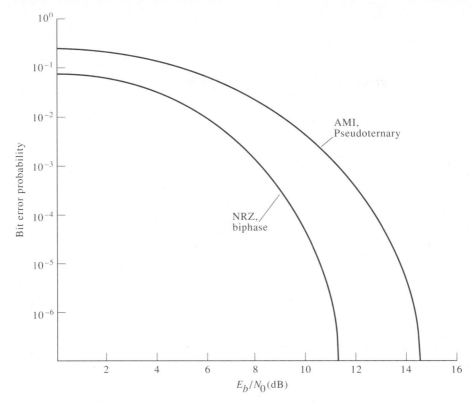

FIGURE 3-4. Theoretical bit error rate for various digital encoding schemes.

In the **Manchester** code, there is a transition at the middle of each bit period. The mid-bit transition serves as a clocking mechanism and also as data: a low-to-high transition represents a 1, and a high-to-low transition represents a 0[3]. In **Differential Manchester,** the mid-bit transition is used only to provide clocking. The encoding of a 0 is represented by the presence of a transition at the beginning of a bit period, and a 1 is represented by the absence of a transition at the beginning of a bit period. Differential Manchester has the added advantage of employing differential encoding.

All of the biphase techniques require at least one transition per bit time and may have as many as two transitions. Thus, the maximum modulation rate is twice that for NRZ; this means that the bandwidth required is correspondingly greater. To compensate for this, the biphase schemes have several advantages:

- *Synchronization:* Because there is a predictable transition during each bit time, the receiver can synchronize on that transition. For this reason, the biphase codes are known as self-clocking codes.

[3]The definition of Manchester presented here conforms to its usage in local area networks. In this definition, a binary 1 corresponds to a low-to-high transition, and a binary 0 to a high-to-low transition. Unfortunately, there is no official standard for Manchester, and a number of respectable textbooks (e.g., [TANE88], [COUC87], [SKLA88], [PEEB87], [BERT87], and the first two editions of this textbook) use the inverse, in which a low-to-high transition defines a binary 0 and a high-to-low transition defines a binary 1. Here, we conform to industry practice and to the definition used in the various LAN standards. For a discussion of this curious discrepancy, see [KESS89].

- *No dc component:* Biphase codes have no dc component, yielding the benefits described earlier.
- *Error detection:* The absence of an expected transition can be used to detect errors. Noise on the line would have to invert both the signal before and after the expected transition to cause an undetected error.

As can be seen from Figure 3-3, the bulk of the energy in biphase codes is between one-half and one times the bit rate. Thus, the bandwidth is reasonably narrow and contains no dc component. However, it is wider than the bandwidth for the multilevel binary codes.

Biphase codes are popular techniques for data transmission. The more common Manchester code has been specified for the IEEE 802.3 standard for baseband coaxial cable and twisted-pair CSMA/CD bus LANs. It has also been used for MIL-STD-1553B, which is a shielded twisted-pair bus LAN designed for high-noise environments. Differential Manchester has been specified for the IEEE 802.5 token ring LAN, using shielded twisted pair.

Modulation Rate

When signal encoding techniques are used, a distinction needs to be made between data rate and modulation rate. The data rate, or bit rate, is $1/t_B$, where t_B = bit duration. However, the modulation rate is the rate at which signal elements are generated. Consider, for example, Manchester encoding. The minimum size signal element is a pulse of one-half the duration of a bit interval. For a string of all binary 0's or all binary 1's, a continuous stream of such pulses is generated. Hence the maximum modulation rate for Manchester is $2/t_B$.

One way of characterizing the modulation rate is to determine the average number of transitions that occur per bit time. In general, this will depend on the exact sequence of bits being transmitted. Table 3-2 compares transition rates for various techniques. It indicates the signal transition rate in the case of a data stream of alternating 1's and 0's, and for the data stream that produces the minimum and maximum modulation rate.

Scrambling Techniques

Although the biphase techniques have achieved widespread use in local-area-network applications at relatively high data rates (up to 10 Mbps), they have not been

TABLE 3-2 Normalized Signal Transition Rate of Various Digital Signal Encoding Rates

	Minimum	101010. . .	Maximum
NRZ-L	0 (all 0's or 1's)	1.0	1.0
NRZI	0 (all 0's)	0.5	1.0 (all 1's)
Binary-AMI	0 (all 0's)	1.0	1.0
Pseudoternary	0 (all 1's)	1.0	1.0
Manchester	1.0 (1010 . . .)	1.0	2.0 (all 0's or 1's)
Differential Manchester	1.0 (all 1's)	1.5	2.0 (all 0's)

widely used in long-distance applications. The principal reason for this is that they require a high signaling rate relative to the data rate. This sort of inefficiency is more costly in a long-distance application.

Another approach is to make use of some sort of scrambling scheme. The idea behind this approach is simple: sequences that would result in a constant voltage level on the line are replaced by filling sequences that will provide sufficient transitions for the receiver's clock to maintain synchronization. The filling sequence must be recognized by the receiver and replaced with the original data sequence. The filling sequence is the same length as the original sequence, so there is no data rate increase. The design goals for this approach can be summarized as follows:

- No dc component.
- No long sequences of zero-level line signals.
- No reduction in data rate.
- Error detection capability.

Two techniques are in use in long-distance transmission services; these are illustrated in Figure 3-5.

A coding scheme that is commonly used in North America is known as **bipolar with 8-zeros substitution (B8ZS).** The coding scheme is based on a bipolar-AMI. We have seen that the drawback of the AMI code is that a long string of zeros may result in loss of synchronization. To overcome this problem the encoding is amended with the following rules (Figure 3-5):

- If an octet of all zeros occurs and the last voltage pulse preceding this octet was positive, then the eight zeros of the octet are encoded as **000 + − 0 − +.**

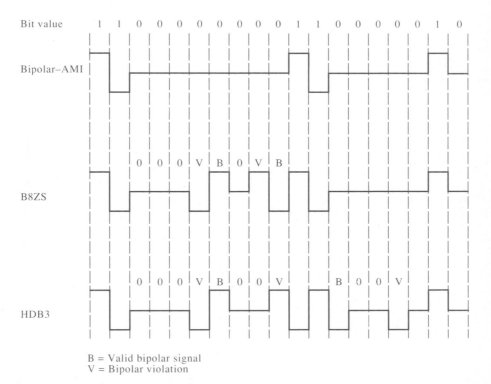

B = Valid bipolar signal
V = Bipolar violation

FIGURE 3-5.   Encoding rules for B8ZS and HDB3.

TABLE 3-3   HDB3 Substitution Rules

Polarity of Preceding Pulse	Number of Bipolar Pulses (Ones) Since Last Substitution	
	Odd	Even
$-$	$000-$	$+00+$
$+$	$000+$	$-00-$

- If an octet of all zeros occurs and the last voltage pulse preceding this octet was negative, then the eight zeros of the octet are encoded as $000 - +0+ -$.

This technique forces two code violations of the AMI code, an event unlikely to be caused by noise or other transmission impairment. The receiver recognizes the pattern and interprets the octet as consisting of all zeros.

A coding scheme that is commonly used in Europe and Japan is known as the **high-density bipolar $-$ 3 zeros (HDB3)** code (Table 3-3). As before, it is based on the use of AMI encoding. In this case, the scheme replaces strings of four zeros with sequences containing one or two pulses. In each case, the fourth zero is replaced with a code violation. In addition, a rule is needed to ensure that successive violations are of alternate polarity so that no dc component is introduced. Thus, if the last violation was positive, this violation must be negative and vice versa. The table shows that this condition is tested for by knowing whether the number of pulses since the last violation is even or odd and the polarity of the last pulse before the occurrence of the four zeros.

Figure 3-3 shows the spectral properties of these two codes. As can be seen, neither has a dc component. Most of the energy is concentrated in a relatively sharp spectrum around a frequency equal to one-half the data rate. Thus, these codes are well-suited to high data rate transmission.

3-2

DIGITAL DATA, ANALOG SIGNALS

We turn now to the case of transmitting digital data using analog signals. The most familiar use of this transformation is for transmitting digital data through the public telephone network. The telephone network was designed to receive, switch, and transmit analog signals in the voice-frequency range of about 300 to 3400 Hz. It is not at present suitable for handling digital signals from the subscriber locations (although this is beginning to change). Thus digital devices are attached to the network via a *modem* (modulator-demodulator), which converts digital data to analog signals, and vice versa.

For the telephone network, modems are used which produce signals in the voice-frequency range. The same basic techniques are used for modems that produce signals at higher frequencies (e.g., microwave). This section introduces these techniques and provides a brief discussion of the performance characteristics of the alternative approaches.

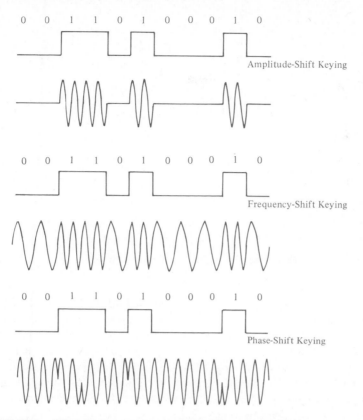

FIGURE 3-6. **Modulation of analog signals for digital data.**

Encoding Techniques

We mentioned that modulation involves operation on one or more of the three characteristics of a carrier signal: amplitude, frequency, and phase. Accordingly, there are three basic encoding or modulation techniques for transforming digital data into analog signals, as illustrated in Figure 3-6.

- Amplitude-shift keying (ASK).
- Frequency-shift keying (FSK).
- Phase-shift keying (PSK).

In all these cases, the resulting signal occupies a bandwidth centered on the carrier frequency.

In ASK, the two binary values are represented by two different amplitudes of the carrier frequency. Commonly, one of the amplitudes is zero; that is, one binary digit is represented by the presence, at constant amplitude, of the carrier, the other by the absence of the carrier. The resulting signal is

$$s(t) = \begin{cases} A \cos(2\pi f_c t + \theta_c) & \text{binary 1} \\ 0 & \text{binary 0} \end{cases}$$

where the carrier signal is $A \cos(2\pi f_c t + \theta_c)$. ASK is susceptible to sudden gain changes and is a rather inefficient modulation technique. On voice-grade lines, it is typically used only up to 1200 bps.

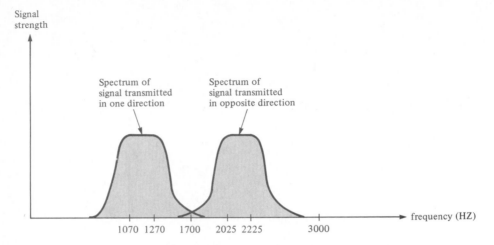

FIGURE 3-7.   Full-duplex FSK transmission on a voice-grade line.

The ASK technique is used to transmit digital data over optical fiber [WERN86]. For LED transmitters, the equation above is valid. That is, one signal element is represented by a light pulse while the other signal element is represented by the absence of light. Laser transmitters normally have a fixed "bias" current that causes the device to emit a low light level. This low level represents one signal element, while a higher-amplitude lightwave represents another signal element.

In FSK, the two binary values are represented by two different frequencies near the carrier frequency. The resulting signal is

$$s(t) = \begin{cases} A \cos(2\pi f_1 t + \theta_c) & \text{binary 1} \\ A \cos(2\pi f_2 t + \theta_c) & \text{binary 0} \end{cases}$$

where f_1 and f_2 are typically offset from the carrier frequency f_c by equal but opposite amounts.

Figure 3-7 shows an example of the use of FSK for full-duplex operation over a voice-grade line. The figure is a specification for the Bell System 108 series modems. Recall that a voice-grade line will pass frequencies in the approximate range 300 to 3400 Hz, and that full-duplex means that signals are transmitted in both directions at the same time. To achieve full-duplex transmission, this bandwidth is split at 1700 Hz. In one direction (transmit or receive), the frequencies used to represent 1 and 0 are centered on 1170 Hz, with a shift of 100 Hz on either side. The effect of alternating between those two frequencies is to produce a signal whose spectrum is indicated as the shaded area on the left in Figure 3-7. Similarly, for the other direction (receive or transmit) the modem uses frequencies shifted 100 Hz to each side of a center frequency of 2125 Hz. This signal is indicated by the shaded area on the right in Figure 3-7. Note that there is little overlap and thus little interference.

FSK is less susceptible to error than ASK. On voice grade lines, it is typically used up to 1200 bps. It is also commonly used for high-frequency (3 to 30 MHz) radio transmission. It can also be used at even higher frequencies on local networks that use coaxial cable.

In PSK, the phase of the carrier signal is shifted to represent data. Figure 3-6c is an example of a two-phase system. In this system, a binary 0 is represented by sending a signal burst of the same phase as the previous signal burst sent. A binary 1 is represented by sending a signal burst of opposite phase to the preceding one. This is known as differential PSK, since the phase shift is with reference to the previous bit transmitted rather than to some constant reference signal. The resulting signal is

$$s(t) = \begin{cases} A \cos(2\pi f_c t + \pi) & \text{binary 1} \\ A \cos(2\pi f_c t) & \text{binary 0} \end{cases}$$

with the phase measured relative to the previous bit interval.

More efficient use of bandwidth can be achieved if each signaling element represents more than one bit. For example, instead of a phase shift of 180°, as allowed in PSK, a common encoding technique, known as *quadrature phase-shift keying* (QPSK) uses phase shifts of multiples of 90°.

$$s(t) = \begin{cases} A \cos(2\pi f_c t + 45°) & 11 \\ A \cos(2\pi f_c t + 135°) & 10 \\ A \cos(2\pi f_c t + 225°) & 00 \\ A \cos(2\pi f_c t + 315°) & 01 \end{cases}$$

Thus each signal element represents two bits rather than one.

This scheme can be extended. It is possible to transmit bits three at a time using eight different phase angles. Further, each angle can have more than one amplitude. For example, a standard 9600 bps modem uses 12 phase angles, four of which have two amplitude values (Figure 3-8). A thorough review of these and other techniques can be found in [OETT79].

This latter example points out very well the difference between the data rate R (in bps) and the modulation rate D (in bauds) of a signal. Let us assume that this scheme is being employed with NRZ-L digital input. The data rate is $R = 1/t_B$ where t_B is the width of each NRZ-L bit. However, the encoded signal contains $l = 4$ bits in each signal element using $L = 16$ different combinations of amplitude and phase. The modulation rate can be seen to be $R/4$, since each change of signal

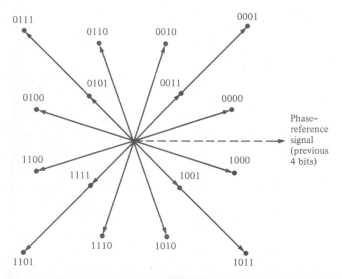

FIGURE 3-8. Phase angles for 9600 bit-per-second transmission.

element communicates four bits. Thus the line signaling speed is 2400 bauds, but the data rate is 9600 bps. This is the reason that higher bit rates can be achieved over voice-grade lines by employing more complex modulation schemes.

In general,

$$D = \frac{R}{l} = \frac{R}{\log_2 L}$$

where

   D = modulation rate, bauds
   R = data rate, bps
   L = number of different signal elements
   l = number of bits per signal element

The above is complicated when an encoding technique other than NRZ is used. For example, we saw that the maximum modulation rate for RZ signals is $2/t_B$. Thus D for RZ is greater than D for NRZ. This to some extent counteracts the reduction in D achieved by using multilevel signal modulation techniques.

Performance

In looking at the performance of various digital-to-analog modulation schemes, the first parameter of interest is the bandwidth of the modulated signal. This depends on a variety of factors; including the definition of bandwidth used and the filtering technique used to create the bandpass signal. We will use some straightforward results from [COUC87]; a more detailed analysis can be found in [AMOR80].

The transmission bandwidth B_T for ASK is of the form

$$B_T = (1 + r)R$$

where R is the bit rate and r is related to the technique by which the signal is filtered to establish a bandwidth for transmission; typically $0 < r < 1$. Thus the bandwidth is directly related to the bit rate. The formula above is also valid for PSK.

For FSK, the bandwidth can be expressed as

$$B_T = 2\Delta F + (1 + r)R$$

where $\Delta F = f_2 - f_c = f_c - f_1$ is the offset of the modulated frequency from the carrier frequency. When very high frequencies are used, the ΔF term dominates. For example, one of the standards for FSK signaling on a coaxial cable multipoint local network uses $\Delta F = 1.25$ MHz, $f_c = 5$ MHz, and $R = 1$ Mbps. In this case $B_T \approx 2\Delta F = 2.5$ MHz. In the example of the preceding section for the Bell 108 modem, $\Delta F = 100$ Hz, $f_c = 1170$ Hz (in one direction), and $R = 300$ bps. In this case $B_T \approx (1 + r)R$, which is the range 300 to 600 Hz.

With multilevel signaling, significant improvements in bandwidth can be achieved. In general

$$B_T = \left(\frac{1 + r}{l}\right)R = \left(\frac{1 + r}{\log_2 L}\right)R$$

where l is the number of bits encoded per signal element and L is the number of different signal elements.

TABLE 3-4 Data Rate to Transmission Bandwidth Ratio for Various Digital-to-Analog Encoding Schemes

	$r = 0$	$r = 0.5$	$r = 1$
ASK	1.0	0.67	0.5
FSK			
Wideband ($\Delta F \gg R$)	~0	~0	~0
Narrowband ($\Delta F \approx f_c$)	1.0	0.67	0.5
PSK	1.0	0.67	0.5
Multilevel signaling			
$L = 4, l = 2$	2.00	1.33	1.00
$L = 8, l = 3$	3.00	2.00	1.50
$L = 16, l = 4$	4.00	2.67	2.00
$L = 32, l = 5$	5.00	3.33	2.50

Table 3-4 shows the ratio of data rate to transmission bandwidth for various schemes. This ratio is also referred to as the bandwidth efficiency. As the name suggests, this parameter measures the efficiency with which bandwidth can be used to transmit data. The advantage of multilevel signaling methods now becomes clear.

Of course, the discussion above refers to the spectrum of the input signal to a communications line. Nothing has yet been said of performance in the presence of noise. Figure 3-9 summarizes some results based on reasonable assumptions concerning the transmission system [COUC87]. Here bit error rate is plotted as a function of the ratio E_b/N_o defined in Chapter 2. Of course, as that ratio increases,

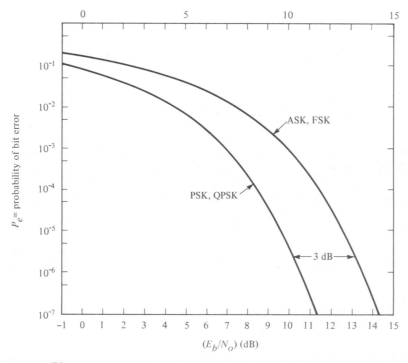

FIGURE 3-9. Bit error rate of various digital-to-analog encoding schemes.

the bit error rate drops. Further, PSK and QPSK are about 3 dB superior to ASK and FSK.

This information can now be related to bandwidth efficiency. Recall that

$$\frac{E_b}{N_0} = \frac{S}{N_0 R}$$

The parameter N_0 is the noise power density in watts/hertz. Hence, the noise in a signal with bandwidth B_T is $N = N_0 B_T$. Substituting, we have

$$\frac{E_b}{N_0} = \frac{S}{N}\frac{B}{R}$$

For a given signaling scheme, the bit error rate can be reduced by increasing E_b/N_0, which can be accomplished by increasing the bandwidth or decreasing the data rate: in other words, by reducing bandwidth efficiency.

EXAMPLE.   What is the bandwidth efficiency for FSK, ASK, PSK, and QPSK for a bit error rate of 10^{-7} on a channel with a S/N of 12 dB?

We have

$$\frac{E_b}{N_0} = 12 \text{ dB} - \left(\frac{R}{B}\right) \text{dB}$$

For FSK and ASK, from Figure 3-8,

$$\frac{E_b}{N_0} = 14.2 \text{ dB}$$

$$\left(\frac{R}{B}\right)\text{dB} = -2.2 \text{ dB}$$

$$\frac{R}{B} = 0.6$$

For PSK, from Figure 3-8

$$\frac{E_b}{N_0} = 11.2 \text{ dB}$$

$$\left(\frac{R}{B}\right)\text{dB} = 0.8 \text{ dB}$$

$$\frac{R}{B} = 1.2$$

The result for QPSK must take into account that the baud rate $D = R/2$. Thus

$$\frac{R}{B} = 2.4$$

    ■

As the example above shows, ASK and FSK exhibit the same bandwidth efficiency, PSK is better, and even greater improvement can be achieved with multilevel signaling.

It is worthwhile to compare these bandwidth requirements with those for digital signaling. A good approximation is

$$B_T = 0.5(1 + r)D$$

where D is the modulation rate. For NRZ, $D = R$, and we have

$$\frac{R}{B} = \frac{2}{1 + r}$$

Thus digital signaling is in the same ballpark, in terms of bandwidth efficiency, as ASK, FSK, and PSK. Significant advantage for analog signaling is seen with multilevel techniques.

3-3

ANALOG DATA, DIGITAL SIGNALS

In this section we examine the process of transforming analog data into digital signals. Strictly speaking, it might be more correct to refer to this as a process of converting analog data into digital data, which process is known as *digitization*. Once analog data have been converted into digital data, a number of things can happen. The three most common:

1. The digital data can be transmitted using NRZ-L. In this case, we have in fact gone directly from analog data to a digital signal.
2. The digital data can be encoded as a digital signal using a code other than NRZ-L. Thus an extra step is required.
3. The digital data can be converted into an analog signal, using one of the modulation techniques discussed in Section 3-2.

This last, seemingly curious, procedure is illustrated in Figure 3-10, which shows voice data that are digitized and then converted to an analog ASK signal. This allows digital transmission in the sense defined in Chapter 2. The voice data, because it has been digitized can be treated as digital data, even though transmission requirements (e.g., use of microwave) dictate that an analog signal be used.

The device used for converting analog data into digital form for transmission, and subsequently recovering the original analog data from the digital is known as a *codec* (coder-decoder). In this section we examine the two principal techniques used in codecs, pulse code modulation and delta modulation. The section closes with a discussion of comparative performance.

Analog data (voice) → Digitizer → Digital data (NRZ – L) → Modulator → Analog signal (ASK)

FIGURE 3-10. **Digitizing analog data.**

Pulse Code Modulation

Pulse Code Modulation (PCM) is based on the sampling theorem, which states [JORD85]:

> "If a signal $f(t)$ is sampled at regular intervals of time and at a rate higher than twice the highest significant signal frequency, then the samples contain all the information of the original signal. The function $f(t)$ may be reconstructed from these samples by the use of a low-pass filter."

For the interested reader, a proof is provided in Appendix 3A. If voice data are limited to frequencies below 4000 Hz, a conservative procedure for intelligibility, 8000 samples per second would be sufficient to completely characterize the voice signal. Note, however, that these are analog samples.

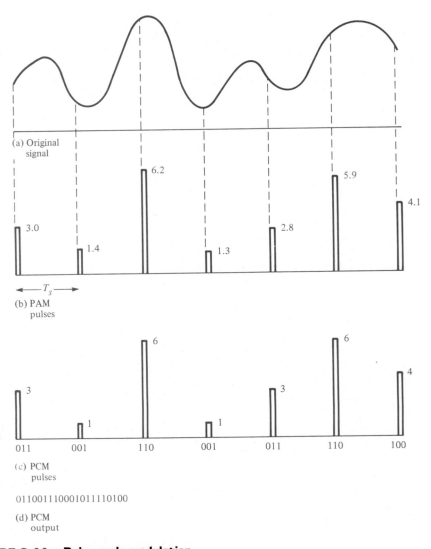

(a) Original signal

(b) PAM pulses

(c) PCM pulses

011 001 110 001 011 110 100

011001110001011110100

(d) PCM output

FIGURE 3-11. Pulse-code modulation.

This is illustrated in Figure 3-11a and b. The original signal is assumed to be bandlimited with a bandwidth of *B*. Samples are taken at a rate 2*B*, or once every 1/2*B* seconds. These samples are represented as narrow pulses whose amplitude is proportional to the value of the original signal. This process is known as *pulse amplitude modulation* (PAM). By itself, this technique has commercial applicability. It is used, for example, in some of AT&T's Dimension PBX products.

However, the most significant fact about PAM is that it is the first step toward PCM, as depicted in Figure 3-11c. To produce PCM data, the PAM samples are quantized. That is, the amplitude of each PAM pulse is approximated by an *n*-bit integer. In the example, $n = 3$. Thus $8 = 2^3$ levels are available for approximating the PAM pulses.

Figure 3-12 illustrates the process, starting with a continuous-time, continuous-amplitude (analog) signal, a digital signal is produced. The digital signal consists of blocks of *n* bits, where each *n*-bit number is the amplitude of a PCM pulse. On reception, the process is reversed to reproduce the analog signal. Notice, however, that this process violates the terms of the sampling theorem. By quantizing the PAM pulse, the original signal is now only approximated and cannot be recovered exactly. This effect is known as *quantizing error* or *quantizing noise*. The signal-to-noise ratio for quantizing noise can be expressed as [JAYA84]:

$$\frac{S}{N} = 6n - a \text{ dB}$$

where *a* is a constant on the order of 0 to 1.

Thus each additional bit used for quantizing increases *S/N* by 6 dB.

Typically, the PCM scheme is refined using a technique known as *nonlinear encoding*, which means, in effect, that the quantization levels are not equally spaced. The problem with equal spacing is that the mean absolute error for each sample is the same, regardless of signal level. Consequently, lower-amplitude values are relatively more distorted. By using a greater number of quantizing steps for signals of low amplitude, and a smaller number of quantizing steps for signals of large amplitude, a marked reduction in overall signal distortion is achieved (e.g., see Figure 3-13).

The same effect can be achieved by using uniform quantizing but *companding* (compressing-expanding) the input analog signal. Companding is a process that compresses the intensity range of a signal by imparting more gain to weak signals than to strong signals on input. At output, the reverse operation is performed. Figure 3-14 is a typical companding function.

Nonlinear encoding can significantly improve the PCM *S/N* ratio. For voice signals, improvements of 24 to 30 dB have been achieved [FREE81].

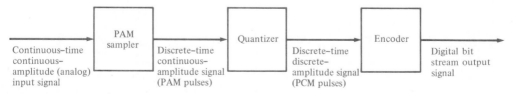

FIGURE 3-12. **Analog-to-digital conversion.**

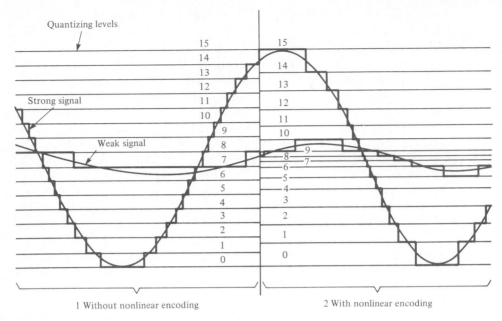

1 Without nonlinear encoding   2 With nonlinear encoding

FIGURE 3-13.   Effect of nonlinear coding.

Delta Modulation (DM)

A variety of techniques have been used to improve the performance of PCM or to reduce its complexity. A discussion of the various approaches that have been taken for voice data can be found in [CROC83]. Here we mention one of the most popular alternatives to PCM: delta modulation (DM).

With DM, the analog data are approximated by a staircase function that moves up or down by one quantization level at each sampling time. An example is shown in Figure 3-15c, where the staircase function is overlaid on the original analog waveform. The important characteristic of this staircase function is that it is binary: At each sampling time, the function moves up or down a constant amount. Thus the output of the DM process is a single binary digit for each sample. In essence, a bit stream is produced by approximating the derivative of an analog signal rather than its amplitude. A 1 is generated if the staircase function is to go up during the next interval; a 0 is generated otherwise.

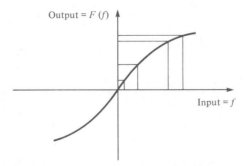

FIGURE 3-14.   Typical companding function.

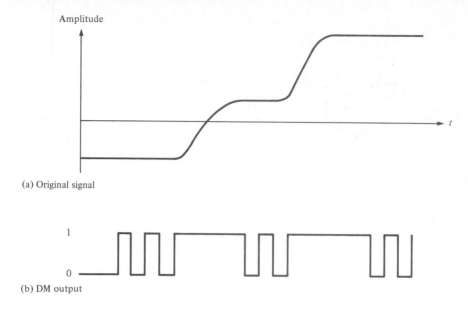

(a) Original signal

(b) DM output

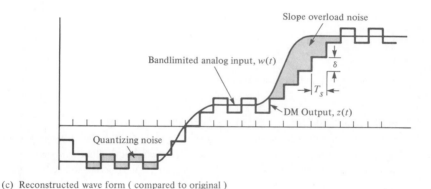

(c) Reconstructed wave form (compared to original)

FIGURE 3-15.   Example of delta modulation (DM).

The transition (up or down) that occurs at each sampling instant is chosen so that the staircase function tracks the original analog waveform as closely as possible. Figure 3-16 illustrates the logic of the process, which is essentially a feedback mechanism. For transmission, the following occurs: At each sampling instant, the analog input is compared to the most recent value of the approximating staircase function. If the value of the sampled waveform exceeds that of the staircase function, a 1 is generated; otherwise, a 0 is generated. This binary value is transmitted as the next output digit. It is also used to determine the next value of the reconstructed waveform or staircase function. The constant value δ is added to the function for a value of 1; the value δ is subtracted for a value of 0. Figure 3-16b shows how the binary stream generated using DM is used at reception to construct the approximating staircase function.

There are two important parameters in a DM scheme, the size of the step assigned to each binary digit, δ, and the sampling rate. As Figure 3-15c illustrates, δ must

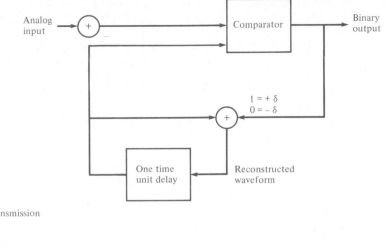

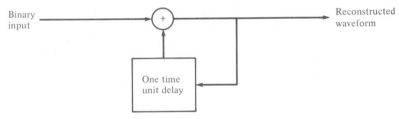

(a) Transmission

(b) Reception

FIGURE 3-16.   Delta modulation.

be chosen to produce a balance between two types of errors or noise. When the analog waveform is changing very slowly, there will be *quantizing noise*. This noise increases as δ is increased. On the other hand, when the analog waveform is changing more rapidly than the staircase can follow, there is *slope overload noise*. This noise increases as δ is decreased.

It should be clear that the accuracy of the scheme can be improved by increasing the sampling rate. However, this increases the data rate of the output signal.

The principal advantage of DM over PCM is the simplicity of its implementation. In general, PCM exhibits better S/N characteristics at the same data rate [COUC83].

Performance

Good voice reproduction via PCM can be achieved with 128 quantization levels, or 7-bit coding ($2^7 = 128$). A voice signal, conservatively, occupies a bandwidth of 4 kHz. Thus, according to the sampling theorem, samples should be taken at a rate of 8000 samples per second. This implies a data rate of $8000 \times 7 = 56$ kbps for the PCM-encoded digital data.

Consider what this means from the point of view of bandwidth requirement. An analog voice signal occupies 4 kHz. A 56-kbps digital signal will require on the order of at least 28 kHz! Even more severe differences are seen with higher bandwidth signals. For example, a common PCM scheme for color television uses 10-bit codes, which works out to 92 Mbps for a 4.6-MHz bandwidth signal. In spite of these numbers, digital techniques continue to grow in popularity for transmitting analog data. The principal reasons for this are:

- Because repeaters are used instead of amplifiers, there is no additive noise.
- As we shall see, time-division multiplexing (TDM) is used for digital signals instead of the frequency-division multiplexing (FDM) used for analog signals. With TDM, there is no intermodulation noise, whereas we have seen that this is a concern for FDM.
- The conversion to digital signaling allows the use of the more efficient digital switching techniques, discussed in Chapter 8.

Furthermore, techniques are being developed to provide more efficient codes. In the case of voice, a reasonable goal appears to be in the neighborhood of 4 kbps [ROBI86], [JAYA86], [JAYA90]. With video, advantage can be taken of the fact that from frame to frame, most picture elements will not change. Interframe coding techniques should allow the video requirement to be reduced to about 15 Mbps, and for slowly changing scenes, such as found in a video teleconference, down to 1.5 Mbps or less [NETR88], [MURA88], [MURA87].

As a final point, we mention that in many instances, the use of a telecommunications system will result in both digital-to-analog and analog-to-digital processing. The overwhelming majority of local terminations into the telecommunications network is analog, and the network itself uses a mixture of analog and digital techniques. Thus digital data at a user's terminal may be converted to analog by a modem, subsequently digitized by a codec, and perhaps suffer repeated conversions before reaching its destination.

Because of the above, telecommunication facilities handle analog signals that represent both voice and digital data. The characteristics of the waveforms are quite different. Whereas voice signals tend to be skewed to the lower portion of the bandwidth (Figure 2-9), analog encoding of digital signals has a more uniform spectral content over the bandwidth and therefore contains more high-frequency components. Studies have shown that, because of the presence of these higher frequencies, PCM-related techniques are preferable to DM-related techniques for digitizing analog signals that represent digital data [ONEA80].

3-4

ANALOG DATA, ANALOG SIGNALS

Modulation has been defined as the process of combining an input signal $m(t)$ and a carrier at frequency f_c to produce a signal $s(t)$ whose bandwidth is (usually) centered on f_c. For digital data, the motivation for modulation should be clear: When only analog transmission facilities are available, modulation is required to convert the digital data to analog form. The motivation when the data are already analog is less clear. After all, voice signals are transmitted over telephone lines at their original spectrum (referred to as baseband transmission). There are two principal reasons:

- A higher frequency may be needed for effective transmission. For unguided transmission, it is virtually impossible to transmit baseband signals; the required antennas would be many kilometers in diameter.

(a) Sinusoidal modulating wave

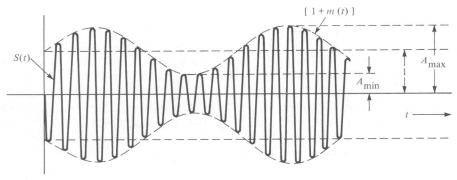

(b) Resulting AM signal

FIGURE 3-17.   Amplitude modulation.

- Modulation permits frequency-division multiplexing, an important technique explored in Chapter 6.

In this section we look at the principle techniques for modulation using analog data: amplitude modulation (AM), frequency modulation (FM), and phase modulation (PM). As before, the three basic characteristics of a signal are used for modulation.

Amplitude Modulation

Amplitude modulation (AM) is the simplest form of modulation, and is depicted in Figure 3-17. Mathematically, the process can be expressed as

$$s(t) = [1 + n_a x(t)] \cos 2\pi f_c t$$

where $\cos 2\pi f_c t$ is the carrier and $x(t)$ is the input signal (carrying data), both normalized to unity amplitude. The parameter n_a, known as the *modulation index,* is the ratio of the amplitude of the input signal to the carrier. Corresponding to our previous notation, the input signal is $m(t) = n_a x(t)$. The "1" in the equation above is a dc component that prevents loss of information, as explained below. This scheme is also known as double sideband transmitted carrier (DSBTC).

EXAMPLE.   Derive an expression for $s(t)$ if $x(t)$ is the amplitude-modulating signal $\cos 2\pi f_m t$.

We have:

$$s(t) = [1 + n_a \cos 2\pi f_m t] \cos 2\pi f_c t$$

By trigonometric identity, this may be expanded to:

$$s(t) = \cos 2\pi f_c t + \frac{n_a}{2} \cos 2\pi (f_c - f_m)t + \frac{n_a}{2} \cos 2\pi (f_c + f_m)t$$

The resulting signal has a component at the original carrier frequency plus a pair of components each spaced f_m hertz from the carrier. ■

From the equation above and Figure 3-16, it can be seen that AM involves the multiplication of the input signal by the carrier. The envelope of the resulting signal is $[1 + n_a x(t)]$ and, as long as $n_a < 1$, the envelope is an exact reproduction of the original signal. If $n_a > 1$, the envelope will cross the time axis and information is lost.

It is instructive to look at the spectrum of the AM signal. An example is shown in Figure 3-18. The spectrum consists of the original carrier plus the spectrum of the input signal translated to f_c. The portion of the spectrum for $|f| > |f_c|$ is the *upper sideband,* and the portion for $|f| < |f_c|$ is the *lower sideband.* Both the upper and lower sidebands are replicas of the original spectrum $M(f)$, with the lower sideband being frequency-reversed. As an example, consider a voice signal with a bandwidth that extends from 300 to 3000 Hz being modulated on a 60-kHz carrier.

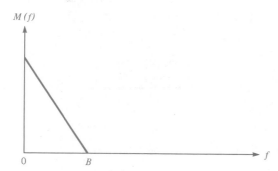

(a) Spectrum of modulating signal

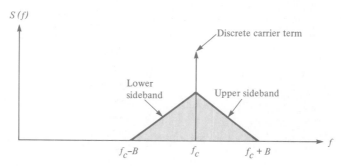

(b) Spectrum of AM signal with carrier at f_c

FIGURE 3-18. Spectrum of an AM signal.

The resulting signal contains an upper sideband of 60.3 to 63 kHz, a lower sideband of 57 to 59.7 kHz, and the 60-Hz carrier. An important relationship is

$$P_t = P_c \left(1 + \frac{n_a^2}{2} \right)$$

where P_t is the total transmitted power in $s(t)$ and P_c is the transmitted power in the carrier. We would like n_a as large as possible so that most of the signal power is used to actually carry information. However, n_a must remain below 1.

It should be clear that $s(t)$ contains unnecessary components, since each of the sidebands contains the complete spectrum of $m(t)$. A popular variant of AM, known as single sideband (SSB), takes advantage of this fact by sending only one of the sidebands, eliminating the other sideband and the carrier. The principal advantages of this approach are:

- Only half the bandwidth is required, that is, $B_T = B$, where B is the bandwidth of the original signal. For DSBTC, $B_T = 2B$.
- Less power is required since no power is used to transmit the carrier or the other sideband. Another variant is double sideband suppressed carrier (DSBSC) which filters out the carrier frequency and sends both sidebands. This saves some power but uses as much bandwidth as DSBTC.

The disadvantage of suppressing the carrier is that the carrier can be used for synchronization purposes. For example, suppose that the original analog signal is an ASK waveform encoding digital data. The receiver needs to know the starting point of each bit time to interpret the data correctly. A constant carrier provides a clocking mechanism by which to time the arrival of bits. A compromise approach is vestigial sideband (VSB), which uses one sideband and a reduced-power carrier.

Angle Modulation

Frequency modulation (FM) and *phase modulation* (PM) are special cases of *angle modulation*. The modulated signal is expressed as

$$s(t) = A_c \cos[2\pi f_c t + \phi(t)]$$

For phase modulation, the phase is proportional to the modulating signal:

$$\phi(t) = n_p m(t)$$

where n_p is the phase modulation index.

For frequency modulation, the derivative of the phase is proportional to the modulating signal:

$$\phi'(t) = n_f m(t)$$

where n_f is the frequency modulation index.

The definitions above may be clarified if we consider the following. The phase of $s(t)$ at any instant is just $2\pi f_c t + \phi(t)$. The instantaneous phase deviation from the carrier signal is $\phi(t)$. In PM, this instantaneous phase deviation is proportional to $m(t)$. Since frequency can be defined as the rate of change of phase of a signal, the instantaneous frequency of $s(t)$ is

$$2\pi f_i(t) = \frac{d}{dt} [2\pi f_c t + \phi(t)]$$

$$f_i(t) = f_c + \frac{1}{2\pi} \phi'(t)$$

and the instantaneous frequency deviation from the carrier frequency is $\phi'(t)$, which in FM is proportional to $m(t)$.

Figure 3-19 illustrates amplitude, phase, and frequency modulation by a sine wave. The shapes of the FM and PM signals are very similar. Indeed, it is impossible to tell them apart without knowledge of the modulation function.

Several observations about the FM process are in order. The peak deviation ΔF can be seen to be

$$\Delta F = \frac{1}{2\pi} n_f A_m \qquad \text{Hz}$$

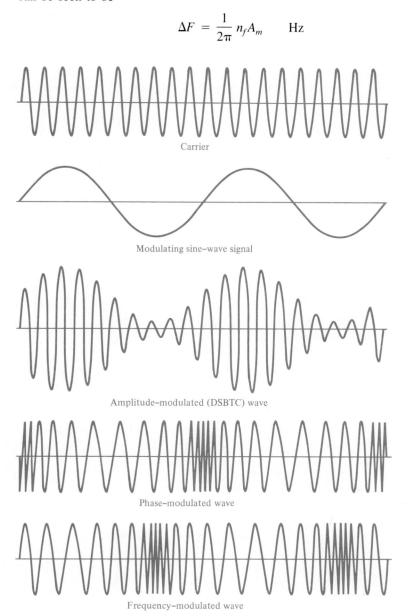

Carrier

Modulating sine–wave signal

Amplitude–modulated (DSBTC) wave

Phase–modulated wave

Frequency–modulated wave

FIGURE 3-19. **Amplitude, phase, and frequency modulation of a sine-wave carrier by a sine-wave signal.**

where A_m is the maximum value of $m(t)$. Thus an increase in the magnitude of $m(t)$ will increase ΔF, which, intuitively, should increase the transmitted bandwidth B_T. However, as should be apparent from Figure 3-19, this will not increase the average power level of the FM signal, which is $A_c^2/2$. This is distinctly different from AM, where the level of modulation affects the power in the AM signal but does not affect its bandwidth.

EXAMPLE.   Derive an expression for $s(t)$ if $\phi(t)$ is the phase-modulating signal $n_p \cos 2\pi f_m t$. Assume that $A_c = 1$. This can be seen directly to be

$$s(t) = \cos[2\pi f_c t + n_p \cos 2\pi f_m t]$$

The instantaneous phase deviation from the carrier signal is $n_p \cos 2\pi f_m t$. The phase angle of the signal varies from its unmodulated value in a simple sinusoidal fashion, with the peak phase deviation equal to n_p.

The expression above can be expanded using Bessel's trigonometric identities:

$$s(t) = \sum_{n=-\infty}^{\infty} J_n(n_p) \cos\left(2\pi f_c t + 2\pi n f_m t + \frac{n\pi}{2}\right)$$

where $J_n(n_p)$ is the nth order Bessel function of the first kind. Using the property

$$J_{-n}(x) = (-1)^n J_n(x)$$

this can be rewritten as

$$s(t) = J_0(n_p) \cos 2\pi f_c t + \sum_{n=1}^{\infty} J_n(n_p)\left[\cos\left(2\pi(f_c + n f_m)t + \frac{n\pi}{2}\right)\right.$$
$$\left. + \cos\left(2\pi(f_c - n f_m)t + \frac{(n+2)\pi}{2}\right)\right]$$

The resulting signal has a component at the original carrier frequency plus a set of sidebands displaced from f_c by all possible multiples of f_m. For $n_p \ll 1$, the higher-order terms fall off rapidly.   ■

EXAMPLE.   Derive an expression for $s(t)$ if $\phi'(t)$ is the frequency-modulating signal $-n_f \sin 2\pi f_m t$. The form of $\phi'(t)$ was chosen for convenience. We have

$$\phi(t) = -\int n_f \sin 2\pi f_m t \, dt = \frac{n_f}{2\pi f_m} \cos 2\pi f_m t$$

Thus

$$s(t) = \cos\left[2\pi f_c t + \frac{n_f}{2\pi f_m} \cos 2\pi f_m t\right]$$
$$= \cos\left[2\pi f_c t + \frac{\Delta F}{f_m} \cos 2\pi f_m t\right]$$

■

The instantaneous frequency deviation from the carrier signal is $-n_f \sin 2\pi f_m t$. The frequency of the signal varies from its unmodulated value in a simple sinusoidal fashion, with the peak frequency deviation equal to n_f rad/s.

The equation for the FM signal has the identical form as for the PM signal, with $\Delta F/f_m$ substituted for n_p. Thus the Bessel expansion is the same.

As with AM, both FM and PM result in a signal whose bandwidth is centered at f_c. However, we can now see that the magnitude of that bandwidth is very different. Amplitude modulation is a linear process and produces frequencies that are the sum and difference of the carrier signal and the components of the modulating signal. Hence, for AM:

$$B_T = 2B$$

However, angle modulation includes a term of the form $\cos(\phi(t))$ which is nonlinear and will produce a wide range of frequencies. In essence, for a modulating sinusoid of frequency f_m, $s(t)$ will contain components at $f_c + f_m$, $f_c + 2f_m$, and so on. In the most general case, infinite bandwidth is required to transmit an FM or PM signal. As a practical matter, a very good rule of thumb, known as Carson's rule [COUC83], is:

$$B_T = 2(\beta + 1)B$$

where

$$\beta = \begin{cases} n_p A_m \text{ for PM} \\ \dfrac{\Delta F}{B} = \dfrac{n_f A_m}{2\pi B} \quad \text{ for FM} \end{cases}$$

We can rewrite the formula for FM as

$$B_T = 2\Delta F + 2B$$

Thus both FM and PM require greater bandwidth than AM.

3-5

RECOMMENDED READING

A good analysis of digital data, digital signal schemes can be found in [PEEB87]. [BENE87], [SKLA88], and [KAMA86] also provide some insights. The latter is concerned with the use of these codes for magnetic tape recording, but the discussion is valid in the data transmission context. A great deal has been written about analog modulation schemes for digital data. [OETT79] is a good survey. [PEEB87] and [SKLA88] contain lengthy analyses. Other worthwhile sources are [FREE81] and [BELL82a].

[MART88] contains a readable introduction to PCM and other techniques for analog-to-digital encoding. More in-depth looks can be found in [COUC87], [JAYA84], [WILL87], and [NETR88]. Two special issues of the IEEE Journal on Selected Areas in Communications report on recent developments in voice coding [AOYA88] and video coding [HASK87]. Finally, the literature on the various analog modulation schemes for analog data is almost limitless. [BELL82a] is a concise overview of the subject.

3-6

PROBLEMS

3-1 Which of the signals of Table 3-1 use differential encoding?

3-2   Develop algorithms for generating each of the codes of Table 3-1 from NRZ-L.

3-3   A modified NRZ code known as *enhanced-NRZ* (E-NRZ) is sometimes used for high density magnetic tape recording. E-NRZ encoding entails separating the NRZ-L data stream into 7-bit words; inverting bits 2, 3, 6, and 7; and adding one parity bit to each word. The parity bit is chosen to make the total number of 1's in the 8-bit word an odd count. What are the advantages of E-NRZ over NRZ-L? Any disadvantages?

3-4   Develop a state diagram (finite state machine) representation of pseudoternary coding.

3-5   Consider the following signal encoding technique. Binary data are presented as input, a_m, $m = 1, 2, 3, \ldots$ Two levels of processing occur.
First, a new set of binary numbers are produced:
$$b_m = a_m + b_{m-1} \bmod 2$$
These are then encoded as
$$c_m = b_m - b_{m-1}$$
On reception, the original data is recovered by
$$a_m = c_m \bmod 2$$
a. Verify that the received values of a_m equal the transmitted values of a_m.
b. What sort of encoding is this?

3-6   For the B8ZS coding scheme to be effective, the probability of occurrences of more than one code violation (two pulses in a row with the same polarity) due to an error must be quite small. What is the probability of the occurrence of more than one code violation in 8 bits for an error rate per bit of 10^{-6}? For an error rate of 10^{-3}?

3-7   For the bit stream 01001110, sketch the waveforms for each of the codes of Table 3-1.

3-8   Consider Figure 3-8. Eight of the phases use only a single level of amplitude. The system shown encodes only 4 bits. How many bits could be encoded if the single amplitude phase were made to be double amplitude?

3-9   Consider a channel using PSK designed with a probability of error of 1 part in 1,000,000. If the signal-to-noise ratio is 1000, what is the bandwidth efficiency?

3-10   Derive an expression for baud rate D as a function of bit rate R for QPSK using the digital encoding techniques of Table 3-1.

3-11   What S/N ratio is required to achieve a bandwidth efficiency of 5.0 for ASK, FSK, PSK, and QPSK? Assume that the required bit error rate is 10^{-6}.

3-12   An NRZ-L signal is passed through a filter with $r = 0.5$ and then modulated onto a carrier. The data rate is 2400 bps. Evaluate the bandwidth for ASK and FSK. For FSK assume that the two frequencies used are 50 kHz and 55 kHz.

3-13 Assume that a telephone line channel is equalized to allow bandpass data transmission over a frequency range of 600 to 3000 Hz. The available bandwidth is 2400 Hz with a center frequency of 1800 Hz. For $r = 1$, evaluate the required bandwidth for 2400 bps QPSK and 4800-bps, eight-level multilevel signaling. Is the bandwidth adequate?

3-14 Why should PCM be preferable to DM for encoding analog signals that represent digital data?

3-15 Are the modem and the codec functional inverses (i.e., could an inverted modem function as a codec, or vice versa)?

3-16 The signal of Problem 2-20 is quantized using 10-bit PCM. Find the signal-to-quantization noise ratio.

3-17 Consider an audio signal with spectral components in the range 300 to 3000 Hz. Assume that a sampling rate of 7 kHz will be used to generate a PCM signal.
a. For $S/N = 30$ dB, what is the number of uniform quantization levels needed?
b. What data rate is required?

3-18 Find the step size δ required to prevent slope overload noise as a function of the frequency of the highest-frequency component of the signal. Assume that all components have amplitude A.

3-19 A PCM encoder accepts a signal with a full-scale voltage of 10 V and generates 8-bit codes using uniform quantization. The maximum normalized quantized voltage is $1 - 2^{-8}$. Determine: (a) normalized step size, (b) actual step size in volts, (c) actual maximum quantized level in volts, (d) normalized resolution, (e) actual resolution, and (f) percentage resolution.

3-20 A carrier with a frequency of 100 kHz is amplitude-modulated with the signal

$$x(t) = 10 \cos 2\pi \times 10^3 t + 8 \cos 4\pi \times 10^3 t + 6 \cos 8\pi \times 10^3 t$$

a. List the frequencies appearing at the output of the modulator.
b. Develop an expression for the DSBTC output $y(t)$. Assume that the carrier has the form $\cos 2\pi \times 10^5 t$.

3-21 An AM broadcast station operates at its maximum allowed total output of 50 kW and 95% modulation ($n_a = 0.95$). How much of its transmitted power conveys information?

3-22 The carrier $c(t) = A_c \sin 2\pi f_c t$ is to be amplitude-modulated by input $m(t) = A_m \sin 2\pi f_m t$. Derive a simplified expression for the modulated signal $s(t)$.

3-23 A modulated RF waveform is given by $s(t) = 500 \cos [2\pi f_c t + 20 \cos 2\pi f_1 t]$, where $f_1 = 1$ kHz and $f_c = 100$ MHz.
a. If the phase modulation index is 100 rad/V, find the expression for the phase modulation voltage $m(t)$. What is its peak value and frequency?
b. If the frequency modulation index is 10^6 rad/V-s, find the frequency modulation voltage $m(t)$. What is its peak value and frequency?

APPENDIX 3A

PROOF OF THE SAMPLING THEOREM

The sampling theorem can be restated as follows. *Given:*

- $x(t)$ is a bandlimited signal with bandwidth f_h.
- $p(t)$ is a sampling signal consisting of pulses at intervals $T_s = 1/f_s$, where f_s is the sampling frequency.
- $x_s(t) = x(t)p(t)$ is the sampled signal.

Then, $x(t)$ can be recovered exactly from $x_s(t)$ if and only if $f_s \geq 2f_h$.

Proof:

Since $p(t)$ consists of a uniform series of pulses, it is a periodic signal and can be represented by a Fourier series:

$$p(t) = \sum_{n=-\infty}^{\infty} P_n e^{j2\pi n f_s t}$$

We have

$$x_s(t) = x(t)p(t)$$

$$= \sum_{n=-\infty}^{\infty} P_n x(t) e^{j2\pi n f_s t}$$

Now consider the Fourier transform of $x_s(t)$:

$$X_s(f) = \int_{-\infty}^{\infty} x_s(t) e^{-j2\pi f t} \, dt$$

Substituting for $x_s(t)$, we have

$$X_s(f) = \int_{-\infty}^{\infty} \sum_{n-\infty}^{\infty} P_n x(t) e^{j2\pi n f_s t} \, e^{-j2\pi f t} \, dt$$

Rearranging yields

$$X_s(f) = \sum_{n=-\infty}^{\infty} P_n \int_{-\infty}^{\infty} x(t) e^{-j2\pi(f-nf_s)t} \, dt$$

From the definition of the Fourier transform, we can write

$$X(f - nf_s) = \int_{-\infty}^{\infty} x(t) e^{-j2\pi(f-nf_s)t} \, dt$$

where $X(f)$ is the Fourier transform of $x(t)$. Substituting this into the preceding equation, we have

$$X_s(f) = \sum_{n=-\infty}^{\infty} P_n X(f - nf_s)$$

This last equation has an interesting interpretation, which is illustrated in Figure 3-20, where we assume without loss of generality that the bandwidth of $x(t)$ is in the range 0 to f_h. The spectrum of $x_s(t)$ is composed of the spectrum of $x(t)$ plus the spectrum of $x(t)$ translated to each harmonic of the sampling frequency. Each

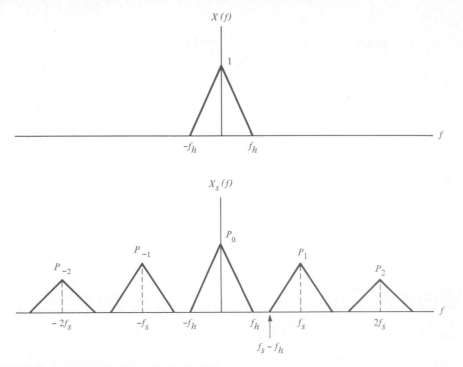

FIGURE 3-20.   Spectrum of a sampled signal.

of the translated spectra is multiplied by the corresponding coefficient of the Fourier series of $p(t)$. Now, if $f_s > 2f_h$, these various translations do not overlap, and the spectrum of $x(t)$, multiplied by P_o, appears in $X_s(f)$. By passing $X_s(f)$ through a bandpass filter with $f < f_s$, the spectrum of $x(t)$ is recovered. In equation form,

$$X_s(f) = P_0X(f) \qquad -f_s < f < f_s$$

CHAPTER 4

Digital Data Communication Techniques

In Chapters 2 and 3, we have been concerned primarily with the attributes of data transmission, such as the characteristics of data signals and transmission media, the encoding of signals, and transmission performance. In this chapter we shift our emphasis from data transmission to data communications.

For two devices linked by a transmission medium to exchange data, a high degree of cooperation is required. Typically, data are transmitted one bit at a time over the medium. The timing (rate, duration, spacing) of these bits must be the same for transmitter and receiver. Two common techniques—asynchronous and synchronous—are explored in Section 4-1. Next, we look at the problem of bit errors. As we have seen, data transmission is not an error-free process and some means of accounting for these errors is needed. In Section 4-2 we look at several error-detection techniques. Finally in this chapter, we look at transmission line interfaces. Typically, digital data devices do not attach to and signal across a transmission medium directly. Rather, this process is mediated through a standardized interface.

Another topic relating to these three is that of data link control. This is sufficiently important to warrant a separate chapter, and is explored in Chapter 5.

4-1

ASYNCHRONOUS AND SYNCHRONOUS TRANSMISSION

In this book we are concerned with serial transmission of data; that is, data are transferred over a single communications path rather than a parallel set of lines, as is sometimes done in I/O devices and internal computer signal paths. With serial transmission, signaling elements are sent down the line one at a time. Each signaling element may be:

- *Less than one bit:* This is the case, for example, with Manchester coding.
- *One bit:* NRZ-L and FSK are digital and analog examples, respectively.
- *More than one bit:* QPSK is an example.

For simplicity in the following discussion, we assume one bit per signaling element unless otherwise stated. The discussion is not materially affected by this assumption.

It was mentioned in Chapter 1 that synchronization is one of the key tasks of data communications. A transmitter is sending a message one bit at a time through a medium to a receiver. The receiver must recognize the beginning and end of a block of bits. It must also know the duration of each bit so that it can sample the line with the proper timing to read each bit.

Suppose that the sender simply transmits a stream of data bits. The sender has a clock that governs the timing of the transmitted bits. For example, if data are to be transmitted at 10,000 bits per second (bps), then one bit will be transmitted every $1/10,000 = 0.1$ millisecond (ms), as measured by the sender's clock. Typically, the receiver will attempt to sample the medium at the center of each bit time. The receiver will time its samples at intervals of one bit time. In our example, the sampling would occur once every 0.1 ms. If the receiver times its samples based on its own clock, then there will be a problem if the transmitter's and receiver's clocks are not precisely aligned. If there is a drift of 1 percent (the receiver's clock is 1 percent faster or slower than the transmitter's clock), then the first sampling will be 0.01 of a bit time (0.001 ms) away from the center of the bit (center of bit is 0.05 ms from beginning and end of bit). After 50 or more samples, the receiver may be in error because it is sampling in the wrong bit time ($50 \times .001 = .05$ ms). For smaller timing differences, the error would occur later, but eventually the receiver will be out of step with the transmitter if the transmitter sends a sufficiently long stream of bits and if no steps are taken to synchronize the transmitter and receiver.

Asynchronous Transmission

Two approaches are common for achieving the desired synchronization. The first is called, oddly enough, asynchronous transmission. The strategy with this scheme is to avoid the timing problem by not sending long, uninterrupted streams of bits. Instead, data are transmitted one character at a time, where each character is five to eight bits in length. Timing or synchronization must only be maintained within each character; the receiver has the opportunity to resynchronize at the beginning of each new character.

The technique is easily explained with reference to Figure 4-1. When no character is being transmitted, the line between transmitter and receiver is in an "idle" state. The definition of idle is equivalent to the signaling element for binary 1. For most interface standards, such as EIA-232-D defined later in this chapter, idle corresponds to the presence of a negative voltage on the line. See also the definition of NRZ-L in the preceding chapter. The beginning of a character is signaled by a *start bit* with a value of binary 0. This is followed by the five to eight bits that

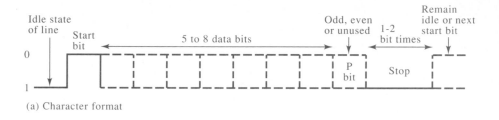

(a) Character format

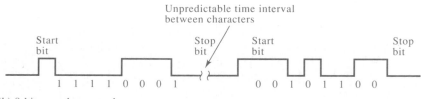

(b) 8-bit asynchronous character stream

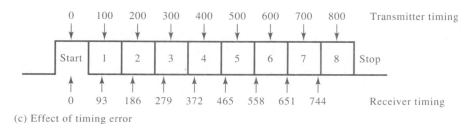

(c) Effect of timing error

FIGURE 4-1.   **Asynchronous transmission.**

actually make up the character.[1] Usually, this is followed by a *parity bit*. The parity bit is set by the transmitter such that the total number of ones in the character, including the parity bit, is even (even parity) or odd (odd parity), depending on the convention being used. The final element is a *stop,* which is a binary 1. A minimum length for the stop is specified, and this is usually 1, 1.5, or 2 times the duration of an ordinary bit. No maximum value is specified. Since the stop is the same as the idle state, the transmitter will continue to transmit the stop signal until it is ready to send the next character.

If a steady stream of characters is sent, the interval between two characters is uniform and equal to the stop element. For example, if the stop bit has unit length and the ASCII characters ABC are sent (without parity bit), the pattern[2] is 01000001100100001101100001111... The start bit (0) starts the timing sequence for the next eight elements, which are the 7-bit ASCII code and the stop bit. In

---

[1]The number of bits that comprise a character depends on the code used. We have already seen one common example, the ASCII code, which uses seven bits per character (Table 2-1). Another common code is the Extended Binary Coded Decimal Interchange Code (EBCDIC), which is an 8-bit character code used on all IBM machines except for their personal computers.

[2]Each character is transmitted starting with the least significant bit (b1 in Table 2-1). In the text above, the transmission is shown from left (first bit transmitted) to right (last bit transmitted).

the idle state, the receiver looks for a transition from 1 to 0 to begin the next character, and then samples the input signal at one-bit intervals for seven intervals. It then looks for the next 1-to-0 transition, which will occur no sooner than one bit time.

The timing requirements for this scheme are modest. For example, ASCII characters are typically sent as 8-bit units, including the parity bit. If the receiver is 5 percent slower or faster than the transmitter, the sampling of the eighth information bit will be displaced by 45 percent and still be correctly sampled. Figure 4-1c shows the effects of a timing error of sufficient magnitude to cause an error in reception. In this example we assume a data rate of 10,000 bits per second (10 kbps); therefore, each bit is of 0.1 millisecond (ms), or 100 nanoseconds (ns), duration. Assume that the receiver is off by 7 percent, or 7 nanoseconds per bit time. Thus, the receiver samples the incoming character every 93 ns (based on the transmitter's clock). As can be seen, the last sample is erroneous.

An error such as this actually results in two errors. First, the last sampled bit is incorrectly received. Second, the bit count may now be out of alignment. If bit 7 is a 1 and bit 8 is a 0, bit 8 could be mistaken for a start bit. This condition is termed a *framing error*, as the character plus start and stop bits is sometimes referred to as a *frame*. A framing error can also occur if some noise condition causes the false appearance of a start bit during the idle state.

Asynchronous communication is simple and cheap but requires an overhead of two to three bits per character. For example, for a 7-bit code, using a 1-bit-long stop bit, two out of every nine bits convey no information but are there merely for synchronization; thus the overhead is 2/9 = 0.22. Of course, the percentage overhead could be reduced by sending larger blocks of bits between the start and stop bits. However, as Figure 4-1c indicates, the larger the block of bits, the greater the cumulative timing error. To use larger blocks of bits successfully, a different form of synchronization, known as synchronous transmission, is used.

Synchronous Transmission

A more efficient means of communication is synchronous transmission. In this mode, blocks of characters or bits are transmitted without start and stop codes, and the exact departure or arrival time of each bit is predictable. To prevent timing drift between transmitter and receiver, their clocks must somehow be synchronized. One possibility is to provide a separate clock line between transmitter and receiver. Otherwise, the clocking information must be embedded in the data signal. For digital signals, this can be achieved with biphase encoding. For analog signals, a number of techniques can be used; the carrier frequency itself can be used to synchronize the receiver based on the phase of the carrier.

With synchronous transmission, there is another level of synchronization required, to allow the receiver to determine the beginning and end of a block of data. To achieve this, each block begins with a *preamble* bit pattern and generally ends with *postamble* bit pattern. These patterns are control information rather than data. In addition, other control information is included that is used in the data link control procedures discussed in Chapter 5. The data plus control information is called a *frame*. The exact format of the frame depends on whether the transmission scheme is character-oriented or bit-oriented.

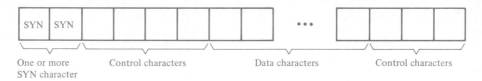

(a) Character – oriented frame

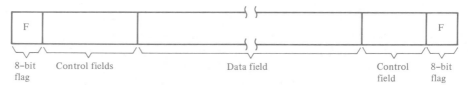

(b) Bit – oriented frame

FIGURE 4-2. **Synchronous transmission.**

With *character-oriented* transmission, the block of data is treated as a sequence of characters (usually 8-bit characters). All control information is in character form. The frame begins with one or more "synchronization characters" (Figure 4-2a). The synchronization character, usually called *SYN*, is a unique bit pattern that signals the receiver that this is the beginning of a block. The postamble is another unique character used in some schemes. The receiver thus is alerted to an incoming block of data by the SYN characters and accepts data until the postamble character is seen. The receiver can then look for the next SYN pattern. Alternatively, another approach is to include frame length as part of the control information. The receiver then looks for a SYN character, determines frame length, reads the indicated number of characters, and then looks for the next SYN character to start the next frame.

With *bit-oriented* transmission, the block of data is treated as a sequence of bits. Neither data nor control information needs to be interpreted in units of 8-bit characters. As with character-oriented schemes, a special bit pattern signals the beginning of a block. In bit-oriented transmission, this preamble is eight bits long and is referred to as a flag. The same flag is also used as a postamble (Figure 4-2b). The receiver looks for the occurrence of the flag pattern to signal start of frame. This is followed by some number of control fields, then a variable-length data field, more control fields, and finally the flag is repeated. The differences between this approach and the character-oriented approach depend on details of the formats and the interpretation of the control information. This subject is explored in Chapter 5.

For sizable blocks of data, synchronous transmission is far more efficient than asynchronous. Asynchronous transmission requires 20% or more overhead. The control information in synchronous transmission is typically less than 100 bits. For example, one of the more common bit-oriented schemes, HDLC, contains 48 bits of control information (including the flags). Thus for a 1000-bit message, the overhead is only $48/1048 \times 100\% = 4.6\%$.

ERROR DETECTION TECHNIQUES

In earlier chapters we talked about transmission impairments and the effect of data rate and S/N on bit error rate. Regardless of the design of the transmission system, there will be errors. And, while thermal noise errors may be reduced to vanishingly small rates, bursty impulse noise may still result in substantial errors.

When a frame is transmitted, three classes of probabilities can be defined at the receiving end:

- *Class 1 (P_1):* A frame arrives with no bit errors.
- *Class 2 (P_2):* A frame arrives with one or more undetected bit errors.
- *Class 3 (P_3):* A frame arrives with one or more detected bit errors but no undetected bit errors.

First consider the case when no means are taken to detect errors. Then the probability of detected errors (P_3) is zero. To express the remaining probabilities, assume that the probability that any given bit is in error, P_B, is constant and independent of bit position. Then we have

$$P_1 = (1 - P_B)^{N_f}$$
$$P_2 = 1 - P_1$$

where N_f is the number of bits per frame.

Figure 4-3a illustrates these equations and shows how the probability of erroneous frames increases drastically with bit error probability. Consider the rather modest requirement that at most one frame with an undetected bit error should occur per day on a continuously-used 300 bps channel. If the frame length is 16 bits, this requirement means that at most one frame out of 1.62×10^6 has an error ($P_2 = 0.6 \times 10^{-6}$). A typical P_B for a public telephone line using a 300 bps modem is 10^{-4}. The resulting value of P_2 can be seen to be about three orders of magnitude too large to meet our requirement.

This is the kind of result that motivates the use of error-detection techniques. All of these techniques operate on the following principle: For a given frame of bits, additional bits that constitute an *error-detecting code*, are added by the transmitter. This code is calculated as a function of the other transmitted bits. The receiver performs the same calculation and compares the two results. A detected error occurs if and only if there is a mismatch. Thus P_3 is the probability that if a frame contains errors, the error-detection scheme will detect that fact. P_2 is known as the *residual error rate*, and is the probability that an error will be undetected despite the use of an error-detection scheme. A number of specific techniques follow this general rule. We will examine the three most common ones:

- Parity bit.
- Longitudinal redundancy check.
- Cyclic redundancy check.

Of course, the detection of an error does no good unless some action is taken to correct the error. One approach is to use an error-detection technique that generates sufficient information that errors can be corrected by the receiver. This technique is known as an error-correcting code, and is reviewed briefly in this

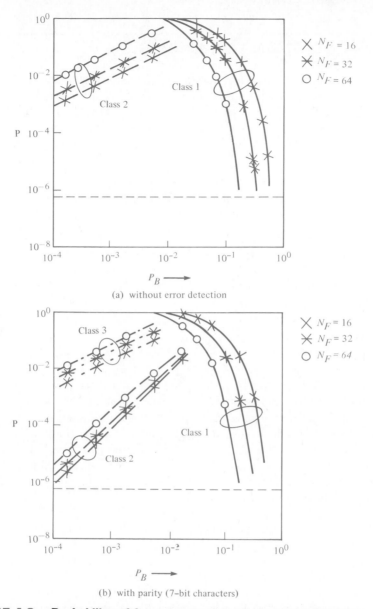

FIGURE 4-3.   **Probability of frame error without and with parity bits.**

section. A far more common procedure is for the receiver to notify the transmitter that an error has been detected and to request a retransmission. This is an element of data link control and will be examined in Chapter 5.

Parity Checks

The simplest bit error detection scheme is to append a parity bit to the end of each word in the frame. A typical example is ASCII transmission, in which a parity bit is attached to each 7-bit ASCII character. The value of this bit is selected so that the word has an even number of 1's (even parity) or an odd number of 1's (odd parity). Typically even parity is used for asynchronous transmission and odd parity for synchronous transmission. So, for example, if the transmitter is transmitting an ASCII *G* (1110001) and using odd parity, it will append a 1 and transmit 11100011. The receiver examines the received character and if the total number of 1's is odd, assumes that no error has occurred. If one bit or any odd number of bits is erroneously inverted during transmission (e.g., 11000011), then, clearly, the receiver will detect an error. Note, however, that if two (or any even number of) bits are inverted, an undetected error occurs!

Again the probabilities are easily expressed:

$$P_1 = (1 - P_B)^{N_B N_C}$$

$$P_2 = \sum_{k=1}^{N_C} \binom{N_C}{k} \left[\sum_{j=2,4,\ldots}^{N_B} \binom{N_B}{j} P_B^j (1 - P_B)^{(N_B - j)} \right]^k$$
$$[(1 - P_B)^{N_B}]^{(N_C - k)}$$

$$P_3 = 1 - P_2 - P_1$$

where

N_B = number of bits per character (including the parity bit)
N_C = number of characters per frame

These three probabilities are illustrated in Figure 4-3b ($N_F = N_B \times N_C$). The parity bit dramatically reduces the probability of accepting a message with undetected errors (P_2), while the probability of receiving a correct message does not change significantly. For a bit error rate of 10^{-4}, the value of P_2 now approaches the requirements of the preceding example. For longer frames, however, this is still not sufficient.

The problem with the use of the parity bit is that noise impulses are often long enough to destroy more than one bit, particularly at high data rates. Figure 4-4 shows the probability of a second error bit within X bits of a first error bit on a

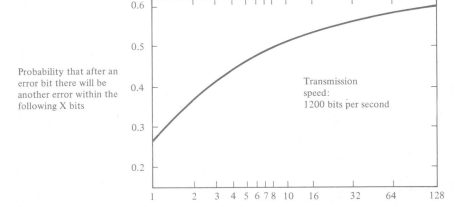

Probability that after an error bit there will be another error within the following X bits

Transmission speed: 1200 bits per second

X

FIGURE 4-4. Probability of a second error bit.

1200-bps voice-grade line. Thus the formulation used above for P_2 is too conservative.

A substantial improvement can be achieved by using a second set of parity bits, as illustrated in Figure 4-5. The frame is viewed as a block of characters arranged in two dimensions. To each character is appended a parity bit, as before. In addition, a parity bit is generated for each bit position across all characters. That is, an additional character is generated in which the *I*th bit of the character is a parity bit for the *I*th bit of all other characters in the block. This can be expressed mathematically using the exclusive-or $\oplus$ operation. The exclusive-or of two binary digits is 0 if both digits are 0 or both are 1. If the digits differ, the result is 1. Let us call the parity bit at the end of each character the row parity bit. Then

$$R_j = b_{1j} \oplus b_{2j} \oplus \cdots b_{nj}$$

where

R_j = parity bit of *j*th character
b_{ij} = *i*th bit in *j*th character
n = number of bits in a character

This equation generates even parity. For the parity check character:

$$C_i = b_{i1} \oplus b_{i2} \oplus \cdots \oplus b_{in}$$

where

C_i = *i*th bit of parity check character
m = number of characters in a frame

In this format, the parity bits at the end of each character are referred to as the vertical redundancy check (VRC), and the parity check character is referred to as the longitudinal redundancy check (LRC).

	bit 1	bit 2		bit n	Parity bit
Character 1	b_{11}	b_{21}		b_{n1}	R_1
Character 2	b_{12}	b_{22}		b_{n2}	R_2
Character m	b_{1m}	b_{2m}		b_{nm}	R_m
Parity check character	C_1	C_2		C_n	C_{n+1}

(a) Format

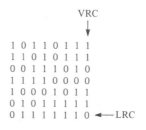

VRC

```
1 0 1 1 0 1 1 1
1 1 0 1 0 1 1 1
0 0 1 1 1 0 1 0
1 1 1 1 0 0 0 0
1 0 0 0 1 0 1 1
0 1 0 1 1 1 1 1
0 1 1 1 1 1 1 0  ←—LRC
```

(b) Example

FIGURE 4-5. Vertical and longitudinal redundancy checks.

Measurements indicate that the use of both VRC and LRC reduces the undetected error rate compared to simple VRC by two to four orders of magnitude [MART70]. However, even this scheme is not foolproof. Consider the case of bits 1 and 3 in character 1 being in error. When the receiver generates the parity bit for character 1, it will match the received parity bit, and no error is detected. However, when it generates the parity check character, bits 1 and 3 will differ from those of the received parity check character, and the error is detected. Now suppose that, in addition, bits 1 and 3 of character 5 are also in error. Not only do the parity bits for character 1 and 5 fail to detect errors, but the parity check character also fails to detect them. Thus some patterns of even numbers of errors remain undetected.

Cyclic Redundancy Checks

To achieve further improvement a very powerful but easily implemented technique, known as *cyclic redundancy check* (CRC), can be used. The procedure can be explained as follows. Given a k-bit frame or message, the transmitter generates an n-bit sequence, known as a *frame check sequence* (FCS), so that the resulting frame, consisting of $k + n$ bits, is exactly divisible by some predetermined number. The receiver then divides the incoming frame by the same number and, if there is no remainder, assumes that there was no error.

To clarify the above, we present the procedure in several ways:

* Modulo 2 arithmetic.
* Polynomials.
* Shift registers and exclusive-or gates.

First, we work with binary numbers and modulo 2 arithmetic. Modulo 2 arithmetic uses binary addition with no carries, which is just the exclusive-or operation.

EXAMPLES

$$
\begin{array}{r}
1111 \\
+\,1010 \\
\hline
0101
\end{array}
\qquad
\begin{array}{r}
11001 \\
\times\quad\ 11 \\
\hline
11001 \\
11001 \\
\hline
101011
\end{array}
$$

Now define:

$T = (k + n)$-bit frame to be transmitted, with $n < k$
$M = k$-bit message, the first k bits of T
$F = n$-bit FCS, the last n bits of T
$P = $ pattern of $n + 1$ bits; this is the predetermined divisor mentioned above

We would like T/P to have no remainder. It should be clear that

$$T = 2^n M + F$$

That is, by multiplying M by 2^n, we have in effect shifted it to the left by n bits and padded out the result with 0's. Adding F gives us the concatenation of M and F, which is T. Now we want T to be exactly divisible by P. Suppose that we divided 2^nM by P:

$$\frac{2^nM}{P} = Q + \frac{R}{P} \tag{4-1}$$

There is a quotient and a remainder. Since division is binary, the remainder is always one bit less than the divisor. We will use this remainder as our FCS. Then

$$T = 2^nM + R$$

Question: Does this R satisfy our condition? To see that it does, consider

$$\frac{T}{P} = \frac{2^nM + R}{P}$$

substituting equation (4-1), we have

$$\frac{T}{P} = Q + \frac{R}{P} + \frac{R}{P}$$

However, any binary number added to itself modulo 2 yields zero. Thus

$$\frac{T}{P} = Q + \frac{R + R}{P} = Q$$

There is no remainder, and therefore T is exactly divisible by P. Thus the FCS is easily generated. Simply divide 2^nM by P and use the remainder as the FCS. On reception, the receiver will divide T by P and will get no remainder if there have been no errors.

A simple example of the procedure is now presented:

1. Given

$$\text{Message } M = 1010001101 \text{ (10 bits)}$$
$$\text{Pattern } P = 110101 \text{ (6 bits)}$$
$$\text{FCS } R = \text{to be calculated (5 bits)}$$

2. The message is multiplied by 2^5, yielding 101000110100000.
3. This product is divided by P:

```
                       1101010110←Q
P→110101|101000110100000←2ⁿM
          110101
           111011
           110101
            111010
            110101
             111110
             110101
              101100
              110101
               110010
               110101
                1110←R
```

4. The remainder ($R = 01110$) is added to 2^nM to give $T = 10100011010110$, which is transmitted.
5. If there are no errors, the receiver receives T intact. The received frame is divided by P:

$$
\begin{array}{r}
1101010110 \\
110101\,\overline{)101000110101110} \\
\underline{110101} \\
111011 \\
\underline{110101} \\
111010 \\
\underline{110101} \\
111110 \\
\underline{110101} \\
101111 \\
\underline{110101} \\
110101 \\
\underline{110101} \\
00
\end{array}
$$

Since there is no remainder, it is assumed that there have been no errors.

The pattern P is chosen to be one bit longer than the desired FCS, and the exact bit pattern chosen depends on the type of errors expected. At minimum, both the high- and low-order bits of P must be 1.

The occurrence of an error is easily expressed. An error results in the reversal of a bit. Mathematically, this is equivalent to taking the exclusive-or of the bit and 1: $0 + 1 = 1$; $1 + 1 = 0$. Thus the errors in an $(n + k)$-bit frame can be represented by an $(n + k)$-bit field with 1's in each error position. The resulting frame T_r can be expressed as

$$T_r = T + E$$

where

$T =$ transmitted frame
$E =$ error pattern with 1's in positions where errors occur
$T_r =$ received frame

The receiver will fail to detect an error if and only if T_r is divisible by P, that is, if and only if E is divisible by P. Intuitively, this seems an unlikely occurrence.

A second way of viewing the CRC process is to express all values as polynomials in a dummy variable X with binary coefficients. The coefficients correspond to the bits in the binary number. Thus for $M = 110011$, we have $M(X) = X^5 + X^4 + X + 1$, and for $P = 11001$, we have $P(X) = X^4 + X^3 + 1$. Arithmetic operations are again modulo 2. The CRC process can now be described as:

1. $\dfrac{X^nM(X)}{P(X)} = Q(X) + \dfrac{R(X)}{P(X)}$
2. $T(X) = X^nM(X) + R(X)$

An error $E(X)$ will only be undetectable if it is divisible by $P(X)$. It can be shown [PETE61] that all of the following are not divisible by $P(X)$ and hence are detectable:

1. All single-bit errors.
2. All double-bit errors, as long as $P(X)$ has a factor with at least three terms.
3. Any odd number of errors, as long as $P(X)$ contains a factor $(X + 1)$.
4. Any burst error for which the length of the burst is less than the length of the FCS.
5. Most larger burst errors.

The first assertion is clear. A single-bit error can be represented by $E(X) = X^i$ for some i. We have said that for $P(X)$ both the first and last terms must be nonzero. Thus $P(X)$ has at least two terms and cannot divide the one-term $E(X)$. Similarly, a two-bit error can be represented by $E(X) = X^i + X^j = X^i(1 + X^{j-i})$ for some i and j with $i < j$. Thus $P(X)$ must divide either X^i or $(1 + X^{j-i})$. We have shown that it does not divide X^i, and it can be shown [PETE61] that it does not divide $(1 + X^{j-i})$ except for very large values of $j - i$, beyond the practical frame length. To see the third assertion, assume that $E(X)$ has an odd number of terms and is

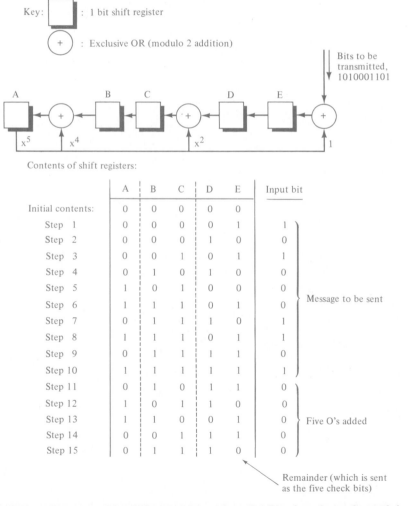

Contents of shift registers:

	A	B	C	D	E	Input bit
Initial contents:	0	0	0	0	0	
Step 1	0	0	0	0	1	1
Step 2	0	0	0	1	0	0
Step 3	0	0	1	0	1	1
Step 4	0	1	0	1	0	0
Step 5	1	0	1	0	0	0
Step 6	1	1	1	0	1	0
Step 7	0	1	1	1	0	1
Step 8	1	1	1	0	1	1
Step 9	0	1	1	1	1	0
Step 10	1	1	1	1	1	1
Step 11	0	1	0	1	1	0
Step 12	1	0	1	1	0	0
Step 13	1	1	0	0	1	0
Step 14	0	0	1	1	1	0
Step 15	0	1	1	1	0	0

Message to be sent (Steps 1–10)

Five 0's added (Steps 11–15)

Remainder (which is sent as the five check bits)

FIGURE 4-6.   **Circuit with shift registers for dividing by the polynomial $(X^5 + X^4 + X^2 + 1)$.**

divisible by $(X + 1)$. Then we can express $E(X)$ as $E(X) = (X + 1)F(X)$. Then $E(1) = (1 + 1)F(1) = 0$ since $1 + 1 = 0$. But $E(1)$ will be 0 if and only if $E(X)$ contains an even number of terms. For the fourth assertion, we define a burst of length j as a string of bits beginning and ending with 1 and containing intervening 1's and 0's. This can be represented as $E(X) = X^i(X^{j-1} + \ldots + 1)$ where i expresses how far the burst is shifted from the right-hand end. We know that $P(X)$ does not divide X^i. For $j < n$, where n is the length of the FCS, $P(X)$ will not divide the second factor, since $P(X)$ is of higher order.

Finally, it can be shown that if all error patterns are considered equally likely, then for a burst of length $r + 1$, the probability that $E(X)$ is divisible by $P(X)$ is $1/2^{r-1}$, and for a longer burst, the probability is $1/2^r$ [PETE61].

Four versions of $P(X)$ are widely used:

$$\text{CRC-12} = X^{12} + X^{11} + X^3 + X^2 + X + 1$$
$$\text{CRC-16} = X^{16} + X^{15} + X^2 + 1$$
$$\text{CRC-CCITT} = X^{16} + X^{12} + X^5 + 1$$
$$\text{CRC-32} = X^{32} + X^{26} + X^{23} + X^{22} + X^{16} + X^{12} + X^{11}$$
$$+ X^{10} + X^8 + X^7 + X^5 + X^4 + X^2 + X + 1$$

The CRC-12 system is used for transmission of streams of 6-bit characters and generates a 12-bit FCS. Both CRC-16 and CRC-CCITT are popular for 8-bit characters, in the United States and Europe respectively, and both result in a 16-bit FCS. This would seem adequate for most applications, although CRC-32 is specified as an option in some point-to-point synchronous transmission standards. The local network standards committee (IEEE-802), evidently a suspicious lot, has specified the use of CRC-32, which generates a 32-bit FCS. This CRC is also used in some DOD applications.

As a final representation, Figure 4-6 shows that the CRC process can easily be implemented as a dividing circuit consisting of exclusive-or gates and a shift register. The circuit is implemented as follows:

1. The register contains n bits, equal to the length of the FCS.
2. There are up to n exclusive-or gates.
3. The presence or absence of a gate corresponds to the presence or absence of a term in the divisor polynomial, $P(X)$.

In this example, we use:

Message $M = 1010001101$; $M(X) = X^9 + X^7 + X^3 + X^2 + 1$
Divisor $P = 110101$; $P(X) = X^5 + X^4 + X^2 + 1$

which were used earlier in the discussion.

The process begins with the shift register cleared (all zeroes). The message, or dividend, is then entered, one bit at a time, starting with the most significant (leftmost) bit. Since no feedback occurs until a 1 dividend bit arrives at the most significant end of the register, the first four operations are simple shifts. Whenever a 1 bit arrives at the left end, a 1 is subtracted (exclusive-or) from the second and fifth bits on the next shift. This is identical to the binary long division process illustrated earlier. The process continues through all the bits of the message, plus four zero bits. These latter bits account for shifting M to the left four positions to accommodate the FCS. After the last bit is processed, the shift register contains the remainder (FCS), which can then be transmitted.

At the receiver, the same logic is used. As each bit of M arrives it is inserted into the shift register at A. If there have been no errors, the shift register should contain the bit pattern for R at the conclusion of M. The transmitted bits of R now begin to arrive, and the effect is to zero out the register so that, at the conclusion of reception, the register contains all 0's.

The shift register implementation makes clear the power of the CRC algorithm. Due to the feedback arrangement, the state of the shift register depends, in a complex way, on the past history of bits presented. Thus it will take an extremely rare combination of errors to fool the system. Further, it is evident that the CRC algorithm is easy to implement in hardware.

Forward Error Correction

In addition to error-detecting codes, there are also error-correcting codes. These are rarely used in data transmission, since retransmission schemes (see Chapter 5) are generally more efficient. Error-correcting codes are used in some situations where retransmission is impractical. Examples are broadcast situations in which there are multiple receivers for one transmission and space probes which essentially use simplex transmission. These codes find more use in applications other than data communication, such as computer memory [STAL90b]. Error-correcting codes are referred to as *forward error correction* to indicate that the receiver, on its own, is correcting the error. Retransmission schemes, in contrast, are referred to as *backward error correction,* since the receiver feeds back information to the transmitter, which then retransmits data found to be in error.

As with error-detecting codes, an error-correcting code is calculated from the bits to be transmitted and is then added to the transmission. To achieve acceptable levels of error correction, the length of the code must be about the same as the length of the data, reducing the effective data rate by 50%. With a code of this relative length, a reduction in error rate by a factor of 10^2 to 10^3 is achieved.

The reader interested in such codes is referred to [BHAR83] and [MIER84]. A deeper analysis of both error-detecting and error-correcting codes is found in [GALL68].

4-3

INTERFACING

Most digital data processing devices are possessed of limited data transmission capability. Typically, they generate only digital signals, and these are usually NRZ-L or a variant. The distance across which they can transmit data is also limited. Consequently it is rare for such a device to attach directly to a transmission medium. The more common situation is depicted in Figure 4-7. The devices we are discussing, which include terminals and computers, are generically referred to as *data terminal equipment* (DTE). A DTE makes use of the transmission system through the mediation of *data circuit-terminating equipment* (DCE). An example of the latter is a modem (a good description of a variety of DCEs can be found in [HELD86]).

On one side, the DCE is responsible for transmitting and receiving bits, one at

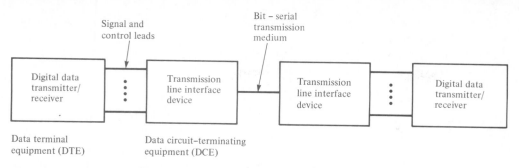

FIGURE 4-7. Generic interface to transmission medium.

a time, over a transmission medium. On the other side, the DCE must interact with the DTE. In general, this requires both data and control information to be exchanged. This is done over a set of wires referred to as *interchange circuits*. For this scheme to work, a high degree of cooperation is required. The two DCEs must understand each other. That is, the receiver of each must use the same encoding scheme (e.g., Manchester, PSK) as the transmitter of the other. In addition, each DTE-DCE pair must be designed to have complementary interfaces and must be able to interact effectively. To ease the burden on data processing equipment manufacturers and users, standards have been developed that specify the exact nature of the interface between the DTE and the DCE. In contemporary parlance, these standards are known as physical layer protocols, and occupy layer 1 of the OSI model referred to in Chapter 1. In this section we examine the nature and functioning of this interface.

The interface has four important characteristics [BERT80]:

- Mechanical.
- Electrical.
- Functional.
- Procedural.

The *mechanical* characteristics pertain to the actual physical connection of the DTE and DCE. Typically, the signal and control leads are bundled into a cable with a terminator plug, male or female, at each end. The DTE and DCE must each present a plug of opposite gender at one end of the cable, effecting the physical connection. This is analogous to the situation for residential electrical power. Power is provided via a socket or wall outlet, and the device to be attached must have the appropriate plug (two-pronged, two-pronged polarized, three-pronged).

The *electrical* characteristics have to do with the voltage levels and timing of voltage changes. Both DTE and DCE must use the same code (e.g., NRZ-L), must use the same voltage levels to mean the same thing, and must use the same duration of signal elements. These characteristics determine the data rates and distances that can be achieved.

Functional characteristics specify the functions that are performed, by assigning meaning to the various interchange circuits. Functions can be classified into the broad categories of data, control, timing, and ground.

Procedural characteristics specify the sequence of events for transmitting data, based on the functional characteristics of the interface. Examples below should clarify this point.

A variety of standards for interfacing exist. This section presents several of the most important:

- EIA-232-D
- EIA-530
- ISDN Physical Interface

EIA-232-D

By far the most common interface standard in the United States is the 232 standard issued by the Electronic Industries Association. The RS-232 standard was first issued in 1962, and its third revision, RS-232-C, was published in 1969. EIA-232-D was introduced in 1987. It is compatible with RS-232-C. The main differences are: EIA-232-D defines a specific cable connector, whereas RS-232-C allows various connectors to be used; and three additional circuits for test operations have been defined. This interface is used to connect DTE devices to voice-grade modems for use on public analog telecommunications systems. It is also widely used for many other interconnection functions.

The **mechanical specification** for EIA-232-D is illustrated in Figure 4-8. It calls for a 25-pin connector, referred to as the DB-25 connector, with a specific arrangement of leads. Thus, in theory, a 25-wire cable could be used to connect the DTE to the DCE. In practice, fewer interchange circuits are used.

The **electrical specification** defines the signaling between DTE and DCE. Digital signaling is used on all interchange circuits. Depending on the function of the interchange circuit, the electrical values are interpreted either as binary or as control signals. The convention specified is that, with respect to a common ground, a voltage more negative than -3 volts is interpreted as binary 1 and a voltage more positive than $+3$ volts is interpreted as binary 0. The interface is rated at a signal rate of <20 kbps and a distance of <15 m. Greater distances and data rates are possible with good design, but it is reasonable to assume that these limits apply in practice as well as in theory. The same voltage levels apply to control signals: a voltage more negative than -3 volts is interpreted as an OFF condition and a voltage more positive than $+3$ volts is interpreted as an ON condition.

Table 4-1 summarizes the **functional specification** of EIA-232-D. The interchange circuits can be grouped into the categories of data, control, timing, and ground. There is one *data circuit* in each direction, so full-duplex operation is possible. In addition, there are two secondary data circuits that are useful when the device operates in a half-duplex fashion. In the case of half-duplex operation, data exchange between two DTEs (via their DCEs and the intervening communications link) is only possible in one direction at a time. However, there may be a need to send a halt or flow control message to a transmitting device. To accommodate this, the communications link is equipped with a reverse channel, usually at a much lower data rate than the primary channel, for this purpose. At the DTE-DCE interface, the reverse channel is carried on a separate pair of data circuits.

There are fourteen *control circuits*. The first eight of these listed in Table 4-1 relate to the transmission of data over the primary channel. For asynchronous transmission, six of these circuits are used (CA, CB, CC, CD, CE, CF). The use of these circuits is explained below, in a discussion of procedural specifications.

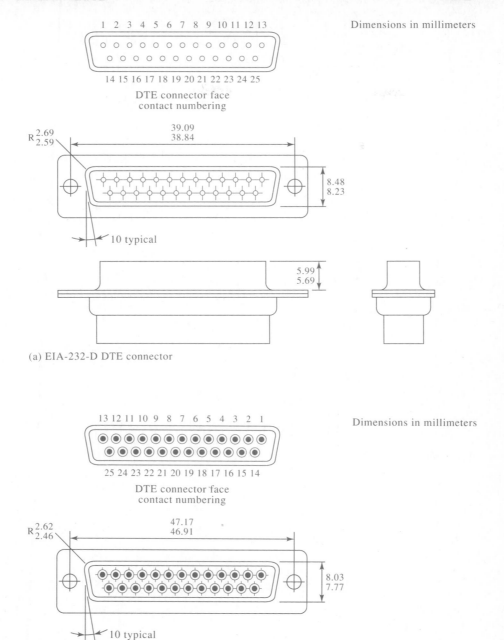

(a) EIA-232-D DTE connector

(b) EIA-232-D DCE connector

FIGURE 4-8. **EIA-232-D connector.**

TABLE 4-1 **EIA-232-D Interchange Circuits**

Pin/ Circuit Label	Name	Direction to:	Function
Data Signals			
2/BA	Transmitted Data	DCE	Data generated by DTE
3/BB	Received Data	DTE	Data received by DTE
14/SBA	Secondary Transmitted Data	DCE	Data generated by DTE on reverse channel
16/SBB	Secondary Received Data	DTE	Data received by DTE on reverse channel
Control Signals			
4/CA	Request to Send	DCE	DTE wishes to transmit
5/CB	Clear to Send	DTE	DCE is ready to receive; response to Request to Send
6/CC	DCE Ready[1]	DTE	DCE is ready to operate
20/CD	DTE Ready[2]	DCE	DTE is ready to operate
22/CE	Ring Indicator	DTE	Indicates that the DCE is receiving a ringing signal on the communication channel
8/CF	Received Line Signal Detector	DTE	Indicates that the DCE is receiving a carrier signal
21/CG	Signal Quality Detector	DTE	Asserted when there is reason to believe there is an error in the received data
23/CH	Data Signal Rate Select	DCE	Asserted to select the higher of two possible data rates
23/CI	Data Signal Rate Select	DTE	Asserted to select the higher of two possible data rates
19/SCA	Secondary Request to Send	DCE	DTE wishes to transmit on reverse channel
13/SCB	Secondary Clear to Send	DTE	DCE is ready to receive on reverse channel
12/SCF	Secondary Received Line Signal Detector	DTE	Indicates that the DCE is receiving a carrier signal on reverse channel
21/RL	Remote Loopback[3]	DCE	Instructs remote DCE to loop back signals
18/LL	Local Loopback[4]	DCE	Instructs DCE to loop back signals from DTE
25/TM	Test Mode[4]	DTE	Indicates if the local DCE is in a test condition
Timing Signals			
24/DA	Transmitter Signal Element Timing	DCE	Clocking signal; transitions to ON and OFF occur at center of each signal element
15/DB	Transmitter Signal Element Timing	DTE	Clocking signal, as above; both circuits relate to signals on BA
17/DD	Receiver Signal Element Timing	DTE	Clocking signal, as above; for circuit BB
Ground/Shield			
7/AB	Signal Ground/Common Return	N/A	Establishes common ground reference for all circuits
1	Shield[5]	N/A	Used for connection to shield on DTE side to provide shield continuity in cases where several cables are connected end to end

[1]This circuit was Data Set Ready in RS-232-C
[2]This circuit was Data Terminal Ready in RS-232-C
[3]Remote Loopback was not included in RS-232-C; only the CG interpretation

[4]This circuit was unassigned in RS-232-C
[5]This circuit was protective ground in RS-232-C

In addition to these six circuits, two other control circuits are used in synchronous transmission. The Signal Quality Detector circuit is turned ON by the DCE to indicate that the quality of the incoming signal over the telephone line has deteriorated beyond some defined threshold. Most high-speed modems support more than one transmission rate so that they can fall back to a lower speed if the telephone line becomes noisy. The Data Signal Rate Selector circuit is used to change speeds. Either the DTE or DCE will have the responsibility of selecting the speed. The next three control circuits (SCZ, SCB, SCF) are used to control the use of the secondary channel.

The last group of control signals relate to loopback testing. These circuits allow the DTE to cause the DCE to perform a loopback test (Figure 4-9). These circuits are only valid if in fact the modem or other DCE supports loopback control; this is now a common modem feature. In the local loopback function, the transmitter output of the modem is connected to the receiver input, disconnecting the modem from the transmission line. A stream of data generated by the user device (e.g., computer) is sent to the modem and looped back to the user device. For remote loopback, the local modem is connected to the transmission facility in the usual fashion, and the receiver output of the remote modem is connected to that modem's transmitter input. During either form of test, the DCE turns ON the Test Mode circuit. Table 4-2 shows the settings for all of the circuits related to loopback testing.

Loopback control is a useful fault isolation tool. For example, suppose that a user at a terminal is communicating with a computer by means of a modem and communication suddenly ceases. Among the possible causes:

1. The terminal's modem has malfunctioned.
2. The communications facility between the two modems has failed.
3. The computer's modem has malfunctioned.
4. The remote computer has malfunctioned.

The loopback tests can help the network manager to isolate the fault. Local loopback checks the functioning of the local interface and the local DCE. Remote loopback tests the operation of the transmission channel and the remote DCE.

There are three *timing circuits* that may be used with synchronous transmission; these provide clock pulses. When the DCE is sending data over circuit BB, it also sends 1-0 and 0-1 transitions on DD, with transitions timed to the middle of each BB signal element. When the DTE is sending data, either the DTE or DCE can provide timing pulses.

The final set of circuits deal with *grounding and shielding*. The Signal Ground/Common Return serves as the return circuit for all data leads. Hence, transmission is unbalanced, with only one active wire. The Shield lead is for connection of a shielded cable at the DTE side of the interface. Shielded cables are used to protect against electromagnetic interference.

The **procedural specification** defines the sequence in which the various circuits are used for particular applications. We give a few examples.

The first example is for an asynchronous private line modem, also known as a limited distance modem, used to connect two devises with a point-to-point link. The modem, as a DCE, requires only the following circuits:

- Signal ground (AB)
- Transmitted data (BA)
- Received data (BB)

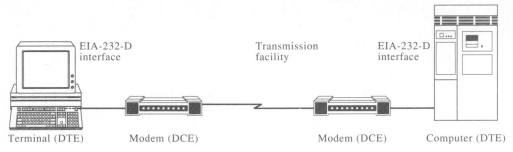

(a) Typical configuration for loopback testing

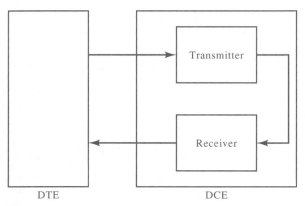

(b) Local loopback testing

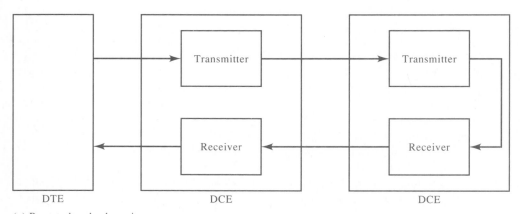

(c) Remote loopback testing

FIGURE 4-9. Local and remote loopback with EIA-232-D.

- Request to send (CA)
- Clear to send (CB)
- DCE ready (CC)
- Received line signal detector (CF)

The first three circuits have been reasonably well explained. When the DTE is ready to send data, it asserts Request to Send. The modem responds, when ready,

TABLE 4-2   Loopback Circuit Settings for EIA-232-D and EIA-530

Local Loopback		Remote Loopback		
Circuit	Condition	Circuit	Local Interface	Remote Interface
DCE Ready	ON	DCE Ready	ON	OFF
Local Loopback	ON	Local Loopback	OFF	OFF
Remote Loopback	OFF	Remote Loopback	ON	OFF
Test Mode	ON	Test Mode	ON	ON

with Clear to Send, thereby indicating that data may be transmitted over circuit BA. If the arrangement is half-duplex, then Request to Send also inhibits the receive mode. The DCE Ready circuit is asserted by the modem when it is ready to operate. The lead should be asserted before the DTE attempts Request to Send. Finally, Received Line Signal Detector indicates that the remote modem is transmitting. Note that it is not necessary to use timing circuits, since this is asynchronous transmission.

The circuits described so far are sufficient for private line modems used point-to-point, but additional circuits are required when the telephone network is used. Now, the initiator of a connection must call the destination station. Two additional leads are required:

- DTE ready
- Ring indicator

With the addition of these two circuits, the DTE-modem system can effectively use the telephone lines in a way analogous to voice telephone usage. Figure 4-10 depicts the steps involved in a dial-up half-duplex operation. In this case, a call is placed from a terminal to a computer. The computer must be available to receive calls, which it indicates to its modem by setting Data Terminal Ready ON. When the call comes in, indicated to the modem by a ringing tone on the line, the modem alerts the computer with a Ring Indicator. Typically, the computer will respond to an incoming connection request with some sort of prompt message to the terminal. First, the computer sets Request to Send ON to indicate to the modem that it would like to transmit. The modem begins to transmit a carrier frequency on the telephone line and sets Clear to Send to signal the computer that it may begin transmitting. The carrier tone alerts the other modem that data is about to arrive. In some configurations, a human operator hears the tone and must press a data on button to be able to receive data. In other configurations, human intervention is not necessary. In any case, the terminal accepts data via the modem until the carrier is dropped. The terminal can now transmit its own message, beginning with a Request-to-Send, Clear-to-Send handshake with its modem. Ultimately, one side hangs up and the exchange terminates.

As an aside, it is instructive to consider situations in which the distances between devices are so close to allow two DTEs to directly signal each other. In this case, the EIA-232-D circuits can still be used, but now no DCE equipment is provided. For the scheme to work, a *null modem* is needed, which interconnects leads in such a way as to fool both DTEs into thinking that they are connected to modems. The reasons for the particular connections in Figure 4-11 should be apparent if the reader has grasped the preceding discussion.

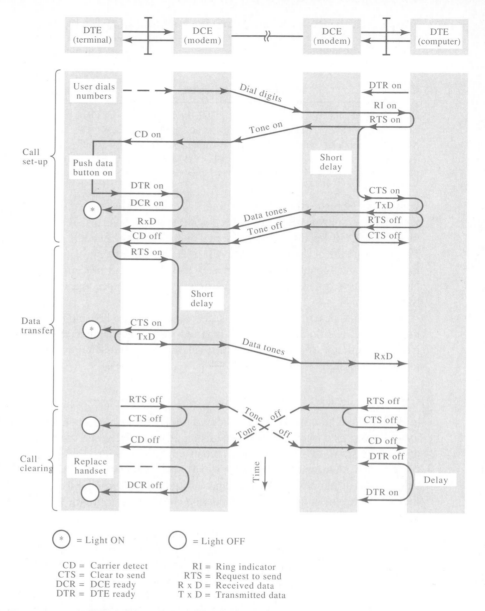

FIGURE 4-10.   EIA-232-D operation. [HALS88]

EIA-530 with RS-422-A and RS-423-A

The limitations of the 232 specification, particularly in the areas of speed and distance, led EIA to introduce the RS-449 specification in 1977, with the intention of replacing RS-232-C. RS-449 makes use of a 37-pin connector, provides more functions, and provides an improved speed and distance capability. However, this specification was not embraced by industry and never made a noticeable dent in the 232 base. This is partially due to the tremendous investment in DB-25 hardware. Also, a given product's surface area can hold fewer 37-pin connectors than 25-pin connectors, allowing fewer ports.

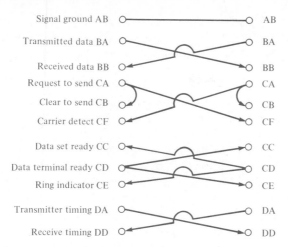

Signal ground AB — AB
Transmitted data BA — BA
Received data BB — BB
Request to send CA — CA
Clear to send CB — CB
Carrier detect CF — CF
Data set ready CC — CC
Data terminal ready CD — CD
Ring indicator CE — CE
Transmitter timing DA — DA
Receive timing DD — DD

FIGURE 4-11. The null modem.

Accordingly, in 1987 EIA-530 was introduced. This standard is intended to operate at data rates from 20 kbps to 2 Mbps using the same 25-pin, DB-25 connector used by EIA-232-D and RS-232-C.

The major improvement in EIA-530 over the 232 family is in the electrical characteristics of the new interface. Actually, EIA-530 does not include an electrical specification; rather it refers to two other EIA standards: RS-422-A and RS-423-A. Whereas RS-232 was designed in the era of discrete electronic components, the new standards take advantage of the superior performance possibilities of integrated circuit technology. To understand these standards, we need to define several modes of transmission.

In a conventional telephone system, and indeed in most uses of twisted pair, signals are carried on a *balanced transmission* line consisting of two conductors. Signals are transmitted as a current that travels down one conductor and returns on the other, the two conductors form a complete circuit. For digital signals this technique is known as *differential signaling,* since the binary value depends on the direction of the voltage difference between the two conductors. *Unbalanced transmission* uses a single conductor to carry the signal, with ground providing the return path.

The balanced mode tolerates more, and produces less, noise than the unbalanced. Ideally, interference on a balanced line will act equally on both conductors and not affect the voltage difference. Because unbalanced transmission does not possess these advantages, it is generally limited to use on coaxial cable; when it is used on interchange circuits, such as EIA-232-D, it is limited to very short distances.

RS-423-A specifies unbalanced transmission. As with EIA-232-D, an NRZ-L encoding scheme is used. In this case, a positive voltage of between 2 and 6 volts, with respect to ground, is interpreted as a binary 0, and a negative voltage of between 4 and 6 volts is interpreted as binary 1. RS-423-A achieves the following rated performance: 3 kbps at 1000 m to 300 kbps at 10 m. This is a significant improvement over EIA-232-D, which is a constant limit of 20 kbps up to 15 m. RS-422-A specifies balanced transmission. Again, an NRL-Z scheme is used; in this case a voltage difference between the two circuits in the range 2 to 6 volts is interpreted as a binary digit, with the direction of the difference determining whether it is interpreted as binary 0 or binary 1. The performance with this standard is 100 kbps at 1200 m to 10 Mbps at 12 m; a graph of the rated performance was shown in Figure 2-19. Although the interface is capable of up to 10 Mbps, EIA-232-D specifies a maximum data rate of 2 Mbps.

Table 4-3 lists the EIA-530 circuits and compares these to the corresponding pin assignments for EIA-232-D. Most of the EIA-530 circuits use RS-422-A and hence require two pins for balanced transmission; these are referred to as Category I circuits. Only the three loopback circuits use RS-423-A; these are referred to as Category II circuits. Thus, some of the functionality of EIA-232-D must be sacrificed to remain within the 25-pin limit. In particular, the following EIA-232-D circuits are not supported on EIA-530: Ring Indicator, Signal Quality Detector, Data Signal Rate Selector, and the five secondary circuits.

TABLE 4-3   EIA-232-D and EIA-530 Interchange Circuits

EIA-530		EIA-232-D	
Signal Name	**Pin Number(s)**	**Signal Name**	**Pin Number**
Shield	1	Shield	1
Transmitted Data*	2, 14	Transmitted Data	2
		Secondary Transmitted Data	14
Received Data*	3, 16	Received Data	3
		Secondary Received Data	16
Request to Send*	4, 19	Request to Send	4
		Secondary Request to Send	19
Clear to Send*	5, 13	Clear to Send	5
		Secondary Clear to Send	13
DCE Ready*	6, 22	DCE Ready	6
		Ring Indicator	22
DTE Ready*	20, 23	DTE Ready	20
		Data Signal Rate Select	23
Signal Ground	7	Signal Ground	7
Received Line Signal Detect*	8, 10	Received Line Signal Detector	8
		Reserved	10
Transmit Signal Element Timing*	15, 12	Transmitter Signal Element Timing	15
(DCE Source)		Secondary Received Line Signal Detector	12
Receiver Signal Element Timing*	17, 9	Receiver Signal Element Timing	17
(DCE Source)		Reserved	9
Local Loopback†	18	Local Loopback	18
Remote Loopback†	21	Remote Loopback/Signal Quality Detector	21
Transmit Signal Element Timing*	24, 11	Transmit Signal Element Timing	24
(DTE Source)		Unassigned	11
Test Mode†	25	Test Mode	25

*Category I circuits (RS-422-A)
†Category II circuits (RS-423-A)

ISDN Physical Connector

The wide variety of functions available with EIA-232D and EIA-530 is provided by the use of a large number of circuits and connections. This is a rather expensive way to achieve results. An alternative would be to provide fewer circuits but to add more logic at the DTE and DCE interfaces. With the dropping costs of logic circuitry, this is an attractive approach. This approach was taken in the X.21 standard for interfacing to public circuit-switched networks, specifying a 15-pin connector. More recently, the trend has been carried further with the specification of an 8-pin physical connector (Figure 4-12) to an Integrated Services Digital

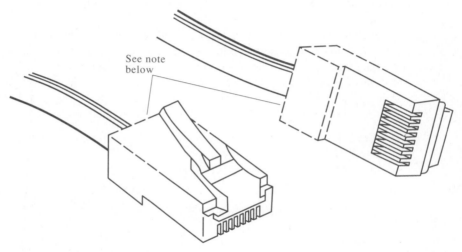

See note
below

NOTE—This portion of the plug illustrates a structure necessary for securing the cordage and is not pertinent to proper mating with the jack.

(a) Plug—8 pole

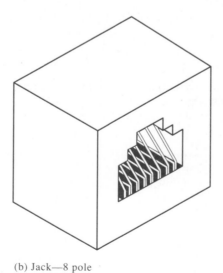

(b) Jack—8 pole

FIGURE 4-12.   ISDN physical connector.

Network (ISDN). ISDN, which is an all-digital replacement for existing public telephone and telecommunications networks, is examined in detail in Part IV. In this section, we look at the physical connector defined for ISDN.

In ISDN terminology, a physical connection is made between terminal equipment (TE) and network-terminating equipment (NT). For purposes of our discussion, these terms correspond, rather closely, to DTE and DCE respectively. The physical connection, defined in ISO standard 8877 (ISO 8877), specifies that the NT and TE cables shall terminate in matching plugs that provide for 4, 6, or 8 contacts. The number of contacts provided depends on usage, as is explained below.

Table 4-4 lists the contact assignments for each of the 8 pins on both the NT and TE sides. Two pins each are needed to provide balanced transmission in each direction. These contact points are used to connect twisted-pair leads coming from the NT and TE devices.

The specification provides for the capability to transfer power across the interface. The direction of power transfer depends on the application. In a typical application, it may be desirable to provide for power transfer from the network side towards the terminals in order to, for example, maintain a basic telephony service in the event of failure of the locally provided power. Two possibilities are seen for the transfer of power from an NT to a TE (Figure 4-13):

- Using the same access leads used for the bidirectional transmission of the digital signal (power source and sink 1)
- On additional wires using access leads 1-2 and 7-8

The remaining two leads are not used in the ISDN configuration but may be useful in other configurations. Thus, the ISDN physical interface consists of just six leads.

Since there are no specific functional circuits, the transmit/receive circuits must be used to carry both data and control signals. The details of this arrangement are deferred until Part IV. For now, suffice it to say that control information is transmitted in the form of messages, and that this information is multiplexed onto the same interface with data using a synchronous TDM technique.

The electrical specification for the interface dictates the use of a pseudoternary coding scheme (Figure 3-2 and Table 3-1). Binary one is represented by the ab-

TABLE 4-4   Contact Assignments for Plugs and Jacks of ISDN Physical Connector (ISO 8877)

Contact Number	TE	NT
1	Power Source 3	Power Sink 3
2	Power Source 3	Power Sink 3
3	Transmit	Receive
4	Receive	Transmit
5	Receive	Transmit
6	Transmit	Receive
7	Power Sink 2	Power Source 2
8	Power Sink 2	Power Source 2

TE = terminal equipment
NT = network-terminating equipment

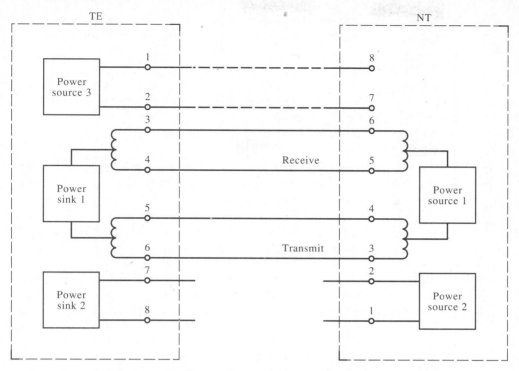

FIGURE 4-13. Reference configuration for signal transmission and power-feeding in normal operating mode of ISDN connector.

sence of voltage, binary zero is represented by a positive or negative pulse of 750 mV ±10%. The data rate is 192 kbps.

4-4

RECOMMENDED READING

An excellent book that covers all of the topics of this chapter is [MCNA88]; the book has somewhat of an electrical engineering orientation but is nevertheless quite approachable and is as thorough as most readers could wish for. [PETE61] is a good presentation of CRC codes; [RAMA88] discusses various CRC software algorithms. [BERT80] discusses various physical-level interfaces. [MCCL83] discusses the physical-level interface from the point of view of its role in an overall communications architecture. [SEYE84] is a detailed presentation of RS-232-C.

4-5

PROBLEMS

4-1 A data source produces 7-bit ASCII characters. Derive an expression for the maximum effective data rate (rate of ASCII data bits) over a B-bps line for the following:

    a. Asynchronous transmission, with a 1.5-unit stop bit and a parity bit.

    b. Bit-synchronous transmission, with a frame consisting of 48 control bits and 128 information bits. The information field contains 8-bit (parity included) ASCII characters.

    c. Same as part (b), except that the information field is 1024 bits.

    d. Character-synchronous transmission, with 9 control characters per frame and 16 or 128 information characters.

    e. Same as part (d), with 12 control characters per frame.

4-2 Demonstrate by example (write down a few dozen arbitrary bit patterns with start and stop bits) that a receiver that suffers a framing error on asynchronous transmission will eventually become realigned.

4-3 Suppose that the sender and receiver agree not to use *any* stop bits. Could this work? If so, explain any necessary conditions.

4-4 Consider a system that is clocked by a master clock running at 8 MHz. This clock has a maximum error of 30 seconds in one month. The system uses asynchronous serial transmission based on characters containing one start bit, seven data bits, one parity bit, and one stop bit. If characters are transmitted in a burst mode, how many characters could be sent before a transmission error caused by the master clock error occurs? Assume that each bit must be sampled within 40% of its center position.

4-5 Many serial terminals have a *break* key. The purpose of this is to allow the receiver to interrupt a sender. There are two ways to implement this break. In the first, a character agreed upon by both sender and receiver is used. This character is reserved and its use always means that the originator of this character wants attention. In the second method the line is held low continuously for a period of time long enough so that the line state is not confused with a character.

    a. For a serial system using 1.5 stop bits, odd parity, and 7 data bits, what is the minimum length of this break sequence?

    b. Under what conditions might a steady stream of ASCII NUL characters accomplish the purpose of a break sequence? Note that a possibility of error must be entertained in order to answer this.

4-6 Suppose that synchronous serial data transmission is clocked by two 8-MHz clocks (one for the sender and one for the receiver) that each have a drift of 1 minute in one year. How long a sequence of bits can be sent before possible clock drift can cause a problem? Assume that a bit waveform will be good if it is sampled within 40% of its center and that the sender and receiver are resynchronized at the beginning of each frame. Consider two cases: (a) 300 bps, and (b) 9600 bps.

4-7 For a constant P_B, Figure 4-3a shows that the class 2 probability increases with the number of bits per frame and the probability of class 1 errors decreases as the number of bits per frame increases. Would you expect this? Why?

4-8 Would you expect that the inclusion of a parity bit would change the probability of receiving a correct message? Why or why not?

4-9 What is the purpose of using modulo 2 arithmetic in computing an FCS rather than binary arithmetic?

4-10 Using Figure 4-4, work out the probability of an undetected error in 7-bit character with one parity bit, given that at least one error has occurred.

4-11 In the VRC/LRC scheme, is the last bit of the parity check character generated horizontally (from the other bits in the character) or vertically (from the parity bit of all other characters)?

4-12 Consider a frame consisting of two characters of four bits each. Assume that the probability of bit error is 10^{-3} and that it is constant and independent for each bit.
   a. What is P, the probability that the frame is received with no undetected errors?
   b. Now add a parity bit to each character, but assume that parity bits are never in error. What is P?
   c. Now add a parity check character, and again assume parity bits are never in error. What is P?

4-13 Using the CRC-CCITT polynomial, generate the 16-bit CRC code for the message consisting of a 1 followed by 15 0's.

4-14 Explain in words why the shift register implementation of CRC will result in all 0's at the receiver if there are no errors. Demonstrate by example.

4-15 For $P = 110011$ and $M = 11100011$, find the CRC.

4-16 A modified CRC procedure is commonly used in communications standards. It is defined as follows:

$$\frac{X^{16} M(X) + X^k L(X)}{P(X)} = Q(X) + \frac{R(X)}{P(X)}$$
$$FCS = L(X) + R(X)$$

where

$L(X) = X^{15} + X^{14} + X^{13} + \ldots X + 1$
$k = $ number of bits in M

   a. Describe in words the effect of this procedure.
   b. Can you explain the potential benefits?
   c. Show a shift register implementation for $P(X) = X^{16} + X^{12} + X^5 + 1$.

4-17 Draw a timing diagram showing the state of all EIA-232-D leads between two DTE-DCE pairs during the course of a data call on the switched telephone network.

4-18 Explain the operation of each null modem connection in Figure 4-10.

4-19 For the EIA-232-D RL circuit to function properly, what circuits must be logically connected?

4-20 Refer to Figure 4-11. The sender's Request to Send is connected to his own Clear to Send and to the receiver's Carrier Detect. What does this accomplish?

CHAPTER 5

Data Link Control

Our discussion so far has concerned *sending signals over a transmission link*. For effective digital data communications much more is needed to control and manage the exchange. We want to convert the procedure above into one of *sending data over a data communications link*. This is done by adding a layer of control in each communicating device above the physical interfacing discussed in Chapter 4, referred to as *data link control* or *data link protocol*. When a data link control procedure is used, the transmission medium between stations is referred to as a *data link*.

To see the need for data link control, we list some of the requirements and objectives for effective data communication between two directly connected transmitting–receiving stations:

- *Frame synchronization:* Data are sent in blocks called frames. The beginning and end of each frame must be clearly identifiable.
- *Use of a variety of line configurations:* These are defined in Section 5-1.
- *Flow control:* The sending station must not send frames at a rate faster than the receiving station can absorb them.
- *Error control:* The bit errors introduced by the transmission system must be corrected.
- *Addressing:* On a multipoint line, the identity of the two stations involved in a transmission must be known.
- *Control and data on same link:* It is usually not desirable to have a separate communications path for control signals. Accordingly, the receiver must be able to distinguish control information from the data being transmitted.
- *Link management:* The initiation, maintenance, and termination of a sustained

data exchange requires a fair amount of coordination and cooperation among stations. Procedures for the management of this exchange are required.

None of these requirements is satisfied by the physical interfacing techniques described in Chapter 4. We shall see in this chapter that a data link protocol that satisfies these requirements is a rather complex affair. To begin, some of the key features of data link control protocols are presented: line configuration control, flow control, and error control. In assessing flow and error control procedures, a novel method of comparing various approaches for various links is presented. This method is based on a parameter a, defined as the ratio of propagation delay to frame transmission time. We will have occasion to employ this parameter again in Part II.

Following these preliminaries, a specific data link protocol, HDLC, is discussed in some detail. HDLC is representative of modern data link protocols that use bit-oriented synchronous transmission.

5-1

LINE CONFIGURATIONS

The three characteristics that distinguish various data link configurations are topology, duplexity, and line discipline.

Topology and Duplexity

The *topology* of a data link refers to the physical arrangement of stations on a link. This was discussed in Chapter 2. If there are only two stations, the link is *point-to-point*. If there are more than two stations, then it is a *multipoint* topology. Traditionally, a multipoint link has been used in the case of a computer (primary station) and a set of terminals (secondary stations). More recently, more complex versions of the multipoint topology are found in local networks (Figure 1-4c).

Traditional multipoint lines are made possible when the terminals are only transmitting a fraction of the time. Figure 5-1 illustrates the advantages of the multipoint configuration. If each terminal has a point-to-point link to its computer, then the computer must have one I/O port for each terminal. Also, there is a separate transmission line from the computer to each terminal. In a multipoint configuration, the computer needs only a single I/O port, saving hardware costs. Only a single transmission line is needed, which also saves costs.

The *duplexity* of a link refers to the direction and timing of signal flow. In *simplex* transmission, the signal flow is always in one direction. For example, an input device such as a card reader or remote sensor could be attached to a host so that the device could only transmit, and never receive. An output device such as a printer or actuator could be configured to only receive. Simplex is not in general use since it is not possible to send error or control signals back down the link to the data source. Simplex is similar to a one-lane, one-way bridge.

A *half-duplex* link can transmit and receive, but not simultaneously. This mode is also referred to as "two-way alternate," suggestive of the fact that two stations on a half-duplex link must alternate in transmitting. This is similar to a one-lane, two-way bridge. On a *full-duplex* link, two stations can simultaneously send and

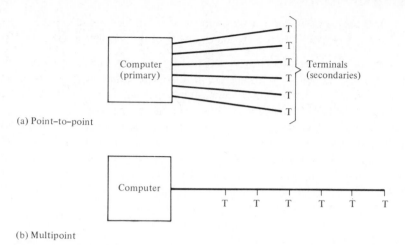

(a) Point–to–point

(b) Multipoint

FIGURE 5-1.   Traditional computer/terminal configurations.

receive data from each other. Thus this mode is known as "two-way simultaneous" and may be compared to a two-lane, two-way bridge.

With digital signaling, which requires guided transmission, full-duplex usually requires two separate transmission paths (e.g., two twisted pair), while half-duplex requires only one. For analog signaling, duplicity depends on frequency, whether guided or unguided transmission is used. If a station transmits and receives on the same frequency, it must operate in half-duplex mode (exception: guided transmission using two separate, isolated conductors). If a station transmits on one frequency and receives on another, it may operate in full-duplex mode (Figure 3-7).

A number of combinations of topology and duplexity are possible. Figure 5-2 depicts the most common configurations. The figure always shows a single primary station (P) and one or more secondary (S) stations (this point is explored when we discuss line discipline). For point-to-point links, the two possibilities are self explanatory. For multipoint links, three configurations are possible:

- Primary full-duplex, secondaries half-duplex (multi-multipoint).
- Both primary and secondaries half-duplex (multipoint half-duplex).
- Both primary and secondaries full-duplex (multipoint duplex).

Line Discipline

Some discipline is needed in the use of a transmission link. On a half-duplex line, only one station at a time should transmit. On either a half- or full-duplex line, a station should only transmit if it knows that the intended receiver is prepared to receive.

Point-to-Point Links.   Line discipline is simple with a point-to-point link. Let us consider first a half-duplex link in which either station may initiate an exchange. An example exchange is depicted in Figure 5-3. If either station wishes to send data to the other, it first performs an enquiry (depicted as enq) of the other station to see if it is prepared to receive. The second station responds with a positive acknowledgment (ack) to indicate that it is ready. The first station then sends some

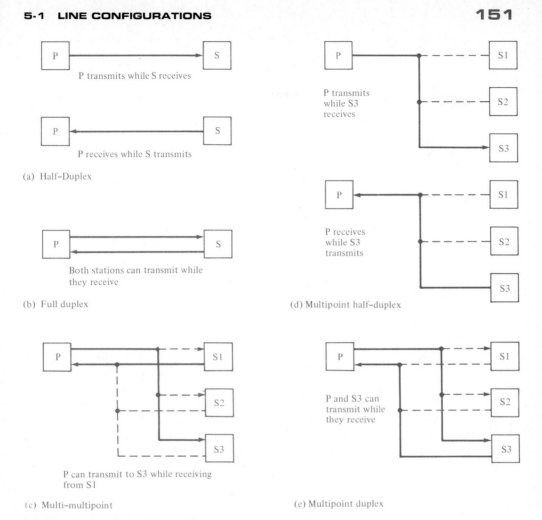

FIGURE 5-2.   **Data link configurations.**

data, which the figure depicts as a frame. In asynchronous communication, the data would be sent as an asynchronous stream of characters. In any case, after some quantum of data is sent, the first station pauses to await results. The second station acknowledges successful receipt of the data (ack). The first station then sends an end of transmission message (eot) which terminates the exchange and returns the system to its initial state.

Several additional features are added to Figure 5-3 to provide for coping with errors. A negative acknowledgment (nak) is used to indicate that a station is not ready to receive, or that data were received in error. A station may fail to respond or respond with an invalid message. The result of these conditions is indicated by light lines in the figure; the heavy line is the normal sequence of communication events. If an unexpected event occurs, such as a nak or invalid reply, a station may retry its last action or may institute some error recovery procedure (erp).

There are three distinct phases in this communication control procedure:

- *Establishment:* This determines which station is to transmit and which to receive, and that the receiver is prepared to receive.

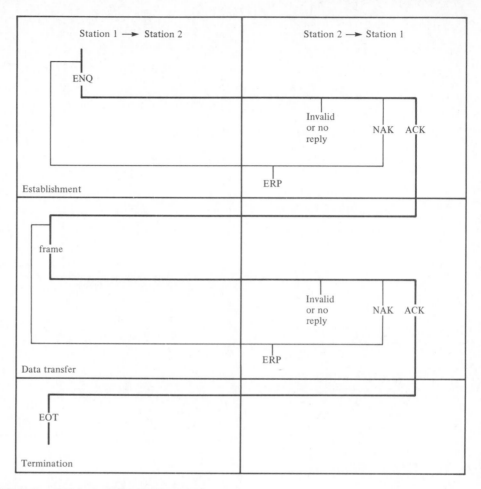

FIGURE 5-3.   Point-to-point link control.

- *Data Transfer:* The data are transferred in one or more acknowledged blocks.
- *Termination:* This terminates the logical connection (transmitter-receiver relationship).

These three phases, in some form, are a part of all line disciplines for both point-to-point and multipoint links.

Several refinements can be added to our discussion. The relationship described above was peer; that is, either station could initiate transmission. A common situation is to have one of the stations designated *primary* and the other *secondary*. The primary has the responsibility of initiating the exchange. This is a common situation when one station is a computer (primary) and the other is a terminal (secondary). Figure 5-3 depicts a sequence in which the primary has data to send to the secondary. If the secondary has data to send, it must wait for the primary to request the data, and only then enter a data transfer phase.

If the link is full-duplex, data and control messages can be transmitted in both directions simultaneously. We shall see the advantages of this when we discuss flow and error control.

Multipoint Links. The choice of line discipline for multipoint links depends primarily on whether there is a designated primary station or not. When there is a primary station, data are exchanged only between the primary and a secondary, not between two secondaries. The most common disciplines used in this situation are all variants of a scheme known as *poll and select*:

- *Poll:* The primary requests data from a secondary.
- *Select:* The primary has data to send and informs a secondary that data are coming.

Figure 5-4 illustrates these concepts. In Figure 5-4a, the primary polls a secondary by sending a brief polling message. In this case, the secondary has nothing to send and responds with some sort of nak message. The timing for this sequence is indicated. The total time is

$$T_N = t_{prop} + t_{poll} + t_{proc} + t_{nak} + t_{prop}$$

where

T_N = total time to poll terminal with nothing to send
t_{prop} = propagation time = $t_1 - t_0 = t_5 - t_4$
t_{poll} = time to transmit a poll = $t_2 - t_1$
t_{proc} = time to process poll before acknowledging = $t_3 - t_2$
t_{nak} = time to transmit a negative acknowledgment = $t_4 - t_3$

Figure 5-4b depicts the case of a successful poll. The time here is

$$T_P = 3t_{prop} + t_{poll} + t_{ack} + t_{data} + 2t_{proc}$$
$$= T_N + t_{prop} + t_{data} + t_{proc}$$

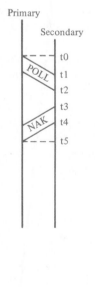

(a) Polled terminal has nothing to send

(b) Polled terminal has Data to send

(c) Select

(d) Fast select

FIGURE 5-4. **Poll and select sequences.**

Here we assume for simplicity that the processing time to respond to any message is a constant.

The most common form of polling is *roll-call polling*, in which the primary selectively polls each secondary in a predetermined sequence. In the simplest case, the primary polls each secondary in a round-robin fashion, $S_1, S_2, \ldots, S_n$, for all n secondaries and then repeats the sequence. The timing can be expressed as

$$T_c = nT_N + kT_D \tag{5-1}$$

where

T_c = time for one complete polling cycle
T_N = average time to poll a secondary exclusive of data transfer
T_D = time to transfer data = $t_{prop} + t_{data} + t_{proc}$
n = number of secondary stations
k = number of secondary stations with data to send during the cycle

Variants of roll-call polling permit priority handling by, for example, polling some stations more than once per cycle.

The select function is shown in Figure 5-4c. Note that four separate transmissions are required to transfer data from the primary to the secondary. An alternative technique is *fast select*. In this case, the selection message includes the data to be transferred (Figure 5-4d). The first reply from the secondary is an acknowledgment that indicates that the station was prepared to receive and did receive the data successfully. Fast selection is particularly well suited for applications where short messages are frequently transmitted and the transfer time for the message is not appreciably longer than the reply time.

The use of roll-call polling for other configurations is easily explained. In the case of multi-multipoint (Figure 5-2c), the primary can be sending a poll to one secondary at the same time that it is receiving a control message or data from another. For multipoint duplex, the primary can engage in full-duplex conversation with any of the secondaries.

It should be clear from Equation (5-1) that the overhead in polling each station can significantly increase response times if there are a large number of terminals (large n) or a long line (large t_{prop}). An improvement can be obtained by using *hub polling* (Figure 5-5). This technique requires secondary stations to participate actively in the polling operation. Two data paths with simultaneous transmission are required, and each secondary must be able to receive on both paths simultaneously. The operation is as follows. The primary sends a poll to the most remote secondary. If the secondary has data to transmit, it transmits the data to the primary, and then

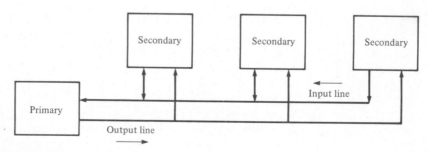

FIGURE 5-5.   Hub polling.

sends a poll to the next secondary in line. If the secondary has no data to send, it immediately sends a poll to the next secondary. The last secondary in line sends a poll to the primary which begins a new cycle. All during this process, the primary can be sending data to the secondaries on the line labeled ''output.''

Another form of line discipline is *contention*. In this mode, there is typically no primary but rather a collection of peer stations. A station can transmit if the line is free; otherwise, it must wait. This technique has found widespread use in local networks and satellite systems.

A characteristic of all multipoint line disciplines is the need for addressing. In the case of roll-call polling, transmissions from the primary must indicate the intended secondary; transmissions from a secondary must identify the secondary. In a peer situation, both transmitter and receiver must be identified. Thus there are three cases:

- *Point-to-point:* no address needed.
- *Primary-secondary multipoint:* one address needed, to identify secondary.
- *Peer multipoint:* two addresses needed, to identify transmitter and receiver.

In practice, the first case is subsumed into the second, so that most data link control protocols require one address even for point-to-point transmission. This simplifies the demands on the station by allowing a single protocol to be used in both circumstances. The peer multipoint case is seen in local networks; this chapter will be concerned only with the first two cases, for which traditional data link control protocols were developed.

5-2

FLOW CONTROL

Flow control is a technique for assuring that a transmitting station does not overwhelm a receiving station with data. The receiver will typically allocate a data buffer with some maximum length. When data are received, it must do a certain amount of processing before it can clear the buffer and be prepared to receive more data. In the absence of flow control, the receiver's buffer may overflow while it is processing old data.

In this section, we examine mechanisms for flow control in the absence of errors. The model we will use is depicted in Figure 5-6a, which is a vertical-time sequence diagram. It has the advantages of showing time dependencies and illustrating the correct send-receive relationship. Each arrow represents a single frame transiting a data link between two stations.

As we discussed previously for synchronous transmission, the data are sent in a sequence of frames with each frame containing a portion of the data and some control information. For now, we assume that all frames that are transmitted are successfully received; no frames are lost and none arrive with errors. Furthermore, frames arrive in the same order in which they are sent. However, each transmitted frame suffers an arbitrary and variable amount of delay before reception.

The simplest form of flow control, known as **stop-and-wait flow control,** works as follows. A source entity transmits a frame. After reception, the destination entity indicates its willingness to accept another frame by sending back an acknowledgment to the frame just received. The source must wait until it receives the ac-

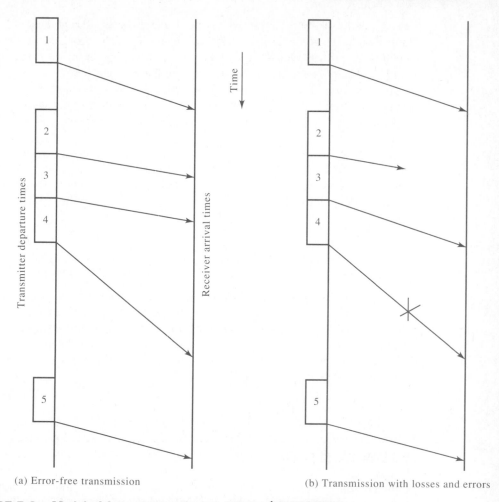

(a) Error-free transmission   (b) Transmission with losses and errors

FIGURE 5-6.   Model of frame transmission. (Based ón [BERT87])

knowledgment before sending the next frame. The destination can thus stop the flow of data by simply withholding acknowledgment. This procedure works fine and, indeed, can hardly be improved upon when a message is sent in a few large frames. However, it is often the case that a source will break up a large block of data into smaller blocks and transmit the data in many frames. This is done for the following reasons:

- The longer the transmission, the more likely that there will be an error, necessitating retransmission of the entire block. With smaller blocks, errors are less likely per block, and fewer data need be retransmitted.
- On a multipoint line, it is usually desirable not to permit one station to occupy the line for very long, thus causing long delays at the other stations.
- The buffer size of the receiver may be limited.

With the use of multiple frames for a single message, the simple procedure described above may be inadequate. We first explore the reason for this inadequacy, then show a technique for overcoming it.

The Effect of Propagation Delay and Transmission Rate

Let us determine the maximum potential efficiency of a half-duplex point-to-point line using the stop-and-wait scheme described above. Suppose that a long message is to be sent as a sequence of frames $f_1, f_2, \ldots, f_n$. For a polling procedure, the following events occur:

- Station S_1 sends a poll of station S_2.
- S_2 responds with f_1.
- S_1 sends an acknowledgment.
- S_2 sends f_2.
- S_1 acknowledges.
   .
   .
   .
- S_2 sends f_n.
- S_1 acknowledges.

The total time to send the data is

$$T_D = T_I + nT_F$$

where

$$T_I = \text{time to initiate sequence} = t_{\text{prop}} + t_{\text{poll}} + t_{\text{proc}}$$
$$T_F = \text{time to send one frame} = t_{\text{prop}} + t_{\text{frame}} + t_{\text{proc}} + t_{\text{prop}} + t_{\text{ack}} + t_{\text{proc}}$$

To simplify matters, we ignore a few terms. For a long sequence of frames, T_I is relatively small and can be dropped. Let us assume that the processing time between transmission and reception is negligible, and that the acknowledgment frame is very small. Then we can express T_D as

$$T_D = n(2t_{\text{prop}} + t_{\text{frame}})$$

Of that time, only $n \times t_{\text{frame}}$ is actually spent transmitting data and the rest is overhead. Thus the utilization or efficiency of the line is

$$U = \frac{n \times t_{\text{frame}}}{n(2t_{\text{prop}} + t_{\text{frame}})}$$

$$U = \frac{t_{\text{frame}}}{2t_{\text{prop}} + t_{\text{frame}}}$$

It is useful to define $a = t_{\text{prop}}/t_{\text{frame}}$. Then

$$U = \frac{1}{1 + 2a} \tag{5-2}$$

This is the maximum possible utilization of the link. We will see that the frame itself contains overhead bits, so actual utilization is lower. The parameter a is a constant if both t_{frame} and t_{prop} are constants. This is typically the case: Fixed-length frames are often used for all except the last frame in a sequence, and the propagation delay is constant for point-to-point links. An approximation for U can be obtained by using the maximum propagation time on a multipoint link.

To get some insight into Equation (5-2), let us derive a different expression for *a.* We have

$$a = \frac{\text{Propagation Time}}{\text{Transmission Time}} \qquad (5\text{-}3)$$

The propagation time is equal to the distance d of the link divided by the velocity of propagation V. For unguided transmission (except through seawater), V is the speed of light, 3×10^8 m/s. A typical value for guided media is 2×10^8 m/sec. The transmission time is equal to the length of the frame L divided by the data rate R, so

$$a = \frac{d/V}{L/R} = \frac{Rd}{VL}$$

Thus a is proportional to the data rate times the length of the medium. This term, $R \times d$, and hence a, is the single most important parameter determining the performance of a data link. A useful way of looking at a is that it represents the length of the medium in bits ($R \times d/V$) compared to the frame length.

With this interpretation of a in mind, Figure 5-7 validates Equation (5-2). In this figure, transmission time is normalized to 1. Hence the propagation time, by Equation (5-3), is a. First consider the case of $a < 1$; this is the case in which the "bit length" of the link is less than that of the frame. A station begins transmitting a frame at time t_0. At $t_0 + a$, the leading edge of the frame reaches the receiving station, while the sending station is still in the process of transmitting the frame. At $t_0 + 1$, the sending station has completed transmission. At $t_0 + 1 + a$, the receiving station has received the entire frame and immediately transmits a small acknowledgment frame. This acknowledgment arrives back at the sending station at $t_0 + 1 + 2a$. Total elapsed time: $1 + 2a$. Total transmission time: 1. Hence utilization or efficiency is $1/(1 + 2a)$. The same result is achieved with $a > 1$, as illustrated in Figure 5-7b.

Let us consider a few examples. At one extreme is a satellite link. The round trip propagation time is about 270 ms. A typical digital transmission service is 56 kbps, and a 4000-bit frame is within the typical range. Thus transmission time equals $4000/56,000 = 71$ ms, and $a = 270/71 = 3.8$. From Equation (5-2) the maximum utilization is $1/(1 + 7.6) = 0.12$. This is about the smallest value of a that one might expect for a satellite link. Recent and proposed satellite services use much shorter transmission times: from 6 ms down to 125µs [EDEL82]. For this range, a is in the range 45 to 2160. Thus for the simple stop-and-wait acknowledgment protocol described above, efficiency could be as low as 0.0002! At the other extreme, in terms of distance, is the local network. Distances range from 0.1 to 10 km, with data rates of 0.1 to 10 Mbps. Using a value of $V = 2 \times 10^8$ m/s and a frame size of 500 bits, the value of a is in the range 10^{-4} to 1. Typical values are 0.01 to 0.1. For the latter range, utilization is in the range 0.83 to 0.98.

We can see that local networks are inherently quite efficient, whereas satellite links are not. As a final example, let us consider digital data transmission via modem over a voice-grade line. A practical upper bound on data rate is 9600 bps. We can again use $V = 2 \times 10^8$ m/s. Again, let us consider a 500-bit frame. Such transmission is used for distances anywhere from a few tens of meters to thousands of kilometers. If we pick, say, as a short distance $d = 100$ m, then $a = (9600 \text{ bps} \times 100 \text{ m})/(2 \times 10^8 \text{ m/s} \times 500 \text{ bits}) = 9.6 \times 10^{-6}$ and utilization

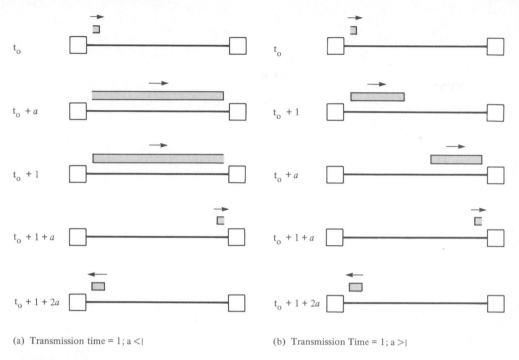

(a) Transmission time = 1; a <| (b) Transmission Time = 1; a >|

FIGURE 5-7. The effect of *a* on utilization.

is effectively unity. Even in a long-distance case, such as $d = 5000$ km, we have $a = (9600 \times 5 \times 10^6)/(2 \times 10^8 \times 500) = 0.48$ and efficiency equals 0.5.

We can conclude that, in some cases, the simple stop-and-wait acknowledgment procedure provides adequate line utilization. For those cases in which this is not the case, a more elaborate procedure is desirable. Such a procedure, universally accepted, is the sliding-window protocol.

The Sliding Window Protocol

The essence of the problem described so far is that only one frame at a time can be in transit. In situations where the bit length of the link is greater than the frame length ($a > 1$), serious inefficiencies result. The obvious solution is to allow multiple frames to be in transit at one time.

Let us examine how this might work for two stations, A and B, connected via a full-duplex link. Station B allocates buffer space for n frames instead of the one discussed above. Thus B can accept n frames, and A is allowed to send n frames without waiting for an acknowledgment. To keep track of which frames have been acknowledged, each is labeled with a sequence number. B acknowledges a frame by sending an acknowledgment that includes the sequence number of the next frame expected. This acknowledgment also implicitly announces that B is prepared to receive the next n frames beginning with the number specified. This scheme can also be used to acknowledge multiple frames. For example, B could receive frames 2, 3, and 4, but withhold acknowledgment until frame 4 has arrived. By then

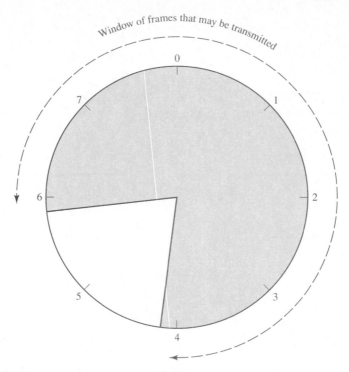

FIGURE 5-8.   Sliding-window depiction.

returning an acknowledgment with sequence number 5, *B* acknowledges frames 2, 3, and 4 at one time. *A* maintains a list of sequence numbers that it is allowed to send and *B* maintains a list of sequence numbers that it is prepared to receive. Each of these lists can be thought of as a *window* of frames. The operation is referred to as **sliding-window flow control.**

An important restriction needs to be noted. Since the sequence number to be used occupies a field in the frame, it is clearly of bounded size. For a k-bit field, the sequence number can range from 0 to $2^k - 1$. Accordingly, frames are numbered modulo 2^k; that is, after sequence number $2^k - 1$, the next number is zero. With this in mind, Figure 5-8 is a useful way of depicting the sliding-window process. It assumes the use of a 3-bit sequence number, so that frames are numbered sequentially from 0 through 7, and then the same numbers are reused for subsequent frames. The shaded portion of the circle represents the window of frames that may be transmitted. The figure indicates that the sender may transmit 7 frames, beginning with frame 6. Each time a frame is sent, the shaded portion will shrink; each time a new acknowledgment is received, the shaded portion will grow.

An example is shown in Figure 5-9. The example assumes a 3-bit sequence number field and a maximum window size of seven. Initially, *A* and *B* have windows indicating that *A* may transmit seven frames, beginning with frame 0 (F0). After transmitting three frames (F0, F1, F2) without acknowledgment, *A* has shrunk its window to four frames. The window indicates that *A* may transmit four frames, beginning with frame number 3. *B* then transmits an ACK 3, which means: "I have received all frames up through frame number 2 and am ready to receive frame number 3; in fact, I am prepared to receive seven frames, beginning with frame number 3." With this acknowledgment, *A* is back up to permission to transmit

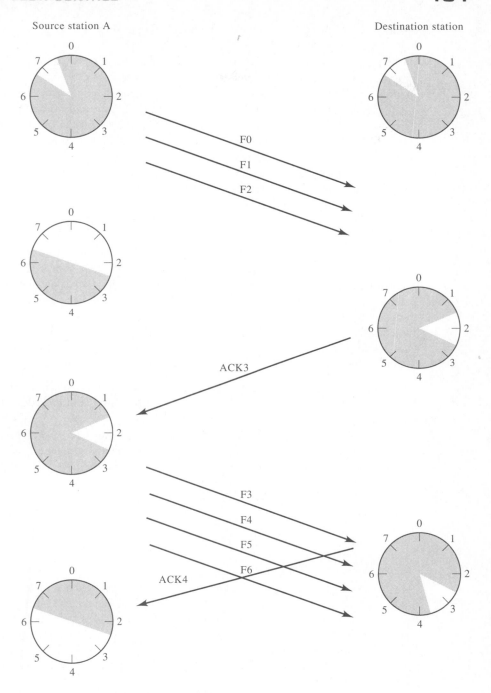

Note: shaded part designates window

FIGURE 5-9. Example of a sliding-window protocol.

seven frames, still beginning with frame 3. *A* proceeds to transmit frames 3, 4, 5, and 6. *B* returns an ACK4, which acknowledges frame 3, and allows the transmission of frames 4 through 2. But, by the time that this acknowledgment reaches *A*, it has already transmitted frames 4, 5, and 6. The result is that *A* may only open its window to permit the transmission of 4 frames, beginning with frame 7.

The mechanism so far described does indeed provide a form of flow control: the receiver must only be able to accommodate *n* frames beyond the one it has last acknowledged. To supplement this, most protocols also allow a station to completely cut off the flow of frames from the other side by sending a Receive Not Ready (RNR) message, which acknowledges former frames but forbids transfer of future frames. Thus, RNR 5 means: "I have received all frames up through number 4 but am unable to accept any more." At some subsequent point, the station must send a normal acknowledgment to reopen the window.

The efficiency of the line now depends on both N, the window size, and a. For convenience, let us again normalize frame transmission time to a value of 1; thus the propagation time is a. Figure 5-10 illustrates the efficiency of a full-duplex point-to-point line. Station *A* begins to emit a sequence of frames at time t_0. The leading edge of the first frame reaches station *B* at $t_0 + a$. The first frame is entirely absorbed by $t_0 + a + 1$. Assuming negligible processing time, station *B* can immediately acknowledge the first frame (ACK1). Let us also assume that the acknowledgment frame is so small that transmission time is negligible. Then the ACK1 reaches station *A* at $t_0 + 2a + 1$. There are two cases:

- *Case 1: $N > 2a + 1$.* The acknowledgment for frame 1 reaches station *A* before it has exhausted its window. Thus *A* can transmit continuously with no pause.
- *Case 2: $N < 2a + 1$.* Station *A* exhausts its window at $t_0 + N$ and cannot send additional frames until $t_0 + 2a + 1$. Thus the line utilization is N time units out of a period of $(2a + 1)$ time units.

From the above, we can state that

$$U = \begin{cases} 1 & N > 2a + 1 \\ \dfrac{N}{2a+1} & N < 2a + 1 \end{cases} \tag{5-4}$$

Typically, the sequence number is provided for in an *n*-bit field and the maximum window size is $N = 2^n - 1$ (not 2^n; this is explained in Section 5-3). Figure 5-11 shows the maximum efficiency achievable for window sizes of 1, 7, and 127 as a function of a. A window size of one, of course, corresponds to the simple stop-and-wait protocol discussed earlier. A window size of seven (3 bits) should be adequate for most applications. A window size of 127 (7 bits) is adequate for some satellite links.

So far, we have discussed transmission in one direction only. If two stations exchange data, each needs to maintain two windows: one for transmit and one for receive. When this is the case, a technique known as *piggybacking* is often used. If a station has data to send and an acknowledgment to send, it sends both together in one frame, thus saving communications capacity. This technique works with either half-duplex or full-duplex links. For a multipoint link, the primary needs to transmit and receive windows for each secondary.

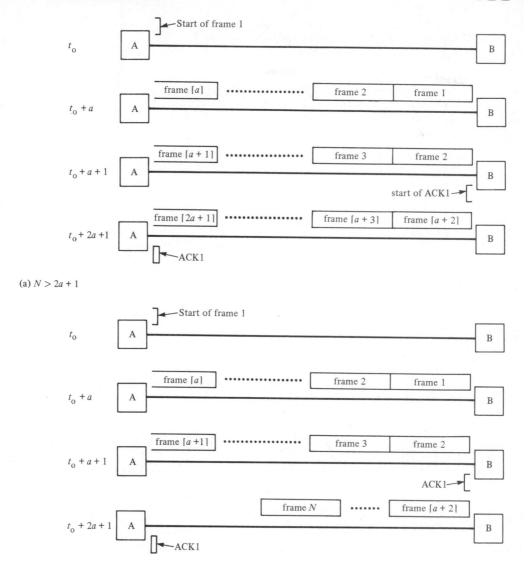

(a) $N > 2a + 1$

(b) $N < 2a + 1$

$\lceil X \rceil$ = smallest integer greater
than or equal to $\lceil X \rceil$

FIGURE 5-10. Timing of a sliding-window protocol.

5-3

ERROR CONTROL

Error control refers to mechanisms to detect and correct errors that occur in the
transmission of frames. The model that we will use, which covers the typical case,
is illustrated in Figure 5-6b. As before, data are sent as a sequence of frames;

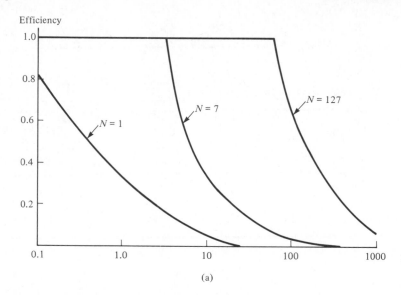

FIGURE 5-11. Line utilization as a function of window size.

frames arrive in the same order in which they are sent; and each transmitted frame suffers an arbitrary and variable amount of delay before reception. In addition, we admit the possibility of two types of errors:

- *Lost frame:* A frame fails to arrive at the other side. A noise burst may damage a frame to the extent that the receiver is not aware that a frame has been transmitted.
- *Damaged frame:* A recognizable frame does arrive but some of the bits are in error (have been altered during transmission).

The most common techniques for error control are based on some or all of the following ingredients:

- *Error Detection:* As discussed in Chapter 4; typically, CRC is used.
- *Positive acknowledgment:* The destination returns a positive acknowledgment to successfully received, error-free frames.
- *Retransmission after timeout:* The source retransmits a frame that has not been acknowledged after a predetermined amount of time.
- *Negative acknowledgment and retransmission:* The destination returns a negative acknowledgment to frames in which an error is detected. The source retransmits such frames.

Collectively, these mechanisms are all referred to as **automatic repeat request (ARQ)**. Three versions of ARQ are in common use:

- Stop-and-wait ARQ
- Go-back-N ARQ
- Selective reject ARQ.

All of these forms are based on the use of the flow control techniques described in Section 5-2. We examine each of these in turn.

Stop-and-Wait ARQ

Stop-and-wait ARQ is based on the stop-and-wait flow control technique outlined previously, and is depicted in Figure 5-12. The source station transmits a single frame and then must await an acknowledgment (ACK). No other data frames can be sent until the destination station's reply arrives at the source station.

The frame transmitted by the source could suffer an error. If the error is detected by the destination, it discards the frame and sends a negative acknowledgment (NAK), causing the source to retransmit the damaged frame. On the other hand, if the transmitted frame is so corrupted by noise as not to be received, the destination will not respond. To account for this possibility, the source is equipped with a timer. After a frame is transmitted, the source waits for an acknowledgment (ACK or NAK). If no recognizable acknowledgment is received during the timeout period; then the frame is retransmitted. Note that this system requires that the source maintain a copy of a transmitted frame until an ACK is received for that frame.

One more refinement is needed. If a frame is sent correctly but the acknowledgment is damaged in transit, then the source will time out and retransmit that frame. The destination will now receive and accept two copies of the same frame. To avoid this problem, frames are alternately labeled with 0 or 1 and positive acknowledgments are of the form ACK0 or ACK1: an ACK0 (ACK1) acknowledges receipt of a frame numbered 1 (0) and indicates that the receiver is ready for a frame numbered 0 (1).

The principal advantage of stop-and-wait ARQ is its simplicity. Its principal disadvantage, as discussed in Section 4.3, is that this is an inefficient protocol. The siding-window flow control technique introduced before can be adapted to provide more efficient line use. In this context, it is referred to as **continuous ARQ.**

Go-back-N ARQ

One variant of continuous ARQ is known as go-back-N ARQ. In this technique, a station may send a series of frames determined by window size, using the sliding window flow control technique. While no errors occur, the destination will acknowledge (ACK) incoming frames as usual.

Consider that station A is sending frames to station B. After each transmission, A sets an acknowledgment timer for the frame just transmitted. The go-back-N technique takes into account the following contingencies:

1. Damaged frame. There are three subcases:
    a. A transmits frame i. B detects an error and has previously successfully received frame $(i - 1)$. B sends a NAK i, indicating that frame i is rejected. When A receives this NAK, it must retransmit frame i and all subsequent frames that it has transmitted.
    b. frame i is lost in transit. A subsequently sends frame $(i + 1)$. B receives frame $(i + 1)$ out of order, and sends a NAK i.
    c. frame i is lost in transit and A does not soon send additional frames. B receives nothing and returns neither an ACK or a NAK. A will time out and retransmit frame i.

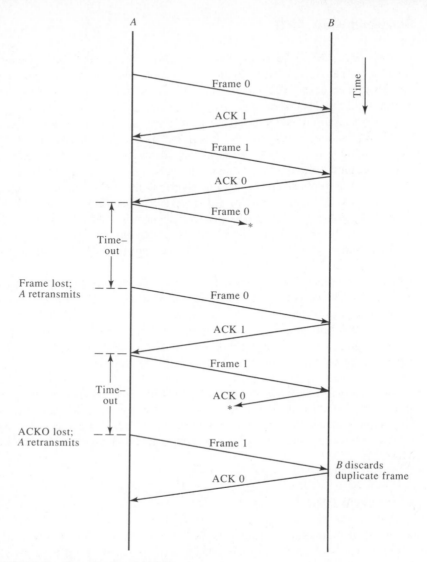

FIGURE 5-12. Stop-and-wait ARQ.

2. Damaged ACK. There are two subcases:
   a. B receives frame i and sends ACK ($i + 1$), which is lost in transit. Since ACKs are cumulative (e.g., ACK 6 means that all frames through 5 are acknowledged), it may be that A will receive a subsequent ACK to a subsequent frame that will do the job of the lost ACK before the associated time expires.
   b. If A's timer expires, A retransmits frame i and all subsequent frames.
3. Damaged NAK. If a NAK is lost, A will eventually time out on the associated frame and retransmit that frame and all subsequent frames.

Figure 5-13a shows the frame flow for go-back-N ARQ on a full-duplex line, assuming a 3-bit sequence number.

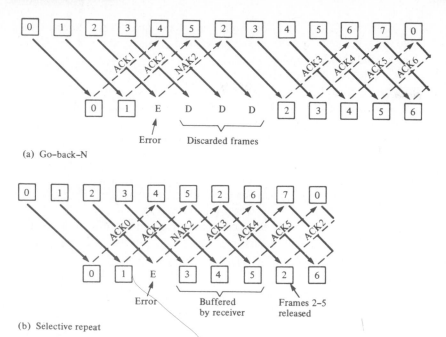

FIGURE 5-13. **Examples of continuous ARQ.**

With go-back-N ARQ, it is not required that each individual frame be acknowledged. For example, station *A* sends frames 0, 1, 2, and 3. Station *B* responds with ACK1 after frame 0, but then does not respond to frames 1 and 2. After frame 3 is received, *B* issues ACK4, indicating that frame 3 and all previous frames are accepted.

We are now in a position to explain why a sequence space of 2^n can support a window size of only $2^n - 1$. It has to do with the interaction of error control and acknowledgment. In most piggyback schemes, a station will send an acknowledgment with a frame, even if the acknowledgment has already been sent. This is because a fixed-length acknowledgment field of *n* bits is incorporated into the frame and some number must be put into the frame. This has the side benefit that in case the first ACK gets lost, the second ACK may get through. Now consider a case in which a station transmits frame 0 and gets an ACK1, and then transmits frame 1, 2, 3, 4, 5, 6, 7, 0 and gets another ACK1. This could mean that all eight frames were received correctly. It could also mean that all eight frames were lost in transit, and the receiving station is repeating its previous ACK1.

Selective-reject ARQ

With selective-reject ARQ, the only frames retransmitted are those that receive a NAK or which time out. Figure 5-13b, which exhibits the same error pattern as Figure 5-13a, illustrates selective repeat. This would appear to be more efficient than the go-back-N approach, since it minimizes the amount of retransmission. On the other hand, the receiver must contain storage to save post-NAK frames until the frame in error is retransmitted, and contain logic for reinserting that frame in the proper sequence. The transmitter, too, will require more complex logic to be able to send frames out of sequence. Because of such complications, the selective-reject ARQ is rarely implemented.

The window size requirement is more restrictive for selective-reject than for go-back-N. We have seen that for a sequence number space of 2^n, the maximum window size for go-back-N is $2^n - 1$. Now consider the case of a 3-bit sequence number size (sequence space is eight) using selective reject. Allow a window size of seven, and consider the following scenario [TANE88]:

1. Station A sends frames 0 through 6 to station B.
2. Station B receives and acknowledges all seven frames.
3. Because of a long noise burst, all seven acknowledgments are lost.
4. Station A times out and retransmits frame 0.
5. Station B has already advanced its receive window to accept frames 7, 0, 1, 2, 3, 4, and 5. Thus it assumes that frame 7 has been lost and that this is a new frame 0, which it accepts.

The problem with the foregoing scenario, for selective reject ARQ, is that there is an overlap between the sending and receiving windows. To overcome the problem, the maximum window size should be no more than half the range of sequence numbers. In the scenario above, if only four acknowledged frames may be outstanding, no confusion can result.

Figure 5-13 compare the two approaches, using a window size of seven. In both cases the third frame (frame 2) is transmitted in error. Because of propagation delays, the error is not reported to the sending station until three subsequent frames (frames 3, 4, and 5) have been sent. For the go-back-N algorithm, these three frames are discarded by the destination and must be retransmitted by the source. For the selective-reject algorithm, these frames are stored by the destination. Note that in this latter case, the frames cannot be acknowledged out of sequence, since any acknowledgment implicitly acknowledges all prior frames. Thus, when frame 2 is successfully retransmitted, the destination returns an ACK 6, acknowledging receipt of the new frame 2 and the frames 3, 4, and 5, which had been stored.

Performance

It would appear that both go-back-N and selective repeat are more efficient than stop-and-wait. Let us develop some approximations to determine the degree of improvement to be expected.

First, consider stop-and-wait ARQ. With no errors, the maximum utilization is $1/(1 + 2a)$ as shown in Equation (5-2). Now, we must take into account the fact that some frames are repeated because of errors. To do this, note that the utilization U can be defined as

$$U = \frac{T_f}{T_t}$$

where

T_f = time for transmitter to emit a single frame
T_t = total time that line is engaged in the transmission of a single frame

For error-free operation using stop-and-wait ARQ, we have

$$U = \frac{T_f}{T_f + 2T_p}$$

where T_p is the propagation time. Dividing by T_f and remembering that $a = T_p/T_f$, we again have Equation (5-2). Now, if errors occur, we must modify Equation (5-2) to

$$U = \frac{T_f}{N_r T_t}$$

where N_r is the expected number of transmissions of a frame. Thus for stop-and-wait ARQ we have

$$U = \frac{1}{N_r (1 + 2a)}$$

A simple expression for N_r can be derived by considering the probability P that a single frame is in error. If we assume that ACKs and NAKs are never in error, the probability that it will take exactly i attempts to transmit a frame successfully is $P^{i-1}(1 - P)$. Thus

$$N_r = \sum_{i=1}^{\infty} iP^{i-1}(1 - P) = \frac{1}{1 - P}$$

and

$$\textit{Stop-and-wait:} \quad U = \frac{1 - P}{1 + 2a}$$

For the sliding window protocol, we developed Equation (5-4) for error free operation, which is repeated here:

$$U = \begin{cases} 1 & N > 2a + 1 \\ \dfrac{N}{2a + 1} & N < 2a + 1 \end{cases}$$

For selective-repeat ARQ, we can use the same reasoning as applied to stop-and-wait ARQ. That is, the error-free equations must be divided by N_r. Again, $N_r = 1/(1 - P)$. So

Selective-repeat:

$$U = \begin{cases} 1 - P & N > 2a + 1 \\ \dfrac{N(1 - P)}{2a + 1} & N < 2a + 1 \end{cases}$$

The same reasoning will still apply for go-back-N ARQ, but we must be more careful in approximating N_r. Each error generates a requirement to retransmit K frames rather than just one frame. Thus

$$N_r = E[\text{number of transmitted frames to successfully transmit one frame}]$$

$$= \sum_{i=1}^{\infty} f(i)P^{i-1}(1 - P)$$

where $f(i)$ is the total number of frames transmitted if the original frame must be transmitted i times. This can be expressed as

$$f(i) = 1 + (i - 1)K$$
$$= (1 - K) + Ki$$

Substituting yields

$$N_r = (1 - K) \sum_{i=1}^{\infty} P^{i-1}(1 - P) + K \sum_{i=1}^{\infty} iP^{i-1}(1 - P)$$
$$= 1 - K + \frac{K}{1 - P}$$
$$= \frac{1 - P + KP}{1 - P}$$

By studying Figure 5-10, the reader should conclude that K is approximately equal to $2a + 1$ for $N > (2a + 1)$, and $K = N$ for $N < (2a + 1)$. Thus

Go-back-N:

$$U = \begin{cases} \dfrac{1 - P}{1 + 2aP} & N > 2a + 1 \\[3ex] \dfrac{N(1 - P)}{(2a + 1)(1 - P + NP)} & N < 2a + 1 \end{cases}$$

Note that for $N = 1$, both selective-repeat and go-back-N reduce to stop and wait. Figure 5-14 compares these three error control techniques for a value of $P = 10^{-3}$. This figure and the equations are only approximations. For example, we have ignored errors in acknowledgment frames and, in the case of go-back-N, errors in retransmitted frames other than the frame initially in error. Nevertheless, the results are very close to those produced by a more careful analysis [MILL81].

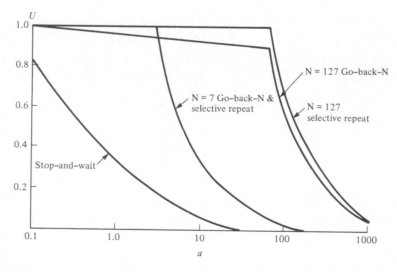

FIGURE 5-14. Line utilization for various error control techniques $(P = 10^{-3})$.

5-4

BIT-ORIENTED LINK CONTROL

Bit-oriented protocols are designed to satisfy a wide variety of data link requirements, including:

- Point-to-point and multipoint links.
- Half-duplex (two-way alternate) and full-duplex (two-way simultaneous) operation.
- Primary-secondary (e.g., host-terminal) and peer (e.g., computer-computer) interaction.
- Links with large (e.g., satellite) and small (e.g., short-distance direct connect) values of a.

In addition, these protocols are intended to satisfy the following objectives:

- *Code independence:* The user should be able to use any code set or bit patterns in the data to be transmitted.
- *Adaptability:* The format should support a variety of link types and an evolving set of requirements.
- *High efficiency:* The format should minimize overhead bits and permit efficient error and flow control.
- *High reliability:* The protocol should have a powerful set of error detection and recovery procedures.

The key to satisfying these requirements and objectives is to rely on positional significance and coded control fields. A structure is positionally significant when it is divided into fields each of which has a particular meaning and whose position is fixed relative to a frame delimiter. A coded control field is one in which different combinations of bits have specific meanings and in which positionally significant subfields are used. We will see that this approach leads to a compact control mechanism. It should be compared with the less efficient character-oriented schemes discussed in Appendix 5A.

A number of very similar bit-oriented protocols have achieved widespread use:

- *High-level data link control (HDLC):* developed by the International Organization for Standardization (ISO 3309).
- *Advanced data communication control procedures (ADCCP):* developed by the American National Standards Institute (ANSI X3.66). With very minor exceptions, ADCCP has been adopted by the U.S. National Bureau of Standards (FIPS PUB 71-1) for use on federal government procurements, and by the Federal Telecommunications Standards Committee (FED-STD- 1003A) as the standard for the national-defense-related National Communications System.
- *Link access procedure, balanced (LAP-B):* adopted by the International Telegraph and Telephone Consultative Committee (CCITT) as part of its X.25 packet-switched network standard.
- *Synchronous data link control (SDLC):* used by IBM. This is not a standard, but is in widespread use.

There are virtually no differences between HDLC and ADCCP. LAP-B is a subset of HDLC. SDLC is also a subset of HDLC, but also includes several minor additional features [BROD83a]. The following discussion is based on HDLC.

Basic Characteristics

To satisfy the variety of requirements listed above, HDLC defines three types of stations, two link configurations, and three data transfer modes of operation. The three station types are:

- *Primary station:* has the responsibility for controlling the operation of the link. Frames issued by the primary are called *commands*.
- *Secondary station:* operates under the control of the primary station. Frames issued by the secondary station(s) are called *responses*. The primary maintains a separate logical link with each secondary station on the line.
- *Combined station:* combines the features of primary and secondary stations. A combined station may issue both commands and responses.

The two link configurations are (Figure 5-15):

- *Unbalanced configuration:* used in point-to-point and multipoint operation. This configuration consists of one primary and one or more secondary stations and supports both full-duplex and half-duplex transmission.
- *Balanced configuration:* used only in point-to-point operation. This configuration consists of two combined stations and supports both full-duplex and half-duplex transmission.

The three data transfer modes of operation are:

- *Normal response mode (NRM):* This is an unbalanced configuration. The primary may initiate data transfer to a secondary, but a secondary may only transmit data in response to a poll from the primary.
- *Asynchronous balanced mode (ABM):* This is a balanced configuration. Either combined station may initiate transmission without receiving permission from the other combined station.
- *Asynchronous response mode (ARM):* This is an unbalanced configuration. In this mode, the secondary may initiate transmission without explicit permission

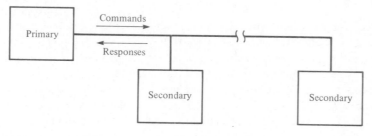

(a) Unbalanced configuration

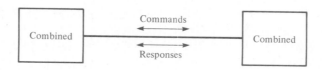

(b) Balanced configuration

FIGURE 5-15.   HDLC link configurations.

of the primary (i.e., send a response without waiting for a command). The primary still retains responsibility for the line, including initialization, error recovery, and logical disconnection.

The normal response mode is used on multidrop lines, in which a number of terminals are connected to a computer. The computer polls each terminal for input. NRM is also often used on point-to-point links, particularly if the link connects a terminal or other peripheral to a computer. The asynchronous balanced mode makes more efficient use of a full-duplex point-to-point link, since there is no polling overhead. The asynchronous response mode is rarely used; it is applicable to hub polling and other special situations in which a secondary may need to initiate transmission.

Frame Structure

HDLC uses synchronous transmission. All transmissions are in frames, and a single frame format suffices for all types of data and control exchanges.

Figure 5-16 depicts the structure of the HDLC frame. The frame has the following fields:

- *Flag:* 8 bits.
- *Address:* One or more octets.
- *Control:* 8 or 16 bits.
- *Information*: variable.
- *Frame check sequence (FCS):* 16 or 32 bits.
- *Flag:* 8 bits.

The flag, address, and control fields that precede the data field are known as a *header*. The FCS and flag fields following the data field are referred to as a *trailer*.

Flag Fields.   Flag fields delimit the frame at both ends with the unique pattern 01111110. A single flag may be used as the closing flag for one frame and the opening flag for the next. All active stations attached to the link are continuously hunting for the flag sequence to synchronize on the start of a frame. While receiving a frame, a station continues to hunt for that sequence to determine the end of the frame. However, since the HDLC frame allows arbitrary bit patterns, there is no assurance that the pattern 01111110 will not appear somewhere inside the frame, thus destroying frame-level synchronization. To avoid this problem, a procedure known as *bit stuffing* is used. The transmitter will always insert an extra 0 bit after each occurrence of five 1's in the frame (with the exception of the flag fields). After detecting a starting flag, the receiver monitors the bit stream. When a pattern of five 1's appears, the sixth bit is examined. If this bit is 0, it is deleted. If the sixth bit is a 1 and the seventh bit is a 0, the combination is accepted as a flag. If the sixth and seventh bits are both 1, the sending station is signaling an abort condition.

With the use of bit stuffing, arbitrary bit patterns can be inserted into the data field of the frame. This property is known as *data transparency*.

Figure 5-17 shows an example of bit stuffing. Note that in the first two cases, the extra 0 is not strictly necessary for avoiding a flag pattern, but is necessary for the operation of the algorithm. The pitfalls of bit stuffing are also illustrated in this

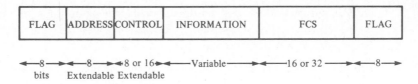

(a) Frame format

	1	2	3	4	5	6	7	8
I: Information	O		N(S)		P/F		N (R)	
S: Supervisory	1	O	S		P/F		N (R)	
U: Unnumbered	1	1	M		P/F		M	

N (S) = Send sequence number
N (R) = Receive sequence number
S = Supervisory function bits
M = Unnumbered function bits
P/F = Poll/final bit

(b) Control field format

```
 1  2  3  4  5  6  7  8  9  10 11 12 13 14 15  16                         8n
[0                      ][0                        ]••••••[1               ]
```

(c) Extended address field

	1	2	3	4	5	6	7	8	9	10	11	12	13	14	15	16
Information	0			N(S)					P/F				N(R)			
Supervisory	1	0	S		0	0	0	0	P/F				N(R)			

(d) Extended control fields

FIGURE 5-16. HDLC frame structure.

figure. When a flag is used as both an ending and starting flag, a 1-bit error merges two frames into one. Conversely, a 1-bit error inside the frame could split it in two.

Address Field.   The address field is used to identify the secondary station that transmitted or is to receive the frame. This field is not needed for point-to-point links, but is always included for the sake of uniformity. An address is normally eight bits long but, by prior agreement, an extended format may be used in which the address length is a multiple of seven bits. The least significant bit in each octet is 1 or 0 according as it is or is not the last octet of the address field. The remaining seven bits form part of the address. The single octet address of 11111111 is interpreted as the all-stations address in both basic and extended formats. It is used to allow the primary to broadcast a frame for reception by all secondaries.

Control Field.   HDLC defines three types of frames, each with a different control field format. *Information frames* (I-frames) carry the data to be transmitted

Original pattern

1 1 1 1 1 1 1 1 1 1 1 0 1 1 1 1 1 0 1 1 1 1 1 0

After bit–stuffing

1 1 1 1 1 0 1 1 1 1 1 0 1 1 0 1 1 1 1 1 0 1 0 1 1 1 1 1 0 1 0

(a) Example

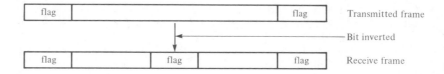

(b) An inverted bit splits a frame in two.

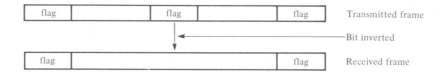

(c) An inverted bit merges two frames.

FIGURE 5-17. Bit stuffing.

for the station, known as *user data*. Additionally, flow and error control data, using the ARQ mechanism, may be piggybacked on an information frame. *Supervisory frames* (S-frames) provide the ARQ mechanism when piggybacking is not used, and *unnumbered frames* (U-frames) provide supplemental link control functions. The first one or two bits of the control field serves to identify the frame type. The remaining bit positions are organized into subfields as indicated in Figure 5-16b and d. Their use is explained in the discussion of HDLC operation, below.

Note that the basic control field for S- and I-frames uses 3-bit sequence numbers. With the appropriate set-mode command, an extended control field can be used for S- and I-frames that employs 7-bit sequence numbers.

Information Field.   The information field is present only in I-frames and some unnumbered frames. The field can contain any sequence of bits. Its length is undefined in the standard, but is generally limited by each implementation to a specified maximum. Frequently, the length must be a multiple of eight bits.

Frame Check Sequence Field.   The frame check sequence is applied to the remaining bits of the frame, exclusive of flags. The normal FCS is the 16-bit CRC-CCITT defined earlier. An optional 32-bit FCS, using CRC-32, may be employed if the frame length or line reliability dictates this choice.

TABLE 5-1   HDLC Commands and Responses

Name	Function	Description
Information (I)	C/R	Exchange user data
Supervisory (S)		
Receive Ready (RR)	C/R	Positive acknowledgment; ready to receive I-frame
Receive Not Ready (RNR)	C/R	Positive acknowledgment; not ready to receive
Reject (REJ)	C/R	Negative acknowledgment; go back N
Selective Reject (SREJ)	C/R	Negative acknowledgment; selective repeat
Unnumbered (U)		
Set Normal Response/ Extended Mode (SNRM/SNRME)	C	Set mode; extended = two-octet control field
Set Asynchronous Response/ Extended Mode (SARM/SARME)	C	Set mode; extended = two-octet control field
Set Asynchronous Balanced/ Extended Mode (SABM/SABME)	C	Set mode; extended = two-octet control field
Set Initialization Mode (SIM)	C	Initialize link control functions in addressed station
Disconnect (DISC)	C	Terminate logical link connection
Unnumbered Acknowledgment (UA)	R	Acknowledges acceptance of one of the above set-mode commands
Disconnected Mode (DM)	R	Secondary is logically disconnected
Request Disconnect (RD)	R	Request for DISC command
Request Initialization Mode (RIM)	R	Initialization needed; request for SIM command
Unnumbered Information (UI)	C/R	Used to exchange control information
Unnumbered Poll (UP)	C	Used to solicit control information
Reset (RSET)	C	Used for recovery; resets N(R), N(S)
Exchange Identification (XID)	C/R	Used to request/report identity and status
Test (TEST)	C/R	Exchange identical information fields for testing
Frame Reject (FRMR)	R	Reports receipt of unacceptable frame

Operation

The operation of HDLC consists of the exchange of I-frames, S-frames, and U-frames between a primary and a secondary or between two primaries. The various commands and responses defined for these frame types are listed in Table 5-1. To describe HDLC operation, we will first discuss these three types of frames, and then give some examples.

Information Frames.   The basic operation of HDLC involves the exchange of information frames (I-frames) containing user data. Each I-frame contains the sequence number of the transmitted frame as well as a piggybacked positive acknowledgment. The acknowledgment is the sequence number of the *next* frame expected. A maximum window size of 7 or 127 is allowed.

The I-frame also contains a poll/final (P/F) bit. The bit is a poll bit for commands (from primary) and a final bit (from secondary) for responses. In normal response mode (NRM), the primary issues a poll giving permission to send by setting the poll bit to 1, and the secondary sets the final bit to 1 on the last I-frame of its response. In asynchronous response mode (ARM) and asynchronous balanced mode (ABM), the P/F bit is sometimes used to coordinate the exchange of S- and U-frames.

Supervisory Frames.   The supervisory frame (S-frame) is used for flow and error control. Both go-back-N ARQ (REJ) and selective-repeat ARQ (SREJ) are allowed. The latter is rarely implemented because of the buffering requirements. A frame may be positively acknowledged with a receive ready (RR) when an I-frame is not available for piggybacking. In addition, a receive not ready (RNR) is used to accept a frame but request that no more I-frames be sent until a subsequent RR is used.

The P/F bit on a supervisory frame may be employed as follows. The primary may set the P bit in an RR frame to poll the secondary. This is done when the primary has no I-frame upon which to piggyback the poll. The secondary responds with an I-frame if it has one; otherwise, it sends an RR with the F bit set to indicate that it has no data to send. The primary (combined station) may set the P bit in the RNR command to solicit the receive status of a secondary/combined station. The response will be an RR with the F bit set if the station can receive I-frames, and an RNR with the F bit set if the station is busy.

Unnumbered Frames.   Unnumbered frames are used for a variety of control functions. As the name indicates, these frames do not carry sequence numbers and do not alter the sequencing or flow of numbered I-frames. We can group these frames into the following categories:

- Mode-setting commands and responses.
- Information transfer commands and responses.
- Recovery commands and responses.
- Miscellaneous commands and responses.

Mode-setting commands are transmitted by the primary/combined station to initialize or change the mode of the secondary/combined station. The secondary/ combined station acknowledges acceptance by responding with an unnumbered acknowledgment (UA) frame; the UA has the F bit set to the same value as the received P bit. Once established, a mode remains in effect at a secondary station until the next mode-setting command is accepted, and at a combined station until the next mode-setting command is either accepted or transmitted and acknowledged.

The commands SNRM, SNRME, SARM, SARME, SABM, and SABME are self-explanatory. Upon acceptance of the command, the I-frame sequence numbers in both directions are set to 0. The set initialization mode (SIM) command is used to cause the addressed secondary/combined station to initiate a station-specified procedure to initialize its data link control functions (e.g., accept a new program or update operational parameters). While in initialization mode, the required information is sent using unnumbered information (UI) frames. The disconnect command (DISC) is used to inform the addressed station that the transmitting station is suspending operation.

In addition to UA, there are several other responses related to mode setting. The disconnected mode (DM) response is sent in response to all commands to indicate that the responding station is logically disconnected. When sent in response to a mode-setting command, DM is a refusal to set the requested mode. The request initialization mode (RIM) response is used in response to a mode-setting command

(a) Point–to point duplex exchange

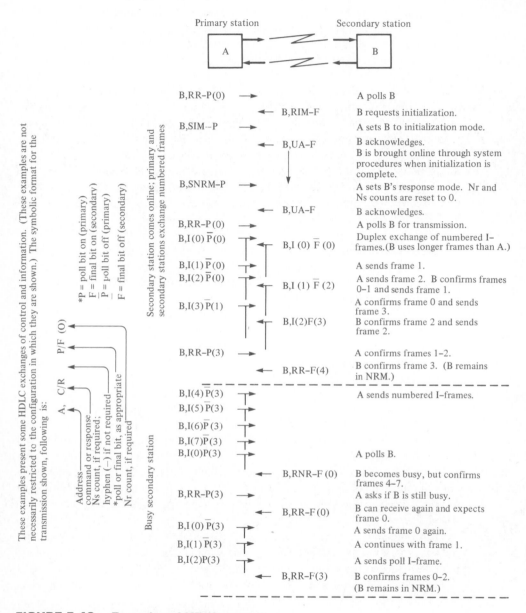

FIGURE 5-18.   Examples of HDLC operation.

when the station is not ready and wishes to initialize. The request disconnect (RD) response is used to request a disconnect of the logical link.

Information transfer commands and responses are used to exchange information between stations. This is done primarily through the unnumbered information (UI) command/response. Examples of UI frame information are higher-level status, operational interruption, time of day, and link initialization parameters. The unnumbered poll (UP) command is used to solicit an unnumbered response, as a way of establishing the status of the addressed station.

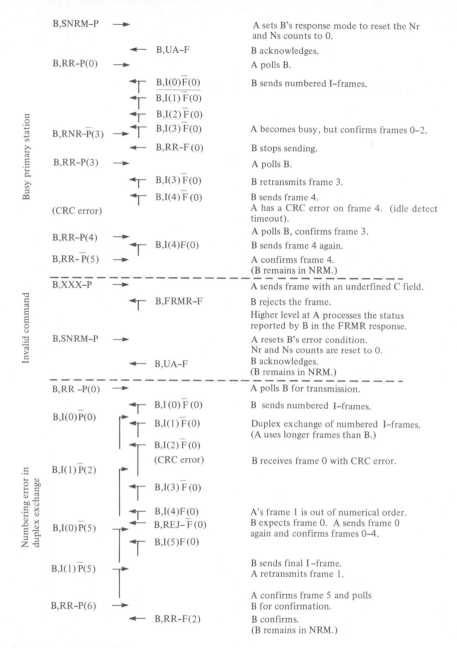

FIGURE 5-18.   (continued)

Recovery commands and responses are used when the normal ARQ mechanism does not apply or will not work. The frame reject (FRMR) response is used to report an error in a received frame, such as:

- Invalid control field.
- Data field too long.
- Data field not allowed with received frame type.
- Invalid receive count (i.e., a frame is acknowledged that has not yet been sent).

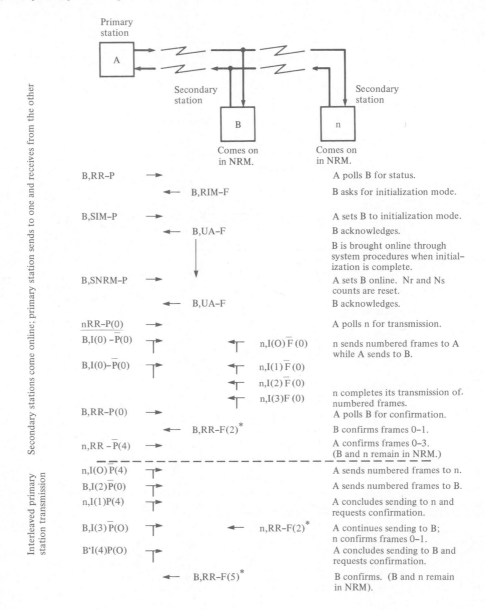

(b) Multipoint duplex exchanges

Primary
station

Secondary
station

Secondary
station

Comes on
in NRM.

Comes on
in NRM.

Secondary stations come online; primary station sends to one and receives from the other

B,RR-P →	A polls B for status.
← B,RIM-F	B asks for initialization mode.
B,SIM-P →	A sets B to initialization mode.
← B,UA-F	B acknowledges.
	B is brought online through system procedures when initialization is complete.
B,SNRM-P →	A sets B online. Nr and Ns counts are reset.
← B,UA-F	B acknowledges.
nRR-P(0) →	A polls n for transmission.
B,I(0) –P̄(0) ⊤ ⊤ n,I(O) F̄ (0)	n sends numbered frames to A while A sends to B.
B,I(0)–P̄(0) ⊤ ⊤ n,I(1) F̄ (0)	
⊤ n,I(2) F̄ (0)	
⊤ n,I(3)F (0)	n completes its transmission of numbered frames.
B,RR-P(0) →	A polls B for confirmation.
← B,RR-F(2)*	B confirms frames 0–1.
n,RR – P̄(4) →	A confirms frames 0–3. (B and n remain in NRM.)

Interleaved primary station transmission

n,I(O) P̄(4) ⊤	A sends numbered frames to n.
B,I(2)P̄(0) ⊤	A sends numbered frames to B.
n,I(1)P(4) ⊤	A concludes sending to n and requests confirmation.
B,I(3) P̄(O) ⊤ ← n,RR–F(2)*	A continues sending to B; n confirms frames 0–1.
B'I(4)P(O) ⊤	A concludes sending to B and requests confirmation.
← B,RR–F(5)*	B confirms. (B and n remain in NRM).

*If a secondary station has information to send, this confirmation may be in the I format.

FIGURE 5-18. (continued)

The reset (RSET) command is used to clear the FRMR condition. RSET announces that the sending station is resetting its send sequence number, and the addressed station should reset its receive sequence number.

Finally, there are two *miscellaneous* command/responses that fit into no neat category. The exchange identification (XID) command/response is used for two stations to exchange station identification and the characteristics of the two stations. The actual information exchanged is implementation dependent. A recently added frame type is the test (TEST) command/response. A test command must be echoed with a test response at the earliest opportunity. This is a simple means of testing that the link and the addressed station are still functioning.

Examples. Figure 5-18 contains a number of examples of HDLC operation for both point-to-point and multipoint links. The reader is urged to study this figure carefully.

5-5

RECOMMENDED READING

There have been a number of survey articles on data link control, of which the following are recommended: [STUT72], [GRAY72], [CONA83], [LAM83]. [MART88], [CYPS78], and [MCNA88] also contain good discussions. Clear discussions of flow control and error control techniques can be found in [MART70] and [BLAC82]. [CONA80] discusses character-oriented protocols, while [CARL80], [BERT87], [WEIS83], and [DONN74] discuss bit-oriented protocols. The latter reference is specifically on SDLC. [BROD83b] is an excellent comparison of IBM's character-oriented (BSC) and bit-oriented (SDLC) protocols.

5-6

PROBLEMS

5-1 Draw a diagram similar to Figure 5-3 for the case in which the primary requests data from the secondary.

5-2 Derive an equation similar to Equation (5-1) for roll-call polling on a multi-multipoint line. Assume that t_0 is constant for all stations and that the primary does not send a poll until it is assured that the response of that poll will not arrive prior to the end of a transmission.

5-3 Derive an equation similar to Equation (5-1) for hub polling.

5-4 Analyze the data link configurations of Figure 5-2. Assume that the primary station and each sender communicate equally (not necessarily a real situation). Further assume that each sender sends messages only 10% of the time on the average. The data links are controlled in such a way that the messages can wait if the line is busy. For each configuration, what percent of the time will the links to and from P be used?

5-5 In the system of Figure 5-3, it would appear that efficiency could be improved by station 1 sending its EOT with the last data frame. Comment on this procedure.

5-6 A computer with many terminals will usually be set up to poll the terminals to see if they have information to send. A computer with only a few terminals will allow the terminals to interrupt it. What are the trade-offs between the two methods of operation?

5-7   Consider a half-duplex point-to-point line using the stop and wait scheme defined
      in Section 5-2. In the derivation of total time required to send data (T_D), the
      assumption is made that the time to initiate the sequence, the processing times,
      and the acknowledgment times are small compared to the propagation time and the
      frame time. Check the validity of this assumption for the following case:
      $t_{prop} = t_{frame}$
      $t_{proc} = t_{poll} = t_{ack} = 0.1 \, t_{prop}$
      $n = 100$
      What percent error does this assumption introduce for this case?

5-8   Consider a half-duplex point-to-point line using a stop and wait scheme.
      a. What is the effect on line utilization of increasing the message size so that fewer
         messages will be required? Other factors remain constant.
      b. What is the effect on line utilization of increasing the number of frames for a
         constant message size?
      c. What is the effect on line utilization of increasing frame size?

5-9   A channel has a data rate of 4 kbps and a propagation delay of 20 ms. For what
      range of frame sizes does stop-and-wait give an efficiency of at least 50%?

5-10 Suppose that a selective-reject ARQ is used where N = 4. Show, by example,
      that a 3-bit sequence number is needed.

5-11 Why is it not necessary to have NAK0 and NAK1 for stop-and-wait ARQ?

5-12 It was stated that multiple-frame acknowledgment could not be used for selective-
      repeat ARQ. What about the following interpretation: ACK i means that frame i
      and all preceding frames are accepted except those that have been explicitly
      NAK'ed?

5-13 Consider the use of 1000-bit frames on a 1-Mbps satellite channel. What is the
      maximum link utilization for:
      a. Stop-and-wait ARQ?
      b. Continuous ARQ with a window size of 7?
      c. Continuous ARQ with a window size of 127?
      d. Continuous ARQ with a window size of 255?

5-14 Consider the following multipoint architecture, which consists of one primary and
      N equally spaced secondaries.

      Let a = (propagation time)/(transmission time), where the propagation time is
      from the primary to the farthest secondary.
      a. Assume roll call polling. Also assume that the transmission time for the poll
         and that primary and secondary processing times are negligible. If every sec-

ondary is always ready to transmit, show that the line utilization is

$$U = \frac{1}{1 + a}$$

If only one station is ready to transmit during any polling cycle show that

$$U = \frac{1}{1 + aN}$$

b. Now consider the same architecture for hub polling. Show that if every secondary is always ready to transmit, the utilization can be approximated by

$$U = \frac{1}{1 + a/2 + a/N}$$

[Hint: Ignore the first station to be polled (from P) and derive the total time it takes for a typical secondary to be polled and transmit.] Now show that if only one station is ready to transmit in each cycle,

$$U = \frac{1}{1 + 2.5a}$$

5-15 In Figure 5-14, line utilization for go-back-N ARQ is greater for $N = 7$ than for $N = 127$ at values of a less than 3. How do you account for this?

5-16 It is clear that bit stuffing is needed for the address, data, and FCS fields of an HDLC frame. Is it needed for the control field?

5-17 Suggest improvements to the bit-stuffing algorithm to overcome the problems of a single-bit error.

5-18 Using the example bit string of Figure 5-17, show the signal pattern on the line using NRZ-L coding. Does this suggest a side benefit of bit stuffing?

5-19 Assume that the primary HDLC station in NRM has sent six I-frames to a secondary. The primary's N(S) count was three (011 binary) prior to sending the six frames. If the poll bit is on in the sixth frame, what will be the N(R) count back from the secondary after the last frame? (Assume error-free operation.)

5-20 Consider that several physical links connect two stations. We would like to use a "multilink HDLC" that makes efficient use of these links by sending frames on a FIFO basis on the next available link. What enhancements to HDLC are required?

CHAPTER 6

Multiplexing

In Chapter 5, we spent a lot of time trying to devise efficient techniques for utilizing a data link under heavy load. Specifically, with two devices connected by a point-to-point link, it was felt to be desirable to have multiple frames outstanding so that the data link not become a bottleneck between the stations. Now consider the opposite problem. Transmission facilities are, by and large, expensive. It is often the case that two communicating stations will not utilize the full capacity of a data link. For efficiency, it should be possible to share that capacity. The generic term for such sharing is multiplexing.

A simple example of multiplexing is the multidrop line. Here, a number of secondary devices (e.g., terminals) and a primary (e.g., host computer) share the same line. This has several advantages:

- The host computer needs only one I/O port for multiple terminals.
- Only one transmission line is needed.

These types of benefits are applicable in other contexts. In long-haul communications, a number of high-capacity fiber, coaxial, terrestrial microwave, and satellite facilities have been built. These facilities can carry large numbers of voice and data transmissions simultaneously using multiplexing.

This chapter concentrates on three types of multiplexing techniques. The first, frequency-division multiplexing (FDM), is the most widespread and is familiar to anyone who has ever used a radio or television set. The second is a particular case of time-division multiplexing (TDM) often known as synchronous TDM. This is commonly used for multiplexing digitized voice streams. The third type seeks to

FIGURE 6-1. Multiplexing.

improve on the efficiency of synchronous TDM by adding complexity to the multiplexer. It is known by a variety of names, including:

- Statistical TDM.
- Asynchronous TDM.
- Intelligent TDM.

We shall refer to it as statistical TDM, since this label points out one of its chief properties.

Figure 6-1 depicts the multiplexing function generically. There are n inputs to a multiplexer. The multiplexer is connected by a single data link to a demultiplexer. The link is able to carry n separate *channels* of data. The multiplexer combines (multiplexes) data from the n input lines and transmits over a higher-capacity data link. The demultiplexer accepts the multiplexed data stream, separates (demultiplexes) the data according to channel, and delivers them to the appropriate output lines.

In addition to the three types of multiplexing listed above, there are other multiplexing techniques more properly termed medium access control techniques. A poll-and-select multipoint line is one example. Other examples are explored in Part II.

6-1

FREQUENCY-DIVISION MULTIPLEXING

Characteristics

Frequency-division multiplexing (FDM) is possible when the useful bandwidth of the medium exceeds the required bandwidth of signals to be transmitted. A number of signals can be carried simultaneously if each signal is modulated onto a different carrier frequency, and the carrier frequencies are sufficiently separated that the bandwidths of the signals do not overlap. A general case of FDM is shown in Figure 6-2a. Six signal sources are fed into a multiplexer, which modulates each signal onto a different frequency ($f_1, \ldots, f_6$). Each modulated signal requires a certain bandwidth centered around its carrier frequency, referred to as a *channel*. To prevent interference, the channels are separated by guard bands, which are unused portions of the spectrum.

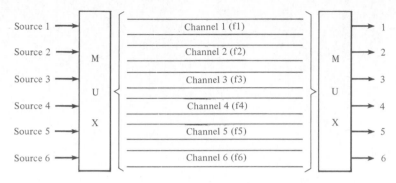

(a) Frequency-Division Multiplexing

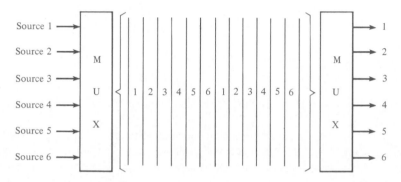

(b) Time-Division Multiplexing

FIGURE 6-2.   FDM and TDM.

The composite signal transmitted across the medium is analog. Note, however, that the input signals may be either digital or analog. In the case of digital input, the techniques of Section 3-2 would be used to produce an analog signal centered at the desired frequency. In the case of analog input, such as voice, the techniques of Section 3-4 apply.

Figure 3-7, which shows full-duplex FSK transmission, is a simple example of FDM. Two signals are carried on the medium, one centered at 1170 Hz, the other at 2125 Hz. In this case, the signals propagate in opposite directions. More typically, FDM is used to refer to a situation in which multiple signals are carried in the same direction.

A familiar example of FDM is broadcast and cable television. The television signal discussed in Chapter 2 fits comfortably into a 6-MHz bandwidth. Figure 6-3 depicts the transmitted TV signal and its bandwidth. The black-and-white video signal is AM modulated on a carrier signal f_{cv}. Since the baseband video signal has a bandwidth of 4 MHz, we would expect the modulated signal to have a bandwidth of 8 MHz centered on f_{cv}. To conserve bandwidth, the signal is passed through a sideband filter so that most of the lower sideband is suppressed. The resulting signal extends from about $f_{cv} - 0.75$ MHz to $f_{cv} + 4.2$ MHz. A separate color subcarrier, f_{cc}, is used to transmit color information. This is spaced far enough from f_{cv} that there is essentially no interference. Finally, the audio portion of the signal is modulated on f_{ca}, outside the effective bandwidth of the other two signals.

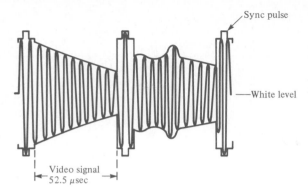

Sync pulse

White level

Video signal
52.5 μsec

(a) Amplitude modulation with video signal

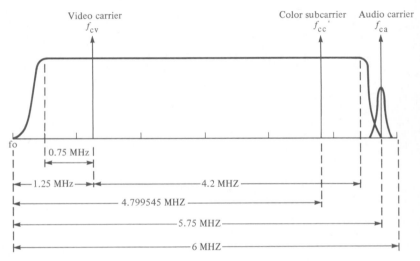

Video carrier
f_{cv}

Color subcarrier
f_{cc}

Audio carrier
f_{ca}

fo

0.75 MHz

1.25 MHz

4.2 MHZ

4.799545 MHZ

5.75 MHZ

6 MHZ

(b) Magnitude spectrum of RF video signal

FIGURE 6-3. Transmitted TV signal.

A bandwidth of 50 kHz is allocated for the audio signal. The composite signal fits into a 6-MHz bandwidth with the video, color, and audio signal carriers at 1.25 MHz, 4.799545 MHz, and 5.75 MHz above the lower edge of the band, respectively. Thus multiple TV signals can be frequency-division multiplexed on a CATV cable, each with a bandwidth of 6 MHz. Given the enormous bandwidth of coaxial cable (as much as 500 MHz), dozens of TV signals can be simultaneously carried using FDM. Table 6-1 shows the most commonly used channel assignments. Of course, using radio-frequency propagation through the atmosphere is also a form of FDM; Table 6-2 shows the frequency allocation in the United States for broadcast television.

A generic depiction of an FDM system is shown in Figure 6-4. A number of analog or digital signals [$m_i(t)$, $i = 1, N$] are to be multiplexed onto the same transmission medium. Each signal $m_i(t)$ is modulated onto a carrier f_{sci}; since multiple carriers are to be used, each is referred to as a *subcarrier*. Any type of modulation may be used. The resulting analog, modulated signals are then summed

TABLE 6-1   Cable TV Channel Frequency Allocation

Channel Designation	Frequency (MHz)
Low Band	
2	54–60
3	60–66
4	66–72
5	76–82
6	82–88
Mid Band	
A	120–126
B	126–132
C	132–138
D	138–144
E	144–150
F	150–156
G	156–162
H	162–168
I	168–174
High Band	
7	174–180
8	180–186
9	186–192
10	192–198
11	198–204
12	204–210
13	210–216
Super Band	
J	216–222
K	222–228
L	228–234
M	234–240
N	240–246
O	246–252
P	252–258
Q	258–264
R	264–270
S	270–276
T	276–282
U	282–288
V	288–294

Source: [CUNN80].

to produce a composite signal $m_c(t)$. Figure 6-4b shows the result. The spectrum of signal $m_i(t)$ is shifted to be centered on f_{sci}. For this scheme to work, f_{sci} must be chosen so that the bandwidths of the various signals do not overlap. Otherwise, it will be impossible to recover the original signals.

The composite signal may then be shifted as a whole to another carrier frequency by an additional modulation step. We will see examples of this below. This second modulation step need not use the same modulation technique as the first.

The composite signal has a total bandwidth B, where $B > \sum\limits_{i=1}^{N} B_{sci}$. This analog

TABLE 6-2 Broadcast Television Channel Frequency Allocation

Channel Number	Band (MHz)	Channel Number	Band (MHz)	Channel Number	Band (MHz)
2	54–60	25	536–542	48	674–680
3	60–66	26	542–548	49	680–686
4	66–72	27	548–554	50	686–692
5	76–82	28	554–560	51	692–698
6	82–88	29	560–566	52	698–704
7	174–180	30	566–572	53	704–710
8	180–186	31	572–578	54	710–716
9	186–192	32	578–584	55	716–722
10	192–198	33	584–590	56	722–728
11	198–204	34	590–596	57	728–734
12	204–210	35	596–602	58	734–740
13	210–216	36	602–608	59	740–746
14	470–476	37	608–614	60	746–752
15	476–482	38	614–620	61	752–758
16	482–488	39	620–626	62	758–764
17	488–494	40	626–632	63	764–770
18	494–500	41	632–638	64	770–776
19	500–506	42	638–644	65	776–782
20	506–512	43	644–650	66	782–788
21	512–518	44	650–656	67	788–794
22	518–524	45	656–662	68	794–800
23	524–530	46	662–668	69	800–806
24	530–536	47	668–674		

signal may be transmitted over a suitable medium. At the receiving end, the composite signal is passed through N bandpass filters, each filter centered on f_{sci} and having a bandwidth B_{sci}, for $1 < i < N$. In this way, the signal is again split into its component parts. Each component is then demodulated to recover the original signal.

Let us consider a simple example of transmitting three voice signals simultaneously over a medium. As was mentioned, the bandwidth of a voice signal is generally taken to be 4 kHz, with an effective spectrum of 300 to 3400 Hz (Figure 6-5a). If such a signal is used to amplitude-modulate a 64-kHz carrier, the spectrum of Figure 6-5b results. The modulated signal has a bandwidth of 8 kHz, extending from 60 to 68 kHz. To make efficient use of bandwidth, we elect to transmit only the lower sideband. Now, if three voice signals are used to modulate carriers at 64, 68, and 72 kHz, and only the lower sideband of each is taken, the spectrum of Figure 6-5c results.

This figure points out two problems that an FDM system must cope with. The first is crosstalk, which may occur if the spectra of adjacent component signals overlap significantly. In the case of voice signals, with an effective bandwidth of only 3100 Hz (300 to 3400), a 4 kHz bandwidth is adequate. The spectra of signals produced by modems for voiceband transmission also fit well in this bandwidth. Another potential problem is intermodulation noise, which was discussed in Chapter 2. On a long link, the nonlinear effects of amplifiers on a signal in one channel could produce frequency components in other channels.

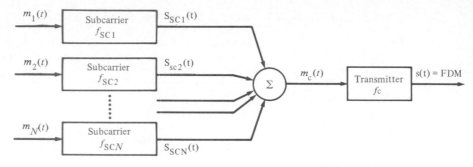

(a) Transmitter

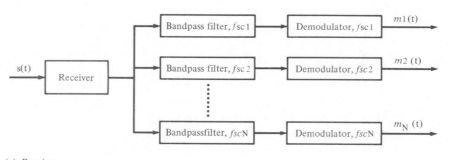

(b) Spectrum of composite signal (positive f)

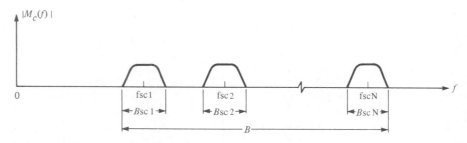

(c) Receiver

FIGURE 6-4.   Frequency division multiplexing. Source: [COUC87]

Carrier Systems

The long-distance carrier system provided in the United States and throughout the world is designed to transmit voiceband signals over high-capacity transmission links, such as coaxial cable and microwave systems. The earliest, and still most common, technique for utilizing high-capacity links is FDM. In the United States, AT&T has designated a hierarchy of FDM schemes to accommodate transmission systems of various capacities. A similar, but unfortunately not identical, system has been adopted internationally under the auspices of CCITT (Table 6-3).

Figure 6-6 shows the first three levels of the AT&T-defined hierarchy. At the first level, 12 voice channels are combined to produce a *group* signal with a bandwidth of 12×4 kHz = 48 kHz, in the range 60 to 108 kHz. The signals are produced in a fashion similar to that described above, using subcarrier frequencies of from 64 to 108 kHz in increments of 4 kHz. The next basic building

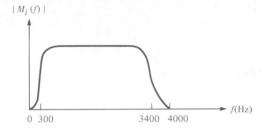

(a) Spectrum of m$_i$(t), positive f

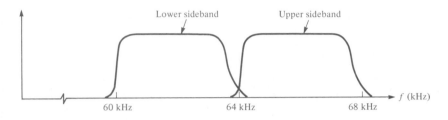

(b) Spectrum of s_{SC1} (t) for f_{SC1} = 64 kHz

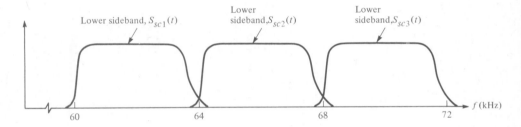

(c) Spectrum of composite signal using subcarriers at
64 kHz, 68kHz, and 72 kHz

FIGURE 6-5. FDM of three voiceband signals.

TABLE 6-3   North American and International FDM Carrier Standards

Number of Voice Channels	Bandwidth	Spectrum	AT&T	CCITT
12	48 kHz	60–108 kHz	Group	Group
60	240 kHz	312–552 kHz	Supergroup	Supergroup
300	1.232 MHz	812–2044 kHz		Mastergroup
600	2.52 MHz	564–3084 kHz	Mastergroup	
900	3.872 MHz	8.516–12.388 MHz		Supermaster group
$N \times 600$			Mastergroup multiplex	
3,600	16.984 MHz	0.564–17.548 MHz	Jumbogroup	
10,800	57.442 MHz	3.124–60.566 MHz	Jumbogroup multiplex	

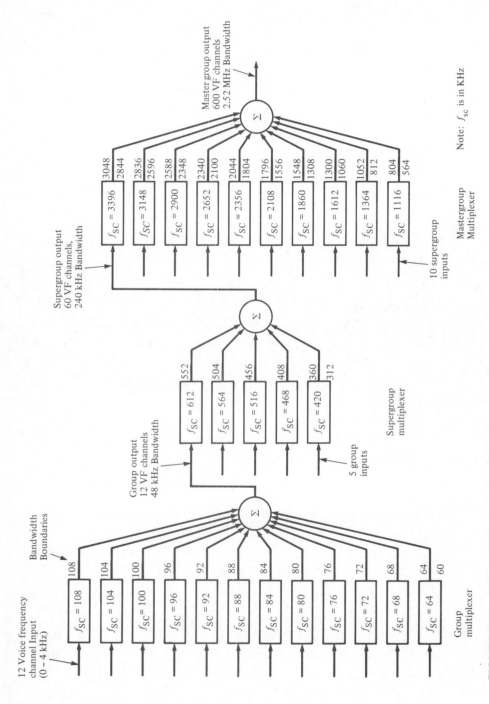

FIGURE 6-6. AT&T FDM hierarchy (first three levels).

block is the 60-channel *supergroup*, which is formed by frequency-division multiplexing five group signals. At this step, each group is treated as a single signal with a 48 kHz bandwidth and is modulated by a subcarrier. The subcarriers have frequencies from 420 to 612 kHz in increments of 48 kHz. The resulting signal occupies 312 to 552 kHz.

There are several variations to supergroup formation. Each of the five inputs to the supergroup multiplexer may be a group channel containing 12 multiplexed voice signals. In addition, any signal up to 48 kHz wide whose bandwidth is contained within 60 to 108 kHz may be used as input to the supergroup multiplexer. As another variation, it is possible to directly combine 60 voiceband channels into a supergroup. This may reduce multiplex costs where an interface with existing group multiplex is not required.

The next level of the hierarchy is the *mastergroup* which combines 10 supergroup inputs. Again, any signal with a bandwidth of 240 kHz in the range 312 to 552 kHz can serve as input to the mastergroup multiplexer. The mastergroup has a bandwidth of 2.52 MHz and can support 600 voice frequency (VF) channels. Higher-level multiplexing is defined above the mastergroup, as shown in Table 6-3.

Note that the original voice or data signal may be modulated many times. For example, a data signal may be encoded using QPSK to form an analog voice signal. This signal could then be used to modulate a 76 kHz carrier to form a component of a group signal. This group signal could then be used to modulate a 516 kHz carrier to form a component of a supergroup signal. Each stage can distort the original data; this is so, for example, if the modulator/multiplexer contains non-linearities or introduces noise.

SYNCHRONOUS TIME-DIVISION MULTIPLEXING

Characteristics

Synchronous time-division multiplexing is possible when the achievable data rate (sometimes, unfortunately, called bandwidth) of the medium exceeds the data rate of digital signals to be transmitted. Multiple digital signals (or analog signals carrying digital data) can be carried on a single transmission path by interleaving portions of each signal in time. The interleaving can be at the bit level or in blocks of bytes or larger quantities. For example, the multiplexer in Figure 6-2b has six inputs which might each be, say, 9.6 kbps. A single line with a capacity of at least 57.6 kbps (plus overhead capacity) could accommodate all six sources.

A generic depiction of a synchronous TDM system is provided in Figure 6-7. A number of signals $[m_i(t), i = 1, N]$ are to be multiplexed onto the same transmission medium. The signals carry digital data and are generally digital signals. The incoming data from each source are briefly buffered. Each buffer is typically one bit or one character in length. The buffers are scanned sequentially to form a composite digital data stream $m_c(t)$. The scan operation is sufficiently rapid so that each buffer is emptied before more data can arrive. Thus the data rate of $m_c(t)$ must at least equal the sum of the data rates of the $m_i(t)$. The digital signal $m_c(t)$ may be transmitted directly, or passed through a modem so that an analog signal is transmitted. In either case, transmission is typically synchronous.

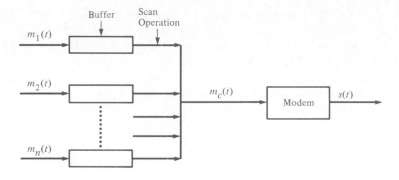

(a) Transmitter

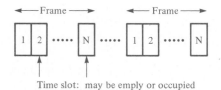

(b) TDM frames

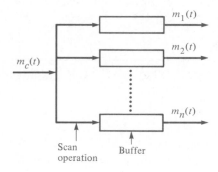

(c) Receiver

FIGURE 6-7. Synchronous time-division multiplexing.

The transmitted data may have a format something like Figure 6-7b. The data are organized into frames. Each frame contains a cycle of time slots. In each frame, one or more slots is dedicated to each data source. The sequence of slots dedicated to one source, from frame to frame, is called a channel. The slot length equals the transmitter buffer length, typically a bit or a character.

The *character-interleaving* technique is used with asynchronous sources. Each time slot contains one character of data. Typically, the start and stop bits of each character are eliminated before transmission and reinserted by the receiver, thus improving efficiency. The *bit-interleaving* technique is used with synchronous sources and may also be used with asynchronous sources. Each time slot contains just one bit.

At the receiver, the interleaved data are demultiplexed and routed to the appropriate destination buffer. For each input source $m_i(t)$, there is an identical output source which will receive the input data at the same rate at which it was generated.

Synchronous TDM is called synchronous not because synchronous transmission is used, but because the time slots are preassigned to sources and fixed. The time slots for each source are transmitted whether or not the source has data to send. This is, of course, also the case with FDM. In both cases, capacity is wasted to achieve simplicity of implementation. Even when fixed assignment is used, however, it is possible for a synchronous TDM device to handle sources of different data rates. For example, the slowest input device could be assigned one slot per cycle, while faster devices are assigned multiple slots per cycle.

TDM Link Control. The reader will note that the transmitted data stream depicted in Figure 6-7 does not contain the headers and trailers that we have come to associate with synchronous transmission. The reason is that the control mechanisms provided by a data link protocol are not needed. It is instructive to ponder this point, and we do so by considering two key data link control mechanisms: flow control and error control. It should be clear that, as far as the multiplexer and demultiplexer (Figure 6-1) are concerned, flow control is not needed. The data rate on the multiplexed line is fixed, and the multiplexer and demultiplexer are designed to operate at that rate. But suppose that one of the individual output lines attaches to a device that is temporarily unable to accept data? Should the transmission of TDM frames cease? Clearly not, since the remaining output lines are expecting to receive data at predetermined times. The solution is for the saturated output device to cause the flow of data from the corresponding input device to cease. Thus, for a while, the channel in question will carry empty slots, but the frames as a whole will maintain the same transmission rate.

The reasoning for error control is the same. It would not do to request retransmission of an entire TDM frame because an error occurs on one channel. The devices using the other channels do not want a retransmission nor would they know that a retransmission had been requested by some other device on another channel. Again, the solution is to apply error control on a per-channel basis.

How are flow control, error control, and other good things to be provided on a per-channel basis? The answer is simple: Use a data link control protocol such as HDLC on a per-channel basis. A simplified example is shown in Figure 6-8. We assume two data sources, each using HDLC. One is transmitting a stream of HDLC frames containing three octets of data, the other is transmitting HDLC frames containing four octets of data. For clarity, we assume that character-interleaved multiplexing is used, although bit interleaving is more typical. Notice what is happening. The octets of the HDLC frames from the two sources are shuffled together for transmission over the multiplexed line. The reader may initially be uncomfortable with this diagram, since the HDLC frames have lost their integrity in some sense. For example, each frame check sequence (FCS) on the line applies to a disjointed set of bits. Even the FCS is not in one piece! However, the pieces are reassembled correctly before they are seen by the device on the other end of the HDLC protocol. In this sense, the multiplexing/demultiplexing operation is transparent to the attached stations; to each communicating pair of stations, it appears that they have a dedicated link.

One refinement is needed in Figure 6-8. Both ends of the line need to be a combination multiplexer/demultiplexer with a full-duplex line in between. Then

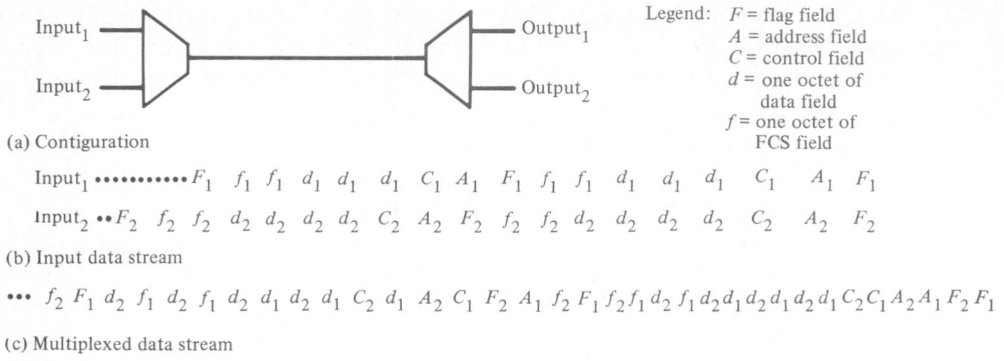

Legend: F = flag field
A = address field
C = control field
d = one octet of data field
f = one octet of FCS field

(a) Configuration

Input$_1$ •••••••••• F_1 f_1 f_1 d_1 d_1 d_1 C_1 A_1 F_1 f_1 f_1 d_1 d_1 d_1 C_1 A_1 F_1

Input$_2$ •• F_2 f_2 f_2 d_2 d_2 d_2 d_2 C_2 A_2 F_2 f_2 f_2 d_2 d_2 d_2 d_2 C_2 A_2 F_2

(b) Input data stream

••• f_2 F_1 d_2 f_1 d_2 f_1 d_2 d_1 d_2 d_1 C_2 d_1 A_2 C_1 F_2 A_1 f_2 F_1 f_2 f_1 d_2 f_1 d_2 d_1 d_2 d_1 d_2 d_1 C_2 C_1 A_2 A_1 F_2 F_1

(c) Multiplexed data stream

FIGURE 6-8. **Use of data link control on TDM channels.**

each channel consists of two sets of slots, one traveling in each direction. The individual devices attached at each end can, in pairs, use HDLC to control their own channel. The multiplexer/demultiplexers need not be concerned with these matters.

Framing. So we have seen that a link control protocol is not needed to manage the overall TDM link. There is, however, a basic requirement for framing. Since we are not providing flag or SYNC characters to bracket TDM frames, some means is needed to assure frame synchronization. It is clearly important to maintain framing synchronization since, if the source and destination are out of step, data on all channels are lost.

Perhaps the most common mechanism for framing is known as *added-digit framing*. In this scheme, typically, one control bit is added to each TDM frame. An identifiable pattern of bits, from frame to frame, is used on this "control channel." A typical example is the alternating bit pattern, 101010. . . This is a pattern unlikely to be sustained on a data channel. Thus to synchronize, a receiver compares the incoming bits of one frame position to the expected pattern. If the pattern does not match, successive bit positions are searched until the pattern persists over multiple frames. Once framing synchronization is established, the receiver continues to monitor the framing bit channel. If the pattern breaks down, the receiver must again enter a framing search mode.

Pulse Stuffing. Perhaps the most difficult problem in the design of a synchronous time-division multiplexer is that of synchronizing the various data sources. If each source has a separate clock, any variation among clocks could cause loss of synchronization. Also, in some cases the data rates of the input data streams are not related by a simple rational number. For both these problems, a technique known as *pulse stuffing* is an effective remedy. With pulse stuffing, the outgoing data rate of the multiplexer, excluding framing bits, is higher than the sum of the maximum instantaneous incoming rates. The extra capacity is used by stuffing extra dummy bits or pulses into each incoming signal until its rate is raised to that of a locally generated clock signal. The stuffed pulses are inserted at fixed locations in the multiplexer frame format so that they may be identified and removed at the demultiplexer.

Example. An example, from [COUC83], illustrates the use of synchronous TDM to multiplex digital and analog sources. Consider that there are 11 sources to be multiplexed on a single link:

- *Source 1:* Analog, 2-kHz bandwidth.
- *Source 2:* Analog, 4-kHz bandwidth.
- *Source 3:* Analog, 2-kHz bandwidth.
- *Sources 4–11:* Digital, 7200 bps synchronous.

As a first step, the analog sources are converted to digital using PCM. Recall from Chapter 4 that PCM is based on the sampling theorem, which dictates that a signal be sampled at a rate equal to twice its bandwidth. Thus the required sampling rate is 4000 samples per second for sources 1 and 3, and 8000 samples per second for source 2. These samples, which are analog (PAM), must then be quantized or digitized. Let us assume that 4 bits are used for each analog sample. For convenience, these three sources will be multiplexed first, as a unit. At a scan rate of 4 kHz, one PAM sample each is taken from sources 1 and 3, and two PAM samples are taken from source 2 per scan. These four samples are interleaved and converted to 4-bit PCM samples. Thus a total of 16 bits is generated at a rate of 4000 times per second, for a composite bit rate of 64 kbps.

For the digital sources, pulse stuffing is used to raise each source to a rate of 8 kbps, for an aggregate data rate of 64 kbps. A frame can consist of multiple cycles of 32 bits, each containing 16 PCM bits and two bits from each of the eight digital sources. Figure 6-9 depicts the result.

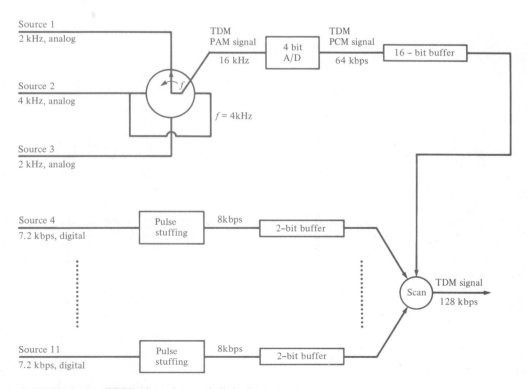

FIGURE 6-9. TDM of analog and digital sources.

Carrier Systems

As with FDM, synchronous TDM is used as part of the long-haul telecommunications system, and a hierarchy of TDM carriers has been developed. Table 6-4 shows the scheme used in North America (also used in Japan) plus the international (CCITT) standard.

The basis of the TDM hierarchy is the DS-1 transmission format (Figure 6-10) which multiplexes 24 channels. Each frame contains eight bits per channel plus a framing bit for $24 \times 8 + 1 = 193$ bits. For voice transmission, the following rules apply. Each channel contains one PCM word. As described earlier, PCM for voice assumes a 4-kHz bandwidth. Therefore, 8000 samples per second are taken. Therefore, each channel slot and hence each frame must repeat 8000 times per second. With a frame length of 193 bits, we have a data rate of $8000 \times 193 = 1.544$ Mbps. For five of every six frames, 8-bit PCM is used. For every sixth frame, each channel contains a 7-bit PCM word plus a signaling bit. The eighth bits form a stream for each voice channel which contains network control and routing information, for example, to establish a connection or terminate a call.

The same overall DS-1 format is used to provide digital data service. For compatibility with voice, the same 1.544-Mbps data rate is used. In this case 23 channels of data are provided. The twenty-fourth channel position is reserved for a special sync byte which allows faster and more reliable reframing following a framing error. Within each channel, seven bits per frame are used for data, with the eighth bit used to indicate whether the channel, for that frame, contains user data or system control data. With seven bits per channel, and since each frame is repeated 8000 times per second, a data rate of 56 kbps can be provided per channel. Lower data rates are provided using a technique known as subrate multiplexing. For this technique, an additional bit is robbed from each channel to indicate which subrate multiplexing speed is being provided. This leaves a total capacity per channel of $6 \times 8000 = 48$ kbps. This capacity is used to multiplex five 9.6-kbps channels, ten 4.8-kbps channels, or twenty 2.4-kbps channels. For example, if channel 2 is used to provide 9.6-kps service, then up to five data subchannels share this channel. The data for each subchannel appears as six bits in channel 2 in every fifth frame.

Finally, the DS-1 format can be used to carry a mixture of voice and data channels. In this case all 24 channels are utilized; no sync byte is provided.

Above this basic data rate of 1.544 Mbps, higher-level multiplexing is achieved

TABLE 6-4 North American and International TDM Carrier Standards

(a) North American			(b) International (CCITT)		
Digital Signal Number	Number of Voice Channels	Data Rate (Mbps)	Level Number	Number of Voice Channels	Data Rate (Mbps)
DS-1	24	1.544	1	30	2.048
DS-1C	48	3.152	2	120	8.448
DS-2	96	6.312	3	480	34.368
DS-3	672	44.736	4	1920	139.264
DS-4	4032	274.176	5	7680	565.148

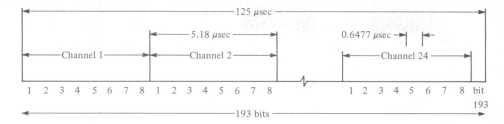

Notes:
1. Bit 193 is a framing bit, used for synchronization.
2. Voice channels:
   . 8–bit PCM used on five of six frames.
   . 7–bit PCM used on every sixth frame, bit 8
     of each channel is a signalling bit.
3. Data channels:
   . Channel 24 used for signaling only in some schemes.
   . Bit 8 is a control bit.
   . Bits 1 – 7 used for 56 kbps service.
   . Bits 2 – 7 used for 9.6 kbps, 4.8 kbps, and 2.4 kbps service.

FIGURE 6-10. DS-1 transmission format.

by interleaving bits from DS-1 inputs. For example, the DS-2 transmission system combines four DS-1 inputs into a 6.312 Mbps stream. Data from the four sources are interleaved 12 bits at a time. Note that $1.544 \times 4 = 6.176$ Mbps. The remaining capacity is used for framing and control bits, and pulse stuffing. The reader interested in the details of this and other digital carrier TDM formats should consult [BELL82a].

As with FDM, a higher level of the TDM hierarchy is formed by multiplexing signals from the next lower level or by combination of those signals plus input at the appropriate data rate from other sources. Figure 6-11 illustrates this hierarchy. First, the DS-1 transmission rate is used to provide both a voice and data service. The data service is known as the Dataphone Digital Service (DDS). The DDS

TABLE 6-5 Capacity of Some Communication Carriers

Transmission Medium	Designation	Transmission	Number of Voice Channels	Operating Frequency (MHz)	Data Rate (Mbps)
Twisted pair	N3	Analog	24	0.172–0.268	
	T1	Digital	24		1.544
	T2	Digital	96		6.312
Coaxial cable	L1	Analog	600	0.006–2.79	
	L4	Analog	3600	0.564–17.55	
	L5	Analog	10,800	3.12–60.5	
	T4	Digital	4032		274.176
Optical fiber	FT3	Digital	672		44.736
Microwave	TD3	Analog	1200	3700–4200	
	TH1	Analog	1800	5925–6425	
	TN1	Analog	1800	10,700–11,700	
	11-GHz	Digital	672		44.736
	18-GHz	Digital	4032		274.176
Satellite	Intelsat V	Analog	~24,000	6/4-GHz band and 14/11-GHz band	

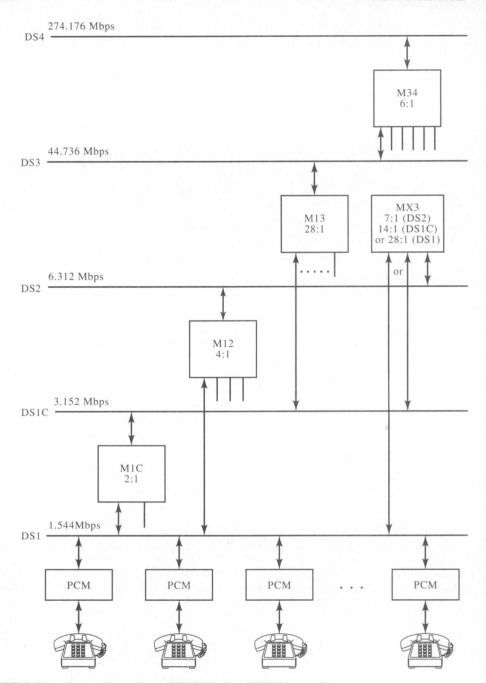

FIGURE 6-11.   North American (AT&T) digital TDM hierarchy.

provides digital transmission service between customer data devices at data rates of from 2.4 to 56 kbps [SLAN81], [ERIK86]. The service is available at customer premises over two twisted-pair lines. The advantage of this service is that it eliminates the need for modems.

Various standardized multiplexers are employed to create higher-capacity transmission facilities. The most commonly-used ones are shown in Figure 6-11. The designations, DS1, DS1C, and so on refer to the multiplexing scheme used for carrying information. AT&T and other carriers supply transmission facilities that support these various multiplexed signals, referred to as carrier systems. These are designated with a "T" label. Thus, the T-1 carrier provides a data rate of 1.544 Mbps and is thus capable of supporting the DS-1 multiplex format, and so on for higher data rates.

Table 6-5 lists some of these TDM facilities for various transmission media. Comparable FDM facilities are also provided. These facilities provide high-capacity transmission for today's long-haul telecommunications systems. Each facility is given a designation that indicates the capacity provided. Thus the *T1 carrier* provides a 1.544-Mbps service, using the DS-1 transmission format. The column labeled transmission denotes whether an analog or digital transmission service is provided. As was mentioned in Chapter 2, analog service implies analog signaling, but a digital transmission service can be provided with either analog or digital service. For example, the T4 service uses digital signaling over coaxial cable, but the FT3 and 11-GHz digital services use analog signaling.

6-3

STATISTICAL TIME-DIVISION MULTIPLEXING

Characteristics

In a synchronous time-division multiplexer, it is generally the case that many of the time slots in a frame are wasted. A typical application of a synchronous TDM involves linking a number of terminals to a shared computer port. Even if all terminals are actively in use, most of the time there is no data transfer at any particular terminal.

An alternative to synchronous TDM is *statistical TDM*, also known as asynchronous TDM and intelligent TDM. The statistical multiplexer exploits this common property of data transmission by dynamically allocating time slots on demand. As with a synchronous TDM, the statistical multiplexer has a number of I/O lines on one side and a higher speed multiplexed line on the other. Each I/O line has a buffer associated with it. In the case of the statistical multiplexer, there are n I/O lines, but only k, where $k < n$, time slots available on the TDM frame. For input, the function of the multiplexer is to scan the input buffers, collecting data until a frame is filled, and then send the frame. On output, the multiplexer receives a frame and distributes the slots of data to the appropriate output buffers.

Because statistical TDM takes advantage of the fact that the attached devices are not all transmitting all of the time, the data rate on the multiplexed line is less than the sum of the data rates of the attached devices. Thus, a statistical multiplexer can use a lower data rate to support as many devices as a synchronous multiplexer. Alternatively, if a statistical multiplexer and a synchronous multiplexer both use a link of the same data rate, the statistical multiplexer can support more devices.

Figure 6-12 contrasts statistical and synchronous TDM. The figure depicts four data sources and shows the data produced in four time epochs (t_0, t_1, t_2, t_3). In the case of the synchronous multiplexer, the multiplexer has an effective output rate of four times the data rate of any of the input devices. During each epoch, data are collected from all four sources and sent out. For example, in the first epoch,

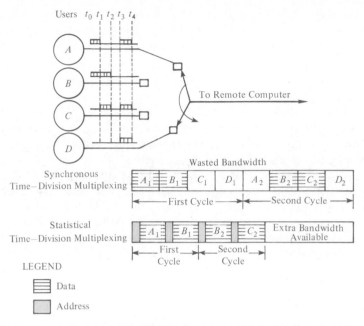

FIGURE 6-12.   Synchronous TDM contrasted with statistical TDM.

sources C and D produce no data. Thus two of the four time slots transmitted by the multiplexer are empty.

In contrast, the statistical multiplexer does not send empty slots if there are data to send. Thus, during the first epoch, only slots for A and B are sent. However, the positional significance of the slots is lost in this scheme. It is not known ahead of time which source's data will be in any particular slot. Since data arrive from and are distributed to I/O lines unpredictably, address information is required to assure proper delivery. Thus there is more overhead per slot for statistical TDM since each slot carries an address as well as data.

The frame structure used by a statistical multiplexer has an impact on performance. Clearly, it is desirable to minimize overhead bits to improve throughput. Generally, a statistical TDM system will use a synchronous protocol such as HDLC. Within the HDLC frame, the data frame must contain control bits for the multiplexing operation. Figure 6-13 shows two possible formats [BACH83]. In the first case, only one source of data is included per frame. That source is identified by an address. The length of the data field is variable, and its end is marked by the end of the overall frame. This scheme can work well under light load, but is quite inefficient under heavy load.

A way to improve efficiency is to allow multiple data sources to be packaged in a single frame. Now, however, some means is needed to specify the length of data for each source. Thus the statistical TDM subframe consists of a sequence of data fields, each labeled with an address and a length. Several techniques can be used to make this approach even more efficient. The address field can be reduced by using relative addressing. That is, each address specifies the number of the current source relative to the previous source, modulo the total number of sources. So, for example, instead of an 8-bit address field, a 4-bit field might suffice.

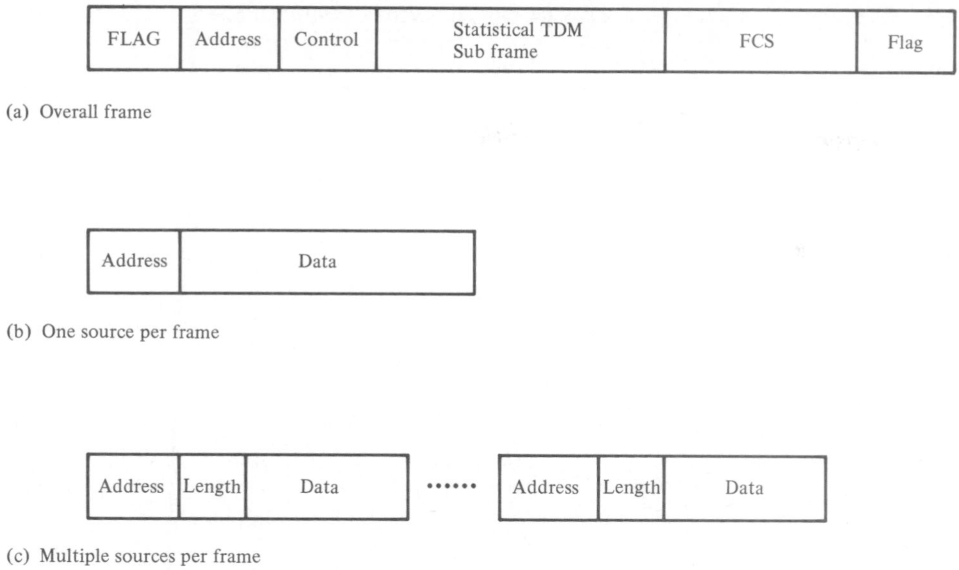

FLAG	Address	Control	Statistical TDM Sub frame	FCS	Flag

(a) Overall frame

Address	Data

(b) One source per frame

Address	Length	Data	••••••	Address	Length	Data

(c) Multiple sources per frame

FIGURE 6-13. Statistical TDM frame formats.

Another refinement is to use a two-bit label with the length field [SEID78]. A value of 00, 01, or 10 corresponds to a data field of one, two, or three bytes; no length field is necessary. A value of 11 indicates that a length field is included.

Performance

We have said that the data rate of the output of a statistical multiplexer is less than the sum of the data rates of the inputs. This is allowable because it is anticipated that the average amount of input is less than the capacity of the multiplexed line. The difficulty with this approach is that, while the average aggregate input may be less than the multiplexed line capacity, there may be peak periods when the input exceeds capacity.

The solution to this problem is to include a buffer in the multiplexer to hold temporary excess input. Table 6-6 gives an example of the behavior of such systems. We assume 10 sources, each capable of 1000 bps, and we assume that the average input per source is 50% of its maximum. Thus, on average, the input load is 5000 bps. Two cases are shown: multiplexers of output capacity 5000 bps and 7000 bps. The entries of the table show the number of bits input from the 10 devices each millisecond and the output from the multiplexer. When the input exceeds the output, backlog develops that must be buffered.

There is a trade-off between the size of the buffer used and the data rate of the line. We would like to use the smallest possible buffer and the smallest possible data rate, but a reduction in one requires an increase in the other. Note that we are not so much concerned with the cost of the buffer—memory is cheap—as we are with the fact that the more buffering there is, the longer the delay. Thus the trade-off is really one between system response time and the speed of the multiplexed line. In this section, we present some approximate measures that examine this

TABLE 6-6   Example of Statistical Multiplexer Performance

Input[a]	Capacity = 5000 bps		Capacity = 7000 bps	
	Output	Backlog	Output	Backlog
6	5	1	6	0
9	5	5	7	2
3	5	3	5	0
7	5	5	7	0
2	5	2	2	0
2	4	0	2	0
2	2	0	2	0
3	3	0	3	0
4	4	0	4	0
6	5	1	6	0
1	2	0	1	0
10	5	5	7	3
7	5	7	7	3
5	5	7	7	1
8	5	10	7	2
3	5	8	5	0
6	5	9	6	0
2	5	6	2	0
9	5	10	7	2
5	5	10	7	0

[a]Input = 10 sources, 1000 bps/source; average input rate = 50% of maximum.

trade-off. These are sufficient for most purposes. A more careful analysis can be found in [CHU73].

Let us define the following parameters for a statistical time-division multiplexer:

N = number of input sources
R = data rate of each source, bps
M = effective capacity of multiplexed line, bps
α = mean fraction of time each source is transmitting,
$\quad 0 < \alpha < 1$
$K = \dfrac{M}{NR}$ = ratio of multiplexed line capacity to total maximum input

In the above, we have defined M taking into account the overhead bits introduced by the multiplexer. That is, M represents the maximum rate at which data bits can be transmitted.

The parameter K is a measure of the compression achieved by the multiplexer. For example, for a given data rate M, if $K = 0.25$, there are four times as many devices being handled as by a synchronous time-division multiplexer using the same link capacity. The value of K can be bounded:

$$\alpha \leq K \leq 1$$

A value of $K = 1$ corresponds to a synchronous time-division multiplexer, since the system has the capacity to service all input devices at the same time. If $K < \alpha$, the input will exceed the multiplexer's capacity.

Some results can be obtained by viewing the multiplexer as a single-server queue. A queueing situation arises when a "customer" arrives at a service facility and, finding it busy, is forced to wait. The delay incurred by a customer is the time spent waiting in the queue plus the time for the service. The delay depends on the pattern of arriving traffic and the characteristics of the server. Table A-3c in the Appendix to this book summarizes results for the case of random (Poisson) arrivals and constant service time. This model is easily related to the statistical multiplexer:

$$\lambda = \alpha\,NR$$
$$S = \frac{1}{M}$$

The average arrival rate λ, in bps, is the total potential input (NR) times the fraction of time α that each source is transmitting. The service time S, in seconds, is the time it takes to transmit one bit, which is $1/M$. Note that:

$$\rho = \lambda\,S = \alpha\,NR/M = \frac{\alpha}{K} = \frac{\lambda}{M}$$

The parameter ρ is the utilization or fraction of total link capacity being used. For example, if the capacity M is 50 kbps and $\rho = 0.5$, the load on the system is 25 kbps. The parameter q is a measure of the amount of buffer space being used in the multiplexer. Finally, t_q is a measure of the average delay encountered by an input source.

Figure 6-14 gives some insight into the nature of the trade-off between system response time and the speed of the multiplexed line. It assumes that data are being transmitted in 1000-bit frames. Part (a) of the figure shows the average number of frames that must be buffered as a function of the average utilization of the multiplexed line. The utilization is expressed as a percentage of the total line capacity. Thus, if the average input load is 5000 bps, the utilization is 100 percent for a line capacity of 5000 bps and about 71 percent for a line capacity of 7000 bps. Part (b) of the figure shows the average delay experienced by a frame as a function of utilization and data rate. Note that as the utilization rises, so do the buffer requirements and the delay. A utilization above 80 percent is clearly undesirable.

Note that the average buffer size being used depends only on ρ, and not directly on M. For example consider the following two cases:

Case I	*Case II*
$N = 10$	$N = 100$
$R = 100$ bps	$R = 100$ bps
$\alpha = 0.4$	$\alpha = 0.4$
$M = 500$ bps	$M = 5000$ bps

In both cases, the value of ρ is 0.8 and the mean buffer size is 2.4. Thus, proportionately, a smaller amount of buffer space per source is needed for multiplexers that handle a larger number of sources. Figure 6-14b also shows that the average delay will be smaller as the link capacity increases, for constant utilization.

So far, we have been considering average queue length, and hence the average amount of buffer capacity needed. Of course, there will be some fixed upper bound on the buffer size available. The variance of the queue size grows with utilization. Thus, at a higher level of utilization, a larger buffer is needed to hold the backlog.

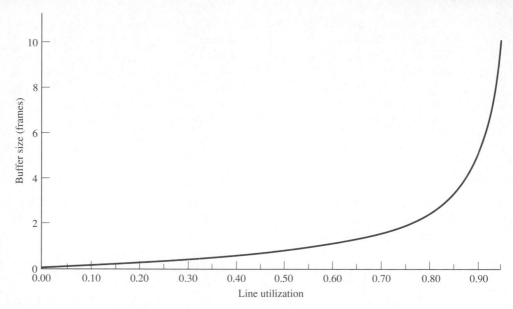

(a) Mean buffer size versus utilization

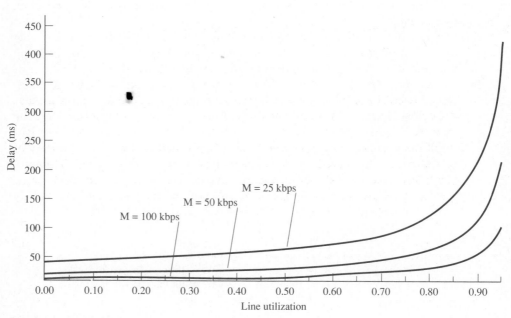

(b) Mean delay versus utilization

FIGURE 6-14.   Buffer size and delay for a statistical multiplexer.

Even so, there is always a finite probability that the buffer will overflow. Figure 6-15, based on [CHU73], shows the strong dependence of overflow probability on utilization. This figure, plus Figure 6-14, suggest that utilization above about 0.8 is undesirable.

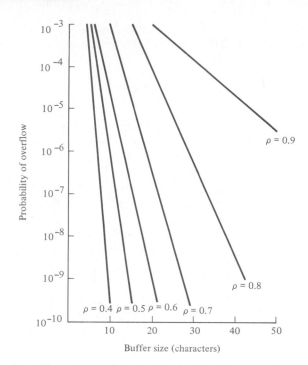

FIGURE 6-15. **Probability of overflow as a function of buffer size.**

6-4

RECOMMENDED READING

A good overall discussion of multiplexing can be found in [DOLL78]. Description of FDM and TDM carrier systems can be found in [BELL82a] and [FREE81]. [SEID78] and [STIF83] are interesting presentations of statistical TDM principles, and [CHU73] provides a detailed mathematical analysis.

6-5

PROBLEMS

6-1 In Figure 6-6, why is it that the frequency of the carrier, f_{sc}, is not within the boundaries of the bandwidth of the modulated signal for group and supergroup inputs?

6-2 The information in four analog signals is to be multiplexed and transmitted over a telephone channel which has a 400- to 3100-Hz bandpass. Each of the analog baseband signals is bandlimited to 500 Hz. Design a communication system (block diagram) that will allow the transmission of these four sources over the telephone channel using
a. Frequency-division multiplexing with SSB subcarriers.
b. Time-division multiplexing using PCM.

Show the block diagrams of the complete system, including the transmission, channel, and reception portions. Include the bandwidths of the signals at the various points in the systems.

6-3   Draw the spectrum of the group signal of Figure 6-6.

6-4   To paraphrase Lincoln: . . . all of the channel some of the time, some of the channel all of the time. . . . Refer to Figure 6-2 and relate the preceding to the figure.

6-5   Consider a transmission system using frequency-division multiplexing. What cost factors are involved in adding one more pair of stations to the system?

6-6   Ten analog signals that are bandlimited to frequencies below 16 kHz are sampled at the Nyquist rate. The digitizing error is to be held below 0.2%. The signals are to travel on a multiplexed channel. What is the bandwidth required for the channel?

6-7   In Synchronous TDM, it is possible to interleave bits, one bit from each channel participating in a cycle. If the channel is using a self-clocking code in order to assist synchronization, would not this bit interleaving introduce problems, since there is not a continuous stream of bits from one source?

6-8   Why is it that the start and stop bits can be eliminated when character interleaving is used in synchronous TDM?

6-9   Explain in terms of data link control and physical layer concepts how error and flow control are accomplished in synchronous time-division multiplexing.

6-10   Bit 193 in the DS-1 transmission format is used for frame synchronization. Explain its use.

6-11   In the DS-1 format, what is the control signal data rate for each voice channel?

6-12   Twenty-four voice signals are to be multiplexed and transmitted over twisted pair. What is the bandwidth required for FDM? Assuming a bandwidth efficiency of 1 bps/Hz, what is the bandwidth required for TDM using PCM?

6-13   Draw a block diagram similar to Figure 6-9 for a TDM PCM system that will accommodate four 300-bps, synchronous, digital inputs and one analog input with a bandwidth of 500 Hz. Assume that the analog samples will be encoded into 4-bit PCM words.

6-14   A character-interleaved time-division multiplexer is used to combine the data streams of a number of 110-bps asynchronous terminals for data transmission over a 2400-bps digital line. Each terminal sends characters consisting of 7 data bits, 1 parity bit, 1 start bit, and 2 stop bits. Assume that one synchronization character is sent every 19 data characters and, in addition, at least 3% of the line capacity is reserved for pulse stuffing to accommodate speed variations from the various terminals.

a. Determine the number of bits per character.
b. Determine the number of terminals that can be accommodated by the multiplexer.
c. Sketch a possible framing pattern for the multiplexer.

6-15 Assume that two 600-bps terminals, five 300-bps terminals, and a number of 150-bps terminals are to be time-multiplexed in a character-interleaved format over a 4800-bps digital line. The terminals send 10 bits/character and one synchronization character is inserted for every 99 data characters. All the terminals are asynchronous and 3% of the line capacity is allocated for pulse stuffing to accommodate variations in the terminal clock rates.
a. Determine the number of 150-bps terminals that can be accommodated.
b. Sketch a possible framing pattern for the multiplexer.

6-16 Find the number of the following devices that could be accommodated by a T1-type TDM line if 1% of the line capacity is reserved for synchronization purposes.
a. 110-bps teleprinter terminals
b. 300-bps computer terminals
c. 1200-bps computer terminals
d. 9600-bps computer output ports
e. 64-kbps PCM voice-frequency lines
How would these numbers change if each of the sources were operational an average of 10% of the time?

6-17 Ten 9600-bps lines are to be multiplexed using TDM. Ignoring overhead bits, what is the total capacity required for synchronous TDM? Assuming that we wish to limit average line utilization of 0.8, and assuming that each line is busy 50% of the time, what is the capacity required for statistical TDM?

6-18 For a statistical time-division multiplexer, define the following parameters

$$F = \text{frame length, bits}$$
$$OH = \text{overhead in a frame, bits}$$
$$L = \text{load of data in the frame, bps}$$
$$C = \text{capacity of link, bps}$$

a. Express F as a function of the other parameters. Explain why F can be viewed as a variable rather than a constant.
b. Plot F versus L for $c = 9.6$ kbps and values of $OH = 40, 80, 120$. Comment on the results and compare to Figure 6-14.
c. Plot F versus L for $OH = 40$ and values of $C = 9.6$ kbps and 7.2 kbps. Comment on the results and compare to Figure 6-14.

6-19 The Clambake Zipper Company has two locations. The international headquarters is located at Cut and Shoot, Texas, while the factory is at Conroe, about 25 miles away. The factory has four 300-bps terminals that communicate with the central computer facilities at headquarters over leased voice grade lines. The company is considering installing time division multiplexing equipment so that only one line will be needed. What cost factors should be considered in the decision?

6-20 In statistical TDM, there may be a length field. What alternative could there be to the inclusion of a length field? What problem might this solution cause and how could it be solved?

6-21 In synchronous TDM, the I/O lines serviced by the two multiplexers may be either synchronous or asynchronous although the channel between the two multiplexers must be synchronous. Is there any inconsistency in this? Why or why not?

PART II

DATA COMMUNICATION NETWORKING

Part I dealt with the transfer of data between devices that are directly connected, generally by a point-to-point link. Often, however, this arrangement is impractical, and a data communication network is required to transmit data between devices. Chapter 7 explains why this is so and provides an overview of the remainder of Part II.

Communication networks can be categorized as follows:

- Switched Networks
  - Circuit-switched networks
  - Packet-switched networks
- Broadcast Networks
  - Packet radio networks
  - Satellite networks
  - Local networks

Packet radio and satellite networks exhibit many similarities and are treated in the same chapter. With that exception, each of these network types is presented and discussed in one chapter of Part II.

CHAPTER 7

Communication Networking Techniques

This chapter serves as an introduction and overview of all of Part II. We begin by showing that the problem of providing communications among a number of devices dictates some kind of communication network solution. Two generic approaches are possible: switched networks and broadcast networks. Following this introductory section the next three sections are devoted to introducing the three principal types of switched networks: circuit-switched, message-switched, and packet-switched. These three are then compared. The final section is an introduction to broadcast networks.

7-1

COMMUNICATION NETWORKS

In its simplest form, data communication takes place between two devices that are directly connected by some form of point-to-point transmission medium. Often, however, it is impractical for two devices to be directly, point-to-point connected. This is so for one (or both) of the following contingencies:

- The devices are very far apart. It would be inordinately expensive, for example, to string a dedicated line between two devices thousands of miles apart.
- There is a set of devices, each of which may require a link to many of the others at various times. Examples are all of the telephones in the world and all of the terminals and computers owned by a single organization.

To see the problem raised by the second point, we need to consider the subject of topology. *Topology*, in this context, refers to the way in which multiple devices

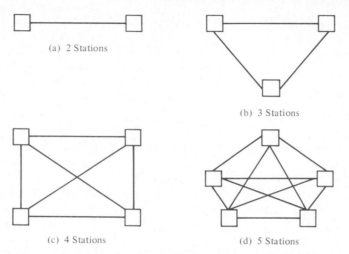

(a) 2 Stations

(b) 3 Stations

(c) 4 Stations

(d) 5 Stations

FIGURE 7-1. The problem with fully connected or mesh topology.

are interconnected via communication links. Consider the situation of multiple devices requiring multiple connections. Why not provide a direct point-to-point link between each pair of devices?

The problem with this approach is illustrated in Figure 7-1. Each device has a point-to-point link with each other device. This is referred to as a *fully connected* or mesh topology. If there are N devices, then $N(N - 1)/2$ full-duplex links are required, and each device requires $(N - 1)$ input/output (I/O) ports. Thus the cost of the system, in terms of cable installation and I/O hardware, grows with the square of the number of devices.

The infeasibility of this approach is clear. The solution to the problem is to attach the devices to a *communication network*. Figure 7-2 illustrates this concept in a

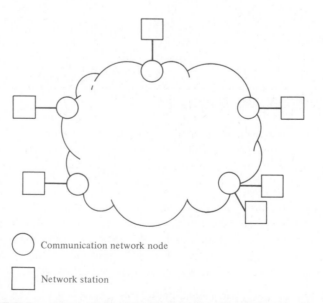

○ Communication network node

□ Network station

FIGURE 7-2. Interconnection via a communication network.

general way. We have a collection of devices that wish to communicate; we will refer to them generically as *stations*. The stations may be computers, terminals, telephones, or other communicating devices. Each station attaches to a network *node*. The set of nodes to which stations attach is the boundary of the communication network, which is capable of transferring data between pairs of attached stations. The communication network is not concerned with the content of the data exchanged between stations; its purpose is simply to move that data from source to destination.

Thus a communication network is a shared resource that addresses the problems cited earlier in this section. The network provides for the sharing of transmission facilities among many stations, which reduces the cost incurred by any pair of stations. Also, a single I/O port is needed by each station, rather than $N - 1$ ports.

Communication networks may be categorized based on the architecture and techniques used to transfer data. The following types of networks are in common use:

- Switched communication network.
  - Circuit-switched network.
  - Message-switched network.
  - Packet-switched network.
- Broadcast communication network.
  - Packet radio network.
  - Satellite network.
  - Local network.

A *switched communication network* consists of an interconnected collection of nodes, in which data are transmitted from source to destination by being routed through the network of nodes. Figure 7-3 is a generic illustration of the concept.

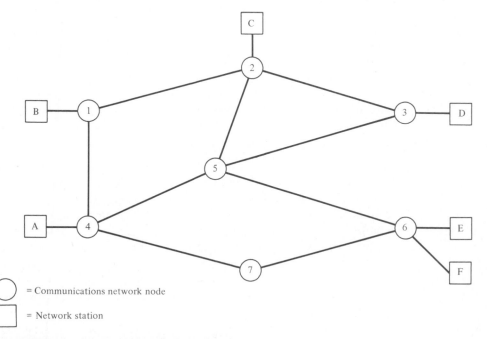

◯ = Communications network node

▢ = Network station

FIGURE 7-3. Generic switching network.

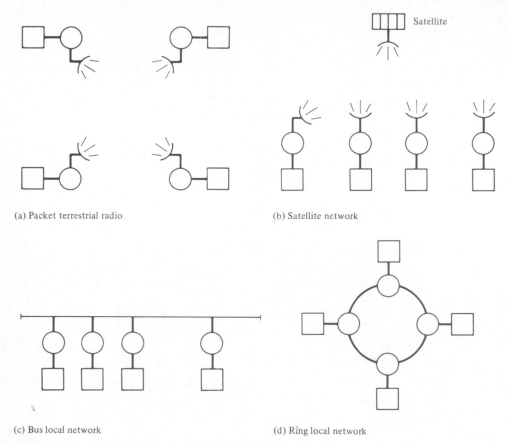

(a) Packet terrestrial radio   (b) Satellite network

(c) Bus local network   (d) Ring local network

FIGURE 7-4. Broadcast communication networks.

The nodes are connected by transmission paths. Data entering the network from a station are routed to the destination by being switched from node to node. For example, data from station *A* intended for station *F* are sent to node 4. They may then be routed via nodes 5 and 6 or nodes 7 and 6 to their destination. The classification of switched networks as circuit, message, or packet refers to the way in which the nodes switch data from one link to another on the way from source to destination. These techniques are discussed later in this chapter.

Several observations are in order:

1. Some nodes connect only to other nodes (e.g., 5 and 7). Their sole task is the internal (to the network) switching of data. Other nodes have one or more stations attached as well. In addition to their switching functions, such nodes accept data from and deliver data to the attached stations.
2. Node-station links are generally dedicated point-to-point links. Node-node links are usually multiplexed links, using either an FDM or TDM technique. For nodes that are some distance apart, the multiplexing significantly reduces transmission costs, as compared to providing dedicated links between each pair of stations.
3. The topology of the network of nodes may be fully connected or partially connected. It is generally the latter, especially for large networks. However,

it is always desirable to have more than one possible path through the network for each pair of stations. This enhances the reliability of the network.

With a *broadcast communication network*, there are no intermediate switching nodes. Each station is attached to a transmitter/receiver that communicates over a medium shared by other stations. In its simplest form, a transmission from any one station is broadcast to and received by all other stations. A simple example of this is a CB radio system, in which all users tuned to the same channel may communicate. Figure 7-4 illustrates types of broadcast networks; these will be discussed later in this chapter.

Again, several observations are in order:

1. Only a single I/O port is needed at each station, as with a switched communication network.
2. Since the transmission facility is shared, only a single station can successfully transmit at a time. This leads to the need for some mechanism for controlling access to the shared medium.
3. Interconnection capability is limited by the nature of the broadcast medium. This will become clear as various specific examples are explored.

Switched communication networks are explored in Sections 7-2 through 7-5 and in Chapters 8 and 9. Broadcast communication networks are explored in Section 7-6 and Chapters 10 and 11.

7-2

CIRCUIT SWITCHING

Communication via circuit switching implies that there is a dedicated communication path between two stations. That path is a connected sequence of links between nodes. On each physical link, a channel is dedicated to the connection. The most common example of circuit switching is the telephone network.

Communication via circuit switching involves three phases, which can be explained with reference to Figure 7-3.

1. *Circuit establishment:* Before any data can be transmitted, an end-to-end (station-to-station) circuit must be established. For example, station A sends a request to node 4 requesting a connection to station E. Typically, the link from A to 4 is a dedicated line, so that part of the connection already exists. Node 4 must find the next leg in a route leading to node 6. Based on routing information and measures of availability and perhaps cost, node 4 selects the link to node 5, allocates a free channel (using TDM or FDM) on that link and sends a message requesting connection to E. So far, a dedicated path has been established from A through 4 to 5. Since a number of stations may attach to 4, it must be able to establish internal paths from multiple stations to multiple nodes. How this is done is explained in Chapter 8. The remainder of the process proceeds similarly. Node 5 dedicates a channel to node 6 and internally ties that channel to the channel from node 4. Node 6 completes the connection to E. In completing the connection, a test is made to determine if E is busy or is prepared to accept the connection.

2. *Data transfer:* Signals can now be transmitted from *A* through the network to *E*. The data may be digital (e.g., terminal to host) or analog (e.g., voice). The signaling and transmission may each be either digital or analog. In any case, the path is: *A*-4 link, internal switching through 4, 4-5 channel, internal switching through 5, 5-6 channel, internal switching through 6, 6-*E* link. Generally, the connection is full duplex, and data may be transmitted in both directions.

3. *Circuit disconnect:* After some period of data transfer, the connection is terminated, usually by the action of one of the two stations. Signals must be propagated to 4, 5, and 6 to deallocate the dedicated resources.

Note that the connection path is established before data transmission begins. Thus channel capacity must be reserved between each pair of nodes in the path, and each node must have available internal switching capacity to handle the requested connection. The switches must have the intelligence to make these allocations and to devise a route through the network.

Circuit switching can be rather inefficient. Channel capacity is dedicated for the duration of a connection, even if no data are being transferred. For a voice connection, utilization may be rather high, but it still does not approach 100%. For a terminal-to-computer connection, the capacity may be idle during most of the time of the connection. In terms of performance, there is a delay prior to data transfer for call establishment. However, once the circuit is established, the network is effectively transparent to the users. Data are transmitted at a fixed data rate with no delay other than the propagation delay through the transmission links. The delay at each node is negligible.

7-3

MESSAGE SWITCHING

Circuit switching is an appropriate and easily-used technique in the case of data exchanges that involve a relatively continuous flow, such as voice (telephone) and some forms of sensor and telemetry input. However, circuit switching does have two rather serious constraints:

- Both stations must be available at the same time for the data exchange.
- Resources must be available and dedicated through the network between the two stations.

An alternative approach, which is generally appropriate to digital data exchange, is to exchange logical units of data, called *messages*. Examples of messages are telegrams, electronic mail, computer files, and transaction queries and responses. If one thinks of data exchange as a sequence of messages being transmitted in both directions between stations, then a very different approach, known as *message switching* can be used.

With message switching, it is not necessary to establish a dedicated path between two stations. Rather, if a station wishes to send a message it appends a destination address to the message. The message is then passed through the network from node to node. At each node, the entire message is received, stored briefly, and then transmitted to the next node.

In a circuit-switching network, each node is an electronic or perhaps electro-mechanical switching device (as described in Chapter 8) which transmits bits as fast as it receives them. A message-switching node is typically a general-purpose minicomputer, with sufficient storage to buffer messages as they come in. A message is delayed at each node for the time required to receive all bits of the message, plus a queueing delay waiting for an opportunity to retransmit to the next node.

Again using Figure 7-3, consider a message to be sent from A to E. Station A appends E's address to the message and sends it to node 4. Node 4 stores the message and determines the next leg of the route (say to 5). Then node 4 queues the message for transmission over the 4-5 link. When the link is available, the message is transmitted to node 5, which will forward the message to node 6, and finally to E. This system is also known as a *store-and-forward* message system. In some cases, the node to which the station attaches, or some central node, also files the message, creating a permanent record.

A number of advantages of this approach over circuit switching are listed in [MART76]:

- Line efficiency is greater, since a single node-to-node channel can be shared by many messages over time. For the same traffic volume, less total transmission capacity is needed. Because messages may be temporarily stored at any point en route, traffic peaks are smoothed out and need not be handled in real time.
- Simultaneous availability of sender and receiver is not required. The network can store the message pending the availability of the receiver.
- When traffic becomes heavy on a circuit-switched network, some calls are blocked; that is, the network refuses to accept any additional connection requests until the load on the network decreases. On a message-switched network, messages are still accepted, but delivery delay increases.
- A message-switching system can send one message to many destinations. Duplicate copies of the message are made, and each is sent to one of the requested destinations. This facility is not easily provided by a circuit-switched network.
- Message priorities can be established. Thus, if a node has a number of messages queued for transmission, it can transmit the higher-priority messages first. These messages will then experience less delay than lower-priority messages.
- Error control and recovery procedures on a message basis can be built into the network. Messages may be numbered and a copy filed for later retrieval in case the original fails to make it through the network.
- A message-switching network can carry out speed and code conversion. Two stations of different data rates can be connected since each connects to its node at its proper data rate. The message-switching network can also easily convert format (e.g., from ASCII to EBCDIC). These features are less often found in a circuit-switched system.
- Messages sent to inoperative terminals may be intercepted and either stored or rerouted to other terminals.

Table 7-1 summarizes the functions of a message-switching node. Note the focus on messages. Each message is treated as a separate entity and is subject to considerable processing.

TABLE 7-1   Functions Performed by a Message-Switching Node

1. The system accepts messages from terminals and computers.
2. On receipt of a message it analyzes the message's header to determine the destination or destinations to which the message must be sent.
3. The system may analyze the header for a priority indication. This will tell the program that certain messages are urgent. They must jump any queues of messages and be sent to their destination immediately.
4. It may analyze the header for an indication that some processing of the message is necessary; for example, statistical information from the message may be gathered by the system.
5. The system detects any errors in transmission of the incoming message and requests a retransmission of faulty messages. This retransmission may be automatic.
6. It detects format errors in incoming messages insofar as possible. Types of format errors that may be picked up include the following:
   (a) *Address invalid:* The address to which the message is to be sent is not included in the computer's directory.
   (b) *Excessive addresses:* There are more than the given maximum number of addresses allowed.
   (c) *Incorrect format:* An invalid character appears in the message in an incorrect location.
   (d) A priority indicator is invalid.
   (e) *Originator code error:* The address of the originator is not included in the computer's list.
   (f) Incorrect character counts.
7. The system stores all the messages arriving and protects them from possible subsequent damage.
8. It takes messages from the store and transmits them to the desired addresses. One message may be sent to many different addresses. In doing this, it does not destroy the message held in the store. The store is thus a queuing area for messages received and messages waiting to be sent as well as a file in which messages are retained.
9. The system redirects messages from the store and sends them to the terminals requesting them. It may, for example, be asked to resend a message with a specified serial number or to send all messages from a given serial number.
10. Systems in use store messages in this manner for several hours or, on some systems, several days. Any message in the store is immediately accessible for this period of time.
11. The system may also maintain a permanent log of messages received. This will probably be done on a relatively inexpensive medium, such as magnetic tape, and not on a random-access file.
12. If messages are sent to a destination at which the terminal is temporarily inoperative, the system intercepts these messages. It may automatically reroute them to alternative terminals that are operative. On the other hand, it may store them until the inoperative terminal is working again.
13. It may intercept messages for other reasons. For example, the system may be programmed to send a message to the location of an important person, although he may be moving from one place to another. The person in question indicates his current location to the computer, and the computer diverts messages for him to that location. The system may handle messages on a priority basis. There may be one urgent priority level so that these messages are sent before any others. Some systems have more than one level of priority, priority level 1 being transmitted before priority level 2, priority level 2 being transmitted before priority level 3, and so on. The system may notify the operator in the event that any priority queue becomes too great. A simple system may have no priority scheme, messages being handled on a first-in, first-out basis.

TABLE 7-1 (Cont.)

14. The system maintains an awareness of the status of lines and terminals. It is programmed to detect faulty operation on terminals where possible, to make a log of excessive noise on lines, and to notify its operator when a line goes out. The system maintains records of any faults it detects.

15. On a well-planned system the messages should be given serial numbers by the operator sending them. The computer checks the serial numbers and places new serial numbers on the outgoing messages. When serial numbers are used, the system can be designed to avoid the loss of any message. This is especially important in the event of a computer failure or of a switchover in a duplex system.

16. At given intervals, perhaps once an hour, the system may send a message to each terminal, quoting the serial number of the last message it received from that terminal. The terminal's operator then knows that the switching system is still on the air.

17. The system may conduct a statistical analysis of the traffic that it is handling.

18. It may be programmed to bill the users for the messages sent. It may, for example, make a small charge per character sent from each terminal and bill the terminal location appropriately.

19. It produces periodic reports of its operation for its operator. These may include reports on the status of all facilities, error statistics, reports giving the number of messages in each queue, message counts, and so on.

Source: [MART76].

The primary disadvantage of message switching is that it is not suited to real-time or interactive traffic. The delay through the network is relatively long and has relatively high variance. Thus it cannot be used for voice connections. Nor is it suited to interactive terminal-host connections.

7-4

PACKET SWITCHING

Packet switching represents an attempt to combine the advantages of message and circuit switching while minimizing the disadvantages of both [HEGG84]. In situations where there is a substantial volume of traffic among a number of stations, this objective is met.

Switching Technique

Packet switching is very much like message switching. The principal external difference is that the length of the units of data that may be presented to the network is limited in a packet-switched network. A typical maximum length is 1000 to a few thousand bits. Message switching systems accommodate far larger messages. From a station's point of view, then, messages above the maximum length must be divided into smaller units and sent out one at a time. To distinguish the two techniques, the data units in the latter system are referred to as *packets*. Another difference from message switching is that packets are typically not filed. A copy of a packet may be temporarily stored for error recovery purposes, but that is all.

Again using Figure 7-3 for an example, consider the transfer of a single packet. The packet contains data plus a destination address. Station *A* transmits the packet to 4, which stores it briefly and then passes it to 5, which passes it to 6, and on to *E*.

On its face, packet switching may seem a strange procedure to adopt, with no particular advantage over message switching. Remarkably, the simple expedient of limiting the maximum size of a data unit to a rather small length has a dramatic effect on performance. Before demonstrating this, we define two common procedures for handling entire messages over a packet-switched network.

The problem is this. A station has a message to send that is of length greater than the maximum packet size. It breaks the message into packets and sends these packets to its node. Question: How will the network handle this stream of packets? There are two approaches: datagram and virtual circuit. (*Note:* This section describes the use of datagrams and virtual circuits *internal* to the network. The somewhat different concept of *external* datagram and virtual-circuit service is introduced in Chapter 9.)

In the *datagram* approach, each packet is treated independently, just as each message is treated independently in a message-switched network. Let us consider the implications of this approach. Suppose that station *A* has a three-packet message to send to *E*. It pops the packets out, 1-2-3, to node 4. On *each* packet, node 4 must make a routing decision. Packet 1 comes in and node 4 determines that its queue of packets for node 5 is shorter than for node 7, so it queues the packet for node 5. Ditto for packet 2. But for packet 3, node 4 finds that its queue for node 7 is shortest and so queues packet 3 for that node. So the packets, each with the same destination address, do not all follow the same route. Furthermore, it is just possible that packet 3 will beat packet 2 to node 6. Thus it is possible that the packets will be delivered to *E* in a different sequence from the one in which they were sent. It is up to *E* to figure out how to reorder them. In this technique each packet, treated independently, is referred to as a datagram.

In the *virtual circuit* approach, a *logical* connection is established before any packets are sent. For example, suppose that *A* has one or more messages to send to *E*. It first sends a Call Request packet to 4, requesting a connection to *E*. Node 4 decides to route the request *and* all subsequent data to 5, which decides to route the request and all subsequent data to 6, which finally delivers the Call Request packet to *E*. If *E* is prepared to accept the connection, it sends out a Call Accept packet to 6. This packet is passed back through nodes 5 and 4 to *A*. Stations *A* and *E* may now exchange data over the logical connection or virtual circuit that has been established. Each packet now contains a virtual circuit identifier as well as data. Each node on the preestablished route knows where to direct such packets; no routing decisions are required. Thus every data packet from *A* intended for E traverses nodes 4, 5, and 6; every data packet from *E* intended for A traverses nodes 6, 5, and 4. Eventually, one of the stations terminates the connection with a Clear Request packet. At any time, each station can have more than one virtual circuit to any other station and can have virtual circuits to more than one station.

So the main characteristic of the virtual-circuit technique is that a route between stations is set up prior to data transfer. Note that this does *not* mean that there is a dedicated path, as in circuit switching. A packet is still buffered at each node, and queued for output over a line. The difference from the datagram approach is that the node need not make a routing decision for each packet. It is made only once for each connection.

If two stations wish to exchange data over an extended period of time, there are certain advantages to virtual circuits. They all have to do with relieving the stations of unnecessary communications processing functions. A virtual circuit facility may provide a number of services, including sequencing, error control, and flow control. We emphasize the word ''may'' because not all virtual circuit facilities will provide all these services completely reliably. With that proviso, we define terms. *Sequencing* refers to that fact that, since all packets follow the same route, they arrive in the original order. *Error control* is a service that assures not only that packets arrive in proper sequence, but that all packets arrive correctly. For example, if a packet in a sequence fails to arrive at node 6, or arrives with an error, node 6 can request a retransmission of that packet from node 4. Finally, *flow control* is a technique for assuring that a sender does not overwhelm a receiver with data. For example, if station *E* is buffering data from *A* and perceives that it is about to run out of buffer space, it can request, via the virtual circuit facility, that *A* suspend transmission until further notice.

One advantage of the datagram approach is that the call setup phase is avoided. Thus if a station wishes to send only one or a few packets, datagram delivery will be quicker. Another advantage of the datagram service is that, because it is more primitive, it is more flexible. For example, if congestion develops in one part of the network, incoming datagrams can be routed away from the congestion. With the use of virtual circuits, packets follow a predefined route, and thus it is more difficult for the network to adapt to congestion. A third advantage is that datagram delivery is inherently more reliable. With the use of virtual circuits, if a node fails all virtual circuits that pass through that node are lost. With datagram delivery, if a node is lost, packets may find alternate routes.

Packet Size

One important design issue is the packet size to be used in the network. There is a significant relationship between packet size and transmission time, as shown in Figure 7-5. In this example, it is assumed that there is a virtual circuit from station *X* through nodes *a* and *b* to station *Y*. The message to be sent comprises 30 octets, and each packet contains 3 octets of control information, which is placed at the beginning of each packet and is referred to as a *header*. If the entire message is sent as a single packet of 33 octets (3 octets of header plus 30 octets of data), then the packet is first transmitted from station *X* to node *a* (Figure 7-5a). When the entire packet is received, it can then be transmitted from *a* to *b*. When the entire packet is received at node *b*, it is then transferred to station *Y*. The total transmission time at the nodes is 99 octet-times (33 octets × 3 packet transmissions).

Suppose now that we break the message up into two packets, each containing 15 octets of the message and, of course, 3 octets each of header or control information. In this case, node *a* can begin transmitting the first packet as soon as it has arrived from *X*, without waiting for the second packet. Because of this overlap in transmission, the total transmission time drops to 72 octet-times. By breaking the message up into 5 packets, each intermediate node can begin transmission even sooner and the savings in time is greater, with a total of 63 octet-times. However, this process of using more and smaller packets eventually results in increased, rather than reduced, delay, as illustrated in Figure 7-5d. This is because each packet contains a fixed amount of header, and more packets means more of these headers.

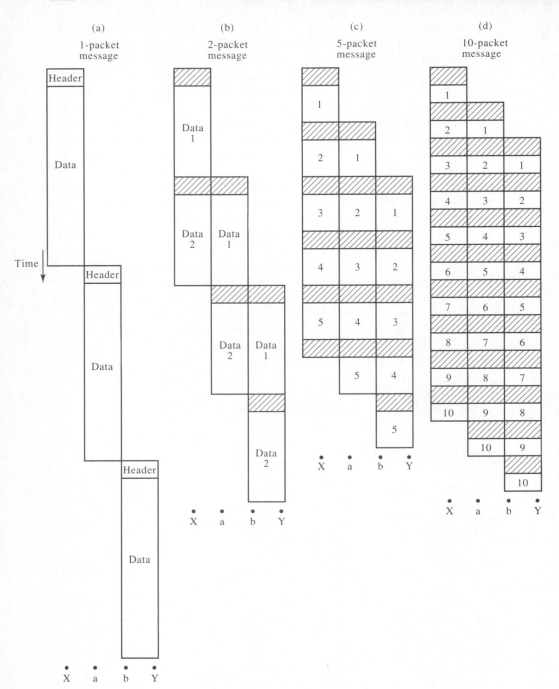

FIGURE 7-5. Effect of packet size on transmission line.

Furthermore, the example does not show the processing and queuing delays at each node. These delays are also greater when more packets are handled for a single message. Thus, packet-switched network designers must consider these factors in attempting to find an optimum packet size.

COMPARISON OF SWITCHED COMMUNICATION TECHNIQUES

We have briefly described three techniques for communication switching: circuit switching, message switching, and packet switching. In this section we present a brief comparison of the three methods, looking first at the important issue of performance, and then examining other characteristics.

Performance

A simple comparison of the various techniques is illustrated in Figure 7-6. The figure depicts the transmission of a message across four nodes, from a source station attached to node 1 to a destination station attached to node 4. In this figure, we are concerned with three types of delay:

- *Propagation delay:* the time it takes a signal to propagate from one node to the next. This time is generally negligible. The speed of electromagnetic signals through a guided medium, for example, is typically 2×10^8 m/s.
- *Transmission time:* the time it takes for a transmitter to send out a block of data. For example, it takes 1 s to transmit a 10,000-bit block of data onto a 10-kbps line.
- *Node delay:* the time it takes for a node to perform the necessary processing as it switches data.

For circuit switching (Figure 7-6a), there is a certain amount of elapsed time before the message can be sent. First, a call request signal is sent through the network, to set up a connection to the destination. If the destination station is not busy, a call accepted signal returns. Note that a processing delay is incurred at each node during the call request; this time is spent at each node setting up the route of the connection. On the return, this processing is not needed since the connection is already set up. After the connection is set up, the message is sent as a single block, with no noticeable delay at the switching nodes.

Message switching (Figure 7-6b) does not require a call setup. However, the entire message must be received at each node before that node begins to retransmit. Thus the total delay using message switching is almost always significantly longer than for circuit switching.

Datagram packet switching (Figure 7-6d) also does not require a call setup. Comparing Figure 7-6b and d, one can see a dramatic improvement in performance. What has changed? The difference is that each node along the route may begin transmission of each packet as soon as that packet arrives. It need not wait for the entire message. Thus datagram packet switching is almost always significantly faster than message switching.

Virtual circuit packet switching (Figure 7-6c) appears quite similar to circuit switching. A virtual circuit is requested using a call-request packet, which incurs a delay at each node. The virtual circuit is accepted with a call-accept packet. In contrast to the circuit-switching case, the call acceptance also experiences node delays, even though the virtual circuit route is now established. The reason is that this packet is queued at each node and must wait its turn before retransmission.

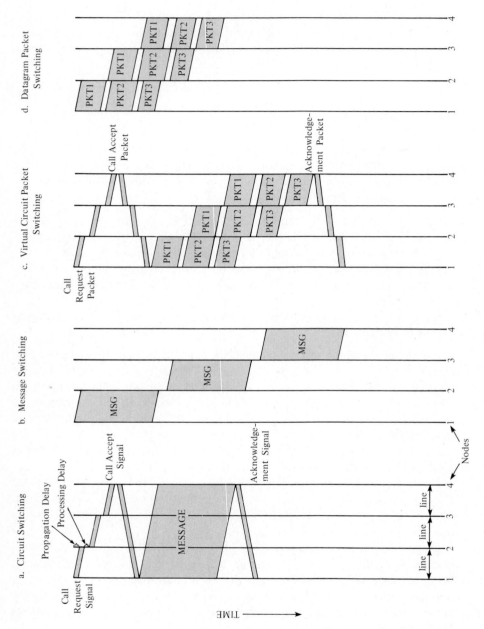

FIGURE 7-6. Event timing for various communication switching techniques.

Once the virtual circuit is established, the message is transmitted in packets. It should be clear that this phase of the operation can be no faster than circuit switching, for comparable networks. This is because circuit switching is an essentially transparent process, providing a constant data rate across the network. Packet switching requires some node delay at each node in the path. Worse, this delay is variable and will increase with increased load.

Figure 7-6 is intended only to suggest what the relative performance of the techniques might be; however, actual performance depends on a host of factors, including:

- Number of stations.
- Number and arrangement of nodes.
- Total load on system.
- Length (in time and data) of typical exchange between two stations.
- Processing speed of the nodes.
- Packet size.

Given the problems of fairly comparing these methods, we will not attempt an analytic comparison. The interested reader is referred to [ROSN82], [SAND80], [KUMM80], and [MIYA75]. For purposes of this discussion, we hazard a few observations.

- For interactive traffic, message switching is not appropriate.
- For light and/or intermittent loads, circuit switching is the most efficient, since the public telephone system can be used, via dial-up lines.
- For very heavy and sustained loads between two stations, a leased circuit-switched line is the most cost effective.
- Packet switching is to be preferred when there is a collection of devices that must exchange a moderate to heavy amount of data; line utilization is most efficient with this technique.
- Datagram packet switching is good for short messages and for flexibility.
- Virtual circuit packet switching is good for long exchanges and for relieving stations of processing burden.

As a final point, we mention one common means of making packet-switched networks cost effective, and that is to provide a public connection service. Examples of such networks in the United States are TELENET and TYMNET. The network consists of nodes owned by the network service provider and linked together by leased channels from common carriers such as AT&T. Subscribers pay fees for attaching to the network and for transmitting packets through it. Whereas individual subscribers may not have sufficient traffic to make a packet switched network economically feasible, the total demand of all subscribers justifies the network. These networks are referred to as *value-added networks* (VANs) because they take a basic long-haul transmission service (e.g., AT&T) and add value (the packet-switching logic). In most other countries, there is a single national-monopoly VAN, called a *public data network* (PDN).

Other Characteristics

Besides performance, there are a large number of other characteristics that may be considered in comparing the four techniques we have been discussing. Table 7-2

TABLE 7-2 Comparison of Communication Switching Techniques

Circuit Switching	Message Switching	Datagram Packet Switching	Virtual-Circuit Packet Switching
Dedicated transmission path	No dedicated path	No dedicated path	No dedicated path
Continuous transmission of data	Transmission of messages	Transmission of packets	Transmission of packets
Fast enough for interactive	Too slow for interactive	Fast enough for interactive	Fast enough for interactive
Messages are not stored	Messages are filed for later retrieval	Packets may be stored until delivered	Packets stored until delivered
The path is established for entire conversation	Route established for each message	Route established for each packet	Route established for entire conversation
Call setup delay Negligible transmission delay	Message transmission delay	Packet transmission delay	Call setup delay Packet transmission delay
Busy signal if called party busy	No busy signal	Sender may be notified if packet not delivered	Sender notified of connection denial
Overload may block call setup; no delay for established calls	Overload increases message delay	Overload increases packet delay	Overload may block call setup; increases packet delay
Electromechanical or computerized switching nodes	Message switch center with filing facility	Small switching nodes	Small switching nodes
User responsible for message loss protection	Network responsible for messages	Network may be responsible for individual packets	Network may be responsible for packet sequences
Usually no speed or code conversion	Speed and code conversion	Speed and code conversion	Speed and code conversion
Fixed bandwidth transmission	Dynamic use of bandwidth	Dynamic use of bandwidth	Dynamic use of bandwidth
No overhead bits after call setup	Overhead bits in each message	Overhead bits in each packet	Overhead bits in each packet

summarizes the most important of these. Most of these characteristics have already been discussed. A few additional comments follow.

As we mentioned, circuit-switching is an essentially transparent service. Once a connection is established, a constant data rate is provided to the connected stations. This is not the case with message and packet switching; these services introduce variable delay so that data arrives in a choppy manner. Indeed, with message switching and datagram packet switching, data may arrive in a different order from the way they were transmitted.

An additional consequence of transparency is that there is no "overhead" required to accommodate circuit switching. Once a connection is established, the analog or digital data are passed through as is from source to destination. For message and packet switching, the data are organized into digital blocks. Thus, analog data must be converted to digital before being transmitted. In addition, each message or packet includes "overhead bits," such as the destination address.

BROADCAST NETWORKS

Types of Broadcast Networks

The principal alternative to the use of a switched communication network is broadcasting. Broadcast networks share the following characteristics:

- For the basic architecture, there are no switching devices (although extended networks might consist of basic networks linked via switches).
- Data transmitted by one station is received by many, and often all, of the other stations on the network.
- Stations share a common transmission medium, and therefore some access control technique is required.

We will be concerned in this book with three types of broadcast networks:

- Packet radio networks (Chapter 10)
- Satellite networks (Chapter 10)
- Local networks (Chapter 11)

Two similar types of broadcast networks are packet radio and satellite networks. In both cases, stations transmit and receive via antenna, and all stations share the same channel or radio frequency. In a *packet radio network* (Figure 7-4a), stations are within transmission range of each other, and broadcast directly (from one station to all other stations). In a *satellite network* (Figure 7-4b), data are not transferred directly from transmitter to receiver but are relayed via satellite: Each station transmits to the satellite; the satellite repeats the transmission and it is received by multiple stations.

A *local network* is a communication network confined to a small area, such as a single building or a small cluster of buildings. In a bus local network (Figure 7-4c), all stations are attached to a common wire or cable in a multipoint configuration. A transmission by any one station propagates the length of the medium in both directions and can be received by all other stations. The ring local network (Figure 7-4d) consists of a closed loop, with each station attached to a simple repeating element. A transmission from any station circulates around the ring past all other stations, and can be received by each station as it goes by.

The two parameters that serve best to differentiate among these three types of networks are the data rate and distances between stations. The reader will recall that these two parameters define a third one, a, which was introduced in Chapter 5 and found to be an important factor in performance. The relevance of a to broadcast networks is explored in Chapter 10. Figure 7-7 depicts the range of data rates and distances applicable to the various broadcast networks. For local networks two subcategories are used, which will be explained in Chapter 11.

Medium Access Control Techniques

With all broadcast networks, the key technical issue is that of access control. Since only one device can successfully transmit on the shared medium at a time, an access control technique is required. The key parameters in any medium access

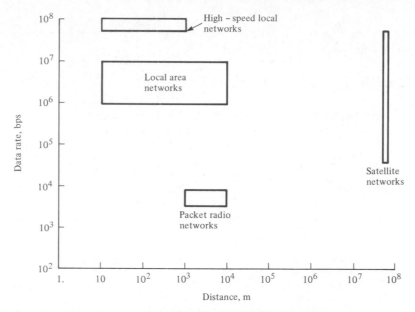

FIGURE 7-7. Data rates and distances for broadcast networks.

control technique are where and how. "Where" refers to whether control is exercized in a centralized or distributed fashion. In a centralized scheme, a controller is designated that has the authority to grant access to the network. A station wishing to transmit must wait until it receives permission from the controller. In a decentralized network, the stations collectively perform a medium access control function to dynamically determine the order in which stations transmit.

A centralized scheme has certain advantages, such as,

- It may afford greater control over access for providing such things as priorities, overrides, and guaranteed bandwidth.
- It allows the logic at each station to be as simple as possible.
- It avoids problems of coordination.

Its principal disadvantages include:

- It results in a single point of failure.
- It may act as a bottleneck, reducing efficiency.
- If propagation delay is high, the overhead may be unacceptable.

The pros and cons for distributed control are mirror images of the points made above.

The second parameter, "how," is constrained by the topology and is a trade-off among competing factors: cost, performance, and complexity. In general, we can categorize access control techniques as being either synchronous or asynchronous. With synchronous techniques, a specific capacity is dedicated to a connection. We see this in circuit switching, FDM, and synchronous TDM. Such techniques are not optimal in broadcast networks because the needs of the stations are generally unpredictable. It is preferable to be able to allocate capacity in an asynchronous (dynamic) fashion, more or less in response to immediate needs. The asynchronous approach can be further subdivided into three categories:

- Round-robin
- Reservation
- Contention

Round-robin techniques are conceptually simple, being based on the philosophy of "give everybody a turn." Each station in turn is given an opportunity to transmit. During that opportunity the station may decline to transmit or may transmit subject to a certain upper bound, usually expressed as a maximum amount of data or time for this opportunity. In any case, the station must then relinquish its turn, and the right to transmit passes to the next station in logical sequence. Control of turns may be centralized or distributed. Polling on a multidrop line is an example of a centralized technique. Various distributed techniques have been used for local networks, and are described in Chapter 11.

When many stations have data to transmit over an extended period of time, round-robin techniques can be very efficient. If only a few stations have data to transmit at any give time, other techniques may be preferable, largely depending on whether the data traffic is "stream" or "bursty." *Stream traffic* is characterized by lengthy and fairly continuous transmissions. Examples are voice communication, telemetry, and bulk file transfer. *Bursty traffic* is characterized by short, sporadic transmissions. Interactive terminal-host traffic fits this description.

For stream traffic, *reservation* techniques are well-suited. In general for these techniques, time on the medium is divided into slots, much as with synchronous TDM. A station wishing to transmit reserves future slots for an extended or indefinite period. Again, reservations may be made in either a centralized or distributed fashion.

For bursty traffic, *contention* techniques are usually appropriate. With these techniques, no control is exercised to determine whose turn it is; all stations contend for time in a way that can be, as we shall see, rather rough and tumble. These techniques are of necessity distributed in nature. Their principal advantage is that they are simple to implement and, under light to moderate load, efficient. For some of these techniques, however, performance tends to collapse under heavy load.

The discussion above has been somewhat abstract, and should become clearer as specific techniques are discussed in Chapters 10 and 11. For future reference, Table 7-3 places the techniques that will be discussed into the classification just outlined. Table 7-4 shows which of these techniques are used with which types of broadcast networks.

TABLE 7-3 Asynchronous Access Control Techniques

	Centralized	**Distributed**
Round-robin	Polling	Token bus
		Token ring
Reservation	Centralized reservation	Distributed reservation
Contention	—	ALOHA
		CSMA
		CSMA/CD

TABLE 7-4   Applicability of Access Control Techniques

Packet radio	Local networks
ALOHA	CSMA/CD
CSMA	Token bus
Satellite	Token ring
ALOHA	Polling
Centralized reservation	
Distributed reservation	

7-7

RECOMMENDED READING

References to most of the topics discussed in this chapter are provided in the remainder of Part II. The exception is message switching, which is not further pursued. [MART76] and [DAVI73] provide good discussions of message switching. A good example of a message-switched network is the U.S. military network, AUTODIN [PAOL75]. An interesting discussion of message switching architectural issues can be found in [HOPE73].

7-8

PROBLEMS

7-1   In what way is channel efficiency greater for message switching than for circuit switching?

7-2   Explain the flaw in the following logic?
Packet switching requires control and address bits to be added to each packet. This causes considerable overhead in packet switching. In circuit switching, a direct circuit is established. No extra bits are added.
a. Therefore there is no overhead in circuit switching.
b. Since there is no overhead in circuit switching, then line utilization in circuit switching must be more effective than in packet switching.

7-3   Study the comparison of switching techniques in Table 7-2. Consider the following application. An expensive printer (such as a laser printer) is to be shared among five personal computers that are all located within 200 feet of the printer. For each switching technique given in the table, rate the importance of each criteria to this application. Then select the switching technique that you consider best fits the application.

7-4   Consider the postal service as a switching network. Compare the operation of the postal service to the functions described in Table 7-2.

7-5   Define the following parameters for a switching network:
   • N: number of hops between two given stations
   • L: message length, bits

- *B*   data rate, in bps, on all links
- *P*: packet size, bits
- *H*: overhead (header) bits per packet
- *S*: call setup time (circuit-switched or virtual circuit) in seconds
- *D*: propagation delay per hop, in seconds

a. For $N = 4, L = 3200, B = 9600, P = 1024, H = 16, S = 0.2, D = 0.001$, compute the end-to-end delay for circuit switching, message switching, virtual circuit packet switching, and datagram packet switching. Assume that there is no node delay.

b. Derive general expressions for the four techniques, taken two at a time (six expressions in all) showing the conditions under which the delays are equal.

7-6   What value of P, as a function of N, B, and H results in minimum end-to-end delay on a datagram network? Assume that L is much larger than P, and that D is zero.

7-7   Two stations communicate via a 1-Mbps satellite link. The satellite serves merely to retransmit data received from one station to the other, with negligible delay. The up-and-down propagation delay for a synchronous orbit is 270 ms. Using HDLC frames of length 1024 bits, what is the maximum possible data throughput (not counting overhead bits)?

7-8   Consider a packet-switched network of N nodes connected by the following topologies
a. Star: one central node with no attached stations; all other nodes attach to the central node.
b. Loop: each node connects to two other nodes to form a closed loop
c. Fully connected.
For each, give the average number of hops between stations.

7-9   Consider a binary tree topology for a packet-switched network. The root node connects to two other nodes. All intermediate nodes connect to one node in the direction toward the root, and two in the direction away from the root. At the bottom are nodes with just one link back toward the root. If there are $2^N - 1$ nodes, derive an expression for the mean number of hops per packet for large N, assuming that all node pairs are equally likely.

7-10   A disadvantage of the contention approach for broadcast networks is the capacity wasted due to multiple stations attempting to access the channel at the same time. Suppose that time is divided into discrete slots with each of N stations attempting to transmit with probability p during each slot. What fraction of the slots are wasted due to multiple transmission attempts?

CHAPTER 8

Circuit Switching

Any treatment of the technology and architecture of circuit-switched networks must of necessity focus on the internal operation of a single switch. This is in contrast to packet-switched networks, which are best explained by the collective behavior of the set of switches that make up a network.

A single switch with a number of attached devices may function as a one-node network. Thus the chapter begins by summarizing the characteristics of such a network. Then we look at the digital switching concepts that underlie this type of network. Next we look at the devices most commonly used to build circuit-switched local networks (although these are rarely thought of as "true" local networks): digital data switches. We are then ready to look at the digital private branch exchange, which supports both digital data devices and telephones. Finally, the concepts of a multinode circuit-switched network are discussed using the public telecommunications network as an example.

8-1

ONE-NODE NETWORKS

A network built around a single circuit-switching node consists of a collection of devices or stations attached to a central switching unit. Circuit switching is used; the central switch establishes a dedicated path between any two devices that wish to communicate.

Figure 8-1 depicts the major elements of such a one-node network. The heart of a modern system is a digital switch. The advent of digital switching technology

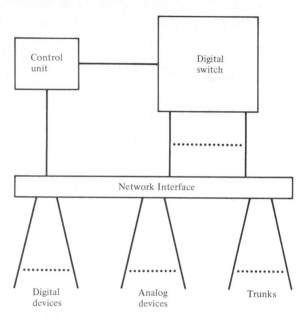

FIGURE 8-1.   Elements of a one-node circuit switch.

has dramatically improved the cost, performance, and capability of circuit-switched networks. Key to the operation of such a system are that (1) all signals are represented digitally, and (2) synchronous time-division multiplexing (TDM) techniques are used.

The network interface element represents the functions and hardware needed to connect digital devices, such as data processing devices and digital telephones, to the network. Analog telephones can also be attached if the network interface contains the logic for converting to digital signals. Trunks to external systems may also be attached. These may include analog voice trunks and digital TDM lines.

The control unit performs three general tasks. First, it establishes connections. This is generally done on demand, that is, at the request of an attached device. To establish the connection, the control unit must handle and acknowledge the request, determine if the intended destination is free, and construct a path through the switch. Second, the control unit must maintain the connection. Since the digital switch uses time-division principles, this may require ongoing manipulation of the switching elements. However, the bits of the communication are transferred transparently. This is in contrast to packet-switching networks, which are sensitive to the transmission protocol (i.e., address and other control information in each packet must be processed) and can be considered content dependent. Third, the control unit must tear down the connection, either in response to a request from one of the parties or for its own reasons.

The switch may be either one-sided or two-sided. In a one-sided system, all attachment points are viewed the same: A connection can be established between any two devices. In a two-sided system, attachment points are grouped into two classes and a connection can be established only between two devices from different classes. A typical application of the latter is the connection of a set of terminals to a set of computer ports; in many cases, only terminal-to-port connections are allowed.

An important characteristic of a circuit-switching device is whether it is blocking or nonblocking. Blocking occurs when the network is unable to connect two stations because all possible paths between them are already in use. A blocking network is one in which such blocking is possible. Hence a nonblocking network permits all stations to be connected (in pairs) at once and grants all possible connection requests as long as the called party is free. When a network is supporting only voice traffic, a blocking configuration is generally acceptable, since it is expected that most phone calls are of short duration and that, therefore, only a fraction of the telephones will be engaged at any time. However, when data processing devices are involved, these assumptions may be invalid. For example, for a data entry application, a terminal may be continuously connected to a computer for hours at a time. [BHUS85] reports that typical voice connections on a PBX have a duration of 120 to 180 seconds, whereas data calls have a range of from 8 seconds to 15 hours. Hence, for data applications, there is a requirement for a nonblocking or ''nearly nonblocking'' (very low probability of blocking) configuration.

8-2

DIGITAL SWITCHING CONCEPTS

The technology of switching has a long history, most of it covering an era when analog signal switching predominated. With the advent of PCM and related techniques, both voice and data can be transmitted via digital signals. This has led to a fundamental change in the design and technology of switching systems. Instead of dumb space-division systems, modern digital switching systems rely on intelligent control of space- and time-division elements.

This section looks at the concepts underlying contemporary digital switching (good discussions can be found in [SKAP79], [JOEL77], and [JOEL79a,b]). We begin with a look at space-division switching, which was originally developed for the analog environment and has been carried over into digital technology. Then the various forms of time-division switching, which were developed specifically to be used in digital switches, are examined. Later sections discuss how these concepts are implemented in digital data switching devices and digital PBXs.

Space-Division Switching

The *space-division switch* is, as its name implies, one in which paths between pairs of devices are divided in space. Each connection requires the establishment of a physical path through the switch that is dedicated solely to the transfer of signals between the two endpoints. The basic building block of the switch is a metallic crosspoint or semiconductor gate [ABBO84] that can be enabled and disabled by a control unit.

Figure 8-2a shows a simple crossbar matrix with *n* inputs and *m* outputs. Interconnection is possible between any input line and any output line by engaging the appropriate crosspoint. The crossbar depicts a bilateral arrangement: There is a distinction between input and output. For example, input lines may connect to terminals, while output lines connect to computer ports. The crossbar switch is

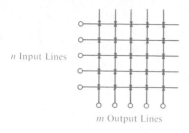

n Input Lines

m Output Lines

(a) Crossbar Matrix

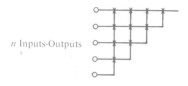

n Inputs-Outputs

(b) Triangular Switch

FIGURE 8-2. **Single-stage space-division switch.**

said to perform concentration, distribution, or expansion according as $n > m$, $n = m$, or $n < m$.

The crossbar matrix makes a distinction between input and output: Any input can connect to any output. It requires $n \times m$ crosspoints. However, if there is no distinction between inputs and outputs, then $n = m$ and the requirement is that any end point can connect to any other endpoint. This requires only a triangular array of $n(n - 1)/2$ crosspoints (Figure 8-2b) and is referred to as a "folded" configuration.

The crossbar switch has a number of limitations or disadvantages:

• The number of crosspoints grows with n^2. This is costly for large n, and results in high capacitive loading on any message path.
• The loss of a crosspoint prevents connection between the two devices involved.
• The crosspoints are inefficiently utilized (at most n out of n^2).

To overcome these limitations, multiple stage switches are employed. The N input lines (inlets) are broken up into N/n groups of n lines. Each group of lines goes into a first-stage matrix. The outputs of the first stage matrices become inputs to a group of second-stage matrices, and so on. Figure 8-3 depicts a three-stage network of switches that is symmetric; that is, the number of inlets to the first stage equals the number of outlets from the last stage. There are k second-stage matrices, each with N/n inlets and N/n outlets. Each first-stage matrix has k outlets so that it connects to all second-stage matrices. Each second-stage matrix has N/n outlets so that it connects to all third-stage matrices.

This type of arrangement has several advantages over the simple crossbar switch:

• The number of crosspoints is reduced (see below), increasing crossbar utilization.
• There is more than one path through the network to connect two endpoints, increasing reliability.

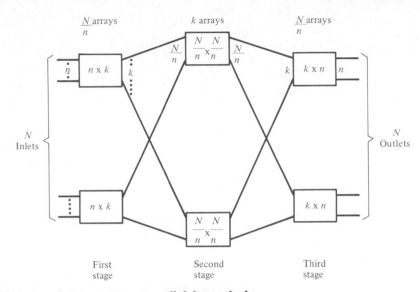

FIGURE 8-3. **Three-stage space-division switch.**

Of course, a multistage network requires a more complex control scheme. To establish a path in a single-stage network, it is only necessary to open a single gate. In a multistage network, a free path through the stages must be determined and the appropriate gates opened.

A consideration with a multistage space-division switch is that it may be blocking. It should be clear from Figure 8-2a that a crossbar matrix is nonblocking; that is, a path is always available to connect an input to an output. That this is not always the case with a multiple-stage switch can be seen in Figure 8-4. The figure shows a three stage switch with $N = 9$, $n = 3$, and $k = 3$. The heavier lines indicate lines that are already in use. In this state, input line 9 cannot be connected to either output line 4 or 6, even though both of these output lines are available.

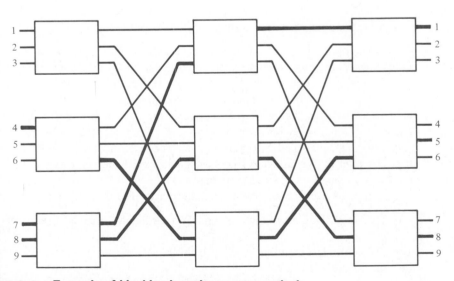

FIGURE 8-4. **Example of blocking in a three-stage switch.**

It should be clear that by increasing the value of k (the number of outlets from each first-stage switch and the number of second stage switches), the probability of blocking is reduced. What value of k is required for a nonblocking three-stage switch? The answer is depicted in Figure 8-5. Consider that we wish to establish a path from input line a to output line b. The worst case situation for blocking occurs if all of the remaining $n - 1$ input lines and $n - 1$ output lines are busy and are connected to different center-stage switches. Thus a total of $(n - 1) + (n - 1) = 2n - 2$ center switches are unavailable for creating a path from a to b. However, if one more center-stage switch exists, the appropriate links must be available for the connection. Thus, a three-stage network will be nonblocking if

$$k = 2n - 1 \qquad (8\text{-}1)$$

We now return to our claim that a multiple-stage switch requires fewer crosspoints than a single-stage switch. From Figure 8-3, the total number of crosspoints N_x in a three-stage switch is

$$N_x = 2Nk + k\left(\frac{N}{n}\right)^2 \qquad (8\text{-}2)$$

Substituting Equation (8-1) into (8-2),

$$N_x = 2N(2n - 1) + (2n - 1)\left(\frac{N}{n}\right)^2 \qquad (8\text{-}3)$$

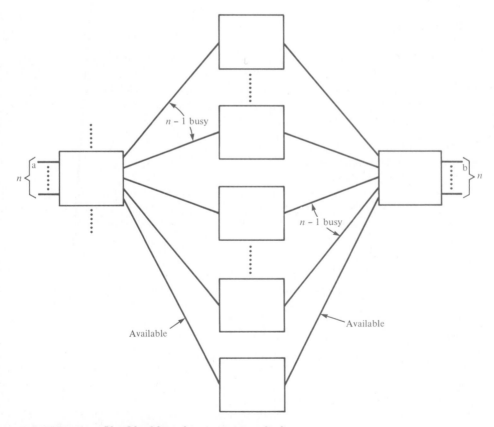

FIGURE 8-5.   Nonblocking three-stage switch.

TABLE 8-1   Number of Crosspoints in a Nonblocking Switch

Number of Lines	Number of Crosspoints for Three-Stage Switch	Number of Crosspoints for Single-Stage Switch
128	7,680	16,384
512	63,488	262,144
3,048	516,096	4.2×10^6
8,192	4.2×10^6	6.7×10^7
32,768	3.3×10^7	1×10^9
131,072	2.6×10^8	1.7×10^{10}

for a nonblocking switch. The actual value as a function of N depends on the number of switches (N/n) in the first and third stages. To optimize, differentiate N_x with respect to n and set the result to 0. For large N, the result converges to $n = (N/2)^{1/2}$. Substituting into (8-3),

$$N_x = 4N(\sqrt{2N} - 1)$$

Table 8.1 compares this value with the number of crosspoints in a single-stage switch. As can be seen, there is a savings that grows with the number of lines.

Time-Division Switching

In contrast to space-division switching, in which dedicated paths are used, *time-division switching* involves the partitioning of a lower-speed data stream into pieces that share a higher-speed data stream with other data pieces. The individual pieces or slots are manipulated by the control logic to route data from input to output. Three concepts comprise the technique of time-division switching

- TDM bus switching
- Time-slot interchange (TSI)
- Time-multiplex switching (TMS)

TDM Bus Switching.   As discussed in Chapter 6, TDM is a technique that allows multiple signals to share a single transmission line by separating them in time. In this chapter, we are concerned primarily with synchronous TDM, that is, a situation in which time slots are preassigned so that few or no overhead bits are required. We will see that this technique permits multiple channels of data to be handled efficiently within switching systems as well as on transmission systems.

Let us briefly review synchronous TDM. As shown in Figure 8-6a, synchronous TDM was designed to permit multiple low-speed streams to share a high-speed line. A set of inputs is sampled in turn. The samples are organized serially into slots (channels) to form a recurring frame of n slots. A slot may be a bit, a byte, or some longer block. An important point to note is that with synchronous TDM, the source and destination of the data in each time slot are known. Hence there is no need for address bits in each slot.

The mechanism for synchronous TDM may be quite simple. For example, each input line deposits data in a buffer; the multiplexer scans these buffers sequentially,

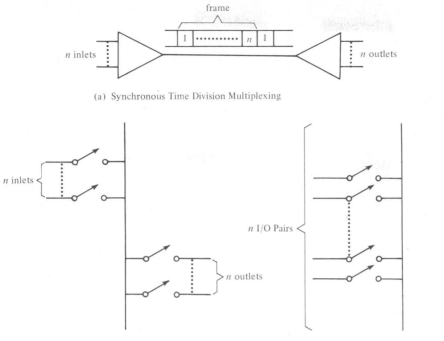

(a) Synchronous Time Division Multiplexing

(b) A Simple Time-Division Switch   (c) A Simple Folded Time-Division Switch

FIGURE 8-6.   TDM bus switching.

taking fixed size chunks of data from each buffer and sending them out on the line. One complete scan produces one frame of data. For output to the lines, the reverse operation is performed, with the multiplexer filling the output line buffers one by one.

The I/O lines attached to the multiplexer may be synchronous or asynchronous; the multiplexed line between the two multiplexers is synchronous and must have a data rate equal to the sum of the data rates of the attached lines. Actually, the multiplexed line must have a slightly higher data rate, since each frame will include some overhead bits (headers and trailers) for synchronization.

The time slots in a frame are assigned to the I/O lines on a fixed, predetermined basis. If a device has no data to send, the multiplexer must send empty slots. Thus the actual data transfer rate may be less than the capacity of the system.

Figure 8-6b shows a simple way in which this technique can be adapted to achieve switching. A set of buffered input and output lines are connected through controlled gates to a high-speed digital bus. Each input line is assigned a time slot. During that time, that line's gate is enabled, allowing a small burst of data onto the bus. For that same time slot, one of the output line gates is also enabled. Since the enabling and disabling of gates is controlled, the sequence of input and output line activations need not be in the same order. Hence a form of switching is possible. Curiously, this technique has no specific name; we shall refer to it as TDM bus switching.

Of course, such a scheme need not be two-sided. As shown in Figure 8-6c, a "folded" switch can be devised by attaching *n* I/O pairs to the bus. Any attached device achieves full duplex operation by transmitting during one assigned time slot and receiving during another. The other end of the connection is an I/O pair for which these time slots have the opposite meanings.

The TDM bus switch has an advantage over a crossbar switch in terms of efficient use of gates. For N devices, the TDM bus switch requires $2N$ gates or switch points, whereas the most efficient multistage crossbar network requires on the order of $N \sqrt{N}$ switch points.

Let us look at the timing involved a bit more closely. First, consider a nonblocking implementation of Figure 8-6c. There must be N repetitively occurring time slots, each one assigned to an input and an output line. We will refer to one iteration for all time slots as a frame. The input assignment may be fixed; the output assignments vary to allow various connections. When a time slot begins, the designated input line may insert a burst of data onto the line, where it will propagate to both ends past all other lines. The designated ouput line will, during that time, copy the data if any as they go by. The time slot, then, must equal the transmission time of the input line plus the propagation delay between input and output lines. In order to keep the successive time slots uniform, time slot length should be defined as transmission time plus the end-to-end bus propagation delay. For efficiency, the propagation delay should be much less than the transmission time, and in practice this is so. Note that only one time slot or burst of data may be on the bus at a time.

To keep up with the input lines, the slots must recur sufficiently frequently. For example, consider a system connecting full-duplex lines at 19.2 kbps. Input data on each line are buffered at the gate. The buffer must be cleared, by enabling the gate, fast enough to avoid overrun. So if there are 100 lines, the capacity of the bus must be at least 1.92 Mbps. Actually, it must be higher than that to account for the wasted time due to propagation delay.

These considerations determine the traffic-carrying capacity of a blocking switch as well. For a blocking switch, there is no fixed assignment of input lines to time slots; they are allocated on demand. The data rate on the bus dictates how many connections can be made at a time. For a system with 200 devices at 19.2 kbps and a bus at 2 Mbps, about half of the devices can be connected at any one time.

The TDM bus switching scheme can accommodate lines of varying data rates. For example, if a 9600-bps line gets one slot per frame, a 19.2-kbps line would get two slots per frame. Of course, only lines of the same data rate can be connected.

Figure 8-7 is an example that suggests how the control for a TDM but switch could be implemented. Let us assume that propagation time on the bus is zero. Time on the bus is organized into 30-μs frames of six 5-μs slots each. A control memory indicates which gates are to be enabled during each time slot. In this example, 6 words of memory are needed. A controller cycles through the memory at a rate of one cycle every 30 μs. During the first time slot of each cycle, the input gate from device 1 and the output gate to device 3 are enabled, allowing data to pass from device 1 to device 3 over the bus. The remaining words are accessed in succeeding time slots and treated accordingly. As long as the control memory contains the contents depicted in Figure 8-7, connections are maintained between 1 and 3, 2 and 5, and 4 and 6.

Several questions may occur to you. For one, is this circuit switching? Circuit switching, recall, was defined as a technique in which a dedicated communications path is established between devices. This is indeed the case in Figure 8-6b and c. To establish a connection between an input and output line, the controller dedicates

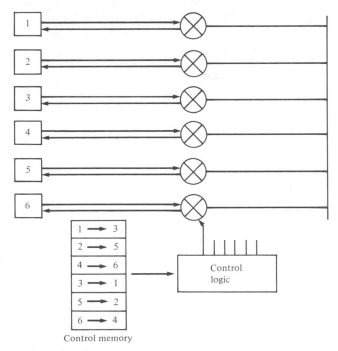

FIGURE 8-7. **Control of a TDM bus switch.**

a certain number of time slots per frame to that connection. The appropriate input and output gates are enabled during those time slots to allow data to pass. Although the bus is shared by other connections, it is nevertheless used to create a dedicated path between input and output. Another question: Is this synchronous TDM? Synchronous TDM is generally associated with creating permanent dedicated time slots for each input line. The scheme depicted in Figure 8-6b and c can assume a dynamic character, with the controller allocating available time slots among connections. Nevertheless, at steady state (a period when no connections are made or broken) a fixed number of slots is dedicated per channel and the system behaves in a manner similar to a synchronous time-division multiplexer.

The control logic for the system described above requires the enabling of two gates to achieve a connection. This logic can be simplified if the input burst into a time slot contains destination address information. All output devices can then always connect to the bus and copy the data from time slots with their address. This scheme blurs the distinction between circuit switching and packet switching.

Time-Slot Interchange. The basic building block of many time-division switches is the *time-slot interchange* (TSI) mechanism. A TSI unit operates on a synchronous TDM stream of time slots, or channels, by interchanging pairs of slots to achieve full-duplex operation. Figure 8-8a shows how the input line of device I is connected to the output line of device J, and vice versa.

We should note several points. The input lines of N devices are passed through a synchronous multiplexer to produce a TDM stream with N slots. To achieve interconnection, the slots corresponding to two inputs are interchanged. This results in a full-duplex connection between two lines. To allow the interchange of any two slots, the incoming data in a slot must be stored until they can be sent out on

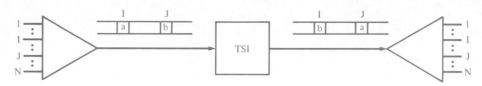

(a) TSI operation

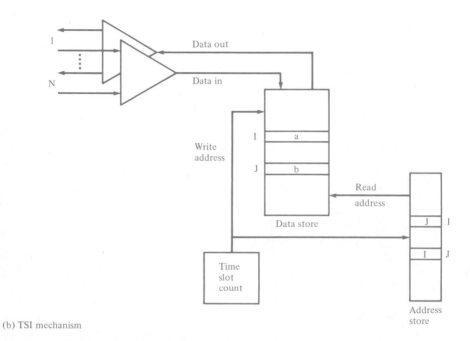

(b) TSI mechanism

FIGURE 8-8.   Time-slot interchange (TSI).

the right channel in the next frame cycle. Hence the TSI introduces a delay and produces output slots in the desired order. These are then demultiplexed and routed to the appropriate output line. Since each channel is provided a time slot in the frame, whether or not it transmits data, the size of the TSI unit must be chosen for the capacity of the TDM line, not the actual data transfer rate.

Figure 8-8b depicts a mechanism for TSI. Individual I/O lines are multiplexed and demultiplexed. These functions can be integrated as part of the switch itself, or they may be implemented remotely, as a device clustering mechanism. A random-access data store whose width equals one time slot of data and whose length equals the number of slots in a frame is used. An incoming TDM frame is written sequentially, slot by slot, into the data store. An outgoing TDM frame is created by reading slots from memory in an order dictated by an address store that reflects the existing connections. In the figure, the data in channels I and J are interchanged, creating a full-duplex connection between the corresponding stations.

TSI is a simple, effective way of switching TDM data. However, the size of such a switch, in terms of number of connections, is limited by the memory access speed. It is clear that, in order to keep pace with the input, data must be read into and out of memory as fast as they arrive. So, for example, if we have 24 sources operating at 64 kbps each, and a slot size of 8 bits, we would have an arrival rate

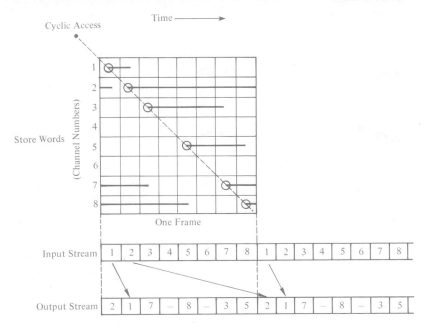

FIGURE 8-9. Operation of TSI store.

of 192,000 slots per second (this is like the structure of the PCM T1 carrier). For each time slot, both a read and a write are required. Thus memory access time would need to be $1/(192,000 \times 2)$, or about 2.6 μs.

Let us look more closely at the operation of the data store; in particular, we need to view it as a function of time. As an example [DAVI73], consider a system with eight input/output lines, in which the following connections exist: 1-2, 3-7, and 5-8. The other two stations are not in use. Figure 8-9 depicts the contents of the data store over the course of one frame (eight slots). During the first time slot, data are stored in location 1 and read from location 2. During the second time slot, data are stored in location 2 and read from location 1. And so on.

As can be seen, the write accesses to the data store are cyclic, that is, accessing successive locations in sequential order, whereas the read accesses are acyclic, requiring the use of an address store. The figure also depicts two frames of the input and output sequences and indicates the transfer of data between channels 1 and 2. Note that in half the cases, data slots move into the next frame.

As with the TDM bus switch, the TSI unit can handle inputs of varying data rates. Figure 8-10 suggests a way in which this may be done. Instead of presenting the input lines to a synchronous multiplexer, they are presented to a selector device. This device will select an input line based on a channel assignment provided from a store controlled by the time slot counter. Hence, instead of sampling equally from each input, it may gather more slots from some channels than others.

Time-Multiplexed Switching. As we have seen, a TSI unit can support only a limited number of connections. Further, as the size of the unit grows, for a fixed access speed, the delay at the TSI grows. To overcome both of these problems, multiple TSI units are used. Now, to connect two channels entering a single TSI unit, their time slots can be interchanged. However, to connect a channel on one

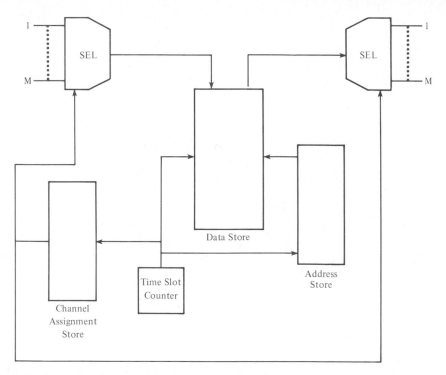

FIGURE 8-10. **TSI operation with variable-rate input.**

TDM stream (going into one TSI) to a channel on another TDM stream (going into another TSI), some form of space division multiplexing is needed. Naturally, we do not wish to switch all of the time slots from one stream to another; we would like to do it one slot at a time. This technique is known as *time-multiplexed switching* (TMS).

Multiple-stage networks can be built up by concatenating TMS and TSI stages. TMS stages, which move slots from one stream to another, are referred to as S, and TSI stages are referred to as T. Systems are generally described by an enumeration of their stages from input to output, using the symbols T and S. Figure 8-11 is an example of a two-stage TS network. Such a network is blocking. For example, if one channel on input stream 1 is to be switched to the third channel in output stream 1, and another channel on input stream 1 is to be switched to the third channel on output stream 2, one of the connections is blocked.

To avoid blocking, three or more stages are used. Some of the more common structures used in commercially available systems are [SKAP79]:

- TST.
- TSSST.
- STS.
- SSTSS.
- TSTST.

The requirements on the TMS unit are stringent. The unit must provide space-division connections between its input and output lines, and these connections must

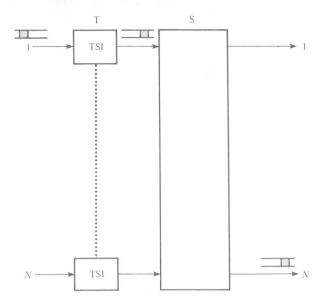

FIGURE 8-11. Two-stage digital switch.

be reconfigured for each time slot. This requires, in effect, a control store whose width is sufficient to handle the number of ingoing and outgoing lines and whose length equals the number of time slots in a frame.

One means of implementing the TMS stage is the crossbar switch discussed earlier. This requires that the crosspoints be manipulated at each time slot. More commonly, the TMS stage is implemented by digital selectors (SEL) which select only one input at a time on a time-slot basis. These SEL devices are the same as those described in the preceding section, except that here each of their inputs is a TDM stream rather than a single line. Figure 8-12 shows STS and TST networks implemented with the SEL units.

In an STS network, the path between an incoming and outgoing channel has multiple possible physical routes equal to the number of TSI units but only one time route. For a fully nonblocking network, the number of TSI units must be double the number of incoming and outgoing TDM streams. On the other hand, the multiple routes between two channels in a TST network are all in the time domain; there is only one physical path possible. Here, too, blocking is a possibility. One way to avoid blocking is by expanding the number of time slots in the space stage. In all multistage networks, whether space- or time-division, a path-search algorithm is needed to determine the route from input to output.

It is interesting to compare the TDM bus switch with TSI and TMS. It does not exactly fit into either category. Compare it to a space switch. The TDM bus switch does connect any input with any output, as in a crossbar or SEL switch. The space switch operates simultaneously on all inputs, whereas the TDM bus switch operates on the inputs sequentially. However, because the frame time on the bus is less than the slot time of any input, the switching is effectively simultaneous. On the other hand, a comparison of Figures 8-8 and 8-6b reveals the similarity between TSI and TDM bus switching.

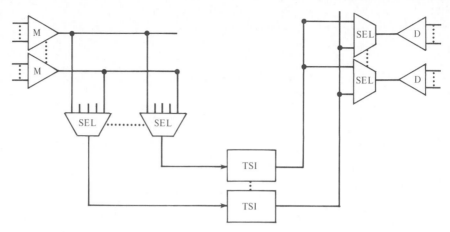

(a) Space-Time-Space Network

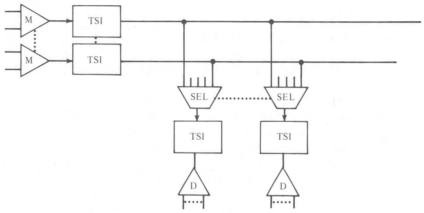

(b) Time-Space-Time Network

FIGURE 8-12.   Three-stage TDM switches.

Modular Switch Architecture

The discussion so far has concerned what might be termed "traditional" digital switch architecture. More recently, a modular switch architecture has been developed based on the use of one module type for all switching stages [KAJI83]. A single module contains both time and space switching.

A major motivation for going to a modular architecture is to overcome some inherent disadvantages of the traditional multistage time-and-space switch. With the traditional switch, the designer must decide in advance the maximum exchange size in order to determine the number of stages and the switch size at each stage. These decisions, in turn, determine a lower size limit. In addition, central control is needed to set up and tear down paths through the switch. As the size of the switch grows, this task becomes increasingly complex. The modular architecture does not possess these disadvantages, as we shall see.

We can contrast the modular switch to the traditional digital switch by listing some of the advantages of the former:

- *Flexible size:* The modules serve as building blocks, allowing a large number of different switch sizes, ranging from very small to very large.
- *Simplified control:* Path setup and tear down is distributed. Each module is intelligent and control is provided via the data path.
- *Simplified manufacturing, testing, and maintenance:* There are fewer parts to build and install.

The principal disadvantage of the modular architecture is potentially increased propagation delay. Each module performs a TSI function. In a large switch, a circuit may pass through multiple modules, and the TSI delays can become substantial.

In the remainder of this section, we briefly describe one example of a modular architecture, the ITT 1240 [COTT81], [KEIS85]. For other examples, the reader is referred to [CHAR79] and [ENOM85].

The basic building block of the ITT switch is depicted in Figure 8-13. This module is a plug-in printed circuit board which carries 16 identical LSI *switch ports* interconnected by a TDM bus switch. Each port has an incoming and an outgoing synchronous TDM line. Each line has a data rate of 4.096 Mbps and carries 32 channels. Each channel is used for either digital data or PCM voice. One TDM frame consists of 16 bits from each of the 32 channels. Eight of these

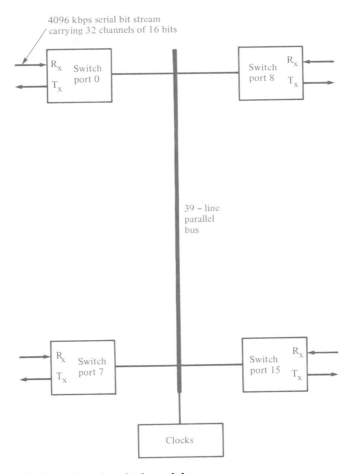

FIGURE 8-13. Digital switch module.

bits are control or unused bits. A little arithmetic reveals that each channel is therefore 64 kbps.

There is no common mechanism or control processor to control the modules. Each module is controlled by the individual switch ports acting together over the TDM bus to make and break connections. The receive (incoming) side of each switch port is in essence a synchronous demultiplexer. It sends the channel data, along with destination port number and channel number, out in 16-bit chunks onto the bus during assigned time slots. The transmit (outgoing) side recognizes its port number on the bus and places each slot of data in the appropriate frame slot of the outgoing line. Since the slots are then transmitted in a (possibly) different order than that in which they were received from the bus, the switch port performs, in effect, a TSI operation. With this architecture, any channel on any of the 16 incoming lines can be connected to any of the 512 (16 × 32) outgoing channels. Thus the module provides a combination of time and space switching.

To begin, let us consider the operation of the simplest switch, depicted in Figure 8-14. Individual terminals (digital data or PCM voice) attach to a *terminal control element* (TCE), which produces two 32-channel TDM streams destined for the switch. Similarly, the TCE receives two 32-channel streams from the switch. Thus the TCE is nothing more than a synchronous TDM multiplexer/demultiplexer. Up to 60 terminals attach to the switch (the extra channels are used for control). The

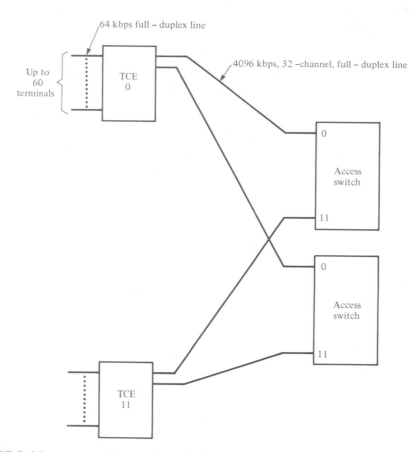

FIGURE 8-14. Single-stage modular switch.

switch in this case consists of two modules which in this context are called *access switches,* with one full-duplex 32-channel link from each TCE going to each module. The use of two modules provides redundancy in the case of failure. Thus any two of the 60 devices on the TCE can be connected via the switch.

Note that one TCE uses up only one port on each of the access switches. The switches support up to 12 TCEs using 12 of the available 16 ports. The remaining ports are unused in this configuration. Thus the simplest one-stage switch consists of two modules and supports 720 terminals. Switching is accomplished as follows. When a terminal requests a connection, and if the destination terminal is attached to the same TCE, the TCE completely implements the connection without involving an access switch. Otherwise, the TCE selects an available outgoing channel (out of the 64) and transmits a path setup request over that channel, which includes the destination address. The access switch responds by selecting an available channel going to the appropriate TCE.

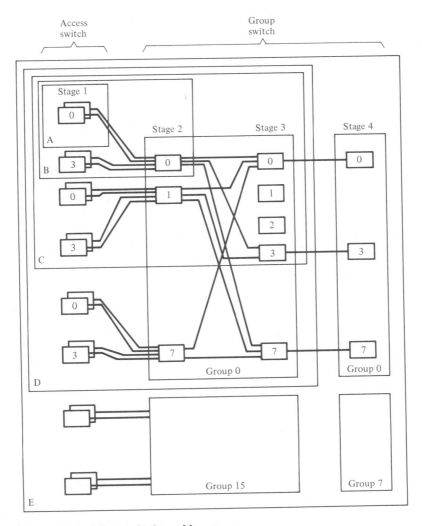

FIGURE 8-15. Modular switch architecture.

The way in which a switch may be expanded, and the operation of a multistage switch, can be explained with reference to Figure 8-15. The single-stage switch is enclosed in a box labeled *A*. For a first expansion, up to three more pairs of access switches may be added to the first stage, all interconnected by a second stage of switching. The four unused ports on each access switch (32 in all) connect to a second-stage switch called a *group switch*. This stage consists of up to four modules, with eight ports on each module utilized. The four ports on each access switch attach, one each, to the four modules of stage 2. Thus full connectivity is achieved. The full switch can now handle a total of 2880 terminals. Switching is accomplished as follows. If two terminals connect via TCEs to the same access switch, a path is set up that "reflects back" through the access switch without going to the second stage. Addresses have a hierarchical format, so it is easy for a module to determine if reflection is allowed. If not, an available channel to the stage 2 switch is selected and that switch in turn reflects back to a different access switch that connects to the TCE of the destination terminal.

The two-step configuration is labeled *B* in the diagram. Further expansion proceeds similarly. The eight unused ports on each second stage module are used to connect to up to eight third-stage switches. Reflection can occur at stage 1, 2, or 3 (boxes *C* and *D*). The maximum configuration consists of four stages and supports over 100,000 terminals.

DIGITAL DATA SWITCHING DEVICES

The techniques discussed in the preceding section have been used to build a variety of digital switching products designed for digital data-only applications. These devices do not provide telephone service and are generally cheaper than a digital PBX for comparable capacity.

The variety of devices is wide and the distinction between types is blurred. For convenience, we categorize them as follows:

- Terminal/port-oriented switch
- Data switch
- Switching statistical multiplexer

In what follows we will look at the functions performed by each type of device, and suggest an architecture that supports those functions. Keep in mind that usually any of the techniques in Section 8-2, or any combination, may be used to implement any of these switches. The discussion here is intended only to give examples.

Before turning to the specific device types, let us look at the requirements for data switching.

Data Switching Requirements

For any circuit-switching system used to connect digital data transmitting devices, certain generic requirements can be defined. These requirements apply both to pure digital data switching devices and to digital PBX systems. We begin first by looking briefly at the data transmission techniques that must be supported by a data switch, and then look at the functions to be performed.

The devices attached to a data switch will use either asynchronous or synchronous transmission. Asynchronous transmission, recall, is character-at-a-time. Each character consists of a start bit, 5 to 8 data bits, a parity bit, and a stop signal, which may be 1, 1.5, or 2 bit times in length. Logic is available which can automatically determine character length, parity, and even bit rate. Hence it is a relatively easy matter for a data switch to handle asynchronous transmission. On input, data are accumulated a character at a time, and transmitted internally using synchronous transmission. At the other end of the connection, they are buffered and transmitted a character at a time to the output line. This applies to any switch using time-division switching techniques. Of course, a pure space-division switch need not concern itself with such matters: A dedicated physical path is set up and bits are transmitted transparently.

Synchronous transmission represents a greater challenge. Synchronous communication requires either a separate clock lead from the transmission point to the reception point or the use of a self-clock encoding scheme, such as Manchester. The latter technique is typical. With synchronous communication, the data rate must be known ahead of time, as well as the synchronization pattern (bits or characters used to signal the beginning of a frame). Thus there can be no universal synchronous interface (until a universal synchronous transmission technique is standardized).

Of course, for either synchronous or asynchronous transmission, full duplex operation is required. Typically, this requires two twisted pairs (known as a twin pair) between a device and the switch, one for transmission in each direction. This is in contrast to the case with analog signaling where a single twisted-pair suffices (see Figure 3-6). Recently, however, some vendors have begun to offer full-duplex digital signaling on a single twisted pair, using a *ping-pong protocol*. In essence, data are buffered at each end and sent across the line at double the data rate with the two ends taking turn. So, for example, two devices may communicate, full duplex, at 56 kbps if they are attached to a 112-kbps line and the line drivers at each end buffer the device data and transmit, alternately, at 112 kbps. In fact, an even higher data rate is required to account for propagation delay and control signals.

We turn now to the functions to be provided by a data switch. The most basic, of course, is the making of a connection between two attached lines. These connections can be preconfigured by a system operator, but more dynamic operation is often desired. This leads to two additional functions: port contention and port selection. *Port contention* is a function that allows a certain number of designated ports to contend for access to a smaller number of ports. Typically, this is used for terminal-to-host connection to allow a smaller number of host ports to service a larger number of terminal ports. When a terminal user attempts to connect, the system will scan through all the host ports in the contention group. If any of the ports is available, a connection is made.

Port selection is an interactive capability. It allows a user (or an application program in a host) to select a port for connection. This is analogous to dialing a number in a phone system. Port selection and port contention can be combined by allowing the selection, by name or number, of a contention group. Port selection devices are becoming increasingly common. A switch without this capability only allows connections that are preconfigured by a system operator. If one knows in advance what interconnections are required, fine. Otherwise, the flexibility of port selection is usually worth the additional cost.

An interactive capability carries with it an additional responsibility: The control unit of the switch must be able to talk to the requesting port. This can be done in two ways. In some cases, the manufacturer supplies a simple keypad device that attaches to and shares the terminal's line. The user first uses the keypad to dial a connection; once the connection is made, communication is via the terminal. As an alternative, the connection sequence can be effected through the terminal itself. A simple command language dialogue is used. However, this technique requires that the system understand the code and protocol being used by the terminal. Consequently, this feature is generally limited to asynchronous ASCII devices.

Terminal/Port-Oriented Switches

The devices discussed in this section were designed to address a specific problem: the connection of interactive terminals to computer ports. In many computer sites with one or more time-sharing systems and a population (usually growing) of terminals, means must be found for interconnection.

One means of connection is simply to assign each terminal to a specific computer port, even when not active. This is expensive in terms of computer ports, since generally only a fraction of the terminals are logged on. Further, the user cannot change to a different computer without making cable changes. Another approach is to use multiple dial-up telephone rotaries, for each computer and each transmission speed. The rotary allows a user to call a single number and gain access to one of several autoanswer modems; if all modems are busy, the rotary returns a busy signal. The approach ties up telephones lines for extended periods and requires the use of modems.

One early solution that avoids some of the expenses mentioned above was the patch panel. This device enabled manual connection of two lines and could also provide some system monitoring and diagnostics. The addition of intelligence to this type of device to eliminate the manual connection function has resulted in a variety of intelligent terminal/port-oriented switches. A variety of names are used, depending partly on function, including intelligent patch panel, port selector, and port contention device.

At a minimum, these devices permit a set of connections to be set up and periodically updated by a system operator. Port selection and port contention functions are also provided on many products.

Figure 8-16 is an example of a noninteractive (without port selection) system. The system allows connection of one I/O port to any other I/O port on the same or a different port card. Connections are set up at system initialization time and may be changed dynamically by the system operator (not the user). The means of establishing connections is simple. Each port has associated with it a destination address register. To connect two ports, the address of each is placed in the other. To transmit data, the sending device puts its data (8 bits) and the destination address (8 bits) on the bus. All devices continually monitor the bus for their own address. The switch is nonblocking, allowing the preassignment of time slots to transmitting devices. Receiving devices need not know the time slot for reception since they are looking for an address. Thus, at the cost of 100% overhead, the control logic is greatly simplified.

Figure 8-17 is an example of a port selection system. A collection of line modules are scanned to produce a TDM stream which is passed over a bus to a switch

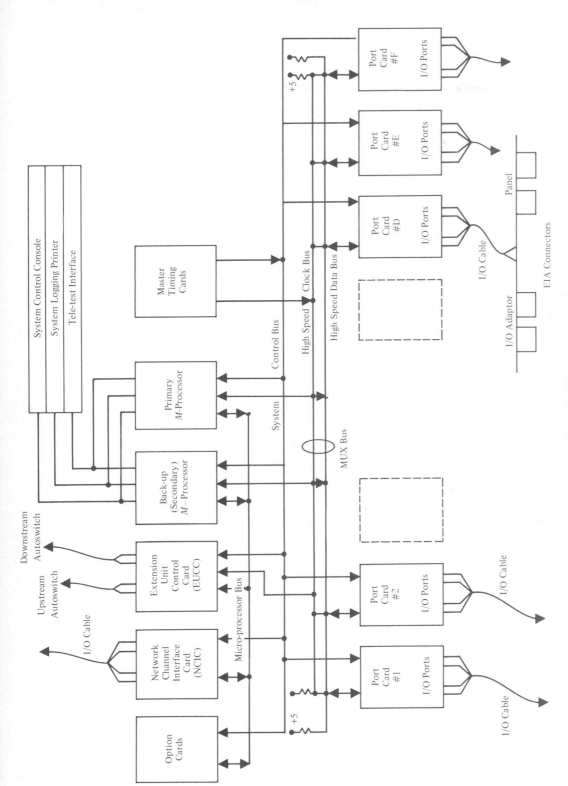

FIGURE 8-16. Example of a port contention system. (From [BYTE85]).

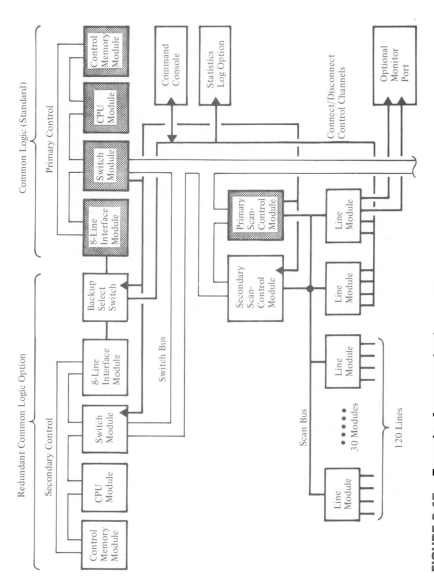

FIGURE 8-17. Example of a port selection system.

module. The output of the switch module is a switched set of time slots that are directed to the proper port. Note the redundant architecture for reliability.

Data Switches

There is little additional that need be said about these devices. No distinction is made between terminal lines and ports. The switch simply has a set of I/O lines and is capable of establishing connections between lines. Any or a combination of the digital switching techniques described in Section 8-2 may be used. Some or all of the functions described above may be provided.

Switching Statistical Multiplexers

There is one device that is quite different from the other types that we have been discussing: the *switching statistical multiplexer*. Unlike the synchronous TDM techniques used in most digital switches, the switching statistical multiplexer uses asynchronous or statistical TDM and has a switching capability [SCHO81].

The switching multiplexer uses the same technique as a statistical multiplexer (Chapter 6), with two additions:

- There may be more than one multiplexed line.
- There is sufficient intelligence to permit any form of routing through the multiplexer.

As with a statistical multiplexer, the switching multiplexer can provide a full-duplex connection between a line and a channel on a multiplexed line (usually referred to as a *trunk*). For line-to-trunk traffic, data are buffered and sent out in fixed-size chunks with an address appended. For trunk-to-line, each slot of incoming data is handled separately; the address is stripped off and the data chunk is routed to the appropriate output line.

This capability is not limited to trunk-line interaction. Two lines can be connected, with data exchanged between them, without addressing. Two channels on separate trunks can be connected; each slot of incoming data on a designated channel is routed, address and all, to the other trunk.

Figure 8-18 summarizes the connection possibilities of the switching multiplexer. Statistical TDM frames are used on the trunks. Connected lines may be synchronous or asynchronous and of varying speeds. Some type of control unit is needed to control the routing.

Figure 8-19 is a conceptual architecture that suggests how a switching multiplexer might be implemented. There are a number of I/O logic units for the lines and trunks. Each unit is capable of receiving and buffering data and transferring it to a data store; on output, it can accept data from the data store and transmit. Areas of the data store serve as dedicated buffers for the I/O units. As data accumulate, they must be transferred to the appropriate I/O unit for transmission. This is done under control of the control unit, which uses information in the routing table to determine the routing.

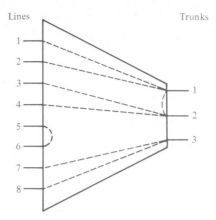

FIGURE 8-18. **Connection possibilities in a switching statistical multiplexer.**

The switching multiplexer can perform all of the data switching functions described in previous sections, although generally on a smaller scale. Preconfigured connections can be set up. The device can have sufficient intelligence to support on-demand port selection and port contention. A mixture of fixed and demand-assigned connections can be provided.

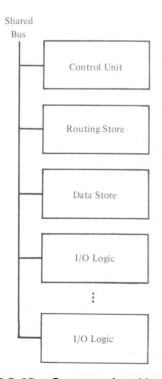

FIGURE 8-19. **Conceptual architecture of a switching statistical multiplexer.**

THE DIGITAL PRIVATE BRANCH EXCHANGE

Evolution of the Digital PBX

The digital PBX is a marriage of two technologies: digital switching and telephone exchange systems. The forerunner of the digital PBX is the private branch exchange (PBX). A PBX is an on-premise facility, owned or leased by an organization, which interconnects the telephones within the facility and provides access to the public telephone system. Typically, a telephone user on the premises dials a three- or four-digit number to call another telephone on the premises, and dials one digit (usually 8 or 9) to get a dial tone for an "outside line," which allows the caller to dial a number in the same fashion as a residential user.

The original private exchanges were manual, with one or more operators at a switchboard required to make all connections. Back in the 1920s, these began to be replaced by automatic systems, called *private automatic branch exchanges* (PABXs), which did not require attendant intervention to place a call. These "first-generation" systems used electromechanical technology and analog signaling. Data connections could be made via modems. That is, a user with a terminal, a telephone, and a modem or acoustic coupler in the office could dial up an on-site or remote number that reached another modem and exchange data.

The "second-generation" PBXs were introduced in the middle 1970s. These systems use electronic rather than electromagnetic technology and the internal switching is digital. Such a system is referred to as digital PBX, or computerized branch exchange (CBX). These systems were designed primarily to handle analog voice traffic, with the codec function built into the switch so that digital switching could be used internally. The systems were also capable of handling digital data connections without the need of a modem.

The "third-generation" systems are touted as "integrated voice/data" systems, although the differences between third generation and upgraded second generation are rather blurred. Perhaps a better term is "improved digital PBX." Some of the characteristics of these systems that differ from those of earlier systems include:

- *The use of digital phones:* This permits integrated voice/data workstations.
- *Distributed architecture:* Multiple switches in a hierarchical or meshed configuration with distributed intelligence provides enhanced reliability.
- *Nonblocking configuration:* Typically, dedicated port assignments are used for all attached phones and devices.

As new features and technologies are employed, incremental improvements make difficult the continuing classification of PBXs into generations. Nevertheless, it is worth noting recent advances in PBX products that, together, might be considered to constitute a fourth generation [JEWE85], [COOV85]:

- *Integrated LAN link:* This capability provides a direct high-speed link to a local area network. This allows an optimum distribution of lower-speed devices (terminals) on the PBX and higher-speed devices (computers) on the LAN in a fashion that is fully transparent to the user.
- *Dynamic bandwidth allocation:* Typically, a PBX offers one or only a small number of different data rate services. The increased sophistication of capacity

allocation within the PBX allows it to offer virtually any data rate to an attached device. This allows the system to grow as user requirements grow. For example, full-motion color video at 448 kbps or advanced codecs at 32 kbps could be accommodated.

* *Integrated packet channel:* This allows the PBX to provide access to an X.25 packet-switched network.

It is worthwhile to summarize the main reasons why the evolution described above has taken place. To the untrained eye, analog and digital PBXs would seem to offer about the same level of convenience. The analog PBX can handle telephone sets directly and uses modems to accommodate digital data devices; the digital PBX can handle digital data devices directly and uses codecs to accommodate telephone sets. Some of the advantages of the digital approach are:

* *Digital technology:* By handling all internal signals digitally, the digital PBX can take advantage of low-cost LSI and VLSI components. Digital technology also lends itself more readily to software and firmware control.
* *Time-division multiplexing:* Digital signals lend themselves readily to TDM techniques, which provide efficient use of internal data paths, access to public TDM carriers, and TDM switching techniques, which are more cost effective than older, crossbar techniques.
* *Digital control signals:* Control signals are inherently digital and can easily be integrated into a digital transmission path via TDM. The signaling equipment is independent of the transmission medium.
* *Encryption:* This is more easily accommodated with digital signals.

Telephone Call Processing Requirements

The characteristic that distinguishes the digital PBX from a digital data switch is its ability to handle telephone connections. Freeman [FREE89] lists eight functions required for telephone call processing:

* Interconnection.
* Control.
* Attending.
* Busy testing.
* Alerting.
* Information receiving.
* Information transmitting.
* Supervisory.

The interconnection function encompasses three contingencies. The first contingency is a call originated by a station bound for another station on the digital PBX. The switching technologies that we have discussed are used in this context. The second contingency is a call originated by a digital PBX station bound for an external recipient. For this, the PBX must not only have access to an external trunk, but must perform internal switching to route the call from the user station to the trunk interface. The PBX also performs a line to trunk concentration function to avoid the expense of one external line per station. The third contingency is a call originated externally bound for a PBX station. Referred to as *direct inward dialing*, this allows an external caller to use the unique phone number of a PBX station to establish a call without going through an operator. This requires trunk-to-line expansion plus internal switching.

The control function includes, of course, the logic for setting up and tearing down a connection path. In addition, the control function serves to activate and control all other functions and to provide various management and utility services, such as logging, accounting, and configuration control.

The PBX must recognize a request for a connection; this is the attending function. The PBX then determines if the called party is available (busy testing) and, if so, alerts that party (alerting). The process of setting up the connection involves an exchange of information between the PBX and the called and calling parties.

Finally, a supervisory function is needed to determine when a call is completed and the connection may be released, freeing the switching capacity and the two parties for future connections.

Let us look more closely at the sequence of events required to complete a call successfully. First, consider an internal call from extension 226 to extension 280. The following steps occur:

1. 226 goes off-hook (picks up the receiver). The control unit recognizes this condition.
2. The control unit finds an available digit receiver and sets up a circuit from 226 to the digit receiver. The control unit also sets up a circuit from a dial-tone generator to 226.
3. When the first digit is dialed, the dial-tone connection is released. The digit receiver accumulates dialed digits (280).
4. After the last digit is dialed, the connection to the digit receiver is released. The control unit examines the number for legitimacy. If it is not, the caller is informed by some means, such as connection to a rapid busy signal generator. Otherwise, the control unit then determines if 280 is busy. If so, 226 is connected to a busy-signal generator.
5. If 280 is free, the control unit sets up a connection between 226 and a ring-back-tone generator and a connection between 280 and a ringer. A connection path between 226 and 280 is reserved.
6. When 280 answers by going off-hook, the ringing and ring-back connections are dropped and a connection is set up between 226 and 280.
7. When either 280 and 226 goes on-hook, the connection between them is dropped.

For outgoing calls, the following steps are required.

1–3. As above. In this case the caller will be dialing an access code number (e.g., the single digit 9) to request access to an outgoing trunk.
4. The control unit releases the connection to the digit receiver and finds a free trunk group and sends out an off-hook signal.
5. When a dial tone is returned from the central office, the control unit repeats steps 2 and 3.
6. The control unit releases the connection to the digit receiver and sends the number out to the trunk and makes a connection from the caller to the trunk.
7. When either the caller or the trunk signals on-hook, the connection between them is dropped.

There are variations on the foregoing sequence. For example, if the PBX performs least-cost routing, it will wait until the number is dialed and then select the appropriate trunk.

Finally, incoming calls, when direct inward dialing is supported, proceed as follows.

1. The control unit detects a trunk seizure signal from the central office, sets up a path from the trunk to a digit receiver, and sends a start-dialing signal out on that trunk.
2. The control unit releases the receiver path and examines the dialed number and checks the called station for busy, in which case a busy signal is returned.
3. If the called number is free, the control unit sets up a ringing connection to the called number and a ring-back connection to the trunk. It monitors the called station for answer and the trunk for abandon.
4. When the called station goes off-hook, the ringing and ring-back connections are dropped and a connection is set up between the trunk and the called station.
5. When either the trunk or called station signals on-hook, the connection between them is dropped.

Data Switching Requirements

The data switching requirements for a digital PBX are the same as those for a digital data switch. Typically, a terminal user will be requesting connection to a computer port. The same issues of speed, asynchronous/synchronous, and calling technique arise.

There are several new wrinkles. The PBX may support a voice/data workstation with one twisted pair for the phone and two pairs for the terminal. In such arrangements, the destination port may be selected from the phone rather than the terminal or a keypad.

The PBX has the advantage of direct connect to outgoing telephone lines. The terminal user who wishes to access an external computer need not have a telephone and a modem; the PBX can provide the link-up service. Typically, the connection is to an outgoing analog voice line. To provide the proper service, the PBX maintains a pool of modems that can be used by any data device to communicate over the external lines.

The exact implementation of the modem pool depends on the architecture of the PBX, but some strange contortions may be required. Consider the case of a PBX whose switching capability consists of a TDM bus switch. Figure 8-20 illustrates this. A device wishing to communicate outside will be connected to an available modem in the pool. The modem produces analog signals which must be switched to an outgoing trunk. But the PBX switches only digital signals! Therefore, the modem output is routed to a codec, which digitizes the data and puts them back onto the TDM bus. They are then routed to a trunk interface, where the signal is converted back to analog and sent on its way.

An important feature of a PBX is the internal integration of data and digitized voice. The same switching mechanism is used for both. It is therefore easier if both conform to common slot size and timing conventions. This is a consideration not faced by the digital switch designer.

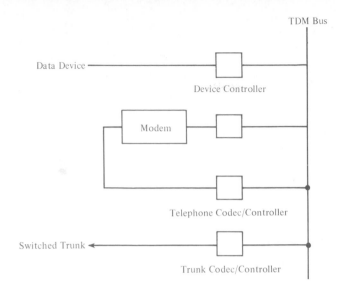

FIGURE 8-20.   Use of a modem in a digital PBX.

Digital PBX Architecture

A variety of architectures have been developed by digital PBX manufacturers. Since these are proprietary, the details are not generally known in most cases. In this section we attempt to present the general architectural features common to all PBX systems.

Digital PBX Components.   Figure 8-21 presents a generic PBX architecture. You should find it quite similar to the data switching architecture that we have discussed. Indeed, since the requirements for the PBX are a superset of those for the data switch, a similar architecture is not surprising.

As always, the heart of the system is some kind of digital switching network. The switch is responsible for the manipulation and switching of time multiplexed digital signal streams, using the techniques described in Section 8-2. The digital switching network consists of some number of space and time switching stages. Many of the PBXs are not sufficiently large, in terms of lines or capacity, to require complex switching networks. Indeed, some have no network as such, but simply use a TDM bus switch.

Attached to the switch are a set of interface units, which provide access to/from the outside world. Typically, an interface unit will perform a synchronous time-division multiplexing function in order to accommodate multiple incoming lines. On the other side, the unit requires two lines into the switch for full duplex operation.

It is important to understand that the interface unit is performing synchronous and not statistical TDM, even though connections are dynamically changing. On the input side, the unit performs a multiplex operation. Each incoming line is sampled at a specified rate. For n incoming lines each of data rate x, the unit must achieve an input rate of nx. The incoming data are buffered and organized into

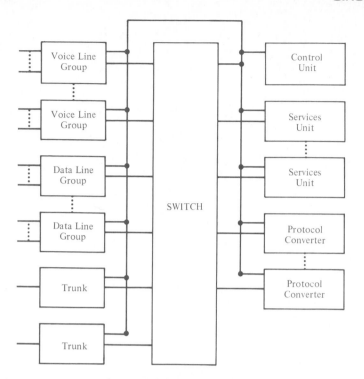

FIGURE 8-21.   Generic digital PBX architecture.

chunks of time-slot size. Then, according to the timing dictated by the control unit, individual chunks are sent out into the switch at the internal PBX data rate, which may be in the range 50 to 100 Mbps. In a nonblocking switch, n time slots are dedicated to the interface unit for transmission, whether or not they are used. In a blocking switch, time slots are assigned for the duration of a connection. In either case, the time-slot assignment is fixed for the duration of the connection, and synchronous TDM techniques may be used.

On the output side, the interface unit accepts data from the switch during designated time slots. In a nonblocking switch these may be dedicated (requiring more than a simple TDM bus switch), but are in any case fixed for the duration of the connection. Incoming data are demultiplexed, buffered, and presented to the appropriate output port at its data rate.

Several types of interface unit are used. A data line group unit handles data devices, providing the functions described in Section 8-3. An analog voice line group handles voice input/output over a number of twisted-pair phone lines. The interface unit must include codecs for digital-to-analog (input) and analog-to-digital (output) conversion. A separate type of unit may be used for integrated digital voice/data workstation, which present digitized voice at 64 kbps and data at the same or a lower rate. The range of lines accommodated by interface units is typically 8 to 24.

In addition to multiplexing interface units that accommodate multiple lines, trunk interface units are used to connect to off-site locations. These may be analog voice trunks or digital trunks, which may carry either data or PCM voice. Whereas a line interface unit must multiplex incoming lines to place on the switch, and de-

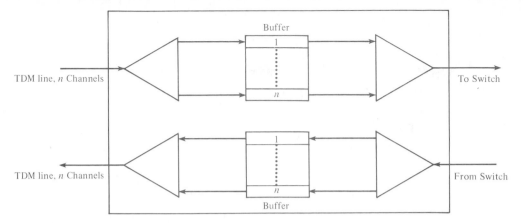

FIGURE 8-22.   Operation of trunk interface unit.

multiplex switch traffic to send to the lines, the trunk unit may have to demultiplex and multiplex in both directions (see Figure 8-22). Consider an incoming digital line with n channels of time-multiplexed data (the argument is the same for an analog trunk, which presents n channels of frequency-multiplexed voice). These data must be demultiplexed and stored in a buffer of length n units. Individual units of the buffer are then transmitted out to the switch at the designated time slots. Question: Why not pass the TDM stream directly from input to the bus, filling n contiguous time slots? Actually, in a nonblocking dedicated port system, this is possible. But for a system with dynamic time-slot assignment, the incoming data must be buffered and sent out on time slots that vary as connections are made and broken.

The other boxes in Figure 8-21 can be explained briefly. The control unit operates the digital switch and exchanges control signals with attached devices. For this purpose, a separate bus or other data path may be used or the control signals may propagate through the switch itself. As part of this or a separate unit, network administration and control functions are implemented. Service units would include such things as tone and busy-signal generators and dialed-digit registers. Some PBX systems provide protocol convertors for connecting dissimilar lines. A connection is made from each line to the protocol convertor.

It should be noted that this generic architecture lends itself to a high degree of reliability. The failure of any interface unit means the loss of only a small number of lines. Key elements such as the control unit can be made redundant.

Distributed Architecture.   For reasons of efficiency and reliability, many PBX manufacturers offer distributed architectures for their larger systems. The PBX is organized into a central switch and one or more distributed modules, with twisted pair, coaxial cable, or fiber optic cable between the central switch and the modules, in a two-level hierarchical star topology.

The distributed modules off-load at least some of the central-switch processor's real-time work load (such as off-hook detection). The degree to which control intelligence is off-loaded varies. At one extreme, the modules may be replicas of the central switch, in which case they function almost autonomously with the exception of certain overall management and accounting functions. At the other extreme, the modules are as limited as possible.

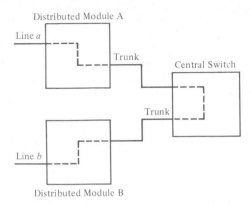

FIGURE 8-23.   **Circuit establishment in a distributed digital PBX.**

A distributed architecture means that it will often be necessary to concatenate several connections to achieve a connection between two devices. Consider Figure 8-23. A connection is desired between lines a and b. In module A, a connection is established between line a and one channel on a TDM trunk to the central switch. In the central switch, that channel is connected to a channel on a TDM trunk to module B. In module B, that channel is connected to line b.

There are several advantages to a distributed architecture:

- It permits growth beyond the practical size of a single digital switch.
- It provides better performance by off-loading of functions.
- It provides higher reliability: the loss of a single module need not disable the entire system.
- It reduces twisted-pair wiring distances.

8-5

ROUTING

In a large circuit-switched network, such as the AT&T long-distance telephone network, many of the circuit connections will require a path through more than one switch. When a call is placed, the network must devise a route through the network from calling subscriber to called subscriber that passes through some number of switches and trunks. There are two main requirements for the network's architecture that bear on the routing strategy: efficiency and resilience. First, it is desirable to minimize the amount of equipment (switches and trunks) in the network, subject to the ability to handle the expected load. The load requirement is usually expressed in terms of a *busy hour traffic load*. This is simply the average load expected over the course of the busiest hour of use during the course of a day. From a functional point of view, it is necessary to handle that amount of load. From a cost point of view, we would like to handle that load with minimum equipment. However, there is another requirement, namely resilience. Although the network may be sized for the busy hour load, it is possible for the traffic to temporarily surge above that level (e.g., during a major storm). It will also be the case that, from time to time, switches and trunks will fail and be temporarily unavailable (unfortunately, maybe during the same storm). We would like the network to provide a reasonable level of service under such conditions.

In the past, the two requirements of efficiency and resilience have been competing. That is, there has been a trade-off between the two. Network efficiency was achieved by minimizing switching and transmission capacity, whereas resilience was achieved by increasing that capacity, in the form of high inter-exchange connectivity. This situation is rapidly changing with the availability of high-bandwidth fiber trunks and high-capacity digital switches capable of handling tens of thousands of trunks. As we will see, all of this is tied to the routing strategy. Traditional routing strategies that have been common in telephone networks are unable to adapt to major network perturbations. Newer, dynamic routing strategies can take advantage of evolving technology to simultaneously improve both network efficiency and network resilience [HURL87].

These concepts are best explained with an example. In the remainder of this section, we look at the evolution of the AT&T network.

Architecture of a Public Telephone Network

The public telecommunications network in the United States consists primarily of the local service offered by the Bell Operating Companies (BOCs) that used to be part of AT&T and the long-distance service still offered by AT&T. There are, of course, a growing number of other providers, particularly of long-distance service. In this section, we look at the architecture of the BOC/AT&T network, which still handles the bulk of telephone traffic in the U.S. Although both the routing and the architecture of this network have and are evolving since divestiture, the overall architecture can still be described as follows.

As with any network, the public telephone network can be described using four generic architectural components:

- *Stations:* generally referred to as *subscribers,* these are the devices that attach to the network.
- *Interfaces:* the interface beween the stations and the network, referred to in the phone system as the *local loop.*
- *Nodes:* the *switching centers* in the network.
- *Links:* the branches between nodes, referred to as *trunks.*

Most of the *subscribers* on the network are telephones. The telephone contains a transmitter and receiver for converting back and forth between analog voice (sound waves) and analog (voice frequency) electrical signals. Some subscribers that transmit digital signals are being incorporated into the network.

The *local loop* is a pair of wires, generally twisted pair, that connects a subscriber to one of the nodes in the network. It is a direct-current (dc) loop that supplies a metallic path for the following [FREE89]:

- Voltage potential for the telephone transmitter. This is supplied over the line from the switching center and is used to convert acoustic energy into electric energy.
- An ac ringing voltage for the bell on the telephone instrument supplied from the switching center.
- Current to flow through the loop when the telephone instrument is taken out of its cradle (off hook), telling the service switch that it requires access.

- Signals generated by the telephone dial or keypad used to communicate to the switch the number of the called subscriber.

The local loop generally covers a distance of a few kilometers to a few tens of kilometers at most.

Each subscriber connects via local loop to a *switching center,* known as an end office. Typically, an end office will support many thousands of subscribers in a localized area. There are over 19,000 end offices in the United States, so it is clearly impractical for each end office to have a direct link to each of the other end offices; this would require on the order of 2×10^8 links. Rather, intermediate switching nodes are used. The function of these intermediate nodes and the manner in which they are interconnected determine the routing mechanism that is used.

The switching centers are linked together by *trunks*. These trunks are designed to carry multiple voice-frequency circuits using either FDM or synchronous TDM. There were referred to as carrier systems in Chapter 6, where they are described.

Alternate Hierarchical Routing

Until recently, the organization of the end offices into a network has involved the use of a hierarchical or tree structure (Figure 8-24), consisting of five classes of switching centers or nodes [REY83]:

- *Class 1:* regional center
- *Class 2:* sectional center
- *Class 3:* primary center
- *Class 4:* toll center
- *Class 5:* end office

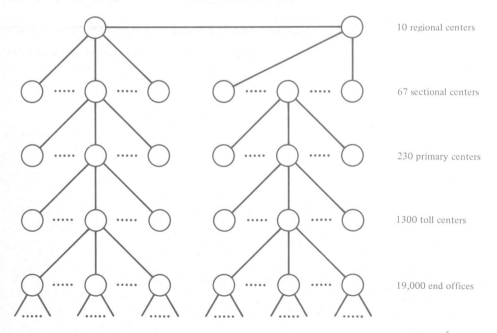

10 regional centers

67 sectional centers

230 primary centers

1300 toll centers

19,000 end offices

$> 150 \times 10^6$ subscribers

FIGURE 8-24.   U.S. public circuit-switched network organization.

Subscribers connect directly to an end office, which must perform the same functions listed earlier for a one-node network. The remaining centers simply serve the function of concentrating traffic so as to reduce transmission facility equipment. This distinction is shown in Figure 8-23. To connect two subscribers attached to the same end office, a circuit is set up between them in the same fashion as described before. If two subscribers connect to different end offices, a circuit between them consists of a concatenation of circuits through one or more intermediate offices. In the figure, a connection is established between lines *a* and *b* by simply setting up the connection through the end office. The connection between *c* and *d* is more complex In *c*'s end office, a connection is established between line *c* and one channel on a TDM trunk to the intermediate switch. In the intermediate switch, that channel is connected to a channel on a TDM trunk to *d*'s end office. In that end office, the channel is connected to line *d*.

The hierarchical structure depicted in Figure 8-24 is actually a set of 10 trees, each rooted in a regional center. The 10 regional centers are meshed together (45 full-duplex links) to provide full connectivity. In the early days of the telephone network, this was the extent of the architecture, and a very simple form or routing, known as *direct routing,* was used. With direct routing, connection establishment follows these rules:

1. If both subscribers attach to the same end office, that end office makes the connection.
2. If the two subscribers attach to different end offices that are attached to the same toll center, a connection is established between the end offices via that toll center.

And so on. The search continues up the hierarchy until a common node is reached. If the two subscribers are under the aegis of different regional centers, the circuit will involve a trunk between regional centers, for a total of nine trunks in the path between the two subscribers.

This architecture and routing strategy has several drawbacks. First, during peak hours, a tremendous amount of traffic must be carried at the upper levels of the hierarchy; accordingly, the facilities at these levels will be inefficiently used most of the time. Second, the loss or saturation of a single switching center decouples the network into isolated subnetworks. Finally, signal quality degrades as the number of switches and trunks increases (for analog transmission).

To compensate for these problems, two additional elements are added to the basic architecture. In addition to the five classes of switching centers, the network is augmented with additional switching nodes called *tandem switches*. These are used to interconnect adjacent end offices. Also, a large number of *high-usage trunks* are used for direct connection between switching centers with high volumes of internode traffic.

With these additions, an *alternate hierarchical routing* algorithm can be used. Traffic is always routed through the lowest available level of the network. Figure 8-25 shows the basic order of selection for alternate routes. The high-usage trunks are depicted as dashed lines, and the backbone hierarchical network is shown with solid lines. With alternate hierarchical routing, connection establishment is as follows. The basic rule is to complete the connection at the lowest possible level of the hierarchy, thus using the fewest trunks in tandem. In the figure, a call placed from telephone 1 to telephone 2 is first handled by the end office of telephone 1. Since telephone 2 is not served by the same end office and is not reachable via a

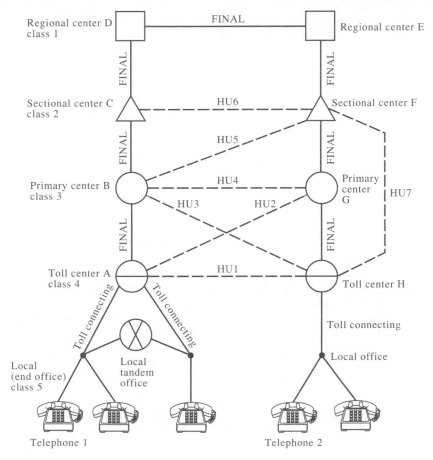

FIGURE 8-25. Alternate hierarchical routing [REY83].

tandem office, the call is routed to toll center A. Toll center A searches for an available high-usage (HU) trunk, first in the HU1 group and then in the HU2 group. If all trunks in these groups are busy, the call overflows to the final trunk group, which moves the call up one level in the hierarchy to primary center B. The primary center again searches for an available HU trunk in the order indicated. This process is dynamic and depends on the availability of high-usage trunks at the time the call is placed. Thus calls between two subscribers might follow different routes at different times. The routing algorithm is driven by the seven- or ten-digit telephone number, which uniquely identifies a subscriber and the centers in its direct hierarchy [FREE89, REY83].

Beginning in the 1940s, when it became possible for an exchange to choose a route based on trunk loading status, alternate hierarchical routing was gradually introduced until it reached the level of complexity just described. The high-usage trunks are sized based on cost in the following way. The requirement to be satisfied is that the probability of blocking during the average busy hour on any of the final paths (see Figure 8-25) is no more than 0.01 [REY83]. For any given high-usage trunk, the capacity of that trunk is optimized by increasing its capacity until the incremental cost of adding further capacity on the high usage trunk would exceed

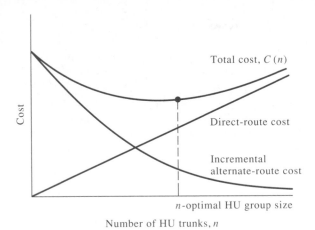

Cost

Total cost, $C(n)$

Direct-route cost

Incremental
alternate-route cost

n-optimal HU group size

Number of HU trunks, n

FIGURE 8-26. Cost function for alternate routing [REY83].

the cost of carrying the incremental traffic on the final route. Figure 8-26 suggests the analysis involved. For a particular high-usage trunk, the cost of that trunk is a linearly-increasing function of capacity. As the capacity of the high-usage trunk increases, the capacity of the final trunks needed to guarantee the 0.01 blocking measure decreases and accordingly the cost of the final trunks decrease. As shown, there is a unique minimum which dictates the size of the high-usage trunk.

The alternate hierarchical routing approach provided significant gains in efficiency over the direct routing approach. More of the traffic is carried at lower levels of the hierarchy. Thus the average length of a connection (number of exchanges and trunks) is decreased for a given level of traffic. Furthermore, the way in which high-usage capacity is determined means that all trunk groups except the final ones are virtually fully loaded.

There are, however, remaining limitations. These limitations are in both the area of efficiency and of resilience. The single measure of the average busy hour is not powerful enough to permit a design that is optimum from the point of view of efficiency. For example, the busy hours for east/west traffic and south/north traffic do not coincide. It is difficult to analyze the effects of this, which leads to oversizing. In terms of resilience, the shortcoming of alternate hierarchical routing is that it is rigid, and assumes no equipment or trunk failure. A major failure will cause a major local congestion near the site of the failure. Over time, various automatic and manual network control procedures have been added to the network, but the basic problem of a rigid hierarchical structure remained. What is required is a more flexible scheme that allows more dynamic routing with a greater ability to adapt to changing conditions in the network. To achieve this, it is necessary to move away from a hierarchical architecture.

Dynamic Nonhierarchical Routing

A nonhierarchical architecture is one in which the circuit-switching nodes have a peer relationship with each other. All nodes are capable of performing the same functions. In such an architecture routing is both more complex and more flexible. It is more complex because the architecture does not provide a ''natural'' path or set of paths based on hierarchical structure. But it is also more flexible since more alternative routes are available.

In general terms, the objective for moving from a hierarchical to a nonhierarchical structure is to exploit both regular (time of day, seasonal) and random traffic variations in choosing a route to improve efficiency and resiliency. Routes are chosen dynamically. With a peer network with a relatively large number of interconnections, very effective load sharing is possible. For example, if a direct path between two switches is fully loaded, blocking new calls, alternate paths may be taken for additional calls, reducing the blocking probability. On the other hand, at times when the load on this direct path is lighter, it may be used as an alternate path or part of an alternate path for other calls to help reduce blocking. Therefore, calls with different source/destination pairs share a larger pool of transmission and switching capacity for connection.

In order to employ dynamic routing of a peer architecture, three capabilities must be added to the network [HURL87]:

- Switches must be enhanced to include the capability to make dynamic routing decisions and to be able to communicate traffic status information to other parts of the network.
- One or more network management centers are needed to determine routes and disseminate routing information.
- A control signaling technique, or protocol, is needed to enable switches to pass traffic status information to the network management centers and for the centers to return routing information to the switches.

The details of the routing capability are, of course, dependent on the architecture. The capability developed by AT&T, referred to as dynamic nonhierarchical routing (DNHR), is an evolution of the existing network. AT&T began the change-over to this capability in 1984, and has substantially completed the initial effort. With DNHR, the network contains a large number (about 100) of regional centers These centers are peer to each other, and make up the DNHR part of the total network. Any call that makes use of the DNHR switches will pass through no more than three switches and two trunks. Routing is based on known historical traffic patterns and on current traffic status.

Figure 8-27 illustrates the DNHR scheme [GLEN86]. There are two or three switches involved in each route. The originating switch is responsible for making the routing decision. The terminating switch is the intended destination. Finally, in some cases, there is an intermediate switch that is part of the route. Each switch, for each destination, is given a set of preplanned routes in order of preference. Usually, the first preference is a direct trunk connection from the originating switch to the terminating switch. These routing sequences reflect the optimal routes for a particular call, based on extensive operational measurement data which is periodically provided by each participating switch to the central network planning system. To take advantage of the differing traffic patterns in different time zones and at different times of day, the day is divided into ten time periods, with a different set of preplanned routes for each time period. In addition to the preplanned routes, additional overflow paths may be assigned. These paths are assigned by a network management center, but the ability to use them depends on the current load. For example, if utilization on a given trunk group is high, no overflow traffic will be allowed on that trunk so that its limited remaining capacity stays available for preplanned routes.

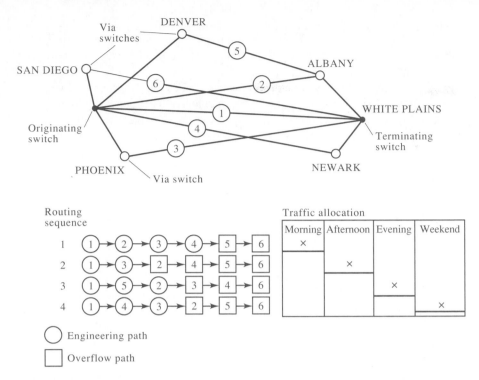

FIGURE 8-27. DNHR routing.

In Figure 8-27, the originating switch has six possible routes to the terminating switch. The direct route (1) will always be tried first. If this trunk is unavailable (busy or out of service), the other routes will be tried in a particular order depending on the time of day. For example, during the morning, route (2) is tried next. If the intermediate switch on a route is unable to complete a requested call, it will send a control message back to the originating switch so that it may try another route. After all preplanned routes have been tried, additional routes (overflow routes) which are not engineered to handle the specific origination-termination traffic may be used if sufficient capacity is available. The distinction between the preplanned and overflow routes is that the capacity of the network (switch and trunk size) is engineered to handle the preplanned traffic at a particular probability of blocking (1 percent).

Control signaling is used to allow the switches to provide traffic information to a network management center. If the network management center determines that an overflow condition exists, it may dynamically change the route sets of any of the switches. The routing updates are communicated back to the switches by control signals.

Below the DNHR network, the remainder of the network is still hierarchical, much as in Figure 8-24. Calls within a particular hierarchy are still handled by alternate hierarchical routing. Each hierarchy attaches to a single regional switch, by which it enters the DNHR network to reach a switch in another hierarchy. This somewhat awkward arrangement is dictated by the need to migrate gradually and with minimum cost and network impact from a hierarchical to a nonhierarchical structure.

The DNHR approach does provide for increased efficiency and resiliency. Because there is more potential for sharing temporarily unused resources in the DNHR network, and because it lends itself to more elaborate, time-dependent routing, fewer trunks are required in the DNHR network than in an equivalent hierarchical network. Because the interconnection structure and routing alternatives are richer, DNHR is more resilient than an equivalent nonhierarchical network. As we move toward ISDN, which will place a greatly increased burden on public circuit-switched networks, the nonhierarchical approach will become more prevalent.

8-6

CONTROL SIGNALING

In a circuit-switched network, control signals are the means by which the network is managed and by which calls are established, maintained, and terminated. Both call management and overall network management require that information be exchanged between subscriber and switch, among switches, and between switch and network management center. For a large public telecommunications network, a relatively complex control signaling scheme is required. In this section, we provide a brief overview of control signal functionality and then look at the technique that is the basis of modern integrated digital networks, common channel signaling.

Signaling Functions

Control signals are necessary for the operation of a circuit-switched network, and involve every aspect of network behavior, including both network services visible to the subscriber and internal mechanisms. As networks become more complex, the number of functions performed by control signaling necessarily grows. The following functions are among the most important:

1. Audible communication with the subscriber, including dial tone, ringing tone, busy signal, and so on.
2. Transmission of the number dialed to switching offices that will attempt to complete a connection.
3. Transmission of information between switches indicating that a call cannot be completed.
4. Transmission of information between switches indicating that a call has ended and that the path can be disconnected.
5. A signal to make a telephone ring.
6. Transmission of information used for billing purposes.
7. Transmission of information giving the status of equipment or trunks in the network. This information may be used for routing and maintenance purposes.
8. Transmission of information used in diagnosing and isolating system failures.
9. Control of special equipment such as satellite channel equipment.

An example of the use of control signaling is shown in Figure 8-28 [REY83], which illustrates a typical telephone connection sequence from one line to another

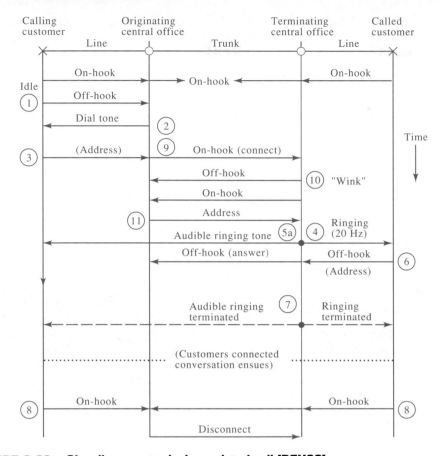

FIGURE 8-28. Signaling on a typical completed call [REY83].

in the same central office. The steps involved appear as circled numbers in the figure:

1. Prior to the call, both telephones are not in use (on-hook). The call begins when one subscriber lifts the receiver (off-hook), which is automatically signaled to switch.
2. The switch responds with an audible dial tone, signaling the subscriber that the number may be dialed.
3. The caller dials the number, which is communicated as a destination address to the switch.
4. If the called subscriber is not busy, the switch alerts the subscriber to an incoming call by sending a ringing signal, which causes the telephone to ring.
5. Feedback is provided to the calling subscriber by the switch:
   a. If the called subscriber is not busy, the switch returns an audible ringing tone to the caller while the ringing signal is being sent to the called subscriber.
   b. If the called subscriber is busy, the switch sends an audible busy signal to the caller (not shown in the figure).

    c. If the call cannot be completed through the switch, the switch sends an audible ''reorder'' message to the caller (not shown in the figure).

6. The called party accepts the call by lifting the receiver (off-hook), which is automatically signaled to the switch.

7. The switch terminates the ringing signal and the audible ringing tone, and establishes a connection between the two subscribers.

8. The connection is released when either subscriber hangs up.

When the called subscriber is attached to a different switch than the calling subscriber, the following switch-to-switch trunk signaling functions are required:

9. The originating switch seizes an idle interswitch trunk, sends an off-hook indication on the trunk, and requests a digit register at the far end, so that the address may be communicated.

10. The terminating switch sends an off-hook followed by an on-hook signal, known as a ''wink.'' This indicates a register-ready status.

11. The originating switch sends the address digits to the terminating switch.

This example gives some idea of the functions that are performed using control signals. The functions performed by control signals can be roughly grouped into the category of supervisory, address, call information, and network management.

The term *supervisory* is generally used to refer to control functions that have a binary character (true/false; on/off), such as request for service, answer, alerting, and return to idle. They deal with the availability of the called subscriber and of the needed network resources. Supervisory control signals are used to determine if a needed resource is available and, if so, to seize it. They are also used to communicate the status of requested resources.

Address signals identify a subscriber. Initially, an address signal is generated by a calling subscriber when dialing a telephone number. The resulting address may be propagated through the network to support the routing function and to locate and ring the called subscriber's phone.

The term *call information* refers to those signals that provide information to the subscriber about the status of a call. This is in contrast to internal control signals between switches used in call establishment and termination. Such internal signals are analog or digital electrical messages. In contrast, call information signals are audible tones that can be heard by the caller or an operator with the proper phone set.

Supervisory, address, and call information control signals are directly involved in the establishment and termination of a call. In contrast, *network management* signals are used for the maintenance, troubleshooting, and overall operation of the network. Such signals may be in the form of messages, such as a list of preplanned routes being sent to a station to update its routing tables. These signals cover a broad scope and it is this category that will expand most with the increasing complexity of switched networks.

Common Channel Signaling

Traditional control signaling in circuit-switched networks has been on a per-trunk or inchannel basis. With *inchannel signaling,* the same channel is used to carry control signals as is used to carry the call to which the control signals relate. Such signaling begins at the originating subscriber and follows the same path as the call itself. This has the merit that no additional transmission facilities are needed for signaling; the facilities for voice trnsmission are shared with control signaling.

Two forms of inchannel signaling are in use: inband and out-of-band. *Inband signaling* uses not only the same physical path as the call it serves, it also uses the same frequency band as the voice signals that are carried. This form of signaling has several advantages. Because the control signals have the same electromagnetic properties as the voice signals, they can go anywhere that the voice signals go. Thus there are no limits on the use of inband signaling anywhere in the network, including places where analog-to-digital or digital-to-analog conversion takes place. In addition, it is impossible to set up a call on a faulty speech path, since the control signals that are used to set up that path would have to follow the same path.

Out-of-band signaling takes advantage of the fact that voice signals do not use the full 4 kHz bandwidth allotted to them. A separate narrow signaling band, within the 4 kHz, is used to send control signals. The major advantage of this approach is that the control signals can be sent whether or not voice signals are on the line, thus allowing continuous supervision and control of a call. However, an out-of-band scheme needs extra electronics to handle the signaling band, and the signaling rates are slower because the signal has been confined to a narrow bandwidth.

As public telecommunications networks become more complex and provide a richer set of services, the drawbacks of inchannel signaling become more apparent. The information transfer rate is quite limited with inchannel signaling. With inband signals, the voice channel being used is only available for control signals when there are no voice signals on the circuit. With out-of-band signals, a very narrow bandwidth is available. With such limits, it is difficult to accommodate, in a timely fashion, any but the simplest form of control messages. However, to take advantage of the potential services and to cope with the increasing complexity of evolving network technology, a richer and more powerful control signal repertoire is needed.

A second drawback of inchannel signaling is the amount of delay from the time a subscriber enters an address (dials a number) and the connection is established. The requirement to reduce this delay is becoming more important as the network is used in new ways. For example, computer-controlled calls, such as with transaction processing, use relatively short messages; therefore, the call setup time represents an appreciable part of the total transaction time.

Both of these problems can be addressed with *common channel signaling,* in which control signals are carried over paths completely independent of the voice channels (Table 8-2). One independent control signal path can carry the signals for a number of subscriber channels, and hence is a common control channel for these subscriber channels.

The principle of common channel signaling is illustrated and contrasted with inchannel signaling in Figure 8-29. As can be seen, the signal path for common channel signaling is physically separate from the path for voice or other subscriber signals. The common channel can be configured with the bandwidth required to carry control signals for a rich variety of functions. Thus, both the signaling protocol and the network architecture to support that protocol are more complex than inchannel signaling. However, the continuing drop in computer hardware costs makes common channel signaling increasingly attractive. The control signals are messages that are passed between switches and between a switch and the network management center. Thus, the control signaling portion of the network is in effect a distributed computer network carrying short messages.

TABLE 8-2 **Signaling Techniques for Circuit-Switched Networks**

Technique	Description	Comment
Inchannel		
Inband	Transmit control signals in the same band of frequencies used by the voice signals.	The simplest technique. It is necessary for call information signals, and may be used for other control signals. Inband can be used over any type of line plant.
Out-of-band	Transmit control signals using the same facilities as the voice signal but a different part of the frequency band.	In contrast to inband, provides continuous supervision during the life of a connection.
Common Channel	Transmit control signals over signaling links that are dedicated to control signals and are common to a number of voice channels.	Reduces call setup time compared to inchannel methods. It is also more adaptable to evolving functional needs.

Two modes of operation are used in common channel signaling (Figure 8-30). In the *associated mode*, the common channel closely tracks along its entire length the interswitch trunk groups that are served between endpoints. The control signals

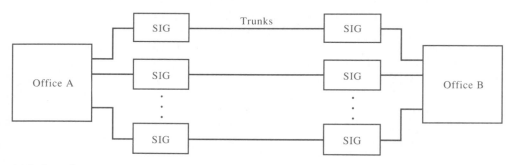

(a) Inchannel

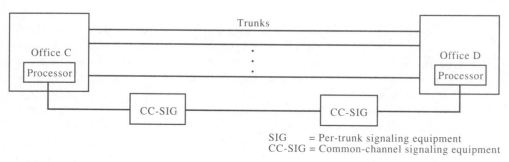

SIG   = Per-trunk signaling equipment
CC-SIG = Common-channel signaling equipment

(b) Common channel

FIGURE 8-29. **Inchannel and common channel signaling.**

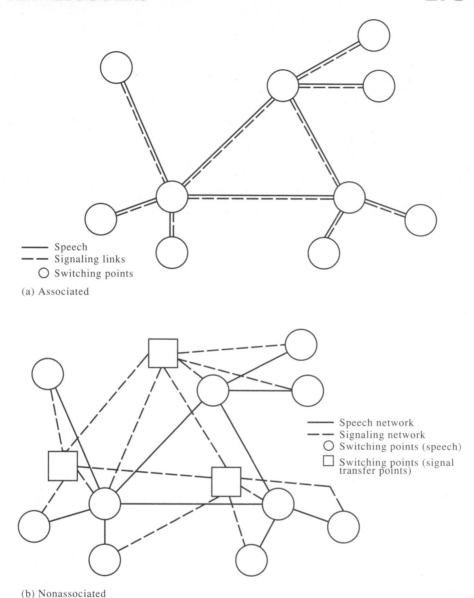

— Speech
– – Signaling links
○ Switching points

(a) Associated

— Speech network
– – Signaling network
○ Switching points (speech)
□ Switching points (signal transfer points)

(b) Nonassociated

FIGURE 8-30.   Common channel signaling modes.

are on different channels from the subscriber signals, and inside the switch, the control signals are routed directly to a control signal processor. A more complex, but more powerful, mode is the *nonassociated mode*. With this mode, the network is augmented by additional nodes, known as signal transfer points. There is now no close or simple assignment of control channels to trunk groups. In effect, there are now two separate networks, with links between them so that the control portion of the network can exercise control over the switching nodes that are servicing the subscriber calls. Network management is more easily exerted in the nonassociated mode since control channels can be assigned to tasks in a more flexible manner. The nonassociated mode is likely to be the mode used in ISDN (see Part IV).

With inchannel signaling, control signals from one switch are originated by a control processor and switched onto the outgoing channel. On the receiving end, the control signals must be switched from the voice channel into the control processor. With common channel signaling, the control signals are transferred directly from one control processor to another, without being tied to a voice signal. This is a simpler procedure, and one that is less susceptible to accidental or intentional interference between subscriber and control signals. This is one of the main motivations for common channel signaling. Another key motivation for common channel signaling is that call setup time is reduced. Consider the sequence of events for call setup with inchannel signaling when more than one switch is involved. A control signal will be sent from one switch to the next in the intended path. At each switch, the control signal cannot be transferred through the switch to the next leg of the route until the associated circuit is established through that switch. With common channel signaling, forwarding of control information can overlap the circuit-setup process.

With nonassociated signaling, a further advantage emerges: One or more central control points can be established. All control information can be routed to a network center where requests are processed and from which control signals are sent to switches that handle subscriber traffic. In this way, requests can be processed with a more global view of network conditions.

Of course, there are disadvantages to common channel signaling. These primarily have to do with the complexity of the technique. However, the dropping cost of digital hardware and the increasingly digital nature of telecommunication networks make common channel signaling the appropriate technology.

All of the discussion in this section has dealt with the use of common channel signaling inside the network, that is, to control switches. Even in a network that is completely controlled by common channel signaling, inchannel signaling is needed for at least some of the communication with the subscriber. For example, dial tone, ringback, and busy signals must be inchannel to reach the user. In general, the subscriber does not have access to the common channel signaling portion of the network and does not employ the common channel signaling protocol.

8-7

RECOMMENDED READING

As befits its age, circuit switching has inspired a voluminous literature. Two good books on the subject are [BELL82b] and [KEIS85]. The first of these is particularly lucid and comprehensive. Worthwhile accounts may also be found in [FREE89] and [DAVI73]. [BROO83] discusses alternative internal organizations for a switch.

[VONA80] describes and discusses port selection and port contention devices. [SCHO81] describes the switching statistical multiplexer. A general survey of digital data switching devices can be found in [KANE80a].

The architecture of a digital PBX is discussed in [KASS79] and [JUNK83]. Descriptive articles on digital PBX products can be found in [JOEL85] and [FREE85]. The subject of routing is covered in [HURL87] and [YUM87]. Discussion of control signaling can be found in [FREE89], [REY83], and [KEIS85].

8-8

PROBLEMS

8-1   Demonstrate why there is a high probability of blocking in a two-stage switch such as Figure 8-11.

8-2   What is the magnitude of delay through a TSI stage?

8-3   Assume that the velocity of propagation on a TDM bus is $0.7c$, its length is 10 m, and the data rate is 500 Mbps. How many bits should be transmitted in a time slot to achieve a bus efficiency of 99%?

8-4   Demonstrate that in a TSI data store, at most, only half of the memory is usefully occupied at any one time. Devise a means of reducing the TSI memory requirement while maintaining its nonblocking property.

8-5   Consider the use of a 500-ns memory in a TSI device. How many full-duplex voice channels can be supported, if the voice is encoded using PCM?

8-6   Determine the number of crosspoints and the total number of memory bits required for a TST switch defined as follows:

- Number of lines = 32.
- Single stage space switch.
- Number of channels per frame = 30.
- Time expansion = 2.

8-7   How many bits of memory are needed in a TSI unit for a 60-channel signal with nine bits per time slot?

8-8   Consider a 3-stage crossbar switch system with 1000 input and 1000 output lines. It is non-blocking. For an optimum design, what is the total number of crosspoints required? How many arrays are needed for each stage and how many input and output lines are there per stage?

8-9   Repeat Problem 8-8 using 2048 as the number of input and output lines.

8-10   Consider the configuration of Figure 8-6b. Suppose that the maximum length of the bus is 1 meter. What is the maximum delay that could occur end-to-end on the bus (assume electricity travels in a copper wire at a rate of 0.8 times the speed of light)?

8-11   For the system of Problem 8-8, how many switch points would be needed if a TDM bus were used?

8-12   Consider a simple non-blocking implementation of Figure 8-6c. Suppose that the bus is 1500 meters long and that 2048 bits of data are to be input in each time slot. The data rate of the bus is 100 Mbps. The maximum number of stations attached to the bus is limited so that a station is guaranteed a slot every 10 milliseconds. Assume that electricity travels in copper wire at 0.8 times the speed of light.

a. What is the guaranteed data rate for a station?

b. What is the maximum sustained data rate of the system?

c. What is the maximum number of stations that can be serviced by this system?

8-13   Consider a simple time-slot interchange switching system. Assume a memory of 50-nsec cycle time. The memory is organized into 16-bit words. Frames are 1024 bits. What is the maximum data rate per channel? What is the data rate of the trunk lines to and from the switch?

8-14   Section 8-4 contains the following sentence: ''The PBX may support a voice/data workstation with one twisted pair for the phone and two pairs for the terminal.'' Why is there one for the phone and two for the terminal? Is not the phone operating with communications both ways also?

8-15   Explain why it is necessary that the interface units for Figure 8-22 perform synchronous TDM rather than statistical TDM.

8-16   Is the ITT switch nonblocking?

8-17   Consider a simple telephone network consisting of two end offices and one toll center with a 1-MHz full-duplex trunk between each end office and the toll center. The average telephone is used to make four calls per 8-hour workday, with a mean call duration of six minutes. Ten percent of the calls are long distance. What is the maximum number of telephones an end office can support?

8-18   If one examines the rate structures of the long-distance telephone services, it would appear that distance, while important, is not the major factor in determining cost. Speculate on the reason for this.

8-19   In Figure 8-20, why is it not possible to route the digital data coming from the device directly to an outgoing trunk, where it will be converted to analog by the codec for transmission?

CHAPTER 9

Packet Switching

In Chapter 7, we introduced the concept of packet switching, and the subordinate concepts of datagrams and virtual circuits. The purpose of this chapter is to explore in more detail the mechanisms by which packet-switched networks provide datagram and virtual-circuit services. The key elements of a packet switched network are these:

- *Routing:* Since the source and destination station are not directly connected, the network must route each packet, from node to node, through the network.
- *Traffic control:* The amount of traffic entering and transiting the network must be regulated for efficient, stable, and fair performance.
- *Error control:* Inevitably, packets will be lost in the network. Some networks ignore this contingency; most take measures to at least partially alleviate the suffering of the attached stations.

The behavior of a packet-switched network is amazingly complex. In this chapter we do not attempt a definitive treatment. Rather the key features in each of the areas above are presented, and the discussion is supported by examples from specific systems currently in operation. Four systems will be repeatedly used throughout the chapter. A discussion of these is presented first.

Throughout this chapter, examples will be given of the operation of various algorithms. Figure 9-1 is a simple instance of a packet-switched network that will be used for many of these examples.

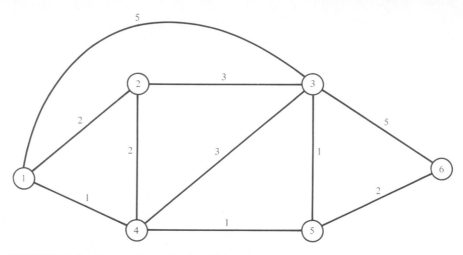

FIGURE 9-1.   Example packet-switched network.

EXAMPLE SYSTEMS

Perhaps the clearest way to present the concepts and techniques of packet switching is by example. In this section we present an overview of four quite different packet-switched systems. The two best-documented communications networks are ARPANET/DDN and TYMNET. In addition, we present two commercially available computer network packages: IBM's SNA and DEC's DNA. These are not pure communications networks, but they are the most widely used computer systems for constructing user-controlled packet-switched networks.

ARPANET/DDN

The ARPA computer network (ARPANET) began under the sponsorship of the Advanced Research Projects Agency (ARPA) to study and demonstrate computer resource sharing [ROBE70, ROBE74]. By 1975, this network had many operational users and was no longer an experimental network, so responsibility for its operation transferred to the Defense Communications Agency. Today ARPANET is an operational network of many nodes and host computers and supports a large number of DOD and non-DOD projects. ARPANET has recently been split into an R&D network, which retains the name ARPANET, and the Defense Data Network (DDN), using the same technology on both. The DDN is designed to meet DOD needs for both a secure command and control communications network and for ordinary unclassified communications [WALK82], [ELSA86].

TYMNET

TYMNET was originally developed to provide cost-effective connection of terminals to central time-sharing computers [TYME71]. Both access and internode speeds were rather limited. As the system grew, higher data rates were provided and the system evolved into TYMNET II [KOPF77]. TYMNET II, although still terminal-oriented, provides a general-purpose packet-switched service for terminal-host and host-host transfers.

SNA

Both ARPANET and TYMNET originally became operational in 1969. Both are, in our terminology, communication networks that are independent of the attached hosts. As the technology of packet switching evolved, computer vendors realized that they could provide not only the endpoint computer functions, but the switching functions as well. The era of computer vendor-based network architectures began with the announcement in 1974 by IBM of its systems network architecture (SNA).

SNA was developed by IBM to protect its customer base and allow its customers to take advantage of new IBM offerings. The problem was that there was a proliferation of communications protocols and user access methods on IBM machines. Customers developed complex applications and were unable to easily incorporate new computers into their operation. Many of the communications techniques were inefficient and a flourishing business in front-end processors developed among minicomputer and communications vendors. These factors led to the development of a network architecture that would provide efficient user access to a network of computers. We will return to SNA in the context of computer network architecture in Part III. For now, we are only concerned with its packet-switching capability.

DNA

In 1975, Digital Equipment Corporation (DEC) announced its digital network architecture (DNA), whose original goals were quite different from those of SNA. SNA was originally concerned with providing uniform, efficient access to host-centered terminal networks. As a minicomputer manufacturer, DEC was concerned with resource sharing in a distributed environment. Thus DNA from the beginning was intended to provide decentralized and distributed networking capability.

9-2

VIRTUAL CIRCUITS AND DATAGRAMS

External and Internal Operation

One of the most important characteristics of a packet-switched network is whether it uses datagrams or virtual circuits. Actually, there are two levels or dimensions of this characteristic, as illustrated in Figure 9-2. At the interface between station and network node, a network may provide either a virtual circuit or datagram service. With a virtual-circuit interface, the user performs a call request to set up a virtual circuit and uses sequence numbers to exercise flow control and error control. The network attempts to deliver the packets in sequence. With datagram service, the network only agrees to handle packets independently. Internally, the

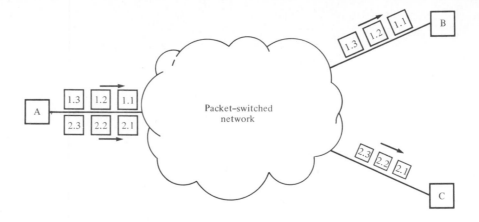

(a) External virtual circuit. A logical connection is set up between two stations.
    Packets are labeled with a virtual circuit number and a sequence number.
    Packets arrive in sequence.

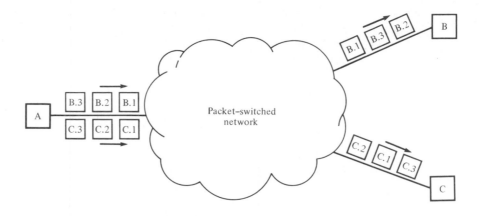

(b) External datagram. Each packet is transmitted independently. Packets are
    labeled with a destination address and may arrive out of sequence.

FIGURE 9-2.   External and internal virtual circuits and datagrams.

network may actually construct a dedicated path between endpoints (virtual circuit)
or not. These internal and external design decisions need not coincide:

- *External virtual circuit, internal virtual circuit:* When the user requests a
  virtual circuit, a dedicated route through the network is constructed. All packets will follow that same route.
- *External virtual circuit, internal datagram:* The network handles each packet
  separately. Thus different packets for the same virtual circuit may take different routes. However, the network endeavors to deliver packets to the destination in sequence. Typically, the network will buffer packets at the destination node so that they may be ordered properly for delivery.

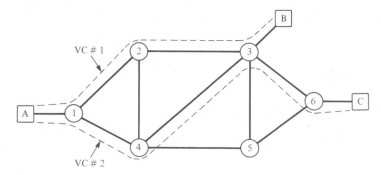

(c) Internal virtual circuit. A route for packets between two stations is defined and labeled. All packets for that virtual circuit follow the same route and arrive in sequence.

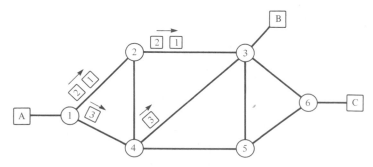

(d) Internal datagram. Each packet is treated independently by the network. Packets are labeled with a destination address and may arrive at the destination node out of sequence.

FIGURE 9-2. (continued)

- *External datagram, internal datagram:* Each packet is treated independently from both the user's and the network's point of view.
- *External datagram, internal virtual circuit:* This combination makes little sense, since one incurs the cost of a virtual circuit implementation but gets none of the benefits.

The question arises as to the choice of virtual circuits or datagrams, both internally and externally. This will depend on the specific design objective of the communication network and the cost factors that prevail. So here we offer only a few general comments.

First, consider internal datagram and virtual circuit mechanisms. A major advantage of a datagram mechanism is its robustness and flexibility. If nodes or links in the network are unavailable, datagrams can be routed around the affected area. On the other hand the loss of a node or link could destroy some virtual circuits. Similarly, the datagram mechanism can react more quickly to congestion by making routing decisions on a per-packet basis. With virtual circuits, routing decisions are usually made only at setup time. Of course, virtual circuit routes can be changed dynamically at the cost of processing overhead. An advantage of the virtual circuit mechanism is that it minimizes per-packet overhead; routing decisions need only be made once per virtual circuit. Also, internal virtual circuits provide sequenced delivery, which is an asset if the external service is virtual circuit.

TABLE 9-1   Virtual Circuit and Datagram Implementations

		Internal Operation	
		Datagram	Virtual Circuit
	Datagram	DNA ARPANET (packet)	—
External Service	**Virtual Circuit**	ARPANET (message, packet)	TYMNET (packet multiplexing) SNA (virtual and explicit routes)

With respect to the external service, the following observations apply. The datagram service allows for efficient use of the network: no call setup or disconnection, and no need to hold up packets while a packet in error is retransmitted. This latter feature is desirable in some real-time applications. The virtual circuit service can provide end-to-end sequencing, flow control, and error control. However, in many cases, these services are provided by a higher-layer protocol and need not be duplicated by the network service.

Again, depending on circumstances, any of the three combinations listed above may be the most appropriate and all have been used. Table 9-1 compares the four example networks in terms of these combinations.

The discussion in Chapter 7 and the treatment in this chapter are concerned with the internal operation of the network. How the network appears to an attached station is determined by the network access protocol that is used. Such protocols will be discussed in Chapter 13.

Example Systems

ARPANET.   Externally, ARPANET offers both datagram and virtual circuit service. When datagram service is used, the attached station (called a host) may transmit packets containing up to 991 bits of data to its local node (called an interface message processor or IMP). The node routes this packet through the network to its destination with no guarantee of delivery or of maintaining sequencing. Using the virtual circuit service, a host may establish a connection with another host and then send a sequence of messages, each containing up to 8063 bits of data. ARPANET guarantees that it will deliver all messages and that they will be delivered in sequence.

Internally, ARPANET functions as a datagram network with an unusual two-level structure. For the datagram service, the network simply treats each incoming datagram independently. For the virtual circuit service, when a message is received by a node for transmission, the message is broken up into as many as eight packets, each containing a maximum of 1008 user data bits. These packets are treated internally as datagrams and are routed independently to the node of the destination station. At the destination node, the packets are buffered until all of the packets of a single message arrive. They are then reassembled into a message and delivered to the destination host. This seemingly curious technique facilitates an effective form of traffic control, as explained below.

TYMNET. TYMNET uses virtual circuits both internally and externally, based on a technique that might be called *packet multiplexing* [RIND79a]. In essence, TYMNET views each station as a source of a character stream rather than a packet stream. As data come in from a station to a local node, they are buffered and then sent along a fixed route to the destination. The amount of data that is packetized for node-to-node hops is variable. Thus an initial burst of data may become spread out across several nodes in transit. Alternatively, characters that are transmitted later by a station may catch up with earlier characters in the network and end up exiting as a block at the destination. Furthermore, a single packet transmitted between two nodes may contain data for more than one virtual circuit.

To support virtual circuits, each node is equipped with a buffer pool, and a number of index vectors, two for each link to an adjacent node. Each of these links supports a fixed number of channels, using a statistical TDM protocol. We use the following notation:

$$R_n(l,c) = \text{read vector of node } n \text{ for channel } c \text{ of link } l$$
$$W_n(l,c) = \text{write vector of node } n \text{ for channel } c \text{ of link } l$$

Figure 9-3 illustrates the use of these vectors to construct a virtual circuit between a terminal attached to node 1000 and a host attached to node 5. When the virtual circuit is constructed, buffer space is allocated in each node along the route and a channel between each pair of these nodes is dedicated to that circuit. Figure 9-3 illustrates the buffers and the write vectors. Data from the terminal are stored in buffer 4 of node 1000. The node has $R_{1000}(112,2)$ set to 4. Thus the node will read data from buffer 4 to transmit on channel 2 to node 112. At node 112, $W_{112}(1000,2) = 200$. This instructs the node to store data on channel 2 from node 1000 in buffer 200. These data are subsequently transmitted to node 5 on channel 1. Finally, the data are directed to buffer 8 of node 5, which is dedicated to output to the attached host.

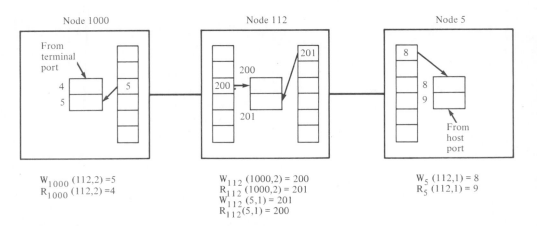

$$W_{1000}(112,2) = 5$$
$$R_{1000}(112,2) = 4$$

$$W_{112}(1000,2) = 200$$
$$R_{112}(1000,2) = 201$$
$$W_{112}(5,1) = 201$$
$$R_{112}(5,1) = 200$$

$$W_5(112,1) = 8$$
$$R_5(112,1) = 9$$

FIGURE 9-3. A virtual circuit in TYMNET.

The assignment of buffers and channels to a virtual circuit is done by a central node, the supervisor. Details are provided below. Note that in this scheme, it is not necessary for the nodes to have knowledge of the overall virtual circuit. They merely need to keep track of local buffer/channel assignments.

Data are transmitted between links in frames, using the format of Figure 9-4. Transmission is done via a character-oriented synchronous protocol, using 3-bit sequence numbers and acknowledgments. Each frame contains one or more packets of data, and each packet contains data for one channel. Note the similarity between Figures 9-4 and 6-13; the internode communication is clearly a form of statistical TDM. Each physical record is formed by picking up data from various channels using the read vector. At the receiving end, the record is unpacked and data are stored in buffers as dictated by the write vector. Note that these data, all of which came in on one link, may now fan out to various links based on the virtual circuit routing. This technique is very similar to that of the switching statistical multiplexer discussed in the preceding chapter. The strength of this technique, in terms of routing and traffic control, will become evident in due course.

SNA.   Initially, SNA was structured with a host-centered, host-controlled philosophy, but it is gradually evolving toward a more flexible approach tailored to true distributed systems [GURU87]. Figure 9-5 presents those aspects of SNA relevant to the present discussion. The communication network is formed by *subarea nodes*, each of which may be a host or a communications controller. *Peripheral nodes*, such as terminals and terminal concentrators, attach to subarea nodes. The link between adjacent subarea nodes consists of one or more transmission groups. A *transmission group* is either a single physical link or multiple links used for parallel transmission. SNA provides a virtual-circuit service using a two-level internal virtual-circuit implementation. Between each pair of subarea nodes, a number of *explicit routes* are predefined. Each route consists of a sequence of transmission groups forming a path between the two nodes. A *virtual route* is simply a source-destination node pair assigned dynamically to an explicit route. The details are provided below, in the discussion of routing.

Note that in Figure 9-5, the identities of nodes and stations have merged. Each subarea node is a communications node capable of performing switching. It may also be a network station that supports users or applications that use the network.

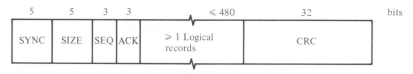

(a) Physical record (frame)

(b) Logical record (packet)

FIGURE 9-4.   TYMNET internode frame format.

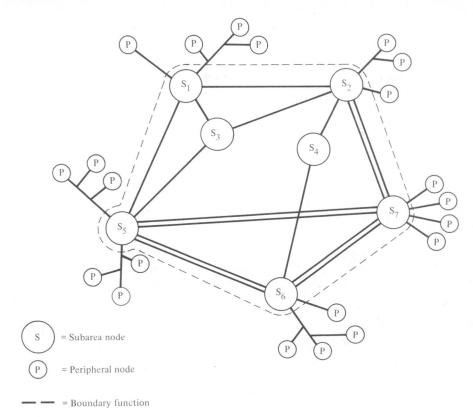

FIGURE 9-5.   An example SNA network configuration.

DNA.   Unlike SNA, DNA does not distinguish node types with respect to the network [WECK80]. The network has no inherent notion of a separate communication network. Each node may perform both switching functions and applications functions. The service provided is datagram, using datagrams internally.

9-3

ROUTING

In Chapter 8 we discussed the function of routing in a circuit-switched telecommunications network. Because of the hierarchical topology of the network and the numbering scheme used, this function was easily explained. With packet-switched networks, the routing function is both more complex and more difficult to explain. The chief reason for this is the relatively undifferentiated nature of the network. Packet-switched networks tend to be flat rather than hierarchical, having a number of alternative routes between endpoints, with no obvious preferred routes. This section will highlight the major elements of the routing function and give examples. The interested reader may pursue the topic in several survey articles [SCHW80], [RUDI76], and in specific chapters on the subject in a number of books [ROSN82], [GERL81], [MART81], [TANE81a], [DAVI79], [CYPS78].

Characteristics

The primary function of a packet-switched network is to accept packets from a source station and deliver them to a destination station. To accomplish this, a path or route through the network must be selected; generally, more than one route is possible. Thus a routing function must be performed. [TANE81a] suggests a number of desirable attributes of the routing function: correctness, simplicity, robustness, stability, fairness, and optimality. To this one might also add efficiency.

The first two items on the list are self-explanatory. Robustness has to do with the ability of the network to deliver packets via some route in the face of localized failures and overloads. Ideally, the network can react to such contingencies without loss of packets or the breaking of virtual circuits. The designer who seeks robustness must cope with the competing claims for stability. Techniques that react to changing conditions have an unfortunate tendency to either react too slowly to events or to experience unstable swings from one extreme to another. For example, the network may react to congestion in one area by shifting most of the load to a second area. Now the second area is overloaded and the first is underutilized, causing a second shift. During these shifts, packets may travel in loops through the network.

A trade-off also exists between fairness and optimality. Some performance criteria may favor the exchange of packets between nearby stations and discourage the exchange between distant stations. This policy will appear unfair to the station which primarily needs to communicate with distant stations. Finally, any routing technique involves some processing overhead at each node and often a transmission overhead as well. The penalty of such overhead needs to be less than the benefit accrued based on some reasonable metric, such as increased robustness or fairness.

With these attributes in mind, we turn to the techniques of routing that can be employed. Table 9-2 lists the elements or dimensions of the routing task. These elements are not completely orthogonal and may not even encompass all aspects of this complex problem. Nevertheless, they serve to clarify and organize routing concepts. First, we comment briefly on each of these dimensions; several are then explored in detail.

TABLE 9-2   Elements of Routing Techniques

Performance criterion	Network information source
Number of hops	None
Cost	Local
Delay	Adjacent nodes
Throughput	Nodes along route
Decision time	All nodes
Packet (datagram)	Routing strategy
Session (virtual circuit)	Fixed
Decision place	Flooding
Each node (distributed)	Random
Central node (centralized)	Adaptive
Originating node	Adaptive routing update time
	Continuous
	Periodic
	Major load change
	Topology change

The selection of a route is generally based on some *performance criterion*. The simplest criterion is to choose the ''shortest'' route (one that passes through the least number of nodes) through the network. This results in the least number of hops per packet (one hop = traversal of one node-to-node link). A generalization of the shortest-route criterion is least-cost routing. In this case, a cost is associated with each link, and the route through the network that accumulates the least cost is sought. For example, the costs in the network of Figure 9-1 are shown as numeric labels on the links. The shortest path from node 1 to node 6 is 1-3-6, but the least cost path is 1-4-5-6. The cost assignment is intended to support one or more design objectives. For example, the cost could be related to the capacity of the link (i.e., the higher the capacity, the lower the cost), or the current queueing delay to use the link. In the first case, the least-cost route should provide the highest throughput. In the second case, the least-cost route should minimize delay.

So, to deliver a packet from one station to another, a routing decision is made based on some performance criterion. Key characteristics of this decision are the time and place of the decision. The *decision time* is either at the packet or virtual-circuit level. When the internal operation of the network is datagram, a routing decision is made individually for each packet. For internal virtual-circuit operation, a routing decision is made at the time that the circuit is established. All subsequent packets using that virtual circuit follow the same route. Note that we are here talking about an internal virtual circuit. For some networks, the routing strategy permits the route of individual packets of an external virtual circuit to vary. This is the case when the network uses datagrams internally but provides an external virtual circuit.

The *decision place* also varies among networks. In some networks, each node has the responsibility of selecting an output link for routing packets as they arrive (distributed routing). The principal alternative is for the routing decision to be made by a central node, such as a network control center (centralized routing). The danger of the latter approach is that the loss of the network control center may block the operation of the network. The distributed approach is perhaps more complex, but is also more robust. An infrequently used alternative is for the originating node to select the route (source node routing). Observe that the decision time and decision place are independent. Again referring to Figure 9-1, suppose that the decision place is each node and that the values depicted are the costs at a given instant in time; the costs may change. If a packet is to be delivered from node 1 to node 6, it might follow the route 1-4-5-6, with each leg of the route determined locally by the transmitting node. Now suppose that the values change such that 1-4-5-6 is no longer the optimum route. In a datagram network, the next packet may follow a different route, again determined by each node along the way. In a virtual circuit network, each node will remember the routing decision that was made when the virtual circuit was established, and simply pass on the packets without making a new decision.

The next element of routing, *network information source*, depends on the performance criterion, decision place, and routing strategy. It is nevertheless worth calling out separately. The information referred to is information about the topology of the network, traffic load, and cost. Surprisingly, some strategies use no information at all and yet manage to get packets through; flooding and some random strategies (discussed below) are in this category. With distributed routing (decision place = each node), the individual node may make use of only local information, such as the cost of each outgoing link or the queue size for each outgoing link.

The node might also collect information from adjacent nodes. Finally, there are algorithms that allow the node to gain information from all nodes on any potential route of interest. Examples of all these are provided below. With centralized routing, the central node may use information obtained from all nodes. As you might expect, the more information used, the more likely the network is to make good routing decisions. On the other hand, the transmission of that information consumes network resources.

A related concept is that of information update time, which is a function of both the information source and the routing strategy. Clearly, if no information is used, there is no update. If the only information used is local, the update is essentially continuous. That is, the local node always knows the current local conditions. For all other information source categories (adjacent nodes, nodes along route, all nodes), the update time is a function of the routing strategy. For a fixed strategy, the information is never updated, except when there is a topology change. For an adaptive strategy, information update time is expressed as an *adaptive routing update time*, as described below. Again, you should expect that increased frequency of update improves the routing decision at the expense of increased overhead.

Finally, a large number of *routing strategies* have evolved. These are discussed below, after an explanation of least-cost routing algorithms.

Least-Cost Algorithms

Virtually all packet-switched networks base their routing decision on some form of least-cost criterion. If the criterion is to minimize the number of hops, each link has a value of 1. More typically, the link value is inversely proportional to the link capacity, proportional to the current load on the link, or some combination. In any case, the assignment of value is of no concern to the *least-cost routing algorithm*, which can be simply stated as:

> Given a network of nodes connected by bidirectional links, where each link has a cost associated with it in each direction, define the cost of a path between two nodes as the sum of the costs of the links traversed. For each pair of nodes find the path with least cost.

Note that the cost of a link may differ in the two directions. This would be true, for example, if the cost of the link equaled the length of the queue of packets awaiting transmission from each of the two nodes on the link. In what follows, we assume for simplicity that the cost of a link is the same in each direction.

Most least-cost routing algorithms in use in packet-switched networks are variations of one of two common algorithms, known as Dijkstra's algorithm and the Bellman-Ford algorithm. These algorithms are defined in this section, using notation similar to that in [BERT87] and an example adapted from [SCHW80]. Later sections will show their application in a variety of routing strategies.

Dijkstra's algorithm [DIJK59] can be stated as: find the shortest paths from a given source node to all other nodes, by developing the paths in order of increasing path length. The algorithm proceeds in stages. By the kth stage, the shortest paths to the k nodes closest to (least cost away from) the source node have been determined; these nodes are in a set M. At the $(k + 1)$st stage, that node not in M that has the shortest path from the source is added to M. As nodes are added to M, their path from the source is defined. The algorithm can be formally described as follows. Define:

N = set of nodes in the network
s = source node
M = set of nodes so far incorporated by the algorithm
d_{ij} = link cost from node i to node j; $d_{ii} = 0$, and $d_{ij} = \infty$ if the nodes are not directly connected
D_n = cost of the least-cost path from node s to node n that is currently known to the algorithm

The algorithm has three steps, which are repeated until $M = N$:

1. Initialize:
   $M = \{s\}$ i.e., set of nodes incorporated is only the source node
   $D_n = d_{sn}$ for $n \neq s$ i.e., initial path costs to neighboring nodes are simply the link costs
2. Find the neighboring node which has the least-cost path from node s and incorporate that node into M:
   Find $w \notin M$ such that $D_w = \displaystyle\min_{j \notin M} D_j$
   Add w to M
3. Update least cost-paths:
   $D_n = \min[D_n, D_w + d_{wn}]$ for all $n \notin M$
   If the latter term is the minimum, the path from s to n is now the path from s to w concatenated with the link from w to n.

Table 9-3a shows the result of applying this algorithm to Figure 9-1, using $s = 1$. Note that at each step the path to each node plus the total of that path is generated. After the final iteration, the least-cost path to each node and the cost of that path has been developed. The same procedures can be used with node 2 as source node, an so on.

The Bellman-Ford algorithm [FORD62] can be stated as: find the shortest paths from a given source node subject to the constraint that the paths contain at most one link, then find the shortest paths with a constraint of paths of at most two links, and so on. This algorithm also proceeds in stages. The algorithm can be formally described as follows. Define:

s = source node
d_{ij} = link cost from node i to node j; $d_{ii} = 0$, and $d_{ij} = \infty$ if the nodes are not directly connected
h = maximum number of links in a path at the current stage of the algorithm
$D_n^{(h)}$ = cost of the least-cost path from node s to node n under the constraint of no more than h links

The algorithm has the following steps, which are repeated until none of the costs change:

1. Initialize:
   $D_n^{(0)} = \infty$, for all $n \neq s$
2. For each successive $h \geq 0$:
   $D_n^{(h+1)} = \displaystyle\min_{j} [D_n^{(h)} + d_{ji}]$
   The path from s to i terminates with the link from j to i.

TABLE 9-3   **Example of Least-Cost Routing Algorithms (using Figure 9-1)**

(a) Dijkstra's Algorithm ($s = 1$)

Iteration	M	D_2	Path	D_3	Path	D_4	Path	D_5	Path	D_6	Path
1	{1}	2	1-2	5	1-3	1	1-4	∞	—	∞	—
2	{1, 4}	2	1-2	4	1-4-3	1	1-4	2	1-4-5	∞	—
3	{1, 2, 4}	2	1-2	4	1-4-3	1	1-4	2	1-4-5	∞	—
4	{1, 2, 4, 5}	2	1-2	3	1-4-5-3	1	1-4	2	1-4-5	4	1-4-5-6
5	{1, 2, 3, 4, 5}	2	1-2	3	1-4-5-3	1	1-4	2	1-4-5	4	1-4-5-6
6	{1, 2, 3, 4, 5, 6}	2	1-2	3	1-4-5-3	1	1-4	2	1-4-5	4	1-4-5-6

(b) Bellman-Ford Algorithm ($s = 1$)

h	$D_2^{(h)}$	Path	$D_3^{(h)}$	Path	$D_4^{(h)}$	Path	$D_5^{(h)}$	Path	$D_6^{(h)}$	Path
0	∞	—	∞	—	∞	—	∞	—	∞	—
1	2	1-2	5	1-3	1	1-4	∞	—	∞	—
2	2	1-2	4	1-4-3	1	1-4	2	1-4-5	10	1-3-6
3	2	1-2	3	1-4-5-3	1	1-4	2	1-4-5	4	1-4-5-6
4	2	1-2	3	1-4-5-3	1	1-4	2	1-4-5	4	1-4-5-6

Table 9-3b shows the result of applying this algorithm to Figure 9-1, using $s = 1$. At each step, the least cost paths with a maximum number of links equal to h are found. After the final iteration, the least-cost path to each node and the cost of that path has been developed. The same procedure can be used with node 2 as source node, and so on. Note that the results agree with those obtained using Dijkstra's algorithm. Figure 9-6 illustrates the results of Table 9-3.

One interesting comparison can be made between these two algorithms, having to do with whether centralized or distributed routing is used: Dijkstra's algorithm seems better suited to centralized routing and the Bellman-Ford to distributed routing. Let us consider the Bellman-Ford algorithm first. If we examine the equation in step 2 of the algorithm, we see that the calculation for node n involves knowledge of the link cost to all neighboring nodes to node n (d_{jn}) plus the total path cost to each of those neighboring nodes from a particular source node s ($D_j^{(h)}$). Each node can maintain a set of costs and associated paths for every other node in the network, and exchange this information with its direct neighbors from time to time. Each node can therefore use the expression in step 2 of the Bellman-Ford algorithm, based only on information from its neighbors and knowledge of its link costs, to update its costs and paths. On the other hand, consider the equation in step 3 of Dijkstra's algorithm. This equation appears to require that, for a distributed algorithm, each node must have complete topological information about that network; that is, it must know the link costs of all links in the network. Thus, for this algorithm, information must be exchanged with all other nodes, increasing the overhead for distributed routing.

Evaluation of the relative merits of the two algorithms should be done with respect to the desirable attributes listed earlier. The evaluation will depend on the implementation approach, as indicated by the various categories in Table 9-1, and the specific implementation.

Finally, we note that these algorithms are known to converge under static conditions of topology and link costs and will converge to the same solution. If the

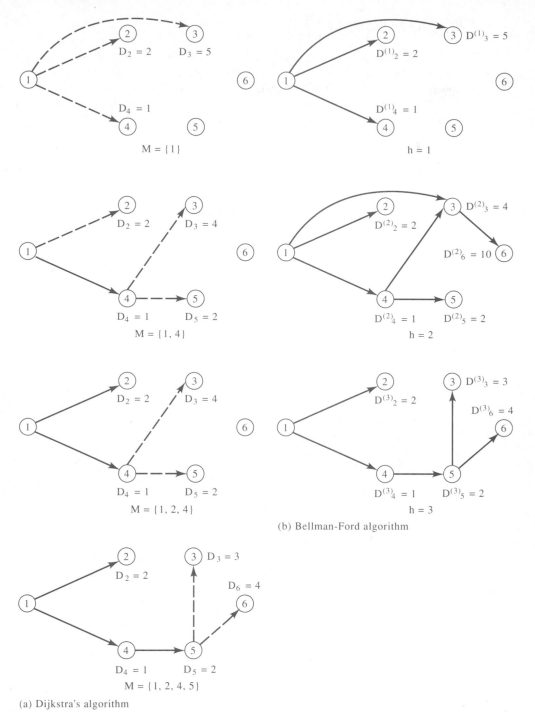

(b) Bellman-Ford algorithm

(a) Dijkstra's algorithm

FIGURE 9-6. Example of least-cost routing algorithm (based on Table 9-3).

link costs change over time, the algorithm will attempt to catch up with these changes. However, if the link cost depends on traffic, which in turn depends on the routes chosen, then a feedback situation exists, and instabilities may result.

Routing Strategies

Fixed Routing.   One of the simplest routing strategies is fixed routing. In this case, a route is selected for each source-destination pair of nodes in the network. Either of the least-cost routing algorithms described above could be used. The routes are fixed, or at least only change when there is a change in the topology of the network. Thus the costs used in designing routes cannot be based on any dynamic variable such as traffic. It could, however, be based on cost or expected traffic.

Figure 9-7 suggests how fixed routing might be implemented. A central routing directory is created, to be stored perhaps at a network control center. Note that it is not necessary to store the route for each possible pair of nodes. Rather, it is sufficient to know, for each pair of nodes, the identity of the first node on the route. To see this, consider that the least-cost route from X to Y begins with the X-A link. Call the remainder of the route, which is the part from A to Y, R_1. Call

CENTRAL ROUTING DIRECTORY

To Node

	1	2	3	4	5	6
1	–	2	4	4	4	4
2	1	–	3	4	4	4
3	5	2	–	5	5	5
4	1	2	5	–	5	5
5	4	4	3	4	–	6
6	5	5	5	5	5	–

From Node

Node 1 Directory

Destination	Next node
2	2
3	4
4	4
5	4
6	4

Node 2 Directory

Destination	Next node
1	1
3	3
4	4
5	4
6	4

Node 3 Directory

Destination	Next node
1	5
2	2
4	5
5	5
6	5

Node 4 Directory

Destination	Next node
1	1
2	2
3	5
5	5
6	5

Node 5 Directory

Destination	Next node
1	4
2	4
3	3
4	4
6	6

Node 6 Directory

Destination	Next node
1	5
2	5
3	5
4	5
5	5

FIGURE 9-7.   Fixed routing (using Fig. 9-1).

the least-cost route for A to Y, R_2. Now, if the cost of R_1 is greater than R_2, then the X-Y route can be improved by using R_2 instead. If the cost of R_1 is less than R_2, then R_2 is not the least-cost route from A to Y. Thus, at each point along a route, it is only necessary to know the identity of the next node, not the entire route. Because of this, each node need only store a single row of the routing directory. The node's directory shows the next node to take for each destination.

With fixed routing, there is no difference between routing for datagrams and virtual circuits. All packets from a given source to a given destination follow the same route. The advantage of fixed routing is its simplicity, and it should work well in a reliable network with a steady load. Its disadvantage is its lack of flexibility. It does not react to network congestion or failures.

A refinement to fixed routing that would accommodate link and node outages would be to supply the nodes with an alternate next node for each direction. For example, the alternate next nodes in the node 1 directory might be 4, 3, 2, 3, 3.

Flooding.   Another simple routing technique is flooding. This technique requires no network information whatsoever, and works as follows. A packet is sent by a source node to every one of its neighbors. At each node, an incoming packet is retransmitted on all outgoing links except for the link that it arrived from. Again as an example, consider Figure 9-1. If node 1 has a packet to send to node 6, it sends a copy of that packet to nodes 2, 3, and 4. Node 2 will send a copy to nodes 3 and 4. Node 4 will send a copy to nodes 2, 3, and 5. And so it goes. Eventually, a number of copies of the packet will arrive at node 6. The packet must have some unique identifier (e.g. source node, sequence number; or virtual circuit number, sequence number) so that node 6 knows to discard all but the first copy.

It is clear that unless something is done to stop the incessant retransmission of packets, the number of packets in circulation just from a single source packet grows without bound. One way to prevent this is for each node to remember the identity of those packets it has already retransmitted. When duplicate copies of the packet arrive, they are discarded. A simpler technique is to include a hop count field with each packet. The count can be originally set to some maximum value, such as the "diameter" of the network. Each time a node passes on a packet, it decrements the count by one. When the count reaches zero, the packet is discarded.

An example of this latter tactic is shown in Figure 9-8. Again, assume that a packet is to be sent from node 1 to node 6. On the first hop, three copies of the packet are created. For the second hop of all these copies, a total of nine copies are created. One of these copies reaches node 6, which absorbs it and does not retransmit. However, the other nodes generate a total of 22 new copies for their third and final hop. Note that if a node is not keeping track of packet identifiers, it may generate multiple copies at this third stage. After the third hop is completed, all packets are destroyed. Node 6 has received four additional copies of the packet.

The flooding technique has two remarkable properties:

* All possible routes between source and destination are tried. Thus, no matter what link or node outages have occurred, a packet will always get through as long as at least one path between source and destination exists.
* Because all routes are tried, at least one copy of the packet to arrive at the destination will have used a minimum-hop route.

Because of the first property, the flooding technique is highly robust and could be used to send high-priority messages. An example application is a military net-

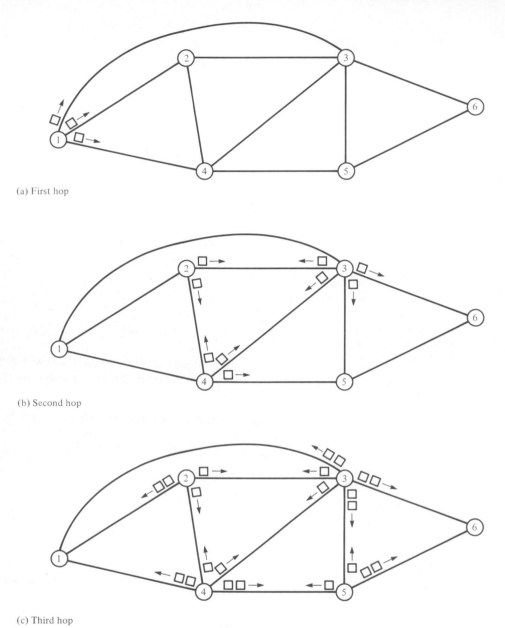

(a) First hop

(b) Second hop

(c) Third hop

FIGURE 9-8. Flooding example (hop count = 3).

work that is subject to extensive damage. Because of the second property, flooding might be used to initially set up the route for a virtual circuit. On the other hand, the principal disadvantage of flooding is the total traffic load that it generates, which is directly proportional to the connectivity of the network. This increased load will increase delay for all subsequent traffic if the network load is nontrivial.

Random Routing. Random routing has the simplicity and robustness of flooding with far less traffic load. With random routing, a node selects only one outgoing path for retransmission of an incoming packet. The outgoing link is chosen at random, generally excluding the link on which the packet arrived. If all links are equally likely to be chosen, then a simple implementation is for a node to utilize outgoing links in a round-robin fashion.

A refinement of this technique is to assign a probability to each outgoing link and to select the link based on that probability. The probability could be based on data rate, in which case we have

$$P_i = \frac{R_i}{\Sigma_j R_j}$$

where

P_i = probability of selecting i
R_j = data rate on link j

The sum is taken over all candidate outgoing links. This scheme should provide good traffic distribution. The probabilities could also be based on fixed link costs.

Like flooding, random routing requires the use of no network information. Because the route taken is a random one, the actual route will typically not be the least-cost route nor the minimum hop-count route. Thus the network must carry a higher than optimal traffic load, although not nearly as high as for flooding. Because of the unpredictability of the delay in delivering packets and the increased traffic load, random routing is not in common use.

Adaptive Routing. The routing strategies discussed so far do not react to changing conditions within the network, or at most react infrequently as the result of some system operator action. This characteristic is not necessarily a bad one. Consider these drawbacks of an adaptive strategy:

- The routing decision is more complex; therefore, the processing burden on the network increases.
- In most cases, adaptive strategies depend on status information that is collected at one place but used at another; therefore, the traffic burden on the network increases.
- An adaptive strategy may react too quickly, causing congestion-producing oscillation, or too slowly, being irrelevant.

Despite these real dangers, adaptive routing strategies are by far the most prevalent, for two reasons:

- An adaptive routing strategy can improve performance as seen by the network user.
- An adaptive strategy can aid in traffic control, discussed later.

These benefits may or may not be realized, depending on the soundness of design and the nature of the load. By and large, it is an extraordinarily complex task to perform properly. Proof of this is seen in the fact that our two example communication networks, ARPANET and TYMNET, have both endured major overhauls of their routing strategy. In the former case the change was largely made to correct design flaws; in the latter it was to adapt to a changing traffic mix.

Adaptive routing strategies can be characterized by the fact that they adapt to measurable changing conditions and by the other elements listed in Table 9-2. Those elements that serve most directly to differentiate the various strategies are

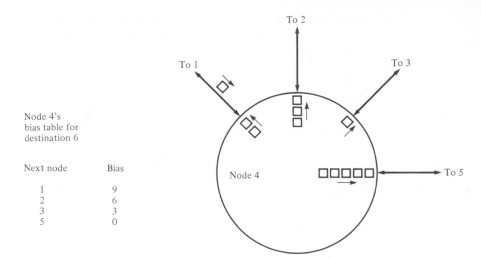

Node 4's
bias table for
destination 6

Next node	Bias
1	9
2	6
3	3
5	0

FIGURE 9-9.   Example of isolated adaptive routing.

the decision place and the network information source. Based on those two parameters, virtually all strategies are in one or a hybrid combination of the following categories:

- *Isolated adaptive:* local information, distributed control.
- *Distributed adaptive:* information from adjacent nodes, distributed control.
- *Centralized adaptive:* information from all nodes, centralized control.

A simple isolated adaptive scheme is for a node to route each packet to the outgoing link with the shortest queue length, Q. This would have the effect of balancing the load on outgoing links. However, outgoing paths may not be headed in the correct general direction. An improvement can be obtained by also taking into account preferred directions, much as with random routing. In this case, each link emanating from the node would have a bias B_i for each destination i. For each

TABLE 9-4   Routing Techniques for Some Networks

	Original ARPANET	Revised ARPANET	TYMNET I	TYMNET II	SNA	DNA
Performance criterion	Delay	Delay	Delay rate, overload	Data rate, load, link and traffic types	User-defined	User-defined
Decision time	Packet	Packet	Session	Session	Session	Packet
Decision place	Each node	Each node	Central node	Central node	Originating node	Each node
Information source	Adjacent nodes	All nodes	All nodes	All nodes	User-defined	Adjacent nodes
Routing strategy	Adaptive	Adaptive	Adaptive	Adaptive	User-defined	Adaptive
Update time	Periodic	Periodic	Load change	Load change	Topology change	Topology change
Routing algorithm	Backward-search	Forward-search	Backward-search	Forward-search	User-defined	Backward-search

incoming packet headed for node i, the node would choose the outgoing link that minimizes $Q + B_i$. Thus a node would tend to send packets in the right direction, with a concession made to current traffic delays.

As an example, Figure 9-9 shows the status of node 4 of Figure 9-1 at a certain point in time. Node 4 has links to four other nodes. A fair number of packets have been arriving and a backlog has built up, with a queue of packets waiting for each of the outgoing links. A packet arrives from node 1 destined for node 6. Question: To which outgoing link should the packet be routed? Based on current queue lengths and the values of bias (B_6) for each outgoing link, the minimum value of $Q + B_6$ is four, on the link to node 3. Thus the packet is routed through node 3.

Isolated adaptive schemes are not in general use since they make little use of available information. The other two adaptive strategies are commonly found. Both take advantage of the information that each node has about the delays and outages that it experiences. In the distributed adaptive case, each node exchanges this delay information with other nodes. Based on this incoming information, a node tries to estimate the delay situation throughout the network, and applies one of the routing algorithms discussed earlier. In the case of a centralized adaptive algorithm, each node reports its information to a central node, which designs routes based on this incoming information and sends the routing information back to the nodes. In the next section we examine several examples of each approach.

Example Systems

Let us now examine the routing techniques used in the four example networks introduced earlier. Table 9-4 summarizes key characteristics of each approach.

ARPANET. The ARPANET routing algorithm is in its third generation. It is instructive to describe these algorithms. The original routing algorithm, designed in 1969, was a distributed adaptive algorithm using estimated delay as the performance criterion and a version of the Bellman-Ford algorithm. For this algorithm, each node maintains two vectors:

$$D_i = \begin{bmatrix} d_{i1} \\ \vdots \\ d_{iN} \end{bmatrix} \qquad S_i = \begin{bmatrix} s_{i1} \\ \vdots \\ s_{iN} \end{bmatrix}$$

where

D_i = delay vector for node i
d_{ij} = current estimate of minimum delay from node i to node j ($d_{ii} = 0$)
N = number of nodes in the network
S_i = successor node vector for node i
s_{ij} = the next node in the current minimum-delay route from i to j

Periodically (every 128 ms), each node exchanges its delay vector with all of its neighbors. On the basis of all incoming delay vectors, a node k updates both of its vectors as follows:

$$d_{kj} = \text{Min}_{i \in A} [d_{ij} + l_{ki}]$$
$$s_{kj} = i \qquad \text{using } i \text{ that minimizes the expression above}$$

(a) Node 1's routing table before update

Destination	Delay	Next Node
1	0	–
2	2	2
3	5	3
4	1	4
5	6	3
6	8	3

D_1 S_1

(b) Delay vectors sent to node 1 from neighbor nodes

D_2	D_3	D_4
2	3	1
0	3	2
3	0	2
2	2	0
3	1	1
5	3	3

(c) Node 1's routing table after update and link costs used in update

Destination	Delay	Next Node
1	0	–
2	2	2
3	3	4
4	1	4
5	2	4
6	4	4

$l_{1,2} = 2$
$l_{1,3} = 5$
$l_{1,4} = 1$

FIGURE 9-10. Original ARPANET routing algorithm.

where

A = set of neighbor nodes for k

l_{ki} = current estimate of delay from k to i

Figure 9-10 provides an example of the original ARPANET algorithm, using the network of Figure 9-11. This is the same network as that of Figure 9-1, with some of the link costs having different values. Figure 9-10a shows the routing table for node 1 at an instant in time that reflects the link costs of Figure 9-11. For each destination, a delay is specified, and the next node on the route that produces that delay. At some point, the link costs change to those of Figure 9-1. Assume that node 1's neighbors (node 2, 3, and 4) learn of the change before node 1. Each of these nodes updates its delay vector and sends a copy to all of its neighbors, including node 1 (Figure 9-10b). Node 1 discards its current routing table and builds a new one, based solely on the incoming delay vector and its own estimate of link delay to each of its neighbors. The result is shown in Figure 9-10c.

The estimated link delay is simply the queue length for that link. Thus in building a new routing table, the node will tend to favor outgoing links with shorter queues. This tends to balance the load on outgoing links. However, because queue lengths vary rapidly with time, the distributed perception of the shortest route could change while a packet is en route. This could lead to a thrashing situation in which a packet continues to seek out areas of low congestion rather than aiming at the destination.

After some years of experience and several minor modifications, the original routing algorithm was replaced by a quite different one in 1979 [MCQU80]. The major shortcomings of the old algorithm were these:

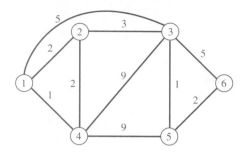

FIGURE 9-11. Network for example of Figure 9-10a.

- The algorithm did not consider line speed, merely queue length. Thus higher-capacity links were not given the favored status they deserved.
- Queue length is, in any case, an artificial measure of delay, since some variable amount of processing time elapses between the arrival of a packet at a node and its placement in an outbound queue.
- The algorithm was not very accurate. In particular, it responded slowly to congestion and delay increases.

The new algorithm is also a distributed adaptive one, using delay as the performance criterion, but the differences are significant. Rather than using queue length as a surrogate for delay, the delay is measured directly. At a node, each incoming packet is timestamped with an arrival time. A departure time is recorded when the packet is transmitted. If a positive acknowledgment is returned, the delay for that packet is recorded as the departure time minus the arrival time plus transmission time and propagation delay. The node must therefore know link data rate and propagation time. If a negative acknowledgment comes back, the departure time is updated and the node tries again, until a measure of successful transmission delay is obtained.

Every 10 s, the node computes the average delay on each outgoing link. If there are any significant changes in delay, the information is sent to all other nodes using flooding. Each node maintains an estimate of delay on every network link. When new information arrives, it recomputes its routing table using Dijkstra's algorithm.

Experience with this new strategy indicated that it was more responsive and stable than the old one. The overhead induced by flooding was moderate since each node does this at most once every 10 seconds. However, as the load on the network grew, a shortcoming in the new strategy began to appear, and the strategy was revised in 1987 [KHAN89].

The problem with the second strategy is the assumption that the measured packet delay on a link is a good predictor of the link delay encountered after all nodes re-route their traffic based on this reported delay. Thus, it is an effective routing mechanism only if there is some correlation between the reported values and those actually experienced after re-routing. This correlation tends to be rather high under light and moderate traffic loads. However, under heavy loads, there is little correlation. Therefore, immediately after all nodes have made routing updates, the routing tables are obsolete!

As an example, consider a network that consists of two regions with only two links, A and B, connecting the two regions (Figure 9-12). Each route between two

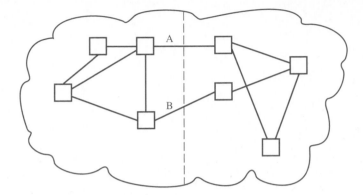

FIGURE 9-12.   Packet-switching network subject to oscillations.

nodes in different regions must pass through one of these links. Assume that a situation develops in which most of the traffic is on link A. This will cause the link delay on A to be significant, and at the next opportunity, this delay value will be reported to all other nodes. These updates will arrive at all nodes at about the same time, and all will update their routing tables immediately. It is likely that this new delay value for link A will be high enough to make link B the preferred choice for most, if not all, inter-region routes. Because all nodes adjust their routes at the same time, most or all inter-region traffic shifts at the same time to link B. Now the link delay value on B will become high, and there will be a subsequent shift to link A. This oscillation will continue until the traffic volume subsides.

There are a number of reasons why this oscillation is undesirable:

1. A significant portion of available capacity is unused at just the time when it is needed most: under heavy traffic load.
2. The over-utilization of some links can lead to the spread of congestion within the network (this will be seen in the discussion of Figure 9-16).
3. The large swings in measured delay values result in the need for more frequent routing update messages. This increases the load on the network at just the time when the network is already stressed.

The ARPANET designers concluded that the essence of the problem was that every node was trying to obtain the best route for all destinations, and that these efforts conflicted. It was concluded that under heavy loads, the goal of routing should be to give the *average* route a good path instead of attempting to give *all* routes the best path.

The designers decided that it was unnecessary to change the overall routing algorithm. Rather, it was sufficient to change the function that calculates link costs. This was done in such a way as to damp routing oscillations and reduce routing overhead. The calculation begins with measuring the average delay over the last 10 seconds. This value is then transformed with the following steps:

1. Using a simple $M/M/1$ queueing model (see Appendix A), the measured delay is transformed into an estimate of link utilization. From queueing theory, utilization can be expressed as a function of delay as follows:

$$\rho = \frac{2(s - t)}{s - 2t}, \text{ where}$$

ρ = link utilization

t = measured delay

s = service time

The service time was set at the network-wide average packet size (600 bits) divided by the data rate of the link.

2. The result is then smoothed by averaging it with the previous estimate of utilization:

$U(n + 1) = 0.5 \times \rho(n + 1) + 0.5 \times U(n)$, where

$U(n)$ = average utilization calculated at sampling time n

$\rho(n)$ = link utilization measured at sampling time n

Averaging increases the period of routing oscillations, thus reducing routing overhead.

3. The link cost is then set as a function of average utilization that is designed to provide a reasonable estimate of cost while avoiding oscillation. Figure 9-13 indicates the way in which the estimate of utilization is converted into a cost value. The final cost value is, in effect, a transformed value of delay. In the figure, delay is normalized to the value achieved on an idle line, which is just propagation delay plus transmission time. One curve on the figure indicates the way in which the actual delay rises as a function of utilization; the increase in delay is due to queueing delay at the node. For the revised algorithm, the cost value is kept at the minimum value until a given level of utilization is reached. This feature has the effect of reducing routing overhead at low traffic levels. Above a certain level of utilization, the cost level is allowed to rise to a maximum value that is equal to three times the minimum value. The effect of this maximum value is to dictate that traffic should not be routed around a heavily utilized line by more than two additional hops.

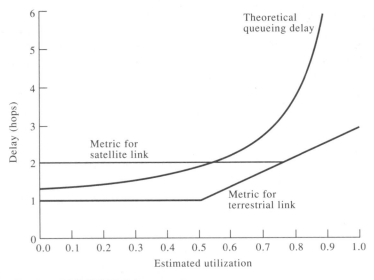

FIGURE 9-13. ARPANET delay metrics.

Note that the minimum threshold is set higher for satellite links. This encourages the use of terrestrial links under conditions of light traffic, since the terrestrial links have much lower propagation delay. Note also that the actual delay curve is much steeper than the transformation curves at high utilization levels. It is this steep rise in link cost which forces all of the traffic on a link to be shed, which in turn causes routing oscillations.

In summary, the revised cost function is keyed to utilization rather than delay. The function acts similar to a delay-based metric under light loads and to a capacity-based metric under heavy loads.

TYMNET Routing.   As with ARPANET, the TYMNET routing algorithm has gone through two major versions. The first version [RIND77, RAJA78], used with TYMNET I, made use of a simple cost allocation based on link capacity and load. The cost table is depicted in Table 9-5. With each link, a fixed cost is associated that is a decreasing function of the data rate of the link. If the link is overloaded in one direction, a penalty cost of 16 is added; if it is overloaded in both directions, a penalty cost of 32 is added. An overload is defined as a condition in which it takes a node more than 0.5 s to service a virtual circuit; this is, in effect, a queueing delay. The last row of the table refers to a composite node made up of individual nodes connected with very high speed DMA links. Such composite nodes are required where large numbers of transmission lines converge.

TYMNET is a centralized network with a central node known as the supervisor responsible for routing. The supervisor knows the fixed cost of each link. When an overload condition exists, this is reported by the affected node to the supervisor which increases the assigned cost to the appropriate link. The cost is decreased when the node reports that the overload condition no longer exists. Thus, with only minor delay, the supervisor has a global picture of network status.

The supervisor performs routing on a virtual-circuit basis. When a virtual circuit is requested, the supervisor determines the least cost route between source and destination using a version of the Bellman-Ford algorithm. The supervisor then passes the necessary routing information for this virtual circuit to each node on the route. When the virtual circuit terminates, the supervisor informs each node on the route. During the life of the virtual circuit, the route is fixed. If an outage occurs, the source and destination stations are required to construct a new virtual circuit. If the supervisor fails, one of three backup nodes assumes responsibility.

The TYMNET I technique had several useful features. Under light loading, the highest-capacity links are preferred. As the load increases, the algorithm tends to spread out the traffic nicely. Also, the processing burden on each node is minimal.

TABLE 9-5   Link Costs in TYMNET

Line Type	Line Not Overloaded	Line Overloaded One Way	Line Overloaded Both Ways
9600 bps	10	26	42
7200 bps	11	27	43
4800 bps	12	28	44
2400 bps	16	32	48
Memory shuffler	1	17	33

As the network grew, the TYMNET designers upgraded the routing function to improve efficiency and handle a wider variety of traffic [TYME81]. Whereas TYMNET I handled primarily interactive traffic over low-speed (up to 9600 bps) lines, TYMNET II also handles computer-to-computer traffic and has higher-speed links, including satellite links. In TYMNET II, link cost is based on data rate, load factor, satellite versus land-based link, and traffic type. For example, if the station is a low-speed interactive terminal, a 9600-bps land link is assigned a lower cost than a 56-kbps satellite link because of the added delay of the satellite. If the virtual circuit is to be used for host-to-host file transfer, the satellite link has the lower cost; throughput is more important than response time.

As before, virtual circuits routes are established by the supervisor, which now uses a version of Dijkstra's algorithm, deemed more efficient. Now, instead of transmitting routing information to each node, the supervisor sends a "needle" to the source node, containing the route as an ordered list of nodes. The needle threads its way along the designated route, depositing routing information as it goes. If an outage is encountered, the needle retraces to the origin and the supervisor is informed. This overcomes a problem in TYMNET I in which proper operation depended on each node successfully receiving routing information from the supervisor.

The recovery procedure is also improved. If an outage destroys a route, the supervisor finds another route for the virtual circuit. Lost packets must be recovered by an end-to-end protocol, but the virtual circuit is not lost.

SNA Routing. The routing function in SNA is to some extent left up to the user. What SNA provides is a foundation upon which a routing technique can be built [ATK180, GURU87, MART87]. To understand SNA routing, four concepts need to be distinguished:

- *Transmission group:* a set of one or more direct links with similar transmission characteristics between adjacent nodes. There may be more than one transmission group between any pair of nodes.
- *Explicit route:* A predefined fixed path between two nodes in an SNA network. The explicit is root defined in terms of the sequence of nodes and transmission groups that constitute the path. This concept corresponds to that of internal vitual circuit, described in Section 9-2.
- *Virtual route:* A logical connection between two nodes, defined by identifying the two nodes. The concept corresponds, roughly, to that of external virtual circuit, described in Section 9-2.
- *Session:* A logical relationship between two network endpoints that supports a user or network application. This concept corresponds roughly to that of a transport connection, which is described in Chapter 15; in essence, a session is a mechanism for providing the reliable exchange of data between endpoint applications.

A transmission group forms a single logical link that has higher capacity than each of the individual links in the group. Load leveling is used so that all of the links in the group share the demand. A group provides enhanced availability: if one of the individual links fails, traffic continues to pass on the remaining links, with no disruption of the network.

Explicit routes must be set up by the network manager. Up to eight explicit routes can be defined between any pair of nodes in the network. The use of multiple explicit routes allows for the balancing of transmission workload: the traffic between any two nodes can be divided up among a number of different explicit routes. In addition, different explicit routes may offer different transmission characteristics, in terms of throughput, response time, and level of security.

Whereas explicit routes have to do with the internal operation of the network, virtual routes are visible to the end systems, and map into explicit routes in a predetermined way. Virtual routes are characterized in two ways. First, a virtual route is assigned one of three priority levels (high, medium, low). Second, a virtual route has one of 48 classes of service. The class of service corresponds to various requirements, such as level or response time, security, or reliability that is desired. When a virtual route is created and assigned to an explicit route, the network administrator associates a particular class of service with the virtual route, based on the administrator's judgement that that particular virtual route will provide that particular class of service.

Finally, a session provides the logical relationship between two user or network applications. A session, when it is created, is assigned to a particular virtual route and therefore to a particular explicit route. Multiple sessions may be assigned to a single virtual route. When initiating a session, a network user can request a particular class of service for that session. Examples of service class are interactive, remote job entry, file transfer, secure, and real time. These are user-visible labels. These are mapped by SNA into particular service class numbers, and each virtual route is associated with a specific service class number.

When a source user requests a session with a destination user, the local node will attempt to assign the session to a virtual route between the corresponding source and destination nodes. The node attempts to match the requested class of service with a virtual route of that service class. Opportunity for load leveling exists by considering the current load (number of sessions) on each eligible virtual route. If an outage occurs during a session, cutting an explicit route and therefore disabling all of the virtual routes on that explicit route, the opportunity exists to reestablish the session by assigning it to a different route within the class.

The distinction between virtual routes and explicit routes provides for flexibility as well as simplicity. Explicit routes are fixed allowing the use of simple, static routing tables. The ability to assign a virtual route to any available explicit route and to assign multiple virtual routes to a single explicit route provides the flexibility needed to react to changing network conditions and to specific user requirements.

Figure 9-14 is an example of a routing table in SNA. Included in the header of each SNA packet (referred to as a path information unit), is the destination address (referred to as the destination subarea) and an explicit route number. This information is used by each intermediate node to look up the address of the next node in the route and the transmission group to be used to get to that next node. Using the routing table in this example, if a packet were destined for node 3 using explicit route 8, it would be sent next to node 7 using transmission group 2. If transmission group 2 includes more than one physical link, the next available link will be used.

The packet (path information unit) header also includes the virtual route number and its priority. When several packets are waiting to be transmitted from one node to another, across the same transmission group, their respective priorities determine the order in which they are transmitted. Thus, even if two virtual routes share the same explicit route, preferential treatment can be given to the session on one of those routes based on priority. The virtual route is also the fundamental element of traffic control, as discussed in Section 9-4.

Destination subarea	Explicit route number	Transmission group number	Next number
3	5	1	7
3	8	2	7
3	12	1	2
4	6	4	5
4	7	1	7
6	15	3	2
.	.	.	.
.	.	.	.
.	.	.	.

FIGURE 9-14.   SNA routing table [MART87].

The SNA approach has some similarity with the TYMENET II approach. In both cases, different types of traffic can be provided with different routes based on link properties. In the case of TYMENET, the supervisor may construct a new route in response to an outage. In SNA, this task is performed by the source node.

DNA Routing.   The DNA routing function is essentially the same as the original ARPANET scheme. As with ARPANET, a distributed adaptive strategy is used. DNA adds a feature designed to test for reachability. Other differences are that the cost function with DNA is user defined, and that updates are triggered only by topology changes.

Table 9-6 depicts the routing tables maintained at each node. There are two matrices:

$$HOPS(i, l)$$
$$COST(i, l)$$

where

i = destination node, $i = 1, N$ for network with N nodes
l = adjacent node, $l \in$ set of adjacent nodes

TABLE 9-6   DNA Routing Tables (for node 1 of Figure 9-1)

		(a) Hops Next Node					(b) Cost Next Node		
		2	3	4			2	3	4
	2	1	2	2		2	2	8	3
	3	2	1	3		3	5	5	3
Destination Node	4	2	3	1	Destination Node	4	4	7	1
	5	3	2	2		5	5	6	2
	6	4	3	3		6	7	8	4

HOPS(i, l) is the estimate of the number of hops required to reach a destination i if node l is the next node on the route, and COST(i, l) is the corresponding cost. Cost is user defined and may be based on such parameters as delay, link data rate, error rate, and node capacity. A node will send its tables to its neighbors whenever an event occurs that potentially changes routes. The primary event causing a change is a link or node going down or coming up. If a node detects such a change, it recomputes its HOPS and COST matrices. If any of the least-cost routes are changed, the node transmits this information to its neighbors, who update their tables. If this new information involves a change, the node that received the new tables must in turn issue its own new tables.

The HOPS information is needed to prevent a loop in the routing algorithm. The problem is this: If a node becomes unreachable, updated delay information will circulate around the network, with each node adding to the delay. By adding a hop count, and setting an upper limit equal to the maximum path length in the network, this condition can be detected.

9-4

TRAFFIC CONTROL

As with routing, the concept of traffic control in a packet-switched network is complex, and a wide variety of approaches have been proposed. Following the pattern of Section 9-3, we present the major elements of traffic control, provide a brief description of the most important strategies, and present examples. The interested reader may pursue the topic in several survey articles [GERL80, POUZ81, HSIE84c], and in specific chapters on the subject in a number of books [GERL81, TANE81a, MART81, DAVI79].

Two related topics should be mentioned. Traffic control, as we use it here, deals with the control of the number of packets entering and using the network. It is concerned with preventing the network from becoming a bottleneck and in using it efficiently. It does not directly serve the end user (i.e., the stations attached to the network). The end users are in need of end-to-end flow control; this is provided at a higher level, and is discussed in Part III. Second, note that many of the adaptive routing techniques attempt to balance traffic throughout the network. This is not traffic control per se and cannot substitute for traffic control. At most, adaptive routing can smooth out temporary problems and defer an overload condition [THAK86].

Table 9-7 summarizes the key elements or characteristics of traffic control in a packet-switched network. We discuss each of these categories, and then look at the approaches taken in our example networks.

TABLE 9-7   Elements of Traffic Control Techniques

Type	Scope	Level
Flow control	Packet (datagram)	Hop
Congestion control	Stream (virtual circuit)	Network access
Deadlock avoidance		Entry-to-exit

Types of Traffic Control

Traffic control mechanisms are of three general types, each with different objectives; flow control, congestion control, and deadlock avoidance.

Flow Control. Flow control is concerned with the regulation of the rate of data transmission between two points. The basic purpose of flow control is to enable the receiver to control the rate at which it receives data, so that it is not overwhelmed. Typically, flow control is exercised with some sort of sliding-window technique, such as is illustrated in Figure 5-9.

We have seen examples of flow control in Chapter 5 for the case of two devices that are directly connected. Flow control can also be used between devices that are indirectly connected, such as two nodes in a packet-switched network that are the endpoints of an internal virtual circuit. It can also be used on a logical connection between two host systems attached to a network. We will see several examples of this latter use in Part III (specifically, in X.25 and in transport protocols).

In considering the internal mechanisms of a packet-switching network, as we are in this chapter, flow control is not so much an end in itself as it is a tool for implementing other types of traffic control policies, as we shall see.

Congestion Control. A quite different type of traffic control is referred to as congestion control. The objective here is to maintain the number of packets within the network below the level at which performance falls off dramatically.

To understand the issue involved in congestion control, we need to look at some results from queueing theory.[1] In essence, a packet-switching network is a network of queues. At each node, there is a queue of packets for each outgoing channel. If the rate at which packets arrive and queue up exceeds the rate at which packets can be transmitted, the queue size grows without bound and the delay experienced by a packet goes to infinity. Even if the packet arrival rate is less than the packet transmission rate, queue length will grow dramatically as the arrival rate approaches the transmission rate. We saw this kind of behavior in Figure 6-14. As a rule of thumb, when the line for which packets are queueing becomes more than 80% utilized, the queue length grows at an alarming rate [MART72].

Consider the queueing situation at a single packet-switching node, such as is illustrated in Figure 9-15. Any given node has a number of transmission links attached to it: one or more to other packet-switching nodes, and zero or more to host systems. On each link, packets arrive and depart. We can consider that there are two buffers at each link, one to accept arriving packets, and one to hold packets that are waiting to depart. In practice, there might be two fixed-size buffers associated with each link, or there might be a pool of memory available for all buffering activities. In the latter case, we can think of each link having two variable-size buffers associated with it, subject to the constraint that the sum of all buffer sizes is a constant.

In any case, as packets arrive, they are stored in the input buffer of the corresponding link. The node examines each incoming packet to make a routing decision, and then moves the packet to the appropriate output buffer. Packets queued up for output are transmitted as rapidly as possible; this is in effect statistical time-division multiplexing. Now, if packets arrive too fast for the node to process them

---

[1] See Appendix A for a brief introduction to queueing theory.

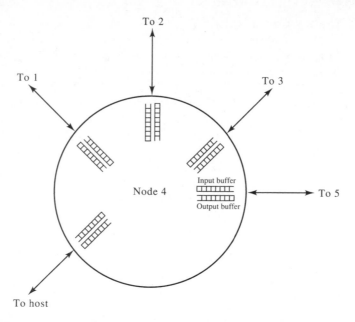

FIGURE 9-15.   Input and output queues at node 4 of Figure 9-1.

(make routing decisions) or faster than packets can be cleared from the outgoing buffers, then eventually packets will arrive for which no memory is available.

When such a saturation point is reached, one of two general strategies can be adopted. The first such strategy is to simply discard any incoming packet for which there is no available buffer space. The alternative is for the node that is experiencing these problems to exercise some sort of flow control over its neighbors so that the traffic flow remains manageable. But, as Figure 9-16 illustrates, each of a nodes neighbors is also managing a number of queues. If node 6 restrains the flow of packets from node 5, this causes the output buffer in node 5 for the link to node 6 to fill up. Thus, congestion at one point in the network can quickly propagate throughout a region or all of the network. While flow control is indeed a powerful tool, we need to use it in such a way as to manage the traffic on the entire network.

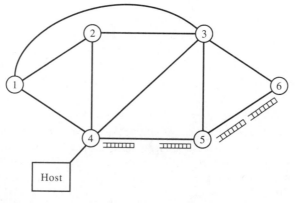

FIGURE 9-16.   The interaction of queues in a packet-switching network.

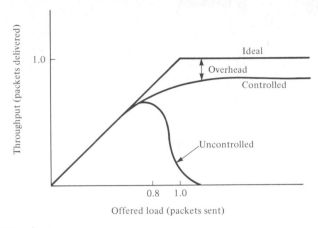

(a) Throughput

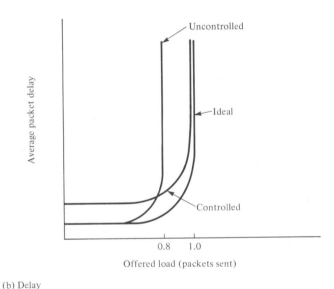

(b) Delay

FIGURE 9-17. The effects of congestion.

Figure 9-17 shows the effect of congestion in general terms. Figure 9-17a plots the throughput of a network (number of packets delivered to destination stations) versus the offered load (number of packets transmitted by source stations). Both axes are normalized to the maximum capacity of the network, which can be expressed as the rate at which the network is theoretically capable of handling packets. In the ideal case, throughput and hence network utilization increases to accommodate an offered load up to the maximum capacity of the network. Utilization then remains at 100%. The ideal case, of course, requires that all stations somehow know the timing and rate of packets that can be presented to the network, which is impossible. If no congestion control is exercised, we have the curve labeled "uncontrolled." As the load increases, utilization increases for a while. Then as the queue lengths at the various nodes begins to grow, throughput actually drops.

The reason for this is that the buffers at each node are of finite size. When a node's buffers are full, it must discard packets. Thus the source stations must retransmit the discarded packets in addition to the new packets. This only exacerbates the situation: As more and more packets are retransmitted, the load on the system grows, and more buffers become saturated. While the system is trying desperately to clear the backlog, stations are pumping old and new packets into the system. Even successfully delivered packets may be retransmitted because it takes so long to acknowledge them: The sender assumes that the packet did not go through. Under these circumstances, the effective capacity of the system is virtually zero.

It is clear that these catastrophic events must be avoided, which is the task of congestion control. The object of all congestion control techniques is to limit queue lengths at the nodes so as to avoid throughput collapse. This control involves some unavoidable overhead. Thus a congestion control technique cannot perform as well as the theoretical ideal. However, a good congestion control strategy will avoid throughput collapse and maintain a throughput that differs from the ideal by an amount roughly equal to the overhead of the control.

Figure 9-17b points out that no matter what technique is used, the average delay experienced by packets grows without bound as the load approaches the capacity of the system. Note that initially the uncontrolled policy results in less delay than a controlled policy, because of its lack of overhead. However, the uncontrolled policy will saturate at lower load.

A number of control mechanisms for congestion control have been suggested and tried. [JAIN88] lists the following:

1. Send a control packet from a congested node to some or all source nodes. This *choke packet* will have the effect of stopping or slowing the rate of transmission from sources and hence limit the total number of packets in the network. This approach requires additional traffic on the network during a period of congestion.

2. Rely on routing information. Routing algorithms, such as ARPANET's provide link delay information to other nodes, which influences routing decisions. This information could also be used to influence the rate at which new packets are produced. Because these delays are being influenced by the routing decision, they may vary too rapidly to be used effectively for congestion control.

3. Make use of an end-to-end probe packet. Such a packet could be time-stamped to measure the delay between two particular endpoints. This has the disadvantage of adding overhead to the network.

4. Allow packet switching nodes to add congestion information to packets as they go by. There are two possible approaches here. A node could add such information to packets going in the direction opposite of the congestion. This information quickly reaches the source node, which can reduce the flow of packets into the network. Alternatively, a node could add such information to packets going in the same direction as the congestion. The destination either asks the source to adjust the load or returns the signal back to the source in the packets (or acknowledgements) going in the reverse direction. A combination of these two approaches is used in SNA, as discussed below.

Deadlock Avoidance.   A problem equally serious to that of congestion is deadlock, a condition in which a set of nodes are unable to forward packets because no buffers are available. This condition can occur even without a heavy load.

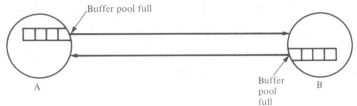

(a) Direct store – and – forward deadlock

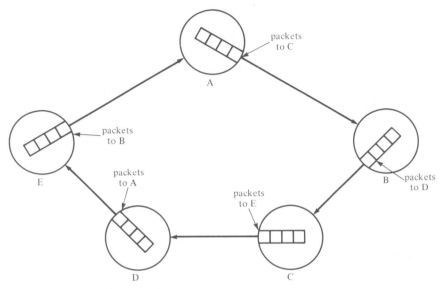

(b) Indirect store – and – forward deadlock

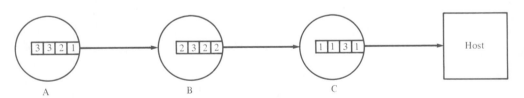

(c) Reassembly deadlock

FIGURE 9-18.   Types of deadlock.

Deadlock avoidance techniques are used to design the network in such a way that deadlock cannot occur. We briefly describe three types of deadlock to which a packet-switched network may be prone.

The simplest form of deadlock is *direct store-and-forward deadlock* and can occur if a node uses a common buffer pool from which buffers are assigned to packets on demand. Figure 9-18a shows a situation in which all of the buffer space in node *A* is occupied with packets destined for *B*. The reverse is true at *B*. Neither node can accept any more packets since their buffers are full. Thus neither node can transmit or receive on any link.

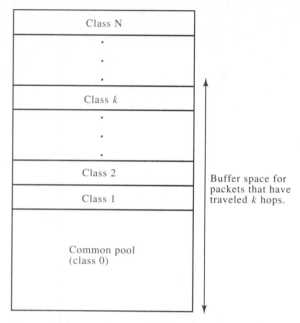

FIGURE 9-19. Structured buffer pool for deadlock avoidance.

Direct store-and-forward deadlock can be avoided by not allowing all buffers to end up dedicated to a single link. Using separate fixed-size buffers, such as illustrated in Figure 9-16, will achieve this prevention. Even if a common buffer pool is used, deadlock is avoided if no single link is allowed to acquire all of the buffer space.

A more subtle form of deadlock, *indirect store-and-forward deadlock,* is illustrated in Figure 9-18b. For each node, the queue to the adjacent node in one direction is full with packets destined for the next node beyond. One simple way to prevent this type of deadlock is to employ a structured buffer pool (Figure 9-19). The buffers are organized in a hierarchical fashion. The pool of memory at level 0 is unrestricted; any incoming packet can be stored there. From level 1 to level N (where N is the maximum number of hops on any network path), buffers are reserved in the following way: Buffers at level k are reserved for packets that have traveled at least k hops so far. Thus, in heavy load conditions, buffers fill up progressively from level 0 to level N. If all buffers up through level k are filled, arriving packets that have covered k or less hops are discarded. It can be shown [GOPA85] that this strategy eliminates direct and indirect store-and-forward deadlocks.

Finally, there is reassembly deadlock, which is peculiar to ARPANET and similar networks. Figure 9-18c shows a situation in which node C has three of four packets from message 1 and one from message 3. All of its buffers are full, so it can accept no more packets. Yet, because it has no complete message, it cannot reassemble packets and deliver them to the host. We will examine a solution to this problem in our discussion of ARPANET, below.

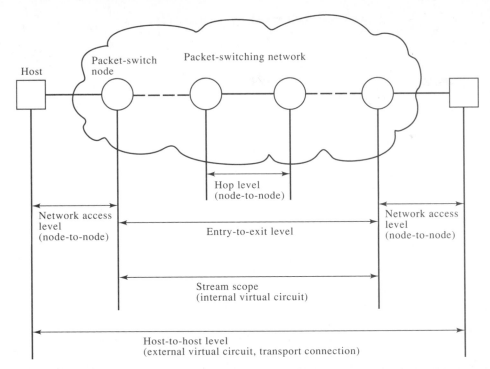

FIGURE 9-20. Scope and level of traffic control. (Based on figure in [GERL81])

Scope and Level of Traffic Control

Traffic control techniques can be categorized by their scope of application. Packet techniques are concerned with controlling the flow of individual packets. This is all that is possible in a datagram network, and is sometime used in virtual circuit networks. Stream techniques have to do with controlling the stream of packets flowing through a virtual circuit.

A third dimension of traffic control is the level, or extent, of application. This is illustrated in Figure 9-20. The hop level is concerned with controls exerted between adjacent nodes. These typically have to do with congestion control or deadlock avoidance. Network access control limits the number of new packets entering the network. These typically are used in congestion control. Finally, entry-to-exit controls are concerned with the flow of packets between two endpoints.

Table 9-8 summarizes the traffic control techniques of our example networks; these are described below. For more detail on traffic control techniques in general, the reader is referred to the references listed above.

Example Systems

ARPANET.   For its virtual-circuit service, ARPANET provides two levels of traffic control [BBN81]. One is an entry-to-entry technique. Recall that a virtual circuit is used to send a sequence of numbered messages between hosts. ARPANET

TABLE 9-8   Traffic Control Techniques for Some Networks

Scope	Hop	Network Access	Entry-to-Exit
Packet	DNA (channel queue limit)	DNA (channel queue limit)	
Stream	TYMNET (quota) SNA (pacing)	TYMNET (quota) ARPANET (RFNM)	ARPANET (window, reassembly buffer allocation) SNA (pacing)

enforces a limit of eight messages in transit between any pair of hosts. This window mechanism with window size of eight is used to prevent any host from flooding the network.

Of more serious concern is a situation of reassembly deadlock, as described earlier. ARPANET's solution is to require that a source node reserve space for each message in advance with a "request for buffer space" packet. When a destination node receives this request, and has available eight buffers for the eight packets that the message might contain, it returns an "allocation" packet. After the entire message is received and reassembled, the receiving node sends back an acknowledgment known as *ready for next message* (RFNM). If the node has buffer space for an additional message, it piggybacks an allocation packet with the RFNM. Thus, during stream transmission, the source node need not send request packets. A time may come when the source has no messages to send but has collected one or more allocation permits. The source node is then obligated to send a "give back" packet to free up buffer space at the destination.

For datagram service, no positive flow control is enforced. Rather, a destination node will discard datagrams for which it has no free buffer space. It is up to the source station to determine from the destination station if the datagram did not get through and to resend it if necessary.

TYMNET.   It is in the area of traffic control that the real strength of the TYMNET approach is seen. The TYMNET traffic control mechanism has the following positive features.

- It is simple.
- It requires very little overhead.
- Deadlocks cannot occur and therefore no mechanisms are needed to avoid it.
- Under conditions of heavy load, virtual circuits with low data rate requirements get all the capacity they need; circuits with high data rate requirements get at least some of what they need. Thus no active circuit is denied service.

Traffic control in TYMNET is on a virtual-circuit basis and includes both network access and hop-level mechanisms [RIND79b, TYME81]. The network access flow control is based on the establishment of the virtual circuit. When the supervisor sets up a virtual circuit, it assigns a quota of buffer space for each channel used along the circuit. The quota is based on throughput class. A node can only transmit data on a particular channel until the quota is exhausted. It must then wait for the next node to refresh its quota. Every half-second, each node sends a "backpressure vector'' to each adjacent node. The vector contains one bit for each channel on the link. If a bit is set to 1, the sending node may reset the quota for the corresponding buffer. Otherwise, the sending node continues to decrement the quota for a particular channel for each character that is transmitted. The result is a backpressure mechanism that eventually works its way back to the sending host.

For example, in Figure 9-3, suppose that the terminal connected to node 1000 is 10 characters per second (cps) and the host is connected to node 5 over a 30-cps virtual-circuit link. As characters arrive from the host they start to flow through the virtual circuit. The characters arrive at node 1000 at 30 cps but can leave at only 10 cps. After the number of characters buffered in node 1000 exceeds the quota of 30, the bit for channel 2 in the backpressure vector is set to zero. Thus node 1000 will have at most 60 characters buffered for this circuit. Now node 112 will go through the same process resulting in at most 60 characters in its buffer. Now the buffer in node 5 begins to grow and, when it reaches 30, the host will be requested to stop transmitting. This request may be in the form of an HDLC RNR (receiver not ready) packet. When the number of characters in node 1000's buffer drops below 30, data again begin to flow from 112 to 1000, from 5 to 112, and finally from the host.

Two refinements help to reduce congestion further. A situation may arise when a station wishes to abort a transmission; for example, a terminal user realizes that what is printing on the screen is of no interest and wishes to stop it with an abort command. To clear out the characters in transit, the host can send a *character gobbler*. This is a PACman-like device that ignores backpressure and goes through the circuit at full speed, gobbling all characters in front of it. A second refinement: When a virtual circuit is terminated, a *circuit zapper* is sent which not only gobbles characters, but releases the buffer pairs and clears the table entries to free up these resources for new circuits.

We have discussed how flow control is performed at the virtual circuit level using a backpressure mechanism. Since TYMNET uses a statistical TDM technique at the hop level (Figure 9-4), there remains the question of how capacity is allocated to the active channels on a link. Frames are constructed using a round robin technique among all active channels. A node sends frames as fast as possible over each link. Each frame contains one or more packets, each corresponding to a different channel. To construct a frame, a node cycles through all channels, picking up packets, until it has a total of 480 bits of data or until it has completed a full cycle. The frame is then sent and a new frame constructed. For each channel visited, the amount of data collected is

$$MIN(Q, D, F)$$

where

Q = quota for that channel
D = amount of data in the read buffer of that channel
F = amount of data space remaining in the frame

Thus, when bandwidth is oversubscribed, channels that only need little get what they want with little or no queueing delay, whereas channels that want all they can get share the remaining bandwidth fairly.

The TYMNET approach is a powerful one that possesses the positive characteristics listed above. The only disadvantage is the packets are torn down and reconstructed at each node, which increases processing requirements.

SNA. Traffic control in SNA [ATKI80], [GEOR82] is an interesting hybrid. The control is exercised on a virtual circuit (virtual route) basis. This control may be triggered by either the destination node, to avoid overflow, or by an intermediate node to reduce congestion. In the case of the endpoint, control is selectively exercised on a particular virtual circuit. In the case of an intermediate node, the node will exercise control on all virtual circuits that pass through a congested link.

The technique is known as pacing, and is a complex version of the sliding-window technique, operating at the virtual-route level. We provide a brief overview here. More detail can be found in [GURU87] and [MEIJ87].

The key elements of the SNA pacing algorithm are listed in Table 9-10. When a virtual route is established, a maximum (WS-MAX) and minimum (WS-MIN) window size are defined. WS-MIN is equal to the hop count of the explicit route selected for this virtual route. This number is based on flow control studies [DEAT79] indicating that this is the minimum window size that provides reasonable throughput. WS-MAX is set at three times WS-MIN. Each sender maintains a window size WS and a pacing count PC, which is the number of additional packets it may send; both are initialized to WS-MIN. Thus, when a virtual route is created, each side is automatically provided with a permission to send WS-MIN.

Each side is responsible for providing the other with permission to send blocks of packets equal to the current window size. The key to the pacing algorithm is the management of the size and rate of arrival of these window permissions.

TABLE 9-10   Elements for SNA Virtual Route Pacing Algorithm

Pacing count (PC)
Number of additional packets that a node may send on a virtual route, before a virtual route pacing response is required.

Window size (WS)
Amount by which pacing count is increased with each virtual route pacing response.

Minimum pacing window size (WS-MIN)
Minimum value that WS may take on. WS is initialized to WS-MIN when a virtual route is created.

Maximum pacing window size (WS-MAX)
Maximum value that WS may take on.

Virtual route pacing count indicator (VRPCI)
Sent with last packet in window to indicate that an additional window is needed.

Virtual route pacing request (VRPRQ)
Sent with first packet in window, to request an additional window.

Virtual route pacing response (VRPRS)
Packet sent from destination back to source, allowing the source to increment its PC by WS.

Virtual route change window reply indicator (CWRI)
Sent by destination back to source to cause WS to be decremented by one.

Virtual route reset window indicator (RWI)
Sent by destination or intermediate system back to source to cause WS to be set to the WS-MIN.

Virtual route change window indicator (CWI)
Sent by intermediate system to destination system to cause the destination system to issue a CWRI back to the source.

First consider the use of pacing for entry-to-exit flow control. The sending node sets a virtual route pacing request (VRPRQ) bit in the first packet of a window (i.e., when PC = WS). When the receiving node gets the request, and when it has buffer space, it returns a virtual route pacing response (VRPRS) packet, which allows the sender to increment PC by WS. Since the sender decrements PC by 1 with each packet sent, the maximum value of PC is 2WS-1. Thus the receiving node can exercise flow control by simply withholding the VRPRS. If a node gets to the point that PC = 1, then it sets the virtual route pacing count indicator (VRPCI) bit in the last packet that it can send. This is a signal to the other side to provide an additional window as soon as possible.

To improve throughput, the sending node is allowed to increment its window size by 1, up to WS-MAX, if its pacing count has gone to 0 by the time it receives VRPRS. The assumption is that the receiving node could handle packets at a faster rate. Unfortunately, the opposite may be true: The receiving node is withholding its VRPRS because it is getting too many packets! To account for this contingency, the receiver may set a change window reply indicator (CWRI) bit or a reset window indicator (RWI) bit on its next VRPRS. The former requests that the sender dec-

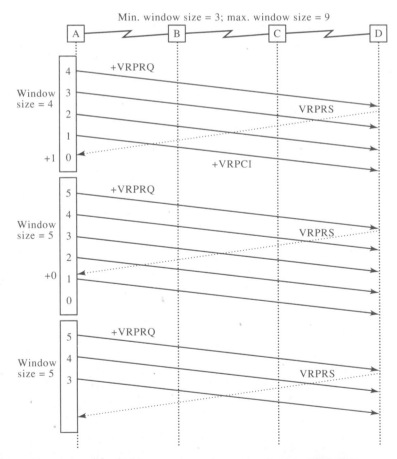

FIGURE 9-21. Virtual route flow control: no congestion [MEIJ87].

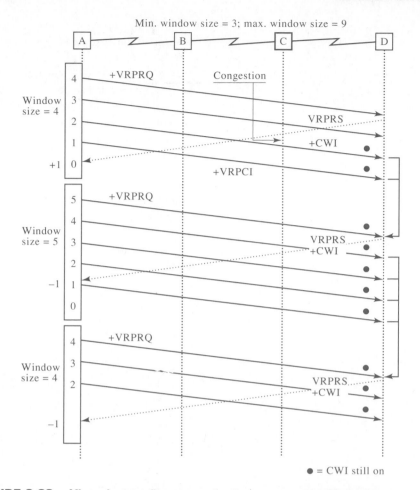

FIGURE 9-22. **Virtual route flow control: minor congestion [MEIJ87].**

rement WS by 1 (down to a minimum of WS-MIN). The latter requests that WS be reset to WS-MIN.

These techniques are also used to relieve congestion in the network. If a node suffers minor congestion on an outgoing link (i.e., queue length is beginning to grow), it sets the change window indicator (CWI) bit on all packets on all virtual routes going out that link. When the receiver gets a packet with CWI set, it sets CRWI on its next VRPRS. Thus, all sending nodes whose virtual routes go through the complaining node will decrement their window size and relieve the congestion. If severe congestion occurs (i.e., buffer saturation), the intermediate node takes more drastic action to relieve the problem. Instead of acting on packets going out the congested link, it sets the RWI bit on all packets coming in on that link. Thus all sending nodes will quickly reset their window sizes to their minimum value.

Each sending node dynamically adjusts its window size based on pacing controls set both in data packets and VRPRS packets. Figures 9-21 through 9-23 provide examples of the algorithm. Thus a single, relatively simple technique provides a unified flow control and congestion control mechanism.

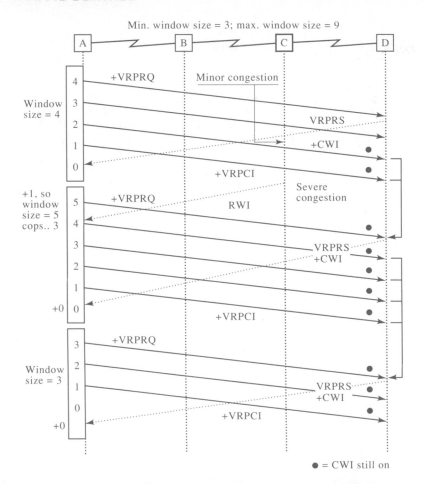

FIGURE 9-23. Virtual route flow control: severe congestion [MEIJ87].

DNA. The principal virtue of the DNA traffic control mechanism is its simplicity. Furthermore, measurements using the mechanism verify that it is effective in preventing buffer saturation and network congestion [WECK80].

The basic mechanism is a channel queue limit technique. When the length of an output channel queue exceeds a specified threshold, input packets (packets originating at this node) are delayed at the user source, and transit packets (this node is neither source nor destination) are discarded. The threshold, proposed in [IRLA78], is equal to the total number of buffers divided by the square root of the number of output lines. Thus no output link ever uses more than that fraction of the buffers. This was found to provide close to optimal performance for the case in which all buffers are pooled and dynamically allocated to output links.

To supplement the foregoing policy, DNA also uses a hop count mechanism. Each time a packet makes a hop, its count is incremented. If the hop count exceeds the maximum allowed, the node discards it. This eliminates packets caught in a temporary loop formed in the routing path.

ERROR CONTROL

Requirements

A final function of packet-switched networks, which we discuss briefly, is error control. A number of contingencies may arise which result in the loss of a packet in the network:

- A packet may be discarded in the aid of traffic control.
- A link may fail.
- A node may fail.
- The destination station may fail.

The latter three contingencies are partially handled by the data link control mechanisms between nodes or between a node and a station. But even this is not enough to ensure that a packet makes it through the network. For example, a node along the route of a packet may accept a packet and return an acknowledgment. If the node then fails before it can forward the packet, the network as a whole does not know that the packet is lost.

Ideally, no packets are lost despite congestion or failures. In relation to this, certain requirements may be placed on the network, in increasing order of difficulty:

1. If a link or node outage occurs, the network can route subsequent packets around the outage.
2. If a link or node fails, all virtual circuits that pass through the outage are automatically rebuilt. Some packets may be lost, and the station is responsible for sorting that out.
3. If a link or node fails, all affected virtual circuits are rebuilt and packets are recovered by the network, not the station.
4. No packet is ever lost in a datagram network.

Virtually all networks satisfy requirement 1. Most networks with a virtual-circuit service satisfy requirement 2, and some satisfy requirement 3. As yet, no network satisfies requirement 4.

Example Systems

We now briefly mention the error control techniques used in our example systems. In ARPANET, no error control is exercised for datagram service. Error control is provided at the message level [BBN81]. When a source node transmits a message (in up to eight packets) it retains a copy of that message, including its sequence number. If the acknowledgment (RFNM) is not received within a certain time, the source node inquires of the destination node whether the full message was received. It might be that the message got through, but the RFNM did not. If the source node gets a negative reply, it retransmits the message. If the source node fails to get a response from the destination node in a reasonable time, it returns an incomplete transmission message to its host. It is then up to the host to decide a course of action. Finally, we note that because ARPANET uses datagrams internally, virtual circuits are maintained as long as there is some route from source to destination.

TYMNET meets requirements 1 and 3 listed above [RIND79a]. When a node or link outage occurs, this fact is reported to the supervisor by neighboring nodes. The supervisor clears out all tables and buffers for each affected virtual circuit and notifies both endpoints. For each destroyed virtual circuit, the originating node automatically requests a new virtual circuit. The supervisor then rebuilds all virtual circuits that were broken. This action preserves all end-to-end connections, but more is needed to preserve the data that were in transit.

Data are preserved in TYMNET in the following fashion. As we described earlier, there is a buffer dedicated to a virtual circuit at each node along its route. The source node is given this information and thus knows the maximum number of characters that may be in transit. The source node maintains two items:

- A circular buffer equal to the maximum number of characters in transit. Once the buffer is full, it always contains the last N characters transmitted, where N is the maximum number of characters in transit.
- A running count of the number of characters transmitted since the virtual circuit was established.

The destination endpoint maintains a running count of the number of characters received. (Of course, virtual circuits are full duplex, so these mechanisms are needed in both directions.) When a failed virtual circuit is rebuilt, the endpoint nodes exchange running count values. Each node then retransmits the lost characters. Thus both the virtual circuit and the data are preserved, with no involvement of the attached stations.

In SNA, the failure of a node or link will destroy an explicit route. The originating node of each affected virtual route is notified, and promptly selects an alternative explicit route to maintain the connection. The responsibility for lost packets is beyond the scope of the communication network function and is handled at a higher (station) level within SNA.

DNA makes no attempt to recover lost datagrams as part of its communications network function. As with SNA, this is left to a higher level.

9-6

RECOMMENDED READING

The literature on packet switching is enormous. We mention here only a few of the many worthwhile references. A number of survey articles were written in the early days of packet switching; among the most interesting are [KIMB75], [GREE77], and [KLEI78]. Surveys of specific networks include [WOOD85], [ROBE78], [QUAR86], and [AMAN86]. Books with good treatments of this subject include [ROSN82] and [DAVI79]. There is also a large body of literature on performance. Good summaries are to be found in [BERT87], [KLEI76], and [SCHW77]. [AHUJ82] provides a mathematical analysis of performance and reliability aspects of traffic control and routing. [MARU83] is an exhaustive analysis of the performance of virtual-circuit-based routing algorithms. [BELL86] and [HSIE84a and b] compare the routing algorithms of ARPANET, TYMENET, SNA, and DNA. [ROBI90] describes ongoing work on congestion control algorithms.

PROBLEMS

9-1   In step 3 of Dijkstra's algorithm, the least-cost path values are only updated for nodes not yet in *M*. Is it not possible that a shorter path could be found to a node already in *M*? If so, demonstrate by example. If not, provide reasoning as to why not.

9-2   Using Dijkstra's algorithm, generate a least-cost route to all other nodes for nodes 2 through 6 of Figure 9-1. Display the results as in Table 9-3a. Do the same for the Bellman-Ford algorithm.

9-3   In Figure 9-1, node 1 sends a packet to node 6 using flooding. Counting the transmission of one packet across one link as a load of one, what is the total load generated if:
a. Each node discards duplicate incoming packets?
b. A hop count field is used and is initially set to 5?

9-4   It was shown that flooding can be used to determine the minimum-hop route. Can it be used to determine the minimum delay route?

9-5   With random routing, only one copy of the packet is in existence at a time. Nevertheless, it would be wise to utilize a hop count field. Why?

9-6   Using Table 9-6 as a model, construct the routing tables for all other nodes of Figure 9-1.

9-7   Another adaptive routing scheme is known as *backward learning*. As a packet is routed through the network, it carries not only the destination address, but the source address plus a running hop count that is incremented for each hop. Each node builds a routing table that gives the next node and hop count for each destination. How is the packet information used to build the table? What are the advantages and disadvantages of this technique?

9-8   Apply Dijkstra's routing algorithm to the networks in Figure 9-24. Provide a table similar to Table 9-3 and a figure similar to Figure 9-6.

9-9   Repeat Problem 9-8 using the Bellman-Ford algorithm.

9-10   Will Dijkstra's algorithm and the Bellman-Ford algorithm always yield the same solutions? Why or why not?

9-11   Both Dijkstra's algorithm and the Bellman-Ford algorithm find the least-cost paths from one node to all other nodes. The Floyd-Warshall algorithm finds the least-cost paths between all pairs of nodes together. Define:

N = set of nodes in the network
d_{ij} = link cost from node i to node j; $d_{ii} = 0$, and $d_{ij} = \infty$ if the nodes are not directly connected

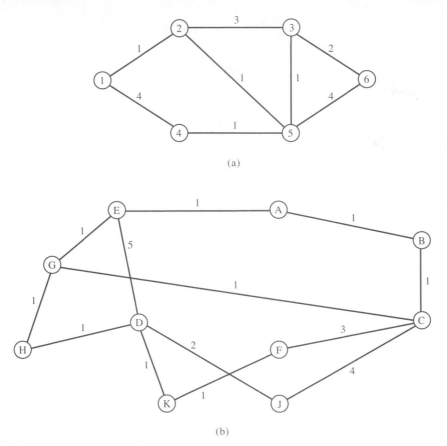

FIGURE 9-24. Packet-switching networks with link costs.

$D_{ij}^{(n)}$ = cost of the least-cost path from node i to node j with the constraint that only nodes 1, 2, . . . , n can be used as intermediate nodes on paths

The algorithm has the following steps:

1. Initialize:
   $D_{ij}^{(0)} = d_{ij}$, for all $i, j, i \neq j$
2. For $n = 0, 1, \ldots, N - 1$
   $D_{ij}^{(n+1)} = \min [D_{ij}^{(n)}, D_{i(n+1)}^{(n)} + D_{(n+1)j}^{(n)}$, for all $i \neq j$

Explain the algorithm in words. Use induction to demonstrate that the algorithm works.

9-12 Build a centralized routing directory for the networks of Problem 9-8.

9-13 Consider a system using flooding with a hop counter. Suppose that the hop counter is originally set to the "diameter" of the network. When the hop count reaches zero, the packet is discarded except at its destination. Does this always ensure that a packet will reach its destination if there exists at least one operable path? Why or why not?

9-14   Prove that the deadlock avoidance strategy illustrated in Figure 9-19 works. Hint: show by induction, starting with $k = N$, that at each node the buffers of class k cannot fill up permanently.

9-15   Suggest an alternative solution to reassembly deadlock.

9-16   What effect does the ARPANET limit of eight messages between hosts have on channel capacity and buffer capacity?

9-17   Suggest a technique for avoiding indirect store-and-forward deadlock.

9-18   Explain why deadlock cannot occur in TYMNET.

9-19   A proposed traffic control measure is known as *isarithmic* control. In this method, the total number of packets in transit is fixed by inserting a fixed number of permits into the network. These permits circulate through the network at random. Whenever a node wants to send a packet just given to it by a station, it must first capture and destroy a permit. When the packet reaches the destination node, that node reissues the permit.
   a. What type of traffic control is this?
   b. List three potential problems with this technique.

9-20   What is the maximum number of packets that may be in transit at any one time on an ARPANET virtual circuit?

9-21   Consider the following network of nodes (Figure 9-25):
   C is the capacity of a link in packets per second. Node A presents a constant load of 0.8 packet per second destined for A'. Node B presents a load λ destined for B'. Node S has a common pool of buffers that it uses for traffic to both A' and B'. When the buffer is full, packets are discarded, and are later retransmitted by the host. Plot the total throughput (i.e., the sum of $A - A'$ and $B - B'$ delivered traffic) as a function of λ. What fraction of the throughput is $A - A'$ traffic for $\lambda > 1$?

9-22   Assuming no malfunction in any of the stations or nodes of a network, is it possible for a packet to be delivered to the wrong destination?

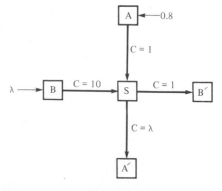

FIGURE 9-25.   Network of nodes.

CHAPTER 10

Radio and Satellite Networks

In this chapter we begin our discussion of packet broadcasting networks. Recall that such networks share the following characteristics:

- Packet transmission.
- No switching.
- Reception by many or all stations.
- Common transmission medium.

In contrast to the case with the packet-switched networks of Chapter 9, issues such as routing, traffic control, and error control are of less concern here. Rather, the key issue is transmission capacity allocation.

This chapter deals with packet radio and satellite networks, which exhibit a number of similarities. The characteristics of local networks are quite different, and that topic is reserved for Chapter 11. For both packet radio and satellite networks, we begin with a discussion of architectural issues, and then look at medium access control protocols. Appendix 10A explores the subject of broadcast network performance, which is relevant to both this chapter and the next.

10-1

PACKET RADIO ARCHITECTURE

The architecture of packet radio networks can be classified as centralized or distributed (Figure 10-1). In a centralized network, there is one central transmitter/receiver, attached to a central resource. All other nodes communicate only with

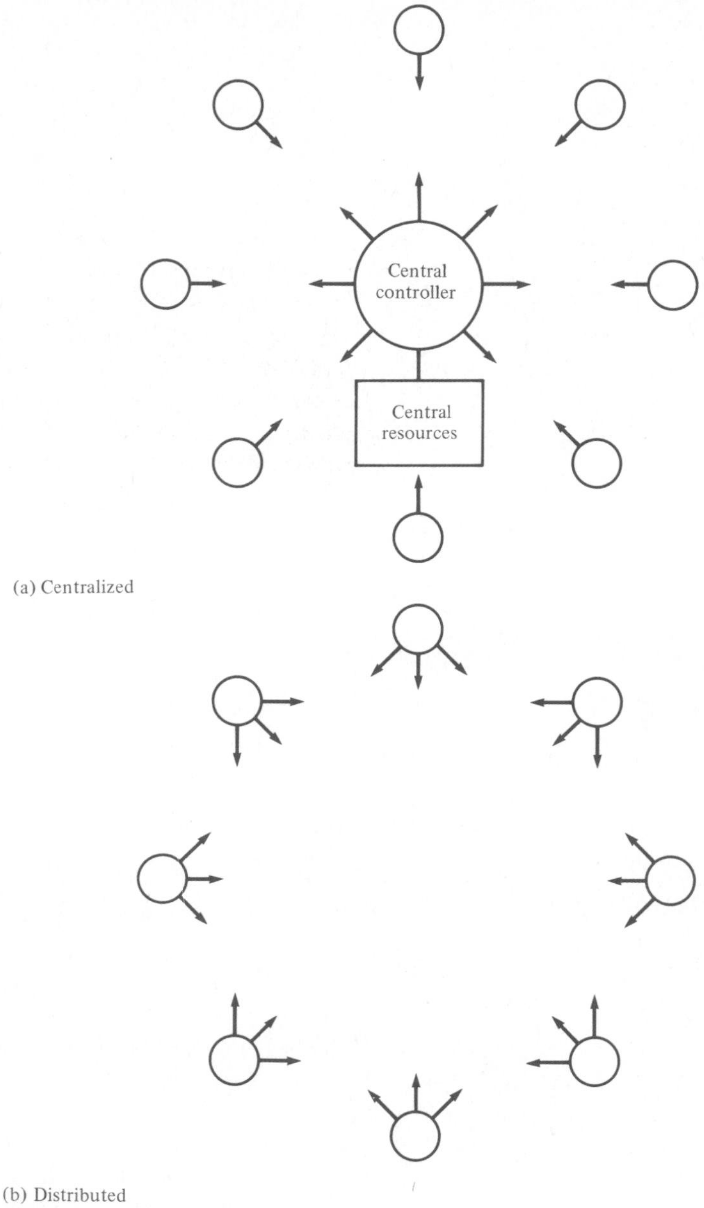

(a) Centralized

(b) Distributed

FIGURE 10-1.   Basic packet radio architecture.

the central node. Node-to-node communication is indirect, mediated by the central
node. The earliest networks followed this model, and were designed primarily to
provide terminal access to a central timesharing system. In a centralized system,
two radio channels are required. Individual nodes send packets to the central node
on one channel, and the central node broadcasts packets on another. Since radio
transmission is omnidirectional, packets transmitted by the central node are heard
by all the other nodes. Thus the configuration is logically equivalent to a multipoint
line with a primary and a number of secondaries (Figure 5-2).

The centralized network is not appropriate for the more common situation today of a collection of microcomputers that wish to exchange data, messages, programs, and so forth. The distributed architecture takes full advantage of the omnidirectional property of radio. One channel is used for all transmissions and each transmission is heard by all other nodes. This configuration is logically equivalent to a local area network (Chapter 11).

Figure 10-1 and the discussion above assume line-of-sight propagation. From Equation (2-1), recall that the maximum distance between transmitter and receiver is slightly more than the line of sight, or a distance of $7.14 \sqrt{Kh}$ in kilometers, where h is the height of both antennas in meters, and K reflects a refraction effect. For example, with two antennas at a height of 10 m, and using a nominal value of $K = 4/3$, the maximum range is 26 km. This represents the maximum radius of a centralized system, and the maximum diameter of a distributed system.

To overcome this geographic limitation, a store-and-forward repeater is used (Figure 10-2). A repeater performs much the same task as a node in a packet-

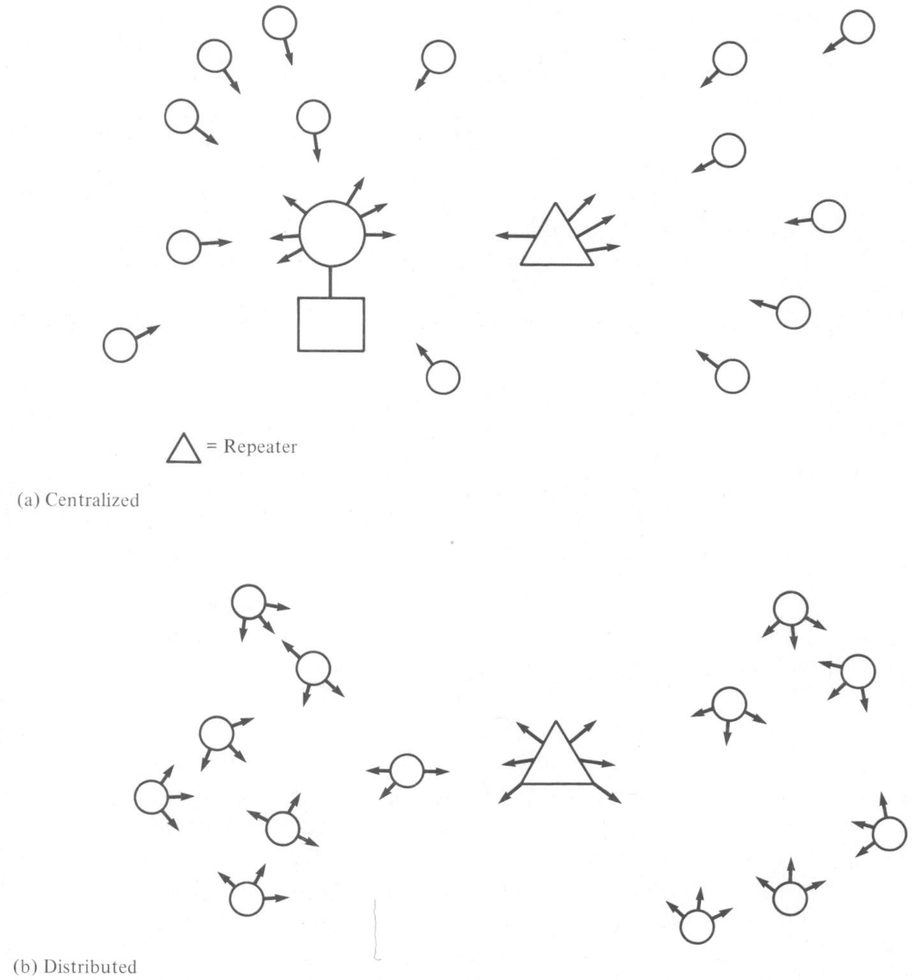

△ = Repeater

(a) Centralized

(b) Distributed

FIGURE 10-2. Packet radio networks with repeaters.

switched network except that it works with broadcast links rather than point-to-point links. In a centralized system, the repeater accepts packets from the central node and retransmits them to remote nodes. It also accepts packets from these remote nodes and forwards them to the central node. In a distributed system, the repeater acts as a switch between two sets of nodes, accepting packets from one set for retransmission to the other, and vice versa.

We now turn to a more detailed description of these two configurations, using ALOHANET [ABRA70], [BIND75a] as our example of a centralized system, and a standard known as AX.25 as our example of a distributed system.

Centralized Networks: ALOHANET

The first packet radio network, ALOHANET, was developed by the University of Hawaii and became operational in 1970. Its principal objective was to allow user terminals in widely scattered locations to access the university computer system. Traffic was primarily terminal-to-host, but terminal-to-terminal traffic could be routed via the central node, called the *menehune* (Hawaiian for "imp"). Remote units were of two types. The *terminal control unit* (TCU) operated with a simple half-duplex terminal and included a buffer, control logic, and transceiver. The *programmable control unit* (PCU) was a microprocessor-based device for terminal concentration and/or a computing station.

As a centralized system, ALOHANET requires two channels. PCU- and TCU-to-menehune traffic are on channel f_1, using a frequency of 407.35 MHz; traffic from the menehune is carried on channel f_2, at a frequency of 413.475 MHz. Both channels have a bandwidth of 100 kHz and, using PSK, a data rate of 9600 bps. Transmission on both channels uses packets with the following format:

- *SYNC (100 bits):* A fairly lengthy synchronization pattern was deemed advisable to minimize errors.
- *Header (32 bits):* The header includes the user address (8 bits), repeater address (6 bits), packet type (3 bits), packet length (8 bits), and various other control bits.
- *CRC (16 bits):* The header is protected with its own error-detecting code.
- *Data (640 bits):* A maximum of 80 characters can be transmitted.
- *CRC (16 bits):* The data are protected with another error-detecting code.

The f_1 (user) channel uses a multiaccess contention protocol known as ALOHA. Each station transmits a packet when it has data to send. It then expects to hear an acknowledgment (ACK) from the menehune. However, since each station transmits at will, it is possible that two transmissions will overlap. This is known as a *collision*; the result is that the menehune receives a garbled transmission. To account for transmission errors and collisions, a user node retransmits a packet if no ACK is received during a random timeout interval. The random time interval avoids a second collision between packets that had originally collided. The time is uniformly distributed in an interval with a minimum of 0.2 s, chosen to allow time for receipt of the ACK, and a maximum of 1.5 s. The lower bound is increased for nodes transmitting through repeaters, to account for the repeater delay in both directions.

The f_2 channel is used primarily for two types of packets: acknowledgment packets and data packets from the central resource. Because the timing of ACKs

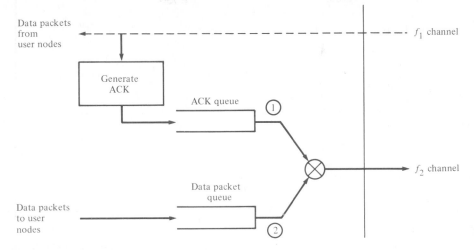

FIGURE 10-3.   **ALOHANET broadcast channel multiplexing.**

is critical, acknowledgment packets have absolute priority. Two queues of packets waiting to be transmitted are maintained by the menehune, one for ACKs and one for all other packets (Figure 10-3). As long as the ACK queue is not empty, the next packet is transmitted from that queue.

In the original implementation, packets from the menehune were not acknowledged by the user nodes, for two reasons. First, since the f_2 channel was noncontention, there was a high probability of successful transmission. Second, ACKs would increase the congestion of the contention-based f_1 channel. Later on, ACKs were added for selected applications, such as file transfer.

The repeaters in ALOHANET also use channels f_1 and f_2. Each repeater has a list of addresses of nodes with which it can communicate. Packets on f_1 from a user node within the address range are repeated on f_1 to the menehune or to the next repeater in the case of cascaded repeaters. Packets on f_2 addressed to a user node within the address range are repeated on f_2 in the opposite direction. The process is depicted in Figure 10-4a, which shows a repeater that communicates with a central controller (C) and a defined set of user nodes (A). Since radio transmission is omnidirectional, it is clear that the menehune and a repeater should not transmit on f_2 at the same time. To avoid this, the menehune will pause after transmission of a packet to a repeater long enough for the packet to be forwarded.

Two more elements of ALOHANET that need to be described are the strategies for routing and flow control. Routing is required if a packet-radio network has more than one repeater. In the case of ALOHANET, a fixed routing strategy is used. The system is set up so that the ranges of addresses for the various repeaters do not overlap. In a system with many repeaters, a more complex routing strategy would be indicated.

Flow control on f_2 requires that the menehune know the input characteristics of the user node. In essence, the menehune waits sufficient time for a node to absorb a packet of data before sending another. Flow control on f_1 is normally not a problem. For lengthy transfers from a PCU, a go-ahead packet mechanism is used. The PCU can only send a certain amount of data and then has to wait for the go-ahead packet.

(a) Centralized network

(b) Distributed network

FIGURE 10-4. Function of a radio packet repeater.

Distributed Networks: The AX.25 Standard

An increasingly common application of distributed packet radio is to provide distributed networking among personal computers, including access to centralized computing resources. In most cases these networks consist of amateur radio stations and are open to any user who conforms to the protocol used on a particular network.

Amateur packet radio networks exist in a number of areas throughout North America, and the number is growing steadily. An effort to standardize these networks has been underway since 1982, under the sponsorship of the American Radio Relay League [KARN85], [BRUN84], which has produced a standard for a link-level protocol suitable for packet-radio networks known as AX.25 [ARRL84].

An ARRL-type network is a distributed network, organized into clusters of stations connected by repeaters. All stations and repeaters share a single frequency for transmission and reception. The AX.25 standard does not specify the frequency to be used. Based on FCC-approved channel availability, the typical network uses the 220-MHz band, using FSK and with a bandwidth of 20 kHz or 100 Khz. A typical data rate is 4800 bps. As with ALOHANET, a fixed routing scheme is used. In this case, the route to be followed is specified by the source station, as explained below.

The link protocol is based on, and very close to, HDLC. The frame format is as follows (compare Figure 5-14):

- *Flag (1 octet):* as in HDLC, 01111110.
- *Address (14 to 70 octets):* explained below.
- *Control:* as in HDLC.

- *Protocol Identifier (1 octet):* specifies what kind of network layer (layer 3) protocol, if any, is in use.
- *Information:* as in HDLC.
- *Frame Check Sequence (2 octets):* as in HDLC.
- *Flag (1 octet):* as in HDLC.

There are two differences between the AX.25 frame format and that of HDLC: the Protocol Identifier (PID) field and the address field. The PID field is used to designate the layer 3 protocol that is using the AX.25 link protocol. This would allow multiple users of the link layer protocol. For example, ARRL is in the process of specifying a network-layer protocol tailored to packet-radio networks. Another alternative is an internet protocol. Typically, the layer 3 protocol within systems on a network is unique and of no concern to the link layer. Thus, at present, the utility of this field is doubtful.

The most important difference between AX.25 and HDLC is in the addressing technique. In HDLC, there are two possible configurations: a point-to-point link with two stations, and a multidrop link with one primary and multiple secondaries. In either case, a single address is sufficient for the operation of the protocol. This is not true in a packet-radio network, for two reasons:

1. Since the network is a peer, distributed network, both the source and destination stations should be identified; neither is unique. For flow control, error control, and sequence numbering, both addresses are needed. To see this, consider a situation in which station *A* is simultaneously engaged in logical connections to two other stations, *B* and *C*. *A* is exchanging AX.25 frames with both *B* and *C*, using the HDLC mechanisms for flow control and error control. Thus, *A* must keep track of the send and receive sequence numbers used for its separate connections to both *A* and *B*. To do this, each incoming frame must identify the sender.
2. If repeaters are involved, these repeaters must be specified. In particular, it is the responsibility of the transmitting station to specify the repeater or repeaters that must be used to get from source to destination.

The AX.25 address field is from 14 to 70 octets long, depending on whether and how many repeaters are used between a particular source–destination pair. If the sending and receiving stations are in the same cluster (within range of each other), then it is only necessary to specify the source and destination station addresses. Each is specified using 7 octets, which contains a call sign of up to 7 characters. If a frame is to go through a repeater, an additional 7-octet address subfield is appended to the end of the address field. This field contains the call sign of the repeater. It also contains two flag bits of interest: the H (has-been-repeated) bit and the address-extension bit. If a station wishes to send a frame to a station that can be reached only through a repeater, it includes not only its address and the destination address, but the repeater address as well. The H bit is set to zero. A repeater will ignore all frames that do not contain its address. If its address is present, the repeater sets the H bit to one and retransmits the packet. A station receiving a frame with a repeater address whose H bit is set to zero will ignore it. This avoids the problem of a station receiving duplicate packets, one from the source and one from the repeater. This is possible since line-of-sight transmission radii of necessity overlap. Figure 10-4b shows the use of a repeater to link two sets of user stations.

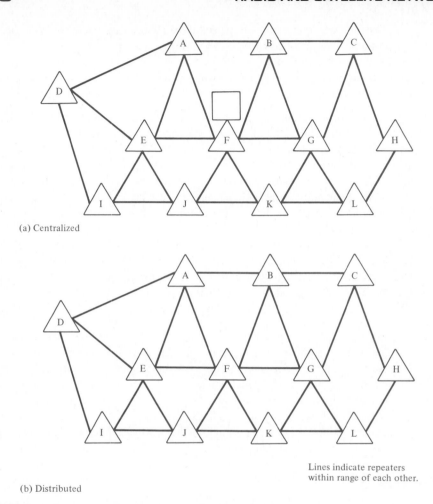

(a) Centralized

(b) Distributed

Lines indicate repeaters
within range of each other.

FIGURE 10-5. Packet radio networks with many repeaters.

- *Variable data rate links:* Data link error detection and control techniques contribute to transmission overhead and thus reduce the effective data rate. Some radio designs allow these techniques, and thus the effective data rate, to vary significantly in response to link quality variations. This affects the selection of minimum delay routes.

- *One-way links:* This would result from different ambient noise levels, jamming, or different antenna characteristics at two radios. Most distributed routing techniques require information from any node to which a packet might be sent, but it is unclear how a sender can even learn the existence of an outgoing one-way link.

Common channel effects are those produced by the fact that all links use the same shared transmission channel. In Figure 10-5, for example, stations *G, K,* and *L* are in range of each other. Only one of the three may transmit at a time. A transmission from one is heard by the other two as well as any other repeaters within range of the transmitter (e.g., *G*'s transmission is heard by *K* and *L,* and also by *B, C,* and *F*). The implications of this situation are:

The AX.25 protocol allows operation through more than one repeater, creating a primitive routing mechanism. Up to eight repeaters may be used by extending the repeater-address subfield. Each address but the last will have the address-extension bit set to zero. The first repeater address designates the first repeater in the chain. As a frame progresses through a chain of repeaters, each successive repeater will set the H bit in its own address, indicating that the frame has been successfully repeated through it.

Whether one or multiple repeaters are employed in a particular transmission, it is the responsibility of the source station to design the route and specify the repeater addresses in the frame.

The operation of the AX.25 protocol is essentially the same as that of HDLC. Functions such as flow control, error control, link establishment, and so forth are identical. One additional requirement in a packet-radio environment is the use of a medium access control technique, several of which are described below (ALOHA, S-ALOHA, CSMA). The AX.25 standard does not specify which such technique to use, but the CSMA technique described below seems the most appropriate for a distributed network.

Routing

In packet radio networks with a small number of repeaters, a fixed routing scheme is adequate. As the use of packet radio grows, we are more likely to see networks with a large number (>10) of repeaters and with at least some of the stations being mobile. Military requirements clearly reflect this architecture. Figure 10-5 illustrates the types of configurations of multirepeater networks. In a centralized network, the routing problem is to find a route between the central node F and all other nodes. In a distributed network, we have the apparently more difficult problem of finding a route between each pair of repeaters. Note also that in a distributed network, one would need some sort of two-level address for each station of the form (repeater, station), where "repeater" identifies the cluster of stations local to a particular repeater. This section presents an overview of the routing problem for such networks and is based primarily on [CARP81].

A multirepeater packet radio network is topologically similar to the type of packet-switched network discussed in Chapter 9. Each repeater is equivalent to a node, and the local cluster of each repeater is equivalent to multiple stations attached to a node. Because of the similarities, one might think that the routing algorithms discussed previously would be applicable to multirepeater packet radio networks. However, there are differences, due to the transmission characteristics of the two networks, and the fact that some packet radio nodes may be mobile. We can group those differences between the two types of networks that affect routing strategy into two categories: link reliability effects and common channel effects.

Link reliability effects are those due to the fact that radio links are less reliable than guided-medium links. They are subject to fading, multipath, and noise interference and, in a hostile environment, to jamming. Lower reliability suggests:

- *More frequent monitoring of link status:* This is required to assure reliable communication. If overhead packets for this purpose are exchanged on a regular basis, routing information could be added (piggybacking).

- *Variable data rate links:* Data link error detection and control techniques contribute to transmission overhead and thus reduce the effective data rate. Some radio designs allow these techniques, and thus the effective data rate, to vary significantly in response to link quality variations. This affects the selection of minimum delay routes.
- *One-way links:* This would result from different ambient noise levels, jamming, or different antenna characteristics at two radios. Most distributed routing techniques require information from any node to which a packet might be sent, but it is unclear how a sender can even learn the existence of an outgoing one-way link.

Common channel effects are those produced by the fact that all links use the same shared transmission channel. In Figure 10-5, for example, stations *G, K,* and *L* are in range of each other. Only one of the three may transmit at a time. A transmission from one is heard by the other two as well as any other repeaters within range of the transmitter (e.g., *G*'s transmission is heard by *K* and *L*, and also by *B, C,* and *F*). The implications of this situation are:

- *Link delays are the same for all output links:* With point to point links, each node has a queue of packets for each link and knows the length of its queues. With broadcast links, these local queues are not independent; there is, in effect, one large distributed queue of packets waiting to use the common channel. This will affect routing strategies that use queueing delay as a parameter.
- *Links are not independent:* The amount of traffic (and hence delay) between one pair of repeaters will affect the delay on other pairwise links. This is not taken into account by most algorithms for globally generating all routes through the network.
- *Routing overhead packets need be sent only once:* Many distributed routing strategies require that routing information be sent by a node to each of its neighbors. This would require only one radio broadcast.

It should be clear that the problem of routing in a packet radio network is even more complex than in a conventional packet-switched network. As yet, there has been little experience or research in this area. As examples, we mention two approaches.

Because of the problems of unreliable links and mobile nodes, it is clear that a highly robust routing algorithm is required. Flooding comes to mind, but is the most wasteful of bandwidth. However, from the point of view of the individual repeater, flooding is required! Even if a packet transmitted by a repeater includes a destination repeater address field, that packet will be received by all other repeaters within range. One way to reduce waste with a flooding approach would be to try to minimize the number of repeaters that actually do retransmit [LIU80]. The procedure works as follows. When a repeater receives a packet to rebroadcast, it waits a random length of time before doing so. If it receives another copy of the packet before its own broadcast, it discards the packet. Thus if two or more neighbors hear the same broadcast, only one of them will relay it. This reduces but does not eliminate packet duplication. In Figure 10-5, for example, if repeater *H* broadcasts a packet, both *C* and *L* will receive it. Since *C* and *L* are not within range of each other, both will rebroadcast it.

Another way to reduce duplicate packets is for each repeater to only forward a packet when it is closer to the destination than the repeater from which it received the packet [GITM76]. Suppose that each repeater knew its hop-count distance from every other repeater. Then the process would work as follows. When a repeater receives a packet from a station for forwarding, it adds a distance field whose value is the number of hops to the destination repeater, and then broadcasts the packet. When a repeater receives a packet from another repeater, it does the following:

- If the packet is for a station in the local cluster, broadcast it.
- If the packet is to be forwarded, check the distance field. If this repeater is closer to the destination than the last repeater, update the distance field and transmit.

In Figure 10-5b, for example, suppose that K broadcasts a packet with a destination of D and a distance of 3. Repeaters J, F, G, and L receive the transmission, but only J and F have a hop count to D of less than 3. They both broadcast a packet with a distance of 2. Repeaters I, E, A, B, G, K, and J get one or two copies of the packet. Of these only I, E, and A are closer to D, and they all send a packet to D.

This seems to work fine. The question is how each repeater may determine its hop count to every other repeater. This could be done in several ways. Each station could maintain a distance table which is periodically exchanged with its neighbors, much like DNA and the original ARPANET algorithm. Another alternative is a backward learning algorithm. When a repeater receives a packet for the first time, that packet will have traversed the shortest route from the original repeater. This information could be used to update the distance table in the destination repeater.

10-2

PACKET RADIO ACCESS PROTOCOLS

As was mentioned in Chapter 7, a medium access control protocol is needed for a multiaccess network. Such protocols are designed to address the problem of how to share a common broadcast channel: the "Who goes next?" problem. The techniques that have been used for packet radio networks can be termed *random access* or *contention* techniques. They are random access in the sense that there is no predictable or scheduled time for any station to transmit: Stations generate packets for transmission at random times. They are contention in the sense that no central control is exercised to determine whose turn it is: All stations contend for time on a network.

In this section we introduce and discuss three contention protocols appropriate for packet radio networks: ALOHA, slotted ALOHA, and *carrier sense multiple access* (CSMA). ALOHA and CSMA have enjoyed extensive use in packet radio networks; slotted ALOHA is a refinement of ALOHA. We will see that these as well as other contention protocols exhibit an inherent instability: as the load on the network increases, a saturation point is reached, beyond which throughput collapses.

ALOHA

The earliest of the contention techniques, known as *ALOHA*, was developed for packet radio networks [ABRA70]. However, it is applicable to any transmission

medium shared by uncoordinated users. ALOHA, or *pure ALOHA* as it is sometimes called, is a true free-for-all. Whenever a station has a packet to send, it does
so. The station then listens for an amount of time equal to the maximum possible
round-trip propagation time on the network (twice the time it takes to send packet
between the two most widely separated stations). If the station hears an acknowledgment during that time, fine; otherwise, it resends the packet. After repeated
failures, it gives up. A receiving station determines the correctness of an incoming
packet by examining the FCS. If the packet is valid, the station acknowledges
immediately. The packet may be invalid, due to noise on the channel or because
another station transmitted a frame at about the same time. In the latter case, the
two frames may interfere with each other so that neither gets through; this is known
as a *collision*. In either case, the receiving station simply ignores the frame.

ALOHA is as simple as can be, and pays a penalty for it. To get at the performance of this protocol, we first present results based on the assumption that
there are an infinite number of stations. This may strike the reader as an absurd
tactic, but, in fact, it leads to analytically tractable equations that are, up to a point,
very close to reality. We will define that point shortly. For now, we state the
infinite-source assumption precisely: There are an infinite number of stations, each
generating an infinitely small rate of packets such that the total number of packets
generated per unit time is finite.

Some additional assumptions are needed. We use the following notation, which
is discussed in some detail in Appendix 10A:

- S: the throughput of the network; the total rate of data being transmitted
  between stations (carried load). S is usually normalized to be expressed
  as a fraction of network capacity.
- G: the total rate of data presented to the network for transmission (offered
  load), also usually normalized.
- I: the total rate of data generated by the stations (input load), also usually
  normalized.
- D: the average delay that occurs between the time a packet or frame is ready
  for transmission from a station, and the completion of successful transmission.

The assumptions are:

1. All packets are of constant length. In general, such packets give better average
   throughput and delay performance than do variable-length packets. In some
   analyses, an exponential distribution of packet length is used.
2. The channel is noise-free.
3. Packets do not collect at individual stations; that is, a station transmits each
   packet before the next arrives, hence $I = S$. This assumption weakens at
   higher loads, where stations are faced with increasing delays for each packet.
4. G, the offered load, is Poisson distributed.[1]

These assumptions do not reflect accurately any actual system. For example,
higher-order moments or even the entire probability distribution of packet length
or G may be needed for accurate results. These assumptions do provide analytic
tractability, enabling the development of closed-form expressions for performance.

[1]See the Appendix to this book for a discussion of the Poisson distribution.

Thus they provide a common basis for comparing a number of protocols and they allow the development of results that give insight into behavior of systems.

To begin, let us consider the centralized network of Figure 10-1a and assume that all stations are equidistant from the central node. Traffic is generated as so many packets per second. It is convenient to normalize this to using the packet transmission time; then we can view S as the number of packets generated per packet time. Since the capacity of the channel is one packet per packet time, S also has a meaning of throughput as a fraction of capacity.

The total traffic on the channel will consist of new packets plus packets that must be retransmitted because of collision:

$$G = S + \text{(number of retransmitted packets per unit time)}$$

Now, a packet must be retransmitted if it suffers a collision. Thus we can express the rate of retransmissions as $G \times \text{Pr}$ [individual packet suffers a collision]. Note that we must use G rather than S in this expression.

To determine the probability of collision, consider Figure 10-6a, which shows three stations that transmit packets at random times. Each transmission takes a normalized transmission time of 1. A packet generated by any station reaches the central node after a constant propagation delay (equidistant stations). Now, if two stations begin to transmit at exactly the same time, their packets will arrive at the controller at the same time and suffer a collision. Moreover, a packet transmitted by station A will suffer a collision if B begins transmission prior to A but within a time period 1 of the beginning of A's transmission, or if B begins transmission after A within a time period 1 of the beginning of A's transmission. Thus the vulnerable period is of length 2.

We have assumed that G is Poisson distributed. For a Poisson process with rate λ, the probability of transmission in a period of time t is $1 - e^{-\lambda t}$. Thus the probability of transmission during the vulnerable period is $1 - e^{-2G}$. Therefore, we have

$$G = S + G(1 - e^{-2G})$$

So

$$\text{ALOHA: } S = Ge^{-2G} \qquad (10\text{-}1)$$

This derivation assumes that G is Poisson, which is not the case even for I Poisson. However, studies indicate that this is a good approximation [SCHW77]. Also, deeper analysis indicates that the infinite population assumption results closely approximate finite population results at reasonably small numbers: say, 50 or more stations [KLEI76].

Another way of deriving (10-1) is to note that S/G is the fraction of offered packets that are transmitted successfully, which is just the probability that for each packet, no additional packets arrive during the vulnerable period, which is e^{-2G}.

One question that might be asked on the basis of Equation (10-1) is: What is the maximum possible throughput using ALOHA? If we differentiate Equation (10-1) with respect to G and set it equal to zero, we find that the maximum occurs at $G = 0.5$ and that $S = 1/2e = 0.18$. That is, the maximum throughput is only 18% of capacity. For example, ALOHANET uses a data rate of 9600 bps. Using the ALOHA scheme, the maximum total throughput (the sum of the data arriving from all user nodes) is only $0.18 \times 9600 = 1728$ bps. Furthermore, this capacity of 1728 bps must be shared among all user nodes.

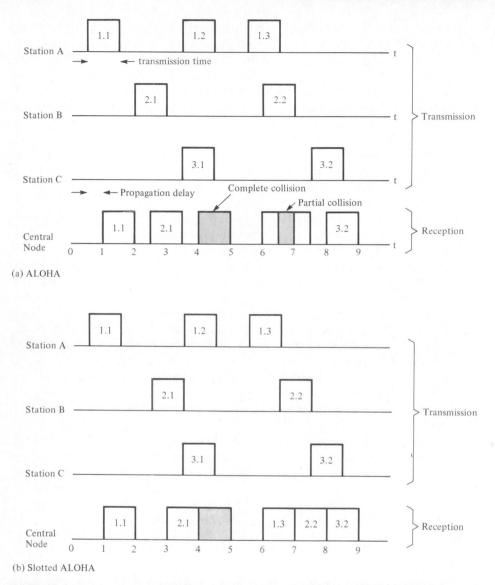

FIGURE 10-6.   Behavior of ALOHA and slotted ALOHA in a centralized packet radio network.

   Delay is more difficult to calculate, but the following reasoning gives a good approximation. We define delay as the time interval from when a user node is ready to transmit a packet until when it is successfully received by the central node. This delay is simply the sum of queueing delay, propagation delay, and transmission time. In ALOHA, the queueing delay is 0; that is, a node transmits immediately when it has a packet to transmit. However, because of collisions, we may consider the queueing delay time to be the total time consumed prior to successful transmission, (i.e., the total time spent in unsuccessful transmissions). To get at this, we need to know the expected number of transmissions per packet. A little thought shows that this is simply G/S. So the expected number of retransmissions per packet is just $G/S - 1 = e^{2G} - 1$. The delay, D, can then be expressed as

$$D = (e^{2G} - 1)\, \delta + a + 1$$

where δ is the average delay for one retransmission and a is the normalized propagation delay (see Appendix 10A). A common normalized algorithm used for ALOHA is to retransmit after a time selected from a uniform distribution of from 1 to K packet-transmission times. This minimizes repeated collisions. The average delay is then $(K + 1)/2$. To this, we must add the amount of time a station must wait to determine that its packet was unsuccessful. This is just time it would take to complete a transmission $(1 + a)$ plus the time it would take for the receiver to generate an acknowledgment (w) plus the propagation time for the acknowledgment to reach the station (a). For simplicity, we assume that acknowledgment packets do not suffer collisions. Thus

$$ALOHA: D = (e^{2G} - 1)\left(1 + 2a + w + \frac{k + 1}{2}\right) + a + 1 \quad (10\text{-}2)$$

Now let us consider the distributed packet radio network. Behavior in this case is slightly different and it will be instructive here for the reader to ponder Figure 10-6a and Appendix 10A. The difference is this: If the propagation delay between stations A and B is a, then a packet transmitted by A will suffer a collision if B begins transmission prior to A but within a time period $1 + a$ of the beginning of A's transmission or if B begins transmission after A within a time period $1 + a$ of the beginning of A's transmission. Thus the vulnerable period is of length $2(1 + a)$. Some calculation reveals that this alters Equations (10-1) and (10-2) as follows:

$$S = Ge^{-2(1+a)G} \quad (10\text{-}3)$$

$$D = (e^{2(1+a)G} - 1)\left(1 + 2a + w + \frac{k + 1}{2}\right) + a + 1 \quad (10\text{-}4)$$

For the typical packet radio network, a is extremely small, 10^{-3} or less. Thus we may safely ignore this refinement. However, we will find that it is relevant in the case of satellite and local networks.

Before attempting to discuss the results obtained so far, let us consider an improved version of ALOHA, namely slotted ALOHA.

Slotted ALOHA

We have seen that the maximum throughput with ALOHA is only 0.18. To improve efficiency, a modification of ALOHA, slotted ALOHA (S-ALOHA), was developed in which time on the channel is organized into uniform slots whose size equals the packet transmission time [ROBE75]. Some central clock or other technique is needed to synchronize all stations. Transmission is permitted only to begin at a slot boundary. Thus packets that do overlap will do so totally (see Figure 10-6b).

Throughput for slotted ALOHA is also easily calculated. All packets begin transmission on a slot boundary. Thus the number of packets that are transmitted during a slot time is equal to the number that was generated during the previous slot and await transmission. So the probability that an individual packet suffers collision is $1 - e^{-G}$. Thus we have:

$$S\text{-}ALOHA: S = Ge^{-G} \quad (10\text{-}5)$$

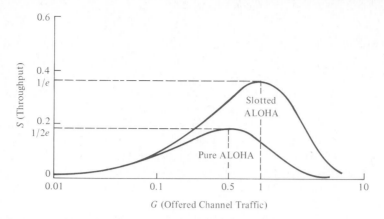

FIGURE 10-7.   **Performance of ALOHA, S-ALOHA with $a = 0$.**

Differentiating (10-5) with respect to G, we have that the maximum possible value for S is $1/e = 0.37$. Thus the effective throughput of a packet radio network is doubled by this simple refinement.

Equations (10-1) and (10-5) are plotted in Figure 10-7, which provides insight into the nature of the instability problem with contention protocols. As offered load increases, so does throughput until, beyond its maximum value, throughput actually declines as G increases. This is because there is an increased frequency of collisions: More packets are offered, but fewer successfully escape collision. Worse, this situation may persist even if the input to the system drops to zero! Consider: For high G, virtually all offered packets are retransmissions and virtually none get through. So, even if no new packets are generated, the system will remain occupied in an unsuccessful attempt to clear the backlog; the effective capacity of the system is virtually zero. Thus, even in a moderately loaded system, a temporary burst of work could move the network into the high-collision region permanently.

Delay for S-ALOHA may be estimated in a similar fashion to that of ALOHA. The main difference now is that there is a delay, averaging half a slot time, between the time a node is ready to send a frame and the time the next slot begins:

$$S\text{-}ALOHA: \quad D = (e^G - 1)\left(1 + 2a + w + \frac{k + 1}{2}\right) + 1.5a + 1.5 \quad (10\text{-}6)$$

These formulas confirm the instability of contention-based protocols under heavy load. As the rate of new packets increases, so does the number of collisions. We can see that both the number of collisions and the average delay grow exponentially with G. Thus there is not only a trade-off between throughput (S) and delay (D), but a third factor enters the trade-off: stability. Figure 10-8 illustrates this point. Figure 10-8a shows that delay increases exponentially with offered load. But Figure 10-8b is perhaps more meaningful. It shows that delay increases with throughput up to the maximum possible throughput. Beyond that point, although throughput declines because of increased numbers of collisions, the delay continues to rise.

It is worth pondering Figures 10-7 and 10-8 to get a better feeling for the behavior of contention channels. Recall that we mentioned that both S and G are ''derived'' parameters, and what we would really like to estimate is the actual traffic generated

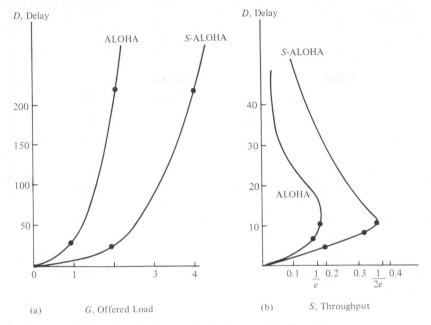

FIGURE 10-8. Delay as a function of **G** and **S** (**a** = 0, **K** = 5).

by network devices, the "input load" I. As long as the input load is less than the maximum potential throughput, $\text{Max}_G(S)$, then $I = S$. That is, the throughput of the system equals the input load. Therefore, all packets get through. However, if $I > \text{Max}_G(S)$, Figures 10-7 and 10-8 no longer apply. The system cannot transmit packets as fast as they arrive. The result: If I remains above the threshold indefinitely, then D goes to infinity, S goes to zero, and G grows without bound.

Figure 10-8b shows that, for a given value of S, there are two possible values of D. How can this be? In both cases, $I = S$, and the system is transmitting all input packets. The explanation is as follows: As the input, $I = S$, approaches the saturation point, the stochastic nature of the input will eventually lead to a period of a high rate of collisions, resulting in decreased throughput and higher packet delays.

Finally, we mention that these results depend critically on the assumptions made. For example, if there is only one station transmitting, the achievable throughput is 1.0, not 0.18 or 0.37. Indeed, with a single user at high data rate and a set of other users at very low data rates, utilization approaching 1 can be achieved. However, the delay encountered by the other users is significantly longer than in the homogeneous case. In general, the more unbalanced the source rates, the higher the throughput [KLEI76].

As before, equations for slotted ALOHA can be derived that take into account the parameter a:

$$S = Ge^{-(1+a)G} \tag{10-7}$$

$$D = (e^{(1+a)G} - 1)\left(1 + 2a + w + \frac{k+1}{2}\right) + 1.5a + 1.5 \tag{10-8}$$

CSMA

We have seen that even with slotted ALOHA, the maximum channel utilization is only 0.37. Both of these protocols fail to take advantage of one of the key properties of packet radio networks, which is that the propagation delay between stations is insignificant compared to packet transmission time (a is very small).

Consider the following observations. If the station-to-station propagation time is large compared to the packet transmission time, then, after a station launches a packet, it will be a long time before other stations know about it. During that time, one of the other stations may transmit a packet; the two packets may interfere with each other, and neither gets through. Indeed, if the distances are great enough, many stations may begin transmitting, one after the other, and none of their packets gets through unscathed. Suppose, however, that the propagation time is extremely small compared to packet transmission time. In that case, when a station launches a packet, all the other stations know it almost immediately. So, if they had any sense, they would not try transmitting until the first station was done. Collisions would be rare since they would occur only when two stations began to transmit almost simultaneously. Another way of looking at it is that the short delay time provides the stations with better feedback about the state of the system; this information can be used to improve efficiency.

The foregoing observations led to the development of a technique known as carrier sense multiple access (CSMA) or listen before talk (LBT). A station wishing to transmit first listens to the medium to determine if another transmission is in progress. If the medium is in use, the station backs off some period of time and tries again, using one of the algorithms explained below. If the medium is idle, the station may transmit. Now, it may happen that two or more stations attempt to transmit at about the same time. If this happens, there will be a collision. To account for this, a station waits a reasonable amount of time after transmitting for an acknowledgment, taking into account the maximum round-trip propagation delay, and the fact that the acknowledging station must also contend for the channel in order to respond. If there is no acknowledgment, the station assumes that a collision has occurred and retransmits.

One can see how this strategy would be effective for systems in which the packet transmission time is much longer than the propagation time. Collisions can occur only when more than one user begins transmitting within a short time (within the period of propagation delay). If a station begins to transmit, and there are no collisions during the time it takes for the leading edge of the packet to propagate to the farthest station, then the station has seized the channel and the remainder of the packet will be transmitted without collision.

With CSMA, an algorithm is needed to specify what a station should do if the medium is found to be busy. Three approaches are depicted in Figure 10-9. One algorithm is *nonpersistent* CSMA. A station wishing to transmit listens to the medium and obeys the following rules:

1. If the medium is idle, transmit.
2. If the medium is busy, wait an amount of time drawn from a probability distribution (the retransmission delay) and repeat step 1.

The use of random retransmission times reduces the probability of collisions. The drawback is that even if several stations have a packet to send, there is likely to be some wasted idle time following a prior transmission.

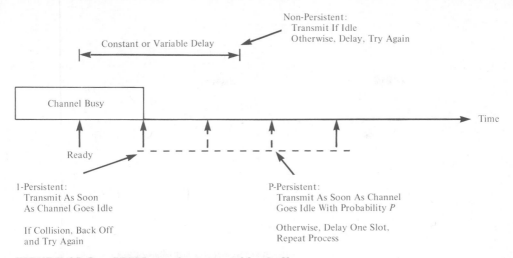

FIGURE 10-9. CSMA persistence and backoff.

To avoid channel idle time, the *1-persistent* protocol can be used. A station wishing to transmit listens to the medium and obeys the following rules:

1. If the medium is idle, transmit.
2. If the medium is busy, continue to listen until the channel is sensed idle, then transmit immediately.
3. If there is a collision (determined by a lack of acknowledgment), wait a random amount of time and repeat step 1.

Whereas nonpersistent stations are deferential, 1-persistent stations are selfish. If two or more stations are waiting to transmit, a collision is guaranteed. Things only get sorted out after the collision.

A compromise that attempts to reduce collisions, like nonpersistent, and reduce idle time, like 1-persistent, is *p-persistent*. The rules are:

1. If the medium is idle, transmit with probability p, and delay one time unit with probability $(1 - p)$. The time unit is typically equal to the maximum propagation delay.
2. If the medium is busy, continue to listen until the channel is idle and repeat step 1.
3. If transmission is delayed one time unit, repeat step 1.

The question arises as to what is an effective value of p. The main problem to avoid is one of instability under heavy load. Consider the case in which n stations have packets to send while a transmission is taking place. At the end of that transmission, the expected number of stations that will attempt to transmit is np. If np is greater than 1, multiple stations will attempt to transmit and there will be a collision. What is more, as soon as all these stations realize that they did not get through, they will be back again, almost guaranteeing more collisions. Worse yet, these retries will compete with new transmissions from other stations, further increasing the probability of collision. Eventually, all stations will be trying to send, causing continuous collisions, with throughput dropping to zero. To avoid this catastrophe, np must be less than one for the expected peaks of n. As p is made

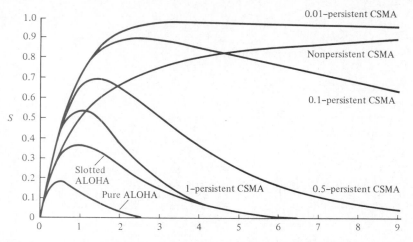

FIGURE 10-10.   Throughput of various contention protocols with $a = 0$.

smaller, stations must wait longer to attempt transmission but collisions are reduced. At low loads, however, stations have unnecessarily long delays.

The performance of CSMA depends on the persistence policy. The easiest to
analyze is nonpersistent CSMA, and we will be content with that. Again, we
assume $a = 0$. Time on the channel consists of two types of intervals. First is a
transmission interval, which lasts a time period 1. Second is an idle period, which
is the time between transmissions. If we assume a Poisson offered load G, the
expected value of the idle period is $1/G$. Total throughput consists of the fraction
of time that the channel is busy:

$$S = \frac{1}{1 + 1/G}$$

$$\text{Nonpersistent CSMA:} \quad S = \frac{G}{G + 1}$$

Figure 10-10 compares the achievable throughput for the various protocols discussed so far, assuming that $a = 0$. It is clear that dramatic improvement can be
achieved using CSMA.

10-3

SATELLITE NETWORK ARCHITECTURE

We mentioned in Part I that a satellite communications link has some unique
properties:

- A satellite in geosynchronous orbit is visible to about one-fourth of the earth's
  surface.
- Transmission cost is independent of distance, within the satellite's area of
  coverage.
- Both broadcast and point-to-point applications are possible.
- Very high bandwidths or data rates are available to users.

- Although satellite links are subject to periodic, short-term outages, the quality of transmission is normally extremely high.
- There is an earth-satellite-earth propagation delay of about one-fourth of a second.
- A transmitting station can in many cases receive its own transmission.

Satellite links are used in a wide variety of configurations, some of which are in the nature of a point-to-point link, others of which are more in the nature of a communication network. Table 10-1 summarizes some of the key characteristics of satellite communication links and groups these into a number of categories. These categories are not independent but interrelated in complex ways. In the remainder of this section we will describe these characteristics and give examples. In doing so, we will need to talk about medium access control. However, a detailed discussion of such protocols is deferred to Section 10-4.

Configurations

The first two categories in Table 10-1 deal with the types of communications configurations that are possible with a satellite link. The variety of configurations that is possible is determined primarily by the nature of the earth stations and the interconnections provided by the satellite link.

Types of Earth Stations. Figure 10-11 depicts three general categories of earth stations; the term earth station refers to a station with a direct communications link to a satellite. By contrast, we use the term "user station" to refer to some endpoint station which indirectly makes use of the satellite link; the distinction should become clear soon. Figure 10-11a indicates the use of a satellite as a link for carrying bulk, long-haul transmission traffic. In this case, the satellite is being used in much the same way as a coaxial cable or terrestrial microwave link. The

TABLE 10-1 Characteristics of Satellite Links

Configurations	Capacity Allocation
Earth stations	Access control
Fixed-assignment carrier	Centralized (satellite)
Multiplexed	Distributed (earth station)
User stations	Allocation strategy
Link configurations	FDM
Point-to-point	FDMA
Point-to-many	SCPC
Many-to-many	DAMA
Many-to-point	TDM
	TDMA
	SS-TDMA
	DAMA
	Multiple-access protocols
	Polling
	Contention
	Reservation

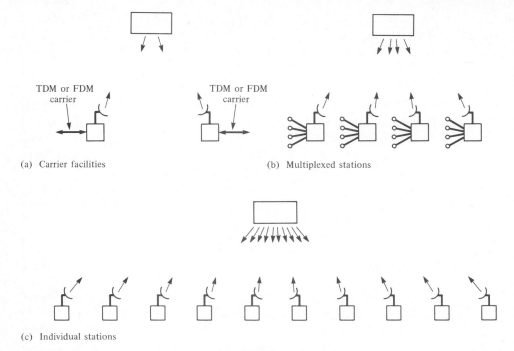

(a) Carrier facilities

(b) Multiplexed stations

(c) Individual stations

FIGURE 10-11.   **Types of satellite earth stations.**

most common application for this type of earth station is as a component of the long-haul telecommunication network. An example of an FDM carrier providing this facility is COMSTAR-2 [BELL82a]. The satellite uses the 4/6-GHz bands and provides a 500-MHz bandwidth which is broken up into 12 40-MHz channels. Actually, the system provides 24 channels (12 full-duplex channels) by means of *frequency reuse*; each frequency assignment is used by two carriers with orthogonal polarization. The 40-MHz channel includes 4 MHz of guard bands, so each channel is actually 36 MHz wide. A total of 1200 voice channels are carried in each 40-MHz channel using a second level of FDM. A similar system could be provided using a synchronous TDM scheme in each of the 40-MHz channels. For example, a 36-MHz channel may be used on the WESTAR satellite to carry one of the following:

- One 50-Mbps data stream.
- 16 channels of 1.544 Mbps each.
- 400 channels of 64 kbps each.
- 600 channels of 40 kbps each.

The discussion above suggests that the satellite is used as an intermediate device providing, in effect, a point-to-point link between two stations. Because of the wide-area coverage of the satellite, this is not necessarily the case. As an example, Figure 10-12 shows seven stations sharing a 36-MHz bandwidth. Station A is assigned the band of 6237.5 to 6242.5 MHz in which it can transmit 60 voice-frequency channels using FDM/FM. That is, FDM is used to carry the 60 channels, and FM is used to modulate the channels onto the carrier frequency, which is in the 6-GHz band. The figure indicates that station A has traffic for other stations as follows: 24 channels to B, 24 channels to D, and 12 channels to E. The remaining

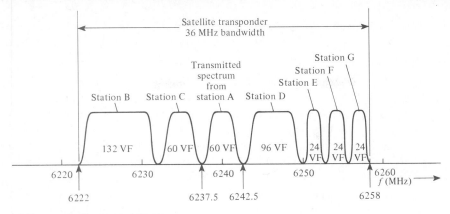

(a) Transponder Frequency Allocation

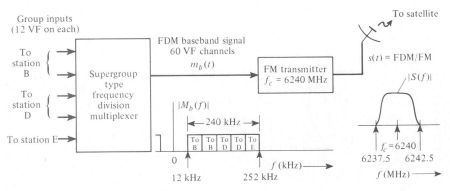

(b) Station A Ground Transmitting Equipment

FIGURE 10-12. A fixed-assignment FDMA configuration.

spectrum of the 36-MHz channel is divided among the other earth stations according to their traffic needs. The last example brings up several instructive points:

- The scheme described is referred to as a fixed-assignment frequency-division multiple access (FDMA) scheme. The term ''fixed assignment'' refers to the fact that the logical links between stations are preassigned. Thus in Figure 10-12, it appears to station A that it has three direct point-to-point links, one each to B (24 channels), D (24 channels), and E (12 channels). FDMA refers to the fact that multiple stations are accessing the satellite link by using different frequency bands.
- Although an earth station may transmit only one carrier up to the satellite (e.g., station A transmits at 6.24 GHz with a bandwidth of 5 MHz), it must be prepared to receive at least one carrier for each distant location with which it wishes to communicate (e.g., station A must receive three carriers, parts of the transmission of B, D, and E).
- The satellite performs no switching function. Although it is receiving portions of the 36-MHz channel from various sources, it simply accepts signals across that spectrum, translates them to the 4 GHz band, and retransmits them.
- Considerable bandwidth is used. For example, station A has 60 voice-frequency channels to transmit, which occupies only 240 kHz. Yet the satellite

bandwidth allocation is 5 MHz. This is due to the use of FM (rather than AM) to maintain signal quality over the long distance of the satellite link and to minimize satellite power requirements.

Skipping next to Figure 10-11c, we see the extreme opposite to the use of a satellite link as a high-capacity carrier trunk. In this case multiple stations communicate directly with the satellite, functioning as both earth stations and user stations. Note the similarity to Figure 10-1a. With individual user stations functioning as earth stations we have a network in which any two stations may communicate via the satellite link. Multiple communication channels are provided with some form of either FDM or TDM. Examples will be discussed in Section 10-4.

An intermediate situation is depicted in Figure 10-10b. In this case, there are user stations, but these do not have direct links to the satellite. Rather, a group of user stations attach to an earth station which multiplexes traffic from all attached stations for transmission. Again, a variety of schemes are used. We mention two general examples.

* Any pair of these stations could have a dedicated channel between them, such as one of the 1.544 Mbps channels on a TDM channel or a 40-MHz FDM channel. This channel could then be used for a statistical TDM scheme.
* A circuit-switching capability could be provided by the satellite. Each earth station then functions in a manner analogous to a data or voice link group on a digital PBX and the satellite functions in a manner analogous to the central switch (Figure 8-21). This technique is examined below.

Satellite Link Configurations.   Figure 10-11 implies a symmetry between uplink and downlink transmission that is not always present. We can characterize satellite links by the number of stations transmitting on the uplink and the number of stations receiving on the downlink. Of course, this characterization depends in part on how much of the spectrum one is talking about. For example, for a satellite with a 500 MHz capacity, it is unlikely that that entire capacity would be used between two points. However, a 40-MHz channel might be so used.

Within a single channel, we have given examples of both point-to-point and many-to-many connections. An example of many-to-point might be a system that collects data from a variety of sources (e.g., sensor data) and delivers them to a single receiver. Far more common is point-to-many, and the prime example of this is TV broadcasting.

Communications satellites have been transmitting commercial broadcast and cable television programs since 1975. The TV signal is frequency modulated onto a carrier in the 6-GHz uplink band; one TV channel occupies one 40-MHz satellite channel using FM. The signal is provided to the satellite by a network or cable TV source and retransmitted on a 4-GHz downlink. The retransmissions are intended primarily for reception by central distribution hubs, such as broadcast stations and cable TV distribution centers. It is possible for people to pick up these signals, but the antennas required are large and expensive.

Another example of point-to-many video transmission, with a more sizable ''many,'' is *direct broadcast satellite* (DBS) [GOUL84], [GOUL85]. During the 1970s DBS was successfully tested on a number of experimental satellites, and this has led to design efforts that should culminate in DBS service in the late 1980s. With this scheme, transmission is in the 12/14-GHz band at higher power; thus smaller (less than 1 meter diameter), less expensive antennas can be used, and it is feasible for people to receive signals for their TV sets directly from rooftop or backyard earth stations.

Capacity Allocation

Typically, a single satellite will handle a rather large bandwidth (e.g., 500 MHz) and divide it into a number of channels of smaller bandwidth (e.g., 40 MHz). Within each of these channels, there is a capacity allocation task to be performed. In some instances, such as TV broadcasting and a single 50 Mbps digital data stream, the entire channel is dedicated to a single user or purpose. With these exceptions, however, the cost-effective use of the satellite requires that each channel be shared by many users. In some cases, the allocation is carried out by centralized control, usually by the satellite; but in most cases, the allocation is a distributed function carried out by the earth station. We will see examples of both.

All of the allocation strategies can be categorized as either frequency-division or time-division strategies. The task is, fundamentally, one of multiplexing, and most of the schemes in use today employ variants of one or the other of the schemes discussed in Chapter 6. In some configurations, however, the satellite link takes on the character of a multipoint medium and some form of multiple access protocol is required. We will survey all these strategies in this section.

FDM.   We have mentioned that FDM is almost always employed, in the sense that a satellite's total bandwidth is divided into channels. Each of these channels is, in turn, usually shared by multiple stations. When each of these stations is assigned a different carrier frequency or group of frequencies on a fixed basis, it is referred to as *frequency-division multiple access* (FDMA). Actually, all of the techniques to be discussed in this section are FDMA, since they involve access to a channel by multiple stations using FDM, but the term is generally reserved for the case of fixed assignment. Further, it is generally assumed for FDMA that each earth station supports multiple user stations on each of its assigned subchannels. Thus some further FDM or TDM technique must be used to allocate subchannel capacity.

The operation of an FDMA system is simple. The example presented earlier (Figure 10-12) is typical. A number of earth stations are assigned transmit carrier frequencies and bands. The satellite accepts signals across the entire spectrum of a channel, translates the entire channel to a different frequency, and retransmits. As an aside, we will see that a midsplit broadband local network works in much the same fashion.

The number of subchannels provided within a satellite channel via FDMA is limited by three factors:

- Thermal noise.
- Intermodulation noise.
- Cochannel interference.

We have seen (Figure 2-21) that the first two factors work in opposite directions. With too little signal strength, the transmitted signal will be corrupted by background noise. With too much signal strength, nonlinear effects in the satellite's amplifiers results in high intermodulation noise. The third factor, cochannel interference, stems from a desire to increase capacity by reusing frequencies, and limits but does not eliminate that practice. A frequency band can be reused if antennas that can radiate two polarized signals of the same frequency (cochannels) in orthogonal planes are employed. Again, if signal strength is too high, cochannel interference becomes significant.

The FDMA scheme just described is not terribly efficient. Typically, in the 6/4-GHz band, each channel has a usable bandwidth of 36 MHz. One standard FDMA scheme [FREE89] divides this into seven 5-MHz blocks, each of which carries a supergroup of 60 voice channels, for a total of 420 voice channels. When the channel is subdivided into 14 2.5-MHz channels, two groups (24 channels) are carried in each subchannel for a total of 336 channels. A more efficient utilization of the bandwidth is to avoid groupings altogether and simply to divide the 36-MHz bandwidth up into individual voice-frequency channels. This technique is known as single-channel per carrier (SCPC).

SCPC is currently provided in the 6/4-GHz band. A single 36-MHz channel is subdivided into 800 45-kHz channels, each dedicated to a simplex voice-frequency link. Analog systems use FM. There is also digital SCPC, using QPSK which provides 64-kbps service, enough for digitized voice. Both schemes use the 45-kHz bandwidth [SHIM85], [FEHE83]. With fixed assignment, pairs of channels (for full duplex) are assigned to pairs of earth stations. Typically, each earth station is multiplexed, supporting a small number of user stations. This corresponds roughly to Figure 10-11b. With multiple user stations per earth station, a high degree of connectivity is achieved even with fixed assignment. As with conventional FDMA, the satellite accepts frequencies across the entire 36-MHz channel, translates them to the 4-GHz band, and broadcasts the channel to all stations.

SCPC is attractive for remote areas where there are few user stations near each site. Whereas FDMA is used as a trunk facility in the long-haul telecommunications system, SCPC provides direct end-user service. Although, SCPC is more efficient than FDMA, it does suffer from the inefficiency of fixed assignment. This is especially unsuitable in very remote areas where it is typical that each earth station would serve one or a very few user stations (such as Figure 10-11c). To achieve greater efficiency, a technique known as demand-assignment multiple access (DAMA) is used. With DAMA, the set of subchannels in a channel is treated as a pool of available links. To establish a full-duplex link between two earth stations, a pair of subchannels is dynamically assigned on demand. This is a form of circuit switching.

The first commercially-available DAMA system was SPADE (*s*ingle channel per carrier, *p*ulse code modulation, multiple-*a*ccess, *d*emand-assignment *e*quipment), introduced in the early 1970s and used on INTELSAT IVA and V satellites [EDEL72], [FREE85a]. As with ordinary SCPC, a 36-MHz bandwidth is divided into 45-kHz subchannels. Each subchannel carries a 64-kbps QPSK signal, which occupies 38 kHz, plus a 7-kHz guardband. Typically, the signal is used to carry PCM voice traffic. With control overhead, explained below, a total of 794 subchannels are available. These subchannels are paired such that two channels 18.045 MHz apart are always used to form a full-duplex circuit (e.g.; 3-404, 4-405, 399-800). In addition, there is a 160-kHz common-signaling channel (CSC) which carries a 128 kbps PSK signal.

Demand assignment is performed in a distributed fashion, by the earth stations, using the CSC. The CSC is used to transmit a repetitive TDM frame as shown in Figure 10-13. The frame is divided into 50 slots, the first of which is devoted to a preamble pattern for synchronization. The remaining slots are permanently as-

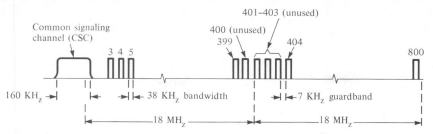

(a) Frequency allocation

(b) CSC frame format

FIGURE 10-13. SPADE system for switched SCPC service.

signed to 49 stations. These stations have the privilege of forming full-duplex circuits on demand. This is accomplished as follows. Assume that station S_i wishes to establish a circuit with S_j. Then S_i selects a subchannel randomly from the available idle channels and transmits the subchannel identifier plus the address of station S_j in the S_i time slot. Station S_j will hear this request on the downlink about 0.25 s later. Assuming that the subchannel is still available and S_j is available, S_j transmits an acknowledgment in its own time slot, which is heard by S_i another quarter second later. When the call is complete, disconnect information is transmitted in the time slot of one of the stations to inform the others that the subchannel is again idle.

Since only 49 stations can participate in this scheme, most of the subchannels are not required. These are used for ordinary fixed-assignment SCPC.

Although the SPADE system did provide the expected advantages of DAMA, the cost and complexity of the equipment at each site was considered too high and the system was discontinued. Recently, however, work has gone forward on other DAMA-SCPC schemes in the 14/12-GHz band and commercial service is likely by the late 1980s [EDEL82]. The basic concept is to develop a system that requires no switching or routing functions in either the satellite or earth stations, but to leave this task to a PBX or telephone company central office. As with fixed-assignment SCPC, each station has two dedicated subchannels for a full-duplex link. In this scheme, however, both subchannels are linked to the central earth station, which performs the circuit-switching function. The only drawback is that two hops are now required between user stations (user station 1 to central office via satellite, central office to user station 2 via satellite).

Finally, we mention that another way to increase utilization and flexibility is to have multiple stations share the same SCPC subchannel. An example of this is the ARPANET satellite IMP [WEIS78]. A number of satellite IMPs are part of the packet-switched network and share a single 64-kbps SCPC channel. Various multiple-access protocols have been tried, including slotted ALOHA and some of the protocols to be discussed in Section 10-4.

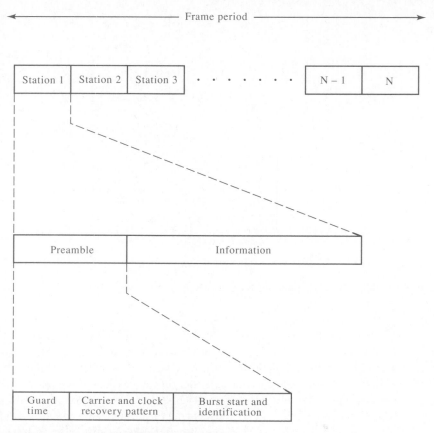

FIGURE 10-14. Example of TDMA frame format.

TDM.   Although FDM techniques are still the most common ones in satellite transmission, TDM techniques are in increasingly widespread use. The future seems to belong to TDM for a number of reasons, including:

- The continuing drop in costs of digital components.
- The advantages of digital techniques, discussed earlier.
- The increased efficiency of TDM due to the lack of intermodulation noise.

As with FDM, all of the techniques to be discussed provide for multiple access, but the fixed-assignment technique is blessed with the name *time-division multiple access* (TDMA). TDMA is in essence the same as synchronous TDM (Section 6.2). Transmission is in the form of a repetitive sequence of frames, each of which is divided into a number of slots. Each slot position across the sequence of frames is dedicated to a particular transmitter. Frame periods range from 125 μs to 15 ms and consist of from 5 to 15 slots [FREE89]; typical frame periods are 750 μs for INTELSAT and 250 μs for the Canadian Telesat. Data rates range from 10 Mbps to over 100 Mbps [JORD85].

Figure 10-14 depicts a typical frame (compare Figure 6-7). Each of the N stations is assigned one or more slots in the frame. Each slot begins with a *preamble* that contains control and timing information. The individual slots are separated by *guard times* to ensure that there is no overlap. The *carrier and clock recovery pattern* is

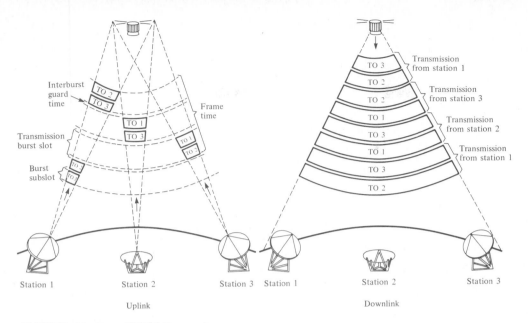

FIGURE 10-15. TDMA operation.

a unique pattern that allows all stations to synchronize to a master clock. The *identification* field identifies the destination station.

The operation of TDMA is depicted in Figure 10-15. Individual stations take turns using the uplink channel and may put a burst of data in the assigned time slot. The satellite repeats all incoming transmissions, which are broadcast to all stations. Thus all stations must know not only which time slot to use for transmissions, but which time slot to use for reception. The satellite is also repeating the reference burst, and all stations synchronize on the reception of that burst.

Each of the repetitive time slots is a subchannel and is independent of the other subchannels. Hence it can be used in any way that is deemed appropriate by the transmitting station. For example, a form of switching can be achieved by including an address field in each time slot. Thus, although the transmitting slot is dedicated, a number of stations could read the data in each slot looking for data addressed to them. Another example of a more sophisticated TDMA scheme is presented in [PONT83].

Ordinary TDMA is more efficient than ordinary FDMA because the guard times and control bits of TDMA utilize less capacity than the guard bands of FDMA. This is illustrated in Figure 10-16. Note the dramatic drop in capacity of FDMA as the number of subchannels increases. By contrast, TDMA drops much more slowly as the number of time slots (subchannels) increases. The use of a long frame time also increases efficiency. For comparison, a SCPC system provides a constant capacity of 800 channels whether its bandwidth is divided among many or a few earth stations.

Even greater efficiencies can be achieved as the newer, higher-frequency (e.g., 14/12-GHz and 30/20-GHz) bands come into use. At these frequencies, satellite transmission beams can be quite narrowly focused, allowing multiple beams on the same frequency to be transmitted to different areas. Thus a satellite can service a number of areas, each containing a number of earth stations. Communication

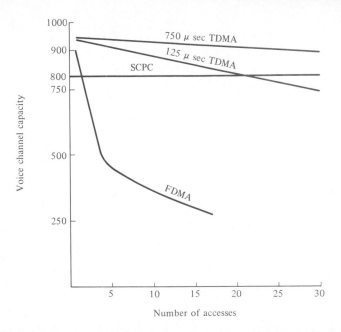

FIGURE 10-16. Relative efficiency of various satellite capacity allocation schemes. Source: [EDEL82]

among stations within a single area could be accomplished with ordinary TDMA. Moreover, communication among stations in different areas can be achieved if the satellite has the capability to switch time slots from one beam to another. This is known as *satellite-switched time-division multiple access* (SS/TDMA) [SCAR83].

Figure 10-17 depicts a simple SS-TDMA system serving two areas, each with two stations. As with ordinary TDMA, only one station at a time may transmit within an area. So within area *A*, either station 1 or 2 may transmit at any one time. However, one station from area *B* may also transmit at any time. Stations from the two areas do not interfere either through the use of polarized signals or different frequencies. At the satellite, data that are received are immediately retransmitted on a downlink frequency. Now, however, two separate downlink beams are used. The station contains a switch for interconnecting input beams and output beams. The connections through the switch may change over time. In the figure, downlink beam *A* repeats uplink beam *A* during periods 1 and 3 and repeats uplink *B* during period 2. Thus any station in any area can send data to any other station in any area.

This technique is a form of time-multiplexed switched, as described in Chapter 8. For a satellite serving *N* areas, there are *N* time-division multiplexed input streams. At any given time, the switch is configured to route these uplink beams in a particular fashion to the *N* downlink beams. Each configuration is referred to as a mode and *N*! modes are required for full connectivity. Table 10-2 shows the modes for a three-area system. For example, stations in area *A* can communicate with each other during modes 1 and 2, communicate with stations in area *B* during modes 3 and 5, and so on. The satellite will switch from mode to mode periodically. At most, a mode change would occur once per slot time. The mode pattern and duration are normally adjustable by ground command to meet changing traffic requirements.

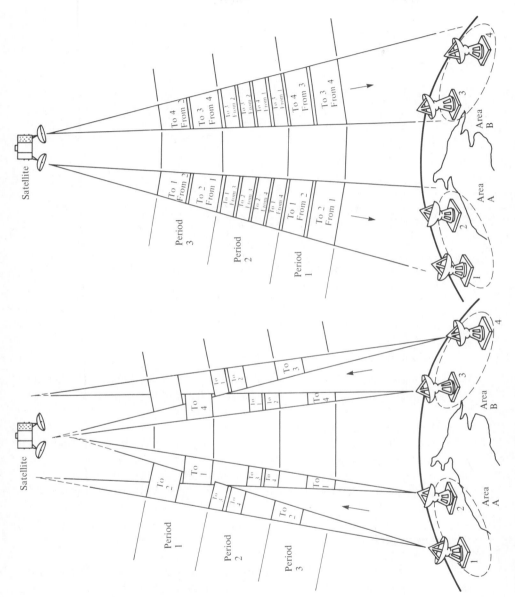

FIGURE 10-17. SS/TDMA operation.

TABLE 10-2   SS/TDMA Modes (three beams)

Input	Output					
	Mode 1	Mode 2	Mode 3	Mode 4	Mode 5	Mode 6
A	A	A	B	C	B	C
B	B	C	A	A	C	B
C	C	B	C	B	A	A

Finally, DAMA techniques are employed with TDM satellite schemes. The SS/TDMA system is to some extent a DAMA system if the mode pattern can be changed by ground command. More commonly DAMA in the TDM context refers to multiple-access techniques for sharing a single channel. This is the subject of our next section.

10-4

SATELLITE CHANNEL ACCESS PROTOCOLS

This section is concerned with TDM-DAMA techniques for use on a single satellite channel. In this situation, there is a single uplink channel and a single downlink channel shared by multiple earth stations. The satellite is essentially passive and performs three tasks:

- Accept all uplink signals.
- Translate signal to downlink frequency.
- Transmit downlink signals.

If two or more stations transmit simultaneously, a collision occurs. The satellite receives and retransmits garbled data. Because the satellite is passive, it is the collective responsibility of the earth stations to allocate channel capacity efficiently to maximize throughput and minimize collisions.

The situation described above is a common one, and considerable research has been done to develop suitable medium access control protocols. We begin by outlining those characteristics of a satellite network that are relevant to access control design, and then review some of the approaches that have been taken.

Characteristics

The design of a medium access control protocol for a satellite network is determined by two principal factors: the nature of the link and the nature of the users.

Let us examine the nature of the link first. The most important thing to note is that the bit length of the link is large. The up-and-down propagation delay is roughly one-fourth of a second, so the bit length is one-fourth of the data rate. SCPC channels are generally 64 kbps, which yields a length of 16,000 bits. At the upper end, a 50-Mbps channel is possible, yielding a length of 12.5 million bits! An immediate implication of the long bit length is that carrier-sense techniques will not work on a satellite network. Recall the CSMA protocol used for distributed packet-radio networks. A station refrains from transmitting if another station is already transmitting. With a satellite, a station will not know that another station is transmitting until a fourth of a second after the other starts, by which time it has long since ceased transmitting.

That's the bad news. The good news is an interesting property that satellites share with broadband local networks: A station receives its own transmissions. Thus an earth station knows, a fourth of a second after it has ceased transmitting, whether its transmission was successful or suffered a collision. This property is exploited in all of the protocols discussed below.

The other determining factor is the nature of the users of the communication service. In general, it is best to assume that there will be a variety of traffic types. For example, some of the stations may generate short, bursty traffic with modest throughput requirements but a need for a short delay time (e.g., transactions). Other stations may generate long streams of traffic that require high throughput, but they may be able to tolerate moderate delays prior to the start of a transmission (e.g., file transfers).

A fair random access scheme will not function well in these circumstances. For example, a stream transmission can cause intolerable delays for bursty traffic. If stream traffic load is stable, one solution is to dedicate certain portions of the bandwidth to various traffic types. This can be done using FDM or by dedicating certain time slots on a TDM system. However, if the stream traffic load varies, as when file transfers are made primarily at night and interactive traffic is high during the day, a fixed-allocation scheme lacks flexibility and is wasteful of bandwidth.

With these factors in mind, we can consider three generic approaches to access control: polling, contention, and reservation. Conventional polling, with a primary station and a number of secondary stations, is clearly inefficient. About a half second would elapse just in sending a poll and waiting for a response. For contention, since CSMA is impractical, ALOHA or S-ALOHA would be used. The performance calculation is the same as for a centralized packet-radio network: The maximum achievable utilization is only 0.37. Thus attention has focused on reservation schemes.

Reservation Protocols

To overcome the inherent disadvantages of polling and contention techniques for DAMA-TDMA, a number of reservation schemes have been proposed, and a few have been implemented. In this section we examine six of these schemes (Figure 10-18). These are representative and should give the reader a feeling for the nature of the trade-offs that must be made. In all of these schemes, a fixed frame length is used, which is divided into a number of time slots. (In what follows, we assume that there are K stations and M slots per frame that may be reserved.) Slots in future frames are reserved in some dynamic fashion for a specific station. The schemes differ primarily in the way in which the reservations are made and released.

Distributed Reservation. The simplest of these schemes is one proposed in [CROW73], called R-ALOHA (Figure 10-19a). In this scheme, there are generally fewer slots per frame than there are stations ($K > M$). Reservations are implicit: Successful transmission in a slot serves as a reservation for the corresponding slot in the next frame. By repeated use of that slot position, a station can transmit a

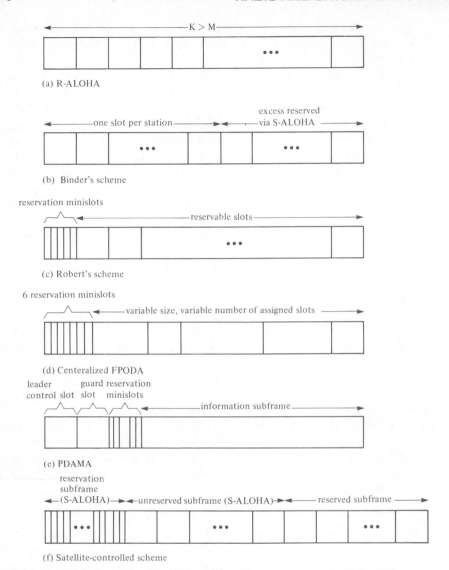

FIGURE 10-18.   Frame format for various satellite reservation protocols.

long stream of data. A station wishing to transmit one or more packets (one packet per slot) of data monitors the slots in the current frame. Any slot that is empty or contains a collision is available for the next frame; the station may contend for that slot using S-ALOHA.

Several observations may be made. First, note that the frame length must be at least as long as the bit length of the link (i.e., 16,000 to 12.5 million bits for data rates of 56 kbps to 50 Mbps). This is so because a station must know the status of each slot in the most recent frame before considering its use in the next frame. Second, this approach allows a dynamic mixture of stream and bursty traffic. If the average message length (number of slots used per reservation) is long, the system behaves like a fixed-assignment TDMA scheme. If most of the traffic is bursty, the performance resembles S-ALOHA. In fact, performance could even be

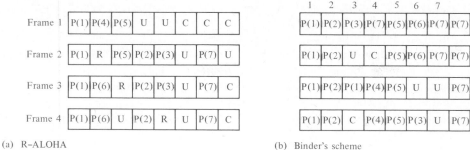

| Frame 1 | P(1) | P(4) | P(5) | U | U | C | C | C |

| Frame 2 | P(1) | R | P(5) | P(2) | P(3) | U | P(7) | U |

| Frame 3 | P(1) | P(6) | R | P(2) | P(3) | U | P(7) | C |

| Frame 4 | P(1) | P(6) | U | P(2) | R | U | P(7) | C |

(a) R–ALOHA

| | 1 | 2 | 3 | 4 | 5 | 6 | 7 | |
| | P(1) | P(2) | P(3) | P(7) | P(5) | P(6) | P(7) | P(7) |

| P(1) | P(2) | U | C | P(5) | P(6) | P(7) | P(7) |

| P(1) | P(2) | P(1) | P(4) | P(5) | U | U | P(7) |

| P(1) | P(2) | C | P(4) | P(5) | P(3) | U | P(7) |

(b) Binder's scheme

Legend　C = Collision
　　　　U = Unused slot
　　　　R = Unused but reserved slot
　　　　P (I) = Packet transmitted by station I

FIGURE 10-19.　Implicit reservation schemes.

worse than S-ALOHA if most messages are one slot in length: After a slot is used, it will remain empty for the next frame because the stations do not realize that it is free. Performance can be improved by including an end-of-use flag with each message [LAM80]. Third, there is a basic fairness problem, since a station can capture most or all of the slots for an indefinite time; if many stations are active with long messages, average delay would be considerable.

The scheme described above will work with an unknown or dynamically varying number of stations. A scheme proposed in [BIND75b] (Figure 10-19b) requires a fixed number of stations less than or equal to the number of time slots in a frame ($K < M$). Each station owns a particular slot position. If there are any extra slots, these are contended for by all stations using S-ALOHA. The owner may use its slot to transmit continuously. If the owner has no data to send, its slot will become empty and available for use by other stations. The owner gets its slot back simply by using it. If the transmission is successful, fine; if not, the collision causes other stations to defer and the station reclaims the slot in the next frame. As before, the frame length must exceed the bit length.

There are two types of slots available for general use in this scheme: slots in excess of fixed-assignment slots (for K strictly less than M) and fixed-assignment slots that were unused in the previous frame. These could be allocated by S-ALOHA. Binder suggests a more complex scheme: Each station includes the length of its queue of slot-sized packets in the header of each packet that it sends. Each station keeps track of the global queue, which is the sum of the individual queues. A round-robin algorithm is used to allocate available slots to queued packets. Thus this scheme has the flavor of both an implicit and an explicit reservation protocol. A station that uses its own slot implicitly reserves it for the next frame. By broadcasting its queue length, a station is explicitly reserving future slots. This technique is superior to R-ALOHA for stream-dominated traffic, since each station is guaranteed one slot of bandwidth. However, when there are a large number of stations, this scheme can lead to a very large average delay because of the required number of slots per frame.

A different approach, proposed in [ROBE73], is to use explicit reservations exclusively. For this scheme, a frame is divided into equal-length slots, one of which is further subdivided into "minislots." The minislots, acquired via

S-ALOHA, function as a common queue for all users. A station wishing to transmit must send a request packet in a minislot specifying the number of slots desired, up to some maximum number. If the reservation is successful (no collision), the station then determines which future slots it has acquired and transmits in them. To do this, the station keeps track of the current global queue length J, which is the sum of outstanding reservations. When each frame is received, the station adds to J the sum of all successful reservations (including its own, if any) and subtracts the number of slots containing data. When a reservation is successful, the station counts off J slots and then sends its data.

Figure 10-20 illustrates the operation. For lengthy streams, this scheme requires a user to contend for slots repeatedly, which results in significant delivery delay variances if there is much traffic. If the maximum reservation size is set high enough to allow complete stream transmissions, delays to begin transmission of other traffic become long. An analysis of the performance of this scheme indicates that it is a significant improvement over S-ALOHA. If the maximum number of slots that can be reserved in a single reservation is R, utilization can approach $R/(R + 1)$ for heavy loads [SCHW77].

Centralized Reservation. All of the protocols discussed so far are distributed reservation schemes. These schemes make few assumptions about traffic mix and avoid the delay that a central controller introduces. However, distributed schemes impose a greater processing burden on stations than do centralized ones, and are more vulnerable to a loss of synchronization. That is, distributed reservation schemes require that all stations share the same perception of the current state (global queue status) of the system. Centralized schemes deal more easily with the problem of synchronization. Furthermore, the extra delay is generally acceptable for stream traffic.

One of the simplest of the centralized reservation schemes is known as fixed priority-oriented demand assignment (FPODA). This scheme is used in the Universe network, which ties together six local networks scattered around the United Kingdom [WATE84]. The data rate used is 1 Mbps and the frame length is 130 ms. Each frame begins with six minislots, one dedicated to each of the six stations. A minislot is 100 bytes in length, and may be used by its station to transmit data or a reservation. Data is in the form of an HDLC frame, expanded to include both source and destination address fields (as was done with AX.25). If a reservation is sent, it is a request for a particular type of service: priority, normal, and bulk. Priority requests specify a particular amount of data to be sent at high priority. Normal requests include an estimate of future throughput requirements (bytes per frame).

One of the six stations acts as master and allocates time on the channel based on reservation requests (including its own). The master splits the remainder of the frame (after the six minislots) into from one to six variable-length slots, with each slot assigned to a particular station. The master maintains a queue of requests and allocates time as follows: priority requests are always put at the front of the queue and filled on a first-come, first-served basis. If there is any time remaining in the frame, it is divided among normal requests proportional to the throughput estimates provided by the stations. If there is any time remaining after that, it is divided equally among all stations with bulk requests. A station that receives a slot allocation in a particular frame may use it to send one of more modified HDLC frames, which allows transmission to one or more destination stations.

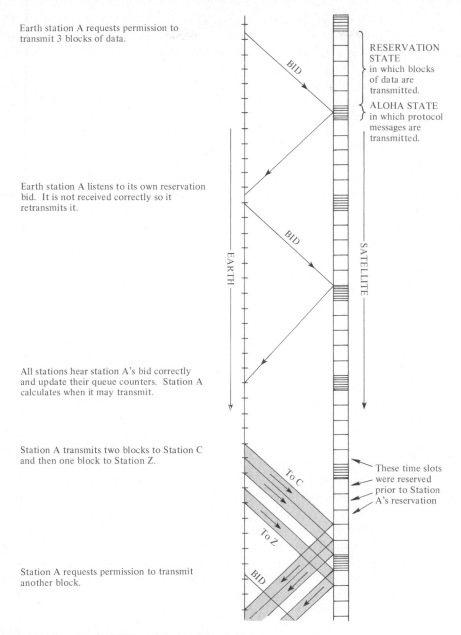

Earth station A requests permission to transmit 3 blocks of data.

BID

RESERVATION STATE in which blocks of data are transmitted.

ALOHA STATE in which protocol messages are transmitted.

Earth station A listens to its own reservation bid. It is not received correctly so it retransmits it.

BID

All stations hear station A's bid correctly and update their queue counters. Station A calculates when it may transmit.

EARTH

SATELLITE

Station A transmits two blocks to Station C and then one block to Station Z.

To C

These time slots were reserved prior to Station A's reservation

To Z

Station A requests permission to transmit another block.

BID

FIGURE 10-20. An ALOHA scheme with explicit reservations.

Once a station has made a normal-service request, it need not repeat that request so long as its throughput requirements remain the same. The master acts as if the same normal-service request was received on each subsequent frame. This frees up the use of the minislot for short blocks of data, such as an acknowledgment to a file transfer.

FPDODA is an effective protocol when there is a small, fixed number of stations sharing the channel. In cases where there is a large or variable number of stations, some other means of placing reservation requests is needed. One such system is the packet-demand assignment multiple access (PDAMA) protocol [PAVE86], [CUMM85] developed for NASA's mobile satellite system, which is a network that provides voice and data communications to mobile users throughout a vast geographical area.

The PDAMA frame format consists of a leader control slot, a guard slot, reservation minislots, and allocated data slots. The frame begins with the leader control slot, whose contents are transmitted by a master station. The slot contains acknowledgments of received reservations and allocations of frame time for other stations. The guard slot is simply an interval that assures that each station hears the leader control slot before attempting further reservations; this interval is 280 ms. The guard slot is also used to allow each station to do ranging. When a station first comes on line, it listens for the next leader subframe. It then transmits a short identification message, which includes the time of transmission, during the guard subframe. If there is no collision (more than one station attempts ranging), the station will hear its own identification message and can determine its round trip time. If there is a collision, the station tries again during subsequent guard subframes, using a random backoff algorithm.

The next subframe consists of a set of minislots used for reservation requests. Stations contend for these minislots using Slotted ALOHA. Three sorts of reservations may be made. Normally, transmission requests are made one packet at a time. If a station has a message to send that is longer than the maximum packet size, it breaks the message up into packets and requests time for each packet. A station may, for a particularly urgent message, request that the message be sent as a unit in a single information subframe. Finally, a station may request an ongoing allocation for a digitized voice exchange.

The information subframe is managed by the master station, which determines which reservation requests are to be honored, based on a prioritized queue of all requests received. The information subframe is of variable length, and is normally allocated to allow a number of stations to send packets in each frame. Two additional modes of operation are supported. A station may request that the system be placed in long message mode. The station granted this allocation uses the entire information subframe until either the long message is completed or until the station is pre-empted by the master for a higher-priority message request. The final mode allows for digitized voice communication. Sufficient capacity is allocated to support full-duplex voice transmission. The master maintains this allocation until it recognizes a hang-up signal or until a higher priority message pre-empts the capacity.

A quite different scheme, proposed in [SUDA83], employs the satellite rather than an earth station to make reservations, and is designed to deal with a mixture of stream and bursty traffic. Each frame consists of three subframes. The *reservation subframe* consists of a set of reservation minislots. The *unreserved subframe* consists of data slots that stations contend for using S-ALOHA (and is intended for bursty traffic). The *reserved subframe* consists of data slots that may be reserved for stream traffic.

To acquire slots in the reserved frame, a station contends for a minislot, using S-ALOHA, to transmit a reservation. A reservation consists of the earth station identifier. If a reservation is successfully received at the satellite, and if at least one unreserved slot is available in the reserved subframe, the satellite immediately sends a confirmation in the same minislot. The confirmation consists of a slot position within the reserved subframe. Upon receipt of the confirmation, the earth station can then use the reserved slot in each succeeding frame until it transmits an end-of-message flag. This informs the satellite to release the slot for future use.

Two timing constraints are associated with this scheme. First, frame retransmission by the satellite is delayed by the time it takes to process a reservation minislot. Second, the unreserved subframe occurs between the reservation subframe and the unreserved subframe and must be longer than the link bit length. In this way, an earth station will know whether its reservation was successful before the beginning of the reserved subframe in the same frame. This results in more efficient use of reserved slots.

Whereas the FPODA and PDAMA schemes are optimized for stream traffic, the scheme in [SUDA83] provides acceptable service for both stream and bursty traffic. A similar philosophy is used in a scheme proposed in [NG77].

10-5

RECOMMENDED READING

The January 1987 issue of the Proceedings of the IEEE is devoted to packet radio [LEIN87]. Worthwhile surveys of packet radio are [SHAC86], [KAHN78], and [NIEL85]. [INGR88] is a practical guide to the use of packet radio. [BIND75a] is a detailed description of ALOHANET plus a commentary on its evolution as lessons were learned. AX.25 is described in [KARN85]. An earlier distributed packet-radio network, MP-Net, is described in [ROUL81]. [KAHN77] is an interesting discussion of various design issues relating to a packet radio network with repeaters.

A readable introduction to satellite communications is [MART78]. Good technical treatments are [HA86] and [SPIL77]. [PICK83b] is a good survey of most of the satellite concepts discussed in this chapter. [BIND81] presents performance results for multiple-access satellite protocols. A more recent treatment is [SKLA88]. [TOBA80] is a survey of performance results for a variety of multiple-access protocols, applicable to satellite, packet radio, and local area networks.

10-6

PROBLEMS

10-1 Assume the usual ALOHANET system, with a data rate of 9600 bps and a packet size of 804 bits. If $G = 0.75$, what is the load on the system in packets/second?

10-2 MP-Net is an early packet-radio network developed and operated by the Montreal Amateur Radio Club. MP-Net uses a sliding-window protocol with a range of 0 to 254. The last frame in a multi-frame transfer (e.g., a file transfer) is given the sequence number 255. Is there any problem with that?

10-3 The MP-Net frame includes both a destination address and a destination repeater address. The latter allows a source to explicitly route a frame through a repeater. When a repeater receives a frame, the repeater checks both the destination repeater address and the destination address to determine whether the packet should be ignored. Would it not be sufficient to just check the destination address?

10-4   A packet is sent from J to C, as depicted in Figure 10-5. What is the total number of packets transmitted between repeaters, assuming no collisions, using each of the two routing techniques described in Section 10-1? For the modified flooding technique, assume a maximum hop count of 3.

10-5   Calculate a value of a for ALOHANET and MP-Net. Assume a maximum radius of 30 km for ALOHANET and a maximum diameter of 60 km for MP-Net. Assume a data rate of 4800 bps for MP-Net.

10-6   Consider a S-ALOHA system with a finite number of stations N and $a = 0$. The offered load from each station is G_i, the throughput S_i. Derive an equation for S_i as a function of G_i. Next, assume that the G_i are identical; what is the equation for $S = \Sigma\, S_i$? Verify that this approaches Ge^{-G} as $N \to \infty$. Above what value of N is the difference negligible?

10-7   A group of N stations shares a 56-kbps ALOHA channel. Each station outputs a 1000-bit packet at an average rate of one every 100 s. What is the maximum useful value of N?

10-8   What is the percent overhead in an ALOHANET packet?

10-9   Why do acknowledgment packets have absolute priority in ALOHANET?

10-10   Figure 10-6 and Equation 10-1 are based on a network configuration similar to that in Figure 10-1a. Does it make any difference to the derivation of the equation as to whether the transmissions are duplex or half-duplex between the central controller and the nodes? Why or why not?

10-11   Calculae the factor a for ALOHANET using a distance of 200 miles.

10-12   Refer to Figure 10-10. With networks using some form of CSMA, it would appear that decreasing p, at least as far as $p = 0.01$, increases the maximum attainable throughput. What penalty, if any, is paid for using a smaller p?

10-13   Calculate the efficiency of the use of bandwidth of station A of Figure 10-12.

10-14   In R-ALOHA, at least one time slot will be wasted after it is relinquished by an owner. Why is this?

10-15   Calculate the frame size in bits and the frame length in meters for FPODA.

10-16   What is the maximum utilization of a packet radio channel for 2 stations that are 100 km apart transmitting at a rate of 32 kbps with packet length of 2000 bits?

10-17   Consider two stations that have been using a terrestrial 4800-bps leased line with a 10^{-5} error rate. Data are transmitted in packets of 1024 bits each, and a selective repeat error control scheme is used. An equivalent satellite link with a 10^{-7} error rate is available. Which of the two has the highest effective throughput?

10-18   Figure 10-12b shows a FDM/FM earth station for a satellite communication system.

Find the peak frequency deviation that achieves the allocated spectral bandwidth for the 6.24-GHz signal.

10-19   For each of the satellite reservation schemes depicted in Figure 10-18, suggest a way in which different stations could be assigned different priorities.

10-20   Consider the satellite-controlled central reservation scheme (Figure 10-18f). Would it not be simpler to divide the bandwidth into two frequency bands, one for slotted ALOHA, and the other for reservations?

APPENDIX 10A

PERFORMANCE CONSIDERATIONS FOR BROADCAST NETWORKS

The key characteristics of packet broadcasting networks that structure the way their performance is analyzed are that there is a shared access medium, requiring a medium access control protocol, and that packet transmission is used. These characteristics are shared by packet radio, satellite, and local networks. It follows that the basic performance considerations, and the approaches to performance analysis, will be the same for all. With the foregoing points in mind, this appendix explores these basic considerations. The section begins by defining the basic measures of performance, then reviews the key parameter for determining performance, which was introduced in Chapter 5. The final topic is a discussion of the interrelationship of the various factors that affect performance.

10A-1   Measures of Performance

Three measures of performance are commonly used:

- D: the delay that occurs between the time a packet is ready for transmission from a station, and the completion of successful transmission.
- S: the throughput of the network; the total rate of data being transmitted between stations (carried load).
- U: the utilization of the medium; the fraction of total capacity being used.

These measures concern themselves with performance within the network. Actual end-to-end performance is also dependent on processing delays within the endpoint stations.

The parameter S is often normalized and expressed as a fraction of capacity. For example, if over a period of 1 s, the sum of the successful data transfers between nodes is 1 Mb on a 10-Mbps channel, then $S = 0.1$. Thus S can also be interpreted as utilization. The analysis is commonly done in terms of the total number of bits transferred, including overhead (headers, trailers) bits; the calculations are a bit easier, and this approach isolates performance effects due to the network alone. One must work backward from this to determine effective throughput.

Results for S and D are generally plotted as a function of the offered load G, which is the actual load or traffic demand presented to the network. We will find that S and G differ. The total load on the network depends in part on the medium

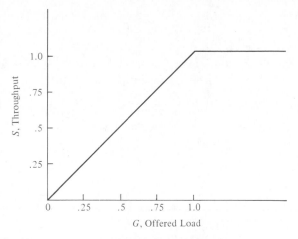

FIGURE 10-21. **Ideal channel utilization.**

access control technique. In some techniques "control packets" are employed; from time to time, packets are transmitted that carry no station data, but are used in the control of the medium. Also, in contention techniques, a "collision" is possible. A collision occurs when two packets are transmitted from two different stations at the same time; the packets interfere with each other and neither is successfully received. Thus S is the normalized rate of data packets successfully transmitted; G is the total number of packets offered to the network, and may include control packets and/or collisions. G, too, is often expressed as a fraction of capacity. Intuitively, we would expect D to increase with G: The more traffic competing for transmission time, the longer the delay for any individual transmission. S should also increase with G, up to some saturation point, beyond which the network cannot handle more load.

Figure 10-21 shows the ideal situation: Channel utilization increases to accommodate load up to an offered load equal to the full capacity of the system; then utilization remains at 100%. Of course, any overhead or inefficiency will cause performance to fall short of the goal. The depiction of S versus G is a reasonable one from the point of view of the network itself. It shows the behavior of the system based on the actual load on it. But from the point of view of the user or the attached station, it may seem strange. Why? Because the offered load includes not only original transmissions but also acknowledgments and, in the case of errors or collisions, retransmissions. The user may want to know the throughput and the delay characteristics as a function of the device-generated data to be put through the system: the "input load." Or if the network is the focus, the analyst may want to know what the offered load is given the input load. We will return to this discussion later.

In summary, we have introduced two additional parameters:

- G: the offered load to the network; the total rate of data presented to the network for transmission.
- I: the input load; the rate of data generated by the stations attached to the network.

Table 10-3 is a very simplified example to show the relationship between these parameters. Here we assume a network with a capacity of 1000 packets/s.

TABLE 10-3 Example Relationship of Broadcast Network Measures of Performance[a]

I	S	G	D	U
100	100	101	0.0505	0.1
500	500	505	0.2525	0.5
990	990	1000	0.5	0.99
1000	990	—	—	0.99
2000	990	—	—	0.99

[a]I, input load (packets/s); S, throughput (packets/s); G, offered load (packets/s) (assumes 1% retransmission rate); D, delay (s); U, utilization (fraction of capacity). Capacity is 1000 packets/s.

For simplicity, I, S, and G are expressed in packets/s. It is assumed that 1% of all transmitted packets are lost and must be repeated. Thus at an input $I = 100$ packets/s, on the average 1 packet/s will be repeated. Thus $S = 100$ and $G = 101$. Assume that the input load arrives in batches, once per second. Hence, on average, with $I = 100$, $D = 0.0505$ s. The utilization is defined as $S/C = 0.1$.

The next two entries are easily seen to be correct. Note that for $I = 990$, the entire capacity of the system is being used ($G = 1000$). If I increases beyond this point, the system cannot keep up. Only 1000 packets/s will be transmitted. Thus S remains at 990 and U at 0.99. But G and D grow without bound as more and more backlog accumulates; there is no steady-state value. This pattern will become familiar in this chapter and Chapter 11.

10A-2 The Effect of Propagation Delay and Transmission Rate

In Chapter 5 we introduced the parameter a defined as

$$a = \frac{\text{Propagation Time}}{\text{Transmission Time}}$$

In that context, we were concerned with a point-to-point link, with a given propagation time between the two endpoints and a transmission time for either a fixed or average frame size. It was shown that a could be expressed as

$$a = \frac{\text{Length of Data Link (Bits)}}{\text{Length of Frame (Bits)}}$$

This parameter is also important in the broadcast network context, and in fact determines an upper bound on the utilization of the network. Consider a perfectly efficient access mechanism that allows only one transmission at a time. As soon as one transmission is over, another station begins transmitting. Furthermore, the transmission is pure data: no overhead bits. What is the maximum possible utilization of the network? It can be expressed as the ratio of total throughput of the system to the capacity or bandwidth:

$$U = \frac{\text{Throughput}}{\text{Capacity}} \tag{10-9}$$

Now define as before (as in Chapter 5):

R = data rate of the channel
d = maximum distance between any two stations
V = velocity of signal propagation
L = average or fixed packet length

The throughput is just the number of bits transmitted per unit time. A packet contains L bits, and the amount of time devoted to that packet is the actual transmission time (L/R) plus the propagation delay (d/V) Thus

$$\text{Throughput} = \frac{L}{d/V + L/R} \tag{10-10}$$

But, by our first definition of a, above:

$$a = \frac{d/V}{L/R} = \frac{Rd}{LV} \tag{10-11}$$

Substituting (10-10) and (10-11) into (10-9)

$$U = \frac{1}{1 + a} \tag{10-12}$$

Note that this differs from Equation (5-2). This is because the latter assumed a half-duplex protocol (no piggybacked acknowledgments).

So utilization varies inversely with a. This can be grasped intuitively by studying Figure 10-22. This figure shows two stations as far apart as possible (worst case) that take turns sending packets. If we normalize time such that the packet transmission time = 1, the sequence of events can be expressed as follows.

1. A station begins transmission at t_0.
2. Reception begins at $t_0 + a$.
3. Transmission is completed at $t_0 + 1$.
4. Reception ends at $t_0 + 1 + a$.
5. The other station begins transmitting.

Event 2 occurs *after* event 3 if $a > 1.0$. In any case the total time for one "turn" is $1 + a$, but the transmission time is only 1, for a utilization of $1/(1 + a)$.

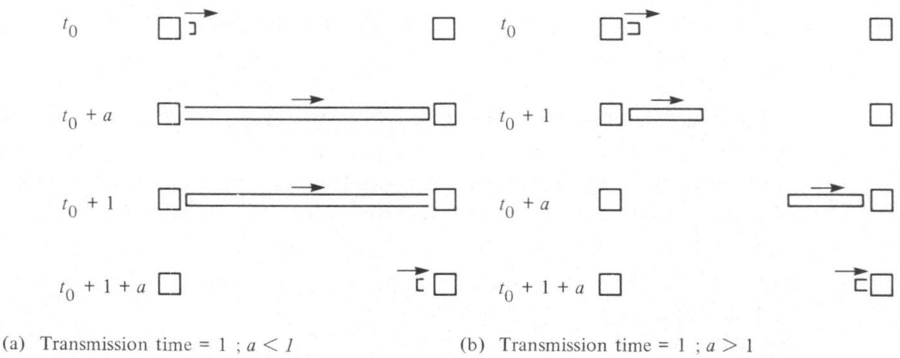

(a) Transmission time = 1 ; $a < 1$ (b) Transmission time = 1 ; $a > 1$

FIGURE 10-22. The effect of a on utilization.

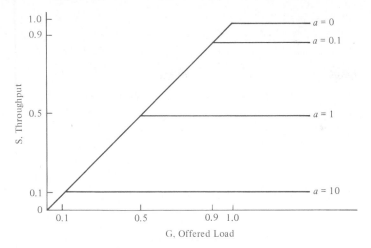

FIGURE 10-23.   **Utilization as a function of a.**

The implication of Equation (10-12) for throughput is shown in Figure 10-23. The ideal case is $a = 0$, which allows 100% utilization. As offered load increases, throughput remains equal to offered load up to the full capacity of the system ($S = G = 1$) and then remains at $S = 1$. For any positive value of a, the system saturates at $S = 1/(1 + a)$.

So we can say that an upper bound on the utilization or efficiency of a broadcast network is $1/(1 + a)$, regardless of the medium access protocol used. Two caveats: First, this assumes that the maximum propagation time is incurred on each transmission. Second, it assumes that only one transmission may occur at a time. These assumptions are not always true; nevertheless, the formula $1/(1 + a)$ is almost always a valid upper bound, because the overhead of the medium access protocol more than makes up for the lack of validity of these assumptions.

The overhead is unavoidable. Frames must include address and synchronization bits. There is administrative overhead for controlling the protocol. In addition, there are forms of overhead peculiar to one or more of the protocols. We highlight these briefly for the most important protocols. (*Note:* On a first reading, some of these terms have not yet been defined. The reader is encouraged to refer back to this section after reading Chapter 11.)

- *Contention protocols (ALOHA, S-ALOHA, CSMA, CSMA/CD):* time wasted due to collisions; need for acknowledgment frames. S-ALOHA requires that slot size equal transmission plus maximum propagation time.
- *Token bus:* token transmission; acknowledgment frames.
- *Token ring:* time waiting for token if intervening stations have no data to send.
- *Explicit reservation:* reservation transmission, acknowledgments.
- *Implicit reservation:* overhead of protocol used to establish reservation, acknowledgments.

There are two distinct effects here. One is that the efficiency or utilization of a channel decreases as a increases. This, of course, affects throughput. The other effect is that the overhead attributable to a protocol wastes bandwidth and hence reduces effective utilization and effective throughput. By and large, we can think of these two effects as independent and additive. However, we shall see that, for contention protocols, there is a strong interaction such that the overhead of these protocols increases as a function of a.

In any case, it would seem desirable to keep a as low as possible. Looking back to the defining formula [Equation 10-11], for a fixed network, a can be reduced by increasing packet size. This will only be useful if the length of messages produced by a station is an integral multiple of the packet size (excluding overhead bits). Otherwise, the large packet size is itself a source of waste. Furthermore, a large packet size increases the delay for other stations. This leads us to the next topic: the various factors that affect performance.

10A-3 Factors That Affect Performance

We list here those factors that affect the performance of a broadcast network. We are concerned here with that part which is independent of the attached devices: those factors that are exclusively under the control of the network designer. The chief factors are:

- Capacity.
- Propagation delay.
- Number of bits per frame.
- Medium access protocol.
- Offered load.
- Number of stations.
- Error rate.

The first three terms have already been discussed; they determine the value of a.

Next is the medium access protocol, which can have a significant effect on network performance. We can think of the first three factors listed above as characterizing the network; they are generally treated as constants or givens. The medium access protocol is the focus of the design effort: the choice that must be made. The next two factors, offered load and the number of stations, are generally treated as the independent variables. The analyst is concerned with determining performance as a function of these two variables. Note that these two variables must be treated separately. Certainly, it is true that for a fixed offered load per station, the total offered load increases as the number of stations increase. The same increase could be achieved by keeping the number of stations fixed but increasing the offered load per station. However, as we shall see, the network performance will be different for these two cases.

A final factor is error rate. An error in packet transmission necessitates a retransmission. Error rates are highly variable and will not be treated directly in any of our estimates of performance.

CHAPTER 11

Local Area Networks

In this chapter we complete our discussion of packet-broadcasting networks by looking at local area networks.

The nature of a local area network is determined primarily by three factors: transmission medium, topology, and medium access control protocol. The bulk of the chapter is devoted to these topics, together with a look at local area network performance. Throughout, reference is made to standards developed for local area networks by two committees: IEEE 802 and ANS X3T9.5. These are described briefly at the end of the chapter.

11-1

LOCAL NETWORK TECHNOLOGY

The principal technology alternatives that determine the nature of a local area network are the topology and transmission medium of the network. Together, they in large measure determine the type of data that may be transmitted, the speed and efficiency of communications, and even the kinds of applications that a network may support.

This section surveys the topologies and transmission media that, within the state of the art, are appropriate for local area networks. Based on these two technologies, three classes of local area networks are defined. The discussion in this section is organized around the common topologies used for local area networks: ring, bus, tree, and star (Figure 11-1).

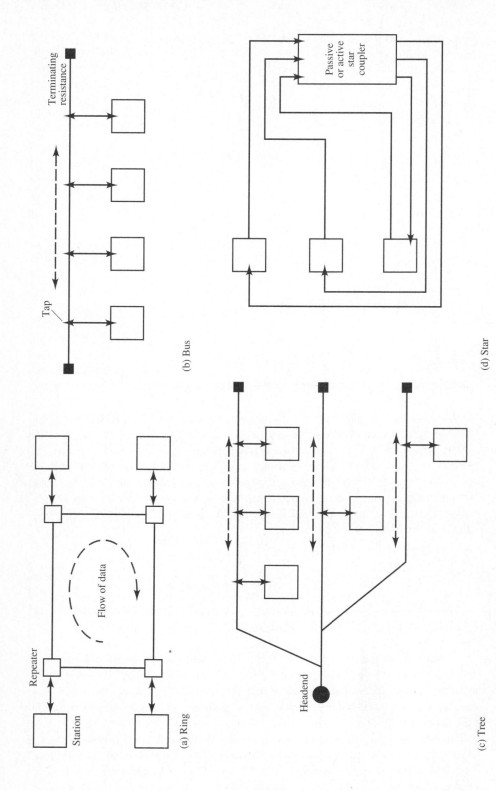

FIGURE 11-1. Local network topologies.

(a) Ring

(b) Bus

(c) Tree

(d) Star

Station

Repeater

Flow of data

Terminating resistance

Tap

Headend

Passive or active star coupler

Ring Topology.   In the ring topology, the network consists of a set of repeaters joined by point-to-point links in a closed loop. Hence each repeater participates in two links on the ring. The repeater is a comparatively simple device, capable of receiving data on one link and transmitting it, bit by bit, on the other link as fast as it is received, with no buffering at the repeater. The links are unidirectional; that is, data are transmitted in one direction only, and all oriented in same way. Thus data circulate around the ring in one direction (clockwise or counter-clockwise).

Each station attaches to the network at a repeater. Data are transmitted in packets inserted onto the ring by the stations. The packet contains source and destination address fields as well as other control information and user data. As a packet circulates, the destination station copies the data into a local buffer. Typically, the packet continues to circulate until it returns to the source station, where it is absorbed, removing it from the ring.

Since multiple devices share the ring, some form of medium access logic is needed to control the order and timing of packet transmissions. This topic is explored later in this chapter.

Virtually any transmission medium can be used with the ring topology. Twisted pair, because of its low cost, is common. Coaxial cable provides greater capacity. Optical fiber is used to achieve very high data transfer rates. Table 11-1 summarizes representative parameters for transmission media for commercially-available ring local area networks.

Bus and Tree Topologies.   Both bus and tree topologies are characterized by the use of a multipoint medium. With the bus topology, all stations attach, through appropriate interfacing hardware, directly to a linear transmission medium, or bus. A transmission from any station propagates the length of the medium in both directions and can be received by all other stations.

The tree topology is a generalization of the bus topology. The transmission medium is a branching cable with no closed loops. The tree layout begins at a point known as the headend. One or more cables start at the headend, and each of these may have branches. The branches in turn may have additional branches to allow quite complex layouts. Again, a transmission from any station propagates throughout the medium, can be received by all other stations, and is absorbed at the endpoints.

As with the ring, transmission is in the form of packets containing addresses and user data. Each station monitors the medium and copies packets addressed to itself. Because all stations share a common transmission link, only one station can successfully transmit at a time, and some form of medium access control technique is needed to regulate access.

Because the ring is constructed as a series of point-to-point links, almost any transmission medium can be used. Twisted pair, at rates up to 10 Mbps, is common. Coaxial cable can be used to achieve higher data rates. Optical fiber is used to achieve very high data transfer rates. Table 11-1 summarizes representative parameters for transmission media for commercially-available ring local networks.

One of the most common communications transmission media, and one that is certainly applicable to bus/tree local networks, is twisted pair wiring. Although typically used for low speed transmission, data rates of up to a few Mbps can be achieved. Twisted pair is relatively low cost and is typically preinstalled in office

TABLE 11-1   Transmission Media for Local Networks: Ring

Transmission Medium	Data Rate (Mbps)	Distance Between Repeaters (km)	Number of Repeaters
Unshielded twisted pair	4	0.1	72
Shielded twisted pair	16	0.3	250
Baseband coaxial cable	16	1.0	250
Optical fiber	100	2.0	240

buildings. It is the most cost-effective choice for single-building, low-traffic requirements.

Higher performance requirements can best be met by coaxial cable, which provides higher throughput, can support a larger number of devices, and can span greater distances than twisted pair. Two transmission methods, baseband and broadband, can be employed on a coax cable; these are explained below. Baseband systems are typically from 1 to 10 Mbps and are generally limited to a single building. However, by limiting the distance covered and the number of devices attached, data rates of 50 Mbps can be achieved. Broadband systems are also typically in the range of 1 to 10 Mbps for a single data path, with 20 Mbps representing a practical upper limit. However, as explained below, broadband can support multiple data paths in contrast to the single data path of baseband. Broadband systems use CATV (Community Antenna Television) cable, which is suitable for outdoor as well as indoor environments. Hence interbuilding and even intracity networks can be supported.

Optical fiber has even greater capacity than coaxial cable and is a promising candidate for future local network installations. However, it has been little used so far due to cost and technical limitations. Optical fiber is well suited to point-to-point configurations which, as described below, are used in ring networks. As the cost of optical fiber transmission components drops, this configuration will become practical. For the more common multipoint configurations, the problem of insertion tap loss must be overcome to exploit fully the tremendous capacity of optical fiber.

Table 11-2 summarizes representative parameters for transmission media for commercially-available bus/tree local networks. Comparing with Table 11-1, one can see that the performance of a given medium is lower for multipoint versus point-to-point configurations. This is because the presence of multiple taps on the multipoint configurations results in higher signal attenuation.

Star Topology.   In the star topology, each station is directly connected to a common central switch. One example of the use of this topology is the case in

TABLE 11-2   Transmission Media for Local Networks: Bus/Tree

Transmission Medium	Data Rate (Mbps)	Range (km)	Number of Taps
Twisted pair	1–10	<2	10's
Baseband coaxial cable	10; 50 with limitations	<3	100's
Broadband coaxial cable	500; 20 per channel	<30	1000's

TABLE 11-3 Transmission Media for Local Networks: Passive or Active Star

Transmission Medium	Data Rate (Mbps)	Distance from Station to Central Switch	Number of Stations
Unshielded twisted pair	1–10 Mbps	0.5 (1 Mbps)–0.1 (10 Mbps)	10's
Baseband coaxial cable	70 Mbps	<1	10's
Optical fiber	10–20 Mbps	<1	10's

which the central switch uses circuit-switching technology. The digital data switch and digital private branch exchange are examples of this approach.

The star topology is also employed for implementing a packet-broadcasting local area network. In this case, each station attaches to a central node, referred to as the star coupler, via two point-to-point links, one for transmission in each direction. A transmission from any one station enters the central node and is retransmitted on all of the outgoing links. Thus, although the arrangement is physically a star, it is logically a bus: a transmission from any station is received by all other stations, and only one station at a time may successfully transmit. Thus, the medium access control techniques used for the packet star topology are the same as for bus and tree.

There are two ways of implementing the star coupler. In the case of the passive star coupler, there is an electromagnetic linkage in the coupler so that any incoming transmission is physically passed to all of the outgoing links. In the case of optical fiber, this coupling is achieved by fusing together a number of fibers, so that incoming light is automatically split among all of the outgoing fibers. In the case of coaxial cable or twisted pair, transformer coupling is used to split the incoming signal.

The other type of star coupler is the active star coupler. In this case, there is digital logic in the central node that acts as a repeater. As bits arrive on any input line, they are automatically regenerated and repeated on all outgoing lines. If multiple input signals arrive simultaneously, a collision signal is transmitted on all outgoing lines.

Any form of guided transmission medium can be used with either the passive or active star coupler. In terms of commercially-available products, the passive star coupler has been used with both baseband coaxial cable and optical fiber products. In both cases, high data rates have been achieved with limited distance and a limited number of devices. Active star couplers have been used in unshielded twisted-pair implementations. Table 11-3 summarizes representative parameters.

11·2

THE BUS/TREE AND STAR TOPOLOGIES

Characteristics of Bus/Tree LANs and HSLNs

The bus/tree topology is a multipoint configuration. That is, there are more than two devices connected to the medium and capable of transmitting on the medium. Because multiple devices share a single data path, only one may transmit at a time.

TABLE 11-4 Bus/Tree Transmission Techniques

Baseband	Broadband
Digital signaling	Analog signaling (requires RF modem)
Entire bandwidth consumed by signal—no FDM	FDM possible—multiple data channels, video, audio
Bidirectional	Unidirectional
Bus topology	Bus or tree topology
Distance: up to a few kilometers	Distance: up to tens of kilometers

A station usually transmits data in the form of a packet containing the address of the destination. The packet propagates throughout the medium and is received by all other stations. The addressed station copies the packet as it goes by.

Two transmission techniques are in use for bus/tree LANs: baseband and broadband. Baseband, using digital signaling, can be employed on twisted pair or coaxial cable. Broadband, using analog signaling in the RF range, employs coaxial cable. Some of the differences are highlighted in Table 11-4, and the following two subsections explore the two methods in some detail. There is also a variant known as carrierband that has the signaling characteristics of broadband but some of the restrictions of baseband; this is also covered below.

The multipoint nature of the bus/tree topology gives rise to several rather stiff problems. First is the problem of determining which station on the medium may transmit at any point in time. With point-to-point links (only two stations on the medium), this is a fairly simple task. If the line is full-duplex, both stations may transmit at the same time. If the line is half-duplex, then a rather simple mechanism is needed to ensure that the two stations take turns. Historically, the most common shared access scheme has been the multidrop line, in which access is determined by polling from a controlling station (discussed in Chapter 5). The controlling station may send data to any other station, or it may issue a poll to a specific station, asking for an immediate response. This method, however, negates some of the advantages of a distributed system and also is awkward for communication between two noncontroller stations. A variety of distributed strategies, referred to as medium access control protocols, have now been developed for bus and tree topologies. These are discussed in Section 11-4.

A second problem has to do with signal balancing. When two devices exchange data over a link, the signal strength of the transmitter must be adjusted to be within certain limits. The signal must be strong enough so that, after attenuation across the medium, it meets the receiver's minimum signal strength requirements. It must also be strong enough to maintain an adequate signal to noise ratio. On the other hand, the signal must not be so strong as to overload the circuitry of the transmitter, which creates harmonics and other spurious signals. Though easily done for a point-to-point link, signal balancing is no easy task for a multipoint line. If any device can transmit to any other device, the signal balancing must be performed for all permutations of stations taken two at a time. For n stations that works out to $n \times (n-1)$ permutations. So, for a 200-station network (not a particularly large system), 39,800 signal strength constraints must be satisfied simultaneously. With interdevice distances ranging from tens to thousands of meters, this is an impossible

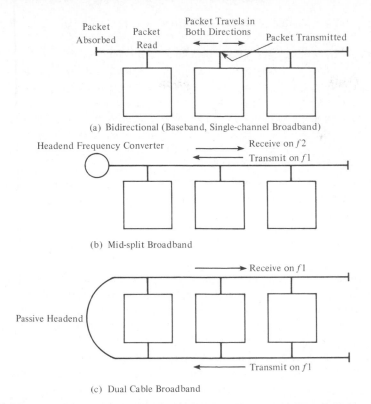

FIGURE 11-2. Baseband and broadband transmission techniques.

task for any but small networks. In systems that use radio-frequency (RF) signals, the problem is compounded because of the possibility of RF signal interference across frequencies. The solution is to divide the medium into segments within which pairwise balancing is possible, using amplifiers or repeaters between segments.

Baseband Systems

A baseband LAN is defined as one that uses digital signaling. Digital signals are inserted on the line as voltage pulses. The entire frequency spectrum of the medium is used to form the signal; hence frequency-division multiplexing (FDM) cannot be used. Transmission is bidirectional. That is, a signal inserted at any point on the medium propagates in both directions to the ends, where it is absorbed (Figure 11-2a). The digital signaling requires a bus topology; unlike analog signals, digital signals can not easily be propagated through the splitters and joiners required for a tree topology. Baseband systems can extend only a limited distance, about a kilometer at most. This is because the attenuation of the signal, which is most pronounced at higher frequencies, causes a blurring of the pulses and a weakening of the signal to the extent that communication over larger distances is impractical.

Baseband Coax. The most popular form of baseband bus LAN uses coaxial cable. Unless otherwise indicated, this discussion is based on the IEEE standard

[IEEE85b] and the almost-identical Ethernet system [METC76], [SHOC82], [DIGI82].

Most baseband coax systems use a special 50-ohm cable rather than the standard CATV 75-ohm cable. This is because, for digital signals, the 50-ohm cable suffers less intense reflections from the insertion capacitance of the taps, and provides better immunity against low-frequency electromagnetic noise.

As with any transmission system, there are engineering trade-offs involving data rate, cable length, number of taps, and the electrical characteristics of the transmit and receive components for a baseband coaxial system. For example, the lower the data rate, the longer the cable can be. That latter statement is true for the following reason: when a signal propagates along a transmission medium, the integrity of the signal suffers due to attenuation, noise, and other impairments. The longer the propagation, the greater the effect, increasing the probability of error. However, at a lower data rate, the individual pulses of a digital signal last longer and can be recovered in the presence of impairments more easily than higher-rate, shorter pulses.

With the above in mind, we give one example that illustrates some of the trade-offs. The Ethernet specification and the original IEEE 802.3 standard specified the use of 50-ohm cable with a 0.4-inch diameter, and a data rate of 10 Mbps. With these parameters, the maximum length of the cable is set at 500 meters. Stations attach to the cable by means of a tap, with the distance between any two taps being a multiple of 2.5 m; this is to ensure that reflections from adjacent taps do not add in phase [YEN83]. A maximum of 100 taps is allowed. In IEEE jargon, this system is referred to as 10BASE5 (10 Mbps, baseband, 500-m segment length). The first two digits give the data rate in megabits per second; the four letters are an abbreviation for the medium (baseband); and the final digit is the maximum cable length in hundreds of meters.

To provide a lower-cost system for personal computer local networks, IEEE later added a 10BASE2 specification. Table 11-5 compares this scheme, dubbed Cheapernet, with the 10BASE5 specification. The key difference is the use of a thinner (0.25 in) cable, which is employed in products such as public address systems. The thinner cable is more flexible; thus it is easier to bend around corners and bring to a workstation rather than installing the cable in the wall and having to provide a drop cable with transmitters and receivers between the main cable and the workstation. The cable is easier to install and requires cheaper electronics than the thicker cable. On the other hand, the thinner cable suffers greater attenuation and lower noise resistance than the thicker cable. Thus it supports fewer taps over a shorter distance.

TABLE 11-5   IEEE Specification for 10-Mbps Baseband Coaxial Bus Local Area Networks

Parameter	10BASE5	10BASE2
Data rate	10 Mbps	10 Mbps
Maximum segment length	500 m	200 m
Network span	2500 m	1000 m
Nodes per segment	100	30
Node spacing	2.5 m	0.5 m
Cable diameter	0.4 in	0.25 in

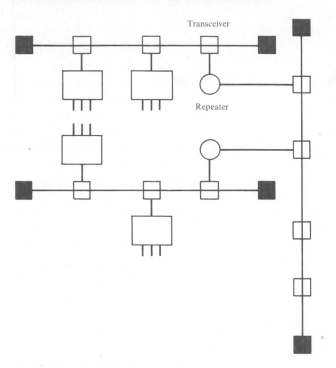

FIGURE 11-3. Baseband configuration.

To extend the length of the network, a repeater may be used. It consists, in essence, of two transceivers joined together and connected to two different segments of coax cable. The repeater passes digital signals in both directions between the two segments, amplifying and regenerating the signals as they pass through. A repeater is transparent to the rest of the system; since it does no buffering, it in no sense isolates one segment from another. So, for example, if two stations on different segments attempt to transmit at the same time, their packets will interfere with each other (collide). To avoid multipath interference, only one path of segments and repeaters is allowed between any two stations. A maximum of four repeaters is allowed in the path between any two stations, extending the effective cable length to 2.5 km. Figure 11-3 is an example of a baseband system with three segments and two repeaters.

Unshielded Twisted Pair Baseband. In recent years, there has been increasing interest in the use of twisted pair as a transmission medium for LANs. From the earliest days of commercial LAN availability, twisted-pair bus LANs have been popular. However, such LANs suffer in comparison with a coaxial cable LAN. First of all, the apparent cost advantage of twisted pair is not as great as it might seem, when a linear bus layout is used. True, twisted-pair cable is less expensive than coaxial cable. On the other hand, much of the cost of LAN wiring is the labor cost of installing the cable, which is no greater for coaxial cable than for twisted pair. Secondly, coaxial cable provides superior signal quality, and therefore can support more devices over longer distances at higher data rates than twisted pair.

The renewed interest in twisted pair, at least in the context of LANs, is in the use of unshielded twisted pair in a star topology arrangement. The reason for the interest is that unshielded twisted pair is simply telephone wire, and virtually all office buildings are equipped with spare twisted pairs running from wiring closets to each office. This yields several benefits when deploying a LAN:

1. There is essentially no installation cost with unshielded twisted pair, since the wire is already there. Coaxial cable has to be pulled. In older buildings, this may be difficult since existing conduits may be crowded.
2. In most office building, it is impossible to anticipate all the locations where network access will be needed. Since it is extravagantly expensive to run coaxial cable to every office, a coaxial-cable based LAN will typically only cover a portion of a building. If equipment subsequently has to be moved to an office not covered by the LAN, a significant expense is involve in extending the LAN coverage. With telephone wire, this problem does not arise, since all offices are covered.

The most popular approach to the use of unshielded twisted pair for a LAN is therefore a star-topology approach. The products on the market use a scheme suggested by Figure 11-4, in which central element of the star is an active element, referred to as the **hub.** Each station is conected to the hub by two twisted pairs (transmit and receive). The hub acts as a repeater: When a single station transmits, the hub repeats the signal, on the outgoing line to each station.

Note that although this scheme is physically a star, it is logically a bus: A transmission from any one station is received by all other stations, and if two stations transmit at the same time there will be a collision.

Multiple levels of hubs can be cascaded in a hierarchical configuration. Figure 11-5 illustrates a two-level configuration. There is one **header hub** (HHUB) and one or more **intermediate hubs** (IHUB). Each hub may have a mixture of stations and other hubs attached to it from below. This layout fits well with building wiring practices. Typically, there is a wiring closet on each floor of an office building, and a hub can be placed in each one. Each hub could service the stations on its floor.

Figure 11-6 shows an abstract representation of the intermediate and header hubs. The header hub performs all the functions described previously for a single-hub configuration. In the case of an intermediate hub, any incoming signal from below

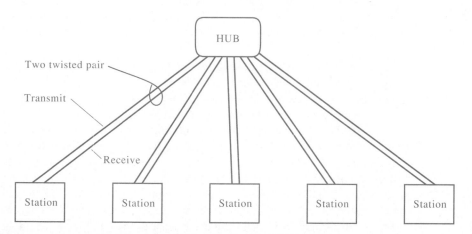

FIGURE 11-4.   Twisted-pair, star-wiring, logical-bus arrangement.

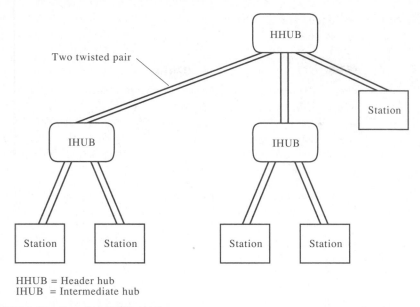

FIGURE 11-5. **Two-level hierarchy.**

is repeated upward to the next higher level. Any signal from above is repeated on all lower-level outgoing lines. Thus, the logical bus characteristic is retained: A transmission from any one station is received by all other stations, and if two stations transmit at the same time there will be a collision.

The initial version of the above scheme employed a data rate of 1 Mbps, and was dubbed StarLAN. More recently, products operating at 10 Mbps have begun to appear. These are intended to be compatible with the 10-Mbps baseband coaxial cable bus systems, requiring only a change of transceiver. Although there is now a fair amount of practical experience with these higher-speed systems, there remains

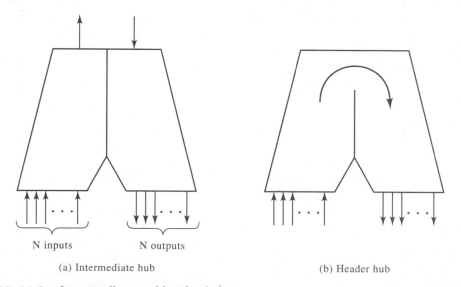

FIGURE 11-6. **Intermediate and header hubs.**

a controversy about their practicality [CLAI88, ORLO88]. Several reasons for this controversy can be stated:

- Existing telephone wire in buildings can be inadequate for data transmission. Problems include twisted pair that isn't twisted, splicing and other connections, and other faults that are not noticeable for voice transmission but that would produce very high error rates at 10 Mbps.
- Twisted-pair cables are rather tightly packed together in conduits. The mutual capacitance from adjacent pairs adversely affects attenuation, crosstalk, and velocity of propagation. The effects on data transmission may not be noticeable at 1 Mbps, but become a problem at 10 Mbps.

These problems can to some extent be overcome by the use of signal processing techniques and by careful design of the transceiver. However, just as we saw with the 10-Mbps coaxial cable bus, there are trade-offs to be made. In this case, IEEE recommends a maximum distance between station and hub of 250 meters at 1 Mbps and 100 meters at 10 Mbps.

Broadband Systems

FDM Broadband LAN.   In the context of local networks, broadband refers to the use of analog signaling. Thus frequency-division multiplexing (FDM) is possible: The frequency spectrum of the cable can be divided into channels or sections of bandwidth. Separate channels can support data traffic, TV, or radio signals. Broadband components allow splitting and joining operations; hence both bus and tree topologies are possible. Much greater distances—tens of kilometers—are possible with broadband compared to baseband. This is because the analog signals that carry the digital data can propagate greater distances before the noise and attenuation damage the data.

As with baseband, stations attach to the cable by means of a tap. Unlike baseband, however, broadband is inherently a unidirectional medium; signals inserted onto the medium can propagate in only one direction. The primary reason for this is that it is infeasible to build amplifiers that will pass signals of one frequency in both directions. This unidirectional property means that only those stations ''downstream'' from a transmitting station can receive its signals. How, then, can full connectivity be achieved?

Clearly, two data paths are needed. These paths are joined at a point on the network known as the headend. For bus topology, the headend is simply one end of the bus. For tree topology, the headend is the root of the branching tree. All stations transmit on one path toward the headend (inbound). Signals received at the headend are then propagated along a second data path away from the headend (outbound). All stations receive on the outbound path.

Physically, two different configurations are used to implement the inbound, outbound paths (Figure 11-2b and c). On a dual-cable configuration, the inbound and outbound paths are separate cables, with the headend simply a passive connector between the two. Stations send and receive on the same frequency.

By contrast, on the split configuration, the inbound and outbound paths are different frequency bands on the same cable. Bidirectional amplifiers pass lower frequencies inbound, and higher frequencies outbound. The headend contains a device, known as a frequency converter, for translating inbound frequencies to

TABLE 11-6   Common Broadband Cable Frequency Splits

Format	Inbound Frequency Band	Outbound Frequency Band	Maximum Two-way Bandwidth
Subsplit	5 to 30 MHz	54 to 400 MHz	25 MHz
Midsplit	5 to 116 MHz	168 to 400 MHz	111 MHz
Highsplit	5 to 174 MHz	232 to 400 MHz	168 MHz
Dual Cable	40 to 400 MHz	40 to 400 MHz	360 MHz

outbound frequencies. The frequency converter at the headend can be either an analog or digital device. The analog device simply translates signals to a new frequency and retransmits them. The digital device recovers the digital data from the headend and then retransmits the cleaned-up data on the new frequency.

Split systems are categorized by the frequency allocation of the two paths, as shown in Table 11-6. Subsplit, commonly used by the cable television industry was designed for metropolitan area television distribution, with limited subscriber-to-central office communication. It provides the easiest way to upgrade existing one-way cable systems to two-way operation. Subsplit has limited usefulness for local area networking because a bandwidth of only 25 MHz is available for two-way communication. Midsplit is more suitable for LANs, since it provides a more equitable distribution of bandwidth. However, midsplit was developed at a time when the practical spectrum of a cable-TV cable was 300 MHz, whereas a spectrum of 400 to 450 MHz is now available. Accordingly, a highsplit specification has been developed to provide greater two-way bandwidth for a split cable system.

The differences between split and dual are minor. The midsplit system is useful when a single cable plant is already installed in a building. Also, the installed system is about 10–15% cheaper than a dual cable system [HOPK79]. On the other hand, a dual cable has over twice the capacity of midsplit. It does not require the frequency translator at the headend, which may need to be redundant for reliability.

Broadband systems use standard, off-the-shelf CATV components, including 75-ohm coaxial cable. All endpoints are terminated with a 75-ohm terminator to absorb signals. Broadband is suitable for tens of kilometers radius from the headend and hundreds or even thousands of devices. For all but very short distances, amplifiers are required.

The broadband LAN can be used to carry multiple channels, some used for analog signals, such as video and voice, and some for digital. Digital channels can generally carry a data rate of somewhere between 0.25 and 1 bps/Hz.

Three kinds of digital data transfer techniques are possible on a broadband cable: dedicated, switched, and multiple access (Figure 11-7). For dedicated service, a small portion of the cable's bandwidth is reserved for exclusive use by two devices. No special protocol is needed. Each of the two devices attaches to the cable through a modem; both modems are tuned to the same frequency. This technique is analogous to securing a dedicated leased line from the telephone company. Transfer rates of up to 20 Mbps are achievable. The dedicated service could be used to connect two devices when a heavy traffic pattern is expected. For example, one computer could be acting as a standby for another, and needs to get frequent updates of state information and file and data base changes.

The switched technique requires the use of a number of frequency bands. Devices are attached through "frequency agile" modems, capable of changing their fre-

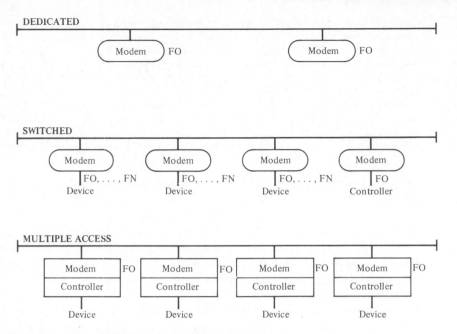

FIGURE 11-7. **Broadband data transfer services.**

quency by electronic command. Initially, all attached devices, together with a controller, are tuned to the same frequency. A station wishing to establish a connection sends a request to the controller, which assigns an available frequency to the two devices and signals their modems to tune to that frequency. This technique is analogous to a dial-up line. Because the cost of frequency-agile modems rises dramatically with data rate, rates of 56 kbps or less are typical. This capability is available in WANG's local network [STAH82], where it is used for terminal-to-host connections. It could also be used for voice service.

Finally, the multiple access service allows a number of attached devices to be supported at the same frequency. As with baseband, some form of medium access control protocol is needed to control transmission. The multiple-access approach is the most common. It provides for distributed, peer communication among many devices, which is the primary motivation for a local network.

Discussions of broadband LANs can be found in [COOP84], [DINE80], and [FORB81].

Carrierband. An abridged form of broadband, known as single-channel broadband or carrierband, is one in which the entire spectrum of the cable is devoted to a single transmission path for analog signals. In general, a single-channel broadband LAN has the following characteristics [KLEI86, RELC87]. Bidirectional transmission, using a bus topology, is employed. Hence there can be no amplifiers, and there is no need for a headend. Some form of FSK is used, generally at a low frequency (a few megahertz). This is an advantage since attenuation is less at lower frequencies.

Because the cable is dedicated to a single task, it is not necessary to take care that the modem output is confined to a narrow bandwidth. Energy can spread over the cable's spectrum. As a result, the electronics are simple and inexpensive. This scheme would appear to give comparable performance, at a comparable price, to baseband.

The single-channel broadband approach is also used in one commercially available HSLN [HOHN80] and is the approach taken by a draft HSLN standard [BURR83]. In both cases, a 50-Mbps data rate is used with phase-shift keying (PSK) on a 150-MHz carrier. The approach should be comparable in performance and cost to HYPERchannel.

Baseband Versus Broadband

One of the silliest aspects of the intense coverage afforded local networks in the trade and professional literature is the baseband versus broadband debate. The fact is that there is room for both technologies in the local network field. The potential customer will find himself faced with a lot of other, more complex, decisions than this one. For the interested reader, thoughtful discussions may by found in [HOPK82] and [KRUT81].

To summarize briefly, baseband has the advantage of simplicity, and, in principle, lower cost. The layout of a baseband cable plant is simple: There are just five rules for trunk layout in the Ethernet specification. A relatively inexperienced local network engineer should be able to cope.

The potential disadvantages of baseband include the limitations in capacity and distance—only disadvantages if your requirements exceed those limitations. Another concern has to do with grounding. Because dc signal components are on the cable, it can be grounded in only one place. Care must be taken to avoid potential shock hazards and antenna effects.

Broadband's strength is its tremendous capacity; it can carry a wide variety of traffic on a number of channels. With the use of active amplifiers, broadband can achieve very wide area coverage. Also, the system is based on a mature CATV technology. Components are reliable and readily available.

Broadband systems are more complex than baseband to install and maintain. The layout design must include cable type selection, and placement and setting of all amplifiers and taps. Maintenance involves periodic testing and alignment of all network parameters. These are jobs for experienced RF engineers. Finally, the average propagation delay between stations for broadband is twice that for a comparable baseband system. This reduces the efficiency and performance of the system.

As with all other network design choices, the selection of baseband or broadband must be based on relative costs and benefits. It is probable that some installations will have both types. Neither is likely to win the LAN war.

11-3

THE RING TOPOLOGY

The major alternative to the bus/tree topology LAN is the ring. The ring has enjoyed considerable popularity in Europe but has only recently gained acceptance in the United States, where Ethernet and MITREnet were largely responsible for shaping the early direction of activity. The current U.S. popularity of the ring LAN dates from the introduction of IBM's product in 1985 [DERF86], [STRO86], which was quickly followed by compatible products from other vendors.

Characteristics of Ring LANs

A ring LAN consists of a number of repeaters, each connected to two others by unidirectional transmission links to form a single closed path. Data are transferred sequentially, bit by bit, around the ring from one repeater to the next. Each repeater regenerates and retransmits each bit.

For a ring to operate as a communication network, three functions are required: data insertion, data reception, and data removal. These functions are provided by the repeaters. Each repeater, in addition to serving as an active element on the ring, serves as a device attachment point. Data insertion is accomplished by the repeater. Data are transmitted in packets, each of which contains a destination address field. As a packet circulates past a repeater, the address field is copied. If the attached station recognizes the address, the remainder of the packet is copied.

Repeaters perform the data insertion and reception functions in a manner not unlike that of taps, which serve as device attachment points on a bus or tree. Data removal, however, is more difficult on a ring. For a bus or tree, signals inserted onto the line propagate to the endpoints and are absorbed by terminators. Hence, shortly after transmission ceases, the bus or tree is clean of data. However, because the ring is a closed loop, a packet will circulate indefinitely unless it is removed. A packet may by removed by the addressed repeater. Alternatively, each packet could be removed by the transmitting repeater after it has made one trip around the loop. This latter approach is more desirable because (1) it permits automatic acknowledgment and (2) it permits multicast addressing: one packet sent simultaneously to multiple stations.

A variety of strategies can be used for determining how and when packets are inserted onto the ring. These strategies are, in effect, medium access control protocols, and are discussed in Section 11-4.

The repeater, then, can be seen to have two main purposes: (1) to contribute to the proper functioning of the ring by passing on all the data that comes its way, and (2) to provide an access point for attached stations to send and receive data. Corresponding to these two purposes are two states (Figure 11-8): the listen state and the transmit state.

In the listen state, each received bit is retransmitted with a small delay, required to allow the repeater to perform required functions. Ideally, the delay should be on the order of one bit time (the time it takes for a repeater to transmit one complete bit onto the outgoing line). These functions are:

- Scan passing bit stream for pertinent patterns. Chief among these is the address or addresses of attached stations. Another pattern, used in the token control strategy explained later, indicates permission to transmit. Note that to perform the scanning function, the repeater must have some knowledge of packet format.
- Copy each incoming bit and send it to the attached station, while continuing to retransmit each bit. This will be done for each bit of each packet addressed to this station.

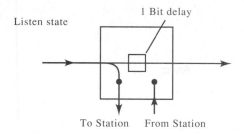

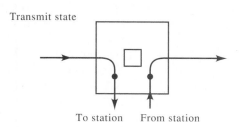

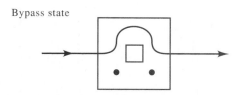

FIGURE 11-8. Ring repeater states.

- Modify a bit as it passes by. In certain control strategies, bits may be modified to, for example, indicate that the packet has been copied. This would serve as an acknowledgment.

When a repeater's station has data to send and when the repeater, based on the control strategy, has permission to send, the repeater enters the transmit state. In this state, the repeater receives bits from the station and retransmits them on its outgoing link. During the period of transmission, bits may appear on the incoming ring link. There are two possibilities, and they are treated differently:

- The bits could be from the same packet that the repeater is still in the process of sending. This will occur if the "bit length" of the ring is shorter than the packet. In this case, the repeater passes the bits back to the station, which can check them as a form of acknowledgment.
- For some control strategies, more than one packet could be on the ring at the same time. If the repeater, while transmitting, receives bits from a packet it did not originate, it must buffer them to be transmitted later.

These two states, listen and transmit, are sufficient for proper ring operation. A third state, the bypass state, is also useful. In this state, a bypass relay can be activated, so that signals propagate past the repeater with no delay other than medium propagation. The bypass relay affords two benefits: (1) it provides a partial solution to the reliability problem, discussed later, and (2) it improves performance by eliminating repeater delay for those stations that are not active on the network.

Twisted pair, baseband coax, and fiber optic cable can all be used to provide the repeater-to-repeater links. Broadband coax, however, could not easily be used. Each repeater would have to be capable, asynchronously, of receiving and transmitting data on multiple channels.

Timing Jitter

The reader will note that the characteristics of transmission media for ring local networks as listed in Table 11-1 are inferior to those listed for point-to-point transmission media in Table 2-3. The reason for this is a phenomenon known as timing jitter.

On a ring transmission medium, some form of clocking is included with the signal, as for example with the use of Differential Manchester encoding (Section 3-1). As data circulate around the ring, each repeater receives the data, and recovers the clocking for two purposes: first, to know when to sample the incoming signal to recover the bits of data, and second, to use the clocking for transmitting the signal to the next repeater. This clock recovery will deviate in a random fashion from the mid-bit transitions of the received signal for several reasons, including noise during transmission and imperfections in the receiver circuitry. The predominant reason, however, is delay distortion (described in Section 2-3). The deviation of clock recovery is known as timing jitter.

As each repeater receives incoming data, it issues a clean signal with no distortion. However, the timing error is not eliminated. Thus the digital pulse width will expand and contract in a random fashion as the signal travels around the ring, and the timing jitter accumulates. The cumulative effect of the jitter is to cause the bit latency or "bit length" of the ring to vary. However, unless the latency of the ring remains constant, bits will be dropped (not retransmitted) as the latency of the ring decreases, or added as the latency increases.

This timing jitter places a limitation on the number of repeaters in a ring. Although this limitation cannot be entirely overcome, several measures can be taken to improve matters [KELL83]; [HONG86]. In essence, two approaches are used in combination. First, each repeater can include a phase-lock loop. This is a device that uses feedback to minimize the deviation from one bit time to the next. Second, a buffer can be used at one or more repeaters. The buffer is initialized to hold a certain number of bits, and expands and contracts to keep the bit length of the ring constant. The combination of phase-locked loops and a buffer significantly increase maximum feasible ring size. The values in Table 11-1 assume the use of these measures.

Potential Ring Problems

One of the principal reasons for the delayed acceptance of the ring LAN in the United States is that there are a number of potential problems with this topology [SALT83]. A break in any link or the failure of a repeater disables the entire network. Installation of a new repeater to support new devices requires the identification of two nearby, topologically adjacent repeaters. Timing jitter must be dealt with. Finally, because the ring is closed, a means is needed to remove circulating packets, with backup techniques to guard against error.

The last problem is a protocol issue, discussed later. The remaining problems can be handled by a refinement of the ring topology, discussed next.

The Star-Ring Architecture

Two observations can be made about the basic ring architecture described above. First, there is a practical limit to the number of repeaters on a ring. This limit is suggested by the jitter, reliability, and maintenance problems just cited and by the accumulating delay of a large number of repeaters. A limit of a few hundred repeaters seems reasonable. Second, the functioning of the ring does not depend on the actual routing of the cables that link the repeaters.

These observations have led to the development of a refined ring architecture, the star-ring, which overcomes some of the problems of the ring and allows the construction of larger local networks [SALW83]. This architecture is the basis of IBM's local network product [STROL83], [DIXO83] and grows out of research done at IBM [BUX83] and M.I.T. [SALT79].

As a first step, consider the rearrangement of a ring into a star. This is achieved by having the interrepeater links all thread through a single site. This *ring wiring concentrator* has a number of advantages. Because there is centralized access to the signal on every link, it is a simple matter to isolate a fault. A message can be launched into the ring and tracked to see how far it gets without mishap. A faulty segment can be disconnected and repaired at a later time. New repeaters can easily be added to the ring: simply run two cables from the new repeater to the site of ring wiring concentration and splice into the ring.

The bypass relay associated with each repeater can be moved into the ring wiring concentrator. The relay can automatically bypass its repeater and two links for any malfunction. A nice effect of this feature is that the transmission path from one working repeater to the next is approximately constant; thus the range of signal levels to which the transmission system must automatically adapt is much smaller.

The ring wiring concentrator permits rapid recovery from a cable or repeater failure. Nevertheless, a single failure could, at least temporarily, disable the entire network. Furthermore, throughput and jitter considerations still place a practical upper limit on the number of stations in a ring, since each repeater adds an increment of delay. Finally, in a spread-out network, a single wire concentration site dictates a lot of cable.

To attack these remaining problems, consider a local network consisting of multiple rings (Figure 11-9). Each ring consists of a connected sequence of wiring concentrators; the set of rings is connected by a *bridge*. The bridge routes data packets from one ring subnetwork to another based on addressing information in the packet so routed. From a physical point of view, each ring operates independently of the other rings attached to the bridge. From a logical point of view, the bridge provides transparent routing between the two rings.

The bridge must perform five functions:

- *Input filtering*: For each ring, the bridge monitors the traffic on the ring and copies all packets addressed to other rings on the bridge. This function can be performed by a repeater programmed to recognize a family of addresses rather than a single address.

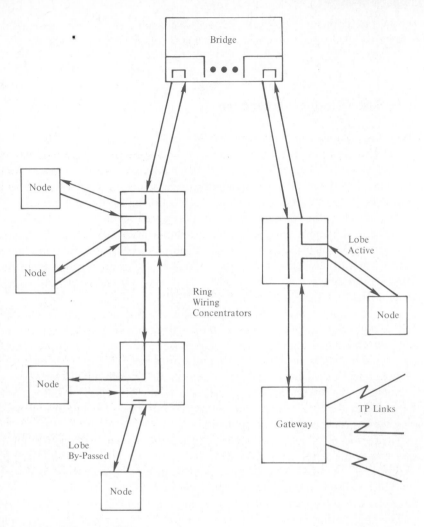

FIGURE 11-9.   Ring bridge.

- *Input buffering:* Received packets may need to be buffered, either because the interring traffic is peaking, or because the target output buffer is temporarily full.
- *Switching:* Each packet must be routed through the bridge to its appropriate destination ring.
- *Output buffering:* A packet may need to be buffered at the threshold of the destination ring, waiting for an opportunity to be inserted.
- *Output transmission:* This function can be performed by an ordinary repeater.

Two principal advantages accrue from the use of a bridge. First, the failure of a ring, for whatever reason, will disable only a portion of the network, and failure of the bridge does not prevent intraring traffic. (This assumes that the bridge is a station attached to a repeater; therefore, the bridge can fail but its repeater remain operational.) Second, multiple rings may be employed to obtain a satisfactory level of performance when the throughput capability of a single ring is exceeded.

There are several pitfalls to be noted. First, the automatic acknowledgment feature of the ring is lost; higher level protocols must provide acknowledgment. Second, performance may not significantly improve if there is a high percentage of interring traffic. If it is possible to do so, network devices should be judiciously allocated to rings to minimize interring traffic.

Bus Versus Ring

For the user with a large number of devices and high capacity requirements, the bus or tree broadband LAN seems the best suited to the requirements. For more moderate requirements, however, the choice between a baseband bus LAN and a ring LAN is not at all clear cut.

The baseband bus is the simpler system. Passive taps rather than active repeaters are used. There is no need for the complexity of bridges and ring wiring concentrators.

The most important benefit or strength of the ring is that it uses point-to-point communication links. There are a number of implications of this fact. First, because the transmitted signal is regenerated at each node, transmission errors are minimized and greater distances can be covered than with baseband bus. Broadband bus/tree can cover a similar range, but cascaded amplifiers can result in loss of data integrity at high data rates. Second, the ring can accommodate optical fiber links, which provide very high data rates and excellent electromagnetic interference (EMI) characteristics. Finally, the electronics and maintenance of point-to-point lines are simpler than for multipoint lines.

A further discussion of ring versus bus is contained in [SALW83] and [SALT81].

11-4

MEDIUM ACCESS CONTROL PROTOCOLS

Bus/Tree Topology

Of all the local network topologies, the bus/tree topologies present the most challenges, and the most options, for medium access control. This section will not attempt to survey the many techniques that have been proposed; good discussions can be found in [LUCZ78] and [FRAN81]. Rather, the emphasis will be on the two techniques that seem likely to dominate the marketplace: CSMA/CD and token bus. Standards for these techniques have been developed by the IEEE 802 committee.

Table 11-7 compares the two techniques on a number of characteristics. The ensuing discussion should clarify its significance.

TABLE 11-7 Bus/Tree Access Methods

	CSMA/CD	Token Bus
Access determination	Contention	Token
Packet-length restriction	Greater than $2\times$ propagation delay	None
Principal advantage	Simplicity	Regulated/fair access
Principal disadvantage	Performance under heavy load	Complexity

CSMA/CD. The most commonly used medium access control technique for bus/tree topologies is *carrier sense multiple access with collision detection* (CSMA/CD), also referred to as *listen while talk* (LWT). The original baseband version of this technique was developed and patented by Xerox [METC77] as part of its Ethernet local network [METC76]. The original broadband version was developed and patented by MITRE [HOPK80] as part of its MITREnet local network [HOPK79].

CSMA/CD is a refinement of the CSMA protocol described in Chapter 10. CSMA/CD attempts to overcome one glaring inefficiency of CSMA. Under CSMA, when two packets collide the medium remains unusable for the duration of transmission of both damaged packets. For packets that are long, compared to propagation time, the amount of wasted capacity can be considerable. This waste can be reduced if a station continues to listen to the medium while it is transmitting. In that case, these rules can be added to the CSMA rules:

1. If a collision is detected during transmission, immediately cease transmitting the packet, and transmit a brief jamming signal to assure that all stations know there has been a collision.
2. After transmitting the jamming signal, wait a random amount of time, then attempt to transmit again using CSMA.

Now, the amount of wasted bandwidth is reduced to the time it takes to detect a collision. Question: How long does that take? Figure 11-10 illustrates the answer for a baseband system. Consider the worst case of two stations that are as far apart as possible. As can be seen, the amount of time it takes to detect a collision is twice the propagation delay. For broadband, the wait is even longer. The worst case is two stations close together and as far as possible from the headend. In this

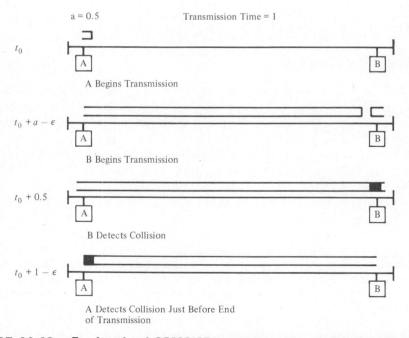

FIGURE 11-10. **For baseband CSMA/CD, packet length should be at least twice the propagation delay ($a \leq 0.5$).**

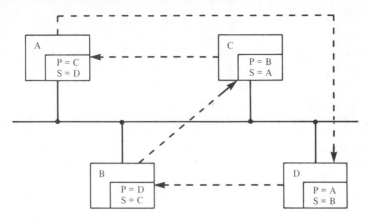

FIGURE 11-12.   Token bus.

Token Bus.   Token bus is a technique in which the stations on the bus or tree form a logical ring; that is, the stations are assigned positions in an ordered sequence, with the last member of the sequence followed by the first. Each station knows the identity of the stations preceding and following it (Figure 11-12).

A control packet known as the token regulates the right of access. When a station receives the token, it is granted control of the medium for a specified time. The station may transmit one or more packets and may poll stations and receive responses. When the station is done, or time has expired, it passes the token on to the next station in logical sequence. This station now has permission to transmit. Hence steady-state operation consists of alternating data transfer and token transfer phases.

Note that non-token-using stations are allowed on the bus. These stations can only respond to polls or requests for acknowledgment. It should also be pointed out that the physical ordering of the stations on the bus is irrelevant and independent of the logical ordering.

This scheme requires considerable maintenance. The following functions, at a minimum, must be performed by one or more stations on the bus:

- *Ring initialization:* When the network is started up, or after the logical ring has broken down, it must be reinitialized. Some cooperative, decentralized algorithm is needed to sort out who goes first, who goes second, and so on.
- *Addition to ring:* Periodically, nonparticipating stations must be granted the opportunity to insert themselves in the ring.
- *Deletion from ring:* A station can voluntarily remove itself from the ring by splicing together its predecessor and successor.
- *Fault management:* A number of errors can occur. These include duplicate address (two stations think it's their turn) and broken ring (no station thinks that it is its turn).

The remainder of this subsection briefly describes the approach taken for these functions in the IEEE 802 standard. To accomplish *addition to ring,* each node in the logical ring has the responsibility of periodically granting an opportunity for new nodes to enter the ring. While holding the token, the node issues a *solicit-successor* packet, inviting nodes with an address between itself and the next node in logical sequence to demand entrance. The transmitting node then waits for one response window or slot time (equal to twice the end-to-end propagation delay of the medium). If there is no response, the node passes the token to its successor as usual. If there is one response, the token holder sets its successor node to be the requesting node and transmits the token to it; the requestor sets its linkages accordingly and proceeds. If more than one node demands to enter the ring, the token holder will detect a garbled response.

The conflict is resolved by an address-based contention scheme. The token holder transmits a *resolve-contention* packet and waits four response windows. Each demander can respond in one of these windows based on the first two bits of its address. If a demander hears anything before its window comes up, it refrains from demanding. If the token holder receives a valid response, it is in business. Otherwise, it tries again, and only those nodes that responded the first time are allowed to respond this time, based on the second pair of bits in their address. This process continues until a valid response is received, no response is received, or a maximum retry count is reached. In the latter two cases, the token holder gives up and passes the token.

Deletion from ring is a much simpler process. If a node wishes to drop out, it waits until it receives the token, then sends a *set-successor* packet to its predecessor, instructing it to splice to its successor.

Fault management by the token holder covers a number of contingencies. First, while holding the token, a node may hear a packet indicating that another node has the token. If so, it immediately drops the token by reverting to listener mode. In this way, the number of token holders drops immediately to 1 or 0. A second problem may arise when, upon completion of its turn, the token holder issues a token packet to its successor. The successor should immediately issue a data or token packet. Therefore, after sending a token, the token issuer will listen for one slot time to make sure that its successor is active. This precipitates a sequence of events:

1. If the successor node is active, the token issuer will hear a valid packet and revert to listener mode.
2. If the issuer does not hear a valid packet, it reissues the token to the same successor one more time.
3. After two failures, the issuer assumes that its successor has failed and issues a *who-follows* packet, asking for the identity of the node that follows the failed node. The issuer should get back a set-successor packet from the second node down the line. If so, the issuer adjusts its linkage and issues a token (back to step 1).
4. If the issuing node gets no response to its who-follows packet, it tries again.
5. If the who-follows tactic fails, the node issues a solicit-successor packet with the full address range (i.e., every node is invited to respond). If this process works, a two-node ring is established and life goes on.
6. If two attempts of step 5 fail, the node assumes that a catastrophe has occurred; perhaps the node's receiver has failed. In any case, the node ceases activity and listens to the bus.

Logical *ring initialization* occurs when one or more stations detect a lack of bus activity of duration longer than a timeout value: The token has been lost. This can be due to a number of causes, such as the network has just been powered up, or a token-holding station fails. Once its timeout expires, a node will issue a *claim-*

token packet. Contending claimants are resolved in a manner similar to the response-window process.

As an option, a token bus system can include classes of service that provide a mechanism of prioritizing access to the bus. Four classes of service are defined, in descending order of priority: 6, 4, 2, 0. Any station may have data in one or more of these classes to send. The object is to allocate network capacity to the higher-priority frames and only send lower-priority frames when there is sufficient capacity. To explain, let us define the following variables:

THT = token holding time. The maximum time that a station can hold the token to transmit class 6 data.

TRT_i = token rotation time for class i (i = 4,2,0). The maximum time that a token can take to circulate and still permit class i transmission.

When a station receives the token, it can transmit classes of data according to the following rules (Figure 11-13): First, the station may transmit class 6 data for a time THT. Hence, for an *n*-station ring, during one circulation of the token, the maximum amount of time available for class 6 transmission is $n \times$ THT. Next, after transmitting class 6 data, or if there were no class 6 data to transmit, it may transmit class 4 data only if the amount of time for the last circulation of the token (including any class 6 data just sent) is less than TRT4. Class 2 and class 0 data are then handled in the same way as class 4.

This scheme, within limits, gives preference to packets of higher priority. More specifically, it guarantees that class 6 data may have a certain portion of the bandwidth. Two cases are possible. If $n \times$ THT is greater than MAX[TRT4, TRT2, TRT0], the maximum possible token circulation time is $n \times$ THT, and class 6 data may occupy the entire cycle to the exclusion of the other classes. If $n \times$ THT is less than MAX[TRT4, TRT2, TRT0], the maximum circulation time is MAX[TRT4, TRT2, TRT0], and class 6 data are guaranteed $n \times$ THT amount of that time.

Figure 11-14, which is adapted from one in [JAYA87], illustrates the average behavior of the IEEE token bus capacity-allocation scheme. That is, the plots ignore temporary load fluctuations, instead depicting the steady-state performance. For convenience, we assume that TRT4 > TRT2 > TRT0 and that the load generated in each class of data is the same.

Figure 11-14a depicts the first case ($n \times$ THT > TRT4). At very low loads, the token circulation time is very short, and all of the data offered in all four classes is transmitted. As the load increases, the average token circulation time reaches TRT0. There is then a range, as indicated in the figure, in which the load continues to increase but the token circulation time remains at TRT0. In this range, the other classes of data increase their throughput at the expense of Class 0 data, whose throughput declines. At some point, the load is such that the token circulation time equals TRT0, but the amount of transmission in Classes 2, 4, and 6 uses up all of that time and no Class 0 data can be transmitted. Further increase in offered load results in renewed increase in the token circulation time. The same pattern repeats for Class 2 and Class 4 data. There is a period when the load increases at a constant token circulation time of TRT2, and during that period, Class 2 data is gradually crowded out. Class 4 data is similarly crowded out at a higher level of load. Finally, a situation is reached in which only Class 6 data is being transmitted, and the token circulation time stabilizes at $n \times$ THT.

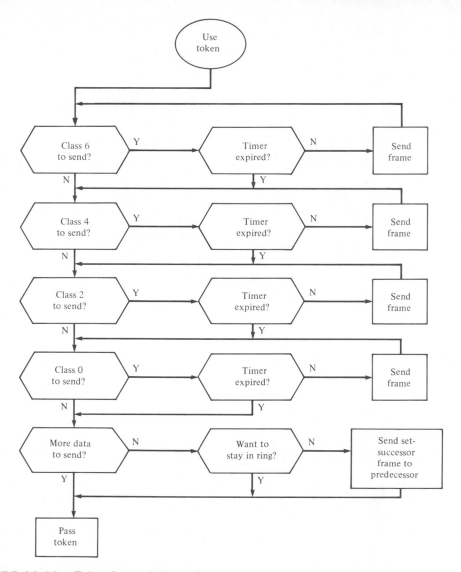

FIGURE 11-13.   Token bus priority scheme.

For the second case just mentioned ($n \times$ THT $<$ TRT4), we need to examine two subcases. Figure 11-14b shows the case in which $\frac{\text{TRT4}}{2} < (n \times \text{THT})$ $<$ TRT4. As before, with increasing load, Class 0 and Class 2 traffic are eliminated and the token circulation time increases. At some point, the increasing load drives the token circulation time to TRT4. Using our simple example, when this point is reached, approximately half of the load is Class 4 data and the other half is Class 6. But, since $n \times$ THT $> \frac{\text{TRT4}}{2}$, if the load on the network continues to increase, the portion of the load that is Class 6 traffic will also increase. This will cause a corresponding decrease in Class 4 traffic. Eventually, a point is reached at which all of the allowable Class 6 traffic is being handled during each token

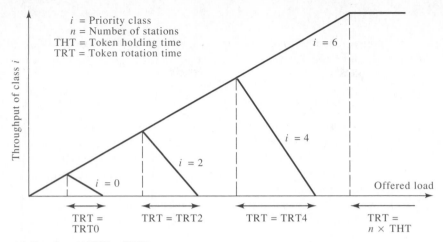

(a) Case I: $n \times$ THT > TRT4

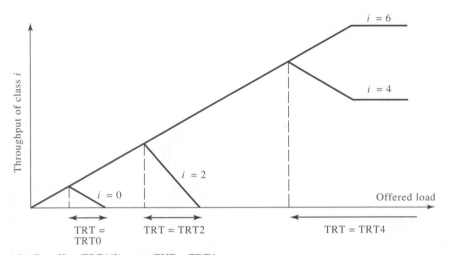

(b) Case IIa: (TRT4/2)< $n \times$ THT < TRT4

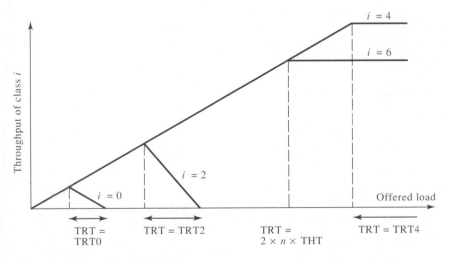

(c) Case IIb: $n \times$ THT < (TRT4/2)

FIGURE 11-14.   Throughput of token bus priority classes.

circulation. This will take an amount of time $n \times$ THT and still leave some time left over for Class 4 data. Thereafter, the total token circulation time remains stable at TRT4.

Finally, Figure 11-14c shows the case in which $n \times \text{THT} < \dfrac{\text{TRT4}}{2}$. As before, increasing load eliminates Class 0 and Class 2 traffic. A point is reached at which the token circulation time is $2 \times n \times$ THT, with half of the traffic being Class 4 and half being Class 6. This is a maximum throughput-per-token-circulation for Class 6. However, the amount of Class 4 data can continue to increase until the token circulation time is TRT4.

It should be obvious that the principal disadvantage of token bus is its complexity. The logic at each station far exceeds that required for CSMA/CD. A second disadvantage is the overhead involved. Under lightly loaded conditions, a station may have to wait through many fruitless token passes for a turn.

Indeed, at first glance it would seem difficult to make a case for this technique. Such a case can be made [MILL82], [STIE81] and it includes the following elements. First, it is possible to regulate the traffic in a number of ways. Multiple priority levels can be used, and different stations can be allowed to hold the token different amounts of time. This type of discrimination is difficult to achieve with CSMA/CD. Second, unlike with CSMA/CD, there is no minimum packet-length requirement with token bus. Third, the necessity for listening while talking imposes physical and electrical constraints on CSMA/CD system; these do not apply to token systems where no station need listen and talk at the same time. Finally, under heavy loads, where it counts, token bus exhibits significantly superior performance to CSMA/CD, as discussed below.

Another advertised advantage of token bus is that it is "deterministic" that is, there is a known upper bound to the amount of time any station must wait before transmitting. This upper bound is known because each station in the logical ring can only hold the token for a specified time. In contrast, with CSMA/CD, the delay time can only be expressed statistically. Furthermore, since every attempt to transmit under CSMA/CD can in principle produce a collision, there is a possibility that a station could be shut out indefinitely. For process-control and other real-time applications, this "nondeterministic" behavior is undesirable. Alas, in the real world, there is always a finite possibility of transmission error, which can cause a lost token. This adds a statistical component to token bus.

Ring Topology

Over the years, a number of different algorithms have been proposed for controlling access to the ring (good surveys are [PENN79] and [LIU78]). In what follows, we look at the most important of these protocols, token ring, and examine its application in two standards.

Token Ring. This is probably the oldest ring control technique, originally proposed in 1969 [FARM69] and referred to as the Newhall ring. This has become the most popular ring access technique in the United States. This technique is the one ring access method selected for standardization by the IEEE 802 Local Network Standards Committee.

The token ring technique is based on the use of a small token packet that circulates around the ring. When all stations are idle, the token packet is labeled as a ''free'' token. A station wishing to transmit must wait until it detects a token passing by. It then changes the token from ''free token'' to ''busy token'' by altering the bit pattern. The station then transmits a packet immediately following the busy token (Figure 11-15).

There is now no free token on the ring, so other stations wishing to transmit must wait. The packet on the ring will make a round trip and be purged by the transmitting station. The transmitting station will insert a new free token on the ring when both of the following conditions have been met:

- The station has completed transmission of its packet.
- The busy token has returned to the station.

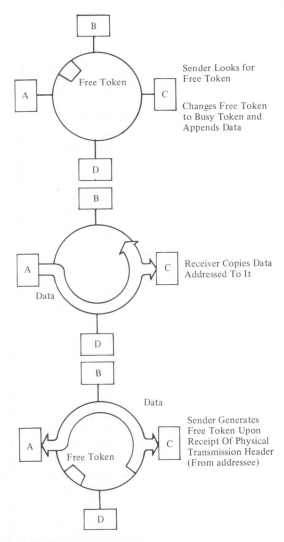

FIGURE 11-15.   Token ring.

If the bit length of the ring is less than the packet length, the first condition implies the second. If not, a station could release a free token after it has finished transmitting but before it receives its own busy token; the second condition is not strictly necessary. However, this might complicate error recovery, since several packets will be on the ring at the same time. In any case, the use of a token guarantees that only one station at a time may transmit.

When a transmitting station releases a new free token, the next station downstream with data to send will be able to seize the token and transmit.

As with token bus, token ring requires fault management techniques. The key error conditions are no token circulating and persistent busy token. To address these problems, one station is designated as active token monitor. The monitor detects the lost-token condition by using a timeout greater than the time required for the longest frame to traverse the ring completely. If no token is seen during this time, it is assumed to be lost. To recover, the monitor purges the ring of any residual data and issues a free token. To detect a circulating busy token, the monitor sets a monitor bit to 1 on any passing busy token. If it sees a busy token with a bit already set, it knows that the transmitting station failed to purge its packet. The monitor changes the busy token to a free token. Other stations on the ring have the role of passive monitor. Their primary job is to detect failure of the active monitor and assume that role. A contention-resolution algorithm is used to determine which station takes over.

The token ring technique shares many of the advantages of token bus. Perhaps its principal advantage is that traffic can be regulated, either by allowing stations to transmit differing amounts of data when they receive the token, or by setting priorities so that higher-priority stations have first claim on a circulating token.

The principal disadvantage of token ring is the requirement for token maintenance. Loss of the free token prevents further utilization of the ring. Duplication of the token can also disrupt ring operation. One station must be elected monitor to assure that exactly one token is on the ring and to reinsert a free token if necessary.

IEEE 802 Ring Standard.   The IEEE 802 token ring standard follows the general scheme outlined above. The major addition is a scheme for capacity allocation using priorities. The 802 specification provides for eight levels of priority. It does this by providing two three-bit fields in each packet and token: a priority field and a reservation field. For clarity, let us define three variables: P_m = priority of message to be transmitted by a station; P_r = received priority; and R_r = received reservation. The scheme works as follows:

1. A station wishing to transmit must wait for a free token with $P_r \leq P_m$.
2. While waiting, a station may reserve a future token at its priority level (P_m). If a packet goes by, it may set the reservation field to its priority ($R_r \leftarrow P_m$) if the reservation field is less than its priority ($R_r < P_m$). If a free token goes by, it sets the reservation field to its priority ($R_r \leftarrow P_m$) if $R_r < P_m$ and $P_m < P_r$. This has the effect of preempting any lower-priority reservations.
3. When a station seizes a token, it sets the reservation field to 0 and leaves the priority field unchanged.
4. Following transmission, a station issues a new token with the priority set to the maximum of P_r, R_r, and P_m, and a reservation set to the maximum of R_r and P_m.

The effect of the above steps is to sort out competing claims and allow the waiting transmission of highest priority to seize the token as soon as possible. A station having a higher priority than the current busy token can reserve the next free token for its priority level as the busy token passes by. When the current transmitting station is finished, it issues a free token at that higher priority. Stations of lower priority cannot seize the token, so it passes to the requesting station of equal or higher priority with data to send.

A moment's reflection reveals that, as is, the algorithm has a ratchet effect on priority, driving it to the highest used level and keeping it there. To avoid this, the station that upgraded the priority level is responsible for downgrading it to its former level when all higher-priority stations are finished. When that station sees a free token at the higher priority, it can assume that there is no more higher-priority traffic waiting, and it downgrades the token before passing it on. Figure 11-16 is an example of the operation of the priority mechanism.

FDDI Ring Standard. The Fiber Distributed Data Interface (FDDI) is a standard for a high-speed ring LAN [ROSS89]. Like the IEEE 802 standard, FDDI employs the token ring algorithm. There are, however, several differences that are intended to allow FDDI to take advantage of the high speed (100 Mbps) of its ring and maximize efficiency.

Figure 11-17 gives an example of ring operation. After station A has seized the token, it transmits frame F1, and immediately transmits a new token. F1 is addressed to station C, which copies it as it circulates past. The frame eventually returns to A, which absorbs it. Meanwhile, B seizes the token issued by A and transmits F2 followed by a token. This action could be repeated any number of times, so that at any one time, there may be multiple frames circulating the ring. Each station is responsible for absorbing its own frames based on the source address field.

Note that in FDDI, a station emits a new token immediately following the frame, where as in IEEE token ring, a station emits a new token only after the leading edge of its transmitted frame returns. The FDDI scheme is thus more efficient, especially in large rings.

Another difference between the IEEE token ring algorithm and that of FDDI is in the area of capacity allocation. The FDDI scheme is designed to be efficient and flexible in meeting a wide range of high-speed requirements. Specifically, FDDI provides support for a mixture of stream and bursty traffic, which is a requirement that was discussed in the context of satellite protocols in Chapter 10.

To accommodate this requirement, FDDI defines two types of traffic: synchronous and asynchronous. The scheme works as follows. A target token rotation time (TTRT) is defined; each station stores the same value for TTRT. Some or all stations may be provided a synchronous allocation (SA_i), which may vary among stations. The allocations must be such that:

$$\text{DMax} + \text{FMax} + \text{TokenTime} + \Sigma\, SA_i \leq \text{TTRT}$$

where

SA_i = allocation for station i
DMax = propagation time for one complete circuit of the ring
FMAX = time required to transmit a maximum-length packet (4500 octets)
TokenTime = time required to transmit a token

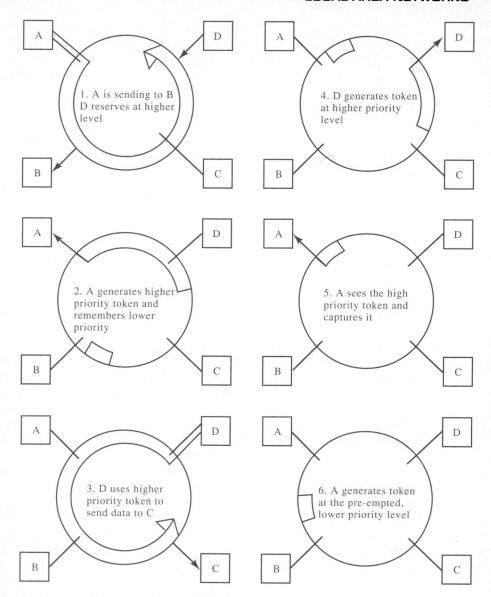

FIGURE 11-16. IEEE token ring priority scheme.

Thus all stations have the same value of TTRT and a separately assigned value of SA_i. In addition, several variables that are required for the operation of the capacity-allocation algorithm are maintained at each station:

- Token-rotation timer (TRT)
- Token-holding timer (THT)
- Late counter (LC)

Each station's TRT is initialized to TTRT; when it is enabled, it counts down until it expires at TRT = 0. It is then reset to TTRT and enabled again. LC is initialized at zero and is incremented when TRT expires. Thus LC records the

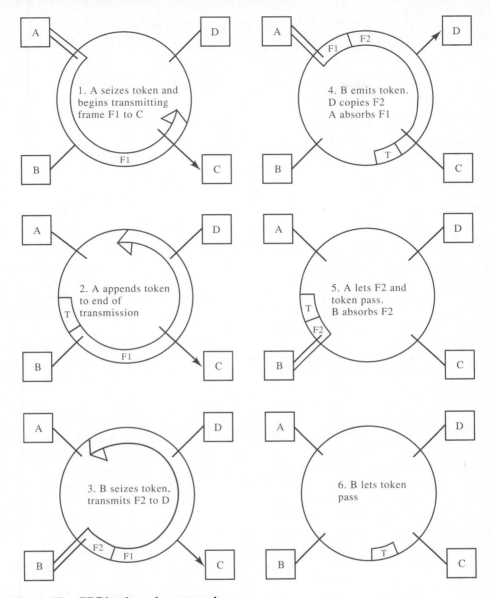

FIGURE 11-17.   FDDI token ring operation.

number of times, if any, that TRT has expired since the token was last received at that station. The token is considered to arrive early if TRT has not expired since the station received the token, that is, if LC = 0.

When a station receives the token, its actions will depend on whether the token is early or late. If the token is early, the station saves the remaining time in TRT in THT; resets TRT, and enables TRT:

THT ⟵ TRT
TRT ⟵ TTRT
enable TRT

The station can then transmit according to the following rules:

1. It may transmit synchronous frames for a time SA_i.
2. After transmitting synchronous frames, or if there were no synchronous frames to transmit, THT is enabled. The station may transmit asynchronous frames only so long as THT > 0.

If a station receives a token and the token is late, then LC is set to zero, and TRT continues to run. The station can then transmit synchronous frames for a time SA_i. The station may not transmit any asynchronous frames.

This scheme is designed to assure that the time between successive sighting of a token is on the order of TTRT or less. Of this time, a given amount is always available for synchronous traffic and any excess capacity is available for asynchronous traffic. Because of random fluctuations in traffic, the actual token circulation time may exceed TTRT [JOHN87, SEVC87], as demonstrated below.

The FDDI algorithm is similar to the 802.4 algorithm with only two classes of data, 6 and 4. Synchronous data corresponds to Class 6, and the value of SA_i in FDDI corresponds to the token holding time in 802.4. Finally, TTRT corresponds to TRT4. Since the sum of the SA_i (all the synchronous allocations) must be less than or equal to TTRT, the FDDI restrictions correspond to Case IIa in Figure 11-14.

Figure 11-18 provides a simplified example of a 4-station ring. We assume that the traffic consists of fixed-length frames, and that TTRT = 100 frame times and SA_i = 20 frame times for all stations. We also assume that the total overhead during one complete token circulation is 4 frame times. The value in the left-hand column is the token circulation time actually experienced at that station for the previous rotation of the token. Thus, when the token arrives early, this value is equal to 100 − TRT. The right-hand value is the number of frames the station transmits; this is broken down into synchronous and asynchronous frames.

The example begins after a period during which no data frames have been sent, so that the token has been circulating as rapidly as possible (4 frame times). Thus, when Station 1 receives the token, it measures a circulation time of 4 (its TRT = 96). It is therefore able to send not only its 20 synchronous frames but also 96 asynchronous frames; recall that THT is not enabled until after the station has sent its synchronous frames. Station 2 experiences a circulation time of 120 (20 frames + 96 frames + 4 overhead frames), but is nevertheless entitled to transmit its 20 synchronous frames. Note that if each station continues to transmit its maximum allowable synchronous frames, then the circulation time surges to 180, but soon

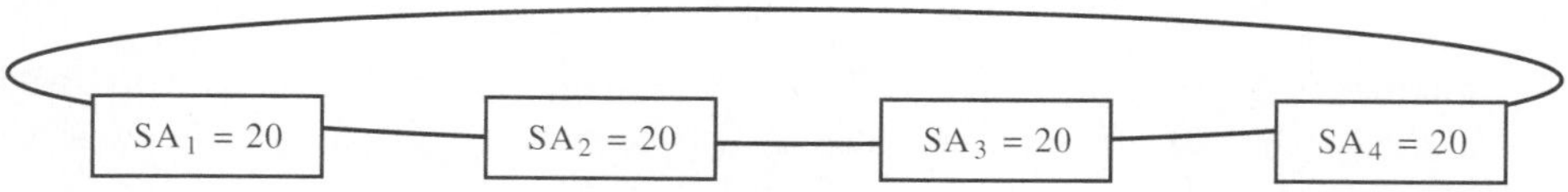

SA$_1$ = 20		SA$_2$ = 20		SA$_3$ = 20		SA$_4$ = 20	
TCT	XMIT	TCT	XMIT	TCT	XMIT	TCT	XMIT
4	20,96	120	20,0	140	20,0	160	20,0
180	20,0	84	20,16	100	20,0	100	20,0
100	20,0	100	20,0	84	20,16	100	20,0
100	20,0	100	20,0	100	20,0	84	20,16
100	20,0	100	20,0	100	20,0	100	20,0
84	20,16	100	20,0	100	20,0	100	20,0
100	20,0	84	20,16	100	20,0	100	20,0

FIGURE 11-18.   Operation of FDDI capacity allocation scheme.

stabilizes at 100. With a total synchronous utilization of 80 and an overhead of 4 frame times, there is an average capacity of 16 frame times available for asynchronous transmission. Note that if all stations always have a full backlog of asynchronous traffic, the opportunity to transmit asynchronous frames rotates among them.

11-5

LAN PROTOCOL PERFORMANCE

The choice of a LAN architecture is based on many factors, but one of the most important is performance. Of particular concern is the behavior (throughput, response time) of the network under heavy load. In this section we provide an introduction to this topic for the two topologies and five medium access control protocols for LANs discussed earlier. A more detailed discussion can be found in [STAL90a].

As in previous chapters, we will see that the parameter a is a determining factor. Table 11-8 gives some idea of the values of a that might be expected for a local network.

Simple Performance Models of Token Passing and CSMA/CD

The purpose of this section is to give the reader some insight into the relative performance of the most important LAN protocols: CSMA/CD, token bus, and token ring, by developing two simple performance models. It is hoped that this exercise will aid in understanding the results of more rigorous analyses, presented later.

For these models we assume a local network with N active stations, and a maximum normalized propagation delay of a. To simplify the analysis, we assume that each station is always prepared to transmit a packet. This allows us to develop an expression for maximum achievable throughput (S). Although this should not be construed to be the sole figure of merit for a local network, it is the single most analyzed figure of merit, and does permit useful performance comparisons.

TABLE 11-8   Representative Values of *a*

Data Rate (Mbps)	Packet Size (bits)	Cable Length (km)	*a*
1	100	1	0.05
	1,000	10	0.05
	100	10	0.5
10	100	1	0.5
	1,000	1	0.05
	1,000	10	0.5
	10,000	10	0.05
50	10,000	1	0.025
	100	1	2.5

First, let us consider token ring. Time on the ring will alternate between data packet transmission and token passing. Refer to a single instance of a data packet followed by a token as a cycle and define:

$$C = \text{average time for one cycle}$$
$$T_1 = \text{average time to transmit a data packet}$$
$$T_2 = \text{average time to pass a token}$$

It should be clear that the average cycle rate is just $1/C = 1/(T_1 + T_2)$. Intuitively,

$$S = \frac{T_1}{T_1 + T_2} \tag{11-1}$$

That is, the throughput, normalized to system capacity, is just the fraction of time that is spent transmitting data.

Refer now to Figure 11-19; time is normalized such that packet transmission time equals 1 and propagation time equals a. Note that the propagation time must include repeater delays. For the case of $a < 1$, a station transmits a packet at time t_0, receives the leading edge of its own packet at $t_0 + a$, and completes transmission at $t_0 + 1$. The station then emits a token, which takes an average time a/N to reach the next station. Thus one cycle takes $1 + a/N$ and the transmission time is 1. So $S = 1/(1 + a/N)$.

For $a > 1$, the reasoning is slightly different. A station transmits at t_0, completes transmission at $t_0 + 1$, and receives the leading edge of its frame at $t_0 + a$. At that point, it is free to emit a token, which takes an average time a/N to reach the next station. The cycle time is therefore $a + a/N$ and $S = 1/(a (1 + 1/N))$.

Summarizing,

$$\text{Token } S = \begin{cases} \dfrac{1}{1 + a/N} & a < 1 \\[2ex] \dfrac{1}{a (1 + 1/N)} & a > 1 \end{cases} \tag{11-2}$$

The reasoning above applies equally well to token bus, where we assume that the logical ordering is the same as the physical ordering and that token-passing time is therefore a/N.

For CSMA/CD, we base our approach on a derivation in [METC76]. Consider time on the medium to be organized into slots whose length is twice the end-to-end propagation delay. This is a convenient way to view the activity on the medium; the slot time is the maximum time, from the start of transmission, required to detect a collision. Again, assume that there are N active stations. Clearly, if each station always has a packet to transmit, and does so, there will be nothing but collisions on the line. So we assume that each station restrains itself to transmitting during an available slot with probability P.

Time on the medium consists of two types of intervals. First is a transmission interval, which lasts $1/2a$ slots. Second is a contention interval, which is a sequence of slots with either a collision or no transmission in each slot. The throughput is just the proportion of time spent in transmission intervals [similar to the reasoning for Equation (11-1)].

To determine the average length of a contention interval, we begin by computing A, the probability that exactly one station attempts a transmission in a slot and

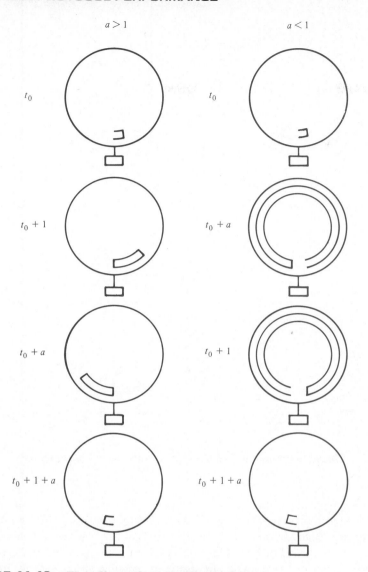

FIGURE 11-19. **The effect of *a* on utilization: ring.**

therefore acquires the medium. This is just the binomial probability that any one station attempts to transmit and the others do not:

$$A = \binom{N}{1} P^1(1 - P)^{N-1}$$

$$A = NP(1 - P)^{N-1}$$

This function takes on a maximum over P when $P = 1/N$:

$$A = (1 - 1/N)^{N-1}$$

Why are we interested in the maximum? Well, we want to calculate the maximum throughput of the medium. It should be clear that this will be achieved if we

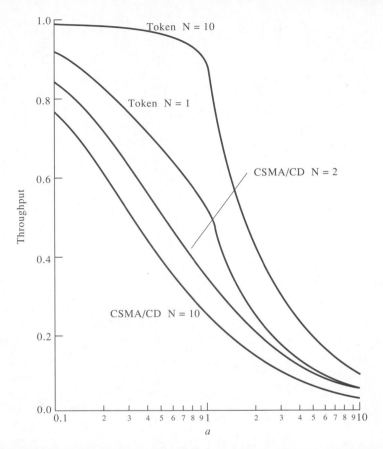

FIGURE 11-20.   Throughput as a function of *a* for token passing and CSMA/CD.

maximize the probability of successful seizure of the medium. This says that the following rule should be enforced: During periods of heavy usage, a station should restrain its offered load to $1/N$. (This assumes that each station knows the value of N. In order to derive an expression for maximum possible throughput, we live with this assumption.) On the other hand, during periods of light usage, maximum utilization cannot be achieved because G is too low; this region is not of interest here.

Now we can estimate the mean length of a contention interval, w, in slots:

$$E[w] = \sum_{i=1}^{\infty} i \, \Pr[i \text{ slots in a row with a collision or no transmission followed by a slot with one transmission}]$$

$$= \sum_{i=1}^{\infty} i(1 - A)^i A$$

The summation converges to

$$E[w] = \frac{1 - A}{A}$$

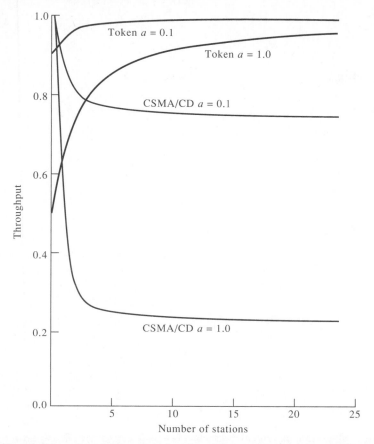

FIGURE 11-21.   Throughput as a function of *N* for token passing and CSMA/CD.

We can now determine the maximum utilization, which is just the length of a transmission interval as a proportion of a cycle consisting of a transmission and a contention interval:

$$\text{CSMA/CD: } S = \frac{1/2a}{1/2a + (1 - A)/A} = \frac{1}{1 + 2a(1 - A)/A} \quad (11\text{-}3)$$

Figure 11-20 shows normalized throughput as a function of *a* for various values of *N* and for both token passing and CSMA/CD. For both protocols, throughput declines as *a* increases. This is to be expected. But the dramatic difference between the two protocols is seen in Figure 11-21, which shows throughput as a function of *N*. Token-passing performance actually improves as a function of *N*, because less time is spent in token passing. Conversely, the performance of CSMA/CD decreases because of the increased likelihood of collision or no transmission.

It is interesting to note the asymptotic value of *S* as *N* increases. For token:

$$\text{Token: } \lim_{N \to \infty} S = \begin{cases} 1 & a < 1 \\ \dfrac{1}{a} & a > 1 \end{cases} \quad (11\text{-}4)$$

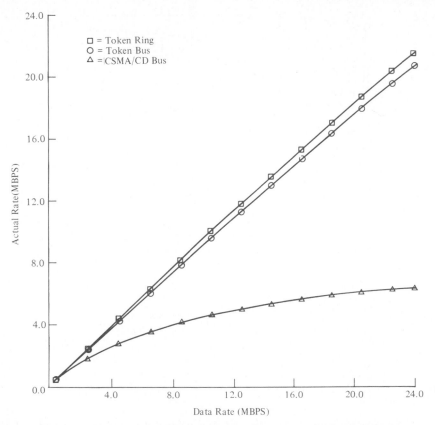

FIGURE 11-22a.   Maximum potential data rate for LAN protocols: 2000 bits per packet; 100 stations active out of 100 stations total.

For CSMA/CD, we need to know that $\lim (1 - 1/N)^{N-1} = 1/e$. Then CSMA/CD:

$$\lim_{N \to \infty} S = \frac{1}{1 + 3.44a} \qquad (11\text{-}5)$$

Comparative Results from Analytic and Simulation Studies

Although there have been a number of performance studies focusing on a single protocol, there have been few systematic attempts to analyze the relative performance of the various local network protocols. In what follows, we look at the results of several carefully done studies that have produced comparative results.

CSMA/CD, Token Bus, and Token Ring.   The first study was done by a group at Bell Labs, under the sponsorship of the IEEE 802 local network standards committee [STUC85]. Naturally enough, the study analyzed the three protocols being standardized by IEEE 802: CSMA/CD, token bus, and token ring. The analysis is based on considering not only mean values but second moments of delay

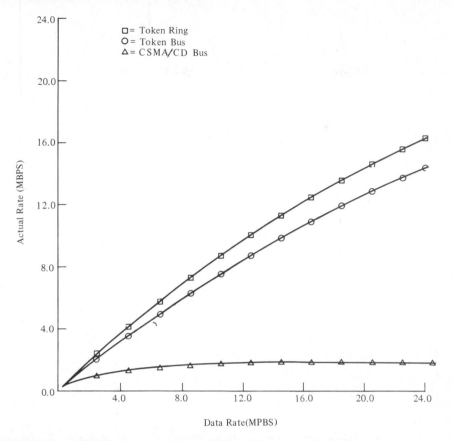

FIGURE 11-22b. 500 bits per packet; 100 stations active out of 100 stations total.

and message length. Two cases of message arrival statistics are employed. In the first, only 1 station out of 100 has messages to transmit, and is always ready to transmit. In such a case, one would hope that the network would not be the bottleneck, but could easily keep up with one station. In the second case, 100 stations out of 100 always have messages to transmit. This represents an extreme of congestion and one would expect that the network may be a bottleneck. In the two cases, the 1 station or 100 stations provide enough input to fully utilize the network. Hence the results are a measure of maximum potential utilization.

The results are shown in Figure 11-22. It shows the actual data transmission rate versus the transmission speed of the medium for the two cases and two packet sizes. Note that the abscissa is not offered load but the actual capacity of the medium. Three systems are examined: token ring with a one-bit latency per repeater, token bus, and CSMA/CD. The analysis yields the following conclusions:

- For the given parameters, the smaller the mean packet length, the greater the difference in maximum mean throughput rate between token passing and CSMA/CD. This reflects the strong dependence of CSMA/CD on a.
- Token ring is the least sensitive to work load.

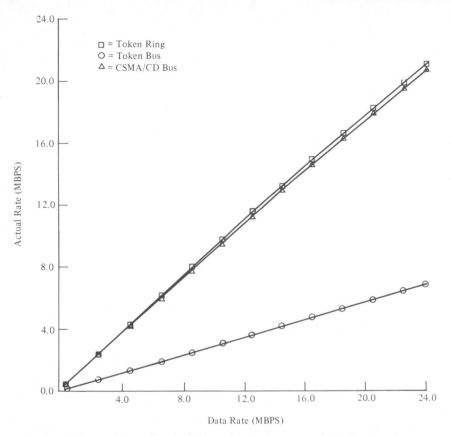

FIGURE 11-22c.   2000 bits per packet; 1 station active out of 100 stations total.

- CSMA/CD offers the shortest delay under light load, while it is most sensitive under heavy load to the work load.

Note also that in the case of a single station transmitting, token bus is significantly less efficient than the other two protocols. This is so because the assumption is made that token-passing time equals the propagation delay, and that the delay in token processing is greater than for token ring.

Another phenomenon of interest is seen most clearly in Figure 11-22b. For a CSMA/CD system under these conditions, the maximum effective throughput at 5 Mbps is only about 1.25 Mbps. If expected load is, say 0.75 Mbps, this configuration may be perfectly adequate. If however, the load is expected to grow to 2 Mbps, raising the network data rate to 10 Mbps or even 20 Mbps will not accommodate the increase! The same conclusion, less precisely, can be drawn from the simple model presented earlier.

The reason for this disparity between CSMA/CD and token passing (bus or ring) under heavy load has to· do with the instability of CSMA/CD. As offered load increases, so does throughput until, beyond its maximum value, throughput actually declines as G increases. This is because there is an increased frequency of collisions: More packets are offered, but fewer successfully escape collision. This same behavior was seen with other contention techniques (ALOHA, CSMA).

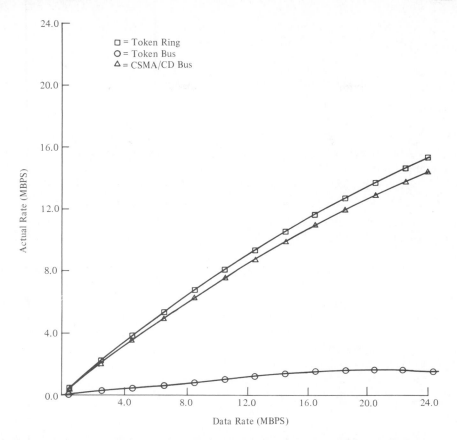

FIGURE 11-22d. 500 bits per packet; 1 station active out of 100 stations total.

11·6

RECOMMENDED READING

The literature on local area networks is vast. The material in this chapter is covered in depth in [STAL90a]. [STAL90d] provides detailed coverage of local network standards. [STAL88a] contains reprints of some of the key articles on local networks as well as an annotated bibliography.

[STUC85], [HAMM86], and [BERT87] provide detailed and rigorous treatments of local area network performance. [SKOV89] looks at other access control protocols for high-speed LANs.

[STAL90f] is a treatment oriented toward managers and end users.

11·7

PROBLEMS

11-1 An alternative to a local network for meeting local requirements for data processing and computer applications is a centralized time-sharing system plus a large number of terminals dispersed throughout the local area. What are the major benefits and pitfalls of this approach compared to a local network?

11-2 Could HDLC be used as a data link control protocol for a local network? If not, what is missing?

11-3 An asynchronous device, such as a teletype, transmits characters one at a time with unpredictable delays between characters. What problems, if any, do you foresee if such a device is connected to a local network and allowed to transmit at will (subject to gaining access to the medium)? How might such problems be resolved?

11-4 Consider the transfer of a file containing one million characters from one station to another. What is the total elapsed time and effective throughput for the following cases:
  a. A circuit-switched, star topology local network. Call setup time is negligible, and the data rate on the medium is 64 kbps.
  b. A bus topology local network with two stations a distance D apart, a data rate of B bps, and a packet size P with 80 bits of overhead. Each packet is acknowledged with an 88-bit packet before the next is sent. The propagation speed on the bus is 200 m/μs. Solve for:
  (1) $D = 1$ km, $B = 1$ Mbps, $P = 256$ bits
  (2) $D = 1$ km, $B = 10$ Mbps, $P = 256$ bits
  (3) $D = 10$ km, $B = 1$ Mbps, $P = 256$ bits
  (4) $D = 1$ km, $B = 50$ Mbps, $P = 10,000$ bits
  c. A ring topology with a total circular length of $2D$, with the two stations a distance D apart. Acknowledgment is achieved by allowing a packet to circulate past the destination station, back to the source station. There are N repeaters on the ring, each of which introduces a delay of one bit time. Repeat the calculation for each of b1 through b4 for $N = 10; 100; 1000$.

11-5 A tree-topology local network is to be provided that spans two buildings. If permission can be obtained to string cable between the two buildings, one continuous tree layout will be used. Otherwise, each building will have an independent tree topology network and a point-to-point link will connect a special communications station on one network with a communications station on the other network. What functions must the communications stations perform? Repeat for ring and star.

11-6 System A consists of a single ring with 300 stations, one per repeater. System B consists of three 100-station rings linked by a bridge. If the probability of a link failure is P_1, a repeater failure is P_r, and a bridge failure is P_b, derive an expression for parts (a) through (d):
  a. Probability of failure of system A.
  b. Probability of complete failure of system B.
  c. Probability that a particular station will find the network unavailable, for systems A and B.
  d. Probability that any two stations, selected at random, will be unable to communicate, for systems A and B.
  e. Compute values for parts (a) through (d) for $P_1 = P_b = P_r = 10^{-2}$.

11-7 The binary exponential backoff algorithm is defined by IEEE 802 thus: "The delay is an integral multiple of slot time. The number of slot times to delay before the nth retransmission attempt is chosen as a uniformly distributed random integer r in the range $0 < r < 2**K$, where $K = \min(n,10)$." Slot time is, roughly, twice the round-trip propagation delay. Assume that two stations always have a frame to send. After a collision, what is the mean number of retransmission attempts before one station successfully transmits? What is the answer if three stations always have frames to send?

11-8 Another medium access control technique for rings is the slotted ring. A number of fixed-length slots circulate continuously on the ring. Each slot contains a leading bit to designate the slot as empty or full. A station wishing to transmit waits until an empty slot arrives, marks the slot full, and inserts a packet of data as the slot goes by. The full slot makes a complete round trip, to be marked empty again by the station that marked it full. In what sense are the slotted ring and token ring protocols the complement of each other?

11-9 For a token ring system, suppose that the destination station removes the data frame and immediately sends a short acknowledgment frame to the sender, rather than letting the original frame return to sender. How will this affect performance?

11-10 Consider a slotted ring of length 10 km with a data rate of 10 Mbps and 500 repeaters, each of which introduces a 1-bit delay. Each slot contains room for one source address byte, one destination address byte, two data bytes, and five control bits for a total length of 37 bits. How many slots are on the ring?

11-11 Compare the capacity allocation schemes for token bus, IEEE 802 token ring, and FDDI. What are the relative pros and cons?

11-12 With continuing improvements in optical fiber transmission components, one might expect to see an HSLN using a fiber bus in the range 100 to 200 Mbps in the foreseeable future. Such a network could support a mix of stream and bursty traffic. Consider the various reservation schemes proposed in Chapter 10. Would any of these be appropriate for a fiber HSLN? Could you suggest a variation in one or more of the protocols that would be better suited?

11-13 Compare equations (10-12), (11-2), and (11-3). Under what circumstances does the throughput for the latter two equations exceed the theoretical maximum of (10-12)? Explain.

11-14 For the graphs in Figure 11-22, determine a and comment on the results.

11-15 Equations (11-2) and (11-4) are valid for token ring and for token baseband bus. What are equivalent equations for broadband bus?

11-16 The maximum distance for a 10-Mbps baseband bus LAN without repeaters is about 500 m. If stations are located at the end of such a system, what is the delay from one station to the other? Does this present a problem? Why or why not?

11-17 In Section 11-4, it was stated that maximum time for collision detection in a broadband system is four times the end-to-end propagation delay. Draw a figure similar to Figure 11-10 that demonstrates this.

11-18 Refer to Figure 11-13. Is it possible that class 0 data might experience starvation (never get a chance to transmit)? Consider two cases:
a. A node that has class 0 and class 6 data to send
b. A node that only has class 0 data to send

11-19 A motivation for using a different capacity allocation scheme for FDDI compared to the IEEE token ring scheme is that the FDDI scheme is more flexible and efficient in allocating capacity for stream and bursty traffic. But it is also the case that the IEEE scheme *cannot* be used on FDDI. Why?

11-20 Rework the example of Figure 11-18 using a TTRT of 12 packets and assume that no station ever has more than 8 asynchronous packets to send.

11-21 Consider a token ring LAN with 12 stations equally spaced around the ring. Assume that each station is always prepared to send a packet. Calculate the throughput normalized to system capacity for the following cases:
a. $a = 3$
b. $a = 0.35$

11-22 Repeat Problem 11-21 substituting a ring version of CSMA/CD for token passing. Assume that each station transmits with a probability 1/N.

APPENDIX 11A

LAN STANDARDS

In recent years, the market for local area network products has come to be dominated by those that conform to standards. The reasons for this are compelling:

1. The published standards are the product of a broad-based effort involving highly knowledgeable individuals from a wide spectrum of vendor and customer organizations. Thus, the specified combinations chosen for standardization reflect a consensus as to which combinations meet typical requirements.
2. The LAN standards have achieved widespread and rapid acceptance both by vendors and customers. Thus, the customer benefits from the cost savings of mass production and has a broad range of compatible products to choose from.

Most of the standards were developed by a committee known as IEEE 802, sponsored by the Institute for Electrical and Electronics Engineers; one of the standards was developed by the American National Standards Institute (ANSI). The IEEE standards were initially issued in 1985. They were subsequently revised and reissued as international standards by the International Organization for Standardization in 1987, with the designation ISO 8802. All of these standards have subsequently been adopted as international standards by the International

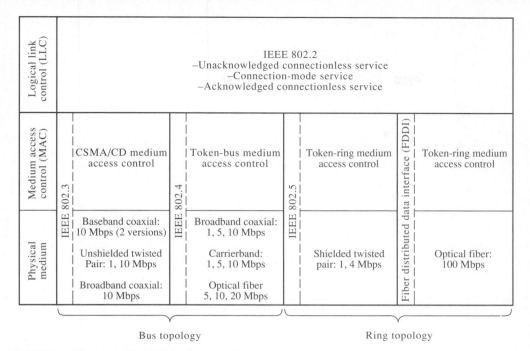

FIGURE 11-23.   Local area network standards.

Organization for Standardization (ISO). The ANSI effort was in the development of the standard for Fiber Distributed Data Interface (FDDI), which was issued in several sections in 1989 and 1990 as an American National Standard. It was adopted by ISO in 1990 as ISO 9314.

The standards that have been issued are illustrated in Figure 11-23. The standards are organized as a three-layer protocol hierarchy. Logical link control (LLC) is responsible for addressing and data link control. It is independent of the topology, transmission medium, and medium access control technique chosen, and was issued as a separate standard. Below logical link control are the medium access control (MAC) and physical layers. Because of the interdependence between medium access control, medium, and topology, these layers were organized into standards based on the medium access control algorithm, with the physical layer specified as part of the medium access control standard.

Logical link control (LLC) is examined in Chapter 13, and much of the detail of the medium access control techniques is covered in the body of this chapter. The remainder of this appendix summarizes some of the details of the medium access control and physical layer specifications.

11A1   CSMA/CD (IEEE 802.3)

Medium Access Control.   The 802.3 medium access control technique is CSMA/CD, as described in this chapter. In order to implement the CSMA/CD algorithm, data is transmitted in the form of packets, referred to as MAC frames, which contain user information and the control information needed for the algorithm. Figure 11-24a shows the format of the IEEE 802.3 MAC frame. The pream-

(a) CSMA/CD

7	1	2, 6	2, 6	2	0-1500		4	octets
Preamble	SFD	DA	SA	Length	Data	Pad	FCS	

(b) Token bus

1	1	1	2, 6	2, 6	≥0	4	1
Preamble	SD	FC	DA	SA	Data	FCS	ED

(c) Token ring

1	1	1	2, 6	2, 6	≥0	4	1	1
SD	AC	FC	DA	SA	Data	FCS	ED	FS

(d) FDDI

8	1	1	2, 6	2, 6	≥0	4	1	1
Preamble	SD	FC	DA	SA	Data	FCS	ED	FS

AC = Access control
DA = Destination address
ED = Ending delimiter
FC = Frame control
FCS = Frame check sequence
FS = Frame status
SA = Source address
SD = Starting delimiter
SFD = Start frame delimiter

FIGURE 11-24.   LAN standard MAC frame formats.

ble is a special 7-octet pattern used by each receiver to establish bit synchronization. This is followed by a start frame delimiter which is a special pattern that signals the beginning of the frame proper. The destination and source addresses specify the transmitting station and the intended receiving station respectively. The length field specifies the number of data octets that follow. The pad field is inserted by the transmitter if needed to assure that the frame is long enough for proper CD operation. Finally, the frame check sequence is a 32-bit cyclic redundancy check for error detection.

Medium Options.   Table 11-9a summarizes the options defined for the IEEE 802.3 medium. The **original 802.3 standard (10BASE5)** specified a 10-Mbps baseband coaxial cable LAN using standard baseband coaxial cable. The maximum length of a segment of cable is 500 meters, with a maximum of 100 taps per segment allowed. The length of the network can be extended using repeaters. The standard allows a maximum of four repeaters in the path between any two stations, extending the effective length of the network to 2.5 km.

This original version, issued in 1985, was soon followed by a new option, sometimes called **Cheapernet (10BASE2).** This provides for the use of a thinner

TABLE 11-9   Physical Layer Specifications for LAN Standards

(a) IEEE 802.3 (CSMA/CD)

	Transmission Medium	Signaling Technique	Data Rate (Mbps)	Maximum Segment Length (m)
10BASE5	Coaxial Cable (50 ohm)	Baseband (Manchester)	10	500
10BASE2	Coaxial Cable (50 ohm)	Baseband (Manchester)	10	185
1BASE5	Unshielded Twisted Pair	Baseband (Manchester)	1	250
10BASE-T	Unshielded Twisted Pair	Baseband (Manchester)	10	100
10BROAD36	Coaxial Cable (75 ohm)	Broadband (DPSK)	10	3600

(b) IEEE 802.4 (Token Bus)

	Transmission Medium	Signaling Technique	Data Rate (Mbps)	Maximum Segment Length (m)
Broadband	Coaxial Cable (75 ohm)	Broadband (AM/PSK)	1, 5, 10	Not specified
Carrierband	Coaxial Cable (75 ohm)	Broadband (FSK)	1, 5, 10	7600
Optical Fiber	Optical Fiber	ASK-Manchester	5, 10, 20	Not specified

(c) IEEE 802.5 (Token Ring)

Transmission Medium	Signaling Technique	Data Rate (Mbps)	Maximum Number of Repeaters	Maximum Distance Between Repeaters (m)
Shielded Twisted Pair	Differential Manchester	1, 4	250	Not specified

(d) Fiber Distributed Data Interface (FDDI)

Transmission Medium	Signaling Technique	Data Rate (Mbps)	Maximum Number of Repeaters	Maximum Distance Between Repeaters (m)
Optical Fiber	ASK-NRZI	100	1000	2000

coaxial cable at the same data rate. The thinner cable results in significantly cheaper electronics, at the penalty of fewer stations and shorter length. Segment length is reduced to 185 meters with a maximum of 30 taps per segment. It is targeted to lower-cost devices, such as UNIX workstations and personal computers.

Another option, known as **StarLAN (1BASE5),** specifies an unshielded twisted-pair version operating at 1 Mbps, using a passive star topology. This option is substantially lower in cost than either of the coaxial cable options and is targeted specifically at personal computer installations that do not require high capacity. This option could be appropriate for a departmental-level LAN. The most recent addition to the standard is the **10BASE-T** option which is also a passive-star-topology LAN using unshielded twisted pair, but operating at 10 Mbps.

A 10-Mbps **broadband (10BROAD36)** option has also been added. This provides for the support of more stations over greater distances than the baseband versions, at greater cost.

11A2   Token Bus (IEEE 802.4)

Medium Access Control. The 802.4 medium access control technique is the token bus algorithm. Figure 11-24 shows the MAC frame format. The only new field, compared to 802.3, is the frame control field. This field contains information needed for the proper operation of the algorithm. One bit indicates whether this frame carries user data or is a control frame. In the latter case, the remaining bits specify which control frame (e.g., token, who-follows).

Medium Options. The token bus standard specifies three physical layer options (Table 11-9b). The first is a **broadband** system, which supports data channels at 1, 5, and 10 Mbps with bandwidths of 1.5, 6, and 12 MHz, respectively. The standard recommends the use of a single-cable split system with a headend frequency translator. The dual cable configuration is also allowed.

The second is a scheme known as **carrierband,** or single-channel broadband. Because carrierband is dedicated to a single data channel, it is not necessary to take care that the modem output be confined to a narrow bandwidth. Energy can spread over the cable's spectrum. As a result, the electronics are simple and inexpensive compared with those for broadband. Carrierband data rates of 1, 5, and 10 Mbps are specified.

The most recent option is one using optical fiber at data rates of 5, 10, and 20 Mbps. Either a passive or active star topology can be used.

11A3   Token Ring (IEEE 802.5)

Medium Access Control. The 802.5 medium access control technique is token passing on a ring topology. Figure 11-24c shows the frame format. The access control field includes a token bit to indicate whether this is a frame or not. In the former case, the remainder of the frame simply consists of the ending delimiter. The access control field also includes a 3-bit priority and a 3-bit reservation, used in the capacity allocation algorithm. The frame control field serves the same function as in the 802.4 MAC frame. The frame status field contains bits that may be set by the receiver to indicate that it has recognized its address and copied the frame; these bits can then be read by the source station when it absorbs the frame.

Medium Option.   The IEEE 802.5 standard specifies **shielded twisted pair** at 1 and 4 Mbps (Table 11-9c).

This standard is supported by IBM, and there is a large number of other vendors with 802.5 products on the market. In addition to providing a shielded twisted-pair product to conform to the IEEE standard, IBM (and other vendors) also offers unshielded twisted pair at 1 and 4 Mbps and shielded twisted pair at 16 Mbps.

11A4   Fiber Distributed Data Interface (FDDI)

Medium Access Control.   The FDDI medium access control technique is also a token-passing ring technique. As explained in the discussion earlier in this chapter, FDDI does not use the priority/reservation scheme of 802.5 for reasons of efficiency. Accordingly, the FDDI MAC frame (Figure 11-24d) is the same as that of 802.5 except that there is no access control field in the FDDI frame.

Medium Option.   The medium specified is 100-Mbps optical fiber (Table 11-9d). The medium specifications specifically incorporates measures designed to ensure high availability.

COMPUTER COMMUNICATIONS ARCHITECTURE

We have dealt, so far, with the technologies and techniques used to exchange data between two devices. Part I dealt with the case in which the two devices share a dedicated transmission link. Part II was concerned with the case in which a *communication network* provides a shared transmission capacity for multiple attached stations.

For voice communication, the above is adequate. However, for communication among data processing devices (computers, terminals), much more is needed. The data processing devices must implement a set of communications functions that will allow them to cooperatively perform some task. This set of functions is organized into a *communications architecture*. With these functions implemented, the network of stations and communications nodes is referred to as a *computer network*.

We begin this part with a detailed but generic look at the elements of a communications architecture (Chapter 12). The open systems interconnection (OSI) model is introduced as a model architecture and a framework for standards. Chapters 13 through 17 examine various aspects of a communications architecture, organized into five broad levels of functionality.

Protocols and Architecture

The purpose of this chapter is to serve as an overview and necessary background to the detailed material that follows in the remainder of Part III. It will also serve to show how the concepts of Parts I and II fit into the broader area of computer networks and computer communications.

We begin with an exposition of the concept of a communications protocol. It is shown that protocols are fundamental to all data communications. Next, we look at a way of systematically describing and implementing the communications function by viewing the communications task in terms of a column of layers, each of which contains protocols. This is the view of the now-famous open systems interconnection (OSI) model.

Although the OSI model is almost universally accepted as the framework for discourse in this area, there is another point of view which grows out of the extensive research and practical experience of ARPANET. This viewpoint, which is characterized by a hierarchy of protocols, is also presented.

Both of the viewpoints above describe the communications function in terms of an architecture, which specifies protocols and their interrelationships. To lend concreteness to the discussion, a commercial architecture is presented: IBM's SNA.

Finally, the standards being developed by various organizations involved in protocol standardization are described briefly in Appendix 12A.

PROTOCOLS

Characteristics

The concepts of distributed processing and computer networking imply that entities in different systems need to communicate. We use the terms "entity" and "system" in a very general sense. Examples of entities are user application programs, file transfer packages, data base management systems, electronic mail facilities, and terminals. Examples of systems are computers, terminals, and remote sensors. Note that in some cases the entity and the system in which it resides are coextensive (e.g., terminals). In general, an *entity* is anything capable of sending or receiving information, and a *system* is a physically distinct object that contains one or more entities.

For two entities to successfully communicate, they must "speak the same language." What is communicated, how it is communicated, and when it is communicated must conform to some mutually acceptable set of conventions between the entities involved. The set of conventions is referred to as a *protocol*, which may be defined as a set of rules governing the exchange of data between two entities. The key elements of a protocol are:

- *Syntax:* includes such things as data format, coding, and signal levels.
- *Semantics:* includes control information for coordination and error handling.
- *Timing:* includes speed matching and sequencing.

HDLC is an example of a protocol. The data to be exchanged must be sent in frames of a specific format (syntax). The control field provides a variety of regulatory functions such as setting a mode and establishing a connection (semantics). Provisions are also included for flow control (timing). Most of Part III will be devoted to discussing other examples of protocols.

Some important characteristics of a protocol are:

- Direct/indirect.
- Monolithic/structured.
- Symmetric/asymmetric.
- Standard/nonstandard.

Communication between two entities may be *direct or indirect*. Figure 12-1 depicts the possible situations. If two systems share a point-to-point link, the entities in these systems may communicate directly; that is, data and control information pass directly between entities with no intervening active agent. The same may be said of a multipoint configuration, although here the entities must be concerned with the issue of access control, making the protocol more complex. If systems connect through a switched communication network, a direct protocol is no longer possible. The two entities must depend on the functioning of other entities to exchange data. A more extreme case is a situation in which two entities do not even share the same switched network, but are indirectly connected through two or more networks. A set of such interconnected networks is termed an *internet*.

An important protocol design consideration is raised by the latter two configurations (Figure 12-1c and d), namely, the extent to which the entities and hence their protocol must be aware of the characteristics of intervening systems. Ideally,

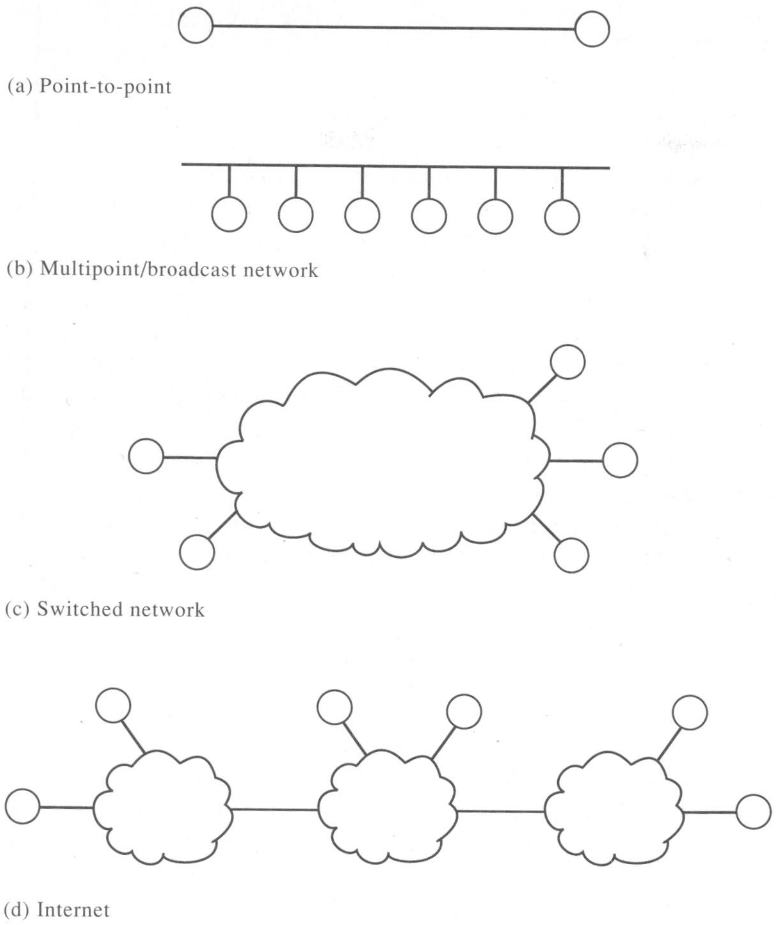

(a) Point-to-point

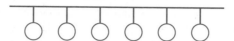

(b) Multipoint/broadcast network

(c) Switched network

(d) Internet

FIGURE 12-1.   Means of connection of communicating systems.

the intervening systems would be transparent and the protocol between the two entities would be the same as for a point-to-point link. We shall see that this ideal cannot be met.

Another characteristic of a protocol is whether it is *monolithic or structured*. It should become clear as Part III proceeds that the task of communication between entities on different systems is too complex to be handled as a unit. For example, consider an electronic mail package running on two computers connected by a synchronous HDLC link. To be truly monolithic, the package would need to include all of the HDLC logic. If the connection were over a packet-switched network, the package would still need the HDLC logic (or some equivalent) to attach to the network. It would also need logic for breaking up mail into packet-sized chunks, logic for requesting a virtual circuit, and so forth. Mail should only be sent when the destination system and entity are active and ready to receive. Logic is needed for that kind of coordination. And, as we shall see, the list goes on. A change in any aspect means that this huge package must be modified, with the risk of introducing difficult-to-find bugs.

An alternative is to use structured design and implementation techniques. Instead of a single protocol, there is a set of protocols that exhibit a hierarchical or layered structure. Lower level, more primitive functions are implemented in lower-level entities that provide services to higher-level entities. For example, there could be an HDLC module (entity) that is invoked by an electronic mail facility when needed. Note that this is just another form of indirection: Higher-level entities rely on lower level entities to exchange data. See the discussion in Section 1.5 for an introduction to the concept of a communications architecture.

When structured protocol design is used, we refer to the hardware and software used to implement the communications function as a *communications architecture*. The remainder of this chapter, after this section, is devoted to this concept.

A protocol may be either *symmetric or asymmetric*. Most of the protocols that we shall study are symmetric. That is, they involve communication between peer entities. Asymmetry may be dictated by the logic of an exchange (e.g., a "user" and a "server" process), or by the desire to keep one of the entities or systems as simple as possible. An example of the latter is the normal response mode of HDLC. Typically, this involves a computer which polls and selects a number of terminals. The logic on the terminal end is quite straightforward.

Finally, a protocol may be either *standard or nonstandard*. A nonstandard protocol is one built for a specific communications situation or, at most, a particular model of a computer. Thus, if K different kinds of information sources have to communicate with L types of information receivers, $K \times L$ different protocols are needed without standards and a total of $2 \times K \times L$ implementations are required (Figure 12-2a). If all systems shared a common protocol, only $K + L$ implementations would be needed (Figure 12-2b). The increasing use of distributed processing and the decreasing inclination of customers to remain locked in to a single vendor dictate that all vendors implement protocols that conform to an agreed-upon standard. Appendix 12A lists the key organizations involved in standards development and outlines the current status of standards development.

Functions

Before turning to a discussion of communications architecture and the various levels of protocols, let us consider a rather small set of functions that form the basis of all protocols. Not all protocols have all functions; this would involve a significant duplication of effort. There are, nevertheless, many instances of the same type of function being present in protocols at different levels.

This discussion will, of necessity, be rather abstract. It does provide an integrated overview of the characteristics and functions of communications protocols. The concept of protocol is fundamental to all of the remainder of Part III, and as we proceed, specific examples of all these functions will be seen.

We can group protocol functions into the following categories:

- Segmentation and reassembly.
- Encapsulation.
- Connection control.
- Ordered delivery.
- Flow control.
- Error control.
- Synchronization.
- Addressing.

Sources   Destinations   Sources   Destinations

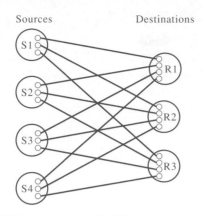
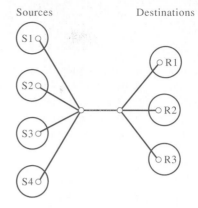

(a) Without standards: 12 different   (b) With standards: 1 protocol,
    protocols, 24 protocol implementations   7 implementations

FIGURE 12-2.   The use of standard protocols.

- Multiplexing.
- Transmission services.

Segmentation and Reassembly.   A protocol is concerned with exchanging streams of data between two entities. Usually, the transfer can be characterized as consisting of a sequence of blocks of data of some bounded size. At the application level, we refer to a logical unit of data transfer as a *message.* Now, whether the application entity sends data in messages or in a continuous stream, lower level protocols may need to break the data up into blocks of some smaller bounded size. This process is called *segmentation,* or *fragmentation.* For convenience, we shall refer to a block of data exchanged between two entities via a protocol as a *protocol data unit* (PDU).

There are a number of motivations for segmentation, depending on the context. Among the typical reasons for segmentation:

- The communications network may only accept blocks of data up to a certain size. DDN, for example, limits messages to 8063 bytes in length [BBN83].
- Error control may be more efficient with a smaller PDU size. For example, fewer bits need to be retransmitted using smaller blocks with the selective repeat technique.
- More equitable access to shared transmission facilities, with shorter delay, can be provided. For example, without a maximum block size, one station could monopolize a multipoint medium.
- A smaller PDU size may mean that receiving entities can allocate smaller buffers (e.g., the ARPANET entry-to-exit protocol).
- An entity may require that data transfer comes to some sort of "closure" from time to time, for checkpoint and restart/recovery operations.

There are several disadvantages to segmentation that argue for making blocks as large as possible:

- Each PDU, as we shall see, contains a fixed amount of control information. Hence the smaller the block, the greater the percentage overhead.

- PDU arrival may generate an interrupt that must be serviced. Smaller blocks result in more interrupts.
- More time is spent processing smaller, more numerous PDUs.

All of these factors must be taken into account by the protocol designer in determining minimum and maximum PDU size.

The counterpart of segmentation is *reassembly*. Eventually, the fragmented data must be reassembled into messages appropriate to the application level. If PDUs arrive out of order, the task is complicated.

The process of segmentation was illustrated in Figure 1-8.

Encapsulation.   Each PDU contains not only data but control information. Indeed, some PDUs consist solely of control information and no data. The control information falls into three general categories:

- *Address:* The address of the sender and/or receiver may be indicated.
- *Error detecting code:* Some sort of frame check sequence is often included for error detection.
- *Protocol control:* Additional information is included to implement the protocol functions listed in the remainder of this section.

The addition of control information to data is referred to as *encapsulation*. Data are accepted or generated by an entity and encapsulated into a PDU containing that data plus control information (See Figures 1-8 and 1-9). An example of this is the HDLC frame (Figure 5-16).

Connection Control.   An entity may transmit data to another entity in an unplanned fashion and without prior coordination. This is known as *connectionless data transfer*; an example is the use of the datagram. While this mode can be useful, it is less common than *connection-oriented data transfer*, of which the virtual circuit is an example [CHAP83].

Connection-oriented data transfer is to be preferred (even required) if stations anticipate a lengthy exchange of data and/or certain details of their protocol must be worked out dynamically. A logical association, or *connection*, is established between the entities. Three phases occur (Figure 12-3):

- Connection establishment.
- Data transfer.
- Connection termination.

With more sophisticated protocols, there may also be connection interrupt and recovery phases to cope with errors and other sorts of interruptions.

During the connection establishment phase, two entities agree to exchange data. Typically, one station will issue a connection request (in connectionless fashion!) to the other. A central authority may or may not be involved. In simpler protocols, the receiving entity either accepts or rejects the request and, in the former case, away they go. In more complex proposals, this phase includes a negotiation concerning the syntax, semantics, and timing of the protocol. Both entities must, of course, be using the same protocol. But the protocol may allow certain optional features and these must be agreed upon by means of negotiation. For example, the protocol may specify a PDU size of *up to* 8000 bytes; one station may wish to restrict this to 1000 bytes.

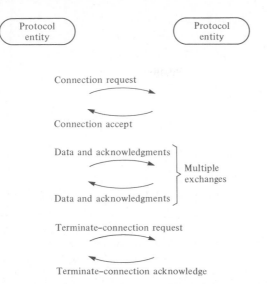

FIGURE 12-3. The phases of a connection-oriented data transfer.

Following connection establishment, the data transfer phase is entered. During this phase both data and control information (e.g., flow control, error control) is exchanged. Finally, one side or the other wishes to terminate the connection and does so by sending a termination request. Alternatively, a central authority might forcibly terminate a connection.

The key characteristic of connection-oriented data transfer is that sequencing is used. Each side sequentially numbers the PDUs that it sends to the other side. Because each side remembers that it is engaged in a logical connection, it can keep track of both outgoing numbers, which it generates, and incoming numbers, which are generated by the other side. Indeed, one can essentially define a connection-oriented data transfer as one in which both sides number PDUs and keep track of both incoming and outgoing numbers. Sequencing supports three main functions: ordered deliver, flow control, and error control.

Ordered Delivery. If two communicating entities are in different hosts connected by a network, there is a risk that PDUs will not arrive in the order in which they were sent, because they may traverse different paths through the network. In connection-oriented protocols, it is generally required that PDU order be maintained. For example, if a file is transferred between two systems, we would like to be assured that the records of the received file are in the same order as those of the transmitted file, and not shuffled. If each PDU is given a unique number, and numbers are assigned sequentially, then it is a logically simple task for the receiving entity to reorder received PDUs on the basis of sequence number. The only hitch in this scheme is that, with a finite sequence number field, sequence numbers repeat (modulo some maximum number). Evidently, the maximum sequence number must be greater than the maximum number of PDUs that could be outstanding at any time. In fact the maximum number may need to be *twice* the maximum number of PDUs that could be outstanding (e.g., selective-repeat ARQ; see Chapter 5).

Flow Control.   Flow control was introduced in Chapter 5 and seen again in Chapter 9. In essence, flow control is a function performed by a receiving entity to limit the amount or rate of data that is sent by a transmitting entity.

The simplest form of flow control is a stop-and-wait procedure, in which each PDU must be acknowledged before the next can be sent. More efficient protocols involve some form of credit provided to the transmitter, which is the amount of data that can be sent without an acknowledgment. The sliding-window technique is an example of this mechanism. Closely related are SNA's pacing algorithm and ARPANET's ready-for-next-message command.

Flow control is a good example of a function that must be implemented in several protocols. Consider again Figure 1-5. Network A will need to exercise flow control over station 1's network services module via the network access protocol, in order to enforce network traffic control. At the same time, station 2's network services module has only limited buffer space and needs to exercise flow control over station 1's network services module via the process-to-process protocol. Finally, even though station 2's network service module can control its data flow, station 2's application may be vulnerable to overflow. For example, the application could be hung up waiting for disk access. Thus flow control is also needed over the application-oriented protocol.

Error Control.   Another previously introduced function is error control. Techniques are needed to guard against loss or damage of data and control information. Most techniques involve error detection, based on a frame check sequence, and PDU retransmission. Retransmission is often activated by a timer. If a sending entity fails to receive an acknowledgment to a PDU within a specified period of time, it will retransmit.

As with flow control, error control is a function that must be performed at various levels of protocol. Consider again Figure 1-5. The network access protocol should include error control to assure that data are successfully exchanged between station and network. However, a packet of data may be lost inside the network, and the process-to-process protocol should be able to recover from this loss.

Synchronization.   It should be apparent from the discussion so far that a protocol entity needs to remember a certain number of parameters (e.g., window size, connection phase, timer value). These parameters can be viewed as state variables and their collection defines the state of the entity. It is occasionally important that two communicating protocol entities be simultaneously in a well-defined state, for example at initialization, checkpointing, and termination. This is termed synchronization.

The difficulty with achieving synchronization is that one entity has knowledge of the state of the other only by virtue of received PDUs. These PDUs do not arrive instantly. They take some time, perhaps a variable amount of time, to traverse from sender to receiver. Furthermore, a PDU may be lost in transit.

An example from [POUZ78] illustrates the problem. Consider two entities, A and B, performing mutual data base updating. Neither should terminate until both are finished updating and the two data bases are synchronized. Question: How can the two entities be sure that both have terminated?

Figure 12-4a shows a state diagram for A. State 1 indicates that A has finished its work. When A has finished, it sends a DONE message to B. When it receives a DONE message back, A is free to terminate and disappear. However, B may

(a) Partial synchronization

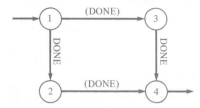

(b) Simple synchronization

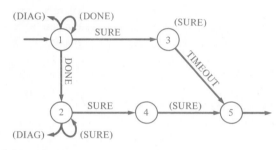

(c) Safe synchronization

(DONE): message sent   DONE: message received

FIGURE 12.4.   Synchronization example.

finish first. To cover this contingency, let us refine the state diagram as shown in Figure 12-4b. When each station has sent and received a DONE message, in either order, it terminates.

Figure 12-4b will only work if no messages are lost. Consider: *A* arrives in state 3 and waits for the DONE message from *B*. *B* sends such a message but it is lost in transit. After waiting a reasonable amount of time, what should *A* do? Going to state 4 and terminating is risky: the two data bases may not agree; *B* may not yet have reached state 1 and may need *A*'s cooperation to complete its task. On the other hand, going back to state 1 could hang *A* up, since *B* may already have gone to state 4 and vanished.

The diagram of Figure 12-4c takes errors into account. When *A* has both transmitted and received a DONE, it issues a SURE message, indicating that it knows that *B* is done. Neither entity can terminate until the other has reached state 2. In case one entity gets hung up in state 2, it at least knows that the other has reached state 1, and possibly state 5. If either entity gets hung up in state 1 or 2, it initializes a diagnostic procedure to resolve the deadlock.

This example is not meant to indicate a generally applicable solution for the synchronization problem. Rather, it serves to illustrate its complexity.

Addressing.   For two entities to communicate, other than over a point-to-point link, they must somehow be able to identify each other. For example, on a broadcast network each station looks for packets that contain its identifier. On a switched network, the network needs to know the identity of the destination station in order to properly route data or set up a connection.

A distinction is generally made among names, addresses, and routes [SHOC78]. A name specifies what an object is; an address specifies where it is; and a route indicates how to get there. For our purposes, it is more useful to draw a distinction suggested in [POUZ78]:

- *Local name:* the name by which an entity is identified within its own system.
- *Global name:* the name by which an entity is known outside its own system.

There are several points of importance here. First, it is desirable to distinguish between local names and global names. Communication may involve a variety of systems of different types and from different vendors. Each system likes to have its own naming convention, and it seems hopeless to attempt to enforce uniform local naming rules. On the other hand, no entity or system can be expected to deal with a variety of name lengths, formats, and global conventions. Thus both local and global names are needed. Second, an address is a form of global name. However, and third, there may not be a unique global name for an entity. If the entity is mobile, its address changes. If it attaches directly to more than one network, each may have its own address for the entity.

The problem of naming and addressing of entities admits of no unique solution. In the remainder of this subsection, we outline some approaches and considerations. During the discussion, we refer to the entities in Figure 12-5. The following topics are considered:

- Name structure.
- Name knowledge.
- Connection names.
- Port names.
- Group names.

The *name structure* used for global names can be either hierarchical or flat. A hierarchical name would have the structure SYSTEM.ENTITY, or in the case of multiple networks, NETWORK.SYSTEM.ENTITY. The fields SYSTEM and NETWORK contain global identifiers of some fixed format. ENTITY must presumably be a name of some fixed maximum length. The name could have global

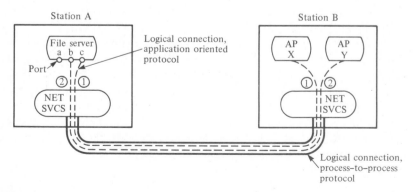

FIGURE 12-5. Example for naming conventions.

significance, in which case the system containing that entity would have to contain a mapping from global entity identifiers to local entity identifiers. Alternatively, if all systems could live with a particular field length, local and global entity identifiers could be the same. As an example, application X in station B is identified as B.X.

A flat name structure is one in which each entity has a global name that is unique throughout the domain of communication. Names could be assigned by preallocation; that is, each system is given a set of global names, which it then assigns to its local entities. Alternatively, a mapping or directory function could be used which globally assigns names to entities.

The hierarchical structure has several advantages. It is easier to add new names to the universe of names with a hierarchical scheme, since entity names need only be unique within a system. With flat names, it must be determined that any new name added to the system is not the same as any previous name. Second, a hierarchical name is an aid to routing since it identifies the system containing the entity. Thus a hierarchical name has more the flavor of an address than does a flat name.

Regardless of name structure, there is a requirement for *name knowledge*. An entity can only send data to or request a connection with an entity whose name it knows. Consider that entity 1 in system A wishes to establish a connection with entity 2 in system B. The possibilities for naming are numerous; we mention only a few. System A could maintain a directory of global names of all entities that might be of interest. Each of these would have some identifier understandable to station A's entities. Another possibility is that entity 1 wishes access to some generic service, such as transaction processing (TP) on system B. Here there are several subpossibilities:

- A network server known to entity 1 maintains a directory mapping generic services by system onto global names.
- There is a ''well-known entity'' on system B. Entity 1 queries this entity for the global name of system B's TP.
- The well-known entity on system B is a log-on facility. Entity 1 logs on to system B and is then allowed access to TP.

At bottom, the problem is this: Entity 1 must know the name of entity 2 to exchange data with it, but how can it get that name unless it already knows it? The preceding should give some feel for the various approaches that can be taken.

For connectionless data transfer, a global name is used with each data transmission. For connection-oriented transfer, it is sometimes desirable to use only a *connection name* during the data transfer phase. The scenario is this: Entity 1 on system A requests a connection to entity 2 on system B, perhaps using the global address B.2. When B.2 accepts the connection, a connection name (usually a number) is provided and is used by both entities for future transmissions. As an example, two connections between applications, labeled ''1'' and ''2,'' are shown in Figure 12-5. The use of a connection name has several advantages:

- *Reduced overhead:* Connection names are generally shorter than global names. For example, in the X.25 protocol (discussed in Chapter 13) used over packet-switched networks, connection request packets contain both source and destination address fields, each with a system-defined length that may be a number of bytes. After a virtual circuit is established, data packets contain just a 12-bit virtual circuit number.

- *Routing:* In setting up a connection, a fixed route may be defined (e.g. SNA and TYMNET, but not ARPANET). The connection name serves to identify the route for handling future PDUs.
- *Multiplexing:* We address this function in more general terms below. Here we note that an entity may wish to enjoy more than one connection simultaneously. Thus incoming PDUs must be identified by connection name.

Another concept often found with protocols is that of *port name*. A port name is a global entity name. If each entity has a single port name, there is not much point to the concept. However, it is often the case that multiple port names are associated with an entity. This can be used to provide multiplexing, as with connection names. For example, a file server module may be able to service a number of users simultaneously. Also, port names can indicate different entry points within an entity. For example, a file server might have a different entry point for users authorized to read and update and for users authorized only to read. In many systems, port names are unique within the system across all entities and entity names are not needed. So, for a hierarchical structure, the form NETWORK.SYSTEM.PORT would be used. For example, the three ports depicted in Figure 12-5 are designated A.a, A.b, and A.c.

Finally, we mention the concept of *group name,* which is a name that refers to more than one entity or port. This term has been used to mean a number of things. One usage is to identify a contention group, as discussed in Chapter 8. A more meaningful use, in the present context, is that a group name identifies multiple simultaneous recipients for data. For example, a user might wish to send a memo to a number of individuals. The network control center may wish to notify all users that the network is going down. A group name may be *broadcast,* intended for all entities within a domain, or *multicast,* intended for a specific subset of entities. Table 12-1 illustrates the possibilities.

Multiplexing.   We have already seen one type of multiplexing that is used with protocols: the multiplexing of data transfers into an entity. This can be accomplished using connection names, which permits multiple simultaneous connection. It can also be accomplished via port names, which also permit multiple simultaneous connections. The latter is shown in Figure 12-5, where the file server in A has two connections active at the same time. Port names also accommodate multiple connectionless transfers from different sources to the same destination. With the use of different port names, interference is avoided.

TABLE 12-1   Multicasting and Broadcasting

Destination	Network Address	System Address	Entity/Port Address
Specific	Specific	Specific	Specific
Multicast	Specific	Specific	Group
	Specific	All	Group
	All	All	Group
Broadcast	Specific	Specific	All
	Specific	All	All
	All	All	All

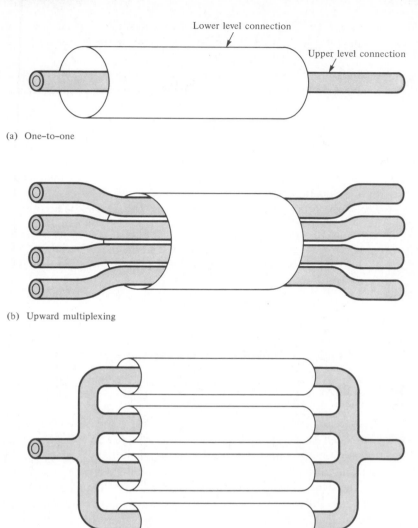

(a) One–to–one

(b) Upward multiplexing

(c) Downward multiplexing

FIGURE 12-6. **Multiplexing and protocol connections.**

Multiplexing is used in another context as well, namely the mapping of connections from one level to another. Consider again Figure 1-5. Network *A* might provide a virtual circuit service. For each process-to-process connection established at the network services level, a virtual circuit could be created at the network access level. This is a one-to-one relationship, but need not be so. Multiplexing can be used in one of two directions (Figure 12-6). *Upward multiplexing* occurs when multiple higher-level connections are multiplexed on, or share, a single lower-level connection. This may be needed to make more efficient use of the lower-level service or to provide several higher-level connections in an environment where only a single lower-level connection exists. Figure 12-5 shows an example of upward multiplexing. *Downward multiplexing,* or *splitting,* means that a single higher-level connection is built on top of multiple lower-level connections, the traffic on the higher connection being divided among the various lower connections. This technique may be used to provide reliability, performance, or efficiency.

Transmission Services.   A protocol may provide a variety of additional services to the entities that use it. We mention here three common examples:

- *Priority:* Certain messages, such as control messages, may need to get through to the destination entity with minimum delay. An example would be a close connection request. Thus priority could be assigned on a message basis. Additionally, priority could be assigned on a connection basis.
- *Grade of service:* Certain classes of data may require a minimum throughput or a maximum delay threshold.
- *Security:* Security mechanisms, restricting access, may be invoked.

All of these services depend on the underlying transmission system and any intervening lower-level entities. If it is possible for these services to be provided from below, the protocol can be used by the two entities to exercise those services.

12-2

THE LAYERED APPROACH: THE OSI MODEL

Motivation

When work is done that involves more than one computer, additional elements must be added to the system: the hardware and software to support the communication between or among the systems. Communications hardware is reasonably standard and generally presents few problems. However, when communication is desired among heterogeneous (different vendors, different models of same vendor) machines, the software development effort can be a nightmare. Different vendors use different data formats and data exchange conventions. Even within one vendor's product line, different model computers may communicate in unique ways.

As the use of computer communications and computer networking proliferates, a one-at-a-time special-purpose approach to communications software development is too costly to be acceptable. The only alternative is for computer vendors to adopt and implement a common set of conventions. For this to happen, a set of international or at least national standards must be promulgated by appropriate organizations. Such standards have two effects:

- Vendors feel encouraged to implement the standards because of an expectation that, because of wide usage of the standards, their products would be less marketable without them.
- Customers are in a position to require that the standards be implemented by any vendor wishing to propose equipment to them.

It should become clear from the ensuing discussion that no single standard will suffice. The task of communication in a truly cooperative way between applications on different computers is too complex to be handled as a unit. The problem must be decomposed into manageable parts. Hence before one can develop standards, there should be a structure or *architecture* that defines the communications tasks.

TABLE 12-2   Purpose of the OSI Model

The purpose of this International Standard Reference Model of Open Systems Inter-connection is to provide a common basis for the coordination of standards development for the purpose of systems interconnection, while allowing existing standards to be placed into perspective within the overall Reference Model.

The term Open Systems Interconnection (OSI) qualifies standards for the exchange of information among systems that are ''open'' to one another for this purpose by virtue of their mutual use of the applicable standards.

The fact that a system is open does not imply any particular systems implementation, technology or means of interconneciton, but refers to the mutual recognition and support of the applicable standards.

It is also the purpose of this International Standard to identify areas for developing or improving standards, and to provide a common reference for maintaining consistency of all related standards. It is not the intent of this International Standard either to serve as an implementation specification, or to be a basis for appraising the conformance of actual implementations, or to provide a sufficient level of detail to define precisely the services and protocols of the interconnection architecture. Rather, this International Standard pro-vides a conceptual and functional framework which allows international teams of experts to work productively and independently on the development of standards for each layer of the Reference Model of OSI.

This line of reasoning led the International Organization for Standardization (ISO) in 1977 to establish a subcommittee to develop such an architecture. The result was the *Open Systems Interconnection* (OSI) reference model, adopted in 1983, which is a framework for defining standards for linking heterogeneous com-puters. The OSI model provides the basis for connecting ''open'' systems for distributed applications processing. The term ''open'' denotes the ability of any two systems conforming to the reference model and the associated standards to connect.

Table 12-2, extracted from the basic OSI document [ISO84] summarizes the purpose of the model.

Concepts

A widely accepted structuring technique, and the one chosen by ISO, is *layering*. The communications functions are partitioned into a vertical set of layers. Each layer performs a related subset of the functions required to communicate with another system. It relies on the next lower layer to perform more primitive functions and to conceal the details of those functions. It provides services to the next higher layer. Ideally, the layers should be defined so that changes in one layer do not require changes in the other layers. Thus we have decomposed one problem into a number of more manageable subproblems.

The task of the ISO subcommittee was to define a set of layers and the services performed by each layer. The partitioning should group functions logically, should have enough layers to make each layer manageably small, but should not have so many layers that the processing overhead imposed by the collection of layers is burdensome. The principles by which ISO went about its task are summarized in Table 12-3. The resulting OSI reference model has seven layers, which are listed

TABLE 12-3   Principles Used in Defining the OSI Layers

1. Do not create so many layers as to make the system engineering task of describing and integrating the layers more difficult than necessary.
2. Create a boundary at a point where the description of services can be small and the number of interactions across the boundary are minimized.
3. Create separate layers to handle functions that are manifestly different in the process performed or the technology involved.
4. Collect similar functions into the same layer.
5. Select boundaries at a point which past experience has demonstrated to be successful.
6. Create a layer of easily localized functions so that the layer could be totally re-designed and its protocols changed in a major way to take advantage of new advances in architectural, hardware or software technology without changing the services expected from and provided to the adjacent layers.
7. Create a boundary where it may be useful at some point in time to have the corresponding interface standardized.
8. Create a layer where there is a need for a different level of abstraction in the handling of data (e.g., morphology, syntax, semantics).
9. Allow changes of functions or protocols to be made within a layer without affecting other layers.
10. Create for each layer boundaries with its upper and lower layer only.

Similar principles have been applied to sublayering:

11. Create further subgrouping and organization or functions to form sublayers within a layer in cases where distinct communication services need it.
12. Create, where needed, two or more sublayers with a common, and therefore minimal functionality to allow interface operation with adjacent layers.
13. Allow bypassing of sublayers.

TABLE 12-4   The OSI Layers

1. Physical	Concerned with transmission of unstructured bit stream over physical medium; deals with the mechanical, electrical, functional, and procedural characteristics to access the physical medium
2. Data link	Provides for the reliable transfer of information across the physical link; sends blocks of data (frames) with the necessary synchronization, error control, and flow control
3. Network	Provides upper layers with independence from the data transmission and switching technologies used to connect systems; responsible for establishing, maintaining, and terminating connections
4. Transport	Provides reliable, transparent transfer of data between end points; provides end-to-end error recovery and flow control
5. Session	Provides the control structure for communication between applications; establishes, manages, and terminates connections (sessions) between cooperating applications
6. Presentation	Provides independence to the application processes from differences in data representation (syntax)
7. Application	Provides access to the OSI environment for users and also provides distributed information services

TABLE 12-5   Justification of the OSI Layers

a. It is essential that the architecture permit usage of a realistic variety of physical media for interconnection with different control procedures (e.g., V.24, V.25, X.21, etc.). Application of principles 3, 5, and 8 [Table 12-3] leads to indentification of a *Physical Layer* as the lowest layer in the architecture.

b. Some physical communication media (e.g., telephone line) require specific techniques to be used in order to transmit data between systems despite a relatively high error rate (i.e., an error rate not acceptable for the great majority of applications). These specific techniques are used in data-link control procedures which have been studied and standardized for a number of years. It must also be recognized that new physical communication media (e.g., fiber optics) will require different data-link control procedures. Application of principles 3, 5, and 8 leads to identification of a *Data Link Layer* on top of the Physical Layer in the architecture.

c. In the open systems architecture, some systems will act as the final destination of data. Some systems may act only as intermediate nodes (forwarding data to other systems). Application of principles 3, 5, and 7 leads to identification of a *Network Layer* on top of the Data Link Layer. Network oriented protocols such as routing, for example, will be grouped in this layer. Thus, the Network Layer will provide a connection path (network-connection) between a pair of transport-entities, including the case where intermediate nodes are involved.

d. Control of data transportation from source end-system to destination end-system (which is not performed in intermediate nodes) is the last function to be performed in order to provide the totality of the transport-service. Thus, the upper layer in the transport-service part of the architecture is the *Transport Layer*, on top of the Network Layer. This Transport Layer relieves higher layer entities from any concern with the transportation of data between them.

e. There is a need to organize and synchronize dialogue, and to manage the exchange of data. Application of principles 3 and 4 leads to the identification of a *Session Layer* on top of the Transport Layer.

f. The remaining set of general interest functions are those related to representation and manipulation of structured data for the benefit of application programs. Application of principles 3 and 4 leads to identification of a *Presentation Layer* on top of the Session Layer.

g. Finally, there are applications consisting of application processes which perform information processing. An aspect of these applications processes and the protocols by which they communicate comprise the *Application Layer* as the highest layer of the architecture.

with a brief definition in Table 12-4. Table 12-5 provides ISO's justification for the selection of these layers.

Table 12-4 defines, in general terms, the functions that must be performed in a system for it to communicate. Of course, it takes two to communicate, so the same set of layered functions must exist in two systems. Communication is achieved by having corresponding (''peer'') entities in the same layer in two different systems communicate via a protocol.

Figure 12-7 illustrates the OSI model. Each system contains the seven layers. Communication is between applications in the systems, labeled AP X and AP Y in the figure. If AP X wishes to send a message to AP Y, it invokes the application layer (layer 7). Layer 7 establishes a peer relationship with layer 7 of the target machine, using a layer 7 protocol. This protocol requires services from layer 6, so

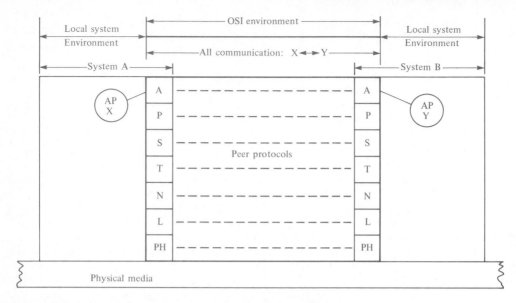

FIGURE 12-7. The OSI environment. Source: [FOLT81]

the two layer 6 entities use a protocol of their own, and so on down to the physical layer, which actually passes the bits through a transmission medium.

Note that there is no direct communication between peer layers except at the physical layer. That is, above the physical layer, each protocol entity sends data *down* to the next lower layer in order to get the data *across* to its peer entity. Even at the physical layer, the OSI model does not stipulate that two systems be directly connected. For example, a packet-switched or circuit-switched network may be used to provide the communications link. This point should become clearer below, when we discuss the network layer.

The attractiveness of the OSI approach is that it promises to solve the heterogeneous computer communications problem. Two systems, no matter how different, can communicate effectively if they have the following in common:

- They implement the same set of communications functions.
- These functions are organized into the same set of layers. Peer layers must provide the same functions, but note that it is not necessary that they provide them in the same way.
- Peer layers must share a common protocol.

To assure the above, standards are needed. Standards must define the functions and services to be provided by a layer (but not how it is to be done—that may differ from system to system). Standards must also define the protocols between peer layers (each protocol must be identical for the two peer layers). The OSI model, by defining a seven-layer architecture, provides a framework for defining these standards.

Some useful OSI terminology is illustrated in Figure 12-8. For simplicity, any layer is referred to as the *(N) layer*, and names of constructs associated with that layer are also preceded by (N). Within a system, there are one or more active entities in each layer. An *(N) entity* implements functions of the (N) layer and also the protocol for communicating with (N) entities in other systems. An example of

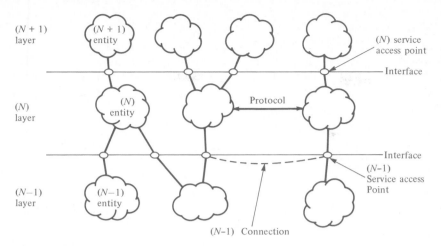

FIGURE 12-8. The layer concept.

an entity is a process in a multiprocessing system. Or it could simply be a subroutine. There might be multiple identical (N) entities, if this is convenient or efficient for a given system. There might also be differing (N) entities, corresponding to different protocol standards at that level.

Each entity communicates with entities in the layers above and below it across an *interface*. The interface is realized as one or more *service access points* (SAPs), which function in the manner of ports, discussed earlier. The (N-1) entity provides *services* to an (N) entity via the invocation of *primitives*. A primitive specifies the function to be performed and is used to pass data and control information. The actual form of a primitive is implementation-dependent. An example is a subroutine call.

The OSI model is connection-oriented. Two (N) entities communicate, using a protocol, by means of an (N-1) connection. This logical connection is provided by (N-1) entities between (N-1) SAPs. ISO is currently at work on a connectionless mode, but this is not yet reflected in the model.

Figure 12-9 illustrates the OSI principles in operation. First, consider the most common way in which protocols are realized. When application X has a message to send to application Y, it transfers those data to an application entity in the application layer. A *header* is appended to the data that contains the required information for the peer layer 7 protocol (encapsulation). The original data, plus the header, is now passed as a unit to layer 6. The presentation entity treats the whole unit as data, and appends its own header (a second encapsulation). This process continues down through layer 2, which generally adds both a header and a trailer (e.g., HDLC). This layer 2 unit, called a *frame*, is then passed by the physical layer onto the transmission medium. When the frame is received by the target system, the reverse process occurs. As the data ascend, each layer strips off the outermost header, acts on the protocol information contained therein, and passes the remainder up to the next layer.

At each stage of the process, a layer may fragment the data unit it receives from the next higher layer into several parts, to accommodate its own requirements. These data units must then be reassembled by the corresponding peer layer before being passed up.

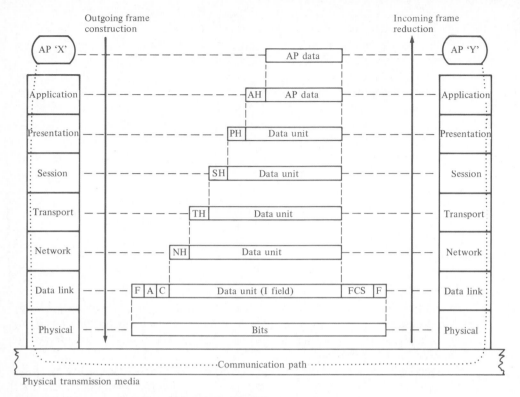

FIGURE 12-9.   OSI operation. Source: [FOLT83]

When two peer entities wish to exchange data, this may be done with or without a prior connection. We have seen an example of this: virtual circuits versus datagrams. A connection can exist at any layer of the hierarchy. In the abstract, a connection is established between two (N) entities by identifying an (N-1) SAP for each (N) entity.

Layers

In this section we discuss briefly each of the layers and, where appropriate, give examples of standards for protocols at those layers.

Physical Layer.   The *physical layer* covers the physical interface between devices and the rules by which bits are passed from one to another. The physical layer has four important characteristics [BERT80, MCCL83]:

- Mechanical.
- Electrical.
- Functional.
- Procedural.

We have already covered physical layer protocols in some detail in Section 4-3. Examples of standards at this layer are EIA-232-D, EIA-530, and portions of ISDN.

Data Link Layer. While the physical layer provides only a raw bit stream service, the *data link layer* attempts to make the physical link reliable and provides the means to activate, maintain, and deactivate the link. The principal service provided by the link layer to the higher layers is that of error detection and control. Thus, with a fully functional data link layer protocol, the next higher layer may assume virtually error-free transmission over the link. However, if communication is between two systems that are not directly connected, the connection will comprise a number of data links in tandem, each functioning independently. Thus the higher layers are not relieved of an error control responsibility.

Chapter 5 was devoted to data link protocols. Examples of standards at this layer are HDLC, ADCCP, and LAP-B.

Network Layer. The basic service of the *network layer* is to provide for the transparent transfer of data between transport entities. It relieves the transport layer of the need to know anything about the underlying data transmission and switching technologies used to connect systems. The network service is responsible for establishing, maintaining, and terminating connections across the intervening communications facility.

It is at this layer that the concept of a protocol becomes a little fuzzy. This is best illustrated with reference to Figure 12-10, which shows two stations that are communicating, not via direct link, but via a packet-switched network. The stations have direct links to the network nodes. The layer 1 and 2 protocols are station-node protocols (local). Layers 4 through 7 are clearly protocols between (N) entities in the two stations. Layer 3 is a little bit of both.

The principal dialogue is between the station and its node; the station sends addressed packets to the node for delivery across the network. It requests a virtual circuit connection, uses the connection to transmit data, and terminates the connection. All of this is done by means of a station-node protocol. However, because packets are exchanged and virtual circuits are set up between two stations, there are aspects of a station-station protocol as well.

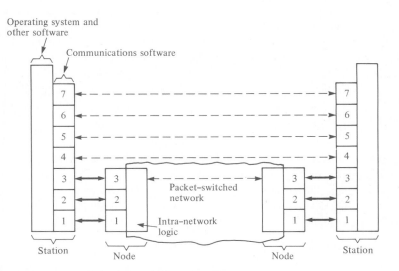

FIGURE 12-10.   Communication across a network.

There is a spectrum of possibilities for intervening communications facilities to be managed by the network layer. At one extreme, the simplest, there is a direct link between stations. In this case, there may be little or no need for a network layer, since the data link layer can perform the necessary functions of managing the link. Between extremes, the most common use of layer 3 is to handle the details of using a communication network. In this case, the network entity in the station must provide the network with sufficient information to switch and route data to another station. At the other extreme, two stations might wish to communicate but are not even connected to the same network. Rather, they are connected to networks which, directly or indirectly, are connected to each other. This situation is explored in some detail in Chapter 14. For now it suffices to say that one approach to providing for data transfer in such a case is to use an Internet Protocol (IP) that sits on top of a network protocol and is used by a transport protocol. IP is responsible for internetwork routing and delivery, and relies on a layer 3 at each network for intranetwork services. IP is sometimes referred to as ''layer 3.5.''

The best known example of layer 3 is the X.25 layer 3 standard, which will be examined in some detail in Chapter 13. The X.25 standard refers to itself as an interface between a station and a node (using our terminology). In the context of the OSI model, it is actually a station-node protocol. Another common example is the I.451 layer 3 standard, also examined in Chapter 13.

Transport Layer.   Layers 4 and above of the OSI model are generally referred to as the higher layers. Protocols at these levels are end-to-end and not concerned with the details of the underlying communications facility.

The purpose of layer 4 is to provide a reliable mechanism for the exchange of data between processes in different systems. The *transport layer* ensures that data units are delivered error-free, in sequence, with no losses or duplications. The transport layer may also be concerned with optimizing the use of network services and providing a requested quality of service to session entities. For example, the session entity might specify acceptable error rates, maximum delay, priority, and security. In effect, the transport layer serves as the user's liaison with the communications facility.

The size and complexity of a transport protocol depends on the type of service it can get from layer 3. For a reliable layer 3 with a virtual circuit capability, a minimal layer 4 is required. If layer 3 is unreliable and/or only supports datagrams, the layer 4 protocol should include extensive error detection and recovery. Accordingly, ISO has defined five classes of transport protocol, each oriented toward a different underlying service. The most complex version is comparable in capability to another transport protocol standard. DOD's Transmission Control Protocol (TCP). All of these standards are discussed in Chapter 15.

Session Layer.   The *session layer* provides the mechanism for controlling the dialogue between applications.

At a minimum, the session layer provides a means for two application processes to establish and use a connection, called a *session*. In addition it may provide the following services:

• *Dialogue type:* This can be two-way simultaneous, two-way alternate, or one-way.
• *Recovery:* The session layer can provide a checkpointing mechanism, so that

if a failure of some sort occurs between checkpoints, the session entity can retransmit all data since the last checkpoint.

A discussion of the principles of session protocols and the ISO standard is presented in Chapter 16.

Presentation Layer.   The *presentation layer* is concerned with the syntax of the data exchanged between application entities. Its purpose is to resolve differences in format and data representation. The presentation layer defines the syntax used between application entities and provides for the selection and subsequent modification of the representation to be used.

Examples of presentation protocols are encryption and virtual terminal protocol. A virtual terminal protocol converts between specific terminal characteristics and a generic or virtual model used by application programs. Virtual terminal protocols are discussed in Chapter 17.

Application Layer.   The *application layer* provides a means for application processes to access the OSI environment. This layer contains management functions and generally useful mechanisms to support distributed applications. Examples of protocols at this level are file transfer and electronic mail, both of which are discussed in Chapter 17.

Summary

Figure 12-11 provides a useful perspective on the OSI architecture. The annotation along the right side suggests viewing the seven layers in three parts, corresponding to the simple 3-layer architecture introduced in Chapter 1. The lower three layers contain the logic for a computer to interact with a network. The host is attached physically to the network, uses a data link protocol to reliably communicate with

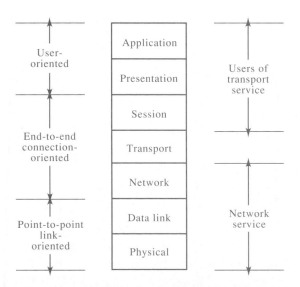

FIGURE 12-11.   Perspectives on the OSI architecture.

the network, and uses a network protocol to request data exchange with another device on the network and to request network services (e.g., priority). The X.25 standard for packet-switching networks encompasses these three layers. Continuing from this perspective, the transport layer provides a reliable end-to-end service regardless of the intervening network facility; in effect, it is the user's liaison to the communications facility. Finally, the upper three layers, taken together, are involved in the exchange of data between end users, making use of a transport service for reliable data transfer.

Another perspective is suggested by the annotation on the left. Again, consider host systems attached to a common network. The lower two layers deal with the link between the host and the network. The next three layers are all involved in transferring data from one host to another: The network layer makes use of the communication network facilities to transfer data from one host to another; the transport layer assures that the transfer is reliable; and the session layer manages the flow of data over the logical connection. Finally, the upper two layers are oriented to the user's concerns, including considerations of the application to be performed and any formatting issues.

12-3

THE TCP/IP PROTOCOL SUITE

In recent years, much of the discussion and development work on communications protocols reported in the open literature has used the terminology and frame of reference of the OSI model. Remarkably, little attention has been given to a communications architecture which predates the OSI model and for which there is far more implementation and practical experience. This architecture is an outgrowth of the development of ARPANET [ROBE70] and the Defense Data Network (DDN) [ELSA86]. Whereas the OSI architecture is intended to guide the future development of protocols, it is the experience already gained in the development and use of protocols within ARPANET that has led to the communications architecture we are about to describe. This architecture has only recently been articulated as such and has no universally accepted name. We refer to it as the TCP/IP protocol suite.

Both OSI and the TCP/IP protocol suite deal with communications among heterogeneous computers. Both are based on the concept of protocol and have many similarities. However, there are philosophical and practical differences between the OSI model and the TCP/IP protocol suite, and the serious student of communications architecture needs to understand both.

In this section we provide an overview of the TCP/IP protocol suite. More detail is provided as various specific topics are pursued in the course of Part III.

Characteristics

The U.S. Department of Defense (DOD) recently has issued standards for a set of communications protocols [STAL90e]. Its motivations are much the same as those of the ISO and any computer system customer. DOD needs to have efficient, cost-effective communications among heterogeneous computers. That DOD has chosen to develop its own protocols and architecture rather than adopt the developing international standards is for three reasons [ENNI82]:

1. The DOD protocols were specified and have enjoyed extensive use prior to ISO standardization of alternative protocols. Because DOD's need was immediate, it was deemed impractical to wait for the ISO protocols to evolve and to stabilize.
2. DOD-specific communications requirements have a major impact on the design of protocols and an architecture. These concerns have not been uppermost in the minds of the ISO developers, and predictably are not reflected in the OSI model.
3. There are philosophic differences concerning the appropriate nature of a communications architecture and its protocols.

The first reason is self-explanatory. The second reason need not concern us in this context. The specific DOD requirements, many of which are also relevant in other contexts, include availability, survivability, security, network interoperability, and the ability to handle surge traffic. The interested reader is referred to [CERF83a].

The third reason is best explained by examining the differences between the TCP/IP protocol suite and the ΘSI model. There are four fundamental differences [ENNI83]:

- The concept of hierarchy versus layering.
- The importance of internetworking.
- The utility of connectionless services.
- The approach to management functions.

Hierarchy Versus Layering. The TCP/IP protocol suite recognizes that the task of communications is too complex and too diverse to be accomplished by a single unit. Accordingly, the task is broken up into modules or entities that may communicate with peer entities in another system. One entity within a system provides services to other entities and, in turn, uses the services of other entities. Good software design practice dictates that these entities be arranged hierarchically (i.e., no entity uses its own services, directly or indirectly).

The OSI model is based on the same reasoning, but takes it one step further. The next step is the recognition that, in many respects, protocols at the same level of the hierarchy have certain features in common. This yields the concept of rows or layers, and the attempt to describe in an abstract fashion what features are held in common by the protocols within a given row.

Now, as an explanatory tool, a layered model has significant value and, indeed, the OSI model is used for precisely that purpose in the remainder of this book. The objection sometimes raised by the designers of the TCP/IP protocol suite and its protocols is that the OSI model is prescriptive rather than descriptive. It dictates that protocols within a given layer perform certain functions. This may not be always desirable. It is possible to define more than one protocol at a given layer, and the functionality of those protocols may not be the same or even similar. Rather, what is common about a set of protocols at the same layer is that they share the same set of support protocols at the next lower layer.

Furthermore, there is the implication in the OSI model that, because interfaces between layers are well defined, a new protocol can be substituted for an old one at a given layer with no impact on adjacent layers (see principle 6, Table 12-3). This is not always desirable or even possible. For example, a local network lends itself easily to multicast and broadcast addressing at the link level. If the IEEE 802 link level were inserted below a network protocol entity that did not support multicasting and broadcasting, that service would be denied to upper layers of the hierarchy. To get around some of these problems, OSI proponents talk of null layers and sublayers (we will see examples). It sometimes seems that these artifacts save the model at the expense of good protocol design.

To make the points above specific, consider the following prescriptions, commonly agreed to be part of the OSI model:

* (N) entities must exchange data using services provided by (N-1) entities. Another way of saying this is that (N-1) entities must be involved in every data transfer between (N) entities.
* (N-1) entities provide their service by exchanging data units which contain (N-1) control information and data from (N) entities.
* (N) control information is passed to the remote side as (N-1) data.

The TCP/IP protocol suite is intended not to be so restrictive. As examples, the following techniques would be allowed:

* An entity may directly use the services of a hierarchically lower entity, even if it is not in an adjacent layer.
* Escape characters can be used to allow the placement of control characters within a data stream (e.g., TELNET, see Chapter 16). This situation is not correctly described by the concept of data units containing both control and higher-level data.
* Separate control and data connections may be used, in which higher-level data and control information do not share a data unit. This is useful, since one might wish to provide different services (priority, reliability) for the different types of connections.
* Lower-level control information can be used to accomplish higher-level control. For example, the closing of a lower-level connection can implicitly close an isomorphic higher-level connection, without requiring the higher-level entity to pass control information.
* Multiple entity cooperation is allowed. For example, an application-level protocol may dictate that the services of a name server entity be employed at the start of a sequence of data transfers, but the latter entity need not be involved after transfer begins.

It may, of course, be possible to provide all of these features within the OSI model, although neither the OSI document [ISO84] nor any of the developing protocols shows any evidence of them. The argument of the TCP/IP protocol suite proponents is not that certain things can be done in the TCP/IP protocol suite that cannot be done in the OSI model. Rather, the argument is that the TCP/IP protocol suite, by simply mandating that protocols be modular and hierarchical, give the designer more freedom to develop efficient, cost-effective, and rich protocols.

Whether the philosophical difference between hierarchy and layering results in any practical difference remains to be seen as more protocols are developed and used.

Internetworking. An historical difference between the TCP/IP protocol suite and the ISO model is the importance that the former places on internetworking. Internetworking occurs when two communicating systems do not attach to the same network. Thus transferred data must traverse at least two networks. Further, these networks may be quite dissimilar.

The requirement for internetworking has led to the development of an Internet Protocol, discussed in Chapter 14. Such a protocol was not originally given a place within the OSI model. The current OSI document makes brief reference to the possibility of networks in tandem, and an internet protocol has emerged as a sub-layer of the network layer (layer 3). This is not a clean solution, but it is the only one possible within the seven-layer architecture.

Connectionless Service. A connectionless service, as the name implies, is one in which data are transferred from one entity to another without the prior mutual construction of a connection (e.g., datagrams). The TCP/IP protocol suite places equal importance on connectionless and connection-oriented services, whereas the OSI model is couched solely in terms of connection-oriented service. It is expected, however, that future versions of the OSI model will incorporate connectionless service [CHAP83].

A primary use of the connectionless service within the TCP/IP protocol suite is in internetworking. Since it is not safe to assume that all intermediate networks are reliable, a connectionless internet protocol is used, with end-to-end connectivity provided at a higher level. A name-address directory server is another example where connectionless service might be desirable.

Management Functions. A final difference between the TCP/IP protocol suite and the OSI model is the way in which various management-related functions are treated. Examples of such functions are the naming (identification) of resources, the control of access to resources, and the accounting for resource and network usage.

The concept of management functions seems not to meld well with the OSI model, partly because these are mostly connectionless services, and partly because there's no ''place'' for them. It would appear that such functions must be classified according to layer and embedded as management entities within each layer. The TCP/IP protocol suite does not preclude this approach but goes further. Within this architecture, a uniform approach is taken to many of these functions and they are provided by protocols that can best be described as ''session layer'' protocols. This description reflects the fact that these protocols make use of transport services. This concept of session will be explored in Chapter 16.

TCP/IP Protocol Architecture

The TCP/IP protocol suite architecture is based on a view of communication that involves three agents: processes, hosts, and networks. *Processes* are the fundamental entities that communicate. Processes execute on *hosts* (stations), which can often support multiple simultaneous processes. Communication between processes takes place across *networks* to which the hosts are attached.

These three concepts yield a fundamental principle of the TCP/IP protocol suite: the transfer of information to a process can be accomplished by first getting it to the host in which the process resides and then getting it to the process within the host. These two levels of demultiplexing can be handled independently. Therefore, a network need only be concerned with routing data between hosts, as long as the hosts agree how to direct data to processes.

With the concepts above in mind, it is natural to organize protocols into four layers. We emphasize here that the important fact is the hierarchical ordering of protocols. The designation of layers is purely for explanatory purposes. An entity in a layer may use the services of another entity in the same layer, or directly use the services of an entity in a lower but not adjacent layer. With that caveat in mind, the DPA organizes protocols into four layers (as suggested by Figure 12-2)

- Network access layer.
- Internet layer.
- Host–host layer.
- Process/application layer.

The *network access layer* contains those protocols that provide access to a communication network. Protocols at this layer are between a communications node and an attached host or its logical equivalent. A function of all these protocols is to route data between hosts attached to the same network. Other services that may be provided are flow control and error control between hosts, and various quality of service features. Examples of the latter are priority and security. A network layer entity is typically invoked by an entity in either the internet or host–host layer, but may be invoked by a process/application layer entity.

The *internet layer* consists of the procedures required to allow data to traverse multiple networks between hosts. Thus it must provide a routing function. This protocol is usually implemented within hosts and gateways. A gateway is a processor connecting two networks whose primary function is to relay data between networks using an internetwork protocol.

The *host–host layer* contains protocol entities with the ability to deliver data between two processes on different host computers. A protocol entity at this level may (or may not) provide a logical connection between higher-level entities. Indeed, it is at this level that explicit connections make the most sense, with a logical connection being one used to exchange data between the ultimate endpoints (processes). Other possible services include error and flow control and the ability to deal with control signals not associated with a logical data connection. Four general types of protocols seem to be needed at this level [MCFA79]: a reliable connection-oriented data protocol, a datagram protocol, a speech protocol, and a real-time data protocol. Each has different services requirements:

- A reliable connection-oriented data protocol is characterized by the need for reliable, sequenced delivery of data. Many data processing applications would use such a service.
- A datagram protocol is a low-overhead, minimum functionality protocol that may be appropriate for some traffic, particularly applications that prefer to implement their own connection-oriented functionality.
- A speech protocol is characterized by the need for handling a steady stream of data with minimum delay variance.
- A real-time data protocol has the demanding characteristics of both a reliable connection-oriented protocol and a speech protocol.

The *process/application layer* contains protocols for resource sharing (e.g., computer-to-computer) and remote access (e.g., terminal-to-computer).

TABLE 12-6 DOD Military Standard Protocols

MIL-STD-1777 Internet Protocol (IP)

Provides a connectionless service for end systems to communicate across one more networks. Does not assume the networks to be reliable.

MIL-STD-1778 Transmission Control Protocol (TCP)

A reliable end-to-end data transfer service. Equivalent to the ISO Class 4 transport protocol.

MIL-STD-1780 File Transfer Protocol (FTP)

A simple application for transfer of ASCII, EBCDIC, and binary files.

MIL-STD-1781 Simple Mail Transfer Protocol (SMTP)

A simple electronic mail facility.

MIL-STD-1782 Telnet Protocol

Provides a simple asynchronous terminal capability.

Within this architecture, DOD has issued the following protocol standards:

- Internet layer: IP (MIL-STD-1777)
- Host-to-host layer: TCP (MIL-STD-1778)
- Process/application layer: FTP (MIL-STD-1780); SMTP (MIL-STD-1781; TELNET (MIL-STD-1782)

These protocol standards are defined briefly in Table 12-6. Note that these standards fit into the upper three layers of the architecture. At the network access layer, systems may be interfaced to a variety of networks. By and large, DOD will rely on national and international standards at this layer, such as X.25 for long-haul packet-switched networks and IEEE 802 for local networks.

Figure 12-12 depicts the way in which specific DOD protocols fit into the four-layer architecture. The shape of the diagram is intended to suggest the way in which various protocols may invoke each other. For example, the file transfer protocol FTP may directly use the transmission control protocol (TCP), which provides reliable connection-oriented service, or it may use some of the services of the TELNET protocol as well. Note that ''ad hoc'' protocols are possible at any level.

Table 12-7 compares the four layers of the TCP/IP protocol suite to the seven of the OSI model.

12-4

EXAMPLE ARCHITECTURE: SNA

It is instructive to compare the standardization efforts underway with an existing communications architecture. For this purpose, we return to an architecture intro-

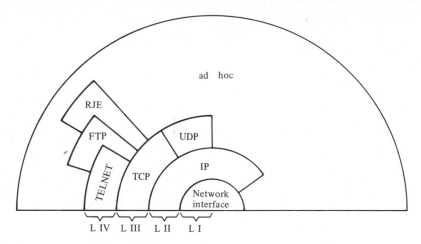

FIGURE 12-12.   TCP/IP protocol architecture.

duced in Chapter 9: IBM's Systems Network Architecture (SNA) [IBM85a,b].
Table 12-7 compares this with the OSI model.

SNA consists of seven layers:

- Physical control.
- Data link control.
- Path control.
- Transmission control.

TABLE 12-7   A Comparison of Communications Architectures

OSI		TCP/IP Protocol Suite		SNA	
7	Applications	7	Process/ application	7	Transaction services
6	Presentations	6		6	Presentation services
5	Session	5	Host-Host	5	Data flow control
4	Transport	4		4	Transmission control
3	Network	3	Internet	3	Path control
2	Data link	2	Network access	2	Data link control
1	Physical	1		1	Physical control

- Data flow control.
- Presentation services.
- Transaction services.

Physical Control

The physical control layer corresponds to OSI layer 1. It specifies the physical interface between nodes. Two types of interface are specified: those for serial communications links and those for parallel links. The interfaces for serial communications links are of the kind discussed in Chapter 4, and are used for most node-to-node connections. SNA networks can also include high-speed parallel links between a mainframe and a front-end communication processor.

Data Link Control

The data link control layer corresponds to OSI layer 2. This layer provides for the reliable transfer of data across a physical link. The protocol specified for serial communications links is SDLC. SDLC is basically a subset of HDLC, which was covered in Chapter 5. The protocol for high-speed parallel links is the S/370 data channel protocol, which is described in [STAL87b].

Path Control

The *path control* layer [ATKI80] creates logical channels between endpoints, referred to as network addressable units (NAUs). An NAU is an application-level entity capable of being addressed and of exchanging data with other entities. Thus key functions of the path control layer are routing and flow control.

Path control is based on the concepts of transmission group, explicit route, and virtual route, introduced in Chapter 9. To recall, a *transmission group* is a set of one or more physical links between adjacent nodes in the network. An *explicit route* is a path between endpoints, defined as an ordered sequence of transmission groups. A *virtual route* is a logical connection between endpoints that is dynamically assigned to an explicit route. Corresponding to these three concepts are three sublayers of the path control layer.

The primary function of the transmission group control sublayer is to make the set of links in a transmission group appear to higher layers as a single physical link. The main advantages of this are increased reliability and capacity for transmission between adjacent nodes. The protocol at this sublayer accepts data units and places them in a FIFO queue. Each data unit is sent out in turn over the next available physical link, using SDLC. Because of errors or differences in propagation delay, units may arrive out of order at the other end of the transmission group. Sequence numbers are used so that the receiving protocol entity can reorder the units. Another function performed at this sublayer is blocking. When a transmission group consists of a single link, the protocol entity may block incoming data units into a larger unit before transmission. This can increase efficiency, for example, by reducing the number of channel I/O operations that data link control needs to execute. The function of this sublayer is unusual and seems to fit best as part of layer 2 of the OSI model.

The explicit route control sublayer is primarily responsible for routing. Explicit routes are predefined in SNA and each node maintains routing information in the form of (explicit route number, next node). Thus, any incoming data must contain an explicit route number. On the basis of that number, the protocol entity selects the next node and passes the data to the transmission group control sublayer.

The virtual route control sublayer provides a logical connection on which traffic from sessions is multiplexed and on which flow control mechanisms are applied. Both entry-to-exit flow control and congestion control are exercised using the pacing algorithm described in Chapter 9. In addition, this sublayer has the ability to segment data units from higher layers to improve efficiency. Segmented data units must be reassembled at the other end. This sublayer and the explicit route control sublayer more or less encompass the functions of OSI's layer 3.

Transmission Control

The next higher layer of SNA is *transmission control*, which corresponds roughly to layer 4 of the OSI model. The transmission control layer is responsible for establishing, maintaining, and terminating SNA sessions. A *session*, which corresponds to OSI's transport connection is a logical relation between endpoints (NAUs). The transmission control layer can establish a session in response to a request from the next higher layer (data flow control), from an application process, or for its own control purposes.

The layer is composed of two modules: the connection point manager (CPMGR), which handles individual data transfers, and session control, which handles session-level matters. The *CPMGR* performs the following functions:

- *Routing:* This is essentially a demultiplexing function. Incoming data units are routed to the appropriate entity, which may be at the same or some higher layer.
- *Encapsulation:* Outgoing messages are encapsulated in a data unit; the header, which is appended to the data, contains control information for expedited delivery, pacing, encryption, and other control functions.
- *Pacing:* This is the same mechanism as is used on virtual routes. In this case, it is used only by the endpoints, to control the flow of data units. A fixed window size is used.

Session control is invoked to activate or deactivate a session. It is also invoked when CPMGR detects a session error, such as a missing sequence number.

Data Flow Control

Within SNA logical connections, called sessions, may be established between applications. SNA has chosen to divide the management of sessions into two layers. The transmission control layer is transmission oriented and, as we have said, corresponds nicely of OSI's layer 4. The *data flow control* layer is end-user oriented and corresponds equally nicely to OSI's layer 5. This layer is responsible for providing session-related services that are visible and of interest to end-user processes and terminals. The principal functions are in the following categories.

- *Send/receive mode:* Three modes may be specified: full duplex, half-duplex flip-flop, and half-duplex contention. The distinction between the latter two roughly corresponds to the distinction between HDLC's normal response mode and asynchronous balanced mode.
- *Chaining:* Chaining is a mechanism to delineate transmission sequences for the purpose of recovery (as discussed under the OSI session layer, above).
- *Bracketing:* Whereas chaining deals with a sequence of data units transmitted in one direction, bracketing deals with a sequence of exchanges. This concept may be used to define and control transaction sequences.
- *Response options:* Three response modes may be specified. For each data unit, (1) do not send a response, (2) send a response only in case of an exception, and (3) always send a response.
- *Quiesce/shutdown:* A temporary or permanent halt to the flow of data may be requested.

Presentation Services

The top two layers of SNA were, until recently, considered as a single layer referred to as the function management data (FMD) services layer [HOBE80]. The FMD services layer comprised a set of functions and services provided to the end user. That layer corresponded to OSI layers 6 and 7. Now, the functions are split into two layers, presentation services and transaction services.

The presentation services layer includes the following services:

- *Format translation:* This service allows each endpoint to have a different view of the exchanged data. For example, it can be used to allow one application to handle multiple terminal types.
- *Compression and compaction:* Data can be compressed at the bit or byte level using specified procedures, to reduce transmission volume.
- *Transaction program support:* This service controls conversation-level communication between transaction programs by (1) loading and invoking transaction programs, (2) maintaining send and receive mode protocols, and (3) enforcing correct verb parameter usage and sequencing restrictions.

Most of these services correspond to OSI layer 6, although some of the transaction program support functions are more in the nature of layer 7.

Transaction Services

This layer is primarily intended to provide network management services. Since these services are directly used by an end user, such as a system manager or network operator, they best fit in OSI's layer 7. The following are included:

- *Configuration services:* allow an operator to start up or reconfigure a network by activating and deactivating links.
- *Network operator services:* include such nonconfiguration operator functions as the collection and display of network statistics, and the communication of data from users and processes to the network operator.

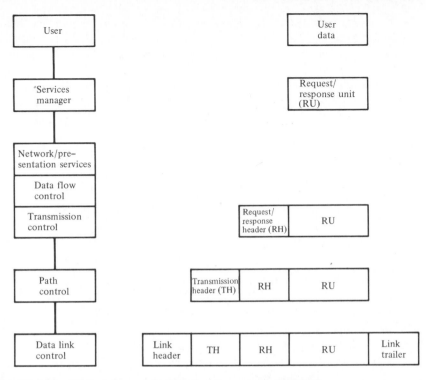

FIGURE 12-13.   SNA data encapsulation. Source: [METZ83]

- *Session services:* support the activation of a session on the behalf of end users and applications. In effect, this is the user interface to the transmission control layer.
- *Maintenance and management services:* provide for the testing of network facilities and assist in fault isolation and identification.

SNA Encapsulation

Unlike the apparent OSI policy, SNA does not require the use of a header at each layer of the hierarchy. Figure 12-13 depicts the overall SNA encapsulation strategy. The most basic piece of data in SNA is the *request/response unit* (RU), which contains either user data or network control information. A services manager creates RUs from user data. The FMD services layer may perform certain transformations on the data to accommodate presentation services or may add control information relating to chains of RUs. The latter are contained in a *FMD header*. This header is optional and, if used, may only appear occasionally (at the start of a chain or bracket); thus it is not shown in the figure.

The transmission control layer then adds a request/response header (RH), containing control information both for itself and the data flow control layer. Rather than create a separate header, the data flow control layer is content to pass parameters to the transmission control layer to include in the header that it constructs. This seems more efficient than the OSI approach, but implies a tighter coupling between layers.

The next two layers add their own headers for their own purposes. Data link control also adds a trailer, as explained in Chapter 5.

12·5

RECOMMENDED READING

An excellent and still valid tutorial on the subject of protocols is [POUZ78]. Other worthwhile surveys are [FALK83], [GREE80], and [MCQU78].

[STAL90c] is a detailed description of the OSI model and of the standards at each layer of the model. The material is also covered in [TANE88], which averages about one chapter per layer. [KNOW87] and [HENS88] cover various OSI-related standards, with emphasis on the upper layers. [SLON87] discusses OSI from the point of view of the practical implementation issues. [STAL87] contains reprints of key articles covering OSI and standards at each layer.

A detailed description of the TCP/IP protocol suite and of the individual standards is contained in [STAL90e]. Two other detailed treatments are [COME88] and [MCCO88]. A more concise, but useful, summary is [DAVI88]. [CLAR88] is an authoritative discussion of the design philosophy behind the TCP/IP architecture.

Three excellent treatments of SNA are [MART87], [GURU87], and [MEIJ87]. All are detailed, complete, and clearly written. [TILL90] provides an interesting analysis of the interconnection of SNA and OSI systems.

12·6

PROBLEMS

12-1 List the major disadvantages with the layered approach to protocols.

12-2 Based on the principles enunciated in Table 12-3, design an architecture with eight layers and make a case for it. Design one with six layers and make a case for that.

12-3 Two blue armies are each poised on opposite hills preparing to attack a single red army in the valley. The red army can defeat either of the blue armies separately but will fail to defeat both blue armies if they attack simultaneously. The blue armies communicate via an unreliable communications system (a foot soldier). The commander, with one of the blue armies, would like to attack at noon. His problem is this: If he sends a message ordering the attack, he cannot be sure it will get through. He could ask for acknowledgment but *that* might not get through. Is there a protocol that the two blue armies can use to avoid defeat?

12-4 In Figure 12-9, exactly one protocol data unit (PDU) in layer N is encapsulated in a protocol data unit at layer (N-1). It is also possible to break one N-level PDU into multiple (N-1)-level PDUs (segmentation) or to group multiple N-level PDUs into one (N-1)-level PDU (blocking). (a) In the case of segmentation, is it necessary that each (N-1)-level segment contain a copy of the N-level header? (b) In the case of blocking, is it necessary that each N-level PDU retain its own header, or can the data be consolidated into a single N-level PDU with a single N-level header?

12-5   Discuss the need or lack of need for a network layer (OSI layer 3) in a broadcast network.

12-6   Compare SNA to the OSI and DPA frameworks. To which is it closest philosophically? Discuss similarities and differences.

12-7   What must be added to the OSI model to reconcile the differences with DPA?

APPENDIX 12A

STANDARDS

Section 1-6 described the most important standard-making organizations and Table 12-8 shows the relationship to the OSI model of some of the most important standards. Remember that the OSI layers are not standards; they merely provide a framework for standards.

ISO, of course, continues to play the key role in the evolution of the OSI model. Their interest in individual standards has focused on layer 3 and above. ISO has issued standards for layers 4 and 5 and is in the process of issuing a variety of standards that cover layers 6 and 7. ISO has also developed a sublayer of layer 3 that deals with internetworking, which involves communication across multiple networks.

CCITT has been concerned with defining access protocols to public communication networks. It has developed standards for connecting *data terminal equipment* (DTE) to a packet-switched network that provides *data circuit-terminating equipment* (DCE). These terms correspond to the stations and nodes of Figure 7-2. The standard, X.25, specifically addresses layer 3 and subsumes standards for layers 2 and 1. Layer 2 is referred to as LAP-B (Link Access Protocol—Balanced) and is almost identical with ISO's HDLC (High-Level Data Link Control) and ANSI's ADCCP (Advanced Data Communication Control Procedures). A corresponding standard, X.21, has been developed for circuit-switched networks.

TABLE 12-8   Some Well-Known Protocol Standards

OSI	ISO	CCITT	DOD	IEEE 802	ASC X3T9.5
7. Application	FTAM	X.400	FTP SMTP		
6. Presentation	VTP		TELNET		
5. Session	ISO Session		TCP		
4. Transport	ISO Transport				
3. Network	ISO IP	ISDN	IP		
2. Data Link		X.25		Logical link control	
1. Physical		X.21		Medium access control Physical	

CCITT is also the controlling organization for developing ISDN standards, discussed in Chapter 18. CCITT is also concerned with the area known as *telematics,* which covers user-oriented information transmission services. Teletex (communication among office word processing systems), videotex (interactive information retrieval), and facsimile (imagery transmission) are included under this term.

NBS works closely with ISO and with interested U.S. organizations. Their intent is to issue federal standards that are compatible with international standards. In some cases, they add or delete features to bring international standards more in line with U.S. standards. NBS has issued a transport standard and endorsed both X.25 and the IEEE 802 (described below) standards for federal standards.

DCA is the issuing agency for communications standards for DOD. They have promulgated the Transmission Control Protocol (TCP) as a transport protocol standard and the Internet Protocol (IP) for internetworking. In addition they have issued standards at higher layers. All of these protocols, unfortunately, differ from planned and issued standards from ISO and NBS.

For the type of local network that we refer to as a *local area network* (LAN), the Institute of Electrical and Electronics Engineers (IEEE), through its 802 committee, has developed a three-layer architecture that corresponds to layers 1 and 2 of the OSI model. A number of standards have been developed by the committee for these layers. Similarly, a subcommittee responsible to the American National Standards Institute (ANSI), known as ANS X3T9.5, has developed standards for the type of local network we refer to as a *high speed local network* (HSLN). These standards, one per layer, correspond nicely to layers 1 and 2 of the OSI model.

This variety may be disheartening, given the alleged benefit of standards, which is to put everyone on the same road. There is certainly room for pessimism. The DOD-NBS disparity makes a uniform federal government position unlikely. For LANs, the 802 committee has produced a number of options and alternatives at each layer, to come up with an astoundingly thick volume for their standard.

The picture, however, is far from bleak. Tremendous progress has been made toward the development and issuance of standards. Most organizations are cooperating to reduce the incidence of duplicate, competing standards. And while vendors and customers are faced in some areas with multiple standards, the customer at least is far better off than in the 1970s, when virtually no standards existed above layer 1, and those that did were frequently ignored.

An interesting discussion of standards and standards-making organizations is [CERN84].

CHAPTER 13

Network Access Protocols

Both the Open Systems Interconnection (OSI) model and the TCP/IP architecture agree that the details of the intervening data transmission system should be kept hidden from the end-to-end protocols that manage communications between stations or endpoints. In the case of the OSI model, these details are handled by layers 1 to 3; in the case of TCP/IP, a network access layer is designated.

For now, let us think of the end-to-end service as being provided by a transport protocol. We would like lower layer protocols to provide the required services for transmitting data between two transport entities, such that the transport protocol can be designed without knowledge of the underlying transmission system. Five cases need to be distinguished. The transport entities may be in separate stations connected by a:

- Circuit-switched network.
- Packet-switched network.
- Broadcast network.
- Point-to-point link.
- Multiple networks.

The first three cases are sufficiently distinct that significantly different approaches are commonly taken. We will examine each by discussing the most widely accepted approach in each case. The fourth case, point-to-point link, is a special case of a broadcast network. Finally, the task of communication across multiple networks is sufficiently complex to warrant a separate chapter.

We begin, however, with a brief examination of the nature of the network interface.

Communication across a network between processes in separate systems can be thought of as involving two kinds of entities:

- The end systems that contain the processes, and implement some sort of communications architecture, such as the seven-layer OSI architecture.
- The node, or switching systems, of the network that manage communication across the network.

In most cases, an end system attaches to a communications device that is considered, from an architectural point of view, to be part of the network. CCITT refers to end systems and the communications devices to which they attach as DTEs and DCEs, respectively.

To understand the protocol implications of the requirement for network attachment, we need to look at the various possible cases. Figure 13-1a depicts the case in which an end system (DTE) attaches to a packet-switching node (DCE) that is part of a packet-switched network. In this case, the DCEs implement layers 1 through 3 of the OSI architecture.

Let us characterize the nature of the interaction between the DTE and DCE in this packet-switching case. In OSI terms, the transport layer is *DTE-DTE oriented,* providing an end-to-end service. The network layer is responsible for making use of the network facilities to route data from source to destination. Thus, this layer is DTE-DCE oriented, since it deals with the interaction between DTE and DCE. Specifically, the layer 3 protocol must allow the DTE to:

- Provide the network with a destination address for data to be transmitted. This information is used by the network to design a route through the network to the destination DTE.
- Request network facilities, such as priority, reverse charging, and so on.

Figure 13-1a depicts the relationship. Note that, in addition to a layer 3 protocol, a data link layer protocol (layer 2) over a physical link (layer 1) between the DTE and DCE is needed. Hence, the DTE-DCE interaction consists of protocols at layers 1, 2, and 3. The local DCE uses a different set of protocols to route data units through the network to the destination DCE, which in turn has a layer 1-3 set of protocols with the destination DTE. The internal operation of the network is transparent to the user, and the internal protocol structure in the network is of no concern to the end systems.

A quite different circumstance is illustrated in Figure 13-1b, which shows two DTEs connected by a point-to-point link. Typically, this configuration also involves the use of DCEs. There is a standardized physical-level interface, such as EIA-232-D between the end system and a DCE (e.g., a modem), and the two DCEs communicate using some other physical protocol across a transmission line (see Figure 4-7). In this case, the DCE operates purely at layer 1 and simply relays the bits from the DTE onto the transmission line and vice versa. Thus, layers 2 and 3, as well as layer 4, are end to end, or DTE to DTE. In this configuration, the layer 3 protocol has very little work to do. There are no network facilities to request, and there is no need for address information to support routing.

A similar situation exists in the case of a circuit-switched network (Figure 13-1c). Once a circuit has been set up between two DTEs across the network, it appears to the two stations that they have a direct point-to-point link. The nodes of the network act simply as layer 1 relays of the bits being transmitted. Again, very little is needed at layer 3.

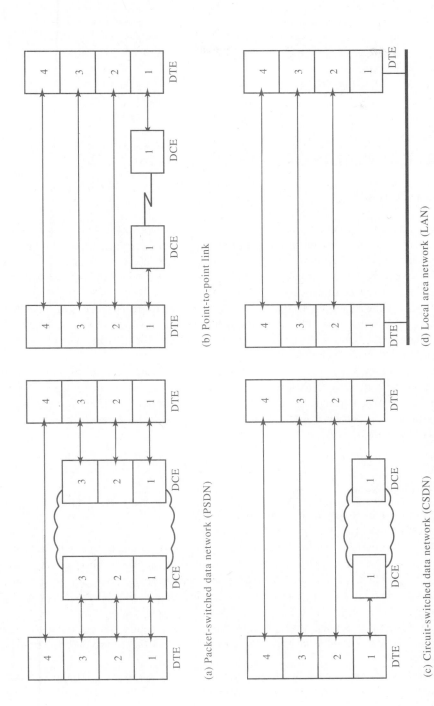

(a) Packet-switched data network (PSDN)

(b) Point-to-point link

(c) Circuit-switched data network (CSDN)

(d) Local area network (LAN)

FIGURE 13-1.   Network interface architecture.

Finally, the architecture of a local area network is depicted in Figure 13-1d. The layer 2 protocols are end to end between attached devices. So, once again, the LAN acts simply as a layer 1 facility for moving bits between two DTEs. In this case, there is no readily-identifiable DCE; the DTEs connect directly to the shared network medium. As in the preceding two cases, there is not a great deal for a layer 3 protocol to do.

13-1

PACKET-SWITCHED NETWORK ACCESS: X.25

Requirements

Unlike a circuit-switched network, a packet-switched network is not transparent to attached stations, even during the data transfer phase. Stations must break up their data into packets. Packets contain not only user data intended for another station on the network, but also control information by means of which the attached station and the network communicate.

Consider the requirements that must be met by the protocols between the attached device and the network. Of course there need to be physical and data link control protocols to move data between the attached device and the network. The remaining functions are at the network layer.

At minimum, the network layer protocol must provide a service for transferring data between stations. This service may be either a virtual-circuit service (connection-oriented) or a datagram service (connectionless). Most public networks provide a virtual-circuit service. Additional functions that must be performed by the network-layer protocol include:

- Flow control.
- Error control.
- Multiplexing.

Flow control is needed in both directions. The network must protect itself from congestion, and to do this may need to limit the flow of packets from the attached stations. Similarly, a station needs to be able to control the rate at which the network delivers packets to it. These considerations did not apply in the case of circuit switching. The circuit-switched network provides a transparent path of constant data rate. The network allocates resources to maintain that data rate. The stations may use flow control end-to-end or at the data link level to limit data flow.

Since station and node are exchanging control information as well as data, some form of *error control* is needed to assure that all of the control information is received properly.

Most packet-switched networks provide a *multiplexing* service. With this service, a station can establish multiple virtual circuits with other stations at the same time. This is needed because, generally, a single physical link attaches a station to a network. It should be possible to sustain multiple connections simultaneously over that link.

Finally, there may be a variety of facilities or services offered by the network. The protocol must include a means for the attached station to request these facilities.

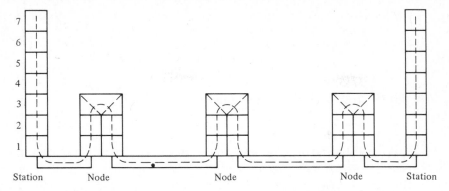

FIGURE 13-2. OSI configuration for circuit-switched communication.

Figure 13-2 depicts the protocol architecture implied by the above requirements. Each node, including intermediate nodes, performs functions up through layer 3. We now turn to a specific example that should help clarify this figure.

A Packet-Switched Network Access Standard: X.25

Perhaps the best known and most widely used protocol standard is X.25, which was originally approved in 1976 (and has been revised three times since: 1980, 1984, and 1988). The standard specifies a DTE-DCE ''interface.'' The standard specifically calls out three levels (Figure 13-3):

- Physical level.
- Link level.
- Packet level.

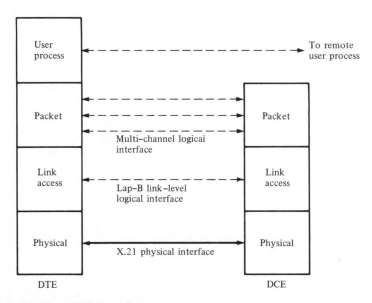

FIGURE 13-3. X.25 interface.

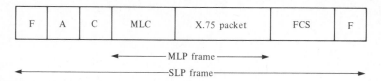

FIGURE 13-4. X.25 multilink frame format.

For the physical level, the physical level portion of X.21 is specified. Optionally (and at present more commonly), X.21 *bis* may be used; this is similar to EIA-232-D. This section will be devoted to a discussion of the link and packet levels.

Link Level. At the link level, X.25 defines both a *single link procedure* (SLP) and a *multilink procedure* (MLP) that allows the interface to operate over multiple lines and achieve greater reliability and throughput. The SLP is defined to be LAP-B, which is a subset of the asynchronous balanced mode (ABM) of HDLC. When multiple links exist between DTE and DCE, each link is governed by the SLP LAP-B.

TABLE 13-1 X.25 Packet Types

Packet Type		Service	
From DCE to DTE	**From DTE to DCE**	**VC**	**PVC**
Call Setup and Clearing			
Incoming call	Call request	X	
Call connected	Call accepted	X	
Clear indication	Clear request	X	
DCE clear confirmation	DTE clear confirmation	X	
Data and Interrupt			
DCE data	DTE data	X	X
DCE interrupt	DTE interrupt	X	X
DCE interrupt confirmation	DTE interrupt confirmation	X	X
Flow Control and Reset			
DCE RR	DTE RR	X	X
DCE RNR	DTE RNR	X	X
	DTE REJ	X	X
Reset indication	Reset request	X	X
DCE reset confirmation	DTE reset confirmation	X	X
Restart			
Restart indication	Restart request	X	X
DCE restart confirmation	DTE restart confirmation	X	X
Diagnostic			
Diagnostic		X	X
Registration			
Registration confirmation	Registration request	X	X

When multiple links exist, the set of links is used as a pooled resource for transmitting packets, regardless of virtual circuit number. When a packet is presented to MLP for transmission, any available link may be chosen. Indeed, the MLP may assign one packet to several links to satisfy throughput or availability constraints.

To keep track of packets, a special MLP frame is defined, which consists of the packet and a 2-octet multilink control (MLC) field (Figure 13-4). The MLC contains a 12-bit sequence number which is unique (modulo 2^{12}) across all links. Once an MLP frame is constructed, it is assigned to a particular link, and further encapsulated in an SLP frame. The SLP frame includes, as usual, a sequence number unique to that link.

There are two principal reasons for needing an MLP sequence number. First, frames sent out over different links may arrive in a different order from that in which they were first constructed by the sending MLP. The destination MLP will buffer incoming frames and reorder them according to MLP sequence number. Second, if repeated attempts to transmit a frame over one link fails, the DTE or DCE will send the frame over one or more other links. The MLP sequence number is needed for duplicate detection in this case.

The MLP mechanism is logically equivalent to the transmission group control mechanism in SNA's path control layer.

Packet Level.   The packet level specifies a *virtual-circuit service*. A variety of packet types are used (Table 13-1), all using the same basic format, with variations (Figure 13-5).

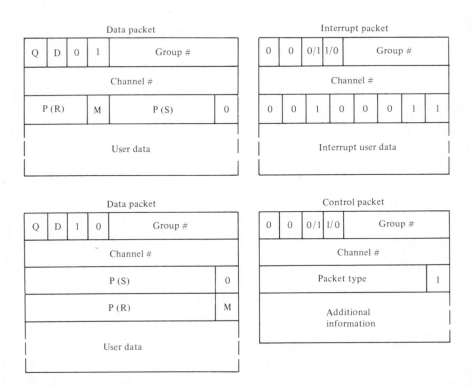

FIGURE 13-5.   X.25 packet formats.

The virtual circuit service of X.25 provides for two types of virtual circuit: virtual call and permanent virtual circuit. A *virtual call* is a dynamically established virtual circuit using a call setup and call clearing procedure analogous to that of X.21. A *permanent virtual circuit* is a permanent, network-assigned virtual circuit. Data transfer occurs as with virtual calls, but no call setup or clearing is required.

The X.25 virtual-circuit service is quite complex. We begin by describing a typical sequence of events for the progress of a virtual call. Then we examine each of the key features of X.25.

Virtual Calls.   Figure 13-6 shows a typical sequence of events in a virtual call. The left-hand part of the figure shows the packets exchanged between DTE A and its DCE; the right-hand part shows the packets exchanged between DTE B and its DCE. The routing of packets between the DCEs is the responsibility of the internal logic of the network.

The sequence of events is as follows:

1. *A* requests a virtual circuit to *B* by sending a Call Request packet to its DCE. The packet includes a virtual circuit number (group, channel), as well as source and destination addresses. Future incoming and outgoing data transfers will be identified by the virtual circuit number.
2. The network routes this call request to *B*'s DCE.
3. *B*'s DCE receives the call request and sends a Call Indication packet to *B*. This packet has the same format as the Call Request packet but a different virtual circuit number, selected by *B*'s DCE from the set of locally unused numbers.
4. *B* indicates acceptance of the call by sending a Call Accepted packet specifying the same virtual circuit number as that of the Call Indication packet.
5. *A* receives a Call Connected packet with the same virtual circuit number as that of the Call Request packet.
6. *A* and *B* send data and control packets using their respective virtual circuit numbers.
7. *A* (or *B*) sends a Clear Request packet to terminate the virtual circuit and receives a local Clear Confirmation packet.
8. *B* (or *A*) receives a Clear Indication packet and transmits a Clear Confirmation packet.

We point out that this DTE-DCE interface is asymmetric. That is, only selected layer 3 protocol information is transferred end-to-end between subscriber DTEs. Much of the information, such as flow control and acknowledgment, usually has only local significance. However, see below.

The way in which data are encapsulated is of some interest. The transmitting DTE must break its data up into units of some maximum length. X.25 specifies that the network must support a maximum user field length of at least 128 octets (i.e., the user data field may be some number of bits up to the maximum). In addition, the network may allow selection of some other maximum field length in the range 16 to 4096 octets. The length may differ for the two ends of the virtual circuit. The DTE constructs control packets and encapsulates data in data packets. These are then transmitted to the DCE via LAP-B. Thus the packet is encapsulated in a layer 2 frame (one packet per frame). The DCE strips off the layer 2 header and trailer and may encapsulate the packet according to some internal network protocol.

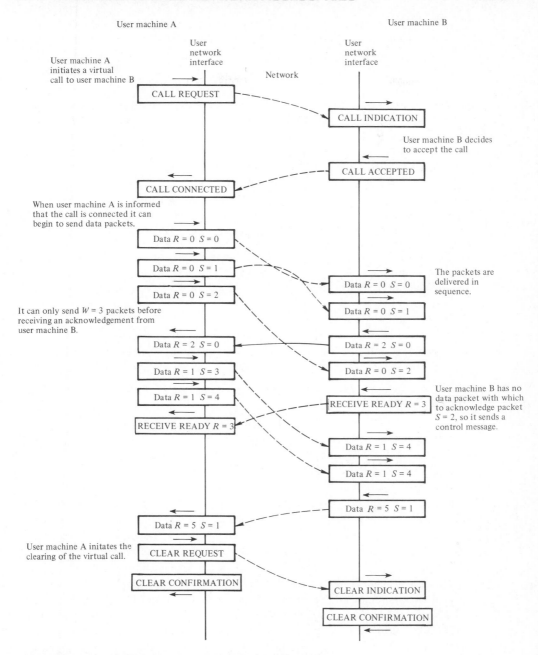

FIGURE 13-6.   Sequence of events—X.25 virtual call.

The description above is the essence of the X.25 virtual circuit service. We now turn to the details, in the following categories:

- Packet format.
- Multiplexing.
- Flow control.
- Packet sequences.
- Reset and restart.

- Interrupt packets.
- Call progress signals.
- User facilities.
- Fast select facility.

Packet Format.   There are two basic types of packet formats, for data packets and control packets (Figure 13-5). In addition to user data, a data packet includes the virtual circuit number, the send and receive sequence numbers, and the M, D, and Q bits. The M and D bits are described below. The Q bit is not defined in the standard, but allows the user to distinguish two types of data. One use of the Q bit, for a PAD, is described in Chapter 17.

Control packets include a virtual circuit number, a packet type identifier, and additional information pertinent to the particular control function. For example, a CALL REQUEST packet includes the following additional fields:

- Calling DTE address length (4 bits): Length of the corresponding address field in semi-octets.
- Called DTE address length (4 bits): Length of the corresponding address field in semi-octets.
- DTE addresses (variable): The calling and called DTE addresses.
- Facility length (16 bits): length of the facilities field in octets.
- Facilities: This field contains a sequence of facility specifications. Each specification consists of an 8-bit facility code and zero or more parameter codes.

Another example of a control packet is the interrupt packet, also shown in Figure 13-5.

Multiplexing.   Perhaps the most important service provided by X.25 is multiplexing. A DTE is allowed by its DCE to establish up to 4095 simultaneous virtual circuits with other DTEs over a single physical DTE-DCE link. The DTE can internally assign these circuits in any way it pleases. Individual virtual circuits could correspond to applications, processes, or terminals for example. The DTE-DCE link provides full-duplex statistical multiplexing. That is, at any time a packet associated with a given virtual circuit can be transmitted in either direction.

To sort out which packets belong to which virtual circuit, each packet contains a 12-bit virtual circuit number (expressed as a 4-bit logical group number plus a 8-bit logical channel number). The assignment of virtual-circuit numbers follows the convention depicted in Figure 13-7. Number zero is always reserved for restart and diagnostic packets common to all virtual circuits. If only a single virtual circuit is allowed (no multiplexing), number 1 is used. Otherwise, contiguous ranges of numbers are allocated for four categories of virtual circuits. Permanent virtual circuits are assigned numbers beginning with 1. The next category is one-way incoming virtual calls. This means that only incoming calls from the network can be assigned these numbers; the circuit, however, is two-way. When a call request comes in, the DCE selects an unused number from this category and places it in the Call Indication packet that it sends to the DTE.

The last category, one-way outgoing virtual calls, is used by the DTE to initiate virtual calls via Call Request packets. Again, the DTE selects an unused number for each new call request. This separation of categories is intended to avoid the simultaneous selection of the same number for two different virtual circuits by the DTE and DCE.

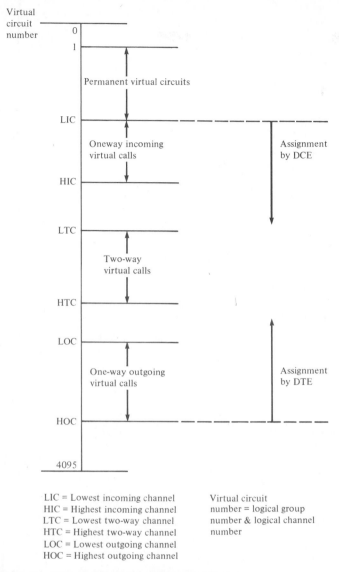

Virtual circuit number

0
1

Permanent virtual circuits

LIC

Oneway incoming virtual calls

HIC

LTC

Two-way virtual calls

HTC

LOC

One-way outgoing virtual calls

HOC

4095

Assignment by DCE

Assignment by DTE

LIC = Lowest incoming channel
HIC = Highest incoming channel
LTC = Lowest two-way channel
HTC = Highest two-way channel
LOC = Lowest outgoing channel
HOC = Highest outgoing channel

Virtual circuit number = logical group number & logical channel number

FIGURE 13-7. Virtual circuit number assignment.

The two-way virtual call category provides an overflow for allocation shared by DTE and DCE. This allows for peak differences in traffic flow.

Flow Control.   Flow control at the X.25 packet level is virtually identical in format and procedure to flow control at the link access layer. A sliding window protocol is used (see Chapter 5). Normally, each data packet includes a 3-bit packet send sequence number, P(S), and a 3-bit packet receive sequence number, P(R). Optionally, a DTE may request, via the user facility mechanism described below, the use of extended 7-bit sequence numbers. In this case, the extended sequence numbers apply to all virtual circuits of the DTE. P(S) is assigned by the DTE on outgoing packets on a virtual circuit basis. The default window size is 2, but it may be set as high as 7 with the 3-bit field or as high as 127 using a 7-bit field.

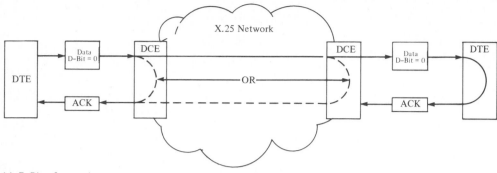

(a) D–Bit = 0 operation

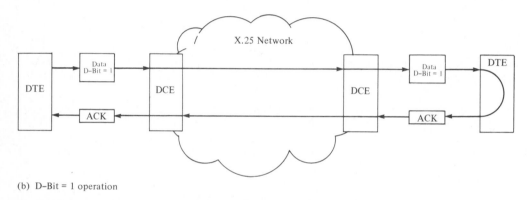

(b) D–Bit = 1 operation

FIGURE 13-8.   Treatment of acknowledgments for data packets.

Incoming data packets on each virtual circuit contain a P(R) which is the number of the next packet expected to be received from the DTE on that virtual circuit. When there are no data packets available for piggybacking, receive ready (RR) and receive not ready (RNR) control packets may be used, with the same meaning as for HDLC. Additionally, X.25 specifies an optional DTE REJ packet.

Acknowledgment (in the form of the P(R) field or RR, RNR packets) and hence flow control may have either local or end-to-end significance, based on the setting of the D bit. When D = 0 (the usual case), acknowledgment is being exercised between the DTE and the network. This is used by the DCE and/or the network to acknowledge receipt of packets and control the flow from the DTE into the network. Note from Figure 13-8a that the acknowledgment may be from the attached DCE or from the remote DCE. In either case, the acknowledgment is said to have "local" (network) significance. When D = 1, acknowledgments come from the remote DTE.

Packet Sequences.   X.25 provides the capability to identify a contiguous sequence of packets, which is called a *complete packet sequence*. This feature has several uses. It can provide a service to higher layers within the DTE. For example, a process may need to fragment messages to get down to the allowable packet size, but wishes to keep track of data on a message basis. This technique is also used when the DCE blocks or fragments data to conform to network packet size restric-

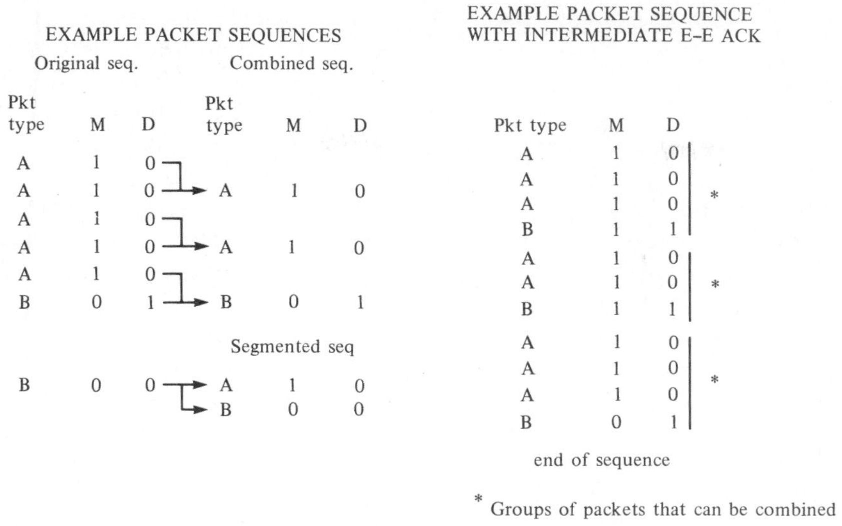

EXAMPLE PACKET SEQUENCES

EXAMPLE PACKET SEQUENCE
WITH INTERMEDIATE E–E ACK

Original seq.   Combined seq.

Pkt type	M	D	Pkt type	M	D
A	1	0			
A	1	0	A	1	0
A	1	0			
A	1	0	A	1	0
A	1	0			
B	0	1	B	0	1

Segmented seq

B	0	0	A	1	0
			B	0	0

Pkt type	M	D	
A	1	0	
A	1	0	
A	1	0	*
B	1	1	
A	1	0	
A	1	0	*
B	1	1	
A	1	0	
A	1	0	
A	1	0	*
B	0	1	

end of sequence

* Groups of packets that can be combined

FIGURE 13-9.   X.25 packet sequences.

tions; this can be useful in internetworking when networks with different packet sizes are connected.

To specify this mechanism, X.25 defines two types of packets: A packets and B packets. An *A packet* is one in which the M bit is set to 1, the D bit is set to zero, and the packet is full (equal to the maximum packet length). A *B packet* is any packet that is not an A packet. Now, a complete packet sequence consists of zero or more A packets followed by a B packet. The network can combine this sequence to make one larger packet. The network may also fragment a B packet into smaller packets to produce a complete packet sequence.

The way in which the B packet is handled depends on the setting of the M and D bits. If D = 1, an end-to-end acknowledgment is sent by the receiving DTE to the sending DTE. This is in effect an acknowledgment of the entire complete packet sequence. M = 1 indicates that there are additional complete packet sequences to follow. This enables the formation of subsequences as part of a larger sequence, so that end-to-end acknowledgment can occur before the end of the larger sequence.

Figure 13-9 shows examples of these concepts. Note that it is the responsibility of the DCEs to reconcile the changes in sequence numbering that fragmentation and assembly cause.

Reset and Restart.   X.25 provides two facilities for recovering from errors. The reset facility is used to reinitialize a virtual circuit. This means that the sequence numbers on both ends are set to zero. Any data or interrupt packets in transit are lost. It is up to a higher-level protocol to recover from the loss of packets.

A reset can be triggered by a number of error conditions including loss of a packet, sequence number error, congestion, or loss of the network's internal virtual circuit. In this latter case, the two DCEs must rebuild the internal virtual circuit to support the still-existing X.25 DTE-DTE virtual circuit.

Either a DTE or DCE can initiate a reset, with a Reset Request or Reset Indication. The recipient responds with a Reset Confirmation. Regardless of who initiated the reset, the DCE is responsible for informing the other end.

A more serious error condition calls for a restart. The issuance of a Restart Request packet, which uses virtual circuit 0, is equivalent to sending a Clear Request on *all* active virtual calls and a Reset Request on all active permanent virtual circuits. Again, either DTE or DCE may initiate action. An example of a condition warranting restart is temporary loss of access of the network.

Interrupt Packets.   A DTE may send an interrupt packet that bypasses the flow control procedures used for data packets. The packet does not contain send and receive sequence numbers and is not blocked by an RNR or a closed window. The interrupt packet carries up to 32 bytes of user data, and is to be delivered to the destination DTE by the network at a higher priority than data packets in transit. Confirmation of interrupt packets is end to end; that is, the sending DTE receives a confirmation of an interrupt packet only after it has been delivered to the remote DTE. A DTE may not send another interrupt packet on any virtual circuit until the outstanding interrupt packet is confirmed. This prevents flooding the network with packets that are not flow controlled. An example of the use of this service is to transmit a terminal break character.

Call Progress Signals.   X.25 includes provision for call progress signals, and these are defined by X.96 (Table 13-2). Call progress signals are not used only during the call establishment phase. The call progress signals fall into two general and overlapping categories for X.25. *Clearing call progress signals* are used to indicate the reason why a CALL REQUEST is denied; they are also used to indicate the reason for a CLEAR REQUEST. In both cases, the signal is carried in a CLEAR INDICATION packet.

Resetting call progress signals are used to indicate the reason why a virtual circuit is being reset or why a restart takes place. The code is contained in a RESET REQUEST, RESET INDICATION, RESTART REQUEST, or RESTART INDICATION PACKET.

User Facilities.   X.25 provides for the use of optional user facilities. These are facilities that may be provided by the network and that may, at the user's option, be employed by a particular user. Some facilities are selectable for use for an agreed period of time. Other facilities are requested on a per-virtual-call basis, as part of the CALL REQUEST packet; with these facilities, the capability or value applies only to the one virtual call.

The facilities that may be provided are defined in X.2, which contains a rather long list. Some of these are termed ''essential.'' Essential facilities must be offered by the network, although their use is optional (Table 13-3). The remaining facilities are termed ''additional,'' and need not be offered by the network.

Finally, a network may provide facilities not specified in X.2 and X.25; these, of course, are beyond the scope of the standard. An example of the latter is the precedence facility available on DDN [BBN83]. A user may include a precedence level from 0 (lowest) to 3 (highest) in a CALL REQUEST packet. The network will attempt to allocate resources accordingly, which may involve pre-empting an existing lower-precedence virtual call.

Fast Select Facility.   The X.25 standard was initially intended to be purely a virtual-circuit service. In response to demand for connectionless network service, two capabilities were included in the 1980 standard: datagram service and the fast

TABLE 13-2 Packet-Switched Call Progress Signals (X.96)

| Signal | Applicable to:[a] | | Usage[b] | Description |
	VC	PVC		
Local Procedure Error	X	X	C, R	Procedure error caused by local DTE
Network Congestion	X	X	C, R	Temporary network congestion or fault
Invalid Facility Request	X		C	Requested user facility not valid
RPOA Out of Order	X		C	Recognized private operating agency unable to forward call
Not Obtainable	X		C	Called DTE address unassigned or unknown
Access Barred	X			
Reverse Charging Acceptance Not Subscribed	X		C	Called DTE will not accept charges on collect call
Fast Select Acceptance Not Subscribed	X		C	Called DTE does not support fast select
Incompatible Destination	X		C, R	The remote DTE does not have a function used or a facility requested
Out of Order	X	X	C, R	Remote DTE out of order
Number Busy	X		C	Called DTE is busy
Remote Procedure Error	X	X	C, R	Procedure error caused by remote DTE
Network Operational		X	R	Network ready to resume after temporary failure or congestion
Remote DTE Operational		X	R	Remote DTE ready after temporary failure
DTE Originated	X	X	C, R	Remote DTE has refused call or requested reset
Ship Absent	X		C	Called ship absent (used with mobile maritime service)
Network Out of Order		X	R	Network temporarily unable to handle data traffic
Registration/Cancellation Confirmed	X	X	R	Facility request confirmed

[a]VC, virtual call; PVC, permanent virtual circuit.
[b]C, clearing call progress signal; R, resetting or restarting call progress signal.

select facility. Because of a complete lack of support for the datagram service, it was subsequently dropped in the 1984 edition of the standard.

The fast select facility is designed to handle transaction-oriented applications in which at least one and sometimes only one inquiry and response take place. The virtual call mechanism is used with the following adjustment. To use fast select, a DTE requests the fast select facility in the facilities field of the Call Request packet. The normal Call Request packet allows only 16 octets of data, but when the fast select facility is employed, 128 octets are allowed. These data are delivered to the destination DTE in a Call Indication packet.

The calling DTE must also specify an unrestricted or restricted response option (Figure 13-10). If the restricted option is selected, the destination DTE must respond to the Call Indication with a Clear Request packet, which may also contain up to 128 octets of user data. Thus a virtual circuit has been created and destroyed with one exchange, and 128 octets have been transmitted in both directions.

TABLE 13-3   **Essential Optional Packet-Switched User Facilities (X.2)**

Assigned for an Agreed Contractual Period

Flow Control Parameter Negotiation

This facility permits negotiation on a per call basis of the window size and maximum user data field length to be used on that call in each directon.

Throughput Class Negotiation

This facility permits negotiation on a per call basis of the number of bits of data that can be transferred on a virtual circuit. The range of values is 75 bps to 48 Kbps.

Closed User Group

This enables the DTE to belong to one or more closed user groups. A closed user group permits the DTEs belonging to the group to communicate with each other but precludes communication with all other DTEs. Thus members are protected by the network from unauthorized access. A DTE may belong to one or more closed user groups.

Fast Select Acceptance

This facility authorizes the DCE to transmit to the DTE incoming Fast Select calls. Without such authorization, the DCE blocks such incoming calls. This is useful to prevent the enlarged Fast Select packets from being delivered to a DTE that has not implemented Fast Select.

Incoming Calls Barred

This facility prevents incoming calls from being presented to the DTE.

Outgoing Calls Barred

This facility prevents the DCE from accepting outgoing virtual calls.

One-way Logical Channel Outgoing

This facility sets the Lowest Outgoing Channel boundary (Figure 13-12). A subscriber reserves a number of logical channels in this fashion to match an expected or desired pattern of calls.

Requested on a Per-Virtual-Call Basis

Flow Control Parameter Negotiation

When a DTE has subscribed to this facility, it may, in a CALL REQUEST packet, separately request user data field sizes and window sizes. The DCE indicates its acceptance or modification of these values in the CALL CONNECTED packet. The DCE may modify window size requests in the direction of $W = 2$, and may modify user data field size requests in the direction of 128 octets.

Throughput Class Negotiation

Operates in a manner similar to Flow Control Parameter Negotiation. The DCE may revise the proposed values in either direction to values smaller than those requested.

Closed User Group Selection

When a DTE has subscribed to this facility, it may, in a CALL REQUEST packet, indicate the closed user group applicable to this call. Similarly, the DCE can indicate the closed user group applicable to an incoming call in a INCOMING CALL packet.

Fast Select

The DTE may employ the fast select facility.

Transit Delay Selection and Identification

The DTE may request a particular transit delay that the network will attempt to meet.

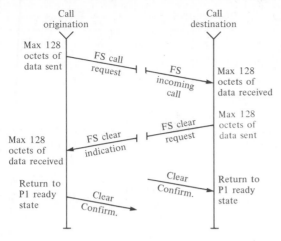

(a) Restricted

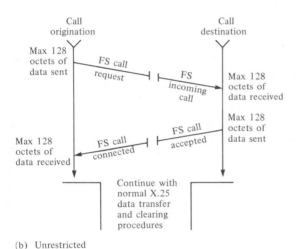

(b) Unrestricted

FIGURE 13-10.   Fast select operation.

If the response is unrestricted, the destination DTE may respond as above. Alternatively, the destination DTE may respond with a Call Accepted packet, augmented with 128 octets of user data. A virtual circuit has now been established and functions as usual.

Summary.   The X.25 standard was developed prior to the OSI model and does not fit cleanly into the model. It is tempting to equate the three levels of X.25 with layers 1 to 3 of the OSI model, but there are difficulties with this assignment.

Levels 1 and 2 of X.25 clearly correspond to layers 1 and 2 of the OSI model. The packet level of X.25 appears to encompass most if not all of the functions of OSI layer 3. However, when the D bit is used, the X.25 packet level provides some end-to-end functionality that appears more typical of a transport protocol. However, we shall see in Chapter 15 that X.25 does not encompass all of the functions one might like in a transport protocol.

NETWORK ACCESS BY COMMON CHANNEL SIGNALING: I.451

Requirements

In Section 8-6, we introduced the concept of common channel control signaling for use with circuit-switched networks. In this scheme, as with packet switching, a station attaches to a network by means of a link that is capable of multiplexing traffic for a number of other stations. There are several key differences:

1. With packet-switching, a number of virtual circuits may be set up between the station and other stations on the network. Traffic is in the form of packets over the physical link between the station and the network. In effect, statistical time-division multiplexing is used; the single link carries packets for various circuits, one at a time. With circuit-switching, two cases are possible. The simplest case, typified by a residential subscriber to a traditional telephone network, is that there is a single physical link between the station and the network that can support a single "real" circuit to some other station. A more complex case, typical of office subscribers, is that there is a single physical link between the station and the network that can support a number of circuits. Each circuit is provided with a separate channel on the physical link using synchronous time-division multiplexing.

2. With packet switching, the dialogue for setting up and tearing down a virtual circuit is carried on the virtual circuit itself (i.e., Call Request and Clear Request packets). With circuit switching using common channel signaling, the dialogue for setting up and tearing down a circuit is carried on a separate channel; this scheme is carried on the same physical link as the other channels, using synchronous TDM.

Let us consider what is required, in terms of functions, for two devices to communicate across a circuit-switched network, and relate that to the OSI model. There are two phases of operation that are of interest: the data transfer phase and the control phase.

For the data transfer phase, recall that a circuit-switched network provides a transparent data path between communicating stations. To the attached stations, it appears that they have a direct full-duplex link over some channel. They are free to use their own fomats, protocols, and frame synchronization. This situation was depicted in Figure 13-1b and is also shown in the top portion of Figure 13-11. Each station is attached to a node of the communications network. The dashed line indicates the path of the data and the elements through which it passes. Data from the source station pass through one or more network nodes to the destination node. Because the connection is transparent, the protocol from station to station is just at the physical level. Each node acts as a relay, passing on data from input to output, performing a simple circuit-switching function.

The control phase is more complex. Both calling and called station have a dialogue with an element of the network:

- *Calling station:* sends a call request to the network identifying the called station; receives call progress signals from the network.

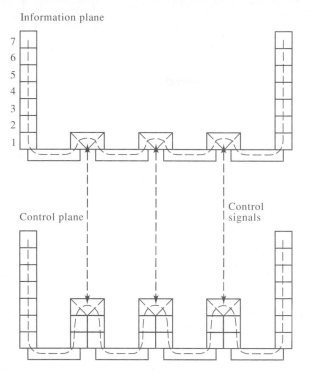

FIGURE 13-11. **OSI configuration for circuit-switched access using common-channel signaling.**

- *Called station:* receives call request from network; sends call acceptance to network.

This dialogue is, in OSI terms, a layer 3 protocol. In addition, internal to the network, control signals are used to set up the circuit. This involves a layer 3 dialogue among the switching nodes of the network.

Thus, the total operation is not covered by the simple diagram of Figure 13-1c. In fact, we need to consider that there are two separate planes of communication, as indicated in Figure 13-11. The transfer of information from one end station to the other involves only the use of layer 1 relaying. The exchange of control information between the user and network supports two general types of functions:

- There is a dialogue between each station and the network to establish the call.
- Call request and call accepted signals are relayed through the network.

In addition, internal control signals are used to set up the circuit and to perform other routing and control functions.

The complete picture is actually even more complex than Figure 13-11 indicates. There is one physical link between the station and the network. A number of logical channels may be used to set up circuits the use the layer 1 relaying indicated in the upper part of the figure. An additional logical channel on that link is used to carry all of the control signals for all of the other channels.

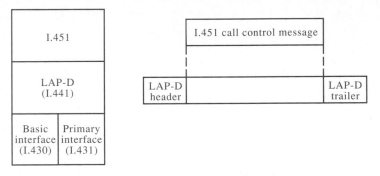

FIGURE 13-12.   Call control communications architecture.

A Standard for Common Channel Signaling: I.451

CCITT has developed a standard, I.451, for common channel signaling. The primary application of this standard is for the Integrated Services Digital Network, which is described in Chapter 18. For purposes of this discussion, we need to know that ISDN is a circuit-switching network that provides for multiple channels be-

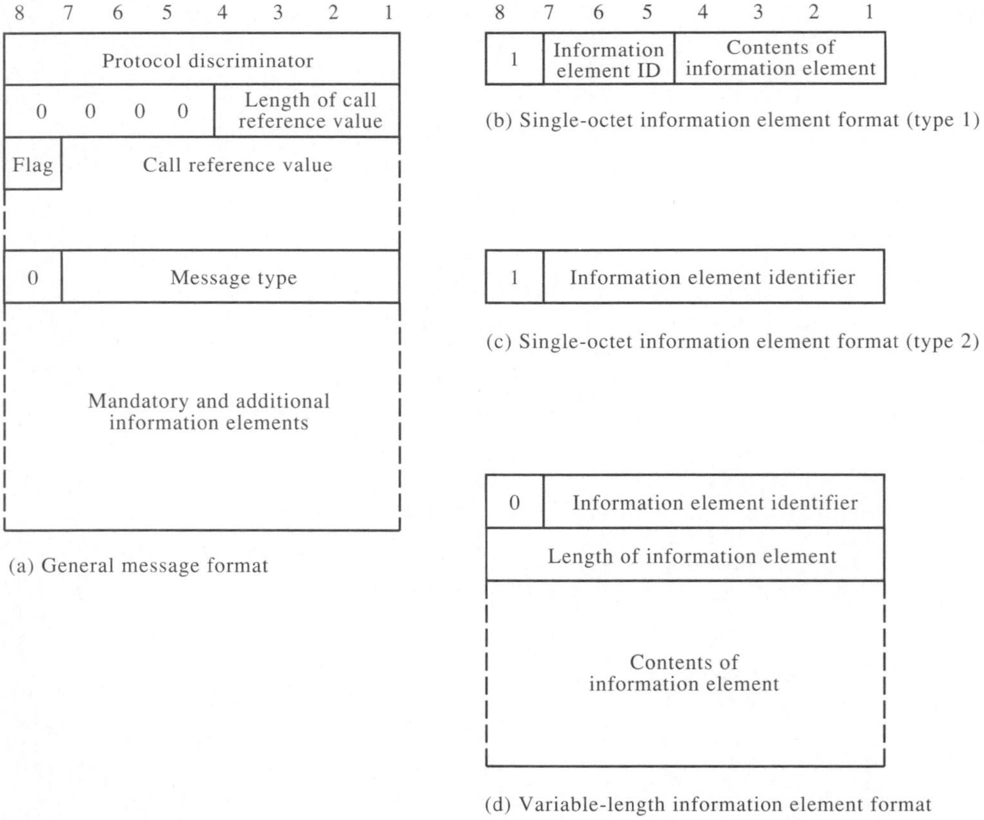

FIGURE 13-13.   I.451 formats.

tween an end station and the network. Channels used to set up end-to-end circuits are referred to as B channels. The channel that is reserved for the transmission of control information is referred to as the D channel I.451 is the control signaling protocol that is used on the D channel.

In OSI terms, I.451 is a layer 3, or network layer, protocol. As Figure 13-12 indicates, I.451 relies on a link layer protocol to transmit messages over the D channel. Each I.451 message is encapsulated in a link-layer frame. The link protocol is I.441, LAP-D; this is very similar to HDLC, discussed in Chapter 5. Finally, the physical layer can be one of two multiplexed TDM structures, referred to as basic and primary, as specified in I.430 and I.431, respectively.

Messages. I.451 specifies procedures for establishing connections on the B channels that share the same physical interface to ISDN as the D channel. It also provides user-to-user control signaling over the D channel.

The process of establishing, controlling, and terminating a call occurs as a result of control signaling messages exchanged between the user and the network over a D channel. A common format is used for all messages defined in I.451, illustrated in Figure 13-13a. Three fields are common to all messages:

- *Protocol discriminator:* used to distinguish messages for user-network call control from other message types. Other sorts of protocols may share the common signaling channel.
- *Call reference:* identifies the user-channel call to which this message refers. As with X.25 virtual circuit numbers, it has only local significance. The call reference field comprises 3 subfields. The length subfield specifies the length of the remainder of the field in octets. This length is one octet for a basic rate interface, and two octets for a primary rate interface. The flag indicates which end of the LAP-D logical connection initiated the call.
- *Message type:* identifies which I.451 message is being sent. The contents of the remainder of the message depend on the message type.

Following these three common fields, the remainder of the message consists of a sequence of zero or more information elements, or parameters. These contain additional information to be conveyed with the message. Thus, the message type specifies a command or response, and the details are provided by the information elements. Some information elements must always be included with a given message (mandatory), and others are optional (additional). Three formats for information elements are used, as indicated in Figures 13-13b through d.

Table 13-4 lists all of the I.451 messages, and the parameters associated with these messages are summarized in Table 13-5. The messages can be grouped along two dimensions. Messages apply to one of four applications: circuit-mode control, packet-mode access connection control, user-to-user signaling not associated with circuit-switched calls, and messages used with the global call reference. In addition messages perform functions in one of four categories: call establishment, call information, call clearing, and miscellaneous.

Circuit-mode control refers to the functions needed to set up, maintain, and clear a circuit-switched connection on a user channel. This function corresponds to call control in existing circuit-switching telecommunications networks. **Packet-mode access connection control** refers to the functions needed to set up a circuit-switched connection (called an access connection in this context) to an ISDN packet-switching node; this connects the user to the packet-switching network pro-

TABLE 13-4   I.451 Messages

Message	Application	Function
Call/Access-Connection Establishment Messages		
ALERTing	C, P, U	Sent by called user and by network to calling user to indicate that called user alerting has been initiated.
CALL PROCeeding	C, P, U	Sent by called user and by network to calling user to indicate that requested establishment has been initiated.
CONNect	C, P, U	Sent by called user and by network to calling user to indicate call/access-connection acceptance by the called user.
CONNect ACKnowledge	C, P, U	Sent by network to called user to indicate the user has been awarded the call/access connection
PROGRESS	C, P	Sent by user or network to indicate progress of a call/access connection in the event of interworking.
SETUP	C, P, U	Sent by calling user and by network to called user to request call/access-connection establishment.
SETUP ACKnowledge	C, U	Sent by network to calling user and called user to network to indicate that call establishment has been initiated but additional information may be required.
Call Information Phase Messages		
RESume	C	Sent by user to request resumption of previously suspended call.
RESume ACKnowledge	C	Sent by network to indicate that requested call has been reestablished.
RESume REJect	C	Sent by network to indicate failure to resume suspended call.
SUSPend	C	Sent by user to request suspension of a call.
SUSPend ACKnowledge	C	Sent by network to indicate that call has been suspended.
SUSPend REJect	C	Sent by network to indicate failure of requested call suspension.
USER INFOrmation	C, U	Sent by user to network and then by network to another user to transfer information between the two users.
Call/Access-Connection Clearing Messages		
DISConnect	C, P	Sent by user or network to indicate call/access connection is completed and the receiver is invited to release the channel and call/access connection reference.
RELease	C, P, U	Sent by either user or network to indicate that the channel and call reference are to be released.
RELease COMplete	C, P, U	Sent by either user or network to indicate acceptance of RELease message and that the channel and call reference are released.
Miscellaneous Messages		
CONgestion CONtrol	C, U	Sent by network or user to set or release flow control on USER INFORMATION messages.
FACility	C	Sent by user to request a network facility and by network when activation of a facility requires user agreement.
INFOrmation	C, U	Sent by network or user to provide additional information.

TABLE 13-4 **(Cont.)**

Message	Application	Function
NOTIFY	C	Sent by user or network to indicate information pertaining to a call.
RESTART	G	Sent by user or network to request the recipient to restart (i.e., return to idle condition) the indicated channel or interface.
RESTART ACKNOWLEDGE	G	Sent by user or network to indicate that the requested restart is complete.
STATUS	C, P, U, G	Sent by user or network in response to a STATUS ENQUIRY or at any time to report an error condition.
STATUS ENQUIRY	C, P, U	Sent by user or network to solicit STATUS message from peer entity.

C = Messages for circuit-mode connection control
P = Messages for packet-mode access connection control
U = Messages for user-to-user signaling not associated with circuit-switched calls
G = Messages used with the global call reference

vided by the ISDN provider. **User-to-user signaling messages** allow two users to communicate without setting up a circuit-switched connection. A temporary signaling connection is established and cleared in a manner similar to the control of a circuit-switched connection. Signaling takes place over the signaling channel and thus does not consume user-channel resources. Finally, **global call reference** refers to the functions that enable user or network to return one or more channels to an idle condition.

Call establishment messages are used to initially set up a call. This group includes messages between the calling terminal and the network (SETUP, SETUP ACK, CALL PROC, CONN, PROGRESS) and between the network and the called terminal (SETUP, ALERT, CONN, CONN ACK, PROGRESS). These messages support the following services:

- Set up a user-channel call in response to user request.
- Provide particular network facilities for this call.
- Inform calling user of the progress of the call establishment process.

Once a call has been set up, but prior to the disestablishment (termination) phase, **call information** phase messages are sent between user and network. One of the messages in this group allows the network to relay, without modification, information between the two users of the call. The nature of this information is beyond the scope of the standard, but it is assumed that it is control signaling information that can't or should not be sent directly over the user-channel circuit. The remainder of the messages allow users to request the suspension and later resumption of a call. When a call is suspended, the network remembers the identity of the called parties and the network facilities supporting the call, but deactivates the call so that no additional charges are incurred and so that the corresponding user channel is freed up. Presumably, the resumption of a call is quicker and cheaper than the origination of a new call.

TABLE 13-5   **Parameters for I.451 Messages**

Bearer Capability

Indicates provision, by the network, of one of the bearer capabilities defined in I.201. Includes specification of rate adaption if used.

Call Identity

Used to identify a suspended call. It is assigned at the start of call suspension.

Call State

Describes the current status of a call, such as active, detached, and disconnect request.

Called Party Number

Identifies called party. The address field includes an indication of numbering plan plus the actual address. Allowable numbering plans include ISDN, X.121, telephony (E.163), and Telex (F.69).

Called Party Subaddress

Identify subaddress of the called party. The subaddress might identify a particular user or piece of equipment at the called number.

Calling Party Number

Identifies calling party.

Calling Party Subaddress

Identify subaddress of the calling party.

Cause

Used to describe the reason for generating certain messages, to provide diagnostic information in the event of procedural errors and to indicate the location of the cause originator. The location is specified in terms of which network originated the cause.

Channel Identification

Identifies channel/subchannel within the interface (e.g., with B channel).

Congestion Level

Describes the congestion status of the call. Currently, only receiver ready and receiver not ready values are defined.

Connected Address

Indicates which address is connected to a call. This may be different from origination or destination address because of changes (e.g., call redirection) during the call. The address field includes an indication of numbering plan plus the actual address. Allowable numbering plans include ISDN, X.121, telephony (E.163), and Telex (F.69).

Date/Time

Indicates date/time when message was generated by network.

Destination Address

Identifies called party. Address structure as indicated for connected address.

Display

Supplies additional information coded in IA5 (International Alphabet 5, also known as ASCII) characters. Intended for display on user terminal.

Facility

Indicates the invocation and operation of supplementary services.

Feature Activation

Invokes a supplementary service.

Feature Indication

Used by network to convey status of supplementary service.

High Layer Compatibility

To be used to check the compatibility at layers 4 though 7 of the caller and called users. The use and coding of this parameter is for further study.

Keypad Facility

Conveys IA5 characters entered by means of a terminal keypad.

Keypad Echo

Conveys to the user characters received by the network via Keypad.

TABLE 13-5 (Cont.)

Low Layer Compatibility

Used for compatibility checking. Includes information transfer capability, information transfer rate, and protocol identification at layers 1 through 3.

More Data

Transferred between users by the network. The use of this flag is not supervised by the network. Its intended use is to permit one user to alert another that more data is coming in an additional USER INFO message.

Network-Specific Facilities

Allows the specification of facilities peculiar to a particular work.

Notification Indicator

Indicate information pertaining to a call: user suspended, user resumed, or bearer service charge.

Progress Indicator

Describes an event which has occurred during the life of a call.

Repeat Indicator

Specifies how repeated information elements shall be interpreted.

Restart Indicator

Identifies the class of the channel or interface to be restarted: single interface, all interfaces, indicated channels.

Segmented Message

Indicates that this transmission is part of a segmented message.

Sending Complete

Indicates completion of called party number.

Signal

Conveys indications causing a stimulus mode terminal to generate tones and alerting signals. Example values are dial tone on, ring back tone on, busy tone on, and tones off.

Switchhook

Indicates the state of the stimulus mode terminal switchhook to the network. Values are on-hook and off-hook.

Transit Network Selection

Identity of a network that connection should use to get to final destination. This parameter may be repeated within a message to select a sequence of networks through which a call must pass.

User-User Information

Used to transfer information between ISDN users that should not be interpreted by the network(s).

Call clearing messages are sent between user and network in order to terminate a call. Finally, there are some **miscellaneous** messages that may be sent between user and network at various stages of the call. Some may be sent during call setup; others may be sent even though no calls exist. The primary function of these messages is to negotiate network features (supplementary services).

Circuit-Switched Call Example. Figure 13-14, taken from I.451, is an example of the use of the protocol to set up a user-channel circuit-switched telephone call. We will follow this example through to give the reader an idea of the use of the I.451 protocol. The example is for the placement of a telephone call, but the

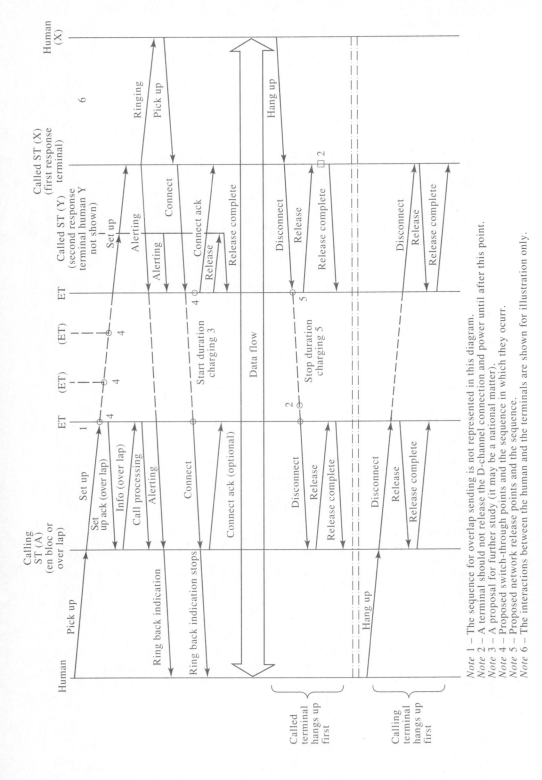

Note 1 – The sequence for overlap sending is not represented in this diagram.
Note 2 – A terminal should not release the D-channel connection and power until after this point.
Note 3 – A proposal for further study (it may be a national matter).
Note 4 – Proposed switch-through points and the sequence in which they ocurr.
Note 5 – Proposed network release points and the sequence.
Note 6 – The interactions between the human and the terminals are shown for illustration only.

FIGURE 13-14. Procedure for an I.451 call.

sequence would be similar for a computer-to-computer or terminal-to-computer data call.

The process begins when a calling subscriber lifts the handset. The ISDN-compatible telephone insures that the signaling channel is active before itself generating a dial tone (not shown). When the subscriber keys in the called number (not shown), the telephone set accumulates the digits, and when all are keyed in, sends a SETUP message over the signaling channel to the exchange. The SETUP message includes the destination number, a channel identification which specifies which user channel is to be used, and any requested network services or facilities (e.g., reverse charging).

The SETUP message triggers two activities at the local exchange. First, using internal control signaling, the local exchange sends a message through the network that results in designating a route for the requested call and allocating resources for that call. Second, the exchange sends back a CALL PROC message indicating that call setup is underway. The exchange may also request more information from the caller (via SETUP ACK and INFO). When the internal control message reaches the remote exchange, it sends a SETUP message to the called telephone. The called telephone accepts the call by sending an ALERT message to the network and generating a ringing tone. The ALERT message is transmitted all the way back to the calling telephone set. When the called party lifts the handset, the telephone sends a CONN message to the network. The local exchange sends a CONN ACK message to its subscriber and forwards the CONN message to the calling exchange, and it in turn forwards it to the calling telephone. The circuit is now available for the called and calling telephone.

Because the call setup process makes use of common channel signaling, other channels are undisturbed, and the fact that all of the user channels are engaged does not prevent the signaling channel dialogue. For example, even if all of a user's channels are assigned to circuits, an incoming call request will be presented to the user via the signaling channel; the user can, if desired, put a call in progress on hold in order to use the corresponding user channel for the new call.

Once the circuit is set up, full duplex 64-kbps data streams are exchanged via the user channel between the two end users. Additional signaling messages, such as call information phase messages, may be transmitted during this period.

Call termination begins when one of the telephone users hangs up. This causes a DISC message to be sent from the telephone to the exchange. The exchange responds with a REL message and when the telephone sends REL COM the user channel is released. The complementary action takes place at the other telephone-network interface.

13-3

BROADCAST NETWORK ACCESS: LLC

We turn now to the third type of network discussed in Part II: broadcast networks. As might be expected, the access method for broadcast networks must reflect requirements that are different from those of either circuit-switched or packet-switched networks. The key difference is that, typically, broadcast networks do not require the routing function. The only systematic work on standards that has been done in this area is for local networks. We will examine one of these standards: the IEEE 802 standard.

IEEE 802 Architecture

The IEEE 802 Committee has developed a three-layer architecture for local network access that, in their view, corresponds to layer 1 and 2 of the OSI model. Before considering their reasoning, let us look at the functions, in terms of OSI layers, that are required to communicate across a local network.

What OSI layers are needed? Layer 1, certainly. Physical connection is required. Layer 2 is also needed. Data transmitted across the network must be organized into frames and control must be exercised. But what about layer 3? The answer is yes and no. If we look at the functions performed by layer 3, the answer would seem to be no. First, there is routing. But with a direct link available between any two points, this is not needed. The other functions (addressing, sequencing, flow control, error control, etc.) are, we learned, also performed by layer 2. The difference is that layer 2 performs these functions across a single link, whereas layer 3 may perform them across the sequence of links required to traverse the network. But since only one link is required to traverse the network, these layer 3 functions are redundant and superfluous!

From the point of view of an attached station, the answer would seem to be yes, the network must provide layer 3. The station sees itself attached to an access point into a network supporting communication with multiple devices. The layer for assuring that a message sent across that access point is delivered to one of a number of end points would seem to be a layer 3 function. So we can say that although the network provides services up through layer 3, the characteristics of the network allow these services to be implemented on two OSI layers. The corollary to this conclusion is that no network layer in the OSI sense is needed, and that the services provided by the network are directly accessible to layer 4 (transport).

With the points made above in mind, let us now think about the functional requirements for controlling a local network and examine these from the top down. We follow the reasoning, illustrated in Figure 13-15, used by the IEEE 802 committee [IEEE85e].

At the highest level are the functions associated with accepting transmissions from and delivering receptions to attached stations. These functions include:

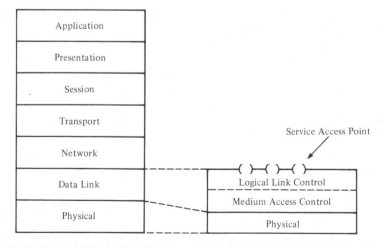

FIGURE 13-15.   IEEE 802 reference model relationship to OSI model.

- Provide one or more service access points. A service access point (SAP), recall, is a logical interface between two adjacent layers.
- On transmission, assemble data into a frame with address and CRC fields.
- On reception, disassemble frame, perform address recognition and CRC validation.
- Manage communication over the link.

These are the functions typically associated with layer 2, the data link layer. The first three, and related functions, are grouped into a logical link control (LLC) layer by IEEE 802. The last function is treated as a separate layer, called medium access control (MAC). This is done for the following reasons:

- The logic required to manage access to a multiple-source, multiple-destination link is not found in traditional layer 2 link control.
- For the same LLC, several MAC options are provided, as was shown in Figure 11-23.

Finally, at the lowest layer, are the functions generally associated with the physical layer. These include:

- Encoding/decoding of signals.
- Preamble generation/removal (for synchronization).
- Bit transmission/reception.

As with the OSI model, these functions are assigned to a physical layer in the IEEE 802 standard.

IEEE 802 Operation

The details of the physical and MAC layers of IEEE 802 were explored in Chapter 11. It remains to examine LLC. Before turning to that topic, it is useful to examine the operation of the overall architecture and the way in which the three layers interact.

Figure 13-16 depicts the relationship. In the figure we show a functioning architecture up through OSI layer 4; the layers above that are not relevant to this discussion. The LLC layer provides a service for moving frames of data from one station on the LAN to another. The transport layer provides end-to-end reliability. Thus, the user of transport is guaranteed that its data will be delivered with no losses and no misorderings. We can trace the operation of this architecture on a single unit of user data in Figure 13-16b, which is keyed to event times marked on Figure 13-16a. At some time t_0, the user of transport presents a block of data to transport. The transport entity encapsulates this data with a transport header and passes the resulting data unit to LLC (t_1). LLC adds its own header and passes the result to MAC (t_2). The LLC header includes the source and destination service access points (plus more; see below). These are needed at the LLC level in order to transfer data to and from higher-level users. In this example, the LLC user is a transport entity, but different LLC SAPs may be associated with different users at the application level, and this information may be used by transport to keep track of different users.

MAC accepts the LLC data unit, appends both a MAC header and a MAC trailer, and passes the resulting frame to the physical layer, which transmits the frame

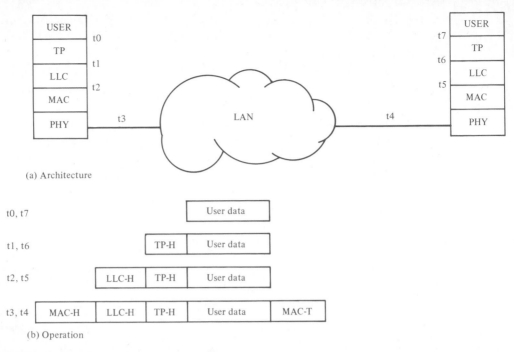

(a) Architecture

FIGURE 13-16.   A LAN communication architecture.

across the LAN (t_3). The MAC header includes destination and source address fields that identify the station or LAN attachment point. This address is needed at the MAC level so that the MAC entity may recognize its own address on frames transmitted to it by other stations. We elaborate on this point below. The MAC trailer includes a frame check sequence field, which is used for error detection. The remaining MAC fields have to do with the control mechanisms within the specific MAC protocol, and need not concern us here (see [STAL90a] or [STAL90d]).

The frame on the LAN will be copied by the station whose address appears in the MAC destination address field (t_4). The user's block of data then moves up through the layers, with the appropriate headers and trailers stripped off at each layer (t_5, t_6, t_7).

Logical Link Control

The IEEE 802 Committee defined not only the LLC protocol, which we may think of as a DCE-DCE protocol, but also an interface for a higher layer. This interface provides the network access mechanism. The logical configuration is depicted in Figure 13-15 and can be seen to be equivalent to Figure 13-1d. That is, access to the network is provided by means of an *interface* to LLC. This is in contrast to X.25, where access is provided by a packet level *protocol* (Figure 13-1a). Thus it is sufficient to examine the interface that LLC provides to higher-level protocols. It is also of some interest to examine the LLC protocol itself, even though this is an intranetwork protocol. We begin by looking at the general link layer requirements for local networks, and then turn to the IEEE 802 specification.

Principles. The link layers for LANs should bear some resemblance to the more common link layers extant. Like all link layers, the LAN link layer is concerned with the transmission of a frame of data between two stations, with no intermediate switching nodes.

It differs from traditional link layers in three ways:

- It must support the multiaccess nature of the link (this differs from multidrop in that there is no primary node).
- It is relieved of some details of link access by the medium access control (MAC) layer.
- It must provide some layer 3 functions.

At a minimum, the link layer should perform those functions normally associated with that layer:

- *Error control:* end-to-end error control and acknowledgment. The link layer should guarantee error-free transmission across the LAN.
- *Flow control:* end-to-end flow control.

These functions can be provided in much the same way as for HDLC and other point-to-point link protocols: by the use of sequence numbers.

It has already been mentioned that because of the lack of intermediate switching nodes, a LAN does not require a separate layer 3; rather, the essential layer three functions can be incorporated into layer 2:

- *Connectionless:* Some form of connectionless service is needed for efficient support of highly interactive traffic.
- *Connection-oriented:* A connection-oriented service is also usually needed.
- *Multiplexing:* Generally, a single physical link attaches a station to a LAN; it should be possible to provide data transfer with multiple endpoints over that link.

Because there is no need for routing, the above functions are easily provided. The connectionless service simply requires the use of source and destination address fields. The station sending the frame must designate the destination address, so that the frame is delivered properly. The source address must also be indicated so that the recipient knows where the frame came from.

Both the connection-oriented and multiplexing capabilities can be supported with the concept of the service access point (SAP), introduced in Chapter 12. An example may make this clear. Figure 13-17 shows three stations attached to a LAN. Each station has an address. Further, the link layer supports multiple SAPs, each with its own address. The link layer provides communication between SAPs. Assume that a process or application X in station A wishes to send a message to a process in station C. X may be a report generator program in minicomputer A. C may be a printer and a simple printer driver. X attaches itself to SAP 1 and requests a connection to station C, SAP 1 (station C may have only one SAP if it is a single printer). Station A's link layer then sends to the LAN a "connection-request" frame which includes the source address $(A,1)$, the destination address $(C,1)$, and some control bits indicating that this is a connection request. The LAN delivers this frame to C, which, if it is free, returns a "connection-accepted" frame. Henceforth, all data from X will be assembled into a frame by A's LLC, which includes source $(A,1)$ and destination $(C,1)$ addresses. Incoming frames addressed to $(A,1)$ will be rejected unless they are from $(C,1)$; these might be

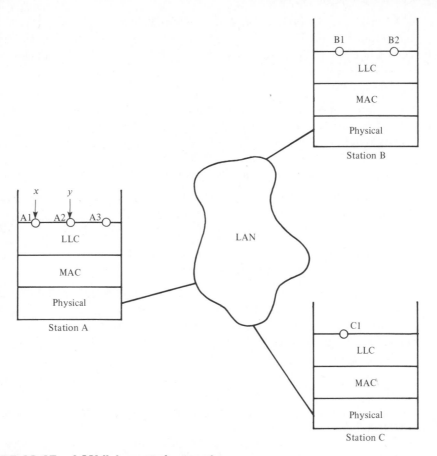

FIGURE 13-17.   LAN link control scenario.

acknowledgment frames, for example. Similarly, station C's printer is declared busy and C will only accept frames from $(A,1)$.

Thus a connection-oriented service is provided. At the same time, process Y could attach to $(A,2)$ and exchange data with $(B,1)$. This is an example of multiplexing. In addition, various other processes in A could use $(A,3)$ to send datagrams to various destinations.

One final function of the link layer should be included, to take advantage of the multiple-access nature of the LAN:

- *Multicast, broadcast:* The link layer should provide a service of sending a message to multiple stations or all stations.

With these requirements in mind, we turn to the 802 specification.

LLC Services.   LLC provides three services:

- *Unacknowledged connectionless service:* This service simply allows for sending and receiving frames. It supports point-to-point, multipoint, and broadcast.
- *Connection-oriented service:* This provides a logical connection between service access points. It provides flow control, sequencing, and error recovery.

TABLE 13-6 Logical Link Control Primitives

UNACKNOWLEDGED CONNECTIONLESS SERVICE

DL-UNITDATA.request (source-address, destination-address, data, priority)
DL-UNITDATA.indication (source-address, destination-address, data, priority)

CONNECTION-MODE SERVICE

DL-CONNECT.request (source-address, destination-address, priority)
DL-CONNECT.indication (source-address, destination-address, priority)
DL-CONNECT.response (source-address, destination-address, priority)
DL-CONNECT.confirm (source-address, destination-address, priority)

DL-DATA.request (source-address, destination-address, data)
DL-DATA.indication (source-address, destination-address, data)

DL-DISCONNECT.request (source-address, destination-address)
DL-DISCONNECT.indication (source-address, destination-address, reason)

DL-RESET.request (source-address, destination-address)
DL-RESET.indication (source-address, destination-address, reason)
DL-RESET.response (source-address, destination-address)
DL-RESET.confirm (source-address, destination-address)

DL-CONNECTION-FLOWCONTROL.request (source-address, destination-address, amount)
DL-CONNECTION-FLOWCONTROL.indication (source-address, destination-address, amount)

ACKNOWLEDGED CONNECTIONLESS SERVICE

DL-DATA-ACK.request (source-address, destination-address, data, priority, service-class)
DL-DATA-ACK.indication (source-address, destination-address, data, priority, service-class)
DL-DATA-ACK-STATUS.indication (source-address, destination-address, priority, service-class, status)
DL-REPLY.request (source-address, destination-address, data, priority, service-class)
DL-REPLY.indication (source-address, destination-address, data, priority, service-class)
DL-REPLY-STATUS.indication (source-address, destination-address, data, priority, service-class, status)

DL-REPLY-UPDATE.request (source-address, data)
DL-REPLY-UPDATE-STATUS.indication (source-address, status)

- *Acknowledged connectionless service:* This service, although connectionless, provides for acknowledgment of individual frames, relieving higher layers of this burden. It supports point-to-point transfers.

These services are specified in terms of primitives which can be viewed as commands or procedure calls with parameters. Table 13-6 summarizes the LLC primitives.

The **Unacknowledged Connectionless Service** is a datagram style of service that simply allows for sending and receiving LLC frames, with no form of acknowledgment to assure delivery. It supports point-to-point, multipoint, and broadcast addressing.

This service provides for only two primitives across the interface between the next higher layer and LLC. DL-UNITDATA.request is used to pass a block of data down to LLC for transmission. DL-UNITDATA.indication is used to pass that block of data up to the destination user from LLC upon reception. The source-address and destination-address parameters specify the local and remote LLC users, respectively. Each of these parameters actually is a combination of LLC service access point and the MAC address. The data parameter is the block of data transmitted from one LLC user to another. The priority parameter specifies the desired parameter. This (together with the MAC portion of the address) is passed down through the LLC entity to the MAC entity, which has the responsibility of implementing a priority mechanism. Token bus (IEEE 802.4) and token ring (IEEE 802.5, FDDI) are capable of this, but the 802.3 CSMA/CD system is not.

The **Connection-Oriented Service** provides a virtual-circuit style connection between service access points (between users). It provides a means by which a user can request or be notified of the establishment or termination of a logical connection. It also provides flow control, sequencing, and error recovery. It supports point-to-point addressing.

This service includes the DL-CONNECT set of primitives (request, indication, response, confirm) to establish a logical connection between SAPs. Once the connection is established, blocks of data are exchanged using DL-DATA.request and DL-DATA.indication. Because the existence of a logical connection guarantees that all blocks of data will be delivered reliably, there is no need for an acknowledgment (via indication and confirm primitives) of individual blocks of data. At any point, either side may terminate the connection with a DL-DISCO-NECT.request; the other side is informed with a DL-DISCONNECT.indication.

The DL-RESET primitives are used to reset a logical connection to an initial state. Sequence numbers are reset, and the connection is reinitialized. Finally, the two flow control primitives regulate the flow of data across the SAP. The flow can be controlled in either direction. This is a local flow control mechanism which specifies the amount of data that may be passed across the SAP.

A diagram might be useful at this point to clarify the relationship of the various primitives (Figure 13-18). A request primitive is passed down from an LLC user to the LLC entity in a station to request that LLC initiate a service. The LLC entity responds by sending a frame across the LAN to the LLC entity in another station, using the protocol explained below. When the frame arrives, the receiving LLC entity uses an indication primitive to pass data or status information up to one of its users. In a connection-oriented service, the receiving LLC user acknowledges receipt by issuing a response primitive down to its LLC entity. The LLC entity sends an acknowledgment frame across the LAN. When this acknowledgment is received, the original LLC entity passes a confirm primitive up to its user.

The **Acknowledged Connectionless Service** provides a mechanism by which a user can send a unit of data and receive an acknowledgment that the data was delivered, without the necessity of setting up a connection.

This service includes DL-DATA-ACK.request and DL-DATA-ACK.indication with meanings analogous to those for the Unacknowledged Connectionless Service, plus DL-DATA-ACK-STATUS.indication to provide acknowledgment to the sending user. The DL-REPLY primitives provide a data exchange service. It allows a user to request that data be returned from a remote station or that data units be exchanged with a remote station. Associated with these primitives are the DL-REPLY-UPDATE primitives. These primitives allow a user to pass data to LLC to be held, and sent out at a later time when requested to do so (by a DL-REPLY primitive) by some other station.

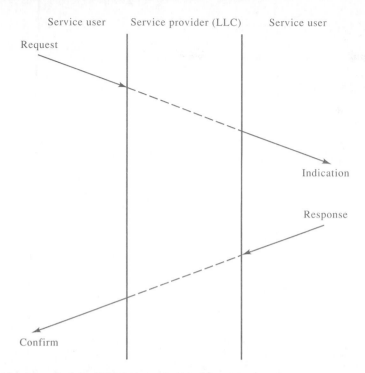

Service user   Service provider (LLC)   Service user

Request

Indication

Response

Confirm

FIGURE 13-18. Relationship among LLC primitives.

LLC Protocol. The LLC frame consists of four fields:

- Destination service access point (1 octet).
- Source service access point (1 octet).
- Control (1–2 octets).
- Data

The source and destination are uniquely specified by a (node, service access point) pair. However, the node address is also used by MAC and is included in the outer MAC frame.

The LLC protocol is modeled after the HDLC balanced mode, and has similar formats and functions. These similarities are summarized briefly in this section. The reader should be able to see how this protocol supports the LLC services defined above.

The first two fields in the LLC frame, the DSAP and SSAP fields, actually contain 7-bit addresses. The least significant bit of DSAP indicates whether this is an individual or group address. The least significant bit of SSAP indicates whether this is a command or response frame.

The format of the LLC control field is identical to that of HDLC (Figure 5-14), using extended (7-bit) sequence numbers. The functioning of LLC is essentially the same as that of HDLC, with four exceptions. First, LLC only makes use of the asynchronous balanced mode of operation, and does not employ normal response mode or asynchronous response mode. This mode is used to support connection-oriented service. The set asynchronous balanced mode (SABM) command is used to establish a connection, and disconnect (DISC) is used to terminate the connection.

Second, LLC supports connectionless service by using the unnumbered information (UI) frame.

Third, LLC permits multiplexing by the use of service access points.

Finally, LLC supports the acknowledge connectionless service by using two new unnumbered frames.

13-4

RECOMMENDED READING

There is a large literature on X.25. [RYBC80], [SIRB85], and [DHAS86] are recommended. [MEIJ82] and [MART81] are additional useful sources. [BURG83] is a discussion of the practical application of X.25.

I.451 is covered in [STAL89].

The IEEE 802 LLC is discussed in more detail in [STAL90a], [STAL90d], and [FIEL86].

An abstract discussion of OSI layer 3 functionality is presented in [WARE83].

13-5

PROBLEMS

13-1 Flow control mechanisms are used at both levels 2 and 3 of X.25. Are both necessary or is this redundant? Explain.

13-2 A DTE wishes to send X octets of data to another DTE using X.25. Its choices are (a) permanent virtual circuit, (b) virtual call, and (c) fast select. What is the total number and percentage of overhead bits? Answer for $X = 128$, 1280, and 12,800 bytes.

13-3 When an X.25 DTE and DCE both decide to put a call through at the same time, a call collision occurs and the incoming call is canceled. When both sides try to clear simultaneously, the clear collision is resolved without canceling either request. Do you think that simultaneous resets are handled like call collisions or clear collisions? Why?

13-4 Figure 13-8 presents two different schemes for packet acknowledgment. Each has certain implications for delay and reliability. Compare the two schemes in these two areas.

13-5 Which of the parameters from Table 13-5 are used by each of the messages in Table 13-4?

13-6 Refer to Figure 13-16. Why is a trailer needed at the MAC layer but not at any of the higher layers?

13-7 Why is there not an LLC primitive L-CONNECTION-FLOWCONTROL.confirm?

13-8 Show, with an example, how the LLC protocol provides LLC services as defined by the LLC primitives.

CHAPTER 14

Internetworking

Packet-switched and packet broadcasting networks grew out of a need to allow the computer user to have access to resources beyond that available in a single system. In a similar fashion, the resources of a single network are often inadequate to meet users' needs. Because the networks that might be of interest exhibit so many differences, it is impractical to consider merging them into a single network. Rather, what is needed is the ability to interconnect various networks so that any two stations on any of the constituent networks can communicate.

Table 14-1 lists some commonly-used terms relating to the interconnection of networks, or internetworking. An interconnected set of networks, from a user's point of view, may appear simply as a larger network. However, if each of the constituent networks retains its identity and special mechanisms are needed for communicating across multiple networks, then the entire configuration is often referred to as an **internet,** and each of the constituent networks as a **subnetwork.**

Each constituent subnetwork in an internet supports communication among the devices attached to that subnetwork. In addition, subnetworks are connected by devices referred to in the ISO documents as **interworking units** (IWUs).[1] IWUs provide a communications path and perform the necessary relaying and routing functions so that data can be exchanged between devices attached to different subnetworks in the internet.

Two types of IWUs of particular interest are bridges and routers. The differences between them have to do with the types of protocols used for the internetworking logic. In essence, a bridge operates at layer 2 of the open systems interconnection

---

[1]The term *gateway* is sometime used to refer to an IWU or to a particular kind of IWU. Because of the lack of consistency in the use of this term, we will avoid it.

TABLE 14-1 Internetworking Terms

Communication Network
  A facility that provides a data transfer service among stations attached to the network.
Internet
  A collection of communication networks interconnected by bridges and/or routers.
Subnetwork
  Refers to a constituent network of an internet. This avoids ambiguity since the entire
  internet, from a user's point of view, is a single network.
Interworking Unit (IWU)
  A device used to connect two subnetworks and permit communication between end
  systems attached to different subnetworks.
Bridge
  An IWU used to connect two LANs that use identical LAN protocols. The bridge acts
  as an address filter, picking up packets from one LAN that are intended for a destination on another LAN and passing those packets on. The bridge does not modify the
  contents of the packets and does not add anything to the packet. The bridge operates at
  layer 2 of the OSI model.
Router
  A device used to connect two networks that may or may not be similar. The router
  employs an internet protocol present in each router and each host of the network. The
  router operates at layer 3 of the OSI model.

(OSI) 7-layer architecture and acts as a relay of frames between like networks. A router operates at layer 3 of the OSI architecture and routes packets between potential networks. Both the bridge and the router assume that the same upper-layer protocols are in use.

We begin our examination with a discussion of the principles underlying various approaches to internetworking. We then examine the three principal architectural approaches to internetworking: bridge, connectionless layer 3 routers, and connection-oriented routers. These three approaches are explored in some detail.

14-1

PRINCIPLES OF INTERNETWORKING

Requirements

Although a variety of approaches have been taken to provide internetwork service, the overall requirements on the internetworking facility can be stated in general. These include:

1. Provide a link between networks. At minimum, a physical and link control connection is needed.
2. Provide for the routing and delivery of data between processes on different networks.
3. Provide an accounting service that keeps track of the use of the various networks and gateways and maintains status information.

4. Provide the services listed above in such a way as not to require modifications to the networking architecture of any of the constituent networks. This means that the internetworking facility must accommodate a number of differences among networks. These include:

a. *Different addressing schemes:* The networks may use different endpoint names and addresses and directory maintenance schemes. Some form of global network addressing must be provided, as well as a directory service.

b. *Different maximum packet size:* Packets from one network may have to be broken up into smaller pieces for another. This process is referred to as segmentation.

c. *Different network access mechanisms:* The network access mechanism between station and network may be different for stations on different networks.

d. *Different timeouts:* Typically, a connection-oriented transport service will await an acknowledgment until a timeout expires, at which time it will retransmit its block of data. In general, longer times are required for successful delivery across multiple networks. Internetwork timing procedures must allow successful transmission that avoids unnecessary retransmissions.

e. *Error recovery:* Intranetwork procedures may provide anything from no error recovery up to reliable end-to-end (within the network) service. The internetwork service should not depend on nor be interfered with by the nature of the individual network's error recovery capability.

f. *Status reporting:* Different networks report status and performance differently. Yet it must be possible for the internetworking facility to provide such information on internetworking activity to interested and authorized processes.

g. *Routing techniques:* Intranetwork routing may depend on fault detection and congestion control techniques peculiar to each network. The internetworking facility must be able to coordinate these to adaptively route data between stations on different networks.

h. *User access control:* Each network will have its own user access control technique (authorization for use of the network). These must be invoked by the internetwork facility as needed. Further, a separate internetwork access control technique may be required.

i. *Connection, connectionless:* Individual networks may provide connection-oriented (e.g., virtual circuit) or connectionless (datagram) service. It may be desirable for the internetwork service not to depend on the nature of the connection service of the individual networks.

These points are worthy of further comment but are best pursued in the context of specific architectural approaches. We outline these approaches next, and then turn to a more detailed discussion of each approach.

Architectural Approaches

In describing the interworking function, two dimensions are important:

• The mode of operation (connection-mode or connectionless)
• The protocol architecture

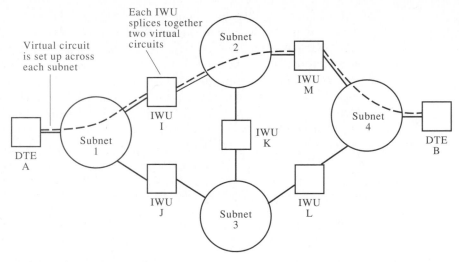

(a) Connection-mode operation

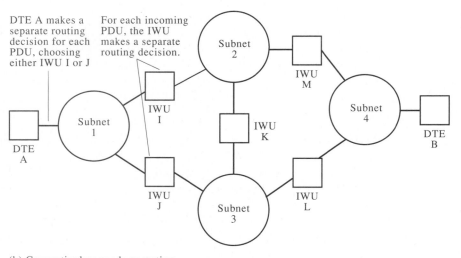

(b) Connectionless-mode operation

FIGURE 14-1. Internetworking approaches.

The mode of operation determines the protocol architecture. ISO has standardized two general approaches [ISRA87,WEIS87], as depicted in Figure 14-1.

Connection-Mode Operation. In the connection-mode operation, it is assumed that each subnetwork provides a connection-mode form of service. That is, it is possible to establish a logical network connection (e.g., virtual circuit) between any two DTEs attached to the same subnetwork. With this in mind, we can summarize the connection-mode approach as follows:

1. Interworking units (IWU) are used to connect two or more subnetworks; each IWU appears as a DTE to each of the subnetworks to which it is attached.
2. When DTE A wishes to exchange data with DTE B, a logical connection is

set up between them. This logical connection consists of the concatenation of a sequence of logical connections across subnetworks. The sequence is such that it forms a path from DTE A to DTE B.

3. The individual subnetwork logical connections are spliced together by IWUs. For example, there is a logical connection from DTE A to IWU I across subnetwork 1, and another logical connection from IWU I to IWU M across subnetwork 2. Any traffic arriving at IWU I on the first logical connection is retransmitted on the second logical connection and vice versa.

Several additional points can be made about this form of operation. First, this approach is suited to providing support for a connection-oriented network access interface, such as X.25. From the point of view of network users in DTEs A and B, a logical network connection is established between them that provides all of the features of a logical connection across a single network.

The second point to be made is that this approach assumes that there is a connection-mode service available from each subnet and that these services are equivalent. Clearly, this may not always be the case. For example, an IEEE 802 or FDDI local area network provides a service defined by the logical link control (LLC). Two of the options with LLC provide only connectionless service. Therefore, in this case, the subnetwork service must be enhanced. An example of how this would be done is for the IWUs to implement X.25 on top of LLC across the LAN.

Figure 14-2a illustrates the protocol architecture for connection-mode operation. Access to all subnetworks, either inherently or by enhancement, is by means of the same network layer protocol. The interworking units operate at layer 3. As was mentioned, layer 3 IWUs are commonly referred to as routers. A connection-oriented router performs the following key functions:

• *Relaying:* Data units arriving from one subnetwork via the network layer protocol are relayed (retransmitted) on another subnetwork. Traffic is over logical connections that are spliced together at the routers.

• *Routing:* When an end-to-end logical connection, consisting of a sequence of logical connections, is to be set up, each router in the sequence must make a routing decision which determines the next hop in the sequence.

Thus, at layer 3, a relaying operation is performed. It is assumed that all of the end systems share common protocols at layer 4 (transport) and above for successful end-to-end communication.

We examine the connection-oriented approach in Section 14.3.

Connectionless-Mode Operation. Figure 14-1b illustrates the connectionless mode of operation. Whereas connection-mode operation corresponds to the virtual circuit mechanism of a packet-switching network (Figure 9-2c), connectionless-mode operation corresponds to the datagram mechanism of a packet-switching network (Figure 9-2d). Each network protocol data unit is treated independently and routed from source DTE to destination DTE through a series of routers and networks. For each data unit transmitted by A, A makes a decision as to which router should receive the data unit. The data unit hops across the internet from one router to the next until it reaches the destination subnetwork. At each router, a routing decision is made (independently for each data unit) concerning the next hop. Thus, different data units may travel different routes between source and destination DTE.

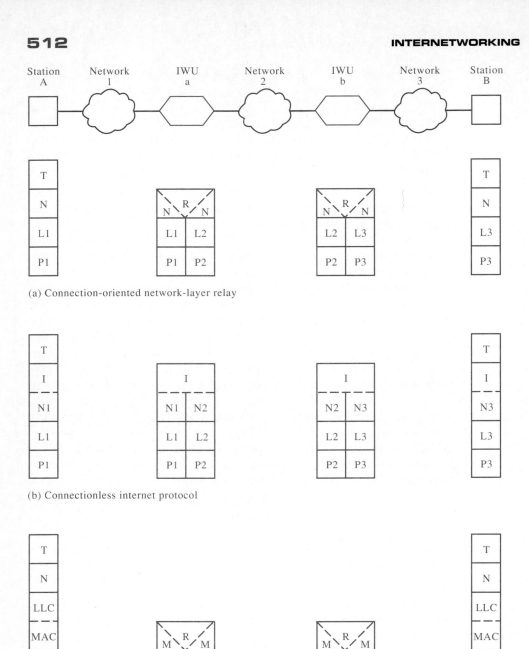

(a) Connection-oriented network-layer relay

(b) Connectionless internet protocol

(c) Bridge

FIGURE 14-2.   Internetwork architectures.

Figure 14-2b illustrates the protocol architecture for connectionless-mode operation. All DTEs and all routers share a common network layer protocol known
generically as the internet protocol (IP). An internet protocol was initially developed for the DARPA internet project, and has been standardized by the U.S.
Department of Defense. The ISO standard, ISO 8473, provides similar functionality. Below this internet protocol, there is needed a protocol to access the particular
subnetwork. Thus, there are typically two protocols operating in each DTE and

router at the network layer: an upper sublayer that provides the internetworking function, and a lower sublayer that provides subnetwork access.

We examine the connectionless internet protocol approach in Section 14.4.

Bridge Approach. A third approach that is quite common is the use of a bridge. The bridge, also known as a MAC-level relay uses a connectionless mode of operation (Figure 14-1b), but does so at a lower level than a router.

The protocol architecture for a bridge is illustrated in Figure 14-2c. In this case, the end systems share common transport and network protocols. In addition, it is assumed that all of the networks use the same protocols at the link layer. In the case of IEEE 802 and FDDI LANs, this means that all of the LANs share a common LLC protocol and a common MAC protocol. For example, all of the LANs are IEEE 802.3 using the unacknowledged connectionless form of LLC. In this case, MAC frames are relayed through bridges between the LANs.

We examine the bridge approach in Section 14.2.

Addressing

In order to transfer data from one DTE to another DTE, there must be some way of uniquely identifying the destination DTE. Thus, with each DTE, we must be able to associate a unique identifier, or address. This address will allow DTEs and IWUs to perform the routing function properly.

In the OSI environment, this unique address is equated to a network service access point (NSAP). An NSAP uniquely identifies a DTE within the internet. A DTE may have more than one NSAP, but each is unique to that particular system. We can refer to such an address as a **global internet address**. Frequently, this address is in the form of (*network, host*), where the parameter *network* identifies a particular subnetwork and the parameter *host* identifies a particular DTE attached to that subnetwork.

Figure 14-3 suggests that another level of addressing may be needed. Each subnetwork must maintain a unique address for each DTE attached to that subnet-

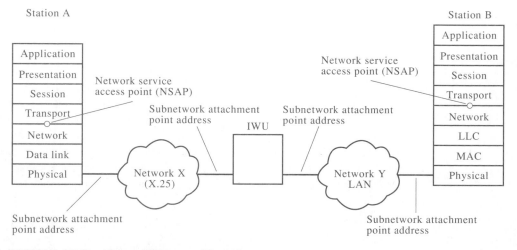

FIGURE 14-3. Network-layer addressing.

work. This allows the subnetwork to route data units through the subnetwork and deliver them to the intended DTE. We can refer to such an address as a **subnetwork attachment point address.**

It would appear convenient for the *host* parameter in the global address to be identical to the subnetwork attachment point address for that DTE. Unfortunately, this may not always be practical. Different networks use different addressing formats and different address lengths. Furthermore, a station may enjoy more than one attachment point into the same network. Accordingly, we must assume that the *host* parameter has global significance and the subnetwork attachment point address has significance only within a particular subnetwork. In this case, the internetworking facility must translate from the global address to the locally-significant address to route data units.

THE BRIDGE

Functions of a Bridge

The simplest of the internetworking devices is the bridge. This device is designed for use between local area networks (LANs) that use identical protocols for the physical and medium access layers (e.g., all conforming to IEEE 802.3 or all conforming to FDDI). Because the devices all use the same protocols, the amount of processing required at the bridge is minimal. The concept of a bridge was introduced in Chapter 11 as a means of linking multiple rings.

Figure 14-4 illustrates the operation of a bridge between two LANs, A and B. The bridge performs the following functions:

- Read all frames transmitted on A, and accept those addressed to stations on B.
- Using the medium access control protocol for B, retransmit the frames onto B.
- Do the same for B-to-A traffic.

In addition to these basic functions, there are some interesting design considerations:

1. The bridge makes no modifications to the content or format of the frames it receives.
2. The bridge should contain enough buffer space to meet peak demands. Over a short period of time, frames may arrive faster than they can be retransmitted.
3. The bridge must contain addressing and routing intelligence. At a minimum, the bridges must know which addresses are on each network in order to know which frames to forward. Further, there may be more than two networks in a sort of cascade configuration. The bridge must be able to pass along frames intended for networks further on. The subject of routing is explored later in this section.

In summary, the bridge provides an extension to the LAN that requires no modification to the communications software in the stations attached to the LANs. It appears to all stations on the two (or more) LANs that there is a single LAN on

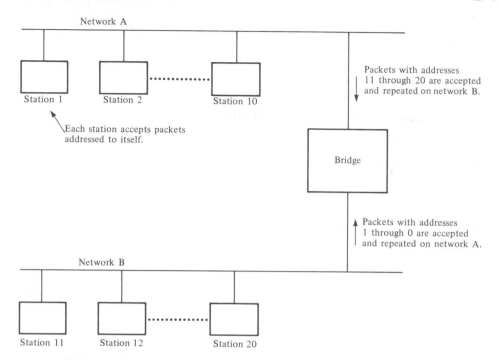

Network A

Station 1

Station 2

Station 10

Packets with addresses
11 through 20 are accepted
and repeated on network B.

Each station accepts packets
addressed to itself.

Bridge

Packets with addresses
1 through 0 are accepted
and repeated on network A.

Network B

Station 11

Station 12

Station 20

FIGURE 14-4. Bridge operation.

which each station has a unique address. The station uses that unique address and need not explicitly discriminate between stations on the same LAN and stations on other LANs; the bridge takes care of that.

Since the bridge is used in a situation in which all of the LANs have the same characteristics, the reader may ask why not simply have one large LAN. Depending on circumstance, there are several reasons for the use of multiple LANs connected by bridges:

- *Reliability:* The danger in connecting all data processing devices in an organization to one network is that a fault on the network may disable communication for all devices. By using bridges, the network can be partitioned into self-contained units.
- *Performance:* In general, performance on a LAN declines with an increase in the number of devices or the length of the medium. A number of smaller LANs will often give improved performance if devices can be clustered so that *intra*-network traffic significantly exceeds *inter*-network traffic.
- *Security*: The establishment of multiple LANs may improve security of communications. It is desirable to keep different types of traffic (e.g., accounting, personnel, strategic planning) that have different security needs on physically separate media. At the same time, the different types of users with different level of security need to communicate through controlled and monitored mechanisms.
- *Geography:* Clearly, two separate LANs are needed to support devices clustered in two geographically distant locations. Even in the case of two buildings separated by a highway, it may be far easier to use a microwave bridge link than to attempt to string coaxial cable between the two buildings. In the case

of widely separated networks, two "half bridges" are needed (see Figures 14-6 and 14-7, below).

The description above has applied to the simplest sort of bridge. More sophisticated bridges can be used in more complex collections of LANs. These would include additional functions, such as:

* Each bridge can maintain status information on other bridges, together with the cost and number of bridge-to-bridge hops required to reach each network. This information may be updated by periodic exchanges of information among bridges. This allows the bridges to perform a dynamic routing function.
* A control mechanism can manage frame buffers in each bridge to overcome congestion. Under saturation conditions, the bridge can give precedence to en-route packets over new packets just entering the internet from an attached LAN, thus preserving the investment in line bandwidth and processing time already made in the enroute frame.

Bridge Protocol Architecture

The IEEE 802 committee has produced two specifications for bridges [IEEE88b, IEEE88c]. In both cases, the devices are referred to as MAC-level relays. In addition, all of the MAC standards suggest formats for a globally administered set of MAC station addresses across multiple homogeneous LANS. In this subsection, we examine the protocol architecture of these bridges.

Within the 802 architecture, the endpoint or station address is designated at the MAC level. At the LLC level, only an SAP address is specified. Thus, it is at the MAC level that a bridge can function. Figure 14-5 shows the simplest case, which

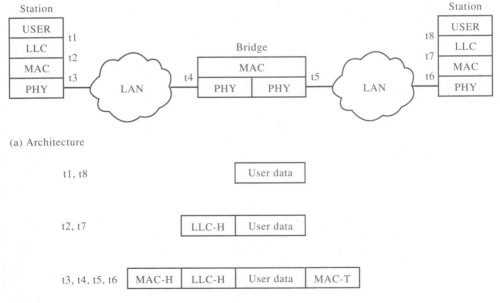

(a) Architecture

t1, t8

t2, t7

t3, t4, t5, t6

(b) Operation

FIGURE 14-5.   Connection of two LANs by a bridge.

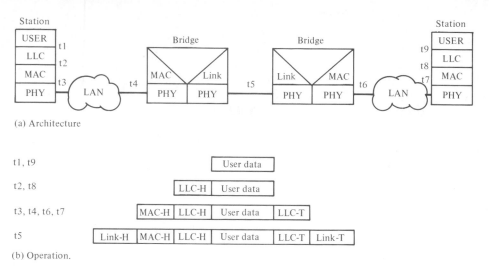

(a) Architecture

t1, t9 | User data |

t2, t8 | LLC-H | User data |

t3, t4, t6, t7 | MAC-H | LLC-H | User data | LLC-T |

t5 | Link-H | MAC-H | LLC-H | User data | LLC-T | Link-T |

(b) Operation.

FIGURE 14-6. Bridge over a point-to-point link.

consists of two LANs connected by a single bridge. The LANs employ the same MAC and LLC protocols. The bridge operates as previously described. A MAC frame whose destination is not on the immediate LAN is captured by the bridge, buffered briefly, and then transmitted on the other LAN. As far as the LLC layer is concerned, there is a dialogue between peer LLC entities in the two endpoint stations. The bridge need not contain an LLC layer since it is merely serving to relay the MAC frames.

Figure 14-5b indicates the way in which data is encapsulated using a bridge. Data is provided by some user to LLC. The LLC entity appends a header and passes the resulting data unit to the MAC entity, which appends a header and a trailer to form a MAC frame. On the basis of the destination MAC address in the frame, it is captured by the bridge. The bridge does not strip of the MAC fields; its function is to relay the MAC frame intact to the destination LAN. Thus the frame is deposited on the destination LAN and captured by the destination station.

The concept of a MAC relay bridge is not limited to the use of a single bridge to connect two nearby LANs. If the LANs are some distance apart, then they can be connected by two bridges that are in turn connected by a communications facility. For example, Figure 14-6 shows the case of two bridges connected by a point-to-point link. In this case, when a bridge captures a MAC frame, it appends a link layer (e.g., HDLC) header and trailer to transmit the MAC frame across the link to the other bridge. The target bridge strips off these link fields and transmits the original, unmodified MAC frame to the destination station.

The intervening communications facility can even be a network, such as a wide-area packet-switching network, as illustrated in Figure 14-7. In this case, the bridge is somewhat more complicated although it performs the same function of relaying MAC frames. The connection between bridges is via an X.25 virtual circuit. Again, the two LLC entities in the end systems have a direct logical relationship with no intervening LLC entities. Thus, in this situation, the X.25 packet layer is operating below an 802 LLC layer. As before, a MAC frame is passed intact between the endpoints. When the bridge on the source LAN receives the frame, it appends an X.25 packet layer header and an X.25 link-layer header and trailer and sends the

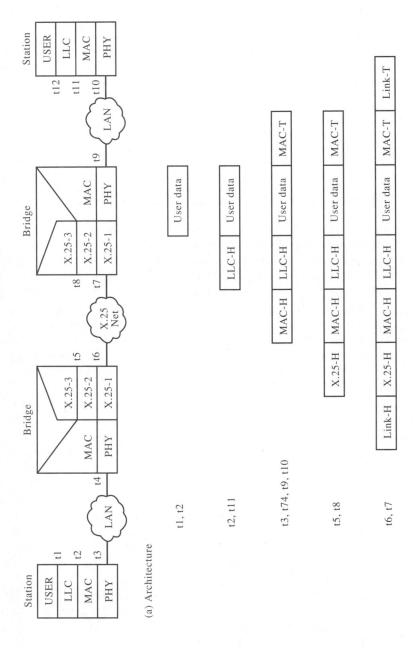

(a) Architecture

(b) Operation

FIGURE 14-7. **Bridge over an X.25 network.**

data to the DCE (packet-switching node) to which it attaches. The DCE strips off the link layer fields and sends the X.25 packet through the network to another DCE. The target DCE appends the link layer field and sends this to the target bridge. The target bridge strips of all the X.25 fields and transmits the original unmodified MAC frame to the destination endpoint.

14-3

ROUTING WITH BRIDGES

In the configuration of Figure 14-4, the bridge makes the decision to relay a frame on the basis of destination MAC address. In a more complex configuration, the bridge must also make a routing decision. Consider the configuration of Figure 14-8. Suppose that station 1 transmits a frame on LAN A intended for station 5. The frame will be read by both bridge 101 and bridge 102. For each bridge, the addressed station is not on a LAN to which the bridge is attached. Therefore, each bridge must make a decision of whether or not to retransmit the frame on its other LAN, in order to move it closer to its intended destination. In this case, bridge 101 should repeat the frame on LAN B, whereas bridge 102 should refrain from retransmitting the frame. Once the frame has been transmitted on LAN B, it will be picked up by both bridges 103 and 104. Again, each must decide whether or not to forward the frame. In this case, bridge 104 should retransmit the frame on LAN E, where it will be received by the destination, station 5.

Thus we see that, in the general case, the bridge must be equipped with a routing capability. When a bridge receives a frame, it must decide whether or not to forward it. If the bridge is attached to more than two networks, then it must decide whether

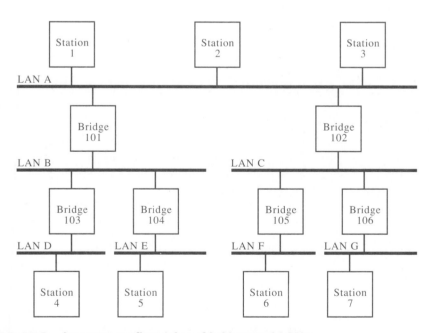

FIGURE 14-8. **Internet configuration of bridges and LANs.**

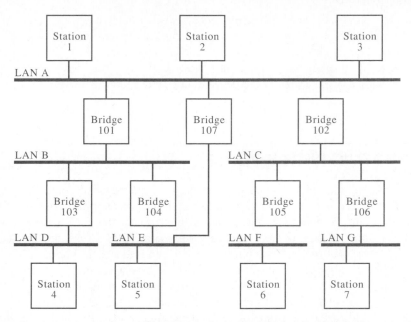

FIGURE 14-9.   Internet configuration of bridges and LANs, with alternate routes.

or not to forward the frame and, if so, on which LAN the frame should be transmitted.

The routing decision may not always be a simple one. In Figure 14-9, bridge 107 is added to the previous configuration, directly linking LAN A and LAN E. Such an addition may be made to provide for higher overall internet availability. In this case, if Station 1 transmits a frame on LAN A intended for station 5 on LAN E, then either bridge 101 or bridge 107 could forward the frame. It would appear preferable for bridge 107 to forward the frame, since it will involve only one "hop," whereas if the frame travels through bridge 101, it must suffer two hops. Another consideration is that there may be changes in the configuration. For example, bridge 107 may fail, in which case subsequent frames from station 1 to station 5 go through bridge 101. So we can say that the routing capability must take into account the topology of the internet configuration and may need to be dynamically altered.

One final point: Figure 14-9 suggests that a bridge knows the identity of each station on each LAN. In a large configuration, such an arrangement is unwieldy. Furthermore, as stations are added to and dropped from LANs, all directories of station location must be updated. It would facilitate the development of a routing capability if all MAC-level addresses were in the form of a network part and a station part. For example, the IEEE 802.5 standard suggests that 16-bit MAC addresses consist of a 7-bit LAN number and an 8-bit station number, and that 48-bit addresses consist of a 14-bit LAN number and a 32-bit station number.[2] In

---

[2]The remaining bit in the 16-bit format is used to indicate whether this is a group or individual address. Of the two remaining bits in the 48-bit format, one is used to indicate whether this is a group or individual address, and the other is used to indicate whether this is a locally-administered or globally-administered address.

the remainder of this discussion, we assume that all MAC addresses include a LAN number and that routing is based on the use of that portion of the address only.

A variety of routing strategies have been proposed and implemented in recent years. The simplest, and most common strategy, is **fixed routing.** This strategy is suitable for small internets and for internets that are relatively stable. More recently, two groups within the IEEE 802 committee and developed specifications for routing strategies. The IEEE 802.1 group has issued a standard for routing based on the use of a **spanning tree** algorithm. The token ring committee, IEEE 802.5, has issued its own specification, referred to as **source routing.** We examine these three strategies in turn.

Fixed Routing

For fixed routing, a route is selected for each source-destination pair of LANs in the internet. If alternate routes are available between two LANs, then typically the route with the least number of hops is selected. The routes are fixed, or at least only change when there is a change in the topology of the internet.

Figure 14-10 suggests how fixed routing might be implemented. A central routing matrix is created, to be stored perhaps at a network control center. The matrix shows, for each source-destination pair of LANs, the identity of the first bridge on the route. So for example, the route from LAN E to LAN F begins by going through bridge 107 to LAN A. Again consulting the matrix, the route from LAN A to LAN F goes through bridge 102 to LAN C. Finally, the route from LAN C to LAN F is directly through bridge 105. Thus the complete route from LAN E to LAN F is bridge 107, LAN A, bridge 102, LAN C, bridge 105.

From this overall matrix, routing tables can be developed and stored at each bridge. Each bridge needs one table for each LAN to which it attaches. The information for each table is derived from a single row of the matrix. For example, bridge 105 has two tables, one for frames arriving from LAN C and one for frames arriving from LAN F. The table shows, for each possible destination MAC address, the identity of the LAN to which the bridge should forward the frame. The table labeled ''from LAN C'' is derived from the row labeled C in the routing matrix. Every entry in that row that contains bridge number 105 results in an entry in the corresponding table in bridge 105.

Once the directories have been established, routing is a simple matter. A bridge copies each incoming frame on each of its LANs. If the destination MAC address corresponds to an entry in its routing table, the frame is retransmitted on the appropriate LAN.

The fixed routing strategy is widely used in commercially-available products. It has the advantage of simplicity and minimal processing requirements. However, in a complex internet, in which bridges may be dynamically added and in which failures must be allowed for, this strategy is too limited. We now turn to two more powerful alternatives.

The Spanning Tree Approach

The spanning tree approach is a mechanism in which bridges automatically develop a routing table and update that table in response to changing topology [BACK88,

Central Routing Matrix

Destination LAN

Source LAN	A	B	C	D	E	F	G
A	–	101	102	101	107	102	102
B	101	–	101	103	104	101	101
C	102	102	–	102	102	105	106
D	103	103	103	–	103	103	103
E	107	104	107	104	–	107	107
F	105	105	105	105	105	–	105
G	106	106	106	106	106	106	–

Bridge 101 table

from LAN A		from LAN B	
Dest	Next	Dest	Next
B	B	A	A
C	–	C	A
D	B	D	–
E	–	E	–
F	–	F	A
G	–	G	A

Bridge 102 table

from LAN A		from LAN C	
Dest	Next	Dest	Next
B	–	A	A
C	C	B	A
D	–	D	A
E	–	E	A
F	C	F	–
G	C	G	–

Bridge 103 table

from LAN B		from LAN D	
Dest	Next	Dest	Next
A	–	A	B
C	–	B	B
D	D	C	B
E	–	E	B
F	–	F	B
G	–	G	B

Bridge 104 table

from LAN B		from LAN E	
Dest	Next	Dest	Next
A	–	A	–
C	–	B	B
D	–	C	–
E	E	D	B
F	–	F	–
G	–	G	–

Bridge 105 table

from LAN C		from LAN F	
Dest	Next	Dest	Next
A	–	A	C
B	–	B	C
D	–	C	C
E	–	D	C
F	F	E	C
G	–	G	C

Bridge 106 table

from LAN C		from LAN G	
Dest	Next	Dest	Next
A	–	A	C
B	–	B	C
D	–	C	C
E	–	D	C
F	–	E	C
G	G	F	C

Bridge 107 table

from LAN A		from LAN E	
Dest	Next	Dest	Next
B	–	A	A
C	–	B	–
D	–	C	A
E	E	D	–
F	–	F	A
G	–	G	A

FIGURE 14-10. Fixed routing (using Figure 14-9).

HART88, IEEE88b, PERL84]. The algorithm consists of three mechanisms: frame forwarding, address learning, and loop resolution.

Frame Forwarding.   In this scheme, a bridge maintains a **forwarding data-base** for each port attached to a LAN. The database indicates the station addresses for which frames should be forwarded through that port. We can interpret this in the following fashion. For each port, a list of stations is maintained. A station is on the list if it is on the ''same side'' of the bridge as the port. For example, for bridge 102 of Figure 14-8, stations on LANs C, F, and G are on the same side of the bridge as the LAN C port, and stations on LANs A, B, D, and E are on the same side of the bridge as the LAN A port. When a frame is received on any port, the bridge must decide whether that frame is to be forwarded through the bridge and out through one of the bridge's other ports. Suppose that a bridge receives a MAC frame on port x. The following rules are applied (Figure 14-11):

1. Search the forwarding database to determine if the MAC address is listed for any port except port x.
2. If the destination MAC address is not found, discard the frame.
3. If the destination address is in the forwarding database for some port y, then determine whether port y is in a blocking or forwarding state. For reasons explained below, a port may sometimes be blocked, which prevents it from receiving or transmitting frames.
4. If port y is not blocked, transmit the frame through port y onto the LAN to which that port attaches.

Address Learning. The above scheme assumes that the bridge is already equipped with a forwarding database that indicates the direction, from the bridge, of each destination station. This information can be preloaded into the bridge, as in static routing. However, an effective automatic mechanism for learning the direction of each station is desirable. A simple scheme for acquiring this information is based on the use of the source address field in each MAC frame (Figure 14-11).

The strategy is this. When a frame arrives on a particular port, it clearly has come from the direction of the incoming LAN. The source address field of the frame indicates the source station. Thus, a bridge can update its forwarding database for that port on the basis of the source address field of each incoming frame. To allow for changes in topology, each element in the database is equipped with a timer. When a new element is added to the database, its timer is set. If the timer expires, then the element is eliminated from the database, since the corresponding direction information may no longer be valid. Each time a frame is received, its source address is checked against the database. If the element is already in the database, the entry is updated (the direction may have changed) and the timer is reset. If the element is not in the database, a new entry is created, with its own timer.

The above discussion indicated that the individual entries in the database are station addresses. If a two-level address structure (LAN number, station number) is used, then only LAN addresses need to be entered in the database. Both schemes work the same. The only difference is that the use of station addresses requires a much larger database than the use of LAN addresses.

Spanning Tree Algorithm. The address learning mechanism described above is effective if the topology of the internet is a tree; that is, if there are no alternate routes in the network. The existence of alternate routes means that there is a closed loop. For example in Figure 14-9, the following is a closed loop: LAN A, bridge 101, LAN B, bridge 104, LAN E, bridge 107, LAN A.

To see the problem created by a closed loop, consider Figure 14-12. At time t_0, station A transmits a frame addressed to station B. The frame is captured by both bridges. Each bridge updates its database to indicate that station A is in the direction of LAN X, and retransmits the frame on LAN Y. Say that bridge α retransmits at time t_1 and bridge β a short time later, t_2. Thus B will receive two copies of the

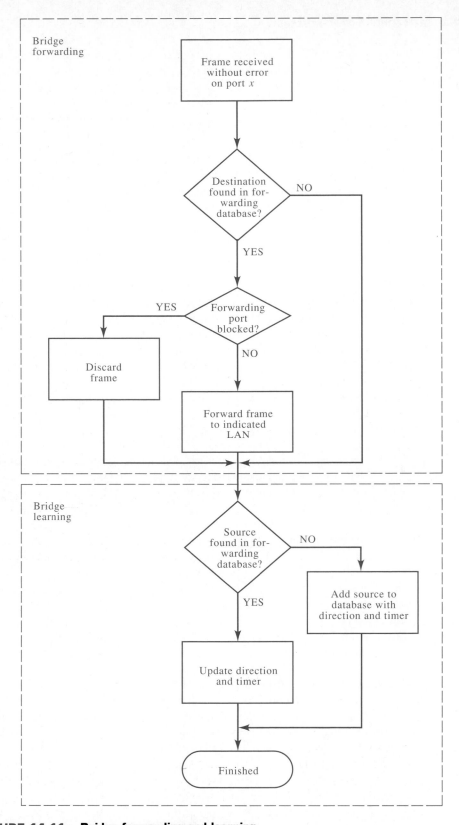

FIGURE 14-11. Bridge forwarding and learning.

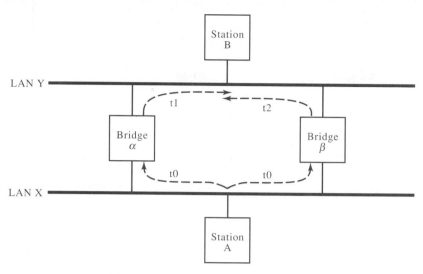

FIGURE 14-12. Loop of bridges.

frame. Furthermore, each bridge will receive the other's transmission on LAY Y. Note that each transmission is a MAC frame with a source address of A and a destination address of B. Thus each bridge will update its database to indicate that station A is in the direction of LAN Y. Neither bridge is now capable of forwarding a frame addressed to station A.

To overcome this problem, a simple result from graph theory is used: For any connected graph, consisting of nodes and edges connecting pairs of nodes, there is a spanning tree of edges that maintains the connectivity of the graph but contains no closed loops. In terms of internets, each LAN corresponds to a graph node, and each bridge corresponds to a graph edge. Thus, in Figure 14-9, the removal of one (and only one) of bridges 107, 101, and 104, results in a spanning tree. What is desired is to develop a simple algorithm by which the bridges of the internet can exchange sufficient information to automatically (without user intervention) derive a spanning tree. The algorithm must be dynamic. That is, when a topology change occurs, the bridges must be able to discover this fact and automatically derive a new spanning tree.

The algorithm is based on the use of the following:

1. Each bridge is assigned a unique identifier; in essence, the identifier consists of a MAC address for the bridge plus a priority level.
2. There is a special group MAC address that means "all bridges on this LAN." When a MAC frame is transmitted with the group address in the destination address field, all of the bridges on the LAN will capture that frame and interpret it as a frame addressed to itself.
3. Each port of a bridge is uniquely identified within the bridge, with a "port identifier."

With this information established, the bridges are able to exchange routing information in order to determine a spanning tree of the internet. We will explain the operation of the algorithm using Figures 14-13 and 14-14 as an example. The following concepts are needed in the creation of the spanning tree:

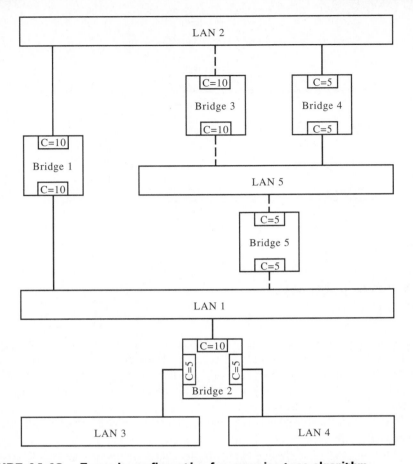

FIGURE 14-13.   Example configuration for spanning tree algorithm.

- *Root bridge:* The bridge with the lowest value of bridge identifier is chosen to be the root of the spanning tree.
- *Path cost:* Associated with each port on each bridge is a path cost, which is the cost of transmitting a frame onto a LAN through that port. A path between two stations will pass through zero or more bridges. At each bridge, the cost of transmission is added to give a total cost for a particular path. In the simplest case, all path costs would be assigned a value of 1; thus the cost of a path would simply be a count of the number of bridges along the path. Alternatively, costs could be assigned in inverse proportion to the data rate of the corresponding LAN, or any other criterion chosen by the network manager.
- *Root port:* Each bridge discovers the first hop on the minimum-cost path to the root bridge. The port used for that hop is labeled the root port.
- *Root path cost:* For each bridge, the cost of the path to the root bridge with minimum cost (the path that starts at the root port) is the root path cost for that bridge.
- *Designated bridge, designated port:* On each LAN, one bridge is chosen to be the designated bridge. This is the bridge on that LAN that provides the minimum cost path to the root bridge. This is the only bridge allowed to forward frames to and from the LAN for which it is the designated bridge.

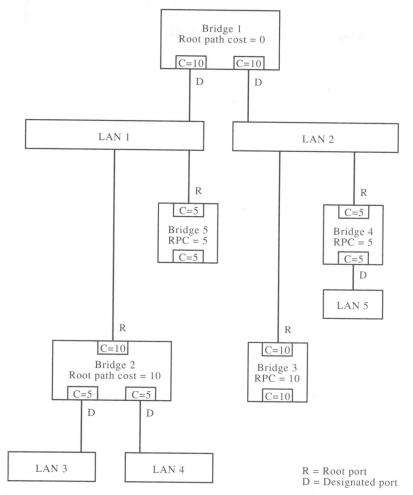

FIGURE 14-14. **Spanning tree for configuration of Figure 14-13.**

The port of the designated bridge that attaches the bridge to the LAN is the designated port. For all LANs to which the root bridge is attached, the root bridge is the designated bridge. All internet traffic to and from the LAN passes through the designated port.

In general terms, the spanning tree is constructed in the following fashion:

1. Determine the root bridge.
2. Determine the root port on all other bridges.
3. Determine the designated port on each LAN. This will be the port with the minimum root path cost. In the case of two or more bridges with the same root path cost, then the highest-priority bridge is chosen as the designated bridge. If the designated bridge has two or more ports attached to this LAN, then the port with the lowest value of port identifier is chosen.

By this process, when two LANs are directly connected by more than one bridge, all of the bridges but one are eliminated. This cuts any loops that involve two

LANs. It can be demonstrated that this process also eliminates all loops involving more than two LANs and that connectivity is preserved. Thus, this process discovers a spanning tree for the given internet. In our example, the solid lines indicate the bridge ports that participate in the spanning tree.

The steps outlined above require that the bridges exchange information. The information is exchanged in the form of bridge protocol data units (BPDUs). A BPDU transmitted by one bridge is addressed to and received by all of the other bridges on the same LAN. Each BPDU contains the following information:

- The identifier of this bridge and the port on this bridge
- The identifier of the bridge that this bridge considers to be the root
- The root path cost for this bridge

To begin, all bridges consider themselves to be the root bridge. Each bridge will broadcast a BPDU on each of its LANs that asserts this fact. On any given LAN, only one claimant will have the lowest-valued identifier and will maintain its belief. Over time, as BPDUs propagate, the identity of the lowest-valued bridge identifier throughout the internet will be known to all bridges. The root bridge will regularly broadcast the fact that it is the root bridge on all of the LANs to which it is attached. This allows the bridges on those LANs to determine their root port and the fact that they are directly connected to the root bridge. Each of these bridges in turn broadcasts a BPDU on the other LANs to which it is attached (all LANs except the one on its root port), indicating that it is one hop away from the root bridge. This activity is propagated throughout the internet. Every time that a bridge receives a BPDU, it transmits BPDUs indicating the identity of the root bridge and the number of hops to reach the root bridge. On any LAN, the bridge claiming to be the one that is closest to the root becomes the designated bridge.

We can trace some of this activity with the configuration of Figure 14-13. At startup time, Bridges 1, 3, and 4 all transmit BPDUs on LAN 2 claiming to be the root bridge. When bridge 3 receives the transmission from bridge 1, it recognizes a superior claimant and defers. Bridge 3 has also received a claiming BPDU from bridge 5 via LAN 5. Bridge 3 recognizes that Bridge 1 has a superior claim to be the root bridge; it therefore assigns its LAN 2 port to be its root port, and sets the root path cost to 10. By similar actions, bridge 4 ends up with a root path cost of 5 via LAN 2; bridge 5 has a root path cost of 5 via LAN 1; and bridge 2 has a root path cost of 20 via LAN 1.

Now consider the assignment of designated bridges. On LAN 5, all three bridges transmit BPDUs attempting to assert a claim to be designated bridge. Bridge 3 defers because it receives BPDUs from the other bridges that have a lower root path cost. Bridges 4 and 5 have the same root path cost, but bridge 4 has the higher priority and therefore becomes the designated bridge.

The results of all this activity are shown in Figure 14-14. Only the designated bridge on each LAN is allowed to forward frames. All of the ports on all of the other bridges are placed in a blocking state. After the spanning tree is established, bridges continue to periodically exchange BPDUs to be able to react to any change in topology, cost assignments, or priority assignment. Any time that a bridge receives a BPDU on a port it makes two assessments:

1. If the BPDU arrives on a port that is considered the designated port, does the transmitting port have a better claim to be designated port?
2. Should this port be my root port?

Source Routing

The source routing approach is a mechanism in which the sending station determines the route that the frame will follow and includes the routing information with the frame; bridges read the routing information to determine if they should forward the frame [DIXO88, HAMN88, PITT87, BEDE86, PITT85, IEEE88c].

Basic Operation. The basic operation of the algorithm can be described with reference to the configuration of Figure 14-15a. A frame from station X can reach station Y by either of the following routes:

- LAN 1, bridge B1, LAN 3, bridge B3, LAN 2
- LAN 1, bridge B2, LAN 4, bridge B4, LAN 2

Station X may choose one of these two routes and place the information, in the form of a sequence of LAN and bridge identifiers, in the frame to be transmitted. When a bridge receives a frame, it will forward that frame if the bridge is on the designated route; all other frames are discarded. In this case, if the first route above is specified, bridges B1 and B3 will forward the frame; if the second route is specified, bridges B2 and B4 will forward the frame.

Note that with this scheme, bridges need not maintain routing tables. The bridge makes the decision whether or not to forwared a frame solely on the basis of the routing information contained in the frame. All that is required is that the bridge know its own unique identifier and the identifier of each LAN to which it is attached. The responsibility for designing the route falls to the source station.

For this scheme to work, there must be a mechanism by which a station can determine a route to any destination station. Before dealing with this issue, we need to discuss different types of routing directives.

Routing Directives and Addressing Modes. The source routing scheme developed by the IEEE 802.5 committee includes four different types of routing directives. Each frame that is transmitted includes an indicator of the type of routing desired. The four directive types are:

- *Null:* No routing is desired. In this case, the frame can only be delivered to stations on the same LAN as the source station.
- *Nonbroadcast:* The frame includes a route, consisting of a sequence of LAN numbers and bridge numbers that defines a unique route from the source station to the destination station. Only bridges on that route forward the frame, and only a single copy of the frame is delivered to the destination station.
- *All-routes broadcast:* The frame will reach each LAN of the internet by all possible routes. Thus each bridge will forward each frame once to each of its ports in a direction away from the source node and multiple copies of the frame may appear on a LAN. The destination station will receive one copy of the frame for each possible route through the network.
- *Single-route broadcast:* Regardless of the destination address of the frame, the frame will appear once, and only once, on each LAN in the internet. For this effect to be achieved, the frame is forwarded by all bridges that are on a spanning tree (with the source node as the root) of the internet. The destination station receives a single copy of the frame.

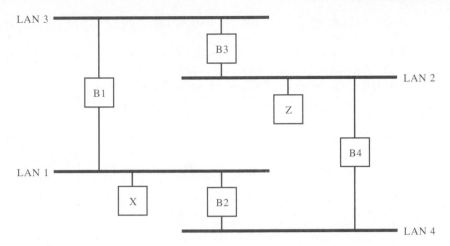

(a) Configuration

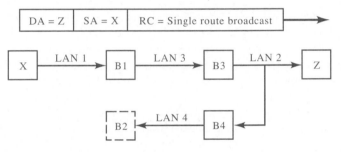

(b) Single-route broadcast request

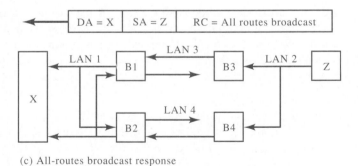

(c) All-routes broadcast response

FIGURE 14-15.   Route discovery example [DIX088].

Let us examine the potential application of each of these four types of routing, and then examine the mechanisms that may be employed to achieve them. First, consider null routing. In this case the bridges that share the LAN with the source station are told not to forward the frame. This will be done if the intended destination is on the same LAN as the source station. Nonbroadcast routing is used when the two stations are not on the same LAN and the source station knows a route that can be used to reach the destination station. Only the bridges on that route will forward the frame.

The remaining two types of routing can be used by the source to discover a route to the destination. For example, the source station can use all-routes broadcasting to send a request frame to the intended destination. The destination returns a response frame, using nonbroadcast routing, on each of the routes followed by the incoming request frame. The source station can pick one of these routes and send future frames on that route. Alternatively, the source station could use single-route broadcasting to send a single request to the destination station. The destination station could send its response frame via all-routes broadcasting. The incoming frames would reveal all of the possible routes to the destination station, and the source station could pick one of these for future transmissions. Finally, single-route broadcasting could be used for group addressing, as discussed below.

Now consider the mechanisms for implementing these various routing directives. Each frame must include an indicator of which of the four types of routing is required. For null routing, the frame is ignored by the bridge. For nonbroadcast routing, the frame includes an ordered list of LAN numbers and bridge numbers. When a bridge receives a nonbroadcast frame, it forwards the frame only if the routing information contains the sequence LAN i, Bridge x, LAN j, where

> LAN i = LAN from which the frame arrived
> Bridge x = this bridge
> LAN j = another LAN to which this bridge is attached

For all-routes broadcasting, the source station marks the frame for this type of routing, but includes no routing information. Each bridge that forwards the frame will add its bridge number and the outgoing LAN number to the frame's routing information field. Thus, when the frame reaches its destination, it will include a sequenced list of all LANs and bridges visited. To prevent the endless repetition and looping of frames, a bridge obeys the following rule: When an all-routes broadcast frame is received, the bridge examines the routing information field. If the field contains the number of a LAN to which the bridge is attached, the bridge will refrain from forwarding the frame on that LAN. Put the other way, the bridge will only forward the frame to a LAN that the frame has not already visited.

Finally, for single-route broadcasting, a spanning tree of the internet must be developed. This can either be done automatically, as in the 802.1 specification, or manually. In either case, as with the 802.1 strategy, one bridge on each LAN is the designated bridge for that LAN, and is the only one that forwards single-route frames.

It is worth noting the relationship between addressing mode and routing directive. There are three types of MAC addresses:

- *Individual:* the address specifies a unique destination station.
- *Group:* the address specifies a group of destination addresses; this is also referred to as *multicast*.
- *All-stations:* the addresses specifies all stations that are capable of receiving this frame; this is also referred to as *broadcast*. We will refrain from using this latter term since it is also used in the source routing terminology.

In the case of a single, isolated LAN, group and all-stations addresses refer to stations on the same LAN as the source station. In an internet, it may be desirable to transmit a frame to multiple stations on multiple LANs. Indeed, since a set

TABLE 14-2   Effects of Various Combinations of Addressing and Source Routing

Addressing Mode	Routing Specification			
	No Routing	**Nonbroadcast**	**All-Routes**	**Single-Route**
Individual	Received by station if it is on the same LAN	Received by station if it is on one of the LANs on the route	Received by station if it is on any LAN	Received by station if it is on any LAN
Group	Received by all group members on the same LAN	Received by all group members on all LANs visited on this route	Received by all group members on all LANs	Received by all group members on all LANs
All-Stations	Received by all stations on the same LAN	Received by all stations on all LANs visited on this route	Received by all stations on all LANs	Received by all stations on all LANs

of LANs interconnected by bridges should appear to the user as a single LAN, the ability to do group and all-stations addressing across the entire internet is mandatory.

Table 14-2 summarizes the relationship between routing specification and addressing mode. If no routing is specified, then all addresses refer only to the immediate LAN. If nonbroadcast routing is specified, then addresses may refer to any station on any LAN visited on the nonbroadcast route. From an addressing point of view, this combination is not generally useful for group and all-stations addressing. If either the all-routes or single-route specification is included in a frame, then all stations on the internet can be addressed. Thus, the total internet acts as a single network from the point of view of MAC addresses. Since less traffic is generated by the single-route specification, this is to be preferred for group and all-stations addressing. Note also that the single-route mechanism in source routing is equivalent to the 802.1 spanning tree approach. Thus, the latter supports both group and all-stations addressing.

Route Discovery and Selection.   With source routing, bridges are relieved of the burden of storing and using routing information. Thus the burden falls on the stations that wish to transmit frames. Clearly, some mechanism is needed by which the source stations can know the route to each destination for which frames are to be sent. Three strategies suggest themselves.

1. Manually load the information into each station. This is simple and effective but has several drawbacks. First, any time that the configuration changes, the routing information at all stations must be updated. Secondly, this approach does not provide for automatic adjustment in the face of the failure of a bridge or LAN.
2. One station on a LAN can query other stations on the same LAN for routing information about distant stations. This approach may reduce the overall

amount of routing messages that must be transmitted, compared to option 3, below. However, at least one station on each LAN must have the needed routing information, so this is not a complete solution.

3. When a station needs to learn the route to a destination station, it engages in a dynamic route discovery procedure.

Option 3 is the most flexible and the one that is specified by IEEE 802.5. As was mentioned earlier, two approaches are possible. The source station can transmit an all-routes request frame to the destination. Thus, all possible routes to the destination are discovered. The destination station can send back a nonbroadcast response on each of the discovered routes, allowing the source to choose which route to follow in subsequently transmitting the frame. This approach generates quite a bit of both forward and backward traffic, and requires the destination station to receive and transmit a number of frames. An alternative is for the source station to transmit a single-route request frame. Only one copy of this frame will reach the destination. The destination responds with an all-routes response frame, which generates all possible routes back to the source. Again, the source can choose among these alternative routes.

Figure 14-15 illustrates the latter approach. Assume that the spanning tree that has been chosen for this internet consists of bridges B1, B3, and B4. In this example, station X wishes to discover a route to station Z. Station X issues a single-route request frame. Bridge B2 is not on the spanning tree and so does not forward the frame. The other bridges do forward the frame and it reaches station Z. Note that bridge B4 forwards the frame to LAN 4, although this is not necessary; it is simply an effect of the spanning-tree mechanism. When Z receives this frame, it responds with an all-routes frame. Two messages reach X: one on the path LAN 2, B3, LAN 3, B1, LAN 1, and the other on the path LAN 2, B4, LAN 4, B2, LAN 1. Note that the frame that arrived by the latter route is received by bridge B1 and forwarded onto LAN 3. However, when bridges B3 receives this frame, it sees in the routing information field that the frame has already visited LAN 2; therefore it does not forward the frame. A similar fate occurs for the frame that follows the first route and is forwarded by bridge B2.

Once a collection of routes have been discovered, the source station needs to select one of the routes. The obvious criterion would be to select the minimum-hop route. Alternatively, a minimum-cost route could be selected, where the cost of a network is inversely proportional to its data rate. In either case, if two or more routes are equivalent by the chosen criterion, then there are several alternatives:

1. Choose the route corresponding to the response message that arrives first. One may assume that that particular route is less congested than the others since the frame on that route arrived earliest.
2. Choose randomly. This should have the effect, over time, of leveling the load among the various bridges.

Another point to consider is how often to update a route. Routes should certainly be changed in response to network failures and perhaps should be changed in response to network congestion. If connection-oriented logical link control is used (see Chapter 13), then one possibility is to rediscover the route with each new connection. Another alternative, which works with either connection-oriented or connectionless service, is to associate a timer with each selected route, and rediscover the route when its time expires.

CONNECTION-ORIENTED INTERNETWORKING

ISO standard ISO/TR 10029 specifies the architecture and functioning of a connection-mode internetworking facility, using ISO 8208 (X.25) as the network layer protocol. We examine the protocol architecture of this approach, and then look at the functions that must be performed by the routers.

Protocol Architecture for Connection-Oriented Internetworking

Figure 14-16 illustrates the protocol activity for transferring data from a DTE attached to a packet-switching network, through a router, to a DTE attached to a LAN which has been enhanced with the use of X.25. The lower portion of the figure shows the format of the data unit being processed at various points during the transfer.

To begin, from the network layer's point of view, data is presented to the network layer by the transport layer (t1). This is in the form of a data unit consisting of a transport protocol header and data from the transport layer user. This block of data is received by the packet level protocol of X.25, which appends a packet header (t2) to form an X.25 packet. The header will include the virtual circuit number of the virtual circuit that connects host A to the router. The packet is handed down to the data link layer protocol (LAP-B), which appends a link header and trailer (t3), and transmits the resulting frame to DCE X (t4). At the DCE, the link header and trailer are stripped off and the result is passed up to the packet level (t5). The packet is transferred across the network and through DCE Y to the router, which appears as just another DTE to the network. Eventually, we reach the packet level at t9 in the router. At this point, the packet is relayed onto the LAN. This will involve going through the LAN protocol layers (logical link control, medium access control) on transmission and reception. Note that on this hop, an X.25 virtual circuit is set up on top of LLC.

Several points are worth noting:

- There is no encapsulation by the router. The same layer 3 header format is reused.
- There is no true end-to-end protocol. Each hop constitutes a single virtual circuit controlled by X.25.
- Because of the 12-bit virtual circuit number field in X.25, the router can handle a maximum of 4096 connections.

Operation of an X.25 Router

We can describe the operation of the router by considering the following areas:

- Virtual call setup
- Data and interrupt transfer
- Virtual call clearing
- Reset
- Restart

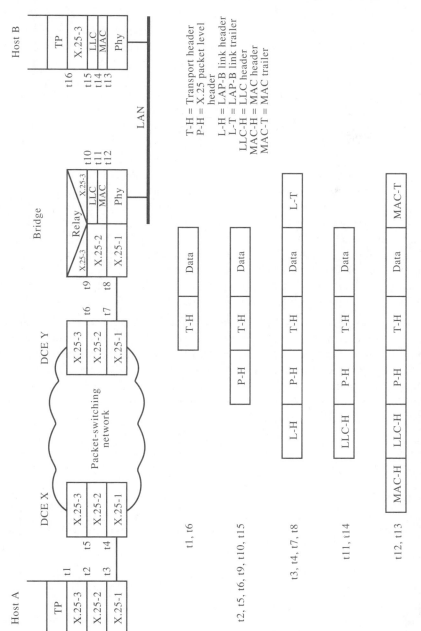

FIGURE 14-16. X.25 internetwork relay operation.

Virtual Call Setup. Let us consider the configuration of Figure 14-16 and suppose that DTE A wishes to set up a logical network connection to DTE B. The process begins when the transport layer isues a request to the network layer for a virtual circuit to DTE B. This request is mapped into a Call Request packet. It is at this point that we see the distinction between global addresses and subnetwork attachment point addresses. The request from the transport layer will refer to the global internet address. It will be conveyed as an optional user facility known as *called address extension* in the Call Request packet. In addition, the Call Request packet includes as a parameter *called DTE address*; this parameter appears in the packet header. In this case, the called DTE address is the subnetwork attachment point address for the router on network X.

What has happened is this. The network service user has requested a logical connection to DTE B. This request passes down to the network-level entity in A, which is an X.25 packet level module. The network entity makes a routing decision that the connection can be set up through the router. So, the X.25 protocol sets up a virtual circuit to the router, using the Call Request packet. The called DTE address parameter of the Call Request packet is used by the local DCE to set up a virtual circuit to the remote DCE, which then issues an Incoming Call packet to the router.

When an Incoming Call packet arrives at a DTE, it will normally accept or reject the connection promptly. If the connection is accepted, a Call Accepted packet is issued. In the case of the router, however, this activity must be deferred until it can be determined if the virtual call can be set up all the way to DTE B. Therefore, upon receipt of the Call Request packet, the router performs the following tasks:

1. Makes a routing decision on the basis of the calling address parameter. This parameter was generated as part transport request primitive in A, and carried in the call user data field of the Incoming Call packet. In this case, there is no need for a hop to another router. Rather, the destination DTE is B, which is attached to a subnetwork to which this router is attached.
2. Select a free virtual circuit number on the LAN side and associate it with the virtual circuit number of the incoming call on the packet-switching network side.
3. Issue a Call Request packet onto the LAN with the subnetwork attachment point address of B in the called DTE address field. A match is made of optional user facilities.
4. If DTE B accepts the call, the router will soon receive a Call Connected packet on the virtual circuit across the LAN. It then transmits a Call Accepted packet on the logical channel corresponding to the original Incoming Call packet on the packet-switching network side.

Data and Interrupt Transfer. Once the virtual call is set up, the router peforms a mapping function between the virtual circuit numbers on the two sides. Incoming data packets on one virtual circuit are relayed and retransmitted on the other virtual circuit. The router may need to perform segmentation if there is a difference in maximum packet size. When a packet must be segmented, it is broken up into two or more smaller packets forming a complete packet sequence, using the M bit.

When an Interrupt packet is received by a DTE, it responds with an Interrupt Confirmation packet. The originating DTE may not send another Interrupt packet until it receives a confirmation to the outstanding one. Since this confirmation is end-to-end, the router must obey the following procedure:

1. When an Interrupt packet is received on one virtual circuit, an Interrupt packet is transmitted on the matching virtual circuit.
2. When an Interrupt Confirmation packet is received on the second virtual circuit, the router transmits an Interrupt Confirmation packet on the first virtual circuit.

Virtual Call Clearing. The virtual call clearing process is not a cooperative function between DTEs. Rather, either DTE may clear the virtual circuit; the other side is merely informed that the clearing has occurred. Accordingly, the router behaves as follows: When a Clear Indication packet is received on a virtual circuit, the router issues a Clear Confirmation packet on that virtual circuit and issues a Clear Request packet on the matching virtual circuit.

Reset. A reset may be initiated by either a DTE or a router. In the former case, the router will receive a Reset Indicator packet on a virtual circuit. It will respond by issuing a DTE Reset Confirmation on that virtual circuit and a Reset Request on the matching virtual circuit.

If the router needs to reset a virtual call, it issues a Reset Request on both of the virtual circuits that are part of that virtual call.

Restart. When a router receives a Restart Indication on the interface to one network it responds as follows:

1. The router issues a DTE Restart Confirmation on that interface.
2. For each virtual circuit that had existed on that interface, the router issues a Clear Request packet on the matching virtual circuit on the other network interface.

Similarly, a router may itself initiate a restart by issuing a Restart Request packet on one subnetwork interface. It must then also issue a Clear Request packet on the other interface for each virtual circuit that was destroyed by the restart.

14·5

CONNECTIONLESS INTERNETWORKING

The Internet Protocol (IP) is the name given to a protocol standard developed by DOD [DOD83a] as part of the DARPA Internet Project. As of late 1986, the DARPA Internet consisted of over 150 interconnected networks (Figure 14-17). Table 14-3 lists characteristics of some of the constituent networks [HIND83]. A protocol similar to IP has been developed by ISO. [CALL83, PISC84]. Both protocols are generically referred to as IP in the following discussion, unless otherwise noted. We begin with a description of the operation of IP and a discussion of key design issues, before turning to specific protocol details.

Operation of an IP Internet

IP provides a connectionless or datagram service between stations. This contrasts with the connection-oriented service. There are a number of advantages to the connectionless approach:

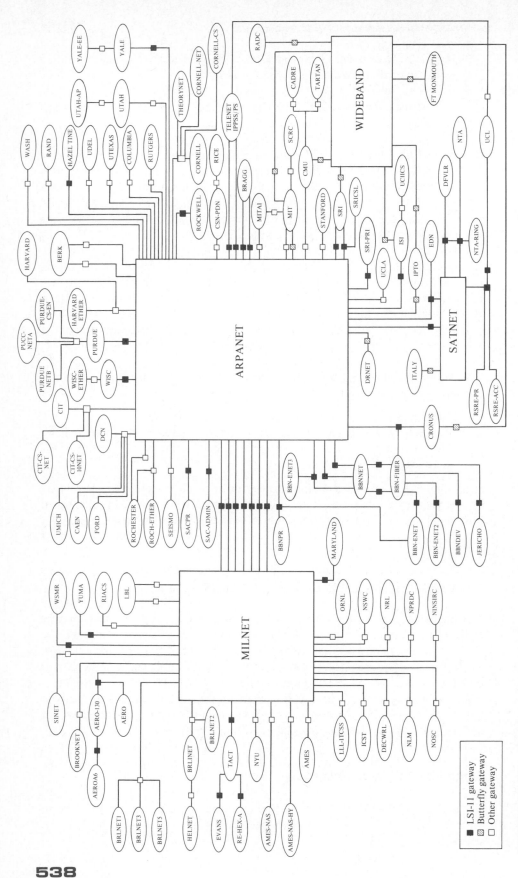

FIGURE 14-17. DARPA internet system.

Legend:
- ■ LSI-11 gateway
- ▨ Butterfly gateway
- ☐ Other gateway

TABLE 14-3 DARPA INTERNET Network Characteristics

Network Type	Message Size (Octets)	Speed[a]	Delay[b]	Guaranteed Delivery	Notes
ARPANET	1008	Medium	Medium	Yes	
SATNET	256	Low	High	No	Satellite network
Pronet	2048	High	Low	Yes	Local area network
Ethernet	1500	High	Low	Yes	Local area network
Telenet	128	Low	Medium	Yes	
Packet radio	254	Medium	Medium	No	Varying topology
Wideband	2000	High	High	No	Satellite Network

[a]Low speed is <100 kbps; medium speed is 100 kbps to 1 Mbps; high speed is >1 Mpbs.
[b]Low delay is <50 ms; medium delay is 50 to 500 ms; high delay is >500 ms.

- A connectionless internet facility is flexible. It can deal with a variety of networks, some of which are themselves connectionless. In essence, IP requires very little of the constituent networks.
- A connectionless internet service can be made highly robust. This is basically the same argument made for a datagram network service versus a virtual circuit service. For a further discussion, the reader is referred to Section 9-2.
- A connectionless internet service is best for connectionless transport protocols. The use of such protocols is discussed in Chapter 15.

As an example, Figure 14-18 depicts the operation of IP for data exchange between host A on a packet-switching network and host B on a LAN, connected by a router. The data to be sent by A are encapsulated in an internet protocol data unit, referred to as a **datagram,** with an IP header specifying the global internet address of B. This datagram is then encapsulated in the X.25 packet and link fields and transmitted to the router. The router strips of the X.25 fields to expose the IP datagram. This is then wrapped in the IEEE 802 protocol fields and sent to B.

With this example in mind, we describe briefly the sequence of steps involved in sending a datagram between two stations on different networks. The process starts in the sending station. The station wants to send an IP datagram to a station in another network. The IP module in the station constructs the datagram with a global network address and recognizes that the destination is on another network. So the first step is to send the datagram to a router (example: station *A* to the router in Figure 14-18). To do this, the IP module appends to the IP datagram a header appropriate to the network that contains the address of the router. For example, for an X.25 network, a layer 3 packet encapsulates the IP datagram to be sent to the router.

Next, the packet travels through the network to the router, which receives it via a DCE-DTE protocol. The router unwraps the packet to recover the original datagram. The router analyzes the IP header to determine whether this datagram contains control information intended for the router, or data intended for a station farther on. In the latter instance, the router must make a routing decision. There are four possibilities:

1. The destination station is attached directly to one of the networks to which the router is attached. This is referred to as ''directly connected.'' For example, in Figure 14-19, all stations labeled S0 are directly connected to the router G1.

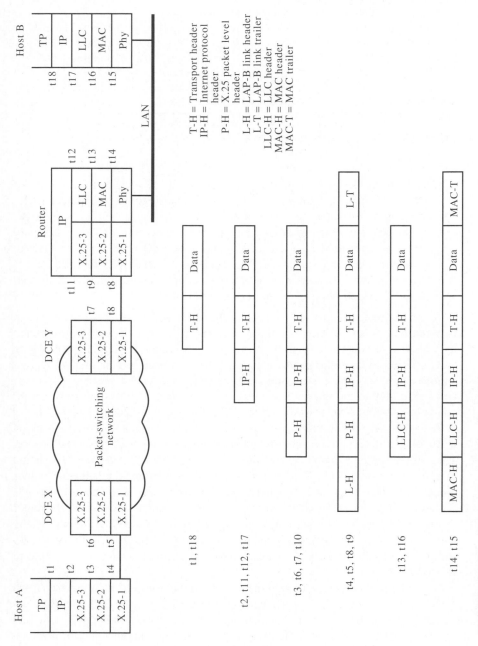

FIGURE 14-18. Internet protocol operation.

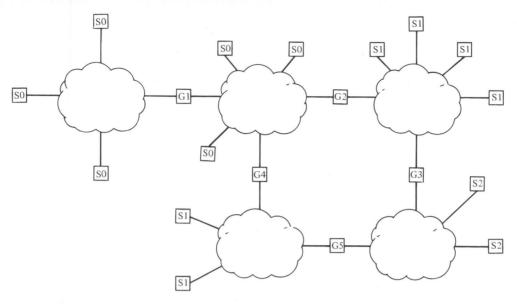

FIGURE 14-19. **Example of internet connectivity.**

2. The destination station is on a network that has a router that directly connects to this router. This is known as a "neighbor router." In Figure 14-19, G2 is a neighbor router of G1, and all stations labeled S1 are one "hop" from G1.
3. To reach the destination station, more than one additional router must be traversed. This is known as a "multiple-hop" situation. In Figure 14-19, all stations labeled S2 are in this category.
4. The router does not know the destination address.

In case 4, the router returns an error message to the source of the datagram. For cases 1 through 3, the router must select the appropriate route for the data, and insert them into the appropriate network with the appropriate address. For case 1, the address is the destination station address. For cases 2 and 3, the address is a router address. Remember, we are speaking here of a lower layer address, usually a layer 3 address or, in the case of local networks, a layer 2 address.

Before actually sending data, however, the router may need to segment the datagram to accommodate a smaller maximum packet size limitation on the outgoing network. Each segment becomes an independent IP datagram. Each new datagram is wrapped in a lower layer packet for transmission. The router then queues each packet for transmission. It may also enforce a maximum queue-length size for each network to which it attaches to avoid having a slow network penalize a faster one. In any case, once the queue limit is reached, additional datagrams are simply dropped.

The process described above continues through zero or more routers until the datagram reaches the destination station. As with a router, the destination station recovers the IP datagram from its network wrapping. If segmentation has occurred, the IP module in the destination station buffers the incoming data until the original data field is reassembled. It then passes this block of data to a higher layer. The higher layer (e.g., transport) is responsible for the proper sequencing of a stream of datagrams and for end-to-end error and flow control.

Design Issues

With that thumbnail sketch of the operation of an IP-controlled internet, we can now go back and examine some design issues in greater detail:

- Routing.
- Datagram lifetime
- Segmentation and reassembly.
- Error control.
- Flow control.

As we proceed with this discussion, the reader will note many similarities with the design issues and techniques relevant to packet-switched networks. To see the reason for this, consider Figure 14-20 [HIND83], which compares an internet architecture with a packet-switched network architecture. The routers (G1, G2, G3) in the internet correspond to the packet-switched nodes (P1, P2, P3) in the network, and the networks (N1, N2, N3) in the internet correspond to the transmission links (T1, T2, T3) in the networks. The routers perform essentially the same functions as packet-switched nodes, and use the intervening networks in a manner analogous to transmission links.

Routing.   Routing is generally accomplished by maintaining a routing table in each station and router that gives, for each possible destination network, the next router to which the IP datagram should be sent.

Table 14-4 shows the routing table for the BBN router, which is part of the DARPA internet. If a network is directly connected, it is so indicated. Otherwise,

TABLE 14-4   INTERNET Routing Table[a]

Network Name	Net Address	Route[b]
SATNET	4	Directly connected
ARPANET	10	Directly connected
BBN-NET	3	1hop via RCC 10.3.0.72 (ARPANET 3/72)
Purdue-Computer Science	192.5.1	2 hops via Purdue 10.2.0.37 (ARPANET 2/37)
INTELPOST	43	2 hops via Mills 10.3.0.17 (ARPANET 3/17)
DECNET-TEST	38	3 hops via Mills 10.3.0.17 (ARPANET 3/17)
Wideband	28	3 hops via RCC 10.3.0.72 (ARPANET 3/72)
BBN-Packet Radio	1	2 hops via RCC 10.3.0.72 (ARPANET 3/72)
DCN-COMSAT	29	1 hop via Mills 10.3.0.17 (ARPANET 3/17)
FIBERNET	24	3 hops via RCC 10.3.0.72 (ARPANET 3/72)
Bragg-Packet Radio	9	1 hop via Bragg 10.0.0.38 (ARPANET 0/38)
Clark Net	8	2 hops via Mills 10.3.0.17 (ARPANET 3/17)
LCSNET	18	1 hop via MIT LCS 10.0.0.77 (ARPANET 0/77)
BBN-Terminal Concentrator	192.1.2	3 hops via RCC 10.3.0.72 (ARPANET 3/72)
BBN-Jericho	192.1.3	3 hops via RCC 10.3.0.72 (ARPANET 3/72)
UCLNET	11	1 hop via UCL 4.0.0.60 (SATNET 60)
RSRE-NULL	35	1 hop via UCL 4.0.0.60 (SATNET 60)
RSRE-PPSN	25	2 hops via UCL 4.0.0.60 (SATNET 60)
San Francisco-Packet Radio-2	6	1 hop via C3PO 10.1.0.51 (ARPANET 1/51)

[a]Network table for BBN router.
[b]Names and acronyms identify routers in the INTERNET system.
Source: [SHEL82].

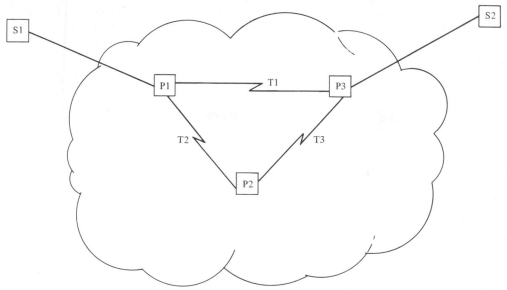

(a) Packet–switched network architecture

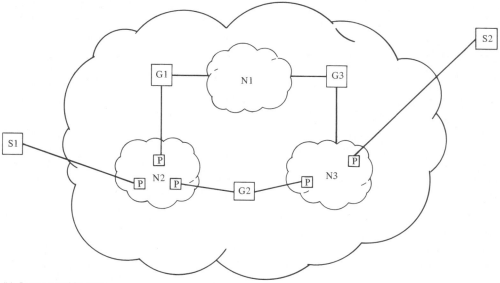

(b) Internet architecture

FIGURE 14-20. The internet as a network. From [HIND83]

the datagram must be directed through one or more routers (one or more hops). The table indicates the identity of the next router on the route (which must share a common network with this router or host) and the number of hops to the destination.

The routing table may be static or dynamic. A static table, however, could contain alternate routes if a router is unavailable. A dynamic table is more flexible in responding both to error and congestion situations. In the DARPA internet, for example, when a router goes down, all of its neighbors will send out a status report, allowing other routers and hosts to update their routing tables. A similar scheme can be used to control congestion. This latter is particularly important because of the mismatch in capacity between local and long-haul networks. The interested reader may consult [DARP81], which specifies a variety of internet control messages used to facilitate routing.

Routing tables may also be used to support other internet services, such as security and priority. For example, individual networks might be classified to handle data up to a given security classification. The routing mechanism must assure that data of a given security level is not allowed to pass through networks not cleared to handle such data.

Another routing technique is source routing. The source station specifies the route by including a sequential list of routers in the datagram. This, again, could be useful for security or priority requirements.

Finally, we mention a service related to routing: route recording. To record a route, each router appends its address to a list of addresses in the datagram. This feature is useful for testing and debugging purposes.

Datagram Lifetime.   If dynamic or alternate routing is used, the potential exists for a datagram or some of its fragments to loop indefinitely through the internet. This is undesirable for two reasons. First, an endlessly circulating datagram consumes resources. Second, we will see in Chapter 15 that a transport protocol may depend on there being an upper bound on datagram lifetime. To avoid these problems, each datagram can be marked with a lifetime. Once the lifetime expires, the datagram is discarded.

A simple way to implement lifetime is to use a hop count. Each time that a datagram passes through a router, the count is decremented. Alternatively, the lifetime could be a true measure of time. This requires that the routers must somehow know how long it has been since the datagram or segment last crossed a router, in order to know by how much to decrement the lifetime field. This would seem to require some global clocking mechanism.

The advantage of using a true time measure is that it can be used in the reassembly algorithm, described next.

Segmentation and Reassembly.   Individual networks within an internet will generally be diverse and, in particular, specify different maximum (and sometimes minimum) packet sizes. It would be inefficient and unwieldy to try to dictate uniform packet size across networks. Thus routers may need to segment incoming datagrams into smaller pieces before transmitting on to the next network.

If datagrams can be segmented (perhaps more than once) in the course of their travels, the question arises as to where they should be reassembled. The easiest solution is to have reassembly performed at the destination only. The principal disadvantage of this approach is the packets can only get smaller as data moves through the internet. This may seriously impair the efficiency of some networks (e.g., CSMA/CD LANs). On the other hand, if intermediate router reassembly is allowed, the following disadvantages result:

1. Large buffers are required at routers, and there is a potential for reassembly deadlock.
2. All segments of a datagram must pass through the same router. This inhibits the use of dynamic routing.

Both DOD and ISO IP specify an efficient technique for segmentation. The technique requires the following fields in the datagram header:

- ID.
- Data Length.
- Offset.
- More flag.

The *ID* is some means of uniquely identifying a station-originated datagram. In DOD IP, it consists of the source and destination addresses, an identifier of the protocol layer that generated the data, and a sequence number supplied by that protocol layer. The *Data Length* is the length of the data field in octets, and the *Offset* is the position of a segment in the original datagram in multiples of 64 bits.

The source station IP layer creates a datagram with Data Length equal to the entire length of the data field, with Offset = 0, and a More Flag set to False. To segment a long packet, an IP module in a router performs the following tasks:

1. Create two new datagrams and copy the header fields of the incoming datagram into both.
2. Divide the data into two approximately equal portions along a 64-bit boundary, placing one portion in each new datagram. The first portion must be a multiple of 64 bits.
3. Set the Data Length field of the first datagram to the length of the inserted data, and set the More Flag to True. The Offset field is unchanged.
4. Set the Data Length field of the second datagram to the length of the inserted data, and add the length of the first data portion divided by eight to the Offset field. The More Flag remains the same.

Table 14-5 gives an example. The procedure can be generalized to an *n*-way split.

To reassemble a datagram, there must be sufficient buffer space at the reassembly point. As segments with the same ID arrive, their data fields are inserted in the proper position in the buffer until the entire datagram is reassembled, which is achieved when a contiguous set of data exists starting with an *Offset* of zero and ending with data from a segment with a false *More Flag*.

TABLE 14-5   Segmentation Example

Original datagram
      Data Length = 472
      Offset   = 0
      More   = 0

First segment
      Data Length = 240
      Offset   = 0
      More   = 1

Second segment
      Data Length = 232
      Offset   = 30
      More   = 0

One eventuality that must be dealt with is that one or more of the segments may not get through; the IP connectionless service does not guarantee delivery. Some means is needed to decide to abandon a reassembly effort in order to free up buffer space. The ISO IP standard suggests two possibilities. First, assign a reassembly lifetime to the first segment to arrive. This is a local, real time which is assigned by the reassembly function and decremented while some, but not all segments of the PDU are being buffered. If the timer expires, all received segments are discarded. The second possibility is that the destination IP entity can make use of the datagram lifetime, which is part of the incoming PDU. The lifetime field continues to be decremented by the reassembly function as if the PDU were still in transit (in a sense, it still is).

Error Control.   The internetwork facility does not guarantee successful delivery of every datagram. When a datagram is discarded by a router, the router should attempt to return some information to the source, if possible. The source internet protocol entity may use this information to modify its transmission strategy and may notify higher layers. To report that a specific datagram has been discarded, some means of datagram identification is needed.

Datagrams may be discarded for a number of reasons, including lifetime expiration, congestion, and FCS error. In the latter case, notification is not possible since the source address field may have been damaged.

Flow Control.   Internet flow control allows routers and/or receiving stations to limit the rate at which they receive data. For the connectionless type of service we are describing, flow control mechanisms are limited. The best approach would seem to be to send flow control packets, requesting reduced data flow, to other routers and source stations.

14-6

CONNECTIONLESS INTERNETWORK PROTOCOL STANDARDS

ISO Internetwork Protocol Standard

In this subsection, we look at the IP standard developed by ISO [CALL83], [PISC84], [PISC86]). As with any protocol, IP can be described in two parts:

- The interface with a higher layer (e.g., ISO TP), specifying the services that IP provides.
- The IP protocol, specifying protocol data unit format and station-router and router-router interaction.

ISO IP Services.   IP provides a connectionless data transfer service to IP users (e.g., ISO TP) in stations attached to networks of the internet. Two primitives are defined at the user-IP interface. The IP user requests transmission of a unit of data with N-UNITDATA.request. N-UNITDATA.indication is used by IP to notify a user of the arrival of a data unit. For both primitives, the following parameters are used:

- *Source address:* internetwork address of sending IP entity.
- *Destination address:* internetwork address of IP entity that is to receive the data.
- *Quality of service:* options requested by the IP user.
- *NS-user-data:* user data to be transmitted.

The quality of service feature allows the user to specify additional services (beyond simple data transfer). The IP entity will endeavor, within the limitations of the network services available to it, to provide these additional services:

- *Transit delay:* the elapsed time between an N-UNITDATA.request at the source and the corresponding N-UNITDATA.indication at the destination.
- *Protection from unauthorized access:* prevention of unauthorized monitoring or manipulation of the user-originated information.
- *Cost determinants:* specification of cost considerations for the IP entity to use in selection of a route for the data.
- *Residual error probability:* the likelihood that a particular unit of data will be lost, duplicated, or delivered incorrectly.
- *Priority:* relative priority of user data.
- *Source routing:* Sequenced list of router addresses that specifies the route.

IP Protocol. The IP protocol is designed to provide the IP services described above. It is best explained by describing the IP data unit format (Figure 14-21). The header consists of four parts. The fixed part is always present and is of fixed length. It contains the following fields:

- *Protocol identifier:* When the source and destination stations are connected to the same network, an internet protocol is not needed. In that case, the internet layer is null and the header consists of this single field of 8 bits.
- *Length indicator:* length of the header in octets.
- *Version:* included to allow evolution of the protocol. Either header format or semantics might change.
- *PDU Lifetime:* Expressed as a multiple of 500 ms. It is determined and set by the source station. Each router that the IP data unit visits decrements this field by 1 for each 500 ms of estimated delay for that hop (transmit time to this router plus processing time).
- *Flags:* The SP flag indicates whether segmentation is permitted. The MS flag is the more flag described earlier. The ER flag indicates whether an error report is desired by the source station if an IP data unit is discarded.
- *Type:* Indicates whether this is a Data (contains user data) or Error (contains error report) PDU.
- *PDU Segment Length:* total data unit length, including header, in octets.
- *PDU checksum:* result of a checksum algorithm (defined in an appendix to this chapter) computed on the entire header. Since some header fields may change (e.g., time to live, segmentation-related fields), this is reverified and recomputed at each router.

The address part of the header is a variable length and is always present. Since addresses may be of variable length, an address length field precedes both the source and destination addresses.

If the SP flag is set to one, then the header includes a segmentation part, with the following fields:

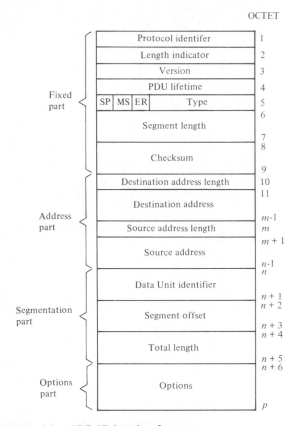

FIGURE 14-21.   ISO IP header format.

- *Data unit identifier:* intended to uniquely identify the PDU. Thus, the station IP entity must assign values that are unique for the PDU's destination and for the maximum time that the PDU may remain in the internet.
- *Segment offset:* indicates where in the initial PDU this segment belongs, measured in 64-bit units. This implies that segments other than the last one must contain user data fields that are a multiple of 64 bits in length.
- *Total length:* specifies the total length of the original PDU, including header and data.

Finally, an optional part may be included in the header, and is used to convey optional parameters. Each option is encoded in three fields: parameter code, parameter length, and parameter value. The parameters that may be specified include: Security, defined by the user; Source Routing, which list the routers to be visited; Recording of Route, which traces the route the PDU has taken so far; Quality of service, which specifies reliability and delay values; and Priority.

DOD Internetwork Protocol Standard

DOD has also issued an internetwork protocol standard [POST81]. Actually, DOD's IP predates ISO's, and the latter is based on the DOD standard.

DOD IP Services. Two primitives are defined at the user-IP interface. The Send primitive is used to request transmission of a data unit. The Deliver primitive is used by IP to notify a user of the arrival of a data unit. Although not part of the standard, IP is expected to use some sort of Error primitive to notify a user of failure in providing the requested service. This service is not assumed to be reliable; that is, there is no guarantee that errors will be reported.

The Send primitive includes the following parameters:

- *Source address:* internetwork address of sending IP entity.
- *Destination address:* internetwork address of IP entity to receive data.
- *Protocol:* identifies the recipient protocol entity (an IP user).
- *Type of service indicators:* used to specify the treatment of the data unit in its transmission through component networks. The indicators are precedence (eight levels), reliability (two levels), delay (two levels), and throughput (two levels). *Precedence* attempts preferential treatment for high importance datagrams. *Reliability* attempts to minimize data loss and error rate. *Delay* and *throughput* attempt to minimize delay or maximize throughput, respectively. To the extent possible, these parameters are passed on to the individual networks for their use. Of course, if a particular network supports only a single grade of service, this parameter has no effect for that leg of the journey.
- *Identifier:* is used, along with the source and destination addresses and user protocol, to identify the data unit uniquely. This parameter is needed for reassembly and error reporting.
- *Don't fragment identifier:* indicates whether IP can segment (called fragment in this standard) data to accomplish delivery.
- *Time to live:* measured in network hops.
- *Data length:* length of data being transmitted.
- *Option data:* options requested by the IP user.
- *Data:* user data to be transmitted.

The *options* feature allows for future extensibility and for inclusion of parameters that are not present with every data unit. The currently defined options are:

- *Security:* The security parameter allows each data unit to be labeled with a security label (e.g., SECRET, CONFIDENTIAL). Compartments are used to specify user groups authorized to access information (i.e., have a ''need to know'').
- *Source routing:* A sequenced list of router addresses specifies the route. Routing may be strict (only identified routers may be visited) or loose (other intermediate routers may also be visited).
- *Record routing:* A field is allocated to record the route of the datagram through a sequence of routers. The field should be large enough to prevent overflow.
- *Stream identification:* Reserved resources used for stream service are named. This service provides special handling for volatile periodic traffic (e.g., voice). IP must endeavor to maintain a constant delay per datagram.
- *Timestamp:* The source internet protocol entity and some or all intermediate routers add a timestamp (accurate to milliseconds) to the data unit as it goes by.

The Deliver primitive includes the following parameters

- Source address.
- Destination address.

- Protocol.
- Type of service indicators.
- Data length.
- Option data.
- Data.

IP Protocol.   The protocol between IP entities is best described by defining the IP datagram format, which is shown in Figure 14-22a. The fields are:

- *Version (4 bits):* version number, included to allow evolution of the protocol. Either header format or semantics might change.
- *Internet header length (IHL) (4 bits):* length of header in 32-bit words. The minimum value is five. Thus a header is at least 20 octets long.
- *Type of service (8 bits):* specifies reliability, precedence, delay, and throughput parameters.
- *Total length (16 bits):* total data unit length, including header, in octets.
- *Identifier (16 bits):* together with source address, destination address, and user protocol, intended to uniquely identify a datagram. Thus the identifier must be unique for the datagram's source, destination, and user protocol for the time during which the datagram will remain in the catenet.
- *Flags (3 bits):* one bit, the More flag, used for fragmentation (segmentation) and reassembly. Another bit, if set, prohibits fragmentation. This facility may be useful if it is known that the destination does not have the capability to reassemble fragments. An example is to down-line load a small microprocessor. However, if this bit is set, the datagram may be discarded if it exceeds the maximum size of an en route network. When the bit is set, it may be advisable to use source routing to avoid networks with small maximum packet sizes. The third bit is currently not used.

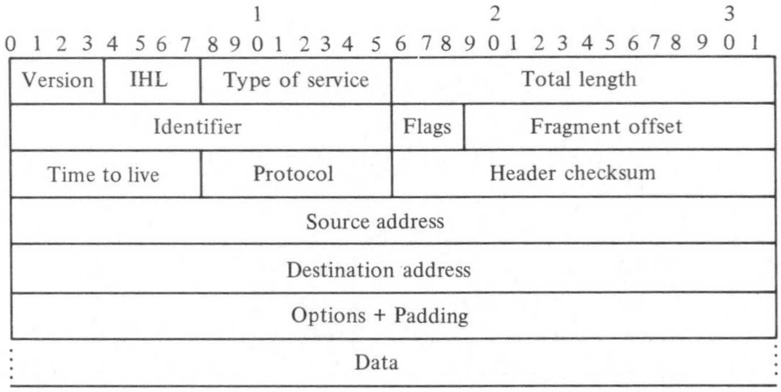

Version	IHL	Type of service	Total length	
Identifier			Flags	Fragment offset
Time to live		Protocol	Header checksum	
Source address				
Destination address				
Options + Padding				
Data				

(a) IP protocol data unit

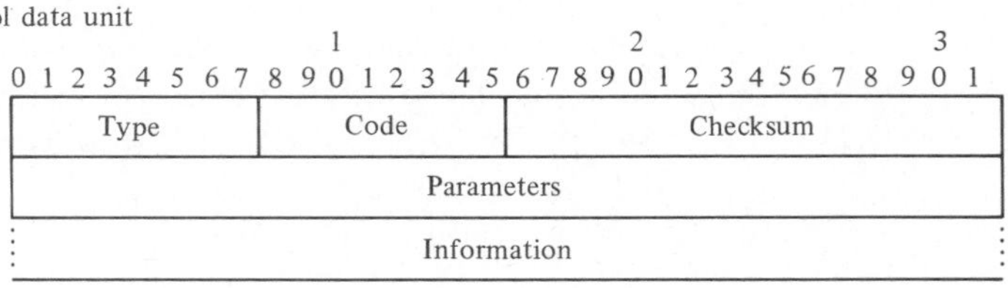

Type	Code	Checksum
Parameters		
Information		

(b) ICMP protocol data unit

FIGURE 14-22.   DOD internet protocol formats.

- *Fragment offset (13 bits):* indicates where in the datagram this fragment belongs. It is measured in 64-bit units. This implies that fragments (other than the last fragment) must contain a data field that is a multiple of 64 bits long.
- *Time to live (8 bits):* measured in router hops.
- *Protocol (8 bits):* indicates the next level protocol which is to receive the data field at the destination.
- *Header checksum (16 bits):* frame check sequence on the header only. Since some header fields may change (e.g., time to live, fragmentation-related fields), this is reverified and recomputed at each router. The checksum field is the 16-bit one's complement addition of all 16 bit words in the header. For purposes of computation, the checksum field itself is considered to have a value of zero.
- *Source address (32 bits):* coded to allow a variable allocation of bits to specify the network and the station within the specified network (7 and 24, 14 and 16, or 21 and 8).
- *Destination address (32 bits):* as above.
- *Options (variable):* encodes the options requested by the sender.
- *Padding (variable):* used to ensure that the internet header ends on a 32-bit boundary.
- *Data (variable):* the data field must be a multiple of eight bits in length. Total length of data field plus header is a maximum of 65,535 octets.

It should be easy to see how the services specified above map into the fields of the IP data units.

Internet Control Message Protocol

DOD has defined an *internet control message protocol* (ICMP) which is a required companion to IP [DARP81]. Basically, ICMP provides feedback about problems in the communication environment. Examples of its use are: When a datagram cannot reach its destination, when the router does not have the buffering capacity to forward a datagram, and when the router can direct the station to send traffic on a shorter route.

Although ICMP is, in effect, at the same level as IP, it is a user of IP. An ICMP message is constructed and then passed on to IP, which encapsulates the message with an IP header and then transmits it to the destination gateway or station. Figure 14-22b shows the general format of ICMP messages. The fields are:

- *Type (8 bits):* specifies the type of ICMP message.
- *Code (8 bits):* used to specify parameters of the message that can be encoded in one or a few bits.
- *Checksum (16 bits):* checksum of the entire ICMP message.
- *Parameters (32 bits):* used to specify more lengthy parameters.
- *Information (variable):* provides additional information related to the message.

In those cases in which the ICMP message refers to a prior datagram, the information field includes the entire IP header plus the first 64 bits of the data field of the original datagram. This enables the source host to match the incoming ICMP message with the prior datagram. The reason for including the first 64 bits of the data field is that this will enable the IP module in the host to determine which upper-level protocol or protocols were involved. In particular, the first 64 bits would include the TCP header or other transport-level header.

Eleven types of messages have been defined:

- Destination unreachable
- Time exceeded
- Parameter problem
- Source quench
- Redirect
- Echo
- Echo reply
- Timestamp
- Timestamp reply
- Information request
- Information reply

The **destination unreachable** message covers a number of contingencies. A router may return this message if it does not know how to reach the destination network. In some networks, an attached router may be able to determine if a particular host is unreachable, and return the message. The destination host itself may return this message if the user protocol or some higher-level service access point is unreachable. This could happen if the corresponding field in the IP header was set incorrectly. If the datagram specifies a source route that is unusable, a message is returned. Finally, if a router must fragment a datagram but the Don't Fragment flag is set, a message is returned.

A router will return a **time exceeded** message if the lifetime of the datagram expires. A host will send this message if it cannot complete reassembly within a time limit.

A syntactic or semantic error in an IP header will cause a **parameter problem** message to be returned by a router or host. For example, an incorrect argument may be provided with an option. The parameter field contains a pointer to the octet in the original header where the error was detected.

The **source quench** message provides a rudimentary form of flow control. Either a router or a destination host may send this message to a source host, requesting that it reduce the rate at which it is sending traffic to the internet destination. On receipt of a source quench message, the source host should cut back the rate at which it is sending traffic to the specified destination until it no longer receives source quench messages. The source quench message can be used by a router or host which must discard datagrams because of a full buffer. In that case, the router or host will issue a source quench message for every datagram that it discards. In addition, a system may anticipate congestion and issue source quench messages when its buffers approach capacity. In that case, the datagram referred to in the source quench message may well be delivered. Thus, receipt of a source quench message does not imply delivery or nondelivery of the corresponding datagram.

A router sends a **redirect** message to a host on a directly connected router to advise the host of a better route to a particular destination. The following is an example of its use. A router, R1, receives a datagram from a host on a network to which the router is attached. The router, R1, checks its routing table and obtains the address for the next router, R2, on the route to the datagram's internet destination network, X. If R2 and the host identified by the internet source address of the datagram are on the same network, a redirect message is sent to the host. The redirect message advises the host to send its traffic for network X directly to router R2, as this is a shorter path to the destination. The router forwards the original datagram to its internet destination (via R2). The address of R2 is contained in the parameter field of the redirect message.

The **echo** and **echo reply** messages provide a mechanism for testing that communication is possible between entities. The recipient of an echo message is obligated to return the message in an echo reply message. An identifier and sequence number are associated with the echo message to be matched in the echo reply message. The identifier might be used like a serviced access point to identify a particular session and the sequence number might be incremented on each echo request sent.

The **timestamp** and **timestamp reply** messages provide a mechanism for sampling the delay characteristics of the internet. The sender of a timestamp message may include an identifier and sequence number in the parameters field and include the time that the message is sent (originate timestamp). The receiver records the time it received the message and the time that it transmits the reply message in the timestamp reply message. If the timestamp message is sent using strict source routing, then the delay characteristics of a particular route can be measured.

The **information request** and **information reply** messages can be used by a host to discover the address of the network to which it is attached, in the following way. The host sends an information request message with the network portion of the source address field of the IP header set to 0. The use of 0 is interpreted as "this network." The replying IP module should send the reply with the addresses fully specified.

14-7

ROUTER-LEVEL PROTOCOLS

The routers in an internet perform much the same function as packet-switching nodes (PSNs) in a packet-switching network (Figure 14-20). As with the nodes of a packet-switching network, the bridges or routers of an internet need to make routing decisions based on knowledge of the topology and conditions of the internet. In simple internets, a fixed routing scheme is possible. However, in more complex internets, a degree of dynamic cooperation is needed among the routers. In particular, the router must avoid portions of the network that have failed and should avoid portions of the network that are congested. In order to make such dynamic routing decisions, routers exchange routing information using a special protocol for that purpose. Information is needed about the status of the internet, in terms of which networks can be reached by which routes, and the delay characteristics of various routes.

In considering the routing function of routers, it is important to distinguish two concepts:

- *Routing information:* information about the topology and delays of the internet.
- *Routing algorithm:* the algorithm used to make a routing decision for a particular datagram, based on current routing information.

A router-router protocol can be used for the purpose of exchanging routing information. In general however, such protocols do not assume or dictate a particular routing algorithm. A general-purpose protocol will provide sufficient information to support a variety of routing algorithms.

Autonomous Systems

In order to proceed in our discussion of router-router protocols, we need to introduce the concept of an **autonomous system.** An autonomous system is an internet connected by homogeneous routers; generally the routers are under the administrative control of a single entity. An **interior router protocol** (IRP) passes routing information between routers within an autonomous system. The protocol used with the autonomous system does not need to be implemented outside of the system. This flexibility allows IRPs to be custom-tailored to specific applications and requirements.

It may happen, however, that an internet will be constructed of more than one autonomous system. For example, all of the local area networks at a site, such as a military base or campus, could be linked by routers to form an autonomous system. This system might be linked through a wide-area network to other autonomous systems. The situation is illustrated in Figure 14-23. In this case, the routing algorithms and routing tables used by routers in different autonomous systems may differ. Nevertheless, the routers in one autonomous system need at least a minimal level of information concerning networks outside the system that can be reached. The protocol used to pass routing information between routers in different autonomous systems is referred to as an **exterior router protocol** (ERP).

We can expect that an ERP will need to pass less information and be simpler than an IRP, for the following reason. If a datagram is to be transferred from a

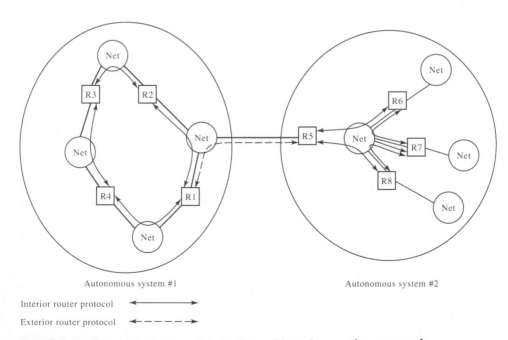

FIGURE 14-23.   Application of exterior and interior routing protocols.

host in one autonomous system to a host in another autonomous system, a router in the first system need only determine the target autonomous system and devise a route to get into that target system. Once the datagram enters the target autonomous system, the routers within that system can cooperate to finally deliver the datagram. For this reason, more progress has been made on standardizing on an ERP than on an IRP. In the next portion of this section, we look at the most widely-used ERP. This will be followed by a discussion of a recently-developed IRP.

Exterior Gateway Protocol

The Exterior Gateway Protocol (EGP) [MILL84] was developed for use in conjunction with internets that employ the TCP/IP protocol suite, although the concepts are applicable to any internet.

Functions. The EGP was designed to allow routers, called gateways, in different autonomous systems to cooperate in the exchange of routing information. The protocol operates in terms of commands and responses, which are sent inside IP datagrams. The repertoire of commands and responses is summarized in Table 14-6.

Three functional procedures are involved in EGP:

- Neighbor acquisition
- Neighbor reachability
- Network reachability

Two routers are considered to be neighbors if they share the same subnetwork. If the two routers are in different autonomous systems, they may wish to exchange routing information. For this purpose, it is necessary to first perform **neighbor acquisition.** In essence, neighbor acquisition occurs when two neighboring routers in different autonomous systems agree to regularly exchange routing information. A formal acquisition procedure is needed since one of the routers may not wish to participate. For example, the router may be overburdened and does not want to be responsible for traffic coming in from outside the system. In the neighbor acqui-

TABLE 14-6   EGP Commands and Responses

	Command		Corresponding Response	
Name	Interpretation		Name	Interpretation
Request	Request gateway become a neighbor		Confirm Refuse	Confirm neighbor relationship Refuse neighbor relationship
Cease	Request termination of neighbor relationship		Cease-ack	Confirm termination
Hello	Request neighbor confirm neighbor reachability		I-H-U	Confirm reachability
Poll	Request neighbor provide network reachability information		Update	Provide network reachability update
			Error	Error

sition process, one router sends a request message to the other, which may either accept or refuse the offer. The protocol does not address the issue of how one router knows the address or even the existence of another router, nor how it decides that it needs to exchange routing information with that particular router. These issues must be dealt with at configuration time or by active intervention of a network manager.

To perform neighbor acquisition, one router sends a Request command to another. If the target router accepts the request, it returns a Confirm response. Otherwise, it returns a Refuse response. After a neighbor relationship has been established, either side may terminate the relationship with a Cease message, for which the appropriate response is a Cease-ack message.

Once a neighbor relationship is established, the **neighbor reachability** procedure is used to maintain the relationship. Each partner needs to be assured that the other partner still exists and is still engaged in the neighbor relationship. For this purpose, the two routers periodically exchange Hello and I-H-U (I heard you) messages. Either router may issue a Hello command, and the partner router is obligated to reply as soon as possible with an I-H-U response.

The final procedure specified by EGP is **network reachability.** As with neighbor reachability, network reachability involves a periodic command/response pair. In this case, one router sends a Poll command, and its partner responds with an Update response. The Update response contains a list of networks that can be reached by the responding router, together with an estimate of the "distance" of each network. This distance typically is expressed in terms of the number of router hops. On the basis of this information, the requesting router can build up a routing table based on determining the shortest path to each destination router.

Formats.   Figure 14-24 illustrates the formats of all of the EGP messages. Each message type begins with a ten-octet header containing the following fields:

- *EGP Version Number:* identifies version of EGP
- *Type:* message type
- *Code:* provides additional information about the message. In effect, it identifies a subtype of message.
- *Status:* provides message-dependent status information.
- *Checksum:* Checksum of the entire EGP message. This is the same checksum used for IP.
- *Autonomous System Number:* assigned number identifying the particular autonomous system.
- *Sequence Number:* used to synchronize commands and responses. A router establishes an initial sequence number during neighbor acquisition, and may increment the number for each subsequent command. Responses contain the last sequence number received.

The **neighbor acquisition** format is used for all of the commands and responses relating to neighbor acquisition and termination (request, confirm, refuse, cease, cease-ack). The Hello Interval and Poll Interval fields specify the minimum intervals between such commands from the partner. This is used to limit the burden of responding to commands for the router. The status field is used to indicate a problem or to declare the mode of operation of the router. A router operating in passive mode will not send Hello commands, and gains neighbor reachability in-

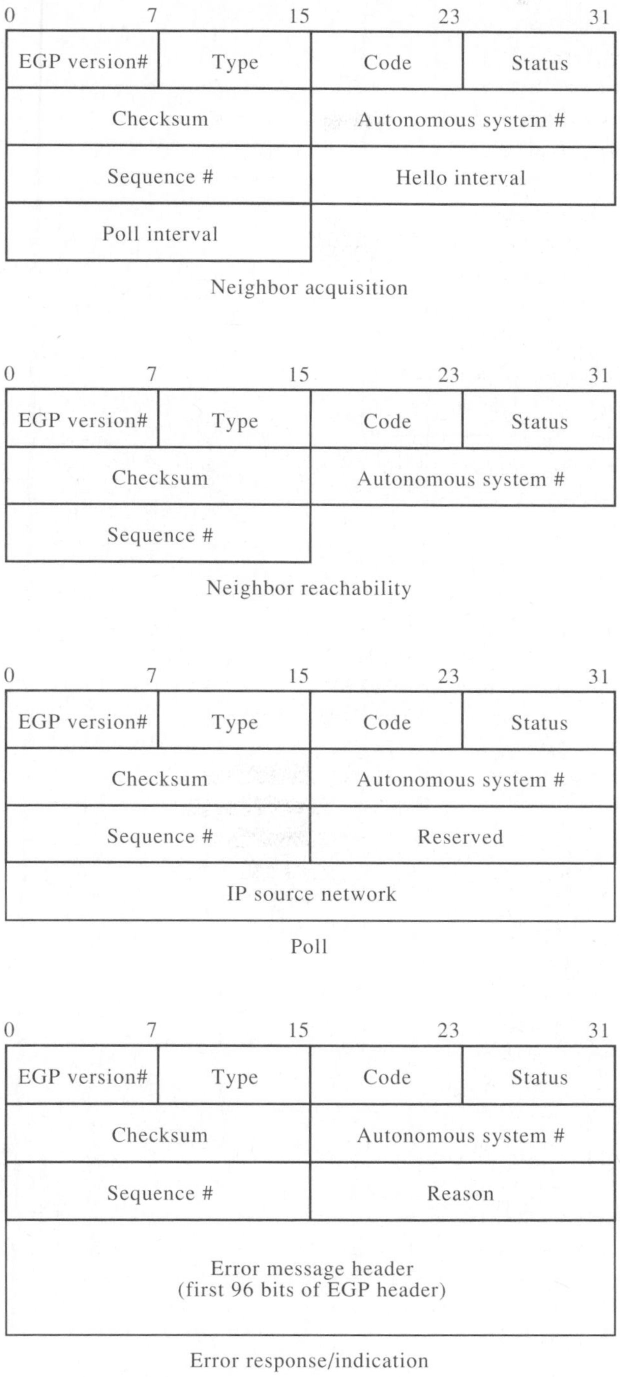

0	7	15	23	31
EGP version#	Type	Code	Status	
Checksum		Autonomous system #		
Sequence #		Hello interval		
Poll interval				

Neighbor acquisition

0	7	15	23	31
EGP version#	Type	Code	Status	
Checksum		Autonomous system #		
Sequence #				

Neighbor reachability

0	7	15	23	31
EGP version#	Type	Code	Status	
Checksum		Autonomous system #		
Sequence #		Reserved		
IP source network				

Poll

0	7	15	23	31
EGP version#	Type	Code	Status	
Checksum		Autonomous system #		
Sequence #		Reason		
Error message header (first 96 bits of EGP header)				

Error response/indication

FIGURE 14-24.   EGP formats.

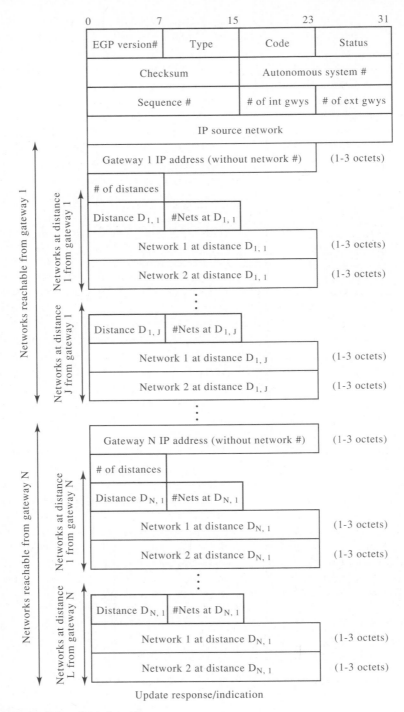

FIGURE 14-24.   (continued).

formation only by responding to Hello commands from the other side. In active mode, a router will periodically issue Hello commands. At least one of the routers in a partnership must be in active mode.

The **neighbor reachability** format is used for the Hello/I-H-U exchange. The status field indicates whether the router is up or down. In the down state, the router is currently unable/unwilling to provide routing information.

The **poll** format is used to solicit network reachability information. The IP Source Network field contains the network number of the network about which reachability information is being requested. This network is one that is common to both autonomous systems and is usually (but not necessarily) a network to which both routers are attached. In effect, the poll message is asking the question: For all routers on the specified network, what networks can be reached by each router and what are the distances involved?

At first glance, the question seems too broad. The requesting router will necessarily want to know which networks are reachable via the responding router, but why ask about other routers? This is best explained with reference to Figure 14-23. In this example, router R1 in autonomous system 1 and router R5 in autonomous system 2 implement EGP and acquire a neighbor relationship. When R5 sends a poll request to R1, R1 responds by indicating which networks it could reach and the distances (network hops) involved. R1 also provides the same information on behalf of R2. That is, R1 tells R5 what networks are reachable via R2 at what distances. In this example, the reason that R5 does not interrogate R2 directly is that R2 does not implement EGP. Typically, most of the routers in an autonomous system will not implement EGP. Only a few routers will be assigned responsibility for communicating with routers in other autonomous systems. A final point: R1 is in possession of the necessary information about R2, since R1 and R2 share an interior router protocol (IRP).

With this background, we can now describe the **update** format. The bulk of the message consists of a number of blocks, one for each router for which a report is provided. The block begins with the internet address of the router that is the subject of that block. The remainder of the block consists of a list of reachable networks grouped according to their distance from this router. First, the number of different distances is specified. The remainder of the block consists of a number of sub-blocks, one for each distance. Each sub-block begins with a field specifying the distance, followed by a field that specifies the number of networks that are reachable at that distance. Finally, the network address of each network at that distance is listed. In Figure 14-24, the notation $D_{i,j}$ has the interpretation: the jth distance in the block for router i.

Two fields in the update message remain to be explained. These fields list the number of internal and external routers provided in this update report. All routers, of course, must directly attach to the network specified in the poll command and repeated in the update response. Internal routers are those that are in the same autonomous system as the responding router. External routers are those in other autonomous systems whose routing information is known to the responding router. This latter situation may arise when one network supports routers from more than two autonomous systems.

The **error** format is used to provide information about a variety of error conditions and may be used in response to any command. The reason field may contain one of the following identifiers:

0   unspecified
1   bad EGP header format
2   bad EGP data field format
3   reachability information unavailable
4   excessive polling rate
5   no response received to a poll

The last field of the error message contains the first 12 octets of the message that caused the error detection.

Open Shortest Path First (OSPF) Protocol

The OSPF protocol was developed as part of the networking research associated with ARPANET and the Defense Advanced Research Projects Agency (DARPA) [MOY89a, MOY89b, BOULE89]. OSPF has also been proposed as in international standard. OSPF is intended for use as an interior routing protocol.

The history of interior routing protocols on the DARPA internet, mirrors that of packet-switching protocols on ARPANET. Recall that ARPANET began with a protocol based on the Bellman-Ford algorithm. The resulting protocol required each node to exchange *path delay information* with its neighbors. Information about a change in network conditions would gradually ripple through the network. A second generation protocol was based on Dijkstra's algorithm and required each node to exchange *link delay information* with all other nodes using flooding. It was found that this latter technique was more effective.

Similarly, the initial interior routing protocol on the DARPA internet was the Routing Information Protocol (RIP), which is essentially the same protocol as the first-generation ARPANET protocol. This protocol requires each router to transmit its entire routing table. Although the algorithm is simple and easy to implement, as the internet expands, routing updates grow larger and consume significantly more network bandwidth. Accordingly, OSPF operates in a fashion similar to the revised ARPANET routing algorithm: each router only transmits descriptions of its local link. This information is transmitted to all of the other routers of which it is aware. Every router receiving the update packet must acknowledge it to the sender. Such updates produce a minimum of routing traffic because link descriptions are small and rarely need to be refreshed.

OSPF provides least-cost routing through a fully user-configurable routing metric that can be set to express any function of delay, data rate, dollar cost, or other factors. OSPF is able to equalize loads over several equal-cost paths.

The topological description of the internet is somewhat more complex than that of a packet-switching network. The database of the topology of an autonomous system, from which routing tables are calculated, is a directed graph. The vertices of the graph are two types: routers and networks. A network vertex is termed transit if it can carry data that neither originates nor terminates on a host on that network; otherwise, it is a stub network. Graph edges are also of two types:

- A graph edge connects two router vertices when they are connected to each other by a direct point-to-point link.
- A graph edge connects a router vertex to a network vertex when the router has an interface on the network.

Figure 14-25 shows an example of an autonomous system, and Figure 14-26 is the resulting directed graph. The mapping is straightforward:

- Two routers joined by a point-to-point line are represented in the graph as being directly connected by a pair of edges, one in each direction (e.g., routers 6 and 10).
- When multiple routers are attached to a network (such as a LAN or a packet-switching network), the directed graph shows all routers bidirectionally connected to the network vertex (e.g., routers 1, 2, 3, and 4 connected to network 3).
- If a single router is attached to a network, the network will appear in the graph as a stub connection (e.g., network 7).
- A host computer can be directly connected to a router, in which case it is depicted in the corresponding graph (e.g., host 1).
- If a router is connected to other autonomous systems, then the path cost to each network in the other systems must be obtained by some exterior routing protocol (ERP). Each such network is represented on the graph by a stub and an edge to the router with the known path cost (e.g., networks 12 through 15).

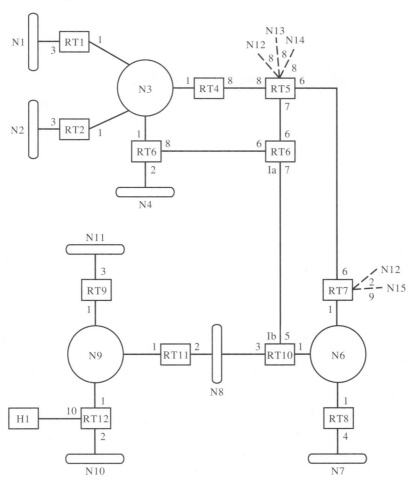

FIGURE 14-25. A sample autonomous system [MOY89].

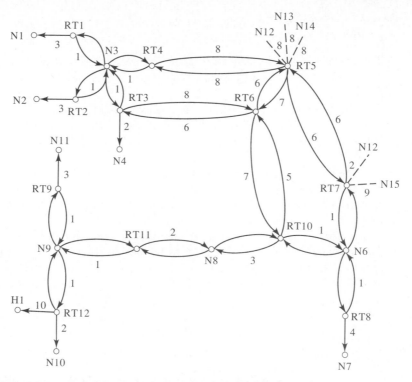

FIGURE 14-26. The resulting directed graph [MOY89].

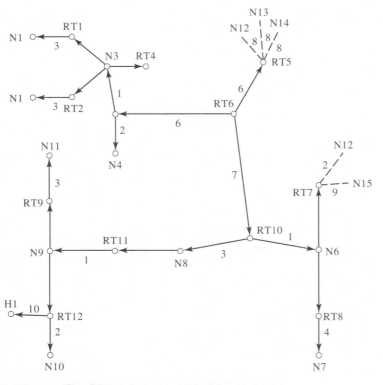

FIGURE 14-27. The SPF tree for router RT6 [MOY89].

TABLE 14-7 Routing Table for Router RT6

Destination	Next Hop	Distance
N1	RT3	10
N2	RT3	10
N3	RT3	7
N4	RT3	8
N6	RT10	8
N7	RT10	12
N8	RT10	10
N9	RT10	11
N10	RT10	13
N11	RT10	14
H1	RT10	21
RT5	RT5	6
RT7	RT10	8
N12	RT10	10
N13	RT5	14
N14	RT5	14
N15	RT10	17

A cost is associated with the output side of each router interface. This cost is configurable by the system administrator. Arcs on the graph are labelled with the cost of the corresponding router output interface. Arcs having no labelled cost have a cost of 0. Note that arcs leading from networks to routers always have cost 0; they are significant nonetheless.

A database corresponding to the directed graph is maintained by each router. It is pieced together from link state messages from other routers in the internet. Using Dijkstra's algorithm, a router calculates the shortest path to all destination networks. The result for routers 6 of Figure 14-26 are shown as a tree in Figure 14-27. The tree gives the entire route to any destination network or host. However, only the next hop to the destination is used in the forwarding process. The resulting routing table for router 6 is shown in Table 14-7. The table includes entries for routers advertising external routes (routers 5 and 7). For external networks whose identity is known, entries are also provided.

14-8

RECOMMENDED READING

Two special issues of the Journal on Selected Areas in Communications provide a number of worthwhile papers on internetworking [GREE90, BUX87]. [GERL88] is a special issue of IEEE Network devoted to bridges. [PARU90] is a thoughtful discussion of the implications of high-speed networking and future trends in distributed processing for internetworking. [CERF87] remains one of the best overall discussions of the design issues related to internetworking. Considerable detail on the ISO internet protocol standard can be found in [BURG89], [ISRA87], and [WEIS87].

Good book-length treatments of the topic are [MCCO88] and [COME88].

14-9

PROBLEMS

14-1 Compare virtual circuit relay and IP. What are the principal strengths and weaknesses of each?

14-2 In Figure 14-16, X.25 is used across a LAN. Note that there are no DCEs, although CCITT has defined X.25 as a DTE-to-DCE protocol. What has happened is this: ISO has issued an extension of X.25 that allows it to be used in a "DTE-to-DTE mode" across a network. What changes are needed in the protocol for this application?

14-3 What are the pros and cons of intermediate reassembly of an internet segmented datagram versus reassembly at the final destination?

14-4 In the case of the ISO internet protocol, the checksum needs to be recalculated at routers because of changes to the internet PDU header, such as a change in PDU lifetime field. In this case, it is certainly possible to recalculate the checksum from scratch. However, because of the nature of the algorithm, some time may be saved by a shorter procedure. Suggest such a procedure. Hint: Suppose that the value in octet k is changed by $Z = $ new_value-old_value. If X and Y denote the checksum values held in octets n and $n + 1$, respectively, then what adjustments must be made to X and Y as a function of Z?

14-5 Repeat the previous problem for the checksum used in the TCP/IP protocol suite.

14-6 Assume a local network is to be attached to a long-haul X.25 network via a single station which appears to the X.25 network as a single DTE. What gateway logic in the station would allow other local network stations to have access to the X.25 network?

14-7 An IP datagram is to be segmented. Which options in the option field need to be copied into the header of each segment, and which need only be retained in the first segment?

14-8 Because of segmentation, an IP datagram can arrive in pieces, not necessarily in the right order. The IP layer at the receiving host must accumulate these segments until the original datagram is reconstituted.
   a. Consider that the IP layer creates a buffer for assembling the datagram. As assembly proceeds the buffer will consist of data and "holes" between the data. Describe an algorithm for reassembly based on this concept.
   b. For the algorithm above, it is necessary to keep track of the holes. Describe a simple mechanism for doing this.

14-9   A transport layer message consisting of 1500 bits of data and 160 bits of header is sent to an internet layer which appends another 160 bits of header. This is then transmitted through two networks, each of which uses a 24-bit packet header. The destination network has a maximum packet size of 800 bits. How many bits, including headers, are delivered to the network layer protocol at the destination?

14-10   The ICMP format includes the first 64 bits of the datagram data field. What might be the purpose of including these bits?

14-11   The architecture suggested by Figure 14-18 is to be used. What functions could be added to the gateways to alleviate some of the problems caused by the mismatched local and long-haul networks?

14-12   Would the spanning tree approach be good for an internet including routers?

14-13   Should internetworking be concerned with a network's internal routing? Why or why not?

APPENDIX 14A

THE ISO CHECKSUM ALGORITHM

The ISO internetwork protocol standard uses an error-detecting code, or checksum, originally specified in [FLET82], and referred to as the Fletcher checksum. This code is also used in the ISO Class 4 transport protocol discussed in Chapter 15. In both cases, a 16-bit checksum is included as a field in each PDU. The checksum is initially calculated by the sender and placed in the outgoing PDU. The receiver applies the same algorithm to the entire header, now including the 16-bit checksum, and should get a zero result if there are no errors.

14A1   Modulo 255 Addition

The Fletcher checksum is based on treating the data to be checked as a sequence of 8-bit unsigned integers and performing mod 255 addition on those integers. With mod 255 addition, the sum of any two numbers is found by performing addition and finding the remainder after division by 255. Thus:

$$254 + 253 \ (\text{mod } 255) = 507 - 255 = 252$$

This scheme is equivalent to performing one's complement addition on the numbers treated as 8-bit unsigned binary integers. With one's complement addition, if there is a carry out of the leftmost digit, then the carry digit is added back to the sum; this is known as *end-around carry*. For example:

$$
\begin{array}{rl}
11111110 & = 254 \\
+\ \underline{11111101} & = 253 \\
111111011 & = 507 \\
\underline{\qquad\qquad 1} & \\
11111100 & = 252
\end{array}
$$

In the original description of the algorithm, Fletcher suggested that either a mod 255 or 256 addition could be used. Because there appears to be a slight advantage, in terms of error-detecting power in using mod 255, this option was chosen for the ISO standards. Unfortunately, mod 255 addition is computationally more complex than mod 256 addition [NAKA88, COCK87].

14A2 Generating the Checksum

The algorithm is based on producing two octets calculated on the octets of the data to be checked (henceforth referred to as *message*). The two values are:

- The sum, modulo 255, of every octet in the message
- The sum, modulo 255, of every octet weighted (reversely) by its position in the message

That is:

$$C0 = \sum_{i=1}^{L} B(i)$$

$$C1 = \sum_{i=1}^{L} (L - i + 1) \times B(i)$$

where:

$$\begin{aligned}
C0 &= \text{first check octet} \\
C1 &= \text{second check octet} \\
L &= \text{length of message in octets} \\
B(i) &= \text{value of } i\text{th octet}
\end{aligned}$$

For convenience, the checksum calculation is performed on the entire message, including the fields that will contain the two check octets. These fields are initialized to zero. Thus, if the two checksum positions are n and $n + 1$, then the two summations above are performed with $B(n) = B(n + 1) = 0$.

Finally, we would like to set the values of the checksum octets so that the results of algorithm is zero. That is, we need:

$$C0' = 0 = \sum_{i=1}^{L} B(i) = C0 + B(n) + B(n + 1)$$

$$C1' = 0 = \sum_{i=1}^{L} (L - i + 1) \times B(i)$$

$$= C1 + (L - n + 1) \times B(n) + (L - n) \times B(n + 1)$$

Where $C0$ and $C1$ are the calculations made with the checksum positions set to zero, and $C0'$ and $C1'$ are the same calculations made after the checksum positions have been set to their proper values. Solving, we obtain

$$B(n) = (L - n) \times C0 - C1$$
$$B(n) = C1 - (L - n + 1) \times C0$$

14A3   Checking the Checksum

Upon receipt of the message, the receiver performs the calculations for $C0$ and $C1$ with the received values, including the received values of the checksum positions. If the result is $C0 = C1 = 0$, then the checksum calculation has succeeded and no errors are assumed.

14A4   Motivation

The most commonly used error-detection algorithm is the cyclic redundancy check (CRC), described in Chapter 4. The CRC has several proven, desirable properties with regard to the kind and number of errors that it can detect. Furthermore, it may be conveniently and efficiently implemented in hardware [SKLO89]. Although the Fletcher checksum is not as powerful, it can be shown that, assuming all bit errors are equally likely, the Fletcher checksum:

- detects all single-bit errors;
- detects all double-bit errors;
- fails to detect only 0.000019% of all burst errors of length not exceeding 16;
- fails to detect only 0.0015% of all larger burst errors.

For the internet and transport protocols, the main drawback of the CRC is that software implementations are relatively inefficient due to the number of computations required. The advantage of the Fletcher checksum is that it is relatively simple to implement and operates relatively efficiently. Nevertheless, it has quite good error-detection properties [FLET82]. Also, in the case of the internet protocol, the recalculation of the checksum after a few octets have been modified is a relatively simple matter. Recalculation with a CRC is considerably more complex.

CHAPTER 15

Transport Protocols

The transport protocol is the keystone of the whole concept of a computer-communications architecture. Lower-layer protocols are needed, to be sure, but they are less important pedagogically and to designers for a number of reasons. For one thing, lower-level protocols are better understood and, on the whole, less complex than transport protocols. Also, standards have settled out quite well for most kinds of layer 1 to 3 transmission facilities, and there is a large body of experience in their use.

Viewed from the other side, upper level protocols are also of lesser importance. The transport protocol provides the basic end-to-end service of transferring data between users. Any process or application can be programmed to access directly the transport services without going through session and presentation layers. Indeed, this is the normal mode of operation for DOD's transport protocols.

The author's conviction of the importance of the transport protocol, together with the remarkable complexity of such protocols, has led to a rather long chapter. For this, the reader's indulgence is begged. We begin by looking at the services that one might expect from a transport protocol. Next, we examine the protocol mechanisms required to provide these services. We find that most of the complexity relates to connection-oriented services. As might be expected, the less the network service provides, the more the transport protocol must do. We then look briefly at the types of network services that might be provided. Then, two sets of protocol standards are examined. Finally, the concept of lightweight transport protocols is introduced.

15-1

TRANSPORT SERVICES

We begin by looking at the kinds of services that a transport protocol can or should provide to higher-level protocols. Figure 15-1 places the concept of transport services in context. In a system, there is a transport entity which provides services to transport users, which might be an application process or a session protocol entity. This local transport entity communicates with some remote transport entity, using the services of some lower layer, such as the network layer.

We have already mentioned that the general service provided by a transport protocol is the end-to-end transport of data in a way that shields the user from the details of the underlying communications systems. To be more specific, we must consider the specific services that a transport protocol can provide. The following categories of service, based on [NBS80b], are useful for describing the transport service:

- Type of service.
- Grade of service.
- Data transfer.
- User interface.
- Connection management.
- Expedited delivery.
- Status reporting.
- Security.

Type of Service

Two basic types of service are possible: connection-oriented and connectionless or datagram service. A connection-oriented service provides for the establishment,

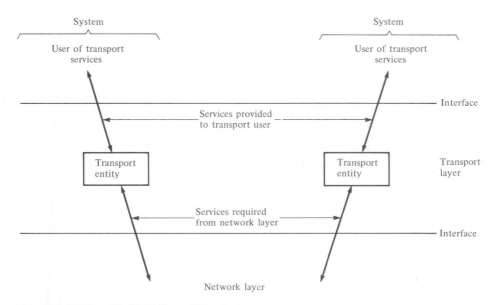

FIGURE 15-1.   **Transport entity context.**

maintenance, and termination of a logical connection between transport users. This has, so far, been the most common type of protocol service available and has a wide variety of applications. The connection-oriented service generally implies that the service is reliable.

The strengths of the connection-oriented approach are clear. It allows connection-related features such as flow control, error control, and sequenced delivery. Connectionless service, however, is more appropriate in some contexts. At lower layers (internet, network), connectionless service is more robust (e.g., see discussion in Section 9-2). In addition, it represents a "least common denominator" of service to be expected at higher layers. Further, even at transport and above there is justification for a connectionless service. There are instances in which the overhead of connection establishment and maintenance is unjustified or even counterproductive. Some examples, listed in [CHAP82]:

- *Inward data collection:* involves the periodic active or passive sampling of data sources, such as sensors, and automatic self-test reports from security equipment or network components. In a real-time monitoring situation, the loss of an occasional data unit would not cause distress, since the next report should arrive shortly.
- *Outward data dissemination:* includes broadcast messages to network users, the announcement of a new node or the change of address of a service, and the distribution of real-time clock values.
- *Request-response:* applications in which a transaction service is provided by a common server to a number of distributed users, and for which a single request-response sequence is typical. Use of the service is regulated at the application level, and lower level connections are often unnecessary and cumbersome.
- *Real-time applications:* such as voice and telemetry, involving a degree of redundancy and/or a real-time transmission requirement. These must not have connection-oriented functions such as retransmission.

Thus, there is a place at the transport level for both a connection-oriented and a connectionless type of service.

Quality of Service

The transport protocol entity should allow the transport user to specify the quality of transmission service to be provided. The transport entity will attempt to optimize the use of the underlying link, network, and internet resources to the best of its ability, to provide the collective requested services.

Examples of services that might be requested:

- Acceptable error and loss levels.
- Desired average and maximum delay.
- Desired average and minimum throughput.
- Priority levels.

Of course, the transport entity is limited to the inherent capabilities of the underlying service. For example, the DOD internet protocol does provide a quality of service parameter. It allows specification of eight levels of precedence or priority, and a binary specification for normal or low delay, normal or high throughput, and normal or high reliability. Thus, the transport entity can "pass the buck" to the internetwork entity, which is still dependent on the underlying transmission facilities. Another example: X.25 provides for throughput class negotiation as an optional user facility. The network may alter flow control parameters and the amount of network resources allocated on a virtual circuit to achieve desired throughput.

The transport layer may also resort to other mechanisms to try to satisfy user requests, such as splitting one transport connection among multiple virtual circuits to enhance throughput.

The user of the quality of service feature needs to recognize that:

- Depending on the nature of the transmission facility, the transport entity will have varying degrees of success in providing a requested grade of service.
- There is bound to be a trade-off among reliability, delay, throughput, and cost of services.

Nevertheless, certain applications would benefit from, or even require, certain qualities of service and, in a hierarchical or layered architecture, the easiest way for an application to extract this quality of service from a transmission facility is to pass the request down to the transport protocol.

Examples of applications that might request particular qualities of service:

- A file transfer protocol might require high throughput. It may also require high reliability to avoid retransmissions at the file transfer level.
- A transaction protocol (e.g., data-base query) may require low delay.
- An electronic mail protocol may require multiple priority levels.

One approach to providing a variety of qualities of service is to include a quality of service facility within the protocol. We have seen this with IP and will see that transport protocols to be discussed later follow the same approach. An alternative is to provide a different transport protocol for different classes of traffic. Four types of transport protocol are suggested in [MCFA79]:

- A reliable connection-oriented protocol.
- A less reliable connectionless protocol.
- A speech protocol, requiring sequenced, timely delivery.
- A real-time protocol that requires high reliability and timeliness.

Data Transfer

The whole purpose, of course, of a transport protocol is to transfer data between two transport entities. Both user data and control data must be transferred, either on the same channel or separate channels. Full-duplex service must be provided. Half-duplex and simplex modes may also be offered to support peculiarities of particular users.

User Interface

It is not clear that the exact mechanism of the user interface to the transport protocol should be standardized. Rather, it should be optimized to the station environment. As examples, a transport entity's services could be invoked by:

- Procedure calls.
- Passing of data and parameters to a process through a mailbox.
- Use of direct memory access (DMA) between a host user and a front-end processor containing the transport entity.

A few characteristics of the interface may be specified however. For example, a mechanism is needed to prevent the user from swamping the transport entity with data. A similar mechanism is needed to prevent the transport entity from swamping a user with data. Another aspect of the interface has to do with the timing and significance of confirmations. Consider: A transport user passes data to a transport entity to be delivered to a remote user. The local transport entity can acknowledge receipt of the data immediately, or it can wait until the remote transport entity reports that the data have made it through to the other end. Perhaps the most useful interface is one that allows immediate acceptance or rejection of requests, with later confirmation of the end-to-end significance.

In discussing the interaction between a transport entity and its user, it is useful to think in terms of primitives and parameters being exchanged, and to depict them as shown in Figure 15-2. The generic primitives shown are:

- *Request:* initiated by the transport user to activate a particular service.
- *Indication:* provided by the transport entity to advise of the activation of a particular service.
- *Response:* provided by a transport user in reply to an indication primitive.
- *Confirmation:* returned to the requesting transport user upon completion of a requested service.

The layout in Figure 15-2 suggest the typical time ordering of these events. We shall have occasion to use this notation in what follows.

Connection Management

When connection-oriented service is provided. The transport entity is responsible for establishing and terminating connections. A symmetric connection establish-

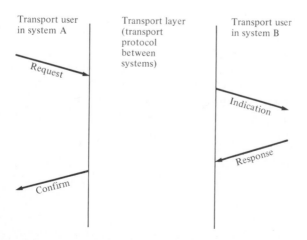

FIGURE 15-2.   Interaction primitives.

ment procedure should be provided, which allows either user to initiate connection establishment. An asymmetric procedure may also be provided to support simplex connections.

Connection termination can be either abrupt or graceful. With an abrupt termination, data in transit may be lost. A graceful termination prevents either side from shutting down until all data have been delivered.

Expedited Delivery

A service similar to that provided by priority classes is the expedited delivery of data. Some data submitted to the transport service may supersede data submitted previously. The transport entity will endeavor to have the transmission facility transfer the data as rapidly as possible. At the receiving end, the transport entity will interrupt the user to notify it of the receipt of urgent data. Thus the expedited data service is in the nature of an interrupt mechanism, and is used to transfer occasional urgent data, such as a break character from a terminal or an alarm condition. In contrast, a priority service might dedicate resources and adjust parameters such that, on average, higher priority data are delivered more quickly.

Status Reporting

A status reporting service allows the transport user to obtain or be notified of information concerning the condition or attributes of the transport entity or a transport connection. Examples of status information:

- Performance characteristics of a connection (e.g., throughput, mean delay).
- Addresses (network, transport).
- Class of protocol in use.
- Current timer values.
- State of protocol "machine" supporting a connection.
- Degredation in requested quality of service.

Security

The transport entity may provide a variety of security services. Access control may be provided in the form of local verification of sender and remote verification of receiver. The transport service may also include encryption/decryption of data on demand. Finally, the transport entity may be capable of routing through secure links or nodes if such a service is available from the transmission facility.

15-2

PROTOCOL MECHANISMS

It is the purpose of this section to make good on our claim that a transport protocol may need to be very complex. For purposes of clarity we present the transport protocol mechanisms in an evolutionary fashion. We begin with a network service that makes life easy for the transport protocol and define the required mechanisms. As the network service is made progressively less capable, the transport protocol becomes progressively more complex.

The ISO has defined three types of network service [ISO86b]:

*   *Type A:* network connections with acceptable residual error rate and acceptable rate of signaled failures.
*   *Type B:* network connections with acceptable residual error rate but unacceptable rate of signaled failures.
*   *Type C:* network connections with residual error rate not acceptable to the transport service user.

In this context, an error is defined as a lost or duplicated network protocol data unit. If the error is caught and corrected by the network service in a fashion that is transparent to the transport entity, no damage is done. If the network service detects an error, cannot recover, and signals the transport entities, this is known as a signaled failure. An example would be the notification by X.25 that a RESET has occurred. Finally, there are residual errors—those which are not corrected and for which the transport entity is not notified.

Type A provides a reliable network service. This makes life easy for the transport protocol designer. It is well to examine this case, because it helps to clarify the basic transport mechanisms. We will then see that most of the complexity of a transport protocol occurs when the underlying service is unreliable.

Following [MCQU78], we consider three subcases of Type A, which present progressively greater difficulties to the transport service:

*   Reliable, sequencing network service with arbitrary message size.
*   Reliable, nonsequencing network service with arbitrary message size.
*   Reliable, nonsequencing network service with maximum message size.

An example of the first case would be reliable X.25 service. The second and third cases might, for example, be reliable datagram services.

In what follows, we will concern ourselves primarily with the most stringent requirement for a transport protocol: The user of the transport service requires a reliable, sequenced, connection-oriented service. It should be clear to the reader what the implications would be of less stringent requirements.

We now consider each of the five types of network service (three subcases of Type A; Type B; Type C).

Reliable Sequencing Network Service

In this case, we assume that the network service will accept messages of arbitrary length and will, with virtually 100% reliability, deliver them in sequence to the destination. These assumptions allow the development of the simplest possible transport protocol. Four issues need to be addressed:

*   Addressing.
*   Multiplexing.
*   Flow Control.
*   Connection establishment/termination.

Addressing.   The issue concerned with addressing is simply this: a user of a given transport entity wishes to either establish a connection with or make a connectionless data transfer to a user of some other transport entity. The target user needs to be specified by all of the following.

- User identification.
- Transport entity identification.
- Station address.
- Network number.

Recalling our discussion in Section 12-1, user addresses can be either flat or hierarchical. Regardless, the transport protocol must be able to derive the information listed above from the user address. Typically, the user address is specified as (*Station*, *Port*). The *Port* variable represents a particular user. Generally, there will be a single transport entity at each station, so a transport entity identification is not needed. If more than one transport entity is present, there is usually only one of each type. In this latter case, the address should include a designation of the type of transport protocol (e.g., TCP, User Datagram). In the case of a single network, *Station* identifies an attached network device. In the case of an internet, *Station* subsumes a network number which can be derived at the internet layer.

Since routing is not a concern of the transport layer, it simply passes the *Station* portion of the address down to the network service. *Port* is included in a transport header, to be used at the destination by the destination transport protocol.

One question remains to be addressed: How does the initiating transport user know the address of the destination transport user? We discussed this problem briefly in Section 12-1, and elaborate here. Two static and two dynamic strategies suggest themselves:

1. The user must know the address it wishes to use ahead of time. This is basically a system configuration function.
2. Some commonly used services are assigned "well-known addresses."
3. A name server is provided. The user requests a service by some generic or global name. The request is sent to the name server, which does a directory lookup and returns an address. The transport entity then proceeds with the connection.
4. In some cases, the target user is to be a process that is spawned at request time. The initiating user can send a process request to a well known address. The user at that address is a privileged system process that will spawn the new process and return an address.

To see that these are distinct cases, we give an example of each:

1. A process may be running that is only of concern to a limited number of transport users. A process in a station may collect statistics on performance. From time to time, a central network management routine connects to the process to obtain the statistics. These processes generally are not, and should not be, well known and accessible to all.
2. Examples of commonly used services are time sharing and word processing.
3. Some services may be commonly used, but their location may change from time to time. For example, a data entry process may be moved from one station to another on a local network to balance load. The names of such "movable" processes can be kept in a directory, with the addresses updated when a move occurs.

4. A programmer has developed a private application (e.g., a simulation program) that will execute on a remote mainframe but be invoked from a local minicomputer. An RJE-type request can be issued to a remote job-management process which spawns the simulation process.

Multiplexing.   We now turn to the concept of multiplexing, which also was discussed in general terms in Section 12-1. With respect to the interface between the transport protocol and higher-level protocols, the transport protocol performs a multiplexing/demultiplexing function. That is, multiple users employ the same transport protocol, and are distinguished by port numbers or service access points.

The transport entity may also perform a multiplexing function with respect to the network services that it uses. Recall that we defined upward multiplexing as the multiplexing of multiple (N) connections on a single (N-1) connection, and downward multiplexing as the splitting of a single (N) connection among multiple (N-1) connections.

Consider, for example, a transport entity making use of an X.25 service. Why should the transport entity employ upward multiplexing? There are, after all, 4095 virtual circuits available. In the typical case, this is more than enough to handle all active transport users. However, most X.25 networks base part of their charge on virtual circuit connect time, since each virtual circuit consumes some node buffer resources. Thus, if a single virtual circuit provides sufficient throughput for multiple transport users, upward multiplexing is indicated.

On the other hand, downward multiplexing or splitting might be used to improve throughput. If, for example, each X.25 virtual circuit is restricted to a 3-bit sequence number, only seven packets can be outstanding at a time. A larger sequence space might be needed for high-delay networks. Of course, throughput can only be increased so far. If there is a single station-node link over which all virtual circuits are multiplexed, the throughput of a transport connection cannot exceed the data rate of that link.

Flow Control.   The OSI document [ISO84] defines flow control as a function for the control of the data flow within a layer or between adjacent layers. Whereas flow control is a relatively simple mechanism at the link layer, it is a rather complex mechanism at the transport layer, for two main reasons:

- Flow control at the transport level involves the interaction of transport users, transport entities, and the network service.
- The transmission delay between transport entities is generally long compared to actual transmission time and, what is worse, variable.

Figure 15-3 illustrates the first point. Transport user A wishes to send data to transport user B over a transport connection. We can view the situation as involving four queues. A generates data and queues it up to send. A must wait to send that data until

- It has permission from B (peer flow control), and,
- It has permission from its own transport entity (interface flow control).

As data flows down from A to transport entity a, a queues the data until it has permission to send it on from b and the network service. The data are then handed to the network layer for delivery to b. The network service must queue the data

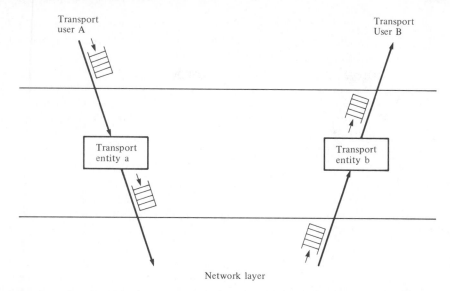

FIGURE 15-3. Queuing representation of connection-oriented data transfer.

until it receives permission from *b* to pass them on. Finally, *b* must await *B*'s permission before delivering the data to their destination.

To see the effects of delay, consider the possible interactions depicted in Figure 15-4. When a user wishes to transmit data, it sends these data to its transport entity (e.g., using a SEND call). This triggers two events. The transport entity generates one or more transport protocol data units (TPDUs) and passes these on to the network service. It also in some way acknowledges to the user that it has accepted the data for transmission. At this point, the transport entity can exercise flow control across the user-transport interface by simply withholding its acknowledgment. The transport entity is most likely to do this if the entity itself is being held up by a flow control exercised by either the network service or the target transport entity.

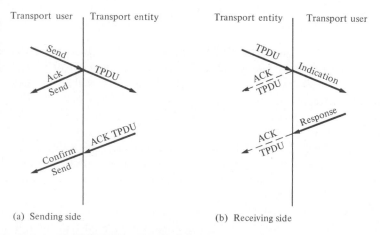

(a) Sending side (b) Receiving side

FIGURE 15-4. User-transport interaction.

In any case, once the transport entity has accepted the data, it sends out a TPDU. Some time later, it receives an acknowledgment that the data have been received at the remote end. It then sends a confirmation to the sender.

At the receiving end, a TPDU arrives at the transport entity. It unwraps the data and sends them on (e.g., by an Indication primitive) to the destination user. When the user accepts the data, it issues an acknowledgment (e.g., in the form of a RESPONSE primitive). The user can exercise flow control over the transport entity by withholding its response.

Now, the target transport entity has two choices regarding acknowledgment. Either it can issue an acknowledgment as soon as it has correctly received the TPDU (the usual practice), or it can wait until it knows that the user has correctly received the data before acknowledging. The latter course is the safer. In the latter case, the send confirmation is in fact a confirmation that the destination user received the data. In the former case, it merely confirms that the data made it through to the remote transport entity.

With the discussion above in mind, we can cite two reasons why one transport entity would want to restrain the rate of TPDU transmission over a connection from another transport entity:

- The user of the receiving transport entity cannot keep up with the flow of data.
- The receiving transport entity itself cannot keep up with the flow of TPDUs.

How do such problems manifest themselves? Well, presumably a transport entity has a certain amount of buffer space. Incoming TPDUs are added to the buffer. Each buffered TPDU is processed (i.e., examine the transport header) and the data are sent to the user. Either of the two problems mentioned above will cause the buffer to fill up. Thus the transport entity needs to take steps to stop or slow the flow of TPDUs to prevent buffer overflow. This requirement is not so easy to fulfill, because of the annoying time gap between sender and receiver. We return to this point in a moment. First, we present four ways of coping with the flow control requirement. The receiving transport entity can:

1. Do nothing.
2. Refuse to accept further TPDUs from the network service.
3. Use a fixed sliding-window protocol.
4. Use a credit scheme.

Alternative 1 means that the TPDUs that overflow the buffer are discarded. The sending transport entity, failing to get an acknowledgment, will retransmit. This is a shame, since the advantage of a reliable network is that one never has to retransmit. Furthermore, the effect of this maneuver is to exacerbate the problem! The sender has increased its output to include new TPDUs plus retransmitted old TPDUs.

The second alternative is a backpressure mechanism that relies on the network service to do the work. When a buffer of a transport entity is full, it refuses additional data from the network service. This triggers flow control procedures within the network that throttle the network service at the sending end. This service, in turn, refuses additional TPDUs from its transport entity. It should be clear that this mechanism is clumsy and coarse-grained. For example, if multiple transport connections are multiplexed on a single network connection (virtual circuit), flow control is exercised only on the aggregate of all transport connections. Remarkably, there is at least one transport protocol that uses this strategy: the EHKP4 protocol standard developed in West Germany [MEIJ82].

The third alternative is already familiar to you from our discussions of link layer protocols. The key ingredients, recall, are:

- The use of sequence numbers on data units.
- The use of a window of fixed size.
- The use of acknowledgments to advance the window.

With a reliable network service, the sliding window technique would actually work quite well. For example, consider a protocol with a window size of 7. Whenever the sender receives an acknowledgment to a particular TPDU, it is automatically authorized to send the succeeding seven TPDUs (of course, some may already have been sent). Now, when the receiver's buffer capacity gets down to seven TPDUs, it can withhold acknowledgment of incoming TPDUs to avoid overflow. The sending transport entity can send at most seven additional TPDUs and then must stop. Since the underlying network service is reliable, the sender will not time out and retransmit. Thus, at some point, a sending transport entity may have a number of TPDUs outstanding for which no acknowledgment has been received. Since we are dealing with a reliable network, the sending transport entity can assume that the TPDUs will get through and that the lack of acknowledgment is a flow control tactic. This tactic would not work well in an unreliable network, since the sending transport entity would not know whether the lack of acknowledgment is due to flow control or a lost TPDU.

The fourth alternative, a credit scheme, provides the receiver with a greater degree of control over data flow. Although it is not strictly necessary with a reliable network service, a credit scheme should result in a smoother traffic flow. Further, it is a more effective scheme with an unreliable network service, as we shall see.

The credit scheme decouples acknowledgment from flow control. In fixed sliding-window protocols, such as X.25, the two are synonymous. In a credit scheme, a TPDU may be acknowledged without granting new credit, and vice versa. Figure 15-5 illustrates the protocol (compare Figure 5-7). For simplicity, we show a data flow in one direction only. In this example, TPDUs are numbered sequentially modulo 8. Initially, through the connection establishment process, the sending and receiving sequence numbers are synchronized and A is granted a credit allocation of 7. A advances the trailing edge of its window each time that it transmits, and advances the leading edge only when it is granted credit.

In both the credit allocation scheme and the sliding window scheme, the receiver needs to adopt some policy concerning the amount of data it permits the sender to transmit. The conservative approach is to only allow new TPDUs up to the limit of available buffer space. If this policy were in effect in Figure 15-5, the first credit message implies that B has five free buffer slots, and the second message that B has seven free slots.

A conservative flow control scheme may limit the throughput of the transport connection in long-delay situations. The receiver could potentially increase throughput by optimistically granting credit for space it does not have. For example, if a receiver's buffer is full but it anticipates that it can release space for two TPDUs within a round-trip propagation time, it could immediately send a credit of 2. If the receiver can keep up with the sender, this scheme may increase throughput and can do no harm. If the sender is faster than the receiver, however, some

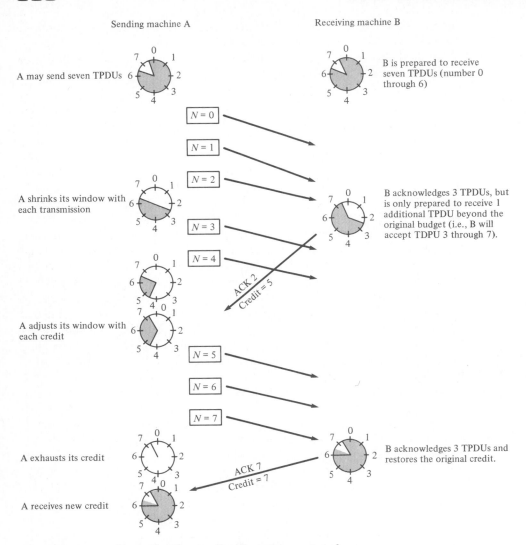

FIGURE 15-5. **Example of a credit allocation protocol.**

TPDUs may be discarded, necessitating a retransmission. Since retransmissions are not otherwise necessary with a reliable network service, an optimistic flow control scheme will complicate the protocol.

Connection Establishment and Termination. Even with a reliable network service, there is a need for connection establishment and termination procedures to support connection-oriented service. Connection establishment serves three main purposes:

- It allows each end to assure that the other exists.
- It allows negotiation of optional parameters (e.g., TPDU size, window size, quality of service).
- It triggers allocation of transport entity resources (e.g., buffer space, entry in connection table).

Connection establishment is by mutual agreement and can be accomplished by a simple set of user commands and control TPDUs, as shown in the state diagram of Figure 15-6. To begin, a user is in an IDLE state (with respect to the transport entity). The user can signal that it will passively wait for a request with a LISTEN command. A server program, such as time sharing or a file transfer application, might do this. The user may change its mind by sending a CLOSE command.

After the LISTEN command is issued, the transport entity creates a connection object of some sort (i.e., a table entry) that is in the LSTN state. If a RFC (request for connection) TPDU is received that specifies the listening user, then a connection is opened. To do this, the transport entity:

- Signals the user that a connection is open.
- Sends an RFC as confirmation to the remote transport entity.
- Puts the connection object in an OPEN state.

A user may open a connection by issuing an OPEN command, which triggers the transport entity to send an RFC. The reception of a matching RFC establishes the connection. The connection is prematurely aborted if the local user issues a

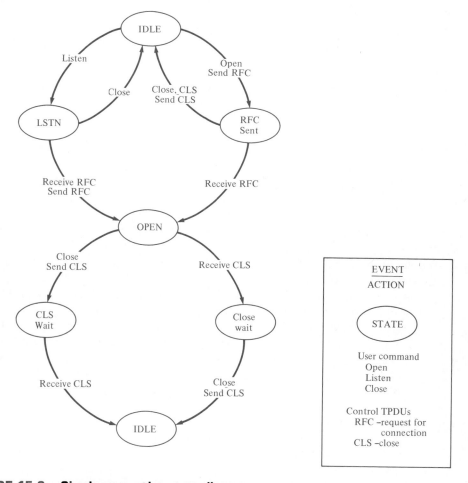

FIGURE 15-6. **Simple connection state diagram.**

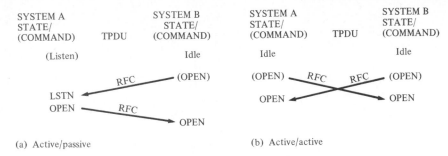

FIGURE 15-7. **Connection establishment sequence of events.**

CLOSE command or the remote transport entity refuses the connection by sending a CLS TPDU.

Figure 15-7 shows the robustness of this protocol. Either side can initiate a connection. Further, if both sides initiate the connection at about the same time, it is established without confusion.

The reader may ask what happens if an RFC comes in while the requested user is idle (not listening). Three courses may be followed:

- The transport entity can reject the request by sending a CLS.
- The request can be queued until a LISTEN is issued by the user.
- The transport entity can interrupt or otherwise signal the user to notify it of a pending request.

Note that if the latter mechanism is used, a Listen command is not strictly necessary, but may be replaced by an Accept command, which is a signal from the user to the transport entity that it accepts the request for connection.

Connection termination is handled similarly. Either side, or both sides, may initiate a close. The connection is closed by mutual agreement. This strategy allows for either abrupt or graceful termination. To achieve the latter, a connection in the CLS WAIT state must continue to accept data TPDUs until a CLS is received.

Reliable Nonsequencing Network Service

In this case, we assume that the network service will accept messages of arbitrary length and will, with virtually 100% reliability, deliver them to the destination. However, we now assume that the TPDUs may arrive out of sequence. This seemingly trivial change has a number of consequences.

The first consequence is that sequence numbers are required on TPDUs for connection-oriented service. We employ them with a reliable sequencing network service for flow control purposes. Here they are required to permit the transport entity to deliver data in sequence.

Equally important, the transport entity must keep track of control TPDUs, both in relationship to each other and to data TPDUs. Examples of this requirement are seen in flow control and in connection establishment and termination.

First, consider flow control. A transport entity may sometimes find it desirable to decrease outstanding offered credit on a connection, because expected resources did not become available, or because resources had to be reallocated to serve another connection. If sequencing is not guaranteed, a situation such as that shown

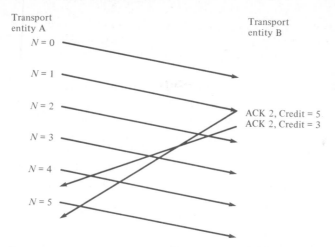

Transport entity A

$N = 0$
$N = 1$
$N = 2$
$N = 3$
$N = 4$
$N = 5$

Transport entity B

ACK 2, Credit = 5
ACK 2, Credit = 3

FIGURE 15-8. Example of flow control with a nonsequenced network service.

in Figure 15-8 might arise. After transport entity A has sent TPDU 1, B responds with a new credit allocation of 5. A short time later, and before additional TPDUs arrive, B discovers a potential shortfall and sends a reduced credit allocation of 3. However, this allocation overtakes the earlier one and arrives first. It appears to A that B has initially granted an allocation of 3 and then obtained additional resources, and increased the allocation to 5. Thus, while B is not prepared to receive any more TPDUs at this point, A feels entitled to send two additional TPDUs. The solution to this problem is to number credit allocations sequentially.

Now consider connection establishment. Figure 15-6 shows that after a transport entity has sent an RFC, it expects to receive either a CLS (connection reject) or RFC (connection accept) from the target entity. The target transport entity, having received the opening RFC, might respond with RFC, followed by a number of TPDUs. One of these TPDUs could arrive back at the initiating entity prior to the RFC. The best policy would seem to be for the initiating transport entity to queue these TPDUs until the RFC is received that confirms the connection.

Just as data may arrive before a connection is officially open, they may also arrive after the connection has closed. The following may occur. After a transport entity has sent its last data TPDU, it sends a CLS. The CLS may arrive before the last data TPDU. One way to avoid a problem is for the CLS TPDU to contain the next sequence number after the last data TPDU sent on this connection. Then, the receiving transport entity, upon receiving a CLS, will wait if necessary for late-arriving data TPDUs before closing the connection.

Reliable Nonsequencing Network Service with Maximum TPDU Size

We now add another limitation to the capability of the network service: It will only accept TPDUs of some maximum size for transfer. Presumably, this size is chosen to optimize network performance.

We need to distinguish two types of data transfer required by the user: stream oriented and block oriented. A stream-oriented interface between transport and the user accepts data as if they were a continuous stream of bits and reproduces the stream at the other end without conveying any information about the breakpoints in the stream submitted by the sender. This interface might serve voice and real-time applications.

A more common occurrence is a transport user that sends data in blocks. For convenience, we refer to a block of data presented to transport as a *letter*. If a letter exceeds the maximum allowable TPDU size, the transport entity must segment the letter before transmission, to be reassembled at reception prior to delivery to the user. Because our network is nonsequencing, segments may arrive out of order. Worse, segments from different letters may be interchanged en route.

A simple solution to this problem is to number each letter sequentially and to number each segment sequentially within each letter. This, however, is an unnecessary duplication of the TPDU sequence numbering function. A moment's thought should make it clear that all that is required is an end-of-letter (EOL) flag. As TPDUs arrive at the destination transport entity, they are reordered. Each sequential set of TPDUs, starting with the first TPDU after an EOL, and including all TPDUs through the next EOL, are treated as a unit. The data from this unit, stripped of transport headers, are delivered as a single letter to the user.

A variation on the foregoing approach is to apply the sequence numbers to the data rather than the TPDUs. An example of this was discussed in Chapter 14, namely the segmentation and reassembly technique for IP.

Failure-Prone Network Service

We now turn to what may strike the reader as an unusual sort of network service. This is a connection-oriented network service and, while it delivers data reliably (though not necessarily in sequence), it suffers from network failures that cause it to reset or restart network connections. Thus TPDUs may be lost, but the loss is reported to the transport entities affected. The reader might visualize an X.25 network service being provided by a relatively unreliable underlying network.

In any case, the transport entity must now cope with the problem of recovering from known loss of data and/or network connections. The sequence numbering scheme provides an effective tool. In the normal course of events, TPDUs need not be acknowledged, since the network service is reliable. However, acknowledgment takes place from time to time in connection with the flow control scheme. We show this mechanism also deals with network failure.

First, consider a connection reset, such as the X.25 RESET command will cause. The network service will signal the transport entity that a reset has occurred on one or more transport connections. The transport entity realizes that it has perhaps lost some incoming TPDUs in transit, and that some already-transmitted TPDUs may not reach their destination. Two actions are indicated:

- Issue a control TPDU to the other end that acknowledges a reset condition and gives the number of the last TPDU received.
- Refrain from issuing new data TPDUs until a corresponding reset control TPDU is received from the other end.

A more serious condition is the loss of an underlying network connection, such as an X.25 RESTART causes. In this case, the side that first initiated the connection should issue a request to the network service for a new network connection and then issue a control TPDU to the other side that identifies the new network connection for the ongoing transport connection. Following this, both sides must resynchronize with the use of reset control TPDUs.

Unreliable Network Service

The most difficult case for a transport protocol is that of an unreliable network service. The problem is not just that TPDUs are occasionally lost, but that TPDUs may arrive out of sequence due to variable transit delays. As we shall see, elaborate machinery is required to cope with these two interrelated network deficiencies. We shall also see that a discouraging pattern emerges. The combination of unreliability and nonsequencing creates problems with every mechanism we have discussed so far. Generally, the solution to each problem raises new problems. Although there are problems to be overcome for protocols at all levels, it seems that there are more difficulties with a reliable connection-oriented transport protocol than any other sort of protocol.

Six issues need to be addressed:

- Retransmission strategy.
- Duplicate detection.
- Flow control.
- Connection establishment.
- Connection termination.
- Crash recovery.

Retransmission Strategy. Two events necessitate the retransmission of a TPDU. First, the TPDU may be damaged in transit but nevertheless arrive at its destination. If a frame check sequence is included with the TPDU, the receiving transport entity can detect the error and discard the TPDU. The second contingency is that a TPDU fails to arrive. In either case, the sending transport entity does not know that the TPDU transmission was unsuccessful. To cover this contingency, we require that a positive acknowledgment (ACK) scheme be used: The receiver must acknowledge each successfully received TPDU. For efficiency, we do not require one ACK per TPDU. Rather, a cumulative acknowledgment can be used, as we have seen many times in this book. Thus the receiver may receive TPDUs numbered 1, 2, and 3, but only send ACK 3 back. The sender must interpret ACK 3 to mean that number 3 and all previous TPDUs have been successfully received.

If a TPDU does not arrive successfully, no ACK will be issued and a retransmission is in order. To cope with this situation, there must be a timer associated with each TPDU as it is sent. If the timer expires before the TPDU is acknowledged, the sender must retransmit.

So the addition of a timer solves that problem. Next problem: At what value should the timer be set? If the value is too small, there will be many unnecessary retransmissions, wasting network capacity. If the value is too large, the protocol will be sluggish in responding to a lost TPDU. The timer should be set at a value a bit longer than the round trip delay (send TPDU, receive ACK). Of course this delay is variable even under constant network load. Worse, the statistics of the delay will vary with changing network conditions.

Two strategies suggest themselves. A fixed timer value could be used, based on an understanding of the network's typical behavior. This suffers from an inability to respond to changing network conditions. If the value is set too high, the service will always be sluggish. If it is set too low, a positive feedback condition can develop, in which network congestion leads to more retransmissions, which increase congestion.

An adaptive scheme has its own problems [ZHAN86]. Suppose that the transport entity keeps track of the time taken to acknowledge data TPDUs and sets its retransmission timer based on the average of the observed delays. This value cannot be trusted for three reasons:

- The peer entity may not acknowledge a TPDU immediately. Recall that we gave it the privilege of cumulative acknowledgments.
- If a TPDU has been retransmitted, the sender cannot know whether the received ACK is a response to the initial transmission or the retransmission.
- Network conditions may change suddenly.

Each of these problems is a cause for some further tweaking of the transport algorithm, but the problem admits of no complete solution. There will always be some uncertainty concerning the best value for the retransmission timer.

Incidentally, the retransmission timer is only one of a number of timers needed for proper functioning of a transport protocol. These are listed in Table 15-1, together with a brief explanation. Further discussion will be found in what follows.

Duplicate Detection. If a TPDU is lost and then retransmitted, no confusion will result. If however, an ACK is lost, one or more TPDUs will be retransmitted and, if they arrive successfully, be duplicates of previously received TPDUs. Thus the receiver must be able to recognize duplicates. The fact that each TPDU carries a sequence number helps but, nevertheless, duplicate detection and handling is no easy thing. There are two cases:

- A duplicate is received prior to the close of the connection.
- A duplicate is received after the close of the connection.

Notice that we say "a" duplicate rather than "the" duplicate. From the sender's point of view, the retransmitted TPDU is the duplicate. However, the retransmitted TPDU may arrive before the original TPDU, in which case the receiver views the original TPDU as the duplicate. In any case, two tactics are needed to cope with a duplicate received prior to the close of a connection:

TABLE 15-1

Retransmission timer	Retransmit an unacknowledged TPDU
Reconnection timer	Minimum time between closing one connection and opening another with the same destination address
Window timer	Maximum time between ACK/CREDIT TPDUs
Retransmit-RFC timer	Time between attempts to open a connection
Persistence timer	Abort connection when no TPDUs are acknowledged
Inactivity timer	Abort connection when no TPDUs are received

- The receiver must assume that its acknowledgment was lost and therefore must acknowledge the duplicate. Consequently, the sender must not get confused if it receives multiple ACKs to the same TPDU.
- The sequence number space must be long enough so as not to "cycle" in less than the maximum possible TPDU lifetime.

Figure 15-9 illustrates the reason for the latter requirement. In this example, the sequence space is of length 8. For simplicity, we assume a sliding-window protocol with a window size of 3. Suppose that A has transmitted TPDUs 0, 1, and 2 and receives no acknowledgments. Eventually, it times out and retransmits TPDU 0. B has received 1 and 2, but 0 is delayed in transit. Thus B does not send any ACKs. When the duplicate TPDU 0 arrives, B acknowledges 0, 1, and 2. Meanwhile, A has timed out again and retransmits 1, which B acknowledges with another ACK 2. Things now seem to have sorted themselves out and data transfer continues. When the sequence space is exhausted, A cycles back to sequence number 0 and continues. Alas, the old TPDU 0 makes a belated appearance and is accepted by B before the new TPDU 0 arrives.

It should be clear that the untimely emergence of the old TPDU would have caused no difficulty if the sequence numbers had not yet wrapped around. The problem is: How big must the sequence space be? This depends on, among other things, whether the network enforces a maximum packet lifetime, and the rate at which TPDUs are being transmitted. Fortunately, each addition of a single bit to the sequence number field doubles the sequence space, so it is rather easy to select

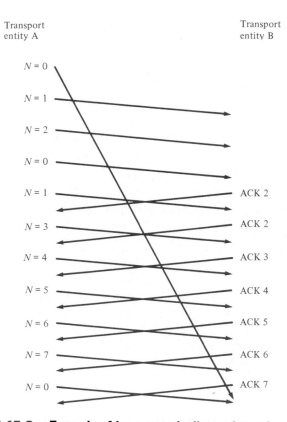

FIGURE 15-9. **Example of incorrect duplicate detection.**

a safe size. As we shall see, the standard transport protocols allow stupendous sequence spaces.

A more subtle problem is posed by TPDUs that continue to rattle around after a transport connection is closed. If a subsequent connection is opened between the same two transport entities, a TPDU from the old connection could arrive and be accepted on the new connection! Similarly, a delayed ACK can enter a new connection and cause problems.

There are a number of approaches to this particular problem. We mention several of the more promising. First, the sequence numbering scheme can be extended across connection lifetimes. This requires that a transport entity remember the last sequence number that it used on transmission for each terminated connection. Then, when a new connection to a transport entity is attempted, the RFC contains the sequence number to be used to begin data transfer. Of course, this procedure is symmetric, with each side responsible for declaring the sequence number with which it will commence transmission.

A second approach is to provide a separate transport connection identifier, and use a new identifier with each new connection.

The procedures above work fine unless a system crash occurs. In that case, the system will not remember what sequence number or connection identifier was used last. An alternative is to simply wait a sufficient time between connections to assure that all old TPDUs are gone. Then, even if one side has experienced a crash, the other side can refuse a connection until the reconnection timer expires. This, of course, may cause unnecessary delays.

Flow Control.   The credit allocation flow control mechanism described earlier is quite robust in the face of an unreliable network service and requires little enhancement. We assume that the credit allocation scheme is tied to acknowledgments in the following way: To both acknowledge TPDUs and grant credit, a transport entity sends a control TPDU of the form (ACK N, CREDIT M), where ACK N acknowledges all data TPDUs through number N, and CREDIT M allows TPDUs number $N + 1$ though $N + M$ to be transmitted. This mechanism is quite powerful. Consider that the last control TPDU issued by B was (ACK N, CREDIT M). Then:

- To increase or decrease credit to X when no additional TPDUs have arrived, B can issue (ACK N, CREDIT X).
- To acknowledge a new TPDU without increasing credit, B can issue (ACK $N + 1$, CREDIT $M - 1$).

If an ACK/CREDIT TPDU is lost, little harm is done. Future acknowledgments will resynchronize the protocol. Further, if no new acknowledgments are forthcoming, the sender times out and retransmits a data TPDU, which triggers a new acknowledgment. However, it is still possible for deadlock to occur. Consider a situation in which B sends (ACK N, CREDIT 0), temporarily closing the window. Subsequently, B sends (ACK N, CREDIT M), but this TPDU is lost. A is awaiting the opportunity to send data and B thinks that it has granted that opportunity. To overcome this problem, a window timer can be used. This timer is reset with each outgoing ACK/CREDIT TPDU. If the timer ever expires, the protocol entity is required to send an ACK/CREDIT TPDU, even if it duplicates a previous one. This breaks the deadlock and also assures the other end that the protocol entity is still alive.

An alternative or supplemental mechanism is to provide for acknowledgments to the ACK/CREDIT TPDU. With this mechanism in place, the window timer can have a quite large value without causing much difficulty.

Connection Establishment. As with other protocol mechanisms, connection establishment must take into account the unreliability of a network service. Recall that a connection establishment calls for the exchange of RFCs, a procedure sometimes referred to as a *two-way handshake*. Suppose that A issues an RFC to B. It expects to get an RFC back, confirming the connection. Two things can go wrong: A's RFC can be lost or B's answering RFC can be lost. Both cases can be handled by use of a retransmit-RFC timer. After A issues an RFC, it will reissue the RFC when the timer expires.

This gives rise, potentially, to duplicate RFCs. If A's initial RFC was lost, there are no duplicates. If B's response was lost, then B may receive two RFCs from A. Further, if B's response was not lost, but simply delayed, A may get two responding RFCs. All of this means that A and B must simply ignore duplicate RFCs once a connection is established.

Now, consider that a duplicate RFC may survive past the termination of the connection. Figure 15-10 depicts the problem that may arise. An old RFC X (request for connection, sequence number begins at X) arrives at B after the connection is terminated. B assumes that this is a fresh request and responds with RFC Y. Meanwhile, A has decided to open a new connection with B and sends RFC Z. B discards this as a duplicate. Subsequently, A initiates data transfer with a TPDU numbered Z. B rejects the TPDU as being out of sequence.

The way out of this problem is for each side to acknowledge explicitly the other's RFC and sequence number. The procedure is known as a *three-way handshake* [TOML75]. The revised connection state diagram is shown in the upper part of Figure 15-11. A new state (RFC Received) is added. In this state, the transport entity hesitates during connection opening to assure that any RFC which was sent has also been acknowledged before the connection is declared open. In addition to the new state, there is a new control TPDU (RST) to reset the other side when a duplicate RFC is detected.

Figure 15-12 illustrates typical three-way handshake operations. Under normal conditions, an RFC includes the sending sequence number. The responding RFC acknowledges that number and includes the sequence number for the other side. The initiating transport entity acknowledges the RFC/ACK in its first data TPDU.

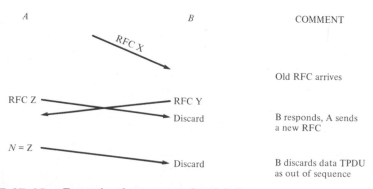

FIGURE 15-10. Example of a two-way handshake.

Next is shown a situation in which an old RFC X arrives at *B* after the close of the relevant connection. *B* assumes that this is a fresh request and responds with RFC Y, ACK X. When *A* receives this message, it realizes that it has not requested a connection and therefore sends a RST, ACK Y. Note that the ACK Y portion of the RST message is essential so that an old duplicate RST does not abort a legitimate connection establishment. The final example shows a case in which an old RFC, ACK arrives in the middle of a new connection establishment. Because of the use of sequence numbers in the acknowledgments, this event causes no mischief.

The upper part of Figure 15-11 does not include transitions in which RST is sent. This was done for simplicity. The basic rule is: Send an RST if connection state is not yet OPEN and an invalid ACK (one which does not reference something

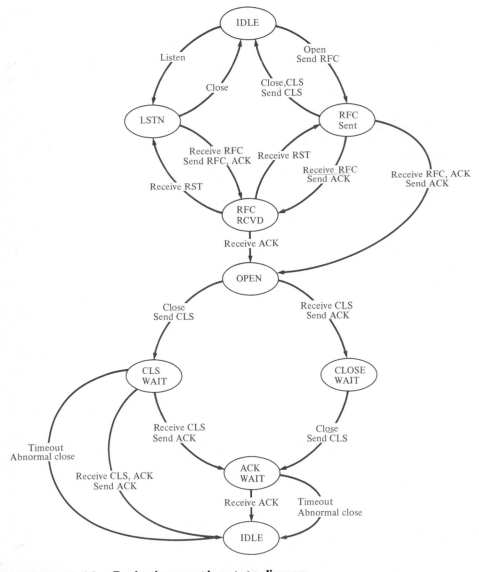

FIGURE 15-11.   Revised connection state diagram.

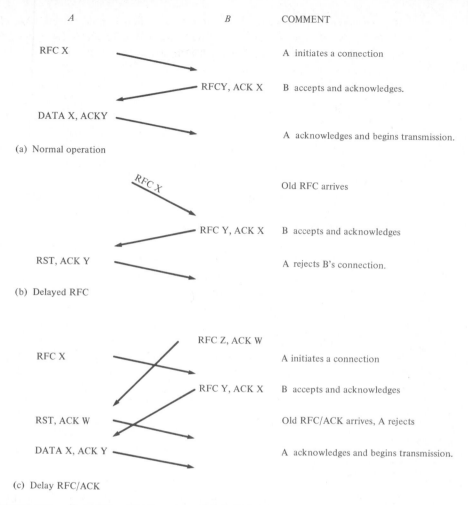

FIGURE 15-12.   Examples of three-way handshake.

that was sent) is received. The reader should try various combinations of events to see that this connection establishment procedure works in spite of any combination of old and lost TPDUs.

Connection Termination.   As with connection establishment, the connection termination procedure must cope with old and lost control TPDUs. Figure 15-11 indicates that a similar solution is adopted. Each side must explicitly acknowledge the CLS TPDU of the other. To avoid confusion, sequence numbers are used as follows:

- CLS contains the sequence number plus one of the last data TPDU sent.
- ACK contains the sequence number received in the CLS.

Timeout procedures are included to allow a transport entity to complete its closing if the other side appears uncooperative. The problem may be lost TPDUs rather than a failure at the other end. Therefore, one or more retransmissions are advisable before signaling an abnormal close.

Crash Recovery. When the system upon which a transport entity is running fails and subsequently restarts, the state information of all active connections is lost. The affected connections become "half-open" since the side that did not fail does not yet realize the problem.

The still active side of a half-open connection can close the connection using a give-up timer. This timer measures the time the transport machine will continue to await an acknowledgment (or other appropriate reply) of a transmitted TPDU after the TPDU has been retransmitted the maximum number of times. When the timer expires, the transport entity assumes that the other transport entity or the intervening network has failed, closes the connection, and signals an abnormal close to the transport user.

In the event that a transport entity fails and quickly restarts, half-open connections can be terminated more quickly by the use of the RST TPDU. The failed side returns a RST X to every TPDU X that it receives. When the RST X reaches the other side, it must be checked for validity based on the sequence number X, since the RST could be in response to an old TPDU. If the reset is valid, the transport entity performs an abnormal termination.

These measures clean up the situation at the transport level. The decision as to whether to reopen the connection is up to the transport users. The problem is one of synchronization. At the time of failure, there may have been one or more outstanding TPDUs in either direction. The transport user on the side that did not fail knows how much data it has received, but the other user may not, if state information were lost. Thus, there is the danger that some user data will be lost or duplicated.

15-3

NETWORK SERVICES

To function, a transport protocol must make use of the services of some lower-level network-oriented protocol, such as X.25 or IP. In this section we look first at the primitives that might be used to implement the transport/network interface, and then discuss the relationship of these primitives to the types of network service provided.

Service Primitives

Table 15-2 lists a set of primitives that might be used to provide a network service to a transport entity. This list is based on that specified by ISO [WARE83].

At minimum, the network service must provide a means of delivering TPDUs to a remote correspondent. The transport entity uses N-DATA.request to transfer data to the network service for transmission. The network service passes up received data using N-DATA.indication. If the service is not connection-oriented, address information must be included in the primitive invocation.

If the network service is connection-oriented, additional primitives are needed: N-CONNECT.request signals a request by a transport entity to open a connection. N-CONNECT.indication presents this request to the correspondent transport entity identified in the connection request. A transport entity signals its willingness to

TABLE 15-2   Network Service Primitives

Required:

    N-DATA.request ([to network address]; [from network address]; data)

    N-DATA.indication ([to network address]; [from network address]; data)

Required for connection-oriented service:

    N-CONNECT.request (to network address; from network address; security; quality of service)

    N-CONNECT.indication (to network address; from network address; security; quality of service)

    N-CONNECT.response ( )

    N-CONNECT.confirm ( )

    N-DISCONNECT.request ( )

    N-DISCONNECT.indication ( )

Additional Useful Primitives:

    N-DATA-ACKNOWLEDGE.request ( )

    N-DATA-ACKNOWLEDGE.indication ( )

    N-EXPEDITED-DATA.request (data)

    N-EXPEDITED-DATA.indication (data)

    N-RESET.request ( )

    N-RESET.indication ( )

    N-RESET.response ( )

    N-RESET.confirmation ( )

accept the connection with N-CONNECT.response. This willingness is communicated to the initiating transport entity with N-CONNECT.confirm. N-DISCONNECT.request and N-DISCONNECT.indication are used to terminate a connection. Please note that these primitives are concerned with the establishment and termination of a network connection (e.g., an X.25 virtual circuit) between two transport entities. These entities may then use this connection to establish one or more transport connections on behalf of transport users.

Additional primitives may be provided by the network service. Although not strictly necessary, these primitives enhance the capability and efficiency of the transport protocol. The N-DATA-ACKNOWLEDGE primitives permit the local exercise of flow control across the transport/network interface in both directions. N-EXPEDITED-DATA provides direct support of the transport expedited data feature. Finally, the N-RESET primitives allow the transport entity to force a reset of the network connection.

Relationship to Type of Network

It is important to realize that there is not a unique correspondence between reliability and whether a network service is connection oriented. A connection-oriented service might be reliable, in which case the techniques described above for a reliable sequencing network service would suffice for the transport protocol. On the other hand, the service might be unreliable, calling for a far more complex transport protocol.

Similarly, an unreliable connectionless service will require a complex transport protocol. However, if the connectionless service is reliable, the transport mechanisms associated with a reliable nonsequencing network service will be adequate.

15-4

THE ISO TRANSPORT STANDARDS

In this section we look at a family of transport protocols developed by ISO as an international standard [ISO86a,b]. This protocol family seems destined to achieve near-universal acceptance outside DOD.

The Transport Protocol Family

In order to handle a variety of user service requirements and available network services, ISO has defined five classes of transport protocol:

- *Class 0:* simple class.
- *Class 1:* basic error recovery class.
- *Class 2:* multiplexing class.
- *Class 3:* error recovery and multiplexing class.
- *Class 4:* error detection and recovery class.

These classes are related to the three types of network service defined in Section 15-2 as follows. Classes 0 and 2 are used with Type A networks; Classes 1 and 3 are used with Type B networks; and Class 4 is used with Type C networks. Table 15-3 lists the functions of the various protocol classes.

Class 0 was developed by CCITT and is oriented for teletex, a text-transmission upgrade to Telex . It provides the simplest kind of transport connection. It provides a connection with flow control based on network-level flow control, and connection release based on the release of the network connection.

Class 1 was also developed by CCITT and is designed to run on an X.25 network and provide minimal error recovery (network-signaled errors). The key difference from Class 0 is that TPDUs are numbered. This allows the protocol to resynchronize after an X.25 RESET and to reassign a transport connection after an X.25 RESTART. Flow control is still provided by the network layer. Expedited data transfer is also provided.

Class 2 is an enhancement to Class 0 that still assumes a highly reliable network service. The key enhancement is the ability to multiplex multiple transport connections onto a single network connection. A corollary enhancement is the provision of explicit flow control, since a single network connection flow control mechanism does not allow individual flow control of transport connections. A credit allocation scheme is used.

Class 3 is basically the union of the Class 1 and 2 capabilities. It provides the multiplexing and flow control capabilities of Class 2. It also contains the resynchronization and reassignment capabilities of Class 1, which are needed to cope with failure-prone networks.

Class 4 assumes that the underlying network service is unreliable. Thus most if not all of the mechanisms described in Section 15-2 must be included.

TABLE 15-3 Functions of ISO Transport Protocol Classes[a]

Protocol Mechanism	Variant	0	1	2	3	4
Assignment to network connection		*	*	*	*	*
TPDU transfer		*	*	*	*	*
Segmenting and reassembling		*	*	*	*	*
Concatenation and separation			*	*	*	*
Connection establishment		*	*	*	*	*
Connection refusal		*	*	*	*	*
Normal release	Implicit	*				
	Explicit		*	*	*	*
Error release		*		*		
Association of TPDUs with transport connection		*	*	*	*	*
DT TPDU numbering	Normal	*	m(1)	m	m	
	Extended		o(1)	o	o	
Expedited data transfer	Network normal		m	(1)	*	*
	Network expedited		ao			
Reassignment after failure			*		*	
Retention until acknowledgment of TPDUs	Conf. receipt		ao			
	AK		m		*	*
Resynchronisation			*		*	
Multiplexing and demultiplexing				*	*	*
Explicit flow control	With			m	*	*
	Without		*	*	o	
Checksum	Use of					*
	Nonuse of		*	*	*	*	o
Frozen references			*		*	*
Retransmission on timeout						*
Resequencing						*
Inactivity control						*
Treatment of protocol errors		*	*	*	*	*
Splitting and recombining						*

[a]Symbols used in this table are as follows:

*   Procedure always included in class.
m   Negotiable procedure whose implementation in equipment is mandatory.
o   Negotiable procedure whose implementation in equipment is optional.
ao Negotiable procedure whose implementation in equipment is optional and where use depends on availability within the network service.
(1) Not applicable in Class 2 when nonuse of explicit flow control is selected.

Transport Services

The transport service specification is the same for all classes [ISO86b]. This is to be expected, since one of the main points of the transport service is to provide end-to-end data transfer independent of the nature of the underlying network. The ISO specification is in the form of just four primitive types and 10 primitives.

TABLE 15-4   ISO Transport Service Primitives

T-CONNECT.request (Called Address, Calling Address, Expedited Data Option, Quality
of Service, Data)
T-CONNECT.indication (Called Address, Calling Address, Expedited Data Option,
Quality of Service, Data)
T-CONNECT.response (Quality of Service, Responding Address, Expedited Data Option,
Data)
T-CONNECT.confirm (Quality of Service, Responding Address, Expedited Data Option,
Data)

T-DISCONNECT.request (Data)
T-DISCONNECT.indication (Disconnect Reason, Data)

T-DATA.request (Data)
T-DATA.indication (Data)

T-EXPEDITED-DATA.request (Data)
T-EXPEDITED-DATA.indication (Data)

These are listed in Table 15-4. The interpretation of the primitive modifiers is
contained in Table 15-5. Figure 15-13 displays the sequences in which these primitives are used. (*Note:* The use of ~ indicates the lack of a defined time relationship
between two primitives.)

The first two primitive types are concerned with connection management. The
T-CONNECT primitives are used to establish a connection. Quality of service
refers to certain characteristics of a transport connection as observed between the
endpoints. The term actually refers to a collection of parameters, having to do with
speed or accuracy/reliability characteristics during the three phases of a connection
(Table 15-6). The transport entity will either provide the requested quality of
service, or indicate in the indication and confirm primitives a lesser quality of
service that can be provided. The quality-of-service parameters related to performance are:

TABLE 15-5   Primitive Types

REQUEST
   A primitive issued by a service user to invoke some service and to pass the parameters
needed to fully specify the requested service.

INDICATION
   A primitive issued by a service provider either:
   (1) to indicate that a procedure has been invoked by the peer service user on the con-
        nection and to provide the associated parameters, or
   (2) to notify the service user of a provider-initiated action.

RESPONSE
   A primitive issued by a service user to acknowledge or complete some procedure previously invoked by an indication to that user.

CONFIRM
   A primitive issued by a service provider to acknowledge or complete some procedure
previously invoked by a request by the service user.

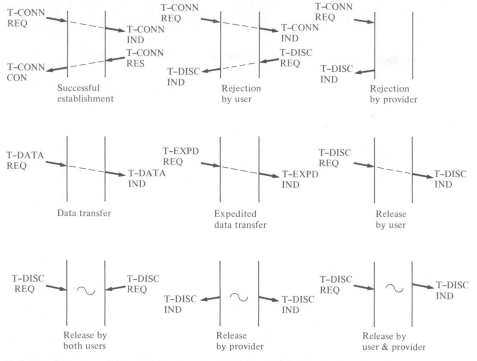

FIGURE 15-13. ISO transport services—primitive sequences.

- *Establishment delay:* maximum acceptable delay between a T-CON-NECT.request and the corresponding T-CONNECT.confirm.
- *Establishment failure probability:* acceptable proportion of connection establishment attempts that fail.
- *Throughput:* maximum and average throughput values that the user expects to produce.
- *Transit delay:* maximum and average delay values desired.
- *Residual error rate:* desired maximum rate of lost data units.
- *Transfer failure probability:* probability that the actual performance will be worse than the expected performance for throughput, transit delay, and residual error rate.

TABLE 15-6   Classification of Quality-of-Service Parameters

	Performance Criterion	
Phase	**Speed**	**Accuracy/Reliability**
TC establishment	TC establishment delay	TC establishment failure probability
Data transfer	Throughput Transit delay	Residual error rate Resilience of the TC Transfer failure probability
TC release	TC release delay	TC release failure probability

- *Release delay:* maximum acceptable delay between issuance of T-DISCON-NECT.request and the successful release of the connection at the peer transport user.
- *Release failure probability:* probability that the release delay will exceed the requested maximum.
- *Resilience:* probability of a connection release initiated by the transport service provider.

In addition, there are two other quality-of-service parameters:

- *Protection:* protection of a connection against passive monitoring and/or modification, replay, addition, or deletion.
- *Priority:* specifies the relative priority of connections with respect to (1) the order in which connections have their quality of service downgraded, if necessary and (2) the order in which connections are broken to recover resources, if necessary.

T-DISCONNECT provides for an abrupt connection termination. Termination can be initiated by either side or by one of the transport entities. T-DISCONNECT can also be used by the local transport entity or the remote addressee to reject a connection attempt.

The remaining primitives are concerned with data transfer. T-DATA and T-EXPEDITED data are used to transfer data over a transport connection. The latter attempts to expedite delivery of the data.

Protocol Formats

The ISO protocol [ISO86a] makes use of 10 types of transport protocol data units (TPDUs):

- Connection request (CR).
- Connection confirm (CC).
- Disconnect request (DR).
- Disconnect confirm (DC).
- Data (DT).
- Expedited data (ED).
- Acknowledgment (AK).
- Expedited acknowledgment (EA).
- Reject (RJ).
- TPDU error (ER).

By this time, the use of these TPDUs should be self-explanatory. In this section we confine ourselves to a discussion of the formats and field values of the various TPDUs. In the next subsection, we discuss the protocol mechanisms that are implemented with these TPDU types.

Each TPDU consists of three parts: a fixed header, a variable header, and a data field. The latter two optionally may not be present in a TPDU. The fixed header contains the frequently occurring parameters (Figure 15-14), and the variable header contains optional or infrequently occurring parameters (Table 15-6).

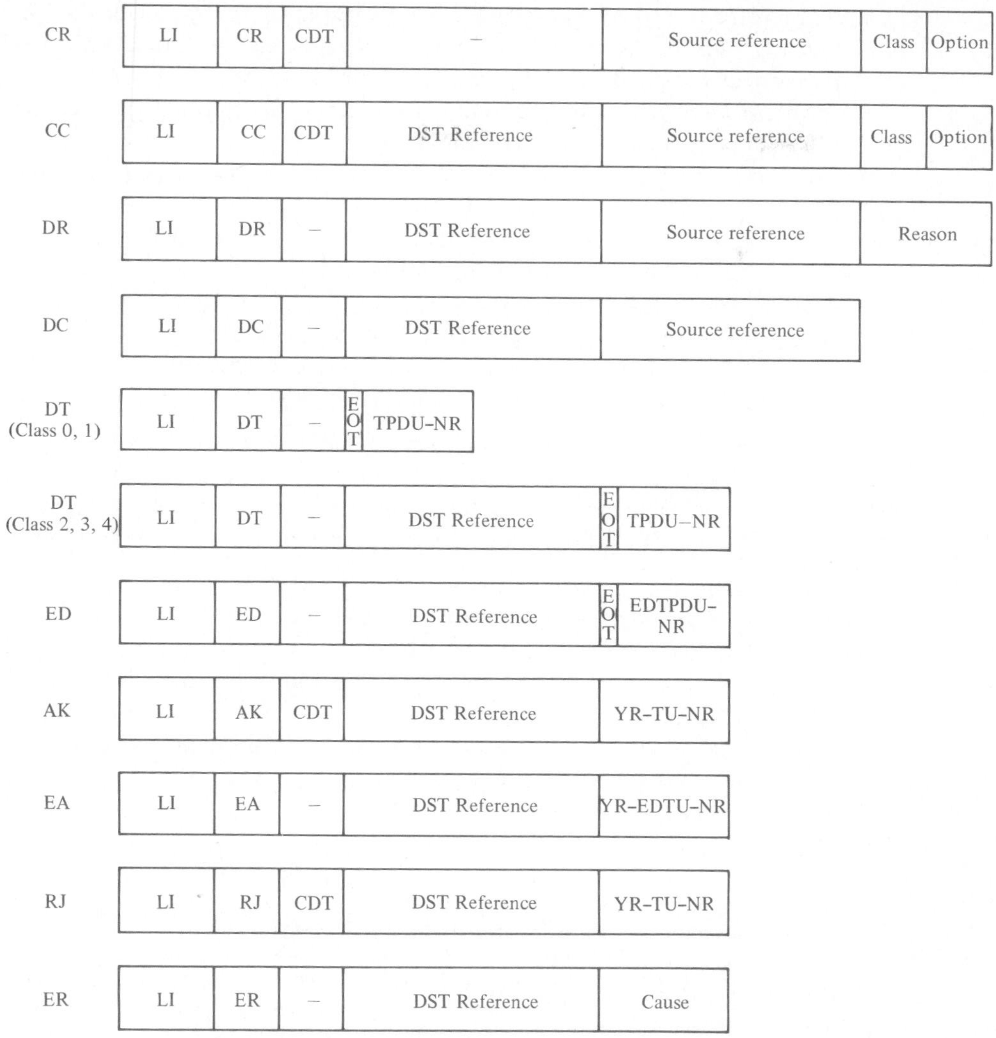

FIGURE 15-14. **ISO transport protocol fixed header formats.**

The fixed headers of the various TPDU types are similar. The fields, not all of which occur in all types, can be defined briefly:

- *Length indicator (LI) (8 bits):* length of the header (fixed plus variable) excluding the LI field, in octets.
- *TPDU code (4 bits):* type of TPDU.
- *Credit (CDT) (4 bits):* flow control credit allocation. Initial credit is granted in CR and CC, subsequent credit is granted in AK. As an option, a 16-bit credit field is used with AK, and is appended after the YR-TU-NR field.
- *Source reference (16 bits):* reference used by the transport entity to identify the transport connection uniquely in its own system.
- *Destination reference (16 bits):* reference used by the peer transport entity to identify the transport connection uniquely in its own system.
- *Class (4 bits):* protocol class.

- *Option (4 bits):* specifies normal (7-bit sequence number, 4-bit credit) or extended (31-bit sequence number, 16-bit credit) flow control fields. Also specifies whether explicit flow control is to be used in Class 2.
- *Reason (8 bits):* reason for requesting a disconnect or rejecting a connection request. The reasons are listed in Table 15-7.
- *EOT (1 bit):* used when a block of user data has been segmented into multiple TPDUs. It is set to 1 on the last TPDU.
- *TPDU-NR (7 bits):* send sequence number of a DT TPDU. It is normally modulo 2^7, but may be extended by three octets to be modulo 2^{31}.
- *EDTPDU-NR (7 bits):* send sequence number of a ED TPDU.
- *YR-TU-NR (8 bits):* the next expected DT sequence number.
- *YR-EDTU-NR (8 bits):* the next expected ED sequence number.
- *Cause (8 bits):* reason for rejection of a TPDU (Table 15-7).

The variable header consists of a sequence of additional parameters. Each parameter field consists of three subfields: a parameter code (8 bits), a parameter length (8 bits), and the parameter value (one or more octets). Most of the parameters are used by CC and CR in the connection establishment process. The parameters are:

- *Calling TSAP ID:* service access point that identifies the calling transport user.
- *Called TSAP ID:* service access point that identifies the called transport user.
- *TPDU size:* maximum TPDU size in octets. The range of options is from 128 to 8192 in powers of 2.
- *Version number:* version of protocol to be followed. This accommodates future revisions to the standard.
- *Security parameter:* user-defined.

TABLE 15-7 ISO Transport Protocol Variable Header Primitives[a]

	CR	CC	DR	DC	DT	ED	AK	EA	RT	ER
Calling TSAP ID	X	X								
Called TSAP ID	X	X								
TPDU size	X	X								
Version number	X	X								
Security parameter	X	X								
Checksum	4	4	4	4	4	4	4	4	4	
Additional option selection	X	X								
Alternative protocol class	X	X								
Acknowledge time	4	4								
Throughput	X	X								
Residual error rate	X	X								
Priority	X	X								
Transmit delay	X	X								
Reassignment time	1, 3	1, 3								
Additional information			X							
Subsequence number							4			
Flow control confirmation							4			
Invalid TPDU										X

[a]4, class 4 only; 1, 3, classes 1 and 3 only.

- *Checksum:* result of checksum algorithm (defined in an appendix to chapter 14) for the entire TPDU. The checksum is used only for Class 4 and, within that class, it is mandatory for all CR TPDUs, and for all TPDUs when the checksum option is selected.
- *Additional option selection:* used to specify use or nonuse of certain options (Table 15-8).
- *Alternative protocol class:* specifies whether only the requested protocol class is acceptable, or that some other class is also acceptable.
- *Acknowledge time:* an estimate of the time taken by the entity to acknowledge a DT TPDU. This helps the other entity select a value for its retransmission timer.
- *Throughput:* specifies the user's throughput requirements in octets per second. Eight values are specified: the target and minimum acceptable values for both maximum throughput and average throughput; in both the calling-called direction and the called-calling direction.
- *Residual error rate:* expresses the target and minimum rate of unreported user data loss.
- *Priority:* priority of this connection.
- *Transit delay:* specifies the user's delay requirements in milliseconds. Four values are specified: the target and maximum acceptable transit delay in both directions.
- *Reassignment time:* amount of time an entity will persist in attempts to reconnect after a network connection is broken.
- *Additional information:* related to the clearing of the connection. User defined.

Subsequence number: number of the AK. It is used to assure that AKs with the same YR-TU-NR are processed in correct sequence.

Flow control confirmation: echoes parameter values in the last AK TPDU received. It contains the values of the YR-TU-NR, CDT, and Subsequence Number fields.

Invalid TPDU: the bit pattern of the rejected TPDU up to and including the octet that caused the rejection.

TABLE 15-8 ISO Transport Parameter Values

Reason for Disconnect Request	**Reason for TPDU Error**
Not specified	Not specified
Congestion at TSAP	Invalid parameter code
Session entity not attached to TSAP	Invalid TPDU error
Address unknown	Invalid parameter value
Normal user-initiated disconnect	
Remote transport entity congestion	**Negotiated Options**
Connection negotiation failed	Network expedited in Class 1
Duplicate source reference	Acknowledgment in Class 1
Mismatch references	Checksum in Class 4
Protocol error	Transport expedited data service
Reference overflow	
Request refused on this network connection	
Header or parameter length invalid	

Protocol Mechanisms

The purpose of this section is to highlight the key transport protocol mechanisms. Much of what was discussed in Section 15-2 is applicable, so only a brief commentary is provided. The following topics are considered:

- Connection establishment.
- Data transfer.
- Connection termination.

Connection Establishment.   The connection establishment phase requires, at minimum, the exchange of a CR and a CC TPDU (Figure 15-13). This two-way handshake suffices for Classes 0 through 3. For Class 4, a third TPDU is needed to acknowledge the CC; this may be an AK, DT, or ED.

The purpose of this phase is to establish a transport connection with agreed-upon characteristics. If the establishment attempt is successful, these characteristics are defined by the parameters of the CC. Prior to success, there may be a period of negotiation. In some cases, the calling entity specifies options (e.g., other classes are acceptable), and the called entity selects one in the CC. In other cases, the calling entity proposes a value (e.g., maximum TPDU size), and the calling entity may accept it (CC) or reject it (DR). The parameters involved in this latter process are listed in Table 15-6.

A transport connection involves four different types of identifiers:

- User identifier (service access point).
- Transport/network address.
- Transport protocol identifier.
- Transport connection identifier.

Since there may be more than one user of the transport entity, a user identifier is needed to allow the transport entity to multiplex data transfers to multiple users. This identifier must be passed down from the transport user, and included in CC and CR TPDUs. The transport/network address identifies the station on which the transport entity is located. This address, or a corresponding name, is passed down from the transport user. The address is not needed in any TPDU, but must be passed down to the network protocol entity for its use. Normally, there will be only one transport protocol entity in a station. However, more than one entity, each of a different type, might be resident in one station. In the latter case, the protocol must be identified to the network service. We saw this facility in use in IP. Finally, each transport connection is given a unique identifier (similar to an X.25 virtual-circuit number) by each of the two transport entities involved. This identifier is used in all TPDUs. It allows the transport entity to multiplex multiple transport connections on a single network connection.

Data Transfer.   Normal data transfer over a connection is accomplished using DTs. Each data unit may be self contained. Alternatively, if the user data plus DT header exceeds the maximum TPDU size, the transport entity may segment the letter and send it out as a sequence of TPDUs. The last TPDU in sequence has the EOT bit set.

DTs are numbered sequentially. This is used in Classes 2 through 4 for flow control. A credit-allocation scheme is used. The initial credit is set in the CC and

CR TPDUs. Subsequent credit is granted with an AK. Note that acknowledgments are in separate TPDUs, and never piggybacked onto DTs. At first glance, this might seem inefficient since an entire TPDU is needed for flow control. This is not so for two reasons:

- The transport entity may choose not to acknowledge every single DT, but only acknowledge in bunches. Thus no overhead for piggybacking is wasted in the DT.
- A sort of piggybacking is possible. A transport entity may concatenate multiple TPDUs (e.g., a DT and an AK) into one unit to be passed to the network service. Thus several TPDUs will be efficiently handled as a single packet by the network.

In Class 4, sequence numbers are also used for resequencing DTs that arrive out of order. Another mechanism unique to Class 4 is the DT checksum. If an error is detected, an ER is returned. Other reasons for ER, for all classes, are listed in Table 15-6.

Expedited data transfer uses the ED and EA data units. Sequence numbers are used, but only one ED may be outstanding at a time. The sender must receive an EA before sending another ED. The reader may ask how a transport entity expedites data. The answer may strike some as clumsy and inefficient, but it is just one more example of the limitations and complexities with which a transport protocol must cope. In Classes 1 through 4, an ED is sent before any DTs queued for that connection. In Class 4, we must contend with the problem that being sent out first does not mean being delivered first. Therefore, the Class 4 entity suspends the transfer of new DTs (although pending DTs will go out) until an EA is received. In effect, the connection is shut down to accommodate this one piece of data.

Connection Termination. An abrupt termination is achieved by the exchange of a DR and a DC. When a transport entity receives a disconnect request from its user, it discards any pending DTs and issues the DR. The entity that receives the DR issues a DC, discards any pending DTs, and informs its user.

15-5

DOD TRANSPORT PROTOCOLS

The DOD transport protocols, together with IP, are the centerpiece of the DOD protocol architecture. The comments made in Chapter 12 concerning the philosophy of that model apply specifically to these protocols.

DOD has defined two transport-level protocols: the Transmission Control Protocol (TCP), which is connection-oriented, and the User Datagram Protocol (UDP), which is connectionless. As yet, UDP is little used. TCP is the principal transport protocol in the DOD world [DOD83b].

TCP Services

TCP is designed to provide reliable communication between pairs of processes (TCP users) across a variety of reliable and unreliable networks and internets.

Functionally, it is equivalent to Class 4 ISO Transport [GROE86]. In contrast to the ISO model, TCP is stream oriented. That is, TCP users exchange streams of data. The data are placed in allocated buffers and transmitted by TCP in segments (TPDUs). TCP supports security and precedence labeling. In addition, TCP provides two useful facilities for labeling data: push and urgent:

- *Data stream push:* Ordinarily, TCP decides when sufficient data has accumulated to form a TPDU for transmission. The TCP user can require TCP to transmit all outstanding data up to and including that labeled with a push flag. On the receiving end, TCP will deliver these data to the user in the same manner. A user might request this if it has come to a logical break in the data.
- *Urgent data signaling:* This provides a means of informing the destination TCP user that significant or "urgent" data is in the upcoming data stream. It is up to the destination user to determine appropriate action.

Tables 15-9 and 15-10 list the TCP service request (user to TCP) and service response (TCP to user) primitives. Several comments are in order.

TABLE 15-9   TCP Service Request Primitives

UNSPECIFIED-PASSIVE-OPEN (source-port, [timeout], [timeout-action], [precedence], [security-range])

  Listen for connection attempts at specified security and precedence levels from any remote user.

FULL-PASSIVE-OPEN (source-port, destination-port, destination-address, [timeout], [timeout-action], [precedence], [security-range])

  Listen for connection attempts at specified security and precedence levels from specified user.

ACTIVE-OPEN (source-port, destination-port, destination-address, [timeout], [timeout-action], [precedence], [security],)

  Request connection at particular security and precedence levels.

ACTIVE-OPEN W/DATA (source-port, destination-port, destination-address, [timeout], [timeout-action], [precedence], [security], data, data-length, push-flag, urgent-flag)

  Request connection at particular security and precedence levels and transmit data with the request.

SEND (local-connection-name, data, data length, push-flag, urgent-flag, [timeout], [timeout-action])

  Causes data to be transferred across named connection.

ALLOCATE (local-connection-name, data length)

  Issue incremental allocation for receive data to TCP.

CLOSE (local-connection-name)

  Close connection gracefully.

ABORT (local-connection-name)

  Close connection abruptly.

STATUS (local-connection-name)

  Report connection status.

TABLE 15-10

OPEN-ID (local-connection-name, source-port, destination-port, destination address)

Informs user of connection name assigned to pending connection requested in an OPEN primitive.

OPEN-FAILURE (local-connection-name)

Reports failure of an active OPEN request.

OPEN-SUCCESS (local-connection-name)

Reports completion of an active OPEN request.

DELIVER (local-connection-name, data, data-length, urgent-flag)

Reports arrival of data.

CLOSING (local-connection-name)

Reports that remote TCP user has issued a CLOSE.

TERMINATE (local-connection-name, description)

Reports that connection has been terminated and no longer exists.

STATUS-RESPONSE (local-connection-name, source-port, source-address, destination-port, destination-address, connection-state, receive-window, send-window, amount-waiting-ack, amount-waiting-receipt, urgent-state, precedence, security, timeout)

Reports current status of connection.

ERROR (local-connection-name, description)

Reports service-request or internal error.

The two passive open commands correspond to the LISTEN command of Figure 15-11. They signal the user's willingness to accept a connection request. The active open with data is analogous to the X.25 fast select facility.

Source port and *destination port* are essentially transport service access points. *Destination address* identifies the network and station address of the remote TCP entity. *Timeout* permits the user to set up a timeout for all data submitted to TCP. If data are not successfully delivered within the timeout, TCP will abort the connection.

TCP Header Format

TCP uses only a single type of TPDU. The header is shown in Figure 15-15a. Because one header must serve to perform all protocol mechanisms, it is rather large. Whereas the ISO fixed header is from five to seven octets long, the TCP header is a minimum of 20 octets long. The fields are:

- *Source port (16 bits):* identifies source service access point.
- *Destination port (16 bits):* identifies destination service access point.
- *Sequence number (32 bits):* sequence number of the first data octet in this TPDU, except when SYN is present. If SYN is present, it is the initial sequence number (ISN) and the first data octet is ISN + 1.

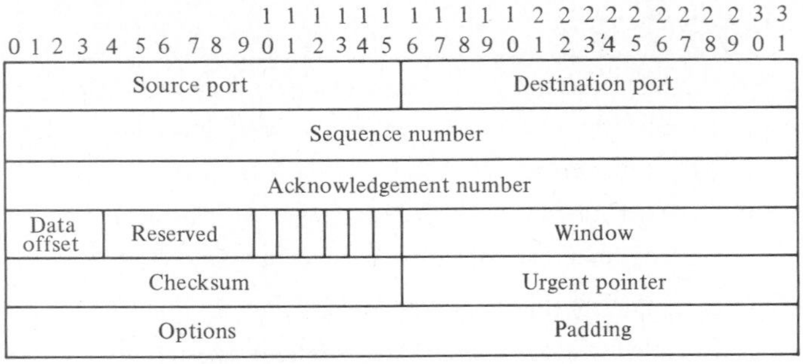

```
                         1 1 1 1 1 1 1 1 1 1 2 2 2 2 2 2 2 2 2 2 3 3
       0 1 2 3 4 5 6 7 8 9 0 1 2 3 4 5 6 7 8 9 0 1 2 3 4 5 6 7 8 9 0 1
```

Source port	Destination port
Sequence number	
Acknowledgement number	

Data offset	Reserved	☐ ☐ ☐ ☐ ☐ ☐	Window
Checksum			Urgent pointer
Options			Padding

(a) Transmission control protocol (TCP)

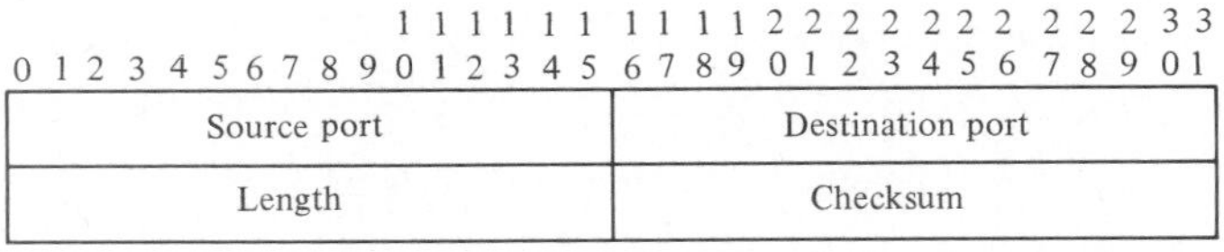

```
                         1 1 1 1 1 1 1 1 1 1 2 2 2 2 2 2 2 2 2 2 3 3
       0 1 2 3 4 5 6 7 8 9 0 1 2 3 4 5 6 7 8 9 0 1 2 3 4 5 6 7 8 9 0 1
```

Source port	Destination port
Length	Checksum

(b) User datagram protocol (UDP)

FIGURE 15-15.   DOD transport protocol header formats.

- *Acknowledgment number (32 bits):* a piggybacked acknowledgment. Contains the sequence number of the next octet that the TCP entity expects to receive.
- *Data offset (4 bits):* number of 32-bit words in the header.
- *Reserved (6 bits):* reserved for future use.
- *Flags (6 bits):*
  URG: urgent pointer field significant.
  ACK: acknowledgment field significant.
  PSH: push function.
  RST: reset the connection.
  SYN: synchronize the sequence numbers.
  FIN: no more data from sender.
- *Window (16 bits):* flow control credit allocation, in octets. Contains the number of data octets beginning with the one indicated in the acknowledgment field which the sender is willing to accept.
- *Checksum (16 bits):* the one's complement of the sum modulo $2^{16} - 1$ of all the 16-bit words in the TPDU.
- *Urgent Pointer (16 bits):* points to the octet following the urgent data. This allows the receiver to know how much urgent data are coming.
- *Options (Variable):* at present, only one option is defined, which specifies the maximum TPDU size that will be accepted.

The reader may feel that some items are missing, and that is indeed the case. TCP is designed specifically and exclusively to work with IP. Hence some user parameters are passed down for inclusion in the IP header. The relevant ones are:

- Precedence: a 3-bit field.
- Normal delay/low delay.
- Normal throughput/high throughput.
- Normal reliability/high reliability.
- Security: an 11-bit field.

It is worth observing that this TCP/IP linkage means that the required minimum overhead for every data unit is actually 40 octets.

TCP Mechanisms

Connection Establishment. Connection establishment in TCP always uses a three-way handshake. When the SYN flag is set, the TPDU is essentially a request for connection (RFC), and functions as explained in Section 15-2. To initiate a connection, an entity sends an RFC X, where X is the initial sequence number. The receiver responds with RFC Y, ACK X by setting both the SYN and ACK flags. Finally, the initiater responds with ACK Y. If both sides issue crossing RFCs, no problem results: Both sides respond with ACKs.

Data Transfer. Although data are transferred in TPDUs over a transport connection, data transfer is viewed logically as consisting of a stream of octets. Hence every octet is numbered, modulo 2^{32}. Each TPDU contains the sequence number of the first octet in the data field. Flow control is exercised using a credit allocation scheme in which the credit is a number of octets rather than a number of TPDUs. In principle, this numbering scheme is more flexible than the ISO/NBS approach and gives the transport entity tighter control over its buffers. In practice, the two seem to provide equivalent performance.

As was mentioned, data are buffered by the transport entity on both transmission and reception. TCP normally exercises its own discretion as to when to construct a TPDU for transmission and when to release received data to the user. The PUSH flag is used to force the data so far accumulated to be sent by the transmitter and passed on by the receiver. This serves an end-of-letter function.

The user may specify a block of data as urgent. TCP will designate the end of that block with an urgent pointer and send it out in the ordinary data stream. The receiving user is alerted that urgent data are being received.

If, during data exchange, a TPDU arrives which is apparently not meant for the current connection, the RST flag is set on an outgoing TPDU. Examples of this situation are delayed duplicate SYNs and an acknowledgment of data not yet sent.

Connection Termination. The normal means of terminating a connection is a graceful close. Each transport user must issue a CLOSE primitive. The transport entity sets the FIN bit on the last TPDU that it sends out, which also contains the last of the data to be sent on this connection.

An abrupt termination occurs if the user issues an ABORT primitive. In this case, the entity abandons all attempts to send or receive data and discards data in its transmission and reception buffers. A RST TPDU is sent to the other side.

User Datagram Protocol

The User Datagram Protocol (UDP) provides a transport-level datagram service. UDP is basically an unreliable service; delivery and duplicate protection are not guaranteed. However, this does reduce the overhead of the protocol and may be adequate in many cases.

Figure 15-15b shows the format of the UDP header. As with TCP, UDP is expected to work with IP. Although it includes a checksum, there is no provision for error reporting. A ''one-way'' handshake is used. That is, UDP assembles a data unit and hands it to IP for transmission. Incoming data units are checked using the checksum. An invalid data unit is discarded. A valid one is passed to the user.

15-6

LIGHTWEIGHT TRANSPORT PROTOCOLS

A Problem with Existing Transport Protocols

As you might expect, a tremendous amount of research, development, and real-world experience have gone into the transport protocols that are currently in widespread use, notable the ISO and TCP/IP versions. However, two trends have led to a need for a new approach:

- The most common configuration for computer networking is now an internet; isolated networks are becoming increasingly rare. Accordingly, the transport protocol is usually supported by an internet protocol.
- The data rates on both LANs (e.g., FDDI) and WANs (e.g., use of T-1 trunks in packet-switching networks, and the approach of broadband ISDN, as described in Chapter 18), are significantly greater than those that existed when current transport protocols were designed.

The upshot is that a conventional transport protocol, especially when bound to an internet protocol, produces a processing overhead that appears to be out of proportion with the high-speed networks that it must traverse. The protocols are too complex to be implemented directly in silicon. As software modules, their performance is severely limited by processor speed, memory access times, buffer management overhead, and packet formats designed for functionality rather than performance.

Note that in the above paragraph, we used the phrase ''appears to be'' rather than ''is.'' Although the problem stated above is generally recognized in the design community, there is a sharp difference of opinion about the best way to proceed. In essence, there are two approaches:

- Improve the performance of existing protocols.
- Design new protocols with the net networking environment clearly in mind.

The former position is advocated by a number of researchers who have demonstrated that improvements in implementation and in integration of communications software with operating-system software can lead to improvements in performance [VAZQ88, HEAT89]. Supporters of this approach feel that the experience gained with existing complex protocols should be retained and that an implementation in silicon unnecessarily retards the evolution and refinement of these protocols. One example of such an approach is the concept of header prediction [CLAR89, STRA89]. Those involved in the project report on a statistical analysis that shows that in specific situations, parts of the packet headers of standard communication protocols follow each other with at least 90 percent certainty. This feature can be used to reduce processing. Once a certain amount of processing is done on one packet, a quick bit comparison with a future packet can determine whether the same processing steps can be skipped for that packet. Such a scheme involves no change to the protocol and no loss of functionality.

Other researchers feel that new protocols that combine internet and transport functionality and that are specifically designed with high-speed networks in mind offer the best hope for providing adequate performance. The resulting protocols have been termed lightweight transport protocols.[1] Examples of experimental lightweight transport protocols include VMTP [CHER89a, WILL89], LNTP [CHAN88], high-speed transport protocol [SABN89], GAM-T [MINE89], Delta-T [WATS89], AND XTP [WHAL89, COHN88, COHN89, CHES88, HIND89, PE89]. In the remainder of this section, we examine XTP, which is the best documented and which is the most likely one of these protocols to become an international standard.

Xpress Transfer Protocol (XTP)

XTP combines the functionality of transport and internet protocols to produce a streamlined protocol that requires minimum processing and that allows for parallel processing of some functions. In this subsection, we highlight some of the key features of XTP.

Frame Design.   As the upper part of Figure 15-16 shows, XTP includes information packets and control packets. A common header format and a common trailer format are used for both packet formats. Both header and trailer are fixed size to simplify processing. The advantage of having some of the control information in a trailer (in contrast to most internet and transport protocols, which only have a header), is that the control bits placed in the trailer correspond to functions that must be performed during or after transmission or reception of the remainder of the packet. For example, error detection codes (one for the header and trailer, one for the body) are in the trailer; on transmission, the code is calculated while the preceding bits of the packet are actually being transmitted and then tacked on to the end of the transmission.

Table 15-11 defines the individual fields of the XTP packets. Table 15-12 lists the individual packet types that can be constructed from the two packet formats.

Receiver Responses.   Most protocols require the receiver to ACK data and allow the receiver some latitude in the timing of issuing ACKs. XTP provides a bit in the trailer for requesting a control packet that reports status (flow, error, and rate parameters). Except for detected errors, when the receiver may autonomously generate advisory control messages, receiver responses are controlled by the peer sender. The sender is thus able to adjust the rate and timing of responses from the receiver to suit the application traffic.

---

[1]It is interesting to note that similar concepts have arisen in the areas of communication protocols, computer architecture, and operating systems at about the same time. In the area of computer architecture, the reduced instruction set computer (RISC) approach has led to improved processor speed by streamlining processor architecture. In the area of operating systems, the lightweight process, or thread, which is a unit of dispatching within a normal process, has led to reduced processing overhead in the operating system. These two concepts are discussed at length in [STAL90b] and [STAL92], respectively.

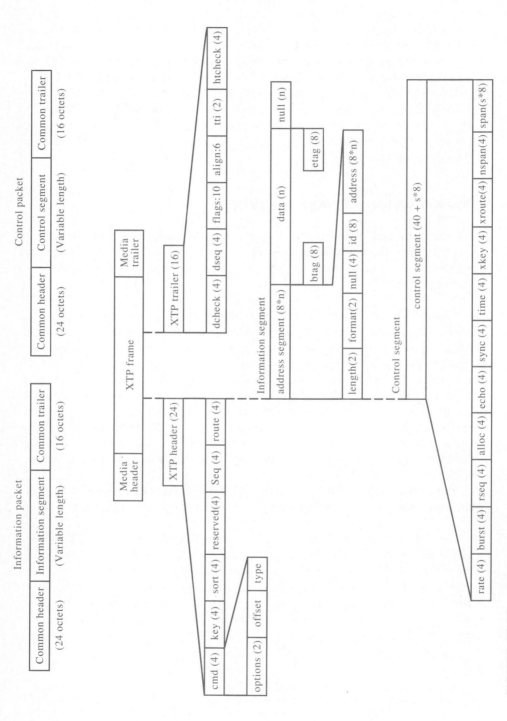

FIGURE 15-16. **XTP packet formats.**

TABLE 15-11 XTP Fields

XTP Header (24 octets)

Command (CMD)
  Options
    Set of options for enabling/disabling various functions, such as error detection, packet retransmission, multicast addressing, and interpretation of Sort field. Also includes bit to indicate whether first 8 octets of user data are tag information.
  Offset
    Specifies the amount of padding, if any, at the beginning of the information segment.
  Type
    Indicates type of packet; see Table 15-12.
Key
  Logical connection identifier. It is an end-to-end value generated at one host and communicated unchanged through internet routers to a destination host. Each side of a connection may assign its own key value to the connection. Once keys have been exchanged (see Xkey, below), each side uses the key of the other side in transmissions.
Sort
  Associates a value with each packet to direct the order of input and output operations. The field represents either a priority or a clock time, which is interpreted as a deadline.
Reserved
  This field in not used in the current version.
Sequence (Seq)
  The 32-bit end-to-end sequence number for the context (connection).
Route
  Provides the basis for packet forwarding through an internet router. The value is used by a router as an index into a routing table. On each hop, the value in the route field is changed for use by the next router.

XTP Trailer (16 octets)

Dcheck
  Error-detection checksum calculated over the information segment or control segment.
Dseq
  Equal to one plus the highest sequence number transferred from XTP to the application.
Flags
  Various control bit flags, including immediate control packet requested, read side closed, end of message, and last packet.
Align
  The number of null octets in the data field that precede the trailer for either alignment or packet padding reasons.
Time to live (TTL)
  Maximum lifetime of the packet in the internet, expressed in 10 millisecond ticks.
HT check
  Error-detection checksum calculated over the header and trailer excluding the Route field.

Information Segment

Address segment
  Length
    Length of the address segment.
  Format
    Network address syntax. Options include ISO standard, TCP/IP standard, and source routing format.

TABLE 15-11   XTP Fields (*continued*)

Null
   Used to pad out address segment to multiple of 8 octets.
Id
   Not used in current version (3.4) of XTP.
Address
   Actual address of host system.
Data
   User data from higher layer.
Null
   May be used for padding.

Control Segment

Rate
   Maximum number of octets receiver will accept in each one second time period.
Burst
   Maximum number of octets receiver will accept per burst of packets.
Rseq
   Highest consecutive sequence number receives without error.
Alloc
   Other side may send packets up to but not including this sequence number.
Echo
   Copy of value in most recently received Sync field.
Sync
   Used to synchronize XTP, in conjunction with Echo field. Sender can transmit a unique number and notice when that value is returned. The sender can conclude that packets sent prior to the one containing the particular sync value have probably had enough time to arrive at the remote receiver.
Time
   Time field of a received control segment is copied to the time field of an outgoing control response. Used by a host to determine round trip delay.
Xkey
   Exchange key. Value assigned to a logical connection by the side that did not originate the connection, and returned to the other side for future use (see Key, above).
Xroute
   Exchange route. Functions in manner similar to Xkey, for internet routers. In this case, the exchange is done on a hop-by-hop basis, rather than end-to-end (see Route, above).
Nspan
   The number of active spans (span = contiguous sequence of packets that has been received).
Span
   Consists of up to 16 pairs of sequence numbers. Each sequence number pair identifies a span of packets that has been successfully received. This selective acknowledgment identifies gaps of packets that must be retransmitted.

Internet Routing.   In a high-speed internet, it is important that the forwarding function of the router be performed rapidly. To aid in this process a route field is included in the XTP header. This has a zero value for logical connections that span a single network. If the connection spans multiple networks and hence goes through

TABLE 15-12   XTP Packet Types

FIRST

Initiates context establishment. Contains address segment and may contain user data.

DATA

Contains user data.

PATH

Consists of header, address segment, and trailer. It is used to thread a path through a internet and may be used to locate a router or to recover from router failure.

DIAG

Indicates error condition at receiver or router (e.g., destination unknown).

MAINT

Gathers end-to-end diagnostic data (e.g., end-to-end route, hop times).

MGMT

Not defined in current version (3.4).

CNTL

Used by receiver to return status (e.g., flow error, and rate parameters). Sent in response to a packet with Sreq trailer command bit set. Used by sender when resynchronizing with the receiver.

SUPER

Allows a router to construct a large packet from small ones for packets using the same route.

ROUTE

Used for route control. Sent by host to request that route be released. Sent by router to acknowledge that route has been released.

RCNTL

Router-generated control packet.

---

one or more routers, the field is used as follows. When an initial connection-opening packet (a FIRST packet; see Table 15-12), arrives at a router from a source (which may be a router), the router analyzes the address field which contains the global destination address and makes a routing decision. An exit port is determined and placed in a routing table. The index to that table is returned to the source in the Xroute field of a control packet. Subsequent DATA packets from the source contained the assigned index in the Route field. As a result, the router can make an immediate routing decision on the basis of a table lookup. If there is a path through several routers, the route value changes at each router.

At any given time, a single route is set up between a source/destination pair. Any number of logical connections may be multiplexed on the same route. Each logical connection is identified by the Key field in the header, which functions in a manner similar to virtual circuit numbers in X.25.

Flow and Error Control.   Flow and error control are applied on a logical-connection basis, end to end. The technique is essentially a sliding-window strategy. However, to improve efficiency, selective retransmission is allowed. At any time, the destination is prepared to accept packets within some window of sequence numbers. If packets are lost or arrive out of order, gaps will develop in the received sequence. The destination is able to inform the source of the existence of such gaps (using the Span field in the Control Segment; see Table 15-11). The source then selectively retransmits the missing packets.

Rate Control. In addition to flow control on a per-connection basis, XTP provides for rate control to be used over each route. The rate may be controlled separately in each direction. XTP routers assign a maximum packet rate to each new router, and return this value to the source computer along with the new Route value in a control packet. The rate is applied to all traffic from the source computer along the route. This feature has a number of benefits:

- If the source system generates a large load on a particular route by initiating more connections, those connections must share the assigned rate, thus avoiding a surge at the router.
- If a source system wants to find a new path through the internet and obtain a new or additional rate, it can do so.
- The router may regulate assigned rates upward or downward in response to the observed load and available resources.
- A rate-based system uses fewer network packets than a scheme that achieves rate control with a moving window flow control scheme.
- The space required in an XTP router to administer rate control in this manner is related to the number of active source/destination pairs through the router. This is a much smaller number than the number of active connections, which would be the case if the protocol architecture required intervention on a connection basis.

Connection Control. In XTP, multi-packet exchange sequences provide user applications with both a transport-level virtual-circuit (connection-oriented) and a transport-level datagram (acknowledged connectionless) service. For the former, connection establishment is illustrated in Figure 15-17a. A connection request is contained in a FIRST packet, which may also include user data. When this is received, the destination replies with a control packet, which either rejects or accepts the connection. In the latter case, the destination may either indicate that the connection is to remain open, or that it is ready to close the connection. If the destination indicates a desire to close the connection, the source will confirm this in a control packet. Otherwise, the two sides may exchange data for a period, and use a three-way handshake to terminate the connection later on.

A two-way handshake is used for a transport-level datagram service or the basis for a simple request/response operation, as illustrated in Figure 15-17b. In this case, the source includes an indication that the connection is to be closed in the FIRST packet. The receiver acknowledges in a control packet. The advantage of this mode is that the destination doesn't have to wait to close the context after issuing the closing control packet.

15-7

RECOMMENDED READING

A good account of transport protocols can be found in [MCQU78]. Other sources are [SUNS81], [GARL77], and a chapter in [TANE88]. [NBS80b] is a good discussion of the types of services and protocol mechanism to be looked for in a transport protocol. The serious student will be amply repayed by the effort of reading the five-volume [NBS83]. The ISO and DOD standards are discussed in detail in [STAL90c] and [STAL90e], respectively.

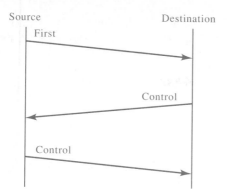

(a) Three-packet connection-mode handshake

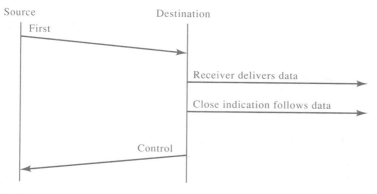

(b) Two-packet transaction-mode handshake

FIGURE 15-17.   XTP operation.

15-8

PROBLEMS

15-1   It is common practice in most transport protocols (indeed, most protocols at all levels) for control and data to be multiplexed over the same logical channel on a per-user-connection basis. An alternative is to establish a single control transport connection between each pair of communicating transport entities. This connection would be used to carry control signals relating to all user transport connections between the two entities. Discuss the implications of this strategy.

15-2   The discussion of flow control with a reliable network service referred to a back-pressure mechanism utilizing a lower-level flow control protocol. Discuss the disadvantages of this strategy.

15-3   Two transport entities communicate across a reliable network. Let the normalized time to transmit a TPDU equal 1. Assume that the end-to-end propagation delay is 3, and that it takes a time 2 to deliver data from a received TPDU to the transport user. The sender initially granted a credit of seven TPDUs. The receiver uses a conservative flow control policy, and updates its credit allocation at every opportunity. What is the maximum achievable throughput?

15-4   Draw diagrams similar to Figure 15-7 for the following (assume a reliable sequenced network service):
       a. Connection termination: active/passive.
       b. Connection termination: active/active.
       c. Connection rejection.
       d. Connection abortion: user issues an OPEN to a listening user, and then issues a CLOSE before any data are exchanged.

15-5   With a reliable sequencing network service, are TPDU sequence numbers strictly necessary? What, if any, capability is lost without them?

15-6   Consider a failure-prone network service that suffers a reset. Should the transport entity allow for the possibility of duplicate TPDUs as a result of the transport-level reset mechanism?

15-7   The discussion of retransmission strategy made reference to three problems associated with dynamic timer calculation. What modifications to the strategy would help to alleviate those problems?

15-8   If a dynamic timer calculation is used for the retransmission strategy, the following moving-average formula is suggested by NBS:

$$\text{SRTD:} = (\text{ALPHA} * \text{SRTD}) + ((1 - \text{ALPHA}) * \text{RTD})$$
$$\text{rtrans:} = \min(\text{UBOUND}, \max(\text{LBOUND}, (\text{BETA} * \text{SRTD})))$$

Where UBOUND and LBOUND are prechosen upper and lower bounds on the timer value, SRTD is the smoothed round-trip delay, and RTD is the last observed round-trip delay. What functions do ALPHA and BETA perform, and what is the effect of higher or lower values of each?

15-9   Consider a transport protocol that uses a connection-oriented network service. Suppose that the transport protocol uses a credit allocation flow control scheme, and the network protocol uses a sliding window scheme. What relationship, if any, should there be between the dynamic window of the transport protocol and the fixed window of the network protocol?

15-10   In a network that has a maximum packet size of 128 bytes, a maximum packet lifetime of 30 s, and an 8-bit packet sequence number, what is the maximum data rate per connection?

15-11   Is a deadlock possible using only a two-way handshake instead of a three-way handshake? Give an example or prove otherwise.

15-12   Why is there not a T-DATA.confirm primitive in Table 15-4?

15-13   In the ISO protocol, why is the Source Reference field included in CR, CC, DR, and DC, but not the other TPDUs?

15-14 Compare the PUSH and URGENT mechanisms of TCP with the expedited data mechanism of ISO. How do they differ?

15-15 Why is UDP needed? Why can't a user program directly access IP?

15-16 Listed below are four strategies that can be used to provide a transport user with the address of the destination transport user. For each one, describe an analogy with the Postal Service user.
  a. Know the address ahead of time.
  b. Make use of a ''well-known address''
  c. Use a name server
  d. Addressee is spawned at request time

15-17 In a credit flow control scheme, what provision can be made for credit allocations that are lost in transit?

15-18 What happens in Figure 15-6 if an RFC comes in while the requested use in IDLE? Is there any way to get the attention of the user when it is not listening?

CHAPTER 16

Session Services and Protocols

The transport layer, as we have seen, presents difficult technical problems. But there is universal agreement that transport protocols are needed, and, fortunately, existing standards are solidifying and being accepted. What do we have above transport? Let us consider this from the top down.

At the application level, users should be able to write their own applications that invoke the computer network functionality through a transport, session, or presentation interface, as appropriate. In addition, certain "utility-grade" applications, such as electronic mail, should be standardized and made available universally. This is widely accepted in principle. Also widely accepted, in principle, is the need for presentation services. A notable example here is a virtual terminal protocol. Some protocols seem to span both application and presentation levels. Examples are electronic mail and file transfer protocols.

Whereas the OSI model calls for the inclusion of a session layer, the DOD reference model (DRM) sets its face against a "session layer" as such, feeling that some of its presumed functions (e.g., graceful close) should be performed by transport and that other functions are peculiar to the processes or applications that wish to communicate. The non-DOD standards organizations have had some trouble pinning down a session layer standard, in part because of the lack of strong motivation for its existence.

This chapter examines the session layer. We begin with a general discussion of session characteristics and requirements. The following two sections examine the standard developed by ISO. In describing this standard, we will notice a marked contrast with the discussion of transport protocols in the preceding chapter. Our primary concern at the transport layer was the complexity of the transport protocol mechanisms required to provide a reliable service. At the session layer, such elaborate mechanisms are not needed; when a session protocol data unit is sent, we are guaranteed that it will be delivered reliably. Instead, the focus at the session layer is with defining a variety of data exchange services that might (or might not!) be useful to applications. Accordingly, although the session protocol is straightforward, the ISO session services are rich and complex.

Finally in this chapter, we examine the SNA approach to session functionality.

16·1

SESSION CHARACTERISTICS

This section discusses session protocols in terms of principles and objectives, rather than a specific standard.

Few session protocols exist at the present time. Much of the original work that has led to the OSI concept of a session layer was done by a group of designers at Honeywell [BACH79], in the context of OSI and Honeywell's own communications architecture [HONE82]. This same general approach was pursued by NBS [NBS81] and ISO [NEUM83], [EMMO83] in developing a specific session protocol standard. What follows is based on the model of the session layer as reflected in the above efforts.

The essential purpose of a session protocol is to provide a user-oriented connection service. The transport protocol is responsible for creating and maintaining a logical connection between endpoints. A session protocol provides a "user interface" by "adding value" to the basic connection service. Let us consider some of the value-added features. We can group them into the following categories:

- Session establishment and maintenance
- Dialogue management.
- Recovery.

Session Establishment and Maintenance

The minimum service that a session protocol entity provides its users is the establishment, maintenance, and termination of sessions. When two users wish to establish a connection, their respective entities will create a session that is mapped onto a transport connection and negotiate the parameters of the session (e.g., data unit size; see below for further examples).

Let us refer to the unit of data exchanged between a session user and a session protocol entity as a record. The session entity accepts records from the user and encapsulates each into a session protocol data unit (SPDU). SPDUs are, in turn, handed over the local transport entity to be sent over a transport connection in a sequence of transport protocol data units (TPDUs). The data are received on the other side and delivered to the user in the proper order. The sending transport entity may, at its discretion, segment SPDUs into multiple TPDUs if the SPDU size is too large. Alternatively, multiple records may be blocked into a single TPDU for efficiency of transmission. In any case, the receiving entity recovers the original records and passes these on to the receiving user.

The simplest relationship between sessions and transport connections is one to one. It might be desirable to multiplex multiple sessions onto a single transport connection. This reduces the processing burden and amount of state information required of the transport entity. However, caution must be observed. For example, a session supporting inquiry/response should not be multiplexed with a session supporting a file transfer, since the sending of the inquiry text may be significantly delayed when entering a long transport queue of file text from the other session. Furthermore, if the receiving session entity is forced, for any reason, to stop receiving the file transfer text, the receiving queue may soon fill up. This will cause the source queue to fill up as well and any text from the inquiry session multiplexed with the halted session may remain trapped in it.

A session might also be split between two transport connections. This could facilitate the transfer of expedited or interrupt data.

Dialogue Management

The session entity may impose a structure on the interaction or dialogue between users. There are three possible modes of dialogue: two-way simultaneous, two-way alternate, and one-way.

The two-way simultaneous mode is a full-duplex type of operation. Both sides can simultaneously send data. Once this mode is agreed upon in the session negotiation phase, there is no specific dialogue management task required. This would probably be the most common mode of dialogue.

Similarly, the one-way mode requires no specific dialogue management mechanism once it is established. All user data flows in one direction only. An example of this is if data are to be sent to a temporarily inactive user, and are accepted by a ''receiver server,'' whose only task is to accept data on behalf of other local users and store them. Note that the characteristic of being one-way is not absolute. There is a two-way dialogue required to establish the session. During data transfer, the receiving session entity may transmit acknowledgments and other control information. Furthermore, the receiving session user may need to send back some interrupt data. For example, the receiver may need to halt reception temporarily because of a local system problem.

The most complex of the three modes is two-way alternate. In this case, the two sides take turns sending data. An example of the use of this mode is for inquiry/response applications. The session entity enforces the alternating interaction by informing each user when it is its turn. This is actually a three-step process:

- The user who has the turn informs its session entity when it has completed its turn.
- The sending session entity sends any outstanding data to the receiving entity and then informs the receiving entity that the turn is being passed.
- The receiving entity passes up any outstanding data to its user and then informs the user that it is its turn.

An economical means of accomplishing this process is to mark the data with a delimiter. Specifically, the sending user includes a delimiter in the last record of its turn. Let us call the sequence of records sent during one user's turn a *session interaction unit*. Then, on the last record of its turn, the user would include an end-of-interaction unit (I) delimiter. This delimiter is, in effect, a token that is passed to the other user.

With two-way alternate, the user is prevented from sending normal data unless it is its turn. However, a user may send interrupt data to, for example, demand the turn. As an example of the use of the demand-turn mechanism, consider a user who has requested data and is viewing them as they scroll onto a screen. The user may wish to abort the transmission once the first few lines have been viewed.

Another form a dialogue management is the *quarantine service*. This service allows a sending session user to supply a number of blocks of data to the session service and request that the session service refrain from delivering any of the data until receiving an explicit release from the user, at which time all of the quarantined data is delivered. The sending user may also request that all currently quarantined data be discarded. An example of the use of this service is for support of terminal-to-host interaction; a screen-full of data may be supplied to session in multiple blocks, but only be delivered for display when all of the data is available. This service places a buffering requirement on the session service, in effect removing that requirement from the application layer.

Recovery

Another potential feature of a session protocol is a recovery support service similar to the checkpoint/restart mechanisms used in file management.

This feature could be provided by defining a *session recovery unit*, which corresponds to the interval between checkpoints. Each user specifies the point at which a recovery unit ends, and the recovery units are numbered sequentially. To recover lost data (e.g., following a disk fault or a paper break on a printer), a user can issue a command to recover, using the recovery unit number to identify the point to which the session should be backed up.

Once a session has been backed up, some form of recovery will generally be attempted. This is a complex function, which would doubtless extend beyond the bounds of the session layer, and will not be pursued in detail here (for a discussion of the issues, see [CHAN72], [STAL76], and [STAL87b]).

One fundamental point does need to be mentioned, namely, the degree of responsibility of the session protocol entities. When the session is backed up to the beginning of a session recovery unit, the session protocol entities may be requested to retransmit all records from that point forward. If so, the session entity must maintain a copy of each record. To avoid unbounded storage requirements, the user should periodically issue a release command, so that some prior session recovery units can be discarded. Alternatively, the session entity might only be required to remember the records of the current recovery unit.

On the other hand, the session entity may only be required to discard outstanding records and back up its recovery-unit counter to the point indicated, with the primary recovery responsibilities being handled at higher levels. In this case, there does not seem much point in having any recovery feature in the session layer. Indeed NBS takes the position that recovery is inherently an application function and, based on the principle of functional separation of layers, should not be visible in the session layer [NBS80b].

Figure 16-1 indicates that a session recovery unit is made up of one or more records. However, there is no need for a defined relationship between session recovery units and session interaction units.

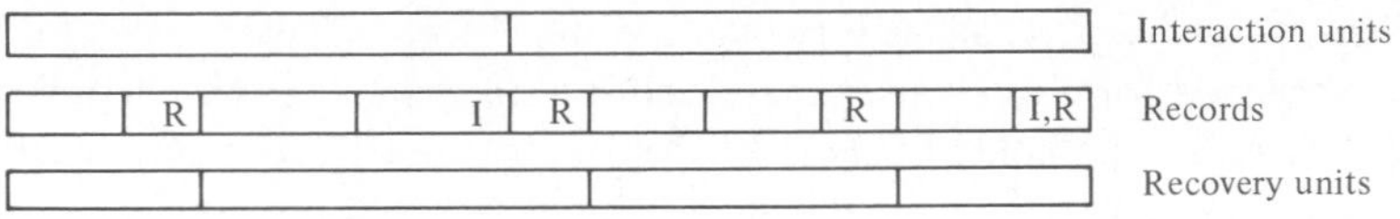

FIGURE 16-1.   Session delimited data units.

16-2

OSI SESSION SERVICE DEFINITION

In this section, we look at the definition of OSI session services developed and standardized by ISO and CCITT. The discussion is based on the most recent version of the standard, which is contained in the 1988 CCITT Recommendation X.215.

Session Services

Table 16-1 lists all of the services provided by OSI session. The OSI document sums up the services provided to a session-service user (SS-user) by the session service as consisting of the following:

1. Establish a connection with another SS-user, exchange data with that user in a synchronized manner, and release the connection in an orderly manner.
2. Negotiate for the use of tokens to exchange data, synchronize and release the connection, and to arrange for data exchange to be half-duplex or full-duplex.
3. Establish synchronization points within the dialogue and, in the event of errors, resume the dialogue from an agreed synchronization point.
4. Interrupt a dialogue and resume it later at a prearranged point.

We will examine the use of tokens in the next subsection. The remainder of the above points are explained in what follows.

As was mentioned in Section 16-1, the minimum service to be provided is the establishment, maintenance, and termination of connections, and the OSI standard certainly includes this service. In addition, OSI session provides a variety of ways of structuring the dialogue that takes place over a session connection. The simplest of these facilities is the ability to choose two-way simultaneous (full-duplex) or two-way alternate (half-duplex) operation.

The OSI session service also provides an optional facility for labeling the data stream with *synchronization points*, which serve two purposes. First, synchronization points can be used to clearly isolate portions of the dialogue. Second, synchronization points can be used in error recovery. Two types of synchronization points are defined: *major synchronization points* and *minor synchronization points*. The relationship is illustrated in Figure 16-2a. Major synchronization points are used to structure the exchange of data into dialogue units. The characteristic of a dialogue unit is that all data within it is completely separated from all data before and after it. When a user defines a major synchronization point, the user may not send more data until that synchronization point is acknowledged by the destination user. For recovery purposes, it is not possible to back up beyond the last major synchronization point. Thus the two purposes mentioned above are achieved. First, since the completion of one dialogue unit must be acknowledged before the next

TABLE 16-1 OSI Session Services

Session Connection Establishment Phase

Session Connection
  Used to establish a connection between two users. Allows users to negotiate tokens and parameters to be used for the connection. Parameters include quality of service and the use of session services.

Data Transfer Phase

Data-Transfer Related

Normal Data Transfer
  Allows the transfer of normal Session Service Data Units (SSDUs) over a session connection, in either half-duplex or full-duplex mode.

Expedited Data Transfer
  Allows the transfer of expedited SSDUs containing up to 14 octets of user data over a session connection, free from the token and flow control constraints of the other data transfer services.

Typed Data Transfer
  Allows the transfer of SSDUs over a session connection, independent of the assignment of the data token. Thus, data may be sent against the normal flow in half-duplex mode.

Capability Data Exchange
  Used when activity services are available. Allows users to exchange data while not within an activity.

Token-Management Related

Give Token
  Used to surrender one or more specific tokens to the other user.

Please Token
  Allows a user to request a token currently assigned to the other user. Thus, this service is only used for a particular token when the other user possesses that token.

Give Control
  Allows a user to surrender all available tokens to the other user. This service is part of the activity management service.

Synchronization Related

Minor Synchronization Point
  Allows the user to define minor synchronization points in the flow of SSDUs. The requestor may request explicit confirmation that the minor synchronization point has been received by the other user.

Major Synchronization Point
  Allows the user to define major synchronization points in the flow of SSDUs, which completely separates the flow before and after the major synchronization point. No additional data SSDUs may be sent until after a confirmation is received.

Resynchronize
  Used to set the session connection to a previous synchronization point, but no further back than the last major synchronization point. The state of the connection at that point is restored.

Exception-Reporting Related

Provider-Initiated Exception Reporting
  Notifies the users of exception conditions or session protocol errors.

TABLE 16-1   OSI Session Services (*continued*)

User-Initiated Exception Reporting
  Allows a user to report an exception condition when the data token is assigned to the other user.

Activity Related

Activity Start
  Used to indicate that a new activity is entered.

Activity Resume
  Used to indicate that a previously interrupted activity is re-entered.

Activity Interrupt
  Allows an activity to be abnormally terminated with the implication that the work so far achieved is not to be discarded and may be resumed later.

Activity Discard
  Allows an activity to be abnormally terminated with the implication that the work so far achieved is to be discarded.

Activity End
  Used to end an activity.

Session Connection Release Phase

Orderly Release
  Allows the session connection to be released after all in-transit data have been delivered and accepted by both users. If the negotiated release option is selected during connection setup, the user receiving a release request may refuse the release and continue the session.

User-Initiated Abort
  Releases a session in a way that will terminate any outstanding service request. This service will cause loss of undelivered SSDUs.

Provider-Initiated Abort
  Used by the session service provider to indicate the release of a connection for internal reasons. This service will cause loss of undelivered SSDUs.

begins, the dialogue unit can be used by the session user to define application-oriented functions. For example, if a sequence of files is to be transferred, each file could be segregated into a separate dialogue unit. Thus the sender could be assured that a particular file had been received and accepted before attempting to send another file. Second, the dialogue units defines the limit of recovery. For example, in a transaction processing application, each transaction could be equated with a dialogue unit. When a transaction is complete and acknowledged, each side can purge any recovery information that had been saved for the purpose of permitting backup to the beginning of that transaction.

Minor synchronization points are used to structure the exchange of data within a dialogue. They provide more flexibility in the recovery facility. A session user may define one or more minor synchronization points within a dialogue unit, and need not wait for acknowledgment before proceeding. At any point, it is possible to resynchronize the dialogue to any previous minor synchronization point within the current dialogue unit, or, of course, to resynchronize to the beginning of the dialogue unit (most recent major synchronization point). This permits the session

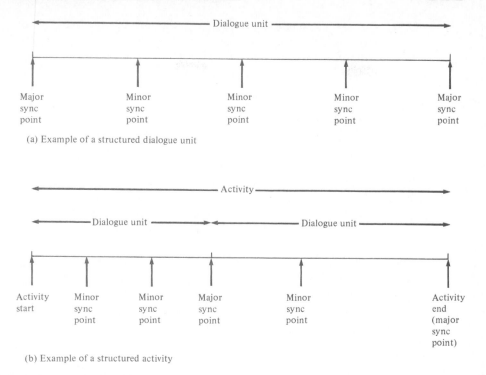

(a) Example of a structured dialogue unit

(b) Example of a structured activity

FIGURE 16-2. **Session interaction structure.**

user to make a tradeoff: With frequent synchronization points, backup and recovery can be speeded up at the expense of saving frequent checkpoints.

Figures 16-3 through 16-5 give some insight into the applicability of minor and major synchronization points. Figure 16-3 shows the use of minor synchronization points in a half-duplex dialogue. At any time, only one session user is transmitting

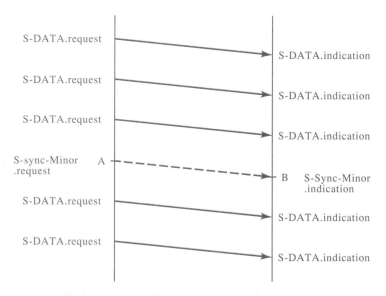

FIGURE 16-3. **Minor synchronization of half-duplex dialogue.**

data. To mark a synchronization point, the sending user issues an S-Sync-Minor.request. This is indicated by point A on the diagram. This results in an S-Sync-Minor.indication being issued to the other session user, indicated by point B. The result is to define a minor synchronization point such that all events prior to A at one end correspond to events prior to B on the other end, and all events after A at one end correspond to events after B on the other end. Thus a clean separation in the dialogue has been defined.

Now consider Figure 16-4, which shows two inadequacies in the use of minor synchronization. One difficulty relates to expedited data. When the transport service provides for expedited data, then the use of session expedited data will result in the transfer of the corresponding session service data unit (SSDU) as transport expedited data. Therefore, it is possible for an expedited SSDU to be issued after an ordinary SSDU but be delivered earlier than the ordinary SSDU. In part (a) of the figure, we see a situation in which the sending user issues an S-Sync-Minor.request followed by an S-Expedited-Data.request. In this case, the expedited data arrives before the S-Sync-Minor.indication. Thus we have an event (expedited data) that occurs after A and prior to B, and the synchronization point does not provide a clean separation of the dialogue.

Figure 16-4b shows the inadequacy of minor synchronization with respect to full-duplex operation. In this case, one user requests a minor synchronization point, which is established at A and B on the two sides. The other user issues an S-DATA.request prior to B which is not received until after A. Again, the separation is not clean.

The use of major synchronization points overcomes both of these problems. Two rules stated in the session service standard are relevant:

1. After making the S-Sync-Major.request, the requestor is not able to initiate any services, except for S-Token-Give.request, S-Activity-Interrupt.request,

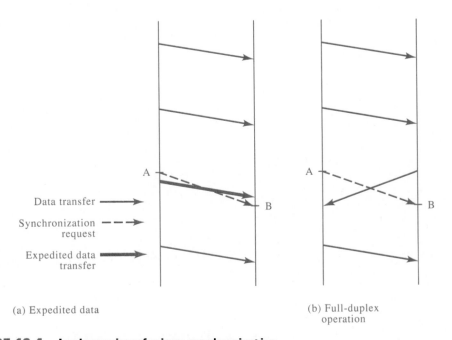

(a) Expedited data   (b) Full-duplex
                                                     operation

FIGURE 16-4.   Inadequacies of minor synchronization.

S-Activity-Discard.request, S-U-Abort.request, or S-Resynchronize.request until the S-Sync-Major.confirm is received.

2. Expedited data transfer services initiated by the acceptor after issuing a S-Sync-Major.response are not indicated before the S-Sync.Major.confirm.

Let us consider the implication of these two rules, using Figure 16-5 (based on a figure in [KNOW87]). When a user requests a major synchronization point (the requestor) with an S-Sync-Major.request, it may not transfer data or expedited data until it receives the corresponding S-Sync.Major.confirm. Thus, there is no danger of expedited data from the requestor overtaking the synchronization request.

Next, consider that the side that receives the S-Sync-Major.indication (the acceptor) issues an S-Sync-Major.response followed by an S-Expedited-Data.request. If the transport expedited data service is available, the expedited data may arrive before the synchronization confirmation. Rule 2 above is designed to prevent this. To explain how this rule is implemented, we must briefly refer to the session protocol, which is examined later in this chapter. When a session user issues an S-Sync-Major.response, the session protocol will issue a corresponding session protocol data unit (SPDU), known as a *major sync point SPDU*. In addition, if transport expedited data service is available, the session protocol will issue a *Prepare SPDU* which will be transferred as transport expedited data. Any session expedited data received by the session protocol on the other side will be held and delivered in an S-Expedited-Data.indication only after the issuance of the S-Sync-Major.confirm. The period of time during which this could occur is indicated by the range E in Figure 16-5.

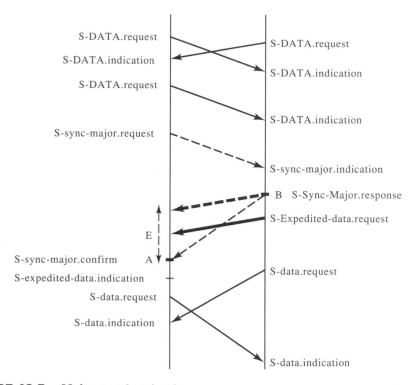

FIGURE 16-5. Major synchronization.

Thus, the major synchronization point capability deals effectively with expedited data. Full-duplex operation is also effectively handled. The requesting user will not issue any data between the S-Sync-Major.request and the S-Sync-Major.confirm, and the accepting user will not issue any data between the S-Sync-Major.indication and the S-Sync-Major.response. Thus, points A and B in the figure define a major synchronization point which cleanly separates the dialogue.

In the OSI standard, it is not the responsibility of the session layer to save any data that has already been transmitted. The session service will simply mark the data stream as requested with a serial number; numbers are assigned sequentially. When resynchronization occurs, the session layer decrements the sequence number back to the point of resynchronization. If it is desired to retransmit data that had been previously transmitted, it is the responsibility of the session user to have saved that data and to present it to the session service again.

One additional level of structuring is available as an option: the activity. An activity is defined as a logical unit of work, consisting of one or more dialogue units (Figure 16-2b). They key feature of an activity is that it can be interrupted and later resumed. For example, if a very long data base transfer is taking place

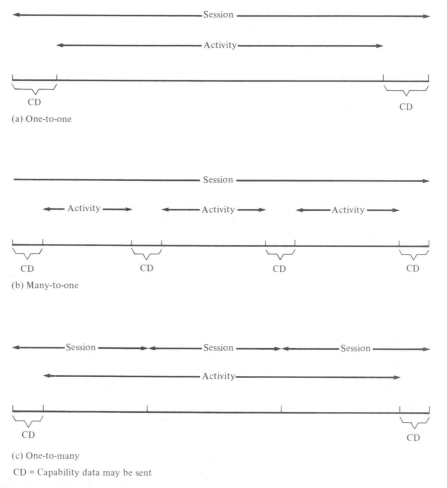

(a) One-to-one

(b) Many-to-one

(c) One-to-many

CD = Capability data may be sent

FIGURE 16-6. **Relationship of activities and sessions.**

and one machine or the other needs to interrupt this process (e.g., to go down for system maintenance or to handle a higher-priority task), then the activity is stopped by the session service, which remembers the last serial number used so that the activity may later be resumed with the same structure of synchronization points intact. Again, it is the responsibility of the session user to save any other context information that will be needed for resumption.

The relationship between an activity and a session connection is not fixed. As indicated in Figure 16-6a, it is possible to make a one-to-one correspondence. In this case, a new activity begins a new session connection, and when the activity is completed, the session connection is terminated. It is also possible to perform multiple activities in sequence over a single session connection (Figure 16-6b). This approach may be desirable if session establishment is time-consuming or resource-consuming. If two session users know that they will engage in a sequence of activities, then it makes sense to maintain the session connection. Finally, a single activity can span multiple session connections (Figure 16-6c). If an activity is interrupted, and it is not anticipated that it will be resumed immediately, then it makes sense to break the connection to free up resources and begin a new connection when the users are prepared to resume the activity.

A final feature illustrated in Figure 16-6 is the use of *capability data*. If two users choose to make use of the activity option, then data may normally only be exchanged when an activity is in progress. Capability data is a mechanism by which such users can exchange a small amount of acknowledged data over a session connection when no activity is in progress. For example, this feature could be used to transmit control information without going through the overhead of setting up an activity.

The Use of Tokens

In the context of the OSI standard, a token is an attribute of a session connection that is dynamically assigned to one user at a time and that grants that user the exclusive right to invoke certain services. Put another way, there are certain services which can only be invoked by the current token holder. A simple example is a token that grants the right to transmit data. As illustrated in Figure 16-7, this token enforces a half-duplex mode of operation. Only the holder of the token can send data. At any time, the token holder can pass the token to the other user, at which time the other user becomes the possessor of the right to transmit.

The token mechanism is used in the ISO session service to structure the dialogue. Four tokens are defined:

- *Data token:* used to manage a half-duplex connection.
- *Synchronize-minor token:* used to govern the setting of minor synchronization points.
- *Major/activity token:* used to govern the setting of major synchronization points and to manage the activity structure.
- *Release token:* used to govern the release of connections.

Associated with the token mechanism are three services. The give-token service allows a user to pass a token to the other user of a session connection. The please-token service allows a user who does not possess a token to request it. The give-control service is used to pass all tokens from one user to another.

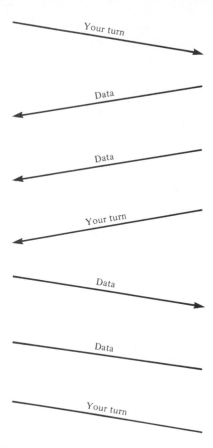

FIGURE 16-7. Simplified token exchange.

Figure 16-8 shows the use of the data token to provide the half-duplex mode of operation. In this example, the token is initially possessed by User A, who is free to transmit data. User B may not transmit normal data, but may transmit a small amount of what is referred to as typed data. An example of typed data would be the transmission of a break character from a terminal to halt the flow of data from an application. User B may request the data token at any time, but the token is relinquished only at User A's discretion.

Each of the four tokens is always in one of two states:

- *Not available:* All four of the tokens are optional and their use must be negotiated during connection establishment. In the case of the data and release tokens, their unavailability means that the corresponding services (data transfer, release) are always available to both users. In the case of the synchronization-minor and major/activity tokens, their unavailability means that the corresponding services (synchronization, activities) are unavailable to both users.
- *Available:* An available token is assigned to one of the two users, who then has the exclusive right to use the associated service.

Table 16-2 summarizes the use of the session tokens and their relationship to session services. Note that, with the exception of the release service, each service

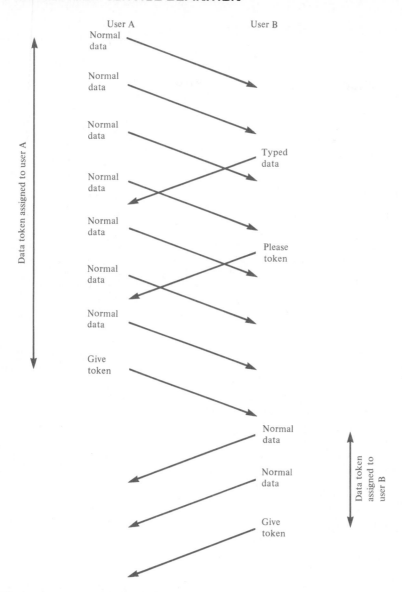

FIGURE 16-8. Two-way alternate service.

listed in the table requires the use of a particular token, and may require the use of additional tokens if they are available. The restrictions appear to be reasonable ones. For example, in the case of half-duplex operation, only the holder of the data token can set synchronization points.

Service Primitives and Parameters

Associated with each of the services listed in Table 16-1 is one type of primitive, as listed in Table 16-3. Like the OSI transport service specification, each type of primitive appears in one or more of variations (request, indication, response, confirm), depending on the requirements of the service (see Table 15-5).

TABLE 16-2   The Use of OSI Session Tokens

Function	Data	Minor Sync	Major Sync	Release
Transfer SSDU (half-duplex)	M	—	—	—
Transfer capability date	I	I	M	—
Set minor sync point	I	M	—	—
Set major sync point	I	I	M	—
Start activity	I	I	M	—
Resume activity	I	I	M	—
Interrupt activity	—	—	M	—
Discard activity	—	—	M	—
End activity	I	I	M	—
Release connection	I	I	I	I

M = Mandatory; token must be available and assigned to user to perform function
I = If available; if token is available, it must be assigned to user to perform function

TABLE 16-3   ISO Session Primitives and Parameters

S-CONNECT.request (identifier, calling SSAP, called SSAP, quality of service, requirements, serial number, token, data)
S-CONNECT.indication (identifier, calling SSAP, called SSAP, quality of service, requirements, serial number, token, data)
S-CONNECT.response (identifier, called SSAP, result, quality of service, requirements, serial number, token, data)
S-CONNECT.confirm (identifier, called SSAP, result, quality of service, requirements, serial number, token, data)

S-DATA.request (data)
S-DATA.indication (data)

S-Expedited-Data.request (data)
S-Expedited-Data.indication (data)

S-Typed-Data.request (data)
S-Typed-Data.indication (data)

S-Capability-Data.request (data)
S-Capability-Data.indication (data)

S-Token-Give.request (Tokens, data)
S-Token-Give.indication (Tokens, data)

S-Token-Please.request (Token, data)
S-Token-Please.indication (Token, data)

S-Control-Give.request (data)
S-Control-Give.indication (data)

S-Sync-Major.request (Type, serial number, data)
S-Sync-Major.indication (Type, serial number, data)
S-Sync-Major.response (serial number, data)
S-Sync-Major.confirm (serial number, data)

TABLE 16-3   ISO Session Primitives and Parameters (*continued*)

S-Sync-Major.request (serial number, data)
S-Sync-Major.indication (serial number, data)
S-Sync-Major.response (data)
S-Sync-Major.confirm (data)

S-Resynchronize.request (type, serial number, tokens, data)
S-Resynchronize.indication (type, serial number, tokens, data)
S-Resynchronize.response (serial number, tokens, data)
S-Resynchronize.confirm (serial number, tokens, data)

S-P-Exception-Report.indication (Reason)

S-U-Exception-Report.request (Reason, data)
S-U-Exception-Report.indication (Reason, data)

S-Activity-Start.request (activity id, data)
S-Activity-Start.indication (activity id, data)

S-Activity-Resume.request (activity id, old activity id, serial number, old session connection id, data)
S-Activity-Resume.indication (activity id, old activity id, serial number, old session connection id, data)

S-Activity-Interrupt.request (reason, data)
S-Activity-Interrupt.indication (reason, data)
S-Activity-Interrupt.response (data)
S-Activity-Interrupt.confirm (data)

S-Activity-Discard.request (reason)
S-Actvity-Discard.indication (reason)
S-Activity-Discard.response
S-Activity-Discard.confirm

S-Activity-End.request (serial number, data)
S-Activity-End.indication (serial number, data)
S-Activity-End.response (data)
S-Activity-End.confirm (data)

S-Release.request (data)
S-Release.indication (data)
S-Release.response (result, data)
S-Release.confirm (result, data)

S-U-Abort.request (data)
S-U-Abort.indication (data)

S-P-Abort.indication (reason)

Figure 16-9 indicates that ways that these variations may be combined in the session service. A service action on the part of one of the session users usually results in action between the two session protocol entities at the two ends of the session connection. This protocol action is invisible to the session user and only manifests itself as a resultant service primitive (indication or confirm). *Confirmed services* are those for which the user invoking the service expects an acknowledgment from the peer user at the other end of the connection. Examples are connection

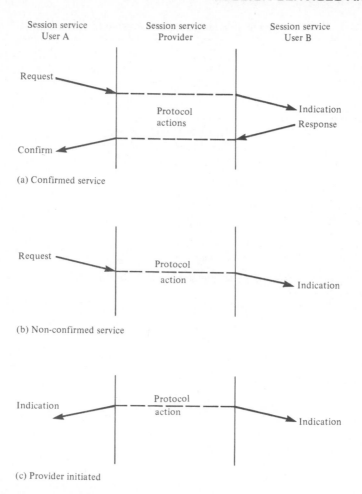

FIGURE 16-9.   Session service primitives.

establishment, synchronization actions, and activity-related actions. In the case of connection establishment, the interaction is used for parameter negotiation as well as acknowledgment. *Nonconfirmed services* require no acknowledgment. An example of this is data transfer. In this case, the data are delivered to the session service provider by a request primitive and delivered by the service provider to the other user by an indication primitive. The session protocol making use of transport guarantees the delivery of the data, and therefore there is no need to confirm that delivery to the sender of the data. *Provider-initiated services* are initiated by the session provider in response to an exception condition that it has detected.

For the connection establishment phase, the S-CONNECT primitives are used. The parameters that are provided are:

- *Identifier;* a unique identifier of this connection.
- *Calling and called SSAP:* service access points that serve as the address of the session users.
- *Quality of service:* a list of parameters that are negotiated as part of the connection establishment process (Table 16-4). For the most part, these parameters are passed down to the transport service, and were defined in Section 15-4.

TABLE 16-4   ISO Session Quality of Service Parameters

Parameter	Negotiate/ Pre-arranged	Performance/ Other	Passed to Transport
SC establishment delay	P	P	Yes
SC establishment failure probability	P	P	Yes
Throughput	N	P	Yes
Transit delay	N	P	Yes
Residual error rate	N	P	Yes
Transfer failure probability	P	P	Yes
SC release delay	P	P	Yes
SC release failure probability	P	P	Yes
SC protection	N	O	Yes
SC priority	N	O	Yes
SC resiliance	P	P	Yes
Extended control	N	O	No
Optimized dialogue transfer	N	O	No

SC = Session connection

The session provider indicates the quality of service that can be provided on the basis of the transport service. There are two additional parameters. The extended-control parameter allows a user to make use of the resynchronize, abort, activity interrupt, and activity discard services when normal flow is congested. The optimized-dialogue parameter permits the session protocol to concatenate multiple session service requests and send them as a unit. These services are provided only if both sides agree. Finally, some parameters are pre-arranged and therefore do not appear in the session connection negotiation.

- *Requirements:* a list of functional options that may be requested; these are summarized below. One side proposes the list in the request primitive; only those that also appear in the response primitive are provided.
- *Serial number:* when synchronization services are to be employed, this is the proposed initial serial number.
- *Token:* a list of the initial side to which the available tokens are assigned.
- *Data:* contains session user data.

The data transfer phase involves primitives for the transfer of data and for the structuring of the dialogue. Each data unit that is delivered to the session service provider is to be delivered to the other user as quickly as possible. Thus, there is no quarantine service provided.

The remainder of the primitives are largely self-explanatory. Several points are worth mentioning. The type parameter in the S-SYNC-Major primitive indicates whether an explicit acknowledgment is required. The activity identifier is used for interrupting and later resuming activities.

Session Functional Units

As you might be able to gather, the session service tries to be all things to all people. The result is that a full-blown implementation of the session standard is not only complex but unnecessary for virtually all applications. Thus, it is likely that only subsets of the session service will be provided by particular implementations. The standard anticipates this and tries to impose some order by introducing the concept of session functional units. The services supported by each of these functional units are indicated in Table 16-5. Note that when a functional unit implies the availability of a token, services concerned with the management of that token are provided in order to be able to request and transfer the available token; the tokens involved are also indicated in the table.

TABLE 16-5 Session Functional Units

Functional Unit	Service(s)	Token Use
Kernel (non-negotiable)	Session connection Normal data transfer Orderly release U-Abort P-Abort	—
Negotiated release	Orderly release Give tokens Please tokens	Release token
Half-duplex	Give tokens Please tokens	Data token
Duplex	No additional services	—
Expedited data	Expedited data transfer	—
Typed data	Typed data transfer	—
Capability data exchange	Capability data exchange	—
Minor synchronize	Minor synchronization point Give tokens Please tokens	Synchronize-minor token
Major synchronize	Major synchronization point Give tokens Please tokens	Major/activity token
Resynchronize	Resynchronize	—
Exceptions	Provider exception reporting User exception reporting	—
Activity management	Activity start Activity resume Activity interrupt Activity discard Activity end Give tokens Please tokens Give control	Major/activity token

Each functional unit is a logical grouping of services. The definition of functional units allows the following:

- Higher-layer entities (applications, presentation entities) may specify which functional units they require. This alerts the session service that it need not attempt to provide other functional units. Furthermore, if the session service is unable to provide the requested functional units, this can be reported to the session user.
- During the session connection establishment phase, the two session entities negotiate the use of functional units, using the Requirements parameter in the S-CONNECT primitive.

The minimum requirement is support of the kernel functional unit, which provides the basic session services required to establish a session connection, transfer normal data, and release the session connection.

There are a few restrictions on the selection of functional units:

- It is not possible to select both the half-duplex and duplex functional units. Clearly, only one mode of operation is possible at a time.
- The capability data exchange functional unit can only be selected when the activity management functional unit has been selected. The reverse is not true; that is, it is not necessary to select the capability data exchange functional unit if the activity management functional unit has been selected.
- The exceptions functional unit can only be selected when the half-duplex functional unit has been selected.

16-3

OSI SESSION PROTOCOL DEFINITION

In the CCITT 1988 blue book, the OSI session service occupies 82 pages, whereas the OSI session protocol occupies 143 pages. This is a clue to the observer that the session protocol, in its full glory, may be quite a bear to implement. However, for our purposes, we are principally concerned with explaining the functionality of the session protocol and its relationship to the session service above and the transport service below. From that point of view, happily, things are reasonably straightforward.

It is the job of the session protocol to bridge the gap between the services provided by the transport layer and those required by the session user. In essence, the transport layer provides three services:

- Establishment, maintenance, and release of a transport service with certain quality-of-service characteristics
- Reliable transfer of data
- Reliable transfer of expedited data

The session service, as we have seen, provides a variety of services relating to the management and structuring of the exchange of data. Hence, it is the job of the session protocol to provide these structuring mechanisms on top of these transport services. In one sense, it appears that the session protocol standard is far more elaborate than the transport protocol standard. For example, the transport protocol includes 10 types of TPDUs while the session protocol includes 36 types of SPDUs. One reason for this complexity is that the session protocol standard has resulted from the merger of various ISO and CCITT endeavors and is anything but cleanly designed.

In another sense, however, this appearance of complexity is misleading. In the transport protocol, elaborate mechanisms are needed to deal with the unreliability and variable-delay problems that are faced. The session protocol is provided with a rather straightforward service. The complexity is in the session service, with its many session service primitives and its abundance of rules for how these primitives are to be used to provide the rich set of session services. The session protocol basically provides a rather straightforward mapping of session service primitives into session protocol data units, and makes use of the comparatively simple, reliable interface to the transport layer to exchange these primitives.

Protocol Data Units and Mechanisms

As with most protocol, the session protocol is best explained by focusing on the collection of PDUs that are used; these are listed in Table 16-6, with an explanation of the parameters in Table 16-7. For the most part, these SPDUs represent a one-to-one mapping with session service primitive pairs (Table 16-8). That is for each request-indication or response-confirm pair (see Figure 16-9), a single SPDU is used to convey the information. There are two classes of exceptions to this rule:

1. In some cases, more than one possible SPDU exists, to reflect more than one possible response to a service request. The exceptions are:
   - S-CONNECT.response, S-CONNECT.confirm: The Accept and Refuse SPDUs indicate acceptance or refusal of a connection request, respectively.
   - S-RELEASE.response, S-RELEASE.confirm: The Disconnect and Not Finished SPDUs indicate acceptance or refusal of an orderly release request, respectively.
2. If the transport protocol imposes a maximum size on the data that it will accept in a single transport service request (maximum TSDU size), then it may be necessary for the session protocol to segment session data into smaller block for transmission. This in turn leads to two cases.
   a. For the following SPDUs, multiple SPDUs of the same type are used to carry the session data:
      - Refuse
      - Finish
      - Disconnect
      - Not Finished
      - Abort
      - Data Transfer
      - Typed Data
      - Capability Data
      - Capability Data ACK
      - Give Tokens
      - Please Tokens
      - Give Tokens Confirm
      - Minor Sync Point
      - Minor Sync ACK

  * Major Sync Point
  * Major Sync ACK
  * Resynchronize
  * Resynchronize ACK
  * Exception Data
  * Activity Start
  * Activity Resume
  * Activity Interrupt
  * Activity Interrupt ACK
  * Activity Discard
  * Activity Discard ACK
  * Activity End
  * Activity End ACK

b. If the S-CONNECT.request primitive, because it includes user data, is too large to be contained in a Connect SPDU, then the Connect SPDU includes a data overflow parameter indicating that more user data is to follow. The called session protocol entity returns an Overflow Accept SPDU, and the calling session protocol entity sends as many Connect Data Overflow SPDUs as are necessary to transfer the user data. Only when all of the data has been transferred will the called entity issue an Accept SPDU to complete the session connection establishment.

Ignoring these complications, the most complex relationship between session service primitives and SPDUs occurs at connection establishment time. Figure 16-10 depicts the possible sequence of events. A request for a connection by a user triggers a Connect SPDU by the user's session protocol entity. The SPDU contains those parameters that were contained in the S-CONNECT.request and that need to be communicated to the other users. These include connection id, serial number, token selections, requirements parameters, calling and called SSAP, and, finally, those quality-of-service parameters that are negotiated between the users (extended control and optimized dialogue), referred to as protocol options. This information is transmitted via the SPDU to the other session protocol entity, which delivers the connection request and associated parameters in an S-CONNECT.indication primitive. The user accepts the connection and negotiates the parameters with a response primitive, which triggers the transmission of an Accept SPDU back to the other side, where a confirm primitive is generated.

A session user may refuse a connection because of congestion, unavailability of the desired application, or other reasons. This is reported to the session protocol entity with a response primitive in which the result parameter indicates the reason for refusal. The session protocol then sends a Refuse SPDU back to the calling side, which sends a confirm primitive to the calling user, indicating that the connection is refused and specifying the reason.

A third alternative sequence is that the called session user accepts the connection request, but proposes session parameters (e.g., no use of synchronization) unacceptable to the calling user. In this case, the calling user will abort the connection as soon as it is confirmed, and the called user will be informed. Note in Figure 16-10c that both an Abort and an Abort Accept SPDU are used. The latter is needed so that the session protocol entity that initiated the abort knows that the other side is ready for a new session connection and, if desired, that the transport connection can now be terminated.

TABLE 16-6 Session Protocol Data Units, Parameters, and Functions

SPDU	Parameters*	Function
Connect	Connection ID, protocol options, maximum TSDU size, version number, initial serial number, token setting, user requirements, calling SSAP, called SSAP, user data, data overflow	Initiate session connection
Accept	Connection ID, protocol options, maximum TSDU size, version number, initial serial number, token setting, token, user requirements, calling SSAP, responding SSAP, enclosure item, user data	Establish session connection
Overflow Accept	Maximum TSDU size, version number	Request remainder of the S-CONNECT.request user data
Connect Data Overflow	Enclosure item, user data	Send subsequent segments of the S-CONNECT.request user data
Refuse	Connection ID, transport disconnect, user requirements, version number, enclosure item, reason	Reject connection request
Finish	Transport disconnect, enclosure item, user data	Initiate orderly release
Disconnect	Enclosure item, user data	Acknowledge orderly release
Not Finished	Enclosure item, user data	Reject orderly release
Abort	Transport disconnect, error code, enclosure item, user data	Abnormal connection release
Abort Accept	—	Acknowledge abort
Data Transfer	Enclosure item, user data	Transfer normal data
Expedited	User data	Transfer expedited data
Typed Data	Enclosure item, user data	Transfer typed data
Capability Data	Enclosure item, user data	Transfer capability data
Capability Data ACK	Enclosure item, user data	Acknowledge capability data
Give Tokens	Token, enclosure item, user data	Transfer tokens
Please tokens	Token, enclosure item, user data	Request token assignment

TABLE 16-6 Session Protocol Data Units, Parameters, and Functions (*continued*)

SPDU	Parameters*	Function
Give Tokens Confirm	Enclosure item, user data	Transfer all tokens
Give Tokens Ack	—	Acknowledge all tokens
Minor Sync Point	Confirm required flag, serial number, enclosure item, user data	Define minor sync point
Minor Sync ACK	Serial number, enclosure item, user data	Acknowledge minor sync point
Major Sync Point	End of activity flag, serial number, enclosure item, user data	Define major sync point
Major Sync ACK	Serial number, enclosure item, user data	Acknowledge major sync point
Resynchronize	Token settings, resync type, serial number, enclosure item, user data	Resynchronize
Resynchronize ACK	Token settings, serial number, enclosure item, user data	Acknowledge resynchronize
Prepare	Type	Notify type SPDU is coming
Exception Report	SPDU bit pattern	Protocol error detected
Exception Data	Reason, enclosure item, user data	Put protocol in error state
Activity Start	Activity ID, enclosure item, user data	Signal beginning of activity
Activity Resume	Connection ID, old activity ID, New activity ID, serial number, enclosure item, user data	Signal resumption of activity
Activity Interrupt	Reason, enclosure item, user data	Interrupt activity
Activity Interrupt ACK	Enclosure item, user data	Acknowledge interrupt
Activity Discard	Reason, enclosure item, user data	Cancel activity
Activity Discard ACK	Enclosure item, user data	Acknowledge cancellation
Activity End	Serial number, enclosure item, user data	Signal activity end
Activity End ACK	Serial number, enclosure item, user data	Acknowledge activity end

*See Table 16-7 for explanation of parameters.

TABLE 16-7   Session Protocol Parameters

Connection ID

Enables SS-users to identify this specific session connection. The value consists of portions defined by the calling and called SS-users.

Protocol Options

Indicates whether or not the initiator is able to receive extended concatenated SPDUs. Certain SPDUs may be concatenated and transmitted as a single unit by the transport layer. Basic concatenation allows two SPDUs to be concatenated. Extended concatenation allows more than two SPDUs to be concatenated.

Maximum TSDU Size

The maximum transport service data unit size. This is the maximum of an SPDU or concatenation of SPDUs.

Version Number

Indicates which versions of this protocol are supported. Version 1 limits the size of user data to 512 octets. Version 2 imposes no restrictions on the length of user data.

Initial Serial Number

Required if minor synchronize, major synchronize, or resynchronize functional unit is proposed.

Token Setting

Initial token position for each token available on this connection.

User Requirements

List of functional units to be supported on this connection.

Calling SSAP

Identifies the calling session user.

Called SSAP

Identifies the called session user.

User Data

Session user data.

Data Overflow

This flag is present if there is more than 10,240 octets of user data to be transmitted with the session connection establishment. The first 10,240 octets are sent in the Connect SPDU; the remainder are sent in one or more Connect Data overflow SPDUs.

Token

Identifies tokens being passed or requested.

Responding SSAP

Identifies the session user that actually responds to a connection request.

Enclosure Item

Used when a session service data unit is segmented into more than one SPDU. This parameter indicates whether the SPDU that contains it is the beginning, an intermediate, or the ending SPDU in the sequence.

Transport Disconnect

Used in the Finish SPDU to indicate whether or not the transport connection is to be retained after the termination of the associated session connection.

Error Code

Contains implementation-defined value related to a protocol error.

TABLE 16-8   Relationship Between Session Service (SS) Primitives and Session Protocol Data Units (SPDUs)

SS Primitive →	SPDU →	SS Primitive
S-CONNECT.request	CONNECT and (0 or 1) OVERFLOW ACCEPT and (0 or more) CONNECT DATA OVERFLOW	S-CONNECT.indication

SS Primitive →	SPDU →	SS Primitive
S-CONNECT.response	ACCEPT or REFUSE	S-CONNECT.confirm
S-DATA.request	DATA TRANSFER	S-DATA.response
S-EXPEDITED-DATA.request	EXPEDITED DATA	S-EXPEDITED-DATA.indication
S-TYPED-DATA.request	TYPED DATA	S-TYPED-DATA.indication
S-CAPABILITY-DATA.request	CAPABILITY DATA	S-CAPABILITY-DATA.indication
S-CAPABILITY-DATA.response	CAPABILITY DATA ACK	S-CAPABILITY-DATA.confirm
S-TOKEN-GIVE.request	GIVE TOKENS	S-TOKEN-GIVE.indication
S-TOKEN-PLEASE.request	PLEASE TOKENS	S-TOKEN-PLEASE.indication
S-CONTROL-GIVE.request	GIVE TOKENS CONFIRM	S-CONTROL-GIVE.indication
S-SYNC-MINOR.request	MINOR SYNC POINT	S-SYNC-MINOR.indication
S-SYNC-MINOR.response	MINOR SYNC ACK	S-SYNC-MINOR.confirm
S-SYNC-MAJOR.request	MAJOR SYNC POINT	S-SYNC-MAJOR.indication
S-SYNC-MAJOR.response	MAJOR SYNC ACK	S-SYNC-MAJOR.confirm
S-RESYNCHRONIZE.request	RESYNCHRONIZE	S-RESYNCHRON-IZE.indication
S-RESYNCHRON-IZE.response	RESYNCHRONIZE ACK	S-RESYNCHRON-IZE.confirm
S-U-EXCEPTION-REPORT.request	EXCEPTION DATA	S-U-EXCEPTION-REPORT.indication
S-ACTIVITY-START.request	ACTIVITY START	S-ACTIVITY-START.indication
S-ACTIVITY-RESUME.request	ACTIVITY RESUME	S-ACTIVITY-RESUME.indication
S-ACTIVITY-INTER-RUPT.request	ACTIVITY INTERRUPT	S-ACTIVITY-INTER-RUPT.indication
S-ACTIVITY-INTER-RUPT.response	ACTIVITY INTERRUPT ACK	S-ACTIVITY-INTER-RUPT.confirm
S-ACTIVITY-DIS-CARD.request	ACTIVITY DISCARD	S-ACTIVITY-DISCARD.indication
S-ACTIVITY-DIS-CARD.response	ACTIVITY DISCARD ACK	S-ACTIVITY-DISCARD.confirm

TABLE 16-8 **Relationship Between Session Service (SS) Primitives and Session Protocol Data Units (SPDUs) (continued)**

SS Primitive →	SPDU →	SS Primitive
S-ACTIVITY-END.request	ACTIVITY END	S-ACTIVITY-END.indication
S-ACTIVITY-END.response	ACTIVITY END ACK	S-ACTIVITY-END.confirm
S-RELEASE.request	FINISH	S-RELEASE.indication
S-RELEASE.response	DISCONNECT or NOT FINISHED	S-RELEASE.confirm
S-U-ABORT.request	ABORT	S-U-ABORT.indication

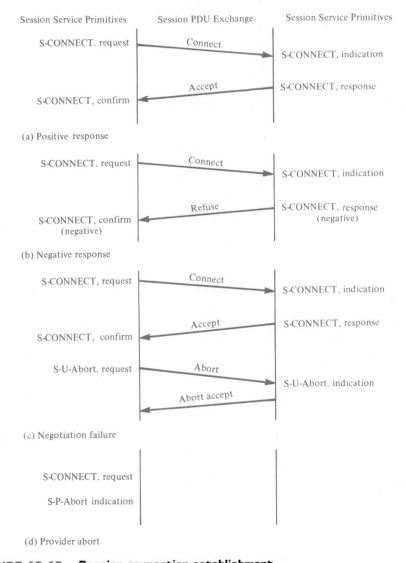

(a) Positive response

(b) Negative response

(c) Negotiation failure

(d) Provider abort

FIGURE 16-10. **Session connection establishment.**

Finally, a session provider can refuse to establish a connection, because of inability to set up a transport connection, inability to provide the desired quality of service, or some other reason. In this case, no SPDUs are employed, since the action is purely local.

Most of the other SPDUs are largely self-explanatory. However, some additional comments will be useful. In the case of the data transfer SPDU, the typical case is that each unit of data (session service data unit, SSDU) received from a session user is encapsulated with a session header and transmitted. If, however, there is a size restriction on data units to be presented to the transport layer (TSDUs), as indicated in the Connect and Accept SPDUs, then the session entity may need to segment the user's data and send it out in two or more Data-transfer SPDUs. In this latter case, the enclosure item parameter is used to indicate whether or not a Data-transfer SPDU is the last one of a group that carries a single SSDU. The receiving session entity will buffer the user data from incoming SPDUs until the last one in a group is received and then transfer all of the data to the user in an S-Data.indication primitive.

The Prepare SPDU is only used when the transport expedited flow option is available. It notifies the recipient session protocol entity of the imminent arrival of a certain SPDU. The SPDUs that may be so signalled include Resynchronize, Activity Interrupt, Activity Discard, and Activity End. In some cases, this alert will allow the session entity to discard some incoming SPDUs which arrive prior to the anticipated SPDU. In all cases, it is useful as a means of preparing the recipient for the occurrence of an important event.

Session Protocol Formats

As can be seen from Table 16-6, the number of parameters that is sent with an SPDU varies widely. Furthermore, the length of parameters is variable. The ISO standard provides a flexible formatting scheme to accommodate these variations. Unfortunately, because the final standard represents the merger of several independent efforts, the scheme is unnecessarily complex.

Figure 16-11 shows the general structure of an SPDU. Each SPDU has up to four fields. The first field is the SPDU identifier (SI), which specifies one of the 34 types of SPDUs. The next field is the length indicator, which specifies the length of the header. If the SPDU contains any parameters, then the next field contains these parameters, using a structure described below. Finally, there may be a field for session user information.

The parameter field may take on one of several general forms, depending on the way in which particular parameters are expressed. In its simplest form, a parameter is expressed with three subfields: a parameter identifier, a length indicator, and the parameter value. This form is known as a PI unit, and the SPDU may contain one or more such units. Alternatively, related parameters may be expressed in a PGI unit, which consists of a parameter group identifier, a length indicator, and either a single parameter value or one or more PI units. As was said, this is a complicated way of achieving a simple purpose, namely, the listing of parameters within a single SPDU. Figure 16-12 gives examples of the formats that appear within the standard.

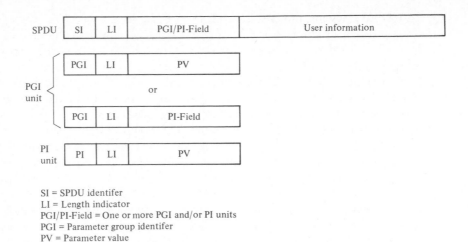

SI = SPDU identifer
LI = Length indicator
PGI/PI-Field = One or more PGI and/or PI units
PGI = Parameter group identifer
PV = Parameter value
PI-Field = One or more PI units
PI = Parameter identifer

FIGURE 16-11. **SPDU format.**

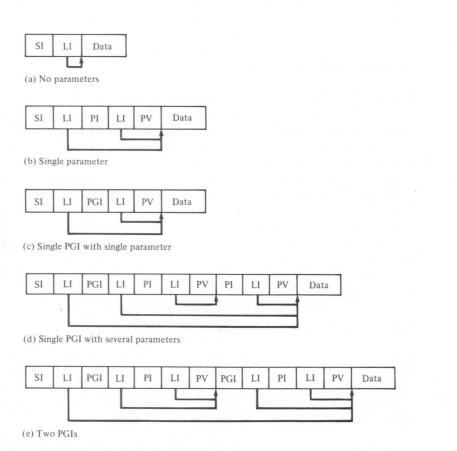

(a) No parameters

(b) Single parameter

(c) Single PGI with single parameter

(d) Single PGI with several parameters

(e) Two PGIs

FIGURE 16-12. **SPDU encoding examples.**

Transport Connections

Session connections must be mapped into transport connections by the session protocol entity. The ISO standard contains specific guidance on the way this is to be done. Most important is the requirement that a transport connection be dedicated to a single session connection. There seems good justification for this restriction. For one thing, different session connections may require different quality of service, which will influence the parameters used to set up the transport connection. Also, if several session connections share a transport connection, neither the session user or the session protocol entity has much control over how the transport service allocates resources to meet the dynamic data transfer demands of several session connections.

If a transport connection provides expedited service, then Abort, Abort Accept, Expedited Data, and Prepare SPDUs are sent using the service. If this service is not available, the Abort and Abort Accept are sent using normal transport data transfer service, and the Expedited Data and the Prepare SPDUs cannot be sent.

Finally, when a session is terminated, the session protocol entity that initially set up the corresponding transport connection has the option of terminating that connection or not. If the transport connection is retained, then it may be used to support a new session connection connection request, provided that it meets the required quality of service.

16-4

THE SNA DATA FLOW CONTROL LAYER

Within SNA, it is the data flow control layer that embodies what we are considering as session functionality. The SNA approach is, in a sense, midway between that of OSI and DPA. Although the session functionality resides in a specific layer of SNA, it consists of a set of functions that act in the nature of agents of the upper layers. Sessions in SNA are actually set up above the data flow control layer, and the services to be used are negotiated at that higher level. The data flow control layer is responsible for enforcing any dialogue discipline that has been agreed to. Otherwise it is transparent. And, when various data flow control functions are employed, they act without benefit of their own header. Rather, there is a single header, the request-response header (RH), which is shared by data flow control and transmission control (see Figure 12-13).

At this point, the reader may wish to review the overall discussion of SNA contained in Chapter 12. We continue here with a summary of the data flow control layer, which is concerned with the following functions:

- Send/receive modes
- Chaining
- Request/response modes
- Bracketing
- Quiescing
- Shutdown

We begin with brief examination of the way in which control and user data are exchanged, and then examine each of these functions in turn.

Requests and Response

Data is transmitted in the form of requests and responses. A request is a data unit that contains either user data or a protocol command. A response is a data unit that acknowledges a particular request. User data is exchanged with the data flow control layer in the form of request or response units. Request units are passed by the data flow control layer to the transmission control layer, which appends a request/response header. The header contains bits that serve the needs of both data flow control and transmission control (Figure 16-13). Commands that initiate at the data flow control layer are also passed to transmission control in the form of a request unit that contains the particular command, and again, transmission control appends the header. Note the contrast with the ISO standard. In ISO session, there are a variety of control and data SPDUs, and control information is passed in the form of a list of parameters in the header. In SNA, data flow control passes control information partly by means of bits in a fixed header format prepared by the next lower layer, and partly by means of commands that are encapsulated with that header.

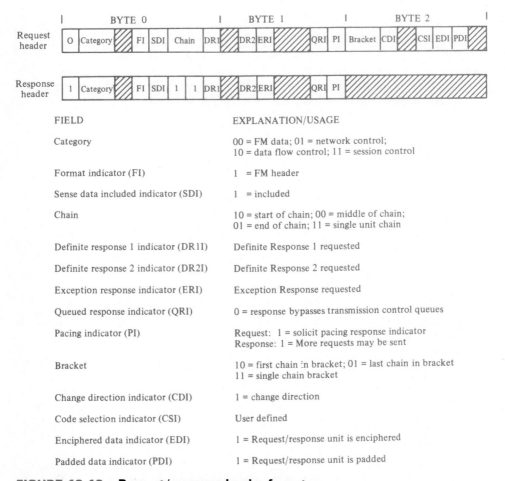

FIELD	EXPLANATION/USAGE
Category	00 = FM data; 01 = network control; 10 = data flow control; 11 = session control
Format indicator (FI)	1 = FM header
Sense data included indicator (SDI)	1 = included
Chain	10 = start of chain; 00 = middle of chain; 01 = end of chain; 11 = single unit chain
Definite response 1 indicator (DR1I)	Definite Response 1 requested
Definite response 2 indicator (DR2I)	Definite Response 2 requested
Exception response indicator (ERI)	Exception Response requested
Queued response indicator (QRI)	0 = response bypasses transmission control queues
Pacing indicator (PI)	Request: 1 = solicit pacing response indicator Response: 1 = More requests may be sent
Bracket	10 = first chain in bracket; 01 = last chain in bracket 11 = single chain bracket
Change direction indicator (CDI)	1 = change direction
Code selection indicator (CSI)	User defined
Enciphered data indicator (EDI)	1 = Request/response unit is enciphered
Padded data indicator (PDI)	1 = Request/response unit is padded

FIGURE 16-13.   Request/response header formats.

Send/Receive Modes

As with the ISO standard, data exchange in SNA can be either full duplex or half-duplex. The simplest mode is *full duplex,* in which both users of a session can send simultaneously. In this case, the data flow control layer does not intervene. The other alternative is half-duplex transmission, and this is handled in one of two ways: half-duplex flip-flop mode, and half-duplex contention mode.

With *half-duplex flip-flop* mode, the two users take turns using the session. One user is designated as the requestor when the session begins, and has the exclusive right to transmit request units. Thereafter, the requestor of the moment can permit the other user to become the requestor by sending a change-direction indicator in the request/response header. If an application program attempts to send data when the other user is designated as the sender, then data flow control will send a request for change of direction, and delay honoring the user's send attempt until the other side has sent a change-direction indicator. Thus, this mechanism is similar to the ISO session data token.

The final mode is the *half-duplex contention* mode. In this mode either user can begin sending a request. That user then retains sole right to transmit requests until it completes a chain of requests (defined below), at which point the two sides are again in contention. If both sides attempt to send at approximately the same time, then each will receive the other's request before receiving the other's response to its own request. In this case, the contention is resolved in accordance with an agreement made at session initiation time: one user is always designated the winner and may proceed to transmit. This mode allows for half-duplex operation without the overhead of exchanging permissions, but introduces the potential for contention. The loser in the contention must be prepared to queue transmission requests until such time as it can gain control.

Chaining

Chaining in SNA corresponds roughly to the use of synchronization points in ISO session. A user may break up a long message or data stream into a chain of requests that are treated as a single unit for purposes of recovery. A chain consists of a sequence of one or more request units. The first unit is marked with a begin-chain indicator, the last unit is marked with an end-chain indicator, and all other units are marked with a middle-of-chain indicator. The sending user retains a copy of all units in the chain until an acknowledgment is received for the entire chain; at that point the sender is assured that the entire chain has been received and may purge its buffer.

Associated with each chain is a response discipline. Three disciplines are defined. In the *definite-response chain,* only the last unit in the chain calls for a positive acknowledgment, called a definite response. Other units are unacknowledged unless an error is detected, in which case a negative acknowledgment, called an exception response, is returned. This is the most common type of chain. The sender is notified of the successful or unsuccessful transmission of an entire chain with minimal network overhead for acknowledgments.

In other cases, an *exception-response* chain is used, for reasons of efficiency. In this case, there is no definite response at the end; the only responses are exception responses. Typical of the use of this discipline is the situation where a user may have multiple inquiries against a static data base. The user requires acknowledgments only if there has been an error, in order to identify which inquiry is in error. Finally, there is the *no-response chain,* in which no acknowledgments of either type are returned. For example, status-updating messages may arrive periodically, so the dialogue required to correct any one message may be a waste of time.

Request/Response Modes

The request and response modes, which are decided at session establishment, control when users send and receive requests and responses over the session connection. Four modes are defined. The *immediate-request mode* requires that the sending user wait for a response before sending any additional requests. If the sender groups the request units into chains, it must wait for the receiver to return a response to the chain. The *delayed-request mode* allows the sending user to send additional requests or chains without waiting for any responses. The immediate request mode would be used for low traffic sessions, such as between a host system and a terminal cluster controller. The delayed request mode would be preferred for high-traffic situations, especially where there may be some delay in some of the responses, such as communication with a communications controller that controls many lines.

The preceding two modes control the timing of requests. In addition, there are two modes that control the timing of responses. The *immediate response mode* requires that the receiving user return responses in the same order in which it received the requests or chains. This mode is useful when there is a series of requests for which exception response only was asked. The user can occasionally request a definite response. When that response is received, the user knows that no more exception reports to previous requests can come in. In the *delayed response mode,* a user may return responses in any order.

Bracketing

A bracket is a set of chains of requests and responses in both directions that together comprise a unit of work. This allows a complex process requiring multiple messages in both directions to go to completion without interruption or the intrusion of unsolicited traffic from unrelated tasks. An example of the use of this feature: A time-sharing system provides services to a terminal user by means of a session. The system also allows message routing between users logged on concurrently. But a message sent to a terminal from another user will not appear on the screen at any random time. It will only appear after the operator responds to the operating system with a transmit key. This is so because a bracket is established at the start of a transmission from the time-sharing system to the user and is terminated when the user's response is received.

A bracket can enclose any series of chains in both directions. It is delimited by use of the begin bracket (BB) indicator in the first request of the first chain, and the end bracket (EB) indicator in the first request of the last chain in the bracket. If brackets are used, the option is selected when the session is established. One user is designated as first speaker and the other as bidder. The first speaker may begin a bracket at any time that a bracket is not underway. The bidder must request permission from the other side to do so.

The bracket is similar to the ISO session activity. In the case of the ISO activity, the relationship is a peer one, with the ability to start an activity governed by the major sync token, whereas the SNA bracket capability is determined by one side, the first speaker.

Quiescing

The quiesce facility allows one user to require that the other user pause in its transmission of data. This facility may be used for various reasons. For example, one user may wish to temporarily stop receiving because it has run low on some resource (like a buffer pool or auxiliary storage), or one user may wish to end the session after it finishes receiving the rest of the current chain.

Three data flow control commands are involved. When one side wishes to halt the flow from the other, it issues a Quiesce At End Of Chain (QEC) command. The receiving side may complete its current chain and then must issue a Quiesce Complete (QC) command. The quiesced side may no longer send requests; however, it can continue to receive requests and issue the appropriate responses. Things remain in this state until the side that issued the QEC issues a Release Request (RQ) command to the other side, at which time normal operation resumes. Note the similarities and differences compared to the activity interrupt facility in ISO session.

Shutdown

The shutdown facility provides a means for the orderly termination of a session. The Shutdown command is issued by the side designated as primary when the primary is ready to end the session. The command requires the secondary to cease transmission as soon as convenient, which might be at the end of the current chain or at the end of the current bracket. When the secondary has sent all its data and performed any end-of-session processing, it sends a Shutdown Complete command. The primary can then end the session.

16-5

RECOMMENDED READING

Very little has been written about session protocols. [NBS80b] is a good general discussion. [EMMO83] summarizes the ISO standard. [CANE86], which explains various obscure points in the ISO standard, is an instructive analysis of the difficulties in interpreting a standards document. The SNA approach is described in [MART87] and MEIJ87].

16-6

PROBLEMS

16-1   Assume that a session layer is making use of a reliable transport layer. The transport layer guarantees that data will be delivered in sequence, but makes no guarantee about timing. Thus multiple session recovery units, as defined in Section 16-1, may be outstanding. Might there be a problem when the sending user requests that the current recovery unit be cancelled?

16-2   A session recovery unit is defined by one of the two session users. Yet it would seem that recovery must involve backing up the data streams of both users. What mechanisms are required to achieve the required cooperation?

16-3   A session user issues an S-Release.request. Before the provider can issue the paired S-Release.indication to the other user, the other user issues an S-Release.request. Eventually, both users receive an S-Release.indication, and both respond with an S-Release.response. However, by this time the session provider has already released the connection, since the standard specifies that the release is to take place if a "release collision" is detected. Is there any problem with this?

16-4   Show the mapping of all session service primitives into session protocol data units, in the manner of Figure 16-10.

16-5   Indicate the restrictions for the session protocol imposed by the token restrictions defined for the session service (Table 16-2).

16-6   It was stated in the chapter that the ISO session standard does not include a quarantine service. But consider the use of the enclosure parameter with the Data Transfer and Typed Data SPDUs. Isn't this a quarantine mechanism?

16-7   The Abort Accept SPDU adds complexity to the protocol which may not be desirable for small systems. Can we do without it?

16-8   The ISO session protocol states that, when a session connection is released, the corresponding transport connection may be maintained and reused provided that transport expedited flow control is not available on the connection. Suggest a reason for the restriction.

16-9   If a transport connection is retained, the standard further states that the side which issues the Connect SPDU to set up a new session connection on an old transport connection must be the same side that originally requested the transport connection. Suggest a reason for this restriction.

CHAPTER 17

Presentation/Application Protocols

Above the session layer, the possibilities for various protocols and services are manifold, and this area is rapidly evolving. In this chapter we will concentrate on three areas:

- Virtual terminal
- File transfer
- Electronic mail

The concept of a virtual terminal protocol addresses many of the issues of the presentation layer. Similarly, file transfer and electronic mail illustrate important application-layer issues. Furthermore, these three areas are the first upper-layer protocols to receive widespread support and to be standardized. Within the DOD protocol architecture, the three upper-layer standards are in these three areas. Within the realm of OSI-related standards, ISO has developed standards for virtual terminal and file transfer, and CCITT has developed standards for electronic mail.

17-1

VIRTUAL TERMINAL PROTOCOLS

Most of our discussion has implicitly assumed that communication is between ''peer'' entities, that is, entities of roughly equal capabilities that wish to do roughly similar kinds of things. There are exceptions to this rule, and perhaps the most significant is the case of terminal-to-application communication.

One's first impression is that this type of communication is outside the scope of a computer-communications architecture. In the case of a terminal directly connected to a computer, the computer will have an I/O driver that handles the terminal and a mechanism for communication between that driver and the application program. If the terminal and computer are connected via a network, the network must transparently pass the data between the terminal and a computer I/O port. This seems to be a requirement since a number of terminal devices do not have the capability of implementing the various OSI layers.

There is, however, a problem in this approach that relates to one of the advertised benefits of a computer network. Specifically, a user at a terminal would like to be able to access resources and applications on a variety of computers. Furthermore, the user does not want to be limited to using the terminals and computers of a single vendor. What does this imply? Usually, in order to be able to use a terminal from one vendor with a host from another vendor, a special host software package must be built to accommodate the foreign terminal. Now consider a network with N types of terminals and M types of hosts. For complete connectivity, each host type must contain a package for handling each terminal type. In the worst case, MN I/O packages must be developed. Furthermore, if a new type of host is acquired, it must be equipped with N new I/O packages. If a new type of terminal is acquired, each host must be equipped with a new I/O package, for a total of M new packages. This is not the type of situation designed to encourage multivendor interoperability.

To solve this problem, a universal terminal protocol is needed—one that can handle all types of terminals. Such a thing exists today in name only: *virtual terminal protocol* (VTP). However, rudimentary versions do already exist. One is the X.28/X.29/X.3 protocol, which is based on a simple parameterized model of an asynchronous terminal. The true VTP is a fundamentally different and more flexible approach. In this section we will provide an overview of both approaches.

Packet Assembler/Disassembler (PAD)

As supplements to the X.25 standard CCITT has developed a set of standards related to a facility known as a *packet assembler/disassembler* (PAD). The PAD is designed to solve the two fundamental problems associated with the attachment of terminals to a network:

1. Many terminals are not capable of implementing the protocol layers for attaching in the same manner as a host. The PAD facility provides the intelligence for communicating with a host using the X.25 protocol.
2. There are differences among terminal types. The PAD facility provides a set of parameters to account for those differences. However, it only deals with asynchronous terminals.

Three standards define the PAD facility:

- *X.3:* describes the functions of the PAD and the parameters used to control its operation.
- *X.28:* describes the PAD-terminal protocol.
- *X.29:* describes the PAD-host protocol.

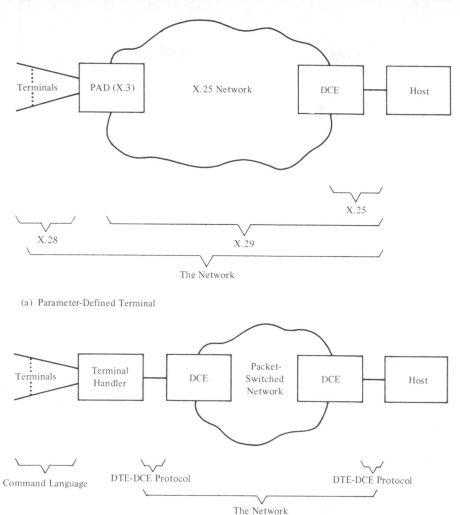

(a) Parameter-Defined Terminal

(b) Virtual Terminal Protocol

FIGURE 17-1. Two views of terminal-network architecture.

Figure 17-1a indicates the architecture for use of the PAD. The terminal attached to the PAD sends characters one at a time. These are buffered in the PAD and then assembled into an X.25 packet, and sent through the network to the host. Host packets are received at the PAD, disassembled by stripping off the X.25 header, and passed to the terminal one character at a time. Simple commands between terminal and PAD (X.28), used to set parameters and establish virtual circuits, consist of character strings. Similar host-PAD control information (X.29) is transmitted in the data field of an X.25 packet, with a bit set in the X.25 header to indicate that this is control information.

Let us look briefly at each of the three standards involved. The PAD itself is defined in X.3, which lists 22 parameters that determine the behavior of the PAD (Table 17-1). Since a PAD may serve more than one terminal (a terminal concentration function), a set of these parameters is maintained for each terminal. Most

TABLE 17-1 PAD Parameters (X.3)

Number	Description	Selectable Values
1 (E)	Whether terminal operator can escape from data transfer to PAD command state	0: not allowed 1: escape character 32–126: graphic characters
2 (E)	Whether PAD echoes back characters received from terminal	0: no echo 1: echo
3 (E)	Terminal characters that will trigger the sending of a partially full packet by the PAD	0: only send full packets 1: alphanumeric 2, 4, 8, 16, 32, 64: other control characters
4 (E)	Timeout value that will trigger the sending of a partially full packet by the PAD	0: no timeout 1–255: multiple of 50 ms
5 (E)	Whether PAD can exercise flow control over terminal output, using X-ON, X-OFF	0: not allowed 1: allowed
6 (E)	Whether PAD can send service signals (control information) to terminal	0: not allowed 1: allowed
7 (E)	Action(s) taken by PAD on receipt of break signal from terminal	0: nothing 1: send interrupt 2: reset 4: send break signal 8: escape 16: discard output
8 (E)	Whether PAD will discard DTE data intended for terminal	0: normal delivery 1: discard
9 (E)	Number of padding characters inserted after carriage return (to terminal)	0: determined by data rate 1–255: number of characters
10 (E)	Whether PAD inserts control characters to prevent terminal line overflow	0: no 1–255: yes, line length
11 (E)	Terminal speed (bps)	0–18: 50 to 64,000
12 (E)	Whether terminal can exercise flow control over PAD, using X-ON, X-OFF	0: not allowed 1: allowed
13 (A)	Whether PAD inserts line feed after carriage return sent or echoed to terminal	0: no line feed 1, 2, 4: various conditions
14 (A)	Number of padding characters inserted after line feed (to terminal)	0: no padding 1–255: number of characters
15 (A)	Whether PAD supports editing during data transfer (defined in parameters 16–18)	0: no 1: yes
16 (A)	Character delete	0–127: selected character
17 (A)	Line delete	0–127: selected character
18 (A)	Line display	0–127: selected character
19 (A)	Terminal type for editing PAD service signals (e.g., character delete)	0: no editing signals 1: printing terminal 2: display terminal
20 (A)	Characters that are not echoed to terminal when echo is enabled	0: no echo mask Each bit represents certain characters
21 (A)	Parity treatment of characters to/from terminal	0: no parity treatment 1: parity checking 2: parity generation
22 (A)	Number of linefeeds from PAD to signal page wait	0: page wait disabled 1–255: number of linefeeds

E = essential parameter
A = additional parameter

of these parameters are self-explanatory, but items 3 and 4 deserve further comment. As the PAD receives characters from a terminal, it places them in a buffer whose length equals the maximum data field size of an X.25 packet. When the buffer is full, the packet is sent. These parameters may also allow the PAD to send a packet when it receives a carriage return, another control character, or when a timeout occurs.

The interface (actually the protocol) between the PAD and a terminal is specified in X.28. There are two phases of operation. In the data transfer phase, the PAD exchanges data between the terminal and the remote DTE. In the control phase, there is a dialogue between the terminal and the PAD. Normally, the control phase is used by the terminal only to request connection to a particular DTE. In response to this request, the PAD sets up a connection to the appropriate DCE, which in turn sets up a virtual circuit to its local DTE. The control phase may also be invoked from a terminal by hitting the break key, if X.3 parameter 7 is set appropriately. Table 17-2 summarizes the terminal commands and PAD responses specified in X.28.

Control information, in *PAD messages*, is exchanged between the PAD and the remote DTE in the data field of an X.25 data packet (see Figure 13-9), as specified in X.29. When the Q bit of a data packet is set, the data are interpreted as one of the messages of Table 17-3. Otherwise, the packet contains data being exchanged between the terminal and the remote DTE. In addition, conventional X.25 packets are exchanged between the DTE and the PAD to manage the virtual circuit.

TABLE 17-2 X.28 Commands and Responses

PAD Command Signal Format	Function	PAD Service Signal Sent in Response[a]
STAT	To request status information regarding a virtual call connected to the DTE	FREE or ENGAGED
CLR	To clear down a virtual call	CLR CONF or CLR ERR (in the case of local procedure error)
PAR? (list of parameter references	To request the current values of specified parameters	PAR (list of parameter references with their current values or INV)
SET? (list of parameter references and corresponding values)	To request changing or setting of the current values of the specified parameters and to request the current values of specified parameters	PAR (list of parameter references with their current values or INV)
PROF (identifier)	To give to PAD parameters a standard set of values	Acknowledgment
RESET	To reset the virtual call	Acknowledgment
INT	To transmit an *interrupt* packet	Acknowledgment
SET (list of parameters with requested values)	To set or change parameter values	Acknowledgment
Selection PAD command signal	To set up a virtual call	Acknowledgment

[a]*PAD service* signals are not sent when parameter 6 is set to 0.

TABLE 17-3 X.29 Messages

Message	Direction	Description
Set PAD	To PAD	Set selected parameters to indicated values
Read PAD	To PAD	Read values of indicated parameters
Set and read PAD	To PAD	Perform set and read functions
Parameter indication	From PAD	List of parameters and values in response to read command
Invitation to clear	To PAD	Requests the PAD to clear the virtual call
Indication of break	To or from PAD	Indication of break from DTE or terminal
Error	To or from PAD	Indicates error in previous message
Reselection PAD	To PAD	Request the PAD to clear the virtual call and establish a call to the selected DTE.

The last message type in Table 17-3, Reselection PAD, accommodates security or directory service applications. For example, the terminal user has established a call to an X.25 DTE that supports a directory service database. Upon completion of the dialogue with the calling user, the X.25 DTE transmits a Reselection PAD message which contains address, facility, and user data information of a new destination. The PAD then clears the call to the directory DTE and transmits a Call Request packet using the new information that is contained in the Reselection PAD message. The originating terminal user receives two service signals. The first indicates the call is being reselected, and the second indicates that the new call has been established.

Generalized Virtual Terminal Protocols

The X.3/X.28/X.29 approach to terminal handling is an effective one for simple asynchronous terminals. Its main defect is a lack of flexibility. As more complex terminals are used, more and more parameters must be defined to deal with them. The alternative is to go to a generalized virtual terminal protocol. In this section we first discuss the characteristics of such protocols and then look at the ISO standard.

Characteristics.   As the name implies, the VTP is a protocol, a set of conventions for communication between peer entities. It includes the following functions:

* Establishing and maintaining a connection between two application-level entities.
* Controlling a dialogue for negotiating the allowable actions to be performed across the connection.
* Creating and maintaining a data structure that represents the ''state'' of the terminal.

- Translating between actual terminal characteristics and a standardized representation.

The first two functions are in the nature of session control (layer 5); the latter two are presentation control (layer 6) functions. Figure 17-1 illustrates the difference in philosophy between this approach and that of the PAD. In the VTP approach, the terminal handler, which implements the terminal side of the protocol, is considered architecturally as a host attached to the network. Thus the protocol is end-to-end in terms of reliability, flow control, and so on. By comparison, the PAD is considered part of the network, not a separate host. From the point of view of the host, the PAD facility is part of its local DCE's X.25 layer 3 functionality. Although the PAD concept affords an easily implemented capability, it does not provide the architectural base for a flexible terminal-handling facility.

The principal purpose of the VTP is to transform the characteristics of a real terminal into a standardized form or virtual terminal. Because of the wide differences in capabilities among terminals, it is unreasonable to attempt to develop a single virtual terminal type. Four classes are of interest:

- *Scroll mode:* These are terminals with no local intelligence, including keyboard-printer and keyboard-display devices. Characters are transmitted as they are entered, and incoming characters are printed or displayed as they come in. On a display, as the screen fills, the top line is scrolled off.
- *Page mode:* These are keyboard-display terminals with a cursor-addressable character matrix display. Either user or host can modify random-accessed portions of the display. I/O can be a page at a time.
- *Form/data entry mode:* These are similar to page mode terminals, but allow definition of fixed and variable fields on the display. This permits a number of features, such as transmitting only the variable part, and defining field attributes to be used as validity checks.
- *Graphics mode:* These allow the creation of arbitrary two-dimensional patterns.

For any VTP, there are basically four phases of operation:

- *Connection management:* includes session-layer-related functions, such as connection request and termination.
- *Negotiation:* used to determine a mutually agreeable set of characteristics between the two correspondents.
- *Control:* exchange of control information and commands (e.g., defining the attributes of a field).
- *Data:* transfer of data between two correspondents.

Figure 17-2 illustrates the process involved. Upon user input, the characteristics of a real terminal are transformed into the agreed format, or "virtual terminal." These formatted data are transmitted over a network to a host system. In the host computer, the virtual terminal structure is translated into the terminal format normally used by the host. The reverse process is performed for host-to-terminal traffic. Thus, a virtual terminal service must understand the virtual terminal format and be able to employ a data-transfer mechanism, such as that provided in the OSI architecture.

A useful feature of a virtual terminal service is the ability to negotiate about the characteristics of the virtual terminal or the details of the data transfer. This allows

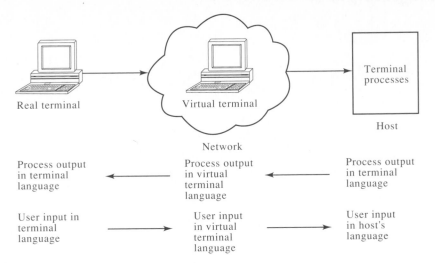

FIGURE 17-2.   Virtual terminal model.

users and processes to define a remote terminal access service that provides service as close as possible to what the terminal user expects.

Figure 17-3 relates the virtual terminal service to the OSI architecture. Terminals are connected locally to a device that may be a terminal cluster controller, some other sort of communications processor, or a general-purpose computer. Some terminal-handler software module is needed to communicate with the terminals; this is usually part of the operating system. The purpose of this module is to link the terminal user to some application in the system. In this case, the user is linked to the virtual terminal service. This service is at the application layer of the OSI architecture and makes use of the lower six layers of OSI to establish a connection with a virtual terminal service module on a remote computer. On the remote computer, the virtual terminal service module provides an interface to various appli-

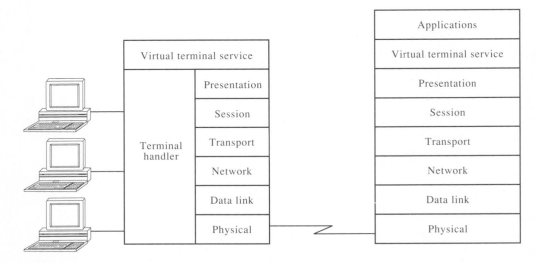

FIGURE 17-3.   Architecture for virtual terminal service.

cations. To the application, terminal traffic coming in through the virtual terminal service module appears to be coming from a local terminal through the usual terminal-handler software. Thus, for both the user and the application, it appears as though the user is locally connected to the remote computer.

The ISO Virtual Terminal Standard

The ISO virtual terminal service is an application-layer service defined within the framework of the open systems interconnection (OSI) model. The standard defines a module for a virtual terminal, which is an abstract representation of a real terminal. The standard defines operations that can be performed, such as reading text from the virtual keyboard, writing text on the virtual screen, and moving a cursor to a particular position on the virtual screen. The standard also defines a virtual terminal protocol for the exchange of data and control messages between a terminal and an application via the virtual terminal service. The protocol standard specifies the display data stream structure and the control messages by which the two sides can agree on the details of the terminal capabilities to be supported.

Rather than defining a single virtual terminal for all possible applications, the standard provides its users with the tools to define a virtual terminal suited to the application at hand and the physical limitations of the terminal. For example, if the physical terminal is monochrome, then the two sides agree not to use color information.

The structure of the ISO standard is suggested by Figure 17-4. A virtual terminal is modeled as being made up of several parts, all of which reside in the conceptual communications area, which is an abstraction used to model the interaction between two systems. A separate copy is maintained by each communicating entity, and it forms the basis for the protocol between the two sides. The Virtual Terminal Protocol (DIS 9041) is specified in terms of interactions between protocol entities in the two systems that affect the objects in the conceptual communications area.

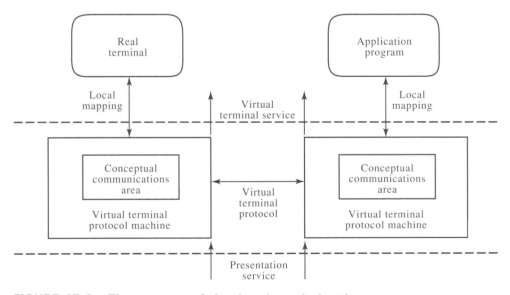

FIGURE 17-4.   The structure of the virtual terminal environment.

TABLE 17-4   Aspects of the ISO Virtual Terminal Service

Classes of Service	**Echo Control**
Basic	Local echo
Forms	Remote echo
Graphics	**Parameters**
Modes of Operation	Display objects
Two-way alternate	Device objects
Two-way simultaneous	Control objects
Delivery Control	
No delivery control	
Simple delivery control	
Quarantine delivery control	

Each entity provides a Virtual Terminal Service (DIS 9040) to its user. The service user can be thought of as a local mapping from a real terminal or application to the virtual terminal context.

Table 17-4 lists some of the key aspects of the ISO standard. We examine each of these in turn.

Classes of Service.   The ISO standard provides different classes of service. Each class meets the needs of a specific range of applications and terminal functions. So far, Basic, Forms, and Graphics classes have been identified. Of these, only the Basic class is fully defined and supported by vendors. We can expect to see the other classes available in the next few years.

The Basic class is a character-oriented service. In its simplest form, it meets the terminal access requirements of applications such as line editing and operating system command language interaction, which can be satisfied with simple scroll-mode terminals. The basic class also supports page-mode terminals and provides for the exchange of data in blocks instead of character-at-a-time. An extension to the basic class provides a primitive set of forms-related services. It allows the definition and addressing of individual fields and the transmission of selected fields. With this capability, the service can transfer just the variable fields on a form. However, there is no facility for defining or using field attributes.

The Forms class is designed to handle all of the operations associated with forms-mode terminals, such as the 3720 terminals. This would allow any forms-mode terminal from any vendor to interact with forms-mode applications on any host from any vendor. Finally, the Graphics class will deal with graphics and image-processing terminals.

Modes of Operation.   The virtual terminal standard supports two modes of operation: two-way alternate (half duplex) and two-way simultaneous (full duplex). When a terminal sets up a connection to a host, the mode of operation is agreed upon between the two virtual service modules.

Recall that the two-way alternate mode enforces the discipline that only one side at a time can transmit. This prevents the situation in which data from the computer begin to appear on the terminal display screen while the user is entering text from the keyboard. The two-way alternate mode is typical of synchronous forms-mode terminals such as the 3270. Most normal enquiry/response applications are naturally two-way alternate, for example.

The two-way simultaneous mode permits both sides to transmit at the same time. An example of the utility of this would be the control terminal for a complex real-time system such as a process control plant. For such an application, the terminal must be capable of being updated rapidly with status changes even if the operator is typing in a command.

Delivery Control.   Delivery control allows one side to control delivery of data to the other side to co-ordinate multiple actions. Normally, any data entered at a terminal are automatically delivered to the application on the other side as soon as possible, and any data transmitted by the application are delivered to the terminal as soon as possible. In some cases, however, one side may require explicit control over when certain data are delivered to its peer.

For example, suppose a user is logged on to a time-sharing system via the virtual terminal service. The time-sharing system may issue a single prompt character (e.g., ''>'') when it is ready for the next command. However, the terminal side of the virtual terminal service may choose to deliver data to the terminal for display only after several characters have been received, rather than one character at a time. Since this single prompt character must be displayed, and since the terminal side cannot reasonably be expected to know what the prompt character is, some mechanism is needed to force delivery. Another example is the use of special ''function keys,'' which are often found on terminals and which can be set up to perform multiple actions, resulting in the transmission of multiple messages to the host. Sometimes it is desirable that all of the functions of the key are presented to the peer user simultaneously.

Three types of delivery control can be specified with any transmission:

- *No delivery control:* This is the default type. In this case data are made available to the peer at the convenience of the implementation of the virtual terminal service.
- *Simple delivery control:* In this case, the service user (terminal or application) can issue a request that all undelivered data be delivered. The invoking side may also, optionally, request acknowledgement of the delivery to the other side.
- *Quarantine delivery control:* This requires that the remote virtual terminal service module hold all incoming data until they are explicitly released for delivery by the other side. For example, an application could send a screenfull of data in several small blocks but instruct the other side to defer delivery so that the entire screen update is displayed at once. Another example is the function key action mentioned previously.

Echo Control.   Echo control is concerned with the control of how characters typed on a keyboard will cause updates to a display (Figure 17-5). In real terminals, characters typed on the keyboard may be displayed on the screen locally by the terminal as they are typed or may be ''echoed back'' to the display by the computer. The former option is less flexible but is often chosen when the communication link is half duplex and echoing back would therefore not be practical. The latter option is used where the communication line is full duplex and where greater control over

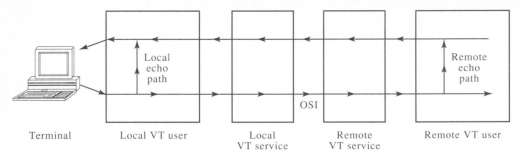

FIGURE 17-5.   Echo paths (ISO 9040).

the screen is required. For example, a time-sharing system may wish to suppress the display of the terminal user's password and identification code but display all other characters.

Virtual Terminal Parameters.   A major feature of the service is the use of terminal parameters. These are similar to those used in X.3 in that they provide a way of defining various characteristics of the terminal. However, the parameters available in the ISO standard are much more complex and powerful than those of X.3. They allow the user to define various characteristics of displayable characters, such as font, size, intensity, color, and so on. Control objects can be defined that are used to control formatting on the display and to trigger various events such as ringing an alarm. Characteristics of other devices such as printers can also be specified.

Figure 17-6 illustrates the parameters that have been defined for the basic class service, and brief definitions are provided in Table 17-5. These parameters can be viewed as being maintained in the conceptual communications area (Figure 17-7), which contains the following components:

- A conceptual data store, containing one or two display objects (two display objects are required for terminal-to-terminal interaction)
- A control, signaling, and status store, containing zero or more control objects, which may be used not only for device but also for signaling and status information.
- An access control store which is used in conjunction with two-way alternate operation.
- Zero or more objects, each of which represents a mapping between a display object and a real device, and provides parameters that enable some control over this mapping. A device object is linked to one display object and to one or more control objects.
- A data structure definition that contains object type definitions for the display, device, and control objects.

17-2

___

FILE TRANSFER PROTOCOLS

The development of computer protocols has been a bottom-up affair. The most used and the most well-defined protocols exist at the lower layers of the hierarchy.

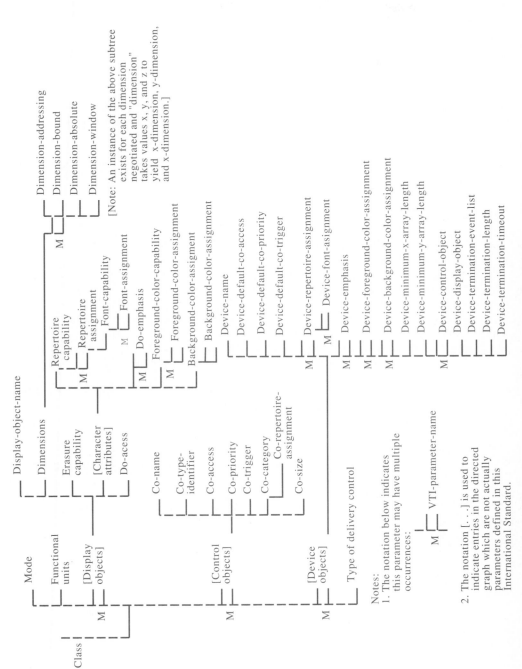

FIGURE 17-6. Directed graph of virtual terminal parameters (ISO 9040).

[Note: An instance of the above subtree exists for each dimension negotiated and "dimension" takes values x, y, and z to yield x-dimension, y-dimension, and x-dimension.]

Notes:
1. The notation below indicates this parameter may have multiple occurrences:

2. The notation [. . .] is used to indicate entries in the directed graph which are not actually parameters defined in this International Standard.

TABLE 17-5   Conceptual Communications Area Object Parameters

Display Objects

Name
  Name assigned to display object.
Dimensions
  One, two, or three. In a typical display object, an X-array may repesent a line, a
  Y-array a page on the terminal screen, and (if used) a Z-array a group of terminal
  screen pages.
Erasure Capability
  Ability to erase characters or not.
Character Attributes
  Specifies the standardized character set or sets supported and associated attributes that
  map to device characteristics.
Access
  Indicates which side may update the display object (side that originated the logical con-
  nection, side that did not originate the logical connection, or both sides).

Control Objects

Name
  Name assigned to control object.
Type Identifier
  Indicates whether this control object is one defined in ISO 9040 or one defined by some
  other agreement.
Access
  Indicates which side may update the control object.
Priority
  Possible values: normal, high, or urgent. This parameter controls the handling of up-
  dates to the control object in relation to updates to other control objects.
Trigger
  Indicates whether this attribute is selected or not. When a control object with the trig-
  ger characteristic is updated, any pending updates to display and control objects must
  be delivered immediately; in S-mode, control is transferred to the peer virtual-terminal
  user.
Category
  Identifies the type of information contained in the control object. Possible values:
  character, boolean, symbolic, integer, and transparent.
Repertoire Assignment
  Relevant only if control object is of category character. Provides same type of informa-
  tion as for a device object.
Size
  Data storage capacity of the control object.

Device Objects

Name
  Name assigned to display object; it also serves as the name of the device object's asso-
  ciated control object.
Default Control Object Values
  Value of the associated control object parameters.
Emphasis
  This parameter is provided to allow negotiation of its use for devices that may have an
  emphasis capability (e.g., highlighted, reverse video). The semantics and values of this
  parameter are not defined in the standard.

**TABLE 17-5 Conceptual Communications Area
Object Parameters (*continued*)**

Foreground and Background Color Assignment
  Specifies colors for character display.
Minimum X-Array and Y-Array Length
  Describes the minimum acceptable imaging area for the device.
Control Object
  List of control objects that are associated with this device object.
Display Object
  Display object associated with this device object.
Termination Event List
  List of termination events that apply to this device. A termination event is one which
  causes input data to be delivered to the peer virtual-terminal user (e.g., carriage return,
  function key, setting a flag).
Termination Length
  Number of characters input by the terminal user that will be considered a termination
  condition.
Termination Timeout
  Expiration of this timeout after the last input from the terminal user will be considered
  a termination condition.

Other Parameters

Mode
  Possible values: S-mode (synchronous), which is two-way alternate; or A-mode (asyn-
  chronous), which is two way simultaneous.
Functional Units
  Sets of optional capabilities which may be provided, including break, urgent data, and
  negotiated release.
Type of Delivery Control
  Possible values: no delivery control, simple delivery control, and quarantine delivery
  control.

At the application level, although there is a great deal of activity, few working
protocols exist. The most notable exception is in the area of file transfer protocols,
examples of which have been around for many years.

Architecture

The purpose of a file transfer protocol (FTP) is to transfer a file or a portion of a
file from one system to another, under command of an FTP user. Depending on
its scope of responsibility, the FTP may be a pure application protocol in the OSI
sense, or it may also have presentation functionality, and even some elements of
a session layer.

  Figure 17-8 shows a view of FTP as an application-level protocol. Here, FTP
is viewed as the top layer of a seven-layer communications architecture that is
supported by the station's operating system. Typically, FTP is used interactively
by an on-line user. The user's communication with FTP is mediated by the operating system, which contains I/O drivers. If the user on system *A* wishes access to
a file on system *B*, then *A*'s FTP establishes a connection to *B*'s FTP. This is, of

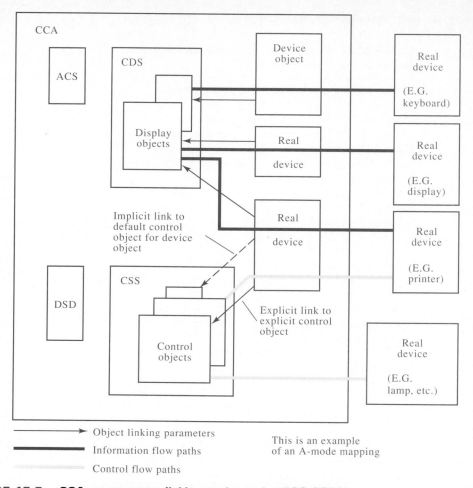

FIGURE 17-7.   CCA components, linking, and mapping (ISO 9040).

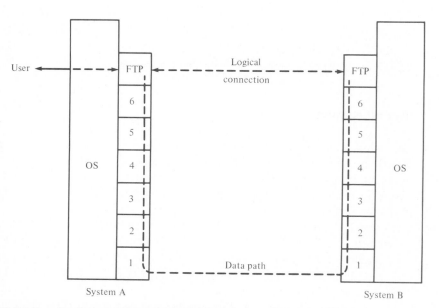

FIGURE 17-8.   Architectural context of a file transfer protocol.

course, a logical connection. The actual path for control and user data is through the layers of the architecture.

The user connects to the local FTP in order to transfer all or part of a file. There are three possibilities. The user at *A* may wish a file at *B* to be transferred to *A*. This would give the user local access to the contents of the file. The user may have prepared a file locally (at *A*) and wish it sent to *B*. Finally, the user may request that a file be exchanged between *B* and a third system, *C*. This is referred to as a third-party transfer and involves the FTP entities at *A*, *B*, and *C*.

FTP must interact with three entities, as depicted in Figure 17-9. First, there must be a user interface to accept requests from an interactive user or, possibly, a program. Of course, this interaction only takes place at the requesting system. The remote FTP in a file transfer event does not interact with a user. Second, FTP must be able to communicate with other FTPs to achieve file transfer. Typically, this is done by interfacing to a lower-level protocol entity. Finally, to transfer a file, FTP must be able to get at the file. For this, an interface is needed to the local file management system.

Consideration of this last interface reminds us that a general-purpose FTP must operate in a heterogeneous environment. Because different systems may have different file formats and structures, FTP must have knowledge of the local file system or, at least, rely on an entity that does. Before suggesting an effective way of handling this situation, let us consider what it is that is to be transferred. There are three possibilities.

- *The data in the file:* If just the actual data in the file are sent, we are not really dealing with a file transfer. This is more in the nature of a message exchange or electronic mail facility.
- *The data plus the file structure:* This, at minimum, is what is usually meant by a file transfer protocol.
- *The data, file structure, and all its attributes:* Examples of attributes are an access control list, an update history, and a list of indices for an indexed sequential file facility.

If the FTP operates somewhere on a spectrum bounded by the last two items, it must have knowledge of the local file structure and format, and it must understand the incoming file structure and format. To avoid the $M \times N$ problem discussed in the section on virtual terminal protocols, a similar solution may be adopted: the virtual file. Thus a general-purpose virtual file structure is defined. Only virtual

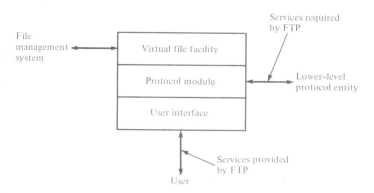

FIGURE 17-9.   Generic FTP structure.

files are exchanged between FTPs. Locally, a transformation is needed between the virtual file format and the local file format. This transformation can be implemented in the FTP or provided by a presentation protocol.

A virtual file structure should be simple enough that files can be exchanged between identical file systems with minimum overhead. On the other hand, it must be complex enough to be able to represent accurately a variety of dissimilar file systems. In general, a virtual file, or any file for that matter, consists of the following:

- A filename, that allows it to be referenced unambiguously.
- Other descriptive attributes which express common properties of the file, such as size, accounting information, history, and so on; these might be referred to as management attributes.
- Attributes describing the logical structure and dimensions of the data stored in the file; these might be referred to as structural attributes.
- Any data forming the contents of the file.

A wide variety of file structures are in common use, including sequential, indexed sequential, hierarchical, network, and relational. A simple example of a hierarchical virtual file structure is shown in Figure 17-10. The key building block of this virtual file is a *file access data unit* (FADU). The FADU is the unit on which operations on the file content are performed. Operations include read, write, insert, and delete. The file exhibits a tree structure, where each node of the tree defines a subtree that is an FADU. The highest-level (level 0) FADU encompasses the entire file. The lowest-level FADUs represent the leaves of the tree. The smallest unit of a file's contents on which filestore operations can be performed is the *data unit* (DU). Each data unit is associated with a node of the file access structure. An example of a data unit is a record in a file. In that case, the internal structure of the data unit (i.e., in terms of fields and groups of fields) is not specified.

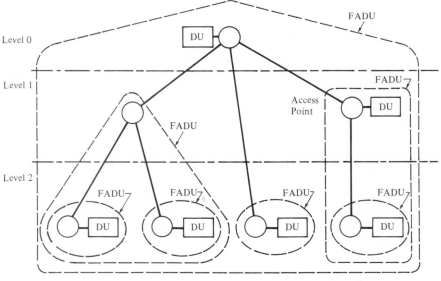

DU = data unit
FADU = file access data unit

FIGURE 17-10. Virtual file structure.

However, certain attributes of the file may be part of the virtual file structure. These may include access control parameters, and the identity of index keys.

Characteristics

As is usually the case with any protocol, file transfer protocols can be characterized by the services they provide and the protocol mechanisms they employ. Table 17-6 contains a list of relevant service and protocol features for file transfer protocols, suggested in [NBS80c]. We will briefly consider each feature in turn.

Service Features.   In the typical computer system, there is some *access control* mechanism to protect the file system. A user must have an ID and password to gain access to the system at all. Then individual files may maintain access control lists with specific permissions (read, write) by user. This capability must be extended across the network. The simplest way, perhaps, is to require the user to do a remote login and be identified at the system. In a controlled network environment, there might be a network-wide access control mechanism. In any case, the mechanism must be mediated by the FTP.

The normal *processing mode* of a file transfer is immediate. That is, when the transfer is requested, FTP will endeavor to achieve the transfer right away and report back. If, however, the transfer is not urgent, the user could indicate that the transfer could take place in a background mode.

A *file naming* facility is needed to identify the source and destination station and the source and destination file. At a minimum, the user must specify the network name of the station and a file name that is locally significant (local to the system on which the file resides). This requires the user to know the syntax and semantics of file naming conventions at each system of interest. A better service is one that involves standardized syntax for file names, although semantics may still differ (e.g., modifiers such as SOURCE and OBJECT may have particular significance). A virtual file name would then be used, to be translated locally by FTP. Again, in a controlled network environment, one might hope for a network-wide file system, with a common syntax and semantics, in which the user need not even know the location of a file.

The basic operation of FTP is to duplicate a file and send it to another system, where it is stored with a new local name. *Alternative operations* include: transfer

TABLE 17-6   File Transfer Protocol Features

Service Features	Protocol Features
Access control	Transmission of commands
Processing mode	File attributes
File naming	Negotiation
Alternative operations	Text formatting
File management	Security
Error recovery	Statistics
Flow control	
File structuring	
Status reports	

of a portion of a file, copy a file only if an empty destination file already exists, and append a file to the contents of a destination file.

An FTP can mediate user access to certain *file management* facilities, either local or remote. Although file management is not properly a part of a file transfer protocol, certain minimal services seem warranted. The following three are found in most file transfer protocols: file allocation (define a new file and allocate space), file deletion, and listing file names in a directory.

An *error recovery* facility would provide for recovery from errors or failure in the file system or operating system. The mechanism to be used is checkpointing. Checkpoint locations are transferred along with the file. The number of unacknowledged checkpoints can be controlled by a sliding window protocol. When an error is detected, the file transfer can be backed up to any acknowledged checkpoint. This mechanism could be implemented entirely in FTP, or rely on the session layer for checkpoint transmission and acknowledgment.

A simple stop-and-wait *flow-control* scheme is a useful addition to an FTP. This mechanism allows the transfer to be temporarily halted and resumed later. This feature provides the ability to mount tapes during the transfer and allows system resources such as disks to be preempted by a higher priority task without aborting a transfer in progress.

We have already discussed the need for a *file structuring* service with an FTP. A hierarchical or tree structure file description will have the most general applicability.

File transfers can be lengthy processes, particularly if performed in background mode. *Status reports* should be provided that indicate the start and completion of a transfer. The user should be able to interrogate FTP to determine the current status of any ongoing file transfer.

Protocol Features.   A fundamental feature of a file transfer protocol is the *transmission of commands*. An FTP entity must communicate with a peer counterpart to coordinate and control the data transfer. Control information could be exchanged over the same session as the file data, or it could be accomplished over a separate session. In a third-party transfer, mechanisms must be in place to provide for the coordination among three FTP entities.

The source FTP must communicate *file attributes* to the recipient system. This is so even if a fully general virtual file structure is used. The reason is that, at the receiving end, the virtual file must be transformed into a local real file. The nature of that transformation may depend on attributes of the original source file. For example, if the destination system only uses the ASCII character code and the source file is non-ASCII text, this attribute needs to be known so that either the source or destination FTP can invoke a conversion function.

A flexible file transfer protocol is bound to have a number of options, for example, use of checkpointing, flow control, buffer size, and so on. A process of *negotiation* is required for two FTP entities to agree on a common level of service.

In text files, there will be certain control codes that affect the format of the text (e.g., vertical and horizontal spacing). A *text formatting* mechanism indicates which control codes are in the file and how they are to be interpreted. Thus systems using different text format control conventions can intelligibly exchange text files.

In addition to specific access control mechanisms that control access to files by identified users, files may be designated with a *security* label. FTP must cooperate with the file system's security mechanism to maintain security. Specifically, FTP must match the security level of the file to the security level of the session.

Finally, *statistics* can be gathered by FTP to provide information to a central control authority and to provide the user with information to be used when allocating local resources.

The ISO FTAM Standard

As an example, we briefly describe a recently adopted ISO standard [ISO87], [LEWA83], known as file transfer, access, and management (FTAM). The FTAM standard is quite complex; this section is intended only to give the reader a general appreciation of its features. The standard is organized into three parts:

- Virtual filestore definition
- File service definition
- File protocol specification

Virtual Filestore Definition. The virtual filestore in FTAM is defined in terms of the structure of files, the attributes that can be assigned to files; and the allowable actions on files and file elements.

There are four aspects of the *structure of a file,* each conveying different information about the file:

- *File access structure:* describes the composition of the file from file access data units (FADUs). The file access structure is that depicted in Figure 17-6. Thus, the current version of the standard is limited to hierarchical or simpler types of file structures. Later revisions may also include network and relational structures.
- *Presentation structure:* describes the abstract syntaxes of the data units (DUs) which are defined within the file access structure. The presentation structure expresses the data unit in terms of the syntactic arrangement of data elements. However, it is not possible to access the individual data elements within a data unit by means of FTAM; the data unit is accessed as a whole. The definition of presentation syntax may be useful for checkpointing and for providing guidance to the presentation layer.
- *Transfer structure:* describes the serialization of the FADUs for communication purposes. The transfer structure specifies the way in which a structured file is transferred as a series of data element values.
- *Identification structure:* describes the naming of the nodes in the file access structure and the identification of FADUs to be transferred.

Each file has associated with it a number of properties, known as *attributes.* Two classes of attributes are defined: file attributes and activity attributes. File attributes represent properties of the file itself, independent of any FTAM action occurring over an ISO session connection. These attributes distinguish a file from bulk data by providing the kind of file management information normally associated with a data base or file management system. Three groups of file attributes are defined in FTAM. The kernel group is the minimum that must be supported; it provides the basic information needed for the act of file transfer. The storage group defines concepts related to the physical storage of files. It is concerned with physical properties of the file, such as size, as well as information about accessors. The security group provides for file-related security information. The attributes are listed in Table 17-7. Some of them merit further definition:

- *Contents type:* indicates the internal structure of the file (unstructured, flat, hierarchical) and the data type (text, binary).
- *Permitted actions:* lists those actions (defined below) which are permitted on this file.
- *Access control:* list of permitted actions by identity of accessor.
- *Encryption name:* name of the algorithm used to encrypt the file contents.
- *Legal qualifications:* character string conveying information about the legal status of the file and its use.

The other class of attributes are activity attributes. These are relevant only to the file service session in progress. There is a different set of values for file activity attributes for each file service connection. As with file attributes, activity attributes are divided into kernel, storage, and security groups. Among these are:

- *Current access context:* indicates the view of the file's access structure for the purpose of communication (hierarchical, flat, unstructured)
- *Current concurrency control:* indicates the restrictions on parallel access to the file for particular actions.

TABLE 17-7   FTAM Attributes

File Attributes	Activity Attributes
Kernel Group	
Filename	Active contents type
Contents Type	Current Access Request
	Current Location
	Current Processing Mode
	Current Application Entity Title
Storage Group	
Storage Account	Current Account
Date and Time of Creation	Current Access Context
Date and Time of Last Modification	Current Concurrency Control
Date and Time of Last Read Access	
Date and Time of Last Attribute Modification	
Identity of Creator	
Identity of Last Modifier	
Identity of Last Reader	
Identity of Last Attribute Modifier	
File Availability	
Permitted Actions	
Filesize	
Future Filesize	
Security Group	
Access Control	Active Legal Qualifications
Encryption Name	Current Initiator Identity
Legal Qualifications	Current Access Passwords

TABLE 17-8   Allowable Actions on FTAM Files

Actions on Complete Files

Create file	Creates new file; establishes its attributes
Select file	Creates relationship between initiator and file
Change attribute	Changes a current file attribute
Read attribute	Gets value of requested attribute
Open file	Establishes suitable regime for the performance of the actions for file access on the selected file. File may be opened for read or read/write.
Close file	Terminates the open regime.
Delete file	Deletes the selected file.
Deselect file	Terminates file selection.

Actions for File Access

Locate	Locates specified FADU
Read	Locates and reads an FADU
Insert	Inserts FADU relative to current location
Replace	Replaces currently located FADU
Extend	Adds data to the end of the DU associated with the root node of the currently located FADU
Erase	Specified FADU is erased

Table 17-8 lists the *allowable actions on files and file elements*. Some actions are defined on a complete file; these fall within the scope of file management. The other actions are related to the access of individual file access data units within a file.

File Service Definition.   Whereas the virtual filestore definition defines the structure of files and the allowable actions on those files, the file service definition defines the services available to users for accessing and manipulating the virtual files.

The FTAM service and its supporting protocol are concerned with creating, in a series of stages, a working environment in which the user's desired activities can take place. The dialogue must, in turn:

- allow the user and the filestore provider to establish each other's identity.
- identify the file which is needed and establish the user's authority to access the file.
- establish the attributes describing the file structure which is to be accessed on this occasion and establish controls on the concurrent access of the file by other users;
- allow the user to access the attributes or contents of the currently selected file.

These steps build up various parts of an operational context. The period for which some part of the contextual information is valid is called a *regime*. As progressively more contextual detail is established, a nest of corresponding regimes is built up; this nesting is shown in Figure 17-11. In essence, the regime determines

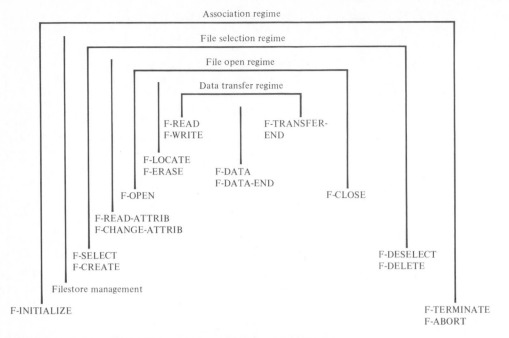

FIGURE 17-11.   FTAM file service regimes and primitives.

the state of the FTAM service provider with respect to a given user connection and therefore the services that can be provided at a given point in time.

As usual, the services provided by FTAM are defined as a set of primitives and parameters. Table 17-9 shows the primitives. They may be grouped as follows:

- *FTAM regime control:* these services are used to create and terminate a connection by which the user can access the virtual file.
- *File selection regime control:* identify a unique file to which subsequent operations will apply. The file may be selected from among existing files, or it may be created.
- *File management:* allows the user to inspect or modify attributes of the selected file.
- *File open regime control:* assigns a file to a user for access purposes. Concurrency controls may be exercised.
- *Grouping control:* allows the user to indicate the start and end of a set of primitives that are to be processed and responded to as a group.
- *Access to file content:* identify a unique location within a file structure (i.e., the position of a particular FADU) to which subsequent operations apply.
- *Bulk data transfer:* used for the transfer of one or more data units. The procedure begins with the user issuing either an F-READ.request or an F-WRITE.request. This causes a sequence of F-DATA.requests followed by an F-DATA-END.request by the sender of the data. The procedure is completed by the user issuing an F-TRANSFER-END.request.
- *Checkpointing and restarting:* allows the sender of data to establish marks in the flow of data for the purpose of subsequent restart. Restarting involves backing up to a checkpoint and retransmitting data from that point.

TABLE 17-9 FTAM Service Primitives

FTAM Regime Control
F-INITIALIZE request/indication/response/confirm
F-TERMINATE request/indication/response/confirm
F-U-ABORT request/indication
F-P-ABORT indication

File Selection Regime Control
F-SELECT request/indication/response/confirm
F-DESELECT request/indication/response/confirm
F-CREATE request/indication/response/confirm
F-DELETE request/indication/response/confirm

File Management
F-READ-ATTRIB request/indication/response/confirm
F-CHANGE-ATTRIB request/indication/response/confirm

File Open Regime Control
F-OPEN request/indication/response/confirm
F-CLOSE request/indication/response/confirm

Grouping Control
F-BEGIN-GROUP request/indication/response/confirm
F-END-GROUP request/indication/response/confirm

Access to File Content
F-LOCATE request/indication/response/confirm
F-ERASE request/indication/response/confirm

Bulk Data Transfer
F-READ request/indication
F-WRITE request/indication
F-DATA request/indication
F-DATA-END request/indication
F-TRANSFER-END request/indication/response/confirm
F-CANCEL request/indication/response/confirm

Checkpointing and Restarting
F-CHECK request/indication/response/confirm
F-RESTART request/indication/response/confirm

File Protocol Specification. The FTAM protocol provides a rather direct support of the FTAM service. By and large, there is a one-to-one mapping from service primitives to protocol data units. The FTAM protocol will set up a session connection and insert checkpoints in the flow of data.

17-3

ELECTRONIC MAIL

One of the deadliest wasters of time in the office is a phenomenon known as "telephone tag." Mr. X calls Ms. Y, who is away from her desk. Some time later Y returns the call but X is out or on another line. X is now "it" and must return

Y's return to X's call. And so on. . . . Independent studies have shown that over 70 percent of all business telephone calls do not reach the intended recipient on the first try [MARI79]. The problem is that the caller and callee must both be at their phones and available to answer at the same time. If the caller could simply write a note and leave it on the callee's desk, the problem could be avoided. Electronic mail provides a way to do this.

Electronic mail addresses another problem as well: the office paper explosion. Offices generate a tremendous amount of paperwork, most of it in the form of internal memos and reports: over 80 percent of all business documents are textual and/or numeric (no graphics) and originate and remain within the same organization [POTT77].

Electronic mail, also known as a computer-based message system (CBMS), is a facility that allows users at terminals to compose and exchange messages. The messages need never exist on paper unless the user (sender or recipient) desires a paper copy of the message. Some electronic mail systems serve only users on a single computer; others provide service across a network of computers. In this section, we briefly look at the functionality of single-system electronic mail, then turn our attention to the more interesting (for this book) case of network electronic mail. Finally, the CCITT X.400 family of standards is described.

Single-System Electronic Mail

The simplest, and by far the most common, form of electronic mail is the single-system facility. This facility allows all the users of a shared computer system to exchange messages. Each user is registered on the system and has a unique identifier, usually the person's last name. Associated with each user is a mailbox. The electronic mail facility is an application program available to any user logged on to the system. A user may invoke the electronic mail facility, prepare a message, and "send" it to any other user on the system. The act of sending simply involves putting the message in the recipient's mailbox. The mailbox is actually an entity maintained by the file management system, and is in the nature of a file directory. One mailbox is associated with each user. Any "incoming" mail is simply stored as a file under that user's mailbox directory. The user may later go and fetch that file to read the message. The user reads messages by invoking the mail facility and "reading" rather than "sending." In most systems, when the user logs on, he or she is informed if there is any new mail in that user's mailbox.

A basic electronic mail system performs four functions:

- *Creation:* A user creates and edits a message, generally using a rudimentary editing capability. Most systems also allow the user to create a message using the system editor or a word processor, and then incorporate the resulting file as the body of the message.
- *Sending:* The user designates the recipient (or recipients) of the message, and the facility stores the message in the appropriate mailbox(es).
- *Reception:* The intended recipient may invoke the electronic mail facility to access and read the delivered mail.
- *Storage:* Both sender and recipient may choose to save the message in a file for more permanent storage.

Because we are interested in the networking aspects of electronic mail, the topic of basic user services will not be further pursued here. More detail can be found in [HIRS85] and [BARC81].

Network Electronic Mail

With a single-system electronic mail facility, messages can only be exchanged among users of that particular system. Clearly, this is too limited. In a distributed environment, we would like to be able to exchange messages with users attached to other systems. Thus, we would like to treat electronic mail as an application-layer protocol that makes use of lower-layer protocols to transmit messages.

Figure 17-12 suggests the internal system architecture required. Let us refer to a single-system mail facility as a *native mail* facility. For native mail, three major modules are needed. Users will interact with native mail via terminals; hence, terminal-handling software is needed. Mail is stored as files in the file system, so file-handling software is needed. Finally, there must be a native mail package that contains all the logic for providing mail-related services to users.

To extend this system to *network mail,* two more modules are needed. Since we are going to communicate across some sort of network or transmission system, communication I/O logic is needed; in the most general case, this would encompass layers 1 through 6 of the OSI model. Mail transfer logic is also needed, that knows how to invoke the communications function, to specify the network address of the recipient, and to request whatever communication services are needed (e.g., priority). Note in the figure that the user does not directly interact with the mail transfer module. Ideally, the user interface for local and remote mail should be the same. If the user designates a local recipient, the message is stored in a local mailbox. If a remote recipient is designated, the native mail module passes the message to the mail transfer module for transmission across the network. Incoming mail from the network is routed to the appropriate mailbox and henceforth treated the same as other messages in the mailbox.

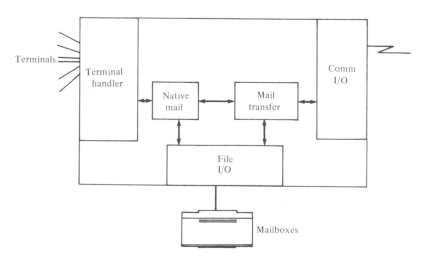

FIGURE 17-12. Conceptual structure of electronic mail system.

Many vendors now offer a network version of their basic electronic mail facility. However, this will only allow the user to send mail to users on systems of the same vendor. As in other areas, standards are needed. It is to these standards that we now turn our attention.

The CCITT X.400 Family of Standards

In 1984, CCITT issued a family of standards for Message Handling Systems (MHS) that encompass the requirements of what we have referred to as network electronic mail; the standards were substantially revised in 1988. The standards do not deal with the user interface or the services available directly to the user (what we have referred to as native mail). They do, however, specify what services are available for use in sending messages across the network and thus provide the base for building the user interface.

TABLE 17-10   The CCITT X.400 Family of Standards for Message Handling Systems

Number	Title	Description
X.400	System Model—Service Elements	Defines the message-handling system model consisting of user agents and message-transfer agents, discusses naming and addressing, defines interpersonal messaging and message transfer services, and discussed protocols for implementation.
X.402	Overall Architecture	Defines the overall architecture and serves as a technical introduction to it.
X.403	Conformance Testing	Specifies the criteria for acceptance of an implementation as conforming to the X.400 family of recommendations.
X.407	Abstract Service Definition Conventions	Defines techniques for formally specifying the distributed information processing tasks that arise in Message Handling.
X.408	Encoded Information Type Conversion Rules	Specifies the conversion between different types of encoded information to allow dissimilar devices to exchange messages. The encoded information types that are handled include Telex, Teletex, ASCII terminals, facsimile, and videotex.
X.411	Message Transfer Layer	Defines the conceptual layer service provided by the message transfer layer and the message transfer protocol.
X.413	Message Store: Abstract Service Definition	Defines the services provided by the message store.
X.419	Protocol Specifications	Defines the protocols for accessing the Message Transfer System, for accessing a Message Store, and that are used between Message Transfer Agents to provide for the distributed operation of the MTS.
X.420	Interpersonal Messaging User Agent Layer	Defines the services provided by Interpersonal Messaging and the procedures for providing those services.

Table 17-10 lists the nine recommendations that comprise the X.400 family. All of the recommendations fit into the framework of an MHS model, which is described in X.400. We describe that model first, and then look at some of the key aspects of the specifications of services and protocols.

MHS Functional Model. X.400 defines a functional model for the message handling system, as shown in Figure 17-13. This model provides a framework for all of the other recommendations. The model defines a number of key components (Table 17-11).

The actual work of message transfer is done in the message transfer system, which consists of an interconnected set of message transfer agents (MTAs). The **message transfer agent** accepts messages from a user agent (UA) for delivery to other UAs or to a message store (MS). Sometimes the MTA that accepts submission of a message delivers it directly to the destination UA or MS. In other cases, it is necessary for the message to be relayed through a series of MTAs to the destination. For example, if only some MTAs have access to the proper long-distance communication paths, a message addressed to a distant UA might be relayed in several

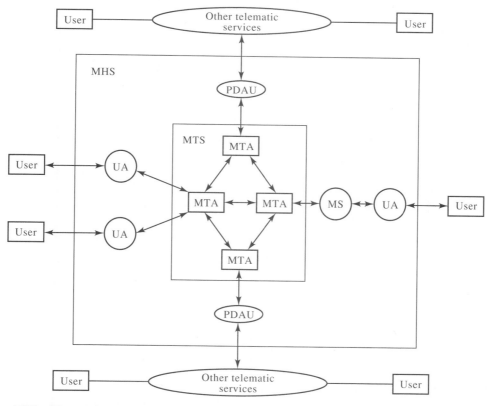

MHS = Message handling system
MTS = Message transfer system
MTA = Message transfer agent
MS = Message store
UA = User agent
AU = Access unit
PDAU = Physical delivery access unit

FIGURE 17-13. X.400 MHS functional model.

TABLE 17-11   Basic Components of a Message Handling System (MHS)

Message Transfer Agent (MTA)

The MTA is a functional entity which, in cooperation with similar entities, conveys messages through the message transfer system. When a message is submitted, the MTA validates the submission envelope and performs housekeeping functions, such as recording submission time and generating a message identifier.

User Agent (UA)

Operates on behalf of the user (person or application program that originates and receives messages). It interacts directly with the user, performs functions for preparing messages and submitting messages for routing to the destination(s). In the process, the source UA interacts with destination UAs, which perform the delivery function. The UAs also assist the user in dealing with other message functions, such as filing, replying, retrieving, and forwarding.

Message Store (MS)

The MS provides a mailbox facility. Messages may be delivered from the message transfer system (MTS) into the MS to be picked up later by a UA.

Access Unit (AU)

An AU provides a gateway between the MHS and an external communications service, such as Telex or Teletex.

Physical Delivery Access Unit (PDAU)

A PDAU is an AU that provides access to a physical delivery system such as the postal system. It produces a hard copy of the message contents together with an envelope addressed using the electronic addressing information provided by the originator.

stages. Using relays also eliminates the need to have all UAs and MTAs available on a 24-hour basis. The store-and-forward action makes it feasible to treat electronic mail components like any other office equipment that gets turned off at night.

The other elements of the message handling system are users of the message transfer system. The **user agent** operates on behalf of a user. The UA submits messages to an MTA for transmission across the network. The X.400 series specifies the interaction of the UA with MTA and other UA entities but does not specify the interaction between the UA and its user.

The **message store** is a concept that was introduced in the 1988 version of the standard. One of the drawbacks of the 1984 scheme, which had no message store, was that if a remote UA was off-line for a period of time, it could be flooded with messages at the log-on stage. Furthermore, a message delivered to the UA is "trapped" in that UA system; it causes problems for users on the move, who may want to access their mailbox from terminals at different locations or from a portable terminal. The MS concept is designed to alleviate these problems.

The functionality defined for the message store can be summarized as follows [CHIL90]:

- One MS acts on behalf of one user (i.e., one originator/response address).
- When a UA subscribes to an MS, all messages destined for the UA are delivered to the MS; when a message is delivered to an MS the role of the message transfer system (MTS) in the transfer process is complete. Note that the MS does not store submitted messages, only delivered messages.
- It is possible to request an alert when a certain message arrives.
- Message submission from the UA to its MTA, via the MS, is transparent.

- Users are provided with general message management facilities such as selective message retrieval, delete, and list.

In effect, the MS specification is just a standardized definition of how otherwise local UA functions have been taken over by a separate system, and accessed via a protocol.

Finally, various **access units** (AUs) allow MHS users to communicate with other message-based systems. The rules for coded information conversion are defined, making it possible to standardize the conversion of message contents for transfer of messages between dissimilar systems.

Figure 17-14 suggests the way in which messages are constructed and transmitted. The user prepares the *body* of a message outside of the scope of X.400, using some sort of word processor or editor. The user presents this body to the user agent software, together with a description, which might include recipient, subject, and priority. The user agent appends a *header* containing this qualifying information to the *message,* forming a complete message. This message is submitted to a message transfer agent. The MTA appends an *envelope* to the message; the envelope contains the source and destination addresses plus other control information needed for relaying the message through the network.

The X.400 Protocol Architecture.   The message-handling protocols defined in the X.400 series are located in the application layer of the OSI model. The X.400 architecture conforms to the OSI concept of the application layer structure, which is summarized briefly in the appendix to this chapter.

The MHS protocols are determined by application contexts which specify combinations of MHS-specific application service elements (ASEs) and other ASEs shared by a number of applications. Table 17-12 lists the ASEs relevant to X.400.

In order to observe how these ASEs interact, refer to Figure 17-15. The figure shows the permissible application contexts: a remote user accessing the MTS; a user accessing the MS, and the basic message transfer operation. In each case, the overall interaction, which involves a number of ASEs, is designated by a particular protocol name (Table 17-13).

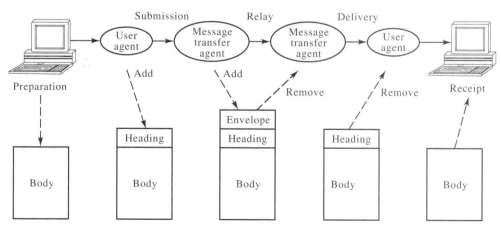

FIGURE 17-14.   X.400 message flow.

TABLE 17-12   **Application Service Elements Relevant to X.400**

MHS ASEs

Message Administration Service Element (MASE)

The MSSE provides protocol operations between MTA and UA and between MS and UA. It covers various administrative tasks, such as changing passwords, and providing information about message status.

Message Delivery Service Element (MDSE)

The MSSE provides protocol operations between MTA and UA. It allows the MTA to deliver messages to the UA.

Message Retrieval Service Element (MRSE)

The MSSE provides protocol operations between MS and UA. It allows the UA to retrieve messages from the message store.

Message Submission Service Element (MSSE)

The MSSE provides protocol operations between MTA and UA and between MS and UA. It provides for the submission of complete messages by the UA, and for submission of a probe, which is a limited envelope to verify delivery parameters.

Message Transfer Service Element (MTSE)

The ony symmetric MHS service element. It provides a set of services to MTA for message transfer.

Common ASEs

Association Control Service Element (ACSE)

Supports the establishment and release of logical connections (called associations) between a pair of application entities. The ACSE contains the parameters that determine the use of the underlying presentation service and indirectly the session service.

Remote Operation Service Element (ROSE)

Supports interactive request/reply operation within the MHS model. It is used with the asymmetric MHS service elements (all but MTSE), to order the interactions between dissimilar open systems.

Remote Transfer Service Element (RTSE)

Supports the reliable transfer of application data. It ensures the reliable transfer of messages without duplication or loss.

TABLE 17-13   **MHS Protocols (X.419)**

Message Transfer Protocol (P1)

P1 provides for relaying messages and other interactions among the various message transfer agents. It thus serves as the backbone switching protocol.

Remote UA Access Protocol (P3)

P3 enables a user agent (UA) that is remote from its message transfer agent (MTA) to obtain access to the message transfer service for submission from the US and retrieval from the MTA. In effect, P3 is a remote procedure call protocol.

MS Access Protocol (P7)

P7 enables a user agent to interact with a message store, providing in effect a mailbox facility.

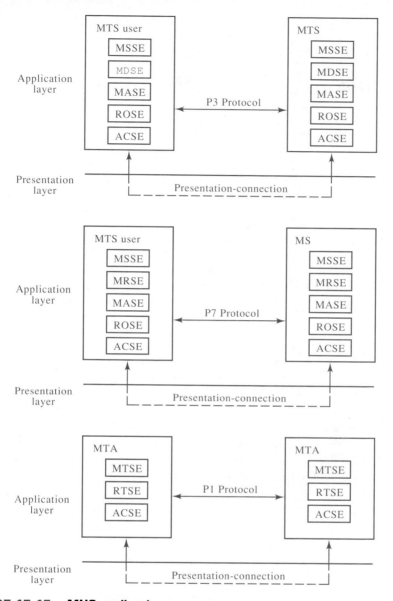

FIGURE 17-15. MHS application contexts.

An example of the use of these protocols is shown in Figure 17-16. User A sends a message to User B and User C. The message is handed over to User A's UA, which *submits* the message after putting it in an envelope. The envelope is, in effect the header of a P3 protocol data unit. The MTAs take over the *transfer* of the message until it reaches an MTA which can make a *delivery* of the message. The routing of the message among the MTAs is accomplished with the P1 protocol. The recipient User B gets delivery directly to B's UA, via protocol P3, where it can be directly read. For recipient User C, a copy of the message is delivered into C's MS from where it can later be retrieved via protocol P7.

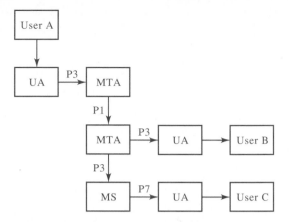

FIGURE 17-16.   Example of how the X.400 protocols can be used [MANR89].

The P1 protocol is used to transfer a message from the originator's MTA to the recipient's MTA through zero or more intermediate MTAs. The protocol is also used, if the service has been requested, for transferring a notification of delivery or nondelivery back to the originator's MTA. Of course, if the originator and recipient share the same MTA, then this protocol is not needed.

Three types of protocol data units are defined: user, delivery report, and probe. The user PDU consists of the user agent sublayer PDU plus a header, known as the *envelope* (Figure 17-17). The envelope contains the information needed for handling the message, including a network name for the recipient that will allow routing, a unique identifier, and information on how to process the PDU, such as the priority and whether a delivery report is required. The delivery report includes a header that consists of a unique identifier, the name of the originator that submitted the message to which this report refers, and trace information, which indicates the route that the delivery report followed. The body of the delivery report PDU includes the identifier of the original user PDU plus information about the delivery. This may include such items as the trace of the original user PDU, billing information, and, of course, whether delivery was successful.

The probe PDU is similar to the envelope portion of a user PDU. Its purpose is to determine if a particular delivery is possible without actually sending a user message. Delivery reports will be returned on probe PDUs.

Figure 17-17 also indicates the presence of a message heading. The heading is transparent to the message transfer agent and to the various protocols (P1, P3, P7). However, the format of the message heading is specified for use by user agents. The heading contains the following fields:

- Message ID
- Originator
- Authorizing users
- Primary recipients
- Copy recipients
- Blind copy recipients
- Replies to message
- Obsoletes messages
- Related messages

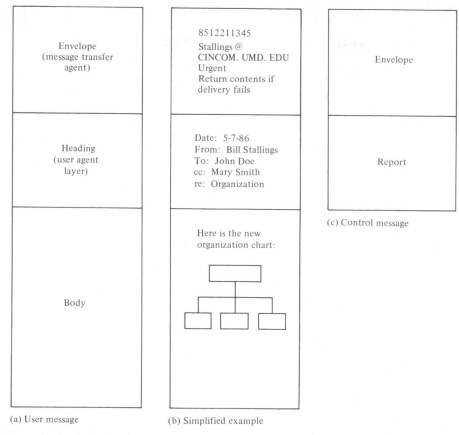

FIGURE 17-17. X.400 message structure.

- Subject
- Expiry time
- Reply time
- Reply recipients
- Importance
- Sensitivity
- Auto forwarded
- Extensions

X.400 Services. As with most communications standards, the X.400 series specifies not only protocols but the services to be provided to users. In this case the users are either terminal users who invoke electronic mail facilities, or application programs that exchange messages. The services are grouped into message transfer services and interpersonal messaging services.

For both sets of services, the services are divided into three categories: basic, essential optional, and additional optional. *Basic* services are inherent in the message handling system and must be implemented. The remaining services are known as optional user facilities which may be invoked at the option of the user, in some cases on a per-message basis and in others for an agreed contractual period. *Essential optional user facilities* must be offered by the service provider; that is, the provider must offer the option, but it is up to the user to select or not select the option. Finally, *additional optional user facilities* may or may not be offered by the provider.

Table 17-14 lists the services provided by the message transfer agent. The layer attempts to deliver messages to one or more intended recipients, and can be asked to notify the originator's UAE of the success or failure of each attempt. This layer may also invoke presentation-layer transformations on behalf of the user agent sublayer. The originator may request that delivery take place no earlier than a specified time. The recipient may request that a message be temporarily held in the system prior to delivery. In addition, the originator may designate a message as urgent.

TABLE 17-14   Message Transfer Layer Services (X.401)

Basic Services

Access management	Enables UA to submit and have messages delivered to it
Content type indication	Specified by originating UA
Converted indication	Specifies any conversions performed on message being delivered
Submission/delivery time stamp	Submission and delivery time are supplied with each message
Message identification	Unique identifier for each message
Nondelivery notification	Message cannot be delivered
Registered encoded information types	Allows UA to specify types that can be delivered to it
Original encoded information types	Specified by submitting UA and supplied to receiving UA

Essential Optional Services

Alternate recipient allowed	Deliver to alternate if designated recipient cannot be found
Deferred delivery	Deliver no sooner than specified date and time
Deferred delivery cancellation	Abort delivery of deferred message
Delivery notification	Notify originator of successful delivery
Disclosure of other recipients	Disclose list of recipients to recipient
Grade of delivery selection	Request urgent, normal, or nonurgent
Multi-destination delivery	Specify more than one recipient
Conversion prohibition	Prevents MTS from conversion
Probe	Determines if a message could be deliverable

Additional Optional Services

Prevention of non-delivery notification	Suppress potential nondelivery notice
Return of contents	Return message contents if nondelivery
Explicit conversion	Specifies particular conversion
Implicit conversion	Perform necessary conversion on all messages without explicit instruction
Alternate recipient assignment	Requests designation of requesting UA as alternate recipient
Hold for delivery	Requests that messages intended for this UA be held in MTS until later time

Interpersonal messaging services are provided by the user agent, and are listed in Table 17-15. In this case optional services receive two designations, one for origination and one for reception. Note that many of the services that are additional (need not be offered) for origination are essential for reception. For example, UAs

TABLE 17-15 **Interpersonal Messaging Services (X.401)**

Basic Services

IP-message identification	Assign reference identifier to each message content sent or received
Typed body	Allows nature and attributes of message body to be conveyed along with body.

Essential Optional Services
(for both origination and reception)

Originator indication	Identifies the user that sent message
Primary and copy recipients indication	Allows UA to specify primary and secondary recipients
Replying IP-message indication	Specifies an earlier message to which this is a reply
Subject indication	Description of message

Additional (for origination) and Essential
(for reception) Optional Services

Blind copy recipient indication	List of recipients whose identities are not to be disclosed to primary or copy recipients
Auto-forwarded indication	Marks a message as containing an automatically-forwarded message
Authorizing users indication	Indicates one or more persons who authorized the message
Expiry date indication	Conveys a date and time after which the originator considers the message invalid
Cross-referencing indication	Specifies one or more other messages related to this one
Importance indication	Specifies low, normal, or high
Obsoleting indication	Specifies previous messages that are obsolete and superseded by this one
Sensitivity indication	Specifies personal, private, or company-confidential
Reply request indication	Asks for response; may also specify date and time and other recipients
Forwarded IP-message indication	Marks a message as containing a forwarded message
Body part encryption indication	Body part of message is encrypted
Multi-part body	Enables sending message with multiple parts, each with its own attributes

Additional Optional Services
(for both orignation and reception)

Nonreceipt notification	Requests that originator be informed if message is not received by its intended recipient
Receipt notification	Requests that originator be notified of receipt of message by intended recipient

are not required to allow a user to mark a message as private, but must be able to appropriately handle a received message marked private. There are many services at this sublayer. Among the most fundamental are specification of primary and secondary recipients and the subject of the message. Other services have to do with how to handle the message and instructions for notification.

17-4

RECOMMENDED READING

A readable discussion of X.3/X.28/X.29 is contained in [MART81]. A lengthy and quite good discussion of terminal handling and virtual terminal protocols is contained in [DAVI79]. The ISO virtual terminal service is discussed in [KNOW87]. For analyses of issues relating to file transfer protocols, see [DAY81] and [NBS80b]. A discussion of the ISO FTAM standard can be found in [LINI89]; it is also well-treated in [KNOW87] and [HENS88]. [HENS88] also provide a good discussion of the 1988 X.400 standards; a somewhat briefer presentation is in [CHIL90]. [MANR89] explains the rather substantial differences between the 1984 and 1988 versions of X.400.

A discussion of the structure of the application layer is found in [STAL90c]. A description of the application-layer protocols of the TCP/IP protocol suite is contained in [STAL90e].

17-5

PROBLEMS

17-1   To which layer of the OSI model would you assign the X.3, X.28, and X.29 standards? Justify your answer in each case.

17-2   Describe how a protocol converter in a digital PBX architecture can be used to implement a virtual terminal protocol.

17-3   What problem may be caused by the fact that a PAD buffers characters from a terminal, rather than sending them immediately? How does X.3 solve these problems?

17-4   User A requests a third-party file transfer between *B* and *C*. What logical connections (e.g., *A-B, B-C, C-A*) are necessary for this transfer?

17-5   There are two file transfer protocols in use on ARPANET: the file transfer protocol (FTP) and the trivial file transfer protocol (TFTP). The former makes use of TELNET, which makes use of TCP. The latter simply makes use of the user datagram protocol (UDP). What features would you expect to be lacking in TFTP?

17-6   Draw a time sequence diagram of FTAM primitives showing the sequence of events in a successful file transfer.

17-7   Indicate how PDUs can be used to implement the FTAM service primitives.

17-8   It is clear from Figure 17-11 that there is not an end-to-end transport connection between the originator and recipient of a message. Why not?

17-9   Protocol P1 provides that a message envelope and its contents be transmitted from one MTAE to another. The standard specifies that the message envelope and the message content be transmitted as a single P1 PDU. Several other mechanisms are possible. The sending MTAE could transmit the message envelope first, wait for approval from the second MTAE, and then transmit the message content. A third method is to transmit the message envelope first, one parameter at a time, waiting for a positive acknowledgment after each parameter. For example, the recipient list might be transmitted first, then handling instructions, and so on. Discuss the relative advantages and disadvantages of each method.

17-10   Electronic mail systems differ in the manner in which multiple recipients are handled. In some systems, the originating UA or MTA makes all the necessary copies and these are sent out independently. An alternative approach is to determine the route for each destination first. Then a single message is sent out on a common portion of the route and copies are only made when the routes diverge; this process is referred to as mail-bagging. Discuss the relative advantages and disadvantages of the two methods.

APPENDIX 17A

APPLICATION LAYER STRUCTURE

As the top layer of the OSI model, the application layer exhibits some differences from the other layers. Specifically, the application layer does not provide services to a higher layer. Accordingly, there is no concept of an application service access point (SAP). The application layer does provide services, but these services are provided to application processes that are outside the seven-layer architecture. The OSI model defines an application process as "an element within an open system which performs the information processing for a particular application." The following examples of application processes are provided:

- A person operating a banking terminal is a manual application process.
- A FORTRAN program executing in a computer center and accessing a remote data base is a computerized application process; the remote database management systems server is also an application process.
- A process control program executing in a dedicated computer attached to some industrial equipment and linked into a plant control system is a physical application process.

Application processes in different open systems that wish to exchange information do so by accessing the application layer. The application layer contains application entities that employ application protocols and presentation services to exchange information. It is these application entities that provide the means for application processes to access the OSI environment. We can think of the application entities as providing useful services that are relevant to one or more application processes.

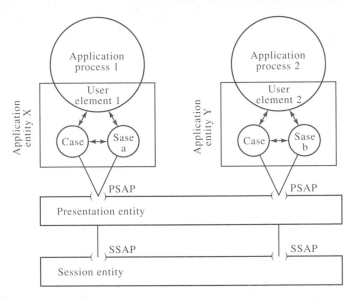

FIGURE 17-18. Upper layer architecture.

The defining OSI document suggests a grouping of functions that clarifies the task of the application layer and also serves as a guide to standardization efforts. This grouping is illustrated in Figure 17-18, and consists of three types of elements:

- User elements: That part of an application process specifically concerned with accessing OSI services. It does this by interfacing with application service elements, which are identifiable collections of functions that provide OSI services.
- Common application service elements (CASE): Provide capabilities that are generally useful to a variety of applications.
- Specific application service elements (SASE): Provide capabilities required to satisfy the particular needs of specific applications.

Several examples of both types of application service elements are listed in Table 17-12.

It should be emphasized that the common and specific application service elements do not form sublayers of the application layer. The application service elements are peer entities and provide a sets of functions that can be assembled to meet the requirements of a particular application.

Each application process is represented to its peer and exchanges data with that peer by means of an application entity. An application entity consists of one user element and a set of application service elements needed to support the particular application. Thus, application service elements are combined in different ways to support different applications. In the application, the user must implement a user element that knows how to access the services of those service elements required for the exchange.

Within an application entity, application service elements may call on each other and on presentation services. The user element does not directly deal with the presentation layer, but may only invoke services of the application service elements within the entity. Each application entity is unambiguously identified by means of a presentation service access point (PSAP), which is, in turn, mapped one-to-one onto a session service access point (SSAP).

If two application entities wish to communicate in a connection-oriented manner, an application connection, referred to as an association, must be established. This association is mapped one-to-one onto a presentation connection. The association is used to exchange protocol information between application service elements in the two application entities. Thus, there may be more than one protocol using the single association (application connection).

PART IV

ISDN

Perhaps the most important development in the computer-communication industry over the next decade will be the evolution of the integrated services digital network (ISDN). The ISDN will have a dramatic effect on communications providers, component manufacturers, and both personal and business users. Although the technology of and standards for ISDN are still evolving, a clear picture of the architecture, design approaches, and services of the ISDN is emerging. A discussion of ISDN ties together many of the concepts used throughout the book and is an appropriate culmination to our study of data and computer communications.

CHAPTER 18

Integrated Services
Digital Network

We have but one more topic to address in this book, and that topic represents in some sense a culmination of all the technologies and techniques that we have explored. The *integrated services digital network* (ISDN) is a projected worldwide public telecommunications network that will service a wide variety of user needs. The ISDN will be defined by the standardization of user interfaces, and will be implemented as a set of digital switches and paths supporting a broad range of traffic types and employing many of the concepts already discussed in this book. Actually, there will be multiple ISDNs, implemented within national boundaries, but from the user's point of view, there will be a single worldwide service.

A number of small-scale ISDN facilities have been developed, but the promised extension of ISDN to encompass worldwide public telecommunications is some years off. Meanwhile, the characteristics of ISDN are defined by an evolving set of standard (being developed on a truly massive scale, both in terms of content and participants. Thus, this chapter provides only a preview of the evolving ISDN.

The chapter begins by looking at a concept that serves as the foundation for ISDN: the integrated digital network (IDN). Next, we provide an overview of ISDN by viewing it from several perspectives. The next two sections concentrate on the two areas that have received the most attention, both technically and in terms of standards; these are the transmission structure and user access to ISDN. This is followed by a discussion of the protocols that have been defined to support user access.

Following this survey of ISDN, two topics remain to be examined. Signaling system number 7 (SS7) is a common-channel signaling scheme designed with ISDN in mind. Finally, the chapter looks at the next, fast approaching, generation of ISDN, known as broadband ISDN.

TABLE 18-1   Use of Digital Technology in Public Telecommunications Networks

Switching
  The circuit-switching nodes of the network make use of digital time-division switching techniques rather than analog space-division switching techniques.

Trunk (Carrier) Transmission
  Digital transmission technology is used on the multiplexed trunks between switches, although either analog or digital signaling may be used. Each trunk carries multiple voice and/or data channels using synchronous time-division multiplexing.

Subscriber Loop
  Digital transmission technology may also be used between the subscriber and the switch to which the subscriber attaches over the "subscriber loop." This implies that digitized voice is employed and that full-duplex digital transmission over the subscriber loop is used.

Control Signaling
  Common channel signaling over a packet-switched network embedded into the public telecommunications network is used. Packets contain messages used for routing, monitoring, and control.

18-1

THE INTEGRATED DIGITAL NETWORK

Public telephone and telecommunications networks are rapidly evolving to the exclusive use of digital technology. The ways in which these networks employ digital technology are listed in Table 18-1. The movement toward digital technology has been "pushed" by the competitive desire to lower cost and improve quality of voice transmission and networking services. As the use of distributed processing and data communications has grown, this evolution of an all-digital network has been "pulled" by the need to provide a framework for ISDN.

The evolution of the existing telecommunications networks and specialized carrier facilities to integrated digital networks is based on two technological developments: digital switching and digital transmission. Both of these developments are, of course, well established. The first T-carrier system was introduced into commercial service by AT&T in 1962, and the first large-scale time-division digital switch, the Western Electric 4ESS, was introduced in 1976. More important than the benefits of either of these two technologies however, was the revolutionary idea that the functions of transmission and switching could be integrated to form an *integrated digital network* (IDN). The idea was proposed as early as 1959 [VAUG59] and is in the process of being implemented worldwide [DORR83, COOK84].

To understand the implications of an IDN, consider Figure 18-1. Traditionally, the transmission and switching systems of a telephone network have been designed and administered by functionally separate organizations. The two systems are referred to by the operating telephone companies as outside plant and inside plant, respectively. In the analog network, incoming voice lines are modulated and multiplexed at the end office and sent out over an FDM line. As you know, the constituent signals may pass through one or more intermediate switching centers before reaching the destination end office (Figure 8-24). At each switching center,

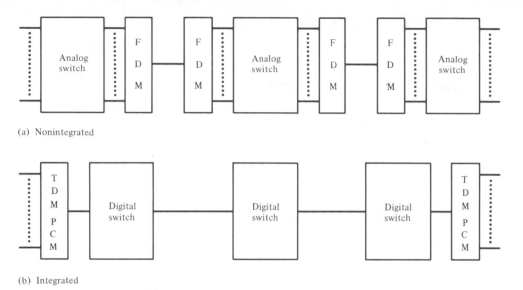

(a) Nonintegrated

(b) Integrated

FIGURE 18-1. The integration of transmission and switching.

the incoming FDM carrier has to be demultiplexed and demodulated by an FDM channel bank before being switched by a space-division switch. After switching, the signals have to be multiplexed and modulated again to be transmitted. This repeated process results in an accumulation of noise, as well as cost.

When both the transmission and switching systems are digital, integration as in Figure 18-1b can be achieved. Incoming voice signals are digitized using PCM and multiplexed using TDM. Time-division digital switches along the way can switch the individual signals without decoding them. Furthermore, separate multiplex/demultiplex channel banks are not needed at the intermediate offices, since that function is incorporated into the switching system.

Figure 18-2 gives a simple example that suggests the architectures that are involved in the analog and digital switching approaches. Consider an intermediate switch in a circuit-switched network that has six voice channels (labeled A, B, C, D, E, F) of data coming in on one trunk (Figure 18-2a). Based on the calls that are currently established, three of the channels are to be switched out on one trunk (A, B, E) and three channels on another trunk (C, D, F). All three trunks link to other switches, and all three trunks are multiplexed to carry multiple channels of data. In the case of a digital system (Figure 18-2b), the voice signals are digitized and transmitted as a stream of bits. On a multiplexed trunk, bits from various voice signals are interleaved using time-division multiplexing (TDM). Thus, the incoming trunk has bits from six different voice channels interleaved in time. Inside the digital switch, a technique such as TDM bus switching, discussed in Chapter 8, is employed to extract the slots of data from the incoming stream and route them to the appropriate outgoing stream.

The architecture for the equivalent analog system is considerably more complex (Figure 18-2c). Each voice signal occupies a frequency band of about 4 kHz. The incoming trunk requires a bandwidth of at least 24 kHz, and each voice signal occupies one channel centered on a unique frequency (f_1 for channel A, f_2 for channel B, etc.). These channels must be fed into a space-division analog switch.

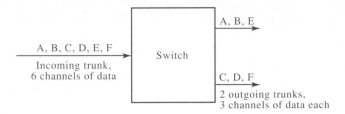

(a) General block diagram

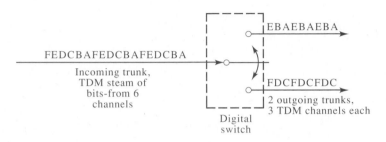

(b) Digital time division switch

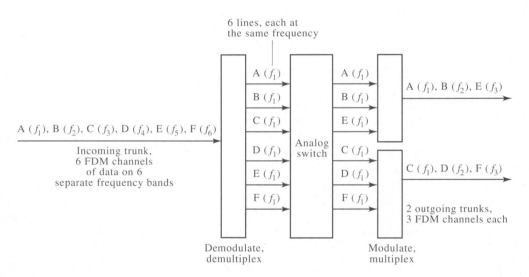

(c) Analog space-division switch

FIGURE 18-2.   Example of digital versus analog switching.

However, such a switch is only capable of switching signals from a collection of input lines to a collection of output lines. For general operation, any input line must be connectable to any output line; therefore, all inputs and outputs must be at the same frequency. Thus, the frequency-division multiplexed (FDM) input must be demultiplexed, and each signal must be returned to the base voice frequency (f_1) to provide input to the switch. The switch routes the incoming data to the appropriate output lines, with each output line dedicated to a particular output trunk.

For each trunk, the associated lines must pass through a modulator/multiplexer to produce an FDM signal for transmission over the outgoing trunk.

The conversion of telecommunications networks to digital transmission and digital switching is well under way. Much less well developed is the extension of digital service to the end user. Telephones are still sending analog data to the end office where they must be digitized. Lower-speed (<56 kbps) end-user digital service is commonly available via leased lines at present, and higher speed leased services are being introduced [HOLM83]. The provision of switched digital service over the local loop [KELC83], [HARR86], [ERIK86] will eventually lead to an end-to-end switched digital telecommunications network.

This evolution has been driven by the need to provide economic voice communications. The resulting network, however, is also well suited to meet the growing variety of digital data service needs. Thus the IDN will combine the coverage of the geographically extensive telephone network with the data carrying capacity of digital data networks in a structure called the *integrated services digital network* (ISDN). In this latter context, the ''integrated'' of ISDN refers to the simultaneous carrying of digitized voice and a variety of data traffic on the same digital transmission links and by the same digital exchanges. The key to ISDN is the small marginal cost for offering data services on the digital telephone network, with no cost or performance penalty for voice services already carried on the IDN.

18-2

OVERVIEW OF ISDN

ISDN Concept

The concept of ISDN is best introduced by considering it from several different viewpoints:

- Principles of ISDN
- Evolution of ISDN
- The user interface
- Objectives
- Benefits
- Services

Principles of ISDN. Standards for ISDN are being defined by CCITT, a topic that we explore later in this section. Table 18-2, which is the complete text one of the ISDN-related standards, states the principles of ISDN from the point of view of CCITT. Let us look at each of these points in turn.

1. *Support of voice and nonvoice applications using a limited set of standardized facilities*. This principle defines both the purpose of ISDN and the means of achieving it. The ISDN will support a variety of services related to voice communications (telephone calls) and nonvoice communications (digital data exchange). These services are to be provided in conformance with standards (CCITT recommendations) that specify a small number of interfaces and data transmission facilities.

TABLE 18-2   CCITT Recommendation I.120 (1988)

1 Principles of ISDN

1.1   The main feature of the ISDN concept is the support of a wide range of voice and non-voice applications in the same network. A key element of service integration for an ISDN is the provision of a range of services (see Part II of the I-Series in this Fascicle) using a limited set of connection types and multipurpose user-network interface arrangements (see Parts III and IV of the I-Series in Fascicle III.8).

1.2   ISDNs support a variety of applications including both switched and non-switched connections. Switched connections in an ISDN include both circuit-switched and packet-switched connections and their concatenations.

1.3   As far as practicable, new services introduced into an ISDN should be arranged to be compatible with 64 kbit/s switched digital connections.

1.4   An ISDN will contain intelligence for the purpose of providing service features, maintenance and network management functions. This intelligence may not be sufficient for some new services and may have to be supplemented by either additional intelligence within the network, or possibly compatible intelligence in the user terminals.

1.5   A layered protocol structure should be used for the specification of the access to an ISDN. Access from a user to ISDN resources may vary depending upon the service required and upon the status of implementation of national ISDNs.

1.6   It is recognized that ISDNs may be implemented in a variety of configurations according to specific national situations.

2 Evolution of ISDNs

2.1   ISDNs will be based on the concepts for telephone IDNs and may evolve by progressively incorporating additional functions and network features including those of any other dedicated networks such as circuit-switching and packet-switching for data so as to provide for existing and new services.

2.2   The transition from an existing network to a comprehensive ISDN may require a period of time extending over one or more decades. During this period arrangements must be developed for the networking of services on ISDNs and services on other networks (see Part V).

2.3   In the evolution towards an ISDN, digital end-to-end connectivity will be obtained via plant and equipment used in existing networks, such as digital transmission; time-division multiplex switching and/or space-division multiplex switching. Existing relevant recommendations for these constituent elements of an ISDN are contained in the appropriate series of recommendations of CCITT and of CCIR.

2.4   In the early stages of the evolution of ISDNs, some interim user-network arrangements may need to be adopted in certain countries to facilitate early penetration of digital service capabilities. Arrangements corresponding to national variants may comply partly or wholly with I-Series Recommendations. However, the intention is that they not be specifically included in the I-Series.

2.5   An evolving ISDN may also include at later stages switched connections at bit rates higher and lower than 64 kbit/s.

2. *Support for switched and nonswitched applications.* ISDN will support both circuit switching and packet switching. In addition, ISDN will support nonswitched services in the form of dedicated lines.

3. *Reliance on 64-kbps connections.* ISDN is intended to provide circuit-switched and packet-switched connections at 64 kbps. This is the fundamental building block of ISDN. This rate was chosen because, at the time, it was the standard rate for digitized voice, and hence was being introduced into the

evolving IDNs. Although this data rate is useful, it is unfortunately restrictive to rely solely on it. Future developments in ISDN will permit greater flexibility.

4. *Intelligence in the network.* An ISDN is expected to be able to provide sophisticated services beyond the simple setup of a circuit-switched call.

5. *Layered protocol architecture.* The protocols being developed for user access to ISDN exhibit a layered architecture and can be mapped into the OSI model. This has a number of advantages:

   • Standards already developed for OSI-related applications may be used on ISDN. An example is X.25 level 3 for access to packet-switching services in ISDN.

   • New ISDN-related standards can be based on existing standards, reducing the cost of new implementations. An example is LAP-D, which is based on LAP-B.

   • Standards can be developed and implemented independently for various layers and for various functions within a layer. This allows for the gradual implementation of ISDN services at a pace appropriate for a given provider or a given customer base.

6. *Variety of configurations.* More than one physical configuration is possible for implementing ISDN. This allows for differences in national policy (single-source versus competition), in the state of technology, and in the needs and existing equipment of the customer base.

Evolution of ISDN.   As we discussed earlier, ISDN evolves from and with the integrated digital network (IDN). The evolution of the IDN has been driven by the need to provide economic voice communications. The resulting network, however, is also well suited to meet the growing variety of digital data service needs. Whereas the ''I'' in IDN refers to the integration of digital transmission and switching facilities, the ''I'' in ISDN refers to the integration of a variety of voice and data transmission services.

Table 18-2 gives the CCITT view of the way in which ISDN will evolve. Let us look at each of these points in turn.

1. *Evolution from telephone IDNs.* The intent is that the ISDN evolve from the existing telephone networks. Two conclusions can be drawn from this point. First, the IDN technology developed for and evolving within existing telephone networks forms the foundation for the services to be provided by ISDN. Second, although other facilities, such as third-party (not the telephone provider) packet-switched networks and satellite links, will play a role in ISDN, the telephone networks will have the dominant role. Although packet switching and satellite providers may be less than happy with this interpretation, the overwhelming prevalence of telephone networks dictates that these networks form the basis of ISDN.

2. *Transition of one or more decades.* The evolution to ISDN will be a slow process. This is true of any migration of a complex application or set of applications from one technical base to a newer one. The introduction of ISDN services will be done in the context of existing digital facilities and existing services. There will be a period of coexistence in which connections and perhaps protocol conversion will be needed between alternative facilities and/or services.

3. *Use of existing networks.* This point is simply an elaboration of point 2. For example, ISDN will provide a packet-switched service. For the time being, the interface to that service will be X.25. With the introduction of fast packet switching (see discussion of broadband ISDN later in this chapter) and more sophisticated virtual call control, there may need to be a new interface in the future.

4. *Interim user-network arrangements.* Primarily, the concern here is that the lack of digital subscriber loops might delay introduction of digital services, particularly in developing countries. With the use of modems and other equipment, existing analog facilities can support at least some ISDN services.

5. *Connections at other than 64 kbps.* The 64-kbps data rate was chosen as the basic channel for circuit switching. With improvements in voice digitizing technology, this rate is unnecessarily high. On the other hand, this rate is too low for many digital data applications. Thus, other data rates will be needed.

The details of the evolution of ISDN facilities and services will vary from one nation to another, and indeed from one provider to another in the same country. These points simply provide a general description, from CCITT's point of view, of the process.

The User Interface. Figure 18-3 is a conceptual view of the ISDN from a user or customer point of view. The user has access to the ISDN by means of a local interface to a "digital pipe" of a certain bit rate. Pipes of various sizes will be available to satisfy differing needs. For example, a residential customer may require only sufficient capacity to handle a telephone and a videotex terminal. An office will undoubtedly wish to connect to the ISDN via an on-premise digital PBX, and will require a much higher capacity pipe.

At any given point in time, the pipe to the user's premises has a fixed capacity, but the traffic on the pipe may be a variable mix up to the capacity limit. Thus a

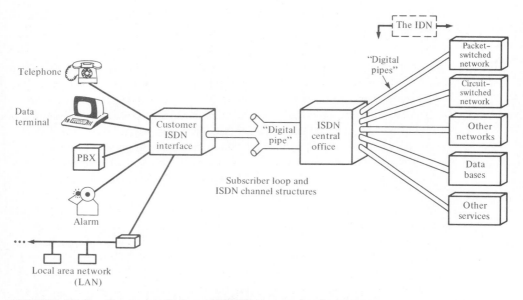

FIGURE 18-3. **Conceptual view of ISDN connection features.**

user may access circuit-switched and packet-switched services, as well as other services, in a dynamic mix of signal types and bit rates. To provide these services, the ISDN will require rather complex control signals to instruct it how to sort out the time-multiplexed data and provide the required services. These control signals will also be multiplexed onto the same digital pipe.

An important aspect of the interface is that the user may, at any time, employ less than the maximum capacity of the pipe, and will be charged according to the capacity used rather than ''connect time.'' This characteristic significantly diminishes the value of current user design efforts that are geared to optimize circuit utilization by use of concentrators, multiplexers, packet switches, and other line sharing arrangements.

Objectives. Activities currently under way are leading to the development of a worldwide ISDN. This effort involves national governments, data processing and communications companies, standards organizations, and others. Certain common objectives are, by and large, shared by this disparate group. We list here the key objectives:

- *Standardization:* It is essential that a single set of ISDN standards be provided to permit universal access and to permit the development of cost-effective equipment.
- *Transparency:* The most important service to be provided is a transparent transmission service. This permits users to develop applications and protocols with the confidence that they will not be affected by the underlying ISDN.
- *Separation of competitive functions:* It must be possible to separate out functions that could be provided competitively as opposed to those that are fundamentally part of the ISDN. In most countries, a single, government-owned entity will provide all services. Some countries desire (in the case of the United States, require) that certain enhanced services be offered competitively (e.g., videotex, electronic mail). Figures 18-4 and 18-5 depict these alternative views.
- *Leased and switched services:* The ISDN should provide dedicated point-to-point services as well as switched services. This will allow the user to optimize his or her implementation of switching and routing techniques.
- *Cost-related tariffs:* The price for ISDN service should be related to cost, and independent of the type of data being carried. One type of service should not be in the position of subsidizing others.
- *Smooth migration:* The conversion to ISDN will be gradual, and the evolving network must coexist with existing equipment and services. Thus ISDN interfaces should evolve from current interfaces, and provide a migration path for users.
- *Multiplexed support:* In addition to providing low-capacity support to individual users, multiplexed support must be provided to accommodate user-owned PBX and local network equipment.

There are, of course, other objectives that could be named. Those listed above are certainly among the most important and widely accepted, and help to define the character of the ISDN.

Benefits. The principal benefits to the user can be expressed in terms of cost savings and flexibility. The integration of voice and a variety of data on a single

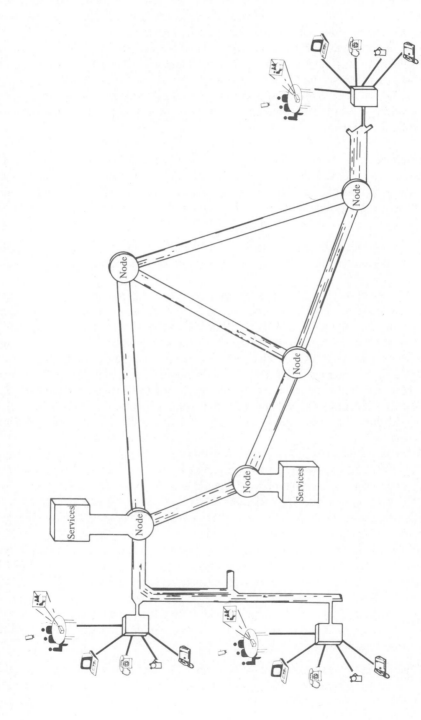

FIGURE 18-4. ISDN in a noncompetitive environment.

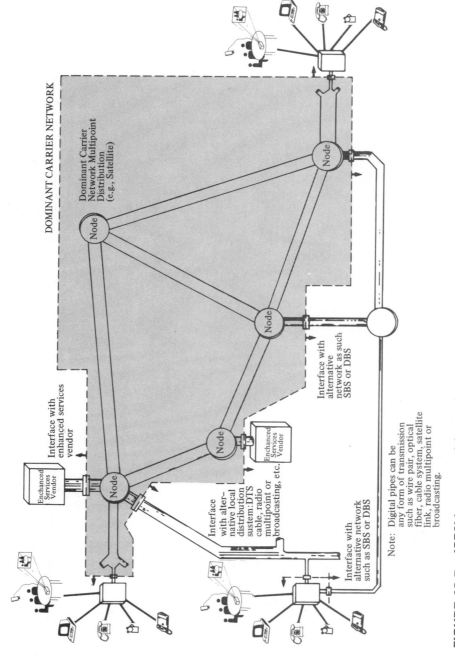

FIGURE 18-5. ISDN in a competitive environment.

DOMINANT CARRIER NETWORK

Dominant Carrier
Network Multipoint
Distribution
(e.g., Satellite)

Interface with enhanced services
vendor

Enchanced
Services
Vendor

Interface
with alter-
native local
distribution
sustem: DTS
cable, radio
multipoint or
broadcasting, etc.

Interface with
alternative network
such as SBS or DBS

Enchanced
Services
Vendor

Interface with
alternative
network as such
SBS or DBS

Note: Digital pipes can be
any form of transmission
such as wire pair, optical
fiber, cable system, satellite
link, radio multipoint or
broadcasting.

707

transport system means that the user does not have to buy multiple services to meet multiple needs. The efficiencies and economies of scale of an integrated network allows these services to be offered at lower cost than if they were provided separately. Further, the user needs to bear the expense of just a single access line to these multiple services.

The requirements of various users can differ greatly in a number of ways: for example, information volume, traffic pattern, response time, and interface types. The ISDN will allow the user to tailor the service purchased to actual needs to a degree not possible at present.

Services.   The ISDN will provide a variety of services, supporting existing voice and data applications as well as providing for applications now being developed. The most important in the latter category are:

- *Facsimile:* service for the transmission and reproduction of graphics, handwritten, and printed material. This type of service has been available for many years, but has suffered from a lack of standardization and the limitations of the analog telephone network. Digital facsimile standards (CCITT Group 3) are now available and can be used to transmit a page of data at 64 kbps in 5 s.
- *Teletex:* service that enables subscriber terminals to exchange correspondence. Communicating terminals are used to prepare, edit, transmit, and print messages. Transmission is at a rate of one page in 2 s at 9.6 kbps.
- *Videotex:* An interactive information retrieval service. A page of data can be transmitted in one second at 9.6 kbps.

Table 18-3 shows the type of services that could be supported by ISDN. These services fall into the broad categories of voice, digital data, text, and image. Most of these services can be provided with a transmission capacity of 64 kbps or less. This rate, as we shall see, will be the standard ISDN rate offered to the user. Some services require considerably higher data rates and may be provided by high speed facilities outside the ISDN (e.g., cable TV distribution plants). However, these higher-speed services may intersect with the ISDN and make use of high-capacity ISDN links for part of a transmission path.

One of the key aspects of the ISDN will be that it is an "intelligent network." By use of a flexible signaling protocol, the ISDN will provide a variety of network facilities for each service. Table 18-4 gives some examples of planned facilities.

Architecture

Figure 18-6 is a block diagram of the ISDN. The ISDN will support a completely new physical connecter for users, a digital subscriber loop (link from end user to central or end office), and modifications to all central office equipment.

The area to which most attention has been paid by standards organizations is that of user access. A *common physical interface* will be defined to provide, in essence, a DTE-DCE connection. The same interface should be usable for telephone, computer terminal, and videotex terminal. Protocols are needed for the exchange of control information between user device and the network. Provision must be made for high-speed interfaces to, for example, a digital PBX or a LAN.

TABLE 18-3 Candidate Services for Integration

Bandwidth	Service			
	Telephony	Data	Text	Image
Digital voice (64 kbps)	Telephone	Packet-switched data Circuit-switched data	Telex Teletex	
	Leased circuits Information retrieval (by voice analysis and synthesis)	Leased circuits Telemetry Funds transfer	Leased circuits Videotex	Facsimile
		Information retrieval Mailbox Electronic mail Alarms	Information retrieval Mailbox Electronic mail	Information retrieval Surveillance
Wide band (>64 kbps)	Music	High-speed computer communication		TV conferencing Teletext Videophone Cable TV distribution

TABLE 18-4 Basic and Additional Facilities for ISDN Services

Telephony	Data	Teletex	Videotex	Facsimile
		Basic		
National toll access	Automatic dialed call	Incoming call not disturbing local mode	Information retrieval by dialogue with a database	Automatic dialed call
International toll access	Manual dialed call	Message printed on operator demand		Manual dialed call
Malicious call blocking	Automatic answer	Message presentation as in the original		Automatic answer
		Day and hour automatic indication		
		Additional		
Transfer call	Direct call	Delayed messages	Transactions (e.g. reservation, shopping)	Delayed delivery
Abbreviated dialing	Closed user group	Abbreviated address		Multiple destination
Rerouting to verbal announcements	Closed user group with outgoing access	Multiple address		
Intermediate call	Calling line identification	Charging indication	Message box service between users	Code, speed, and format conversion for different terminals
Conference call	Called line identification	Telex access		
Camp-on busy	Abbreviated address calling	Graphic mode	Loading of software from a data base to a terminal	
Barring outgoing toll traffic	Barred incoming call			
	Multiaddress calling		Loading of special character set	
Hot line	Detailed billing			
Detailed billing	Transfer call			
Automatic wake-up	Call charging indication			

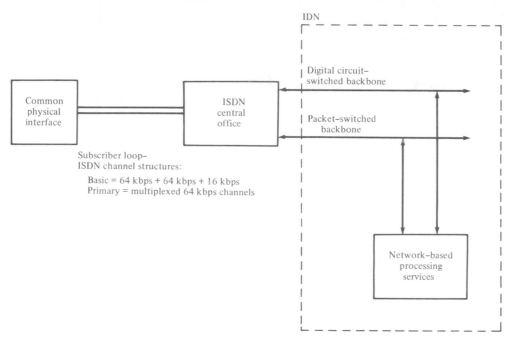

IDN

Common physical interface

ISDN central office

Digital circuit–switched backbone

Packet–switched backbone

Network–based processing services

Subscriber loop–
ISDN channel structures:

Basic = 64 kbps + 64 kbps + 16 kbps
Primary = multiplexed 64 kbps channels

FIGURE 18-6. **Block diagram of ISDN functions.**

The subscriber loop portion of today's telephone network consists of twisted pair links between the subscriber and the central office, carrying 4-kHz analog signals. Under the ISDN, one or two twisted pairs will be used to provide a basic full-duplex digital communications link.

The digital central office will connect the numerous ISDN subscriber loop signals to the IDN. In addition to providing access to the circuit-switched network, the central office will provide subscriber access to dedicated lines, packet-switched networks, and time-shared transaction-oriented computer services. Multiplexed access via digital PBX and LAN must also be accommodated.

Standards

Although a number of standards organizations are involved in various aspects of ISDN, the controlling body is the International Telegraph and Telephone Consultative Committee (CCITT). The development of ISDN is governed by a set of recommendations issued by CCITT, called the I-series of recommendations. These recommendations, or standards, were first issued in 1984. A more complete set was issued in 1988.

It is enlightening to look at the history of CCITT's interest in ISDN. In 1968, CCITT established Special Study Group D (forerunner of today's Study Group XVIII, which has ISDN responsibility within CCITT) to look at a variety of issues related to the use of digital technology in the telephone network. At each Plenary Assembly, the study group was given assignments for the next four-year study period. The first and principal question assigned over this period is shown in Table 18-5. The titles of the first question reflect the evolution of CCITT interest. The focus shifts from digital technology to integrated digital networks (IDN) to ISDN.

TABLE 18-5   Question 1 as Assigned to Special Study Group D (1969–1976) and to Study Group XVIII (1977–1992)

Study Period	Title of Question 1
1969–1972	Planning of digital systems
1973–1976	Planning of digital systems and integration of services
1977–1980	Overall aspects of integrated digital network and integration of services
1981–1984	General network aspects of an integrated services digital network (ISDN)
1985–1988	General question on ISDN
1989–1992	General aspects of ISDN

In 1968, Study Group D was set up to study all questions related to the standardization of transmission of pulse-code-modulated (PCM) voice and to coordinate work going on in other groups relating to digital networking. Even at this early stage, there was a vision of an ISDN. Recommendation G.702, issued in 1972, contained the following definition of an integrated services digital network:

> An integrated digital network in which the same digital switches and digital paths are used to establish for different services, for example, telephony, data.

At this point, there was no information on the type of network that could integrate digital switches and paths, nor how the network could integrate various services. Nevertheless, it was a recognition of the path that could be followed with digital technology.

During the next study period (1973–1976), there were continuing advances in digital transmission technology. In addition, digital switching equipment began to emerge from the laboratory. Thus the construction of integrated digital networks became a real possibility. Accordingly, the 1976 set of recommendations included specifications dealing with digital switching as well as the specification of a new control signaling scheme designed for use in the forthcoming digital networks. The first question for this period also specifically deals with the integration of services.

In planning for the 1977–1980 study period, CCITT recognized that the evolution toward a digital network was under way and was more important than the standardization of individual digital systems and equipment. Thus the focus was on the integration aspects of the digital network and on the integration of services on an IDN. Two key developments that emerged during this study period were:

- The integration of services is based on providing a standardized user-network interface that allows the user to request various services through a uniform set of protocols.
- ISDN will evolve from the digital telephone network.

At the end of this period, the first ISDN standard emerged, entitled Integrated Services Digital Network (ISDN), which was just a general statement of principles and objectives. No other standards on ISDN were issued in 1980; at this point, only the general concept of an ISDN had been developed.

As the next period began (1981–1984), ISDN was declared the major concern of CCITT for the upcoming study period. A set of recommendations was published in 1984. This initial set of specifications was incomplete and, in some cases, internally inconsistent. Nevertheless, the specification of ISDN by 1984 was sufficient for manufacturers and service providers to begin to develop ISDN-related equipment and to demonstrate ISDN-related services and networking configurations. The 1984 series included this definition of ISDN, retained in the 1988 documents:

> An ISDN is a network, in general evolving from a telephony IDN, that provides end-to-end digital connectivity to support a wide range of services, including voice and non-voice services, to which users have access by a limited set of standard multi-purpose user-network interfaces.

Work on the I-series and related recommendations continued in the 1985–1988 period. At the beginning of this period, CCITT was significantly restructured to give a number of its study groups a part of future ISDN work. The dominant function of CCITT became the study of ISDN matters. The 1988 version of the I-series recommendations were sufficiently detailed to make preliminary ISDN implementations possible in the late 1980s.

Table 18-6 lists the 1988 I-series recommendations, indicating which were new in 1988 and which were revisions of 1984 documents. The 1984 standards contained recommendations in series I.100 through I.400. Some updates and expansions occurred in this series in the 1984-1988 period. The I.500 and I.600 series were left for further study in 1984, and some preliminary work was ready for 1988.

TABLE 18-6   The 1988 CCITT ISDN Recommendations

		New/Revision
Part I—General Structure		
I.110	Preamble and General Structure of the I-Series Recommendations	R
I.111	Relationship with Other Recommendations Relevant to ISDNs	R
I.112	Vocabulary of Terms for ISDNs	R
I.113	Vocabulary of terms for Broadband Aspects of ISDN	N
I.120	Integrated Services Digital Networks	R
I.121	Broadband Aspects of ISDN	N
I.122	Framework for Providing Additional Packet Mode Bearer Services	N
I.130	The Method for the Characterization of Telecommunication Services Supported by an ISDN and Network Capabilities of an ISDN	R
I.140	Attribute Technique for the Characterization of Telecommunication Services Supported by an ISDN and Network Capabilities of an ISDN	N
I.141	ISDN Network Charging Capabilities Attributes	N
Part II—Service Capabilities		
I.200	Guidance to the I.200 Series	N
I.210	Principles of Telecommunication Services Supported by an ISDN and the Means to Describe Them	R
I.220	Common Dynamic Description of Basic Telecommunication Services	N
I.221	Common Specific Characteristics of Services	N
I.230	Definition of Bearer Service Categories	N
I.231	Circuit Mode Bearer Service Categories	N

TABLE 18-6   The 1988 CCITT ISDN Recommendations (*Continued*)

		New/Revision
Part II—Service Capabilities		
I.232	Packet Mode Bearer Services Categories	N
I.240	Definition of Teleservices	N
I.241	Teleservices Supported by an ISDN	N
I.250	Definition of Supplementary Services	N
I.251	Number Identification Supplementary Services	N
I.252	Call Offering Supplementary Services	N
I.253	Call Completion Supplementary Services	N
I.254	Multiparty Supplementary Services	N
I.255	Community of Interest Supplementary Services	N
I.256	Charging Supplementary Services	N
I.257	Additional Information Transfer	N
Part III—Overall Network Aspects and Functions		
I.310	ISDN-Network Functional Principles	R
I.320	ISDN Protocol Reference Model	R
I.324	ISDN Network Architecture	N
I.325	Reference Configurations for ISDN Connection Types	N
I.326	Reference Configuration for Relative Network Resource Requirements	N
I.330	ISDN Numbering and Addressing Principles	R
I.331	Numbering Plan for the ISDN Era	R
I.332	Numbering Principles for Interworking Between ISDNs and Dedicated Networks with Different Numbering Plans	N
I.333	Terminal Selection in ISDN	N
I.334	Principles Relating ISDN Numbers/Subaddresses to the OSI Reference Model Network Layer Addresses	N
I.335	ISDN Routing Principles	N
I.340	ISDN Connection Types	R
I.350	General Aspects of Quality of Service and Network Performance in Digital Networks, Including ISDN	N
I.351	Recommendations in Other Series, Including Network Performance Objectives that Apply at Reference Point T of an ISDN	N
I.352	Network Performance Objectives for Connection Processing Delays in an ISDN	R
Part IV—ISDN User-Network Interfaces		
I.410	General Aspects and Principles Relating to Recommendations on ISDN User-Network Interfaces	R
I.411	ISDN User-Network Interfaces—Reference Configurations	R
I.412	ISDN User-Network Interfaces—Interface Structures and Access Capabilities	R
I.420	Basic User-Network Interface	R
I.421	Primary Rate User-Network Interface	R
I.430	Basic User-Network Interface—Layer 1 Specification	R
I.431	Primary Rate User-Network Interface—Layer 1 Specification	R
I.440	ISDN User-Network Interface Data Link Layer—General Aspects	R

TABLE 18-6   The 1988 CCITT ISDN Recommendations (*Continued*)

		New/Revision
Part IV—ISDN User-Network Interfaces		
I.441	ISDN User-Network Interface, Data Link Layer Specification	R
I.450	ISDN User-Network Interface Layer 3—General Aspects	R
I.451	ISDN User-Network Interface Layer 3 Specification for Basic Call Control	R
I.452	Generic Procedures for the Control of ISDN Supplementary Services	N
I.460	Multiplexing, Rate Adaptation, and Support of Existing Interfaces	R
I.461	Support of X.21, X.21 bis and X.20 is Based DTEs by an ISDN	R
I.462	Support of Packet Mode Terminal Equipment by an ISDN	R
I.463	Support of DTEs with V-Series Type Interfaces by an ISDN	R
I.464	Multiplexing, Rate Adaptation, and Support of Existing Interfaces for Restricted 64 kbit/s Transfer Capability	R
I.465	Support by an ISDN of DTEs with V-Series Type Interfaces with Provision for Statistical Multiplexing	N
I.470	Relationship of Terminal Functions to ISDN	N
Part V—Internetwork Interfaces		
I.500	General Structure of the ISDN Interworking Recommendations	N
I.510	Definition and General Principles for ISDN Interworking	N
I.511	ISDN-to-ISDN Layer 1 Internetwork Interface	N
I.515	Parameter Exchange for ISDN Interworking	N
I.520	General Arrangements for Network Interworking between ISDNs	N
I.530	Network Interworking between an ISDN and a Public Switched Telephone Network (PSTN)	N
I.540	General Arrangements for Interworking between Circuit-Switched Public Data Networks (CSPDNs) and ISDNs for the Provision of Data Transmission	N
I.550	General Arrangements for Interworking between Packet Switched Public Data Networks (PSPDNs) and ISDNs for the Provision of Data Transmission	N
I.560	Requirements to be Met in Providing the Telex Service within an ISDN	N
Part VI—Maintenance Principles		
I.601	General Maintenance Principles of ISDN Subscriber Access and Subscriber Installation	N
I.602	Application of Maintenance Principles to ISDN Subscriber Installations	N
I.603	Application of Maintenance Principles to ISDN Basic Accesses	N
I.604	Application of Maintenance Principles to ISDN Primary Rate Accesses	N
I.605	Application of Maintenance Principles to Static Multiplexed ISDN Basic Accesses	N

TABLE 18-7   Study Topics Relating to ISDN for 1989–1992 Study Period (Study Group XVIII)

A   General aspects of ISDN

B   Asynchronous Transfer Mode (ATM)

C   Network aspects of digital hierarchies

D   Network application of Synchronous Digital Hierarchy with reference to the Network Node Interface (NNI)

E   General aspects of Quality of Service and network performance in digital network including ISDNs

F   Network performance objectives for ISDN circuit mode information transfer

G   Performance objectives for timing and controlled slips (synchronization), filter, wander and propagation delay

H   Network performance objectives for ISDN connection, processing and packet mode information transfer

I   Performance objectives for ISDN availability

J   Impact of signal processing on ISDN

K   Interworking of ISDNs with other networks, including compatibility checking and terminal selection

L   Interworking between network using different digital hierarchies—Layer 1 functionality

M   Network capabilities for the support of broadband services in ISDNs

N   ISDN network capabilities for the support of additional and/or new services

O   ISDN packet mode bearer services—services and user-network interface aspects

P   ISDN architecture and functional principles, characterization methods and reference configurations (including user-network interfaces)

Q   ISDN Protocol Reference Model

R   ISDN Connection Types

S   Network capabilities for the integration of mobile network services into ISDN

T   Layer 1 characteristics of ISDN interfaces and ISDN access

U   Vocabulary for ISDNs

V   Broadband ISDN infuence on principles for video encoding

It should be clear from this list that the ISDN standards activity is a massive effort. Table 18-7 lists the key areas of interest for the 1992 set of recommendations.

18-3

TRANSMISSION STRUCTURE

ISDN Channels

The digital pipe between the central office and the ISDN user will be used to carry a number of communication channels. The capacity of the pipe, and therefore the number of channels carried may vary from user to user. The transmission structure of any access link will be constructed from the following types of channels:

- *B channel:* 64 kbps.
- *D channel:* 16 or 64 kbps.
- *H channel:* 384, 1536, and 1920 kbps.

The B channel is the basic user channel. It can be used to carry digital data, PCM-encoded digital voice, or a mixture of lower-rate traffic, including digital data and digitized voice encoded at a fraction of 64 kbps. In the case of mixed traffic, all traffic must be destined for the same endpoint. Three kinds of connections can be set up over a B channel:

- *Circuit-switched:* this is equivalent to switched digital service available today. The user places a call and a circuit-switched connection is established with another network user. An interesting feature is that, unlike X.21, the call establishment dialogue does not take place over the B channel, but is done over the D, as explained below.
- *Packet-switched:* the user is connected to a packet-switching node, and data is exchanged with other users via X.25.
- *Semipermanent:* this is a connection to another user set up by prior arrangement, and not requiring a call establishment protocol. This is equivalent to a leased line.

The designation of 64 kbps as the standard user channel rate highlights the fundamental contradiction in standards activities. This rate was chosen as the most effective for digitized voice, yet the technology has progressed to the point at which 32 kbps or even less will produce equally satisfactory voice reproduction. To be effective, a standard must freeze the technology at some defined point. Yet by the time the standard is approved, it may already be obsolete.

The D channel serves two purposes. First, it carries signalling information to control circuit-switched calls on associated B channels at the user interface. In addition, the D channel may be used for packet-switching or low-speed (e.g., 100 bps) telemetry at times when no signalling information is waiting. Table 18-8 summarizes the types of data traffic to be supported on B and D channels.

H channels are provided for user information at higher bit rates. The user may use such a channel as a high-speed trunk or subdivide the channel according to the user's own TDM scheme. Examples of applications include fast facsimile, video, high-speed data, high-quality audio, and multiple information streams at lower data rates.

These channel types are grouped into transmission structures that are offered as a package to the user. The best-defined structures at this time are the basic channel structure (basic access) and the primary channel structure (primary access), which are depicted in Figure 18-7.

TABLE 18-8   ISDN Channel Functions

B Channel (64 kbps)	D Channel (16 kbps)
Digital voice	Signaling
64 kbps PCM	Basic
Low bit rate (32 kbps)	Enhanced
High-speed data	Low-speed data
Circuit-switched	Videotex
Packet-switched	Teletex
Other	Terminal
Facsimile	Telemetry
Slow-scan video	Emergency services
	Energy management

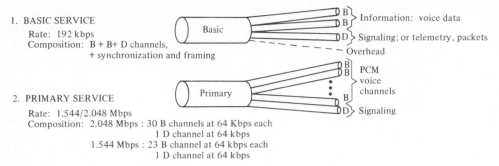

1. BASIC SERVICE

    Rate: 192 kbps
    Composition: B + B+ D channels,
                 + synchronization and framing

2. PRIMARY SERVICE

    Rate: 1.544/2.048 Mbps
    Composition: 2.048 Mbps : 30 B channels at 64 Kbps each
                               1 D channel at 64 kbps
               1.544 Mbps : 23 B channel at 64 kbps each
                              1 D channel at 64 kbps

FIGURE 18-7. ISDN channel structures.

The basic channel structure consists of two full-duplex 64 kbps B channels and a full-duplex 16-kbps D channel. The total bit rate, by simple arithmetic, is 144 kbps. However, framing, synchronization, and other overhead bits bring the total bit rate on a basic access link to 192 kbps [VAN84]. Figure 18-8 shows the frame structure for basic access. Each frame of 48 bits includes 16 bits from each of the B channels and 4 bits from the D channel. The functions of the remaining bits are explained in Section 18-5.

The basic service is intended to meet the needs of most individual users, including residential and very small offices. It allows the simultaneous use of voice and several data applications, such as packet-switched access, a link to a central alarm service, facsimile, videotex, and so on. These services could be accessed through a single multifunction terminal or several separate terminals. In either case, a single physical interface is provided. Most existing two-wire local loops can support this interface [GIFF86].

In some cases one or both of the B channels remain unused. This results in a $B + D$ or D interface, rather than the $2B + D$ interface. However, to simplify the network implementation, the data rate at the interface remains at 192 kbps. Nevertheless, for those subscribers with more modest transmission requirements, there may be a cost savings in using a reduced basic interface.

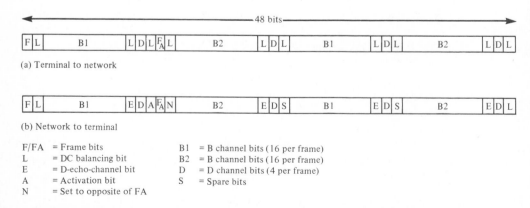

(a) Terminal to network

(b) Network to terminal

F/FA = Frame bits   B1   = B channel bits (16 per frame)
L   = DC balancing bit   B2   = B channel bits (16 per frame)
E   = D-echo-channel bit   D   = D channel bits (4 per frame)
A   = Activation bit   S   = Spare bits
N   = Set to opposite of FA

FIGURE 18-8. Physical layer multiplexed frame format for ISDN basic user-network interface.

The primary service is intended for users with greater capacity requirements, such as offices with a digital PBX or a local network. Because of differences in the digital transmission hierarchies used in different countries, it was not possible to get agreement on a single data rate. The United States, Canada, and Japan make use of a transmission structure based on 1.544 Mbps; this corresponds to the T1 transmission facility using the DS-1 transmission format. In Europe, 2.048 Mbps is the standard rate. Both of these data rates are provided as a primary interface service. Typically, the channel structure for the 1.544-Mbps rate will be 23 B channels plus one 64-kbps D channel and, for the 2.048-Mbps rate, 30 B channels plus one 64-kbps D channel. Again, it is possible for a customer with lower requirements to employ fewer B channels, in which case the channel structure is $nB + D$, where n ranges from 1 to 23 or 1 to 30 for the two primary services. Also, a customer with high data rate demands may be provided with more than one primary physical interface. In this case, a single D channel on one of the interfaces may suffice for all signalling needs, and the other interfaces may consist solely of B channels ($24B$ or $31B$).

The primary interface may also be used to support H channels. Some of these structures include a 64-kbps D channel for control signaling. When no D channel is present, it is assumed that a D channel on another primary interface at the same subscriber location will provide any required signaling. The following structures are recognized:

- *Primary rate interface H0 channel structures:* This interface supports multiple 384-kbps H0 channels. The structures are $3H0 + D$ and $4H0$ for the 1.544-Mbps interface and $5H0 + D$ for the 2.048-Mbps interface.
- *Primary rate interface H1 channel structures:* The H11 channel structure consists of one 1536-kbps H11 channel. The H12 channel structure consists of one 1920-kbps H12 channel and one D channel.
- *Primary rate interface structures for mixtures of B and H0 channels:* Consists of zero or one D channels plus any possible combination of B and H0 channels up to the capacity of the physical interface (e.g., $3H0 + 5B + D$ and $3H0 + 6B$).

Figure 18-9 illustrates the use of B and D channels for setting up calls. The user interface consists of some number of B channels and one D channel. The B channel can be used to support a circuit to another end user or some value-added service provided by a third party (e.g., a data base system). The B channel can also provide a link to a packet-switching network node. In this figure, the packet-switching network is provided by the ISDN provider; it is also possible to set up a circuit across ISDN to a third-party packet-switching network. In all of these cases, the D channel is used to exchange control messages between the user and the ISDN local exchange. These messages set up, maintain, and terminate B-channel connections.

Finally, we elaborate on an earlier reference to the use of a B channel to carry lower-data-rate signals. This capability is needed to support existing terminals that operate at less than 64 kbps. Two techniques are defined in the standards: rate adaption and multiplexing. There are a number of possible cases:

- *Single bit stream of 8, 16, or 32 kbps:* the first 1, 2, or 4 bits, respectively, of each octet in a B channel are used, with the remaining 7, 6, or 4 bits set to 1.

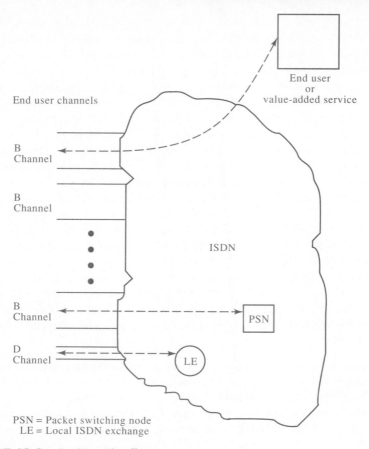

FIGURE 18-9.   B channel calls.

- *Single bit stream at another rate of less than 32 kbps:* the signal is first converted to a bit stream of 8, 16, or 32 kbps by bit padding: superfluous bits are added in a structured fashion. The resulting bit stream is then adapted to 64 kbps as above.
- *Single bit stream of between 32 and 64 kbps:* the signal is converted to 64 kbps by bit padding.
- *Multiple bit streams of 8, 16, and/or 32 kbps:* bits from different streams, up to a total of 64 kbps, are interleaved with each octet.
- *Multiple bit streams of rates other than 8, 16, or 32 kbps:* the signals are first converted into bit streams of 8, 16, or 32 kbps, and then multiplexed as above.

Subscriber Loop Technology

The extension of digital links to the end users is an essential part of ISDN evolution: The subscriber loop must support the channel structure being developed.

One intermediate technique for providing access is *data over voice*. On an analog link, voice occupies the frequency spectrum below 4 kHz. A data rate of 8 to 16 kbps can be supported by appropriate modulation of the digital signal onto a carrier at a band above 4 kHz.

To provide true full-duplex digital service, three approaches are possible. The first makes use of two twisted pairs (four-wire) per subscriber. Each twisted pair is operated in simplex fashion. This technique is technically simple, but doubles the amount of cable needed to serve hundreds of millions of residential subscribers.

What is really desired is a means of transmitting full-duplex digital data over a single twisted pair. This would allow the introduction of ISDN services making use of the large installed base of twisted-pair local loop. Two approaches to achieving this are illustrated in Figure 18-10 [KADE81]. The first method, known as time compression multiplexing [BOSI82], or the ping-pong protocol, was described in Chapter 8. In this technique, data are transmitted in one direction at a time, with transmission alternating between the two directions. To achieve the desired subscriber data rate, the subscriber's bit stream is divided into equal segments, compressed in time to a higher transmission rate, and transmitted in bursts which are expanded at the other end to the original rate. A short quiescent period is used between bursts going in opposite directions to allow the line to settle down; this results in a data rate requirement of 2.25 times the data rate as seen by the subscribers.

The alternative method is known as echo cancellation. In this technique, digital transmission is allowed to proceed in both directions within the same bandwidth simultaneously. This procedure introduces a technical difficulty known as echo. Echo is the feedback of the transmitted signal to the receiver. This echo primarily occurs from the local attachment of the transmitter-receiver to the two-wire local loop. The technique used to overcome this problem is echo cancellation [LIN90], [MURA90], [MESS84], [MESS86]. A replica of the echo signal is generated at the transmitting end and is subtracted from the incoming signal. This effectively cancels the echo. This technique has the disadvantage of requiring complex digital signal processing circuitry, but avoids the need to transmit at a signalling rate more

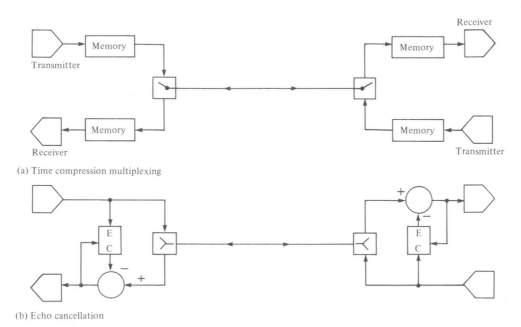

(a) Time compression multiplexing

(b) Echo cancellation

FIGURE 18-10. Techniques for full-duplex digital transmission over the subscriber loop.

than double the subscriber rate. With the continued advances in VLSI circuitry, the cost of echo cancellation is dropping, and has become the preferred technique [GERW84], [LECH86].

The above comments apply to twisted-pair connections. Ultimately, optical fiber connections will be used [FINN89b]. For these, FDM or time-compression multiplexing are the most attractive options.

18-4

USER ACCESS

One of the key objectives of the ISDN is that a uniform user access, both physically and logically, be provided. The details of user access arrangements are still evolving, but the work is sufficiently advanced to present an overview.

User-Network Interfaces

To define the requirements for ISDN user access, an understanding of the anticipated configuration of user premises equipment and of the necessary standard interfaces is critical. The first step is to group functions that may exist on the user's premises. Figure 18-11 shows the CCITT approach to this task, using:

* *Reference points:* conceptual points used to separate groups of functions.
* *Functional groupings:* certain finite arrangements of physical equipment or combinations of equipment.

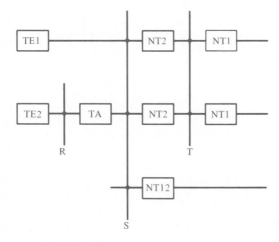

R,S,T – Reference interface points
TE1 – Subscriber terminel type 1
TE2 – Subscriber terminal type 2
TA – Terminal adapter
NT1 – Network termination 1
NT2 – Network termination 2
Nt12 – Combined network termination 1 and 2

FIGURE 18-11.   ISDN reference points and functional groupings.

The architecture on the subscriber's premises is broken up functionally into groupings separated by reference points. This permits interface standards to be developed at each reference point. This effectively organizes the standards work and provides guidance to the equipment providers. Once stable interface standards exist, technical improvements on either side of an interface can be made without impact on adjacent functional groupings. Finally, with stable interfaces, the subscriber is free to procure equipment from different suppliers for the various functional groupings, so long as the equipment conforms to the relevant interface standards.

Network termination 1 (NT1) includes functions associated with the physical and electrical termination of the ISDN on the user's premises; these correspond to OSI layer 1. The NT1 may be controlled by the ISDN provider and forms a boundary to the network. This boundary isolates the user from the transmission technology of the subscriber loop and presents a physical connector interface for user device attachment. In addition, the NT1 performs line maintenance functions such as loopback testing and performance monitoring. The NT1 supports multiple channels (e.g., 2B + D); at the physical level, the bit streams of these channels are multiplexed together, using synchronous time-division multiplexing. Finally, the NT1 interface might support multiple devices in a multidrop arrangement. For example, a residential interface might include a telephone, personal computer, and alarm system, all attached to a single NT1 interface via a multidrop line.

Network termination 2 (NT2) is an intelligent device that can perform switching and concentration functions; it may include functionality up through layer 3 of the OSI model. Examples of NT2 are a digital PBX, a terminal controller, and a LAN. An example of a switching function is the construction of a private network using semipermanent circuits among a number of sites. Each site could include a PBX that acts as a circuit switch or a host computer that acts as a packet switch. The concentration function simply means that multiple devices, attached to a digital PBX, LAN, or terminal controller, may transmit data across ISDN.

Network termination 1, 2 (NT12) is a single piece of equipment that contains the combined functions of NT1 and NT2. This points out one of the regulatory issues associated with ISDN interface development. In many countries, the ISDN provider will own the NT12 and provide full service to the user. In the United States, there is a need for a network termination with a limited number of functions to permit competitive provision of user premises equipment. Hence the user premises network functions are split into NT1 and NT2.

Terminal equipment refers to subscriber equipment that makes use of ISDN. Two types are defined. **Terminal equipment type 1** (TE1) refers to devices that support the standard ISDN interface. Examples are digital telephones, integrated voice/data terminals, and digital facsimile equipment. **Terminal equipment type 2** (TE2) encompasses existing non-ISDN equipment. Examples are terminals with a physical interface such as EIA-232-D and host computers with an X.25 interface. Such equipment requires a **terminal adaptor** (TA) to plug into an ISDN interface.

The definitions of the functional groupings also define, by implication, the reference points. **Reference point T** (terminal) corresponds to a minimal ISDN network termination at the customer's premises. It separates the network provider's equipment from the user's equipment. **Reference point S** (system) corresponds to the interface of individual ISDN terminals. It separates user terminal equipment from network-related communications functions. **Reference point R** (rate) provides a non-ISDN interface between user equipment that is not ISDN-compatible and adaptor equipment. Typically, this interface will comply with an older interface standard, such as EIA-232-D.

Access Configurations

Based on the definitions above, various possible configurations for ISDN user-network interfaces have been proposed by CCITT [GIFF86]. These are shown in Figure 18-12. Note that on the customer's premises there may be interfaces at S and T, at S but not T, at T but not S, or at a combined S–T interface. In the latter

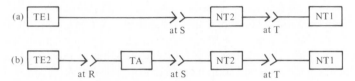

Configurations where ISDN physical interfaces occur at reference points S and T

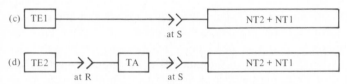

Configurations where ISDN physical interfaces occur at reference point S only

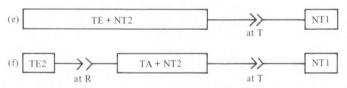

Configurations where ISDN physical interfaces occur at reference point T only

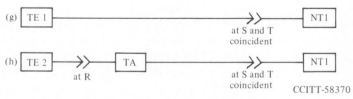

CCITT-58370

Configurations where a single ISDN physical interface occurs at a location where both reference points S and T coincide

$\longrightarrow\!\!\succ\!\!-$ Physical interface at the designated reference point

☐ Equipment implementing functional groups

FIGURE 18-12. Examples of physical configurations.

case, no functions corresponding to NT2 are present. This configuration illustrates a key feature of ISDN interface compatibility: an ISDN subscriber device, such as a telephone, can connect directly to the subscriber loop terminator or into a PBX or LAN, using the same interface specifications and thus ensuring portability.

Figure 18-13 provides examples of the ways in which a customer may implement the NT1 and NT2 functions. These examples illustrate that a given ISDN function can be implemented using various technologies, and that different ISDN functions can be combined in a single device. For example, Figure 18-13c illustrates that a LAN can interface to ISDN using a primary or basic access interface while the user devices make use of a very different interface (e.g., token ring).

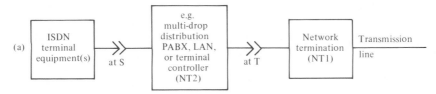

An implementation (see Figure 18-10a) where ISDN physical interfaces occur at reference points S and T.

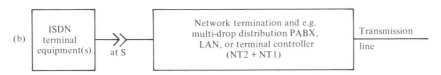

An Implementation (see Figure 18-10c) where ISDN physical interface occurs at reference point S but not T.

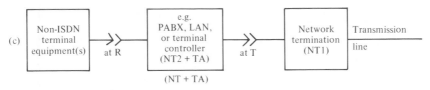

An implementation (see Figure 18-10f) where an ISDN physical interface occurs at reference point T but not S.

An implementation (see Figure 18-10g) where a single ISDN physical interface occurs at a location where both reference points S and T coincide.

FIGURE 18-13.   Examples of implementations of NT1 and NT2 functions.

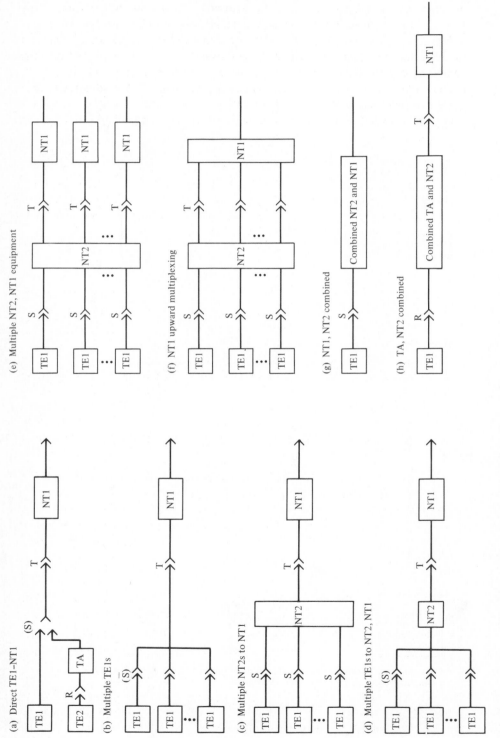

FIGURE 18-14. Possible configurations for ISDN user/network interface.

One additional set of configurations is suggested by ISDN. These cover cases in which the subscriber has more than one device at a particular interface point, but not so many devices that a separate PBX or LAN is warranted. In these cases, it is possible to have multiple physical interfaces at a single reference point. Examples are shown in Figure 18-14. Figure 18-14a and b show multiple terminals connected to the network, either through a multidrop line or through a multiport NT1. These cases are not intended to require that individual terminals can talk to each other, as in a LAN, but rather that each terminal can communicate with the network.

Figure 18-14c and d provide multiple connections between TE1s and NT2. The two figures more or less correspond to PBX and LAN, respectively. Figure 18-14e shows the case of multiple NT1 equipment, whereas Figure 18-14f shows a case in which NT1 provides a layer 1 upward multiplexing of multiple connections.

The final two configurations indicate that either S or T, but not both, need not correspond to a physical interface in a particular instance. We have already referred to the combination of NT1 and NT2 as NT12. In addition, an NT2 can be equipped with the capability to attach TE2 equipment directly.

18-5

ISDN PROTOCOLS

ISDN Protocol Architecture

The development of standards for ISDN includes, of course, the development of protocols for interaction between ISDN users and the network and for interaction between one ISDN user and another. It would be desirable to fit these new ISDN protocols into the OSI framework, and to a great extent this has been done. However, there are certain requirements for ISDN that are not met within the current structure of OSI [DUC85]. Examples of these are:

- *Multiple related protocols:* The primary example of this is the use of a protocol on the D channel to set up, maintain, and terminate a connection on a B channel.
- *Multi-media calls:* ISDN will allow a call to be set up that allows information flow consisting of multiple types, such as voice, data, facsimile, and control signals.
- *Multipoint connections:* ISDN will allow conference calls.

These and other functions are not directly addressed in the current OSI specification. However, the basic 7-layer framework appears valid even in the ISDN context and the issue is more one of specific functionality at the various layers. The issue of the exact relationship between ISDN and OSI remains one for further study.

Figure 18-15 suggests the relationship between OSI and ISDN. As a network, ISDN is essentially unconcerned with user layers 4-7. These are end-to-end layers employed by the user for the exchange of information. As with the networks discussed in Chapter 13, network access is concerned only with layers 1–3. Layer 1, defined in I.430 and I.431, specifies the physical interface for both basic and

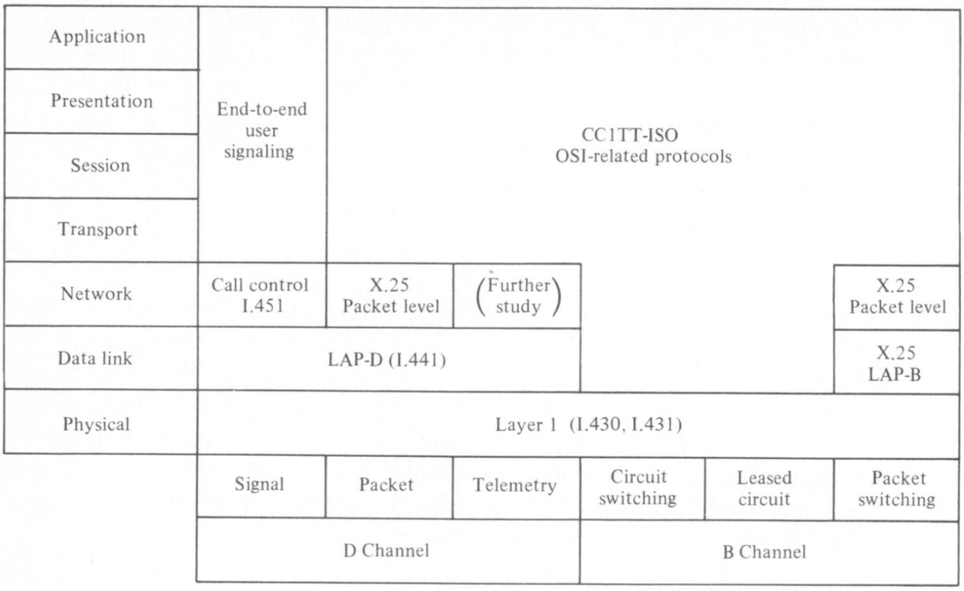

Application	End-to-end user signaling	CCITT-ISO OSI-related protocols					
Presentation							
Session							
Transport							
Network	Call control I.451	X.25 Packet level	(Further study)				X.25 Packet level
Data link	LAP-D (I.441)						X.25 LAP-B
Physical	Layer 1 (I.430, I.431)						
	Signal	Packet	Telemetry	Circuit switching	Leased circuit	Packet switching	
	D Channel			B Channel			

FIGURE 18-15. Layered protocol structure at the ISDN user-network interface (Source: [KANO86]).

primary access. Since B and D channels are multiplexed over the same physical interface, these standards apply to both types of channels. Above this layer, the protocol structure differs for the two channels.

For the D-channel, a new data link layer standard, LAP-D has been defined. All transmission on this channel is in the form of LAP-D frames that are exchanged between the subscriber equipment and an ISDN switching element. Three applications are supported: control signaling, packet-switching, and telemetry. For control signaling, a call control protocol has been defined (I.451). This protocol is used to establish, maintain, and terminate connections on B channels. Thus it is a protocol between the user and the network. I.451 was examined in Chapter 13. Above layer 3, there is the possibility for higher-layer functions associated with user-to-user control signaling. These are a subject for further study. The D channel can also be used to provide packet switching services to the subscriber. In this case, the X.25 level 3 protocol is used, and X.25 packets are transmitted in LAP-D frames. The X.25 level 3 protocol is used to establish virtual circuits on the D channel to other users, and to exchange packetized data. The final application area, telemetry, is a subject for further study.

The B channel can be used for circuit switching, semipermanent circuits, and packet-switching. Let us consider circuit switching first. The D channel is used to set up a circuit between two ISDN users. Once the circuit is set up, it may be used for data transfer between the users. Recall from Chapter 2 that a circuit-switched network provides a transparent data path between communication stations. To the attached stations, it appears that they have a direct full-duplex link with each other. They are free to use their own formats, protocols, and frame synchronization. Hence, from the point of view of ISDN, layers 2–7 are not visible nor specified. The same line of reasoning applies to semipermanent circuits. In the case of packet-switching, a circuit-switched connection is set up on the B channel between the user and a packet-switched node using the D channel control protocol. Once the circuit is set up on the B channel, the user employs X.25 levels 2 and 3 to establish a virtual circuit to another user over that channel and to exchange packetized data.

Some of the issues raised by Figure 18-15 are examined in the remainder of this section. First, we look at the way in which packet-switched and circuit-switched connections are set up. Next we examine LAP-D. Finally, the physical layer specifications are reviewed.

ISDN Connections

Three types of services for end-to-end communication are provided:

- Circuit-switched calls over the B channel
- Packet-switched calls over the B channel
- Packet-switched calls over the D channel

Circuit Switching.   The network configuration and protocols for circuit switching involve both the B and D channels. The B channel is used for the transparent exchange of user data. The communicating users may use any protocols they wish for end-to-end communication. The D channel is used to exchange control information between the user and the network for call establishment and termination, and access to network facilities.

Figure 18-16 depicts the protocol architecture that implements circuit switching. (See Table 18-9 for a key to Figures 18-16 through 18-18.) The B channel is serviced by an NT1 or NT2 using only layer 1 functions. The end users may employ any protocol, although generally layer 3 will be null. On the D channel, a three-layer network access protocol is used, and is explained below. Finally, the process

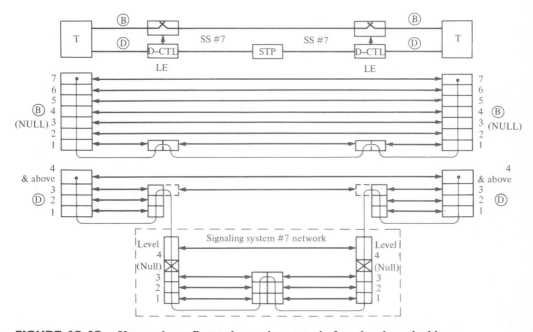

FIGURE 18-16.   Network configuration and protocols for circuit switching.

TABLE 18-9   Key to Figures 18-16 Through 18-18

$$
\begin{aligned}
B &= \text{An ISDN B channel} \\
D &= \text{An ISDN D channel} \\
T &= \text{Terminal} \\
\text{D-CTL} &= \text{D-channel controller} \\
\text{SS 7} &= \text{CCITT signaling system 7} \\
\text{STP} &= \text{Signaling transfer point} \\
\text{(Null)} &= \text{Channel not present} \\
7, 6, 5, 4, 3, 2, 1 &= \text{Layers in ISO basic reference model} \\
\text{LEVEL} &= \text{Levels in SS 7} \\
\text{LE} &= \text{Local exchange} \\
\text{TE} &= \text{Transit exchange} \\
\text{PSF} &= \text{Packed-switching facility} \\
\text{Horizontal line} &= \text{Peer-to-peer protocol} \\
\text{Vertical line} &= \text{Layer-to-layer data flow}
\end{aligned}
$$

of establishing a circuit through ISDN involves the cooperation of switches internal to ISDN to set up the connection. These switches interact using a standard known as *CCITT Common Channel Signaling System No. 7* (SS7) [PHEL86], [ROEH85], [SCHL86], which is examined later in this chapter.

Packet Switching.   The ISDN must also permit user access to packet-switched services for data traffic (e.g., interactive) that is best serviced by packet switching. Figures 18-17 and 18-18 show two possibilities.

The first possibility is high-speed (64 kbps) packet-switched access via the B channel Figure 18-17 depicts a scenario in which the ISDN provides a circuit-switched link to a value-added packet-switching node. The local user interface need

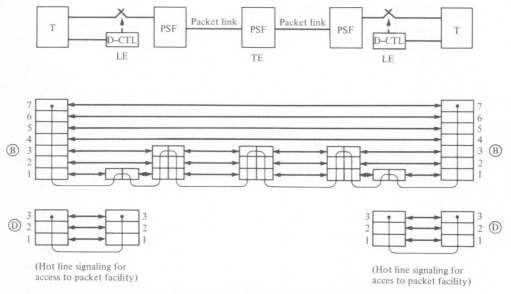

FIGURE 18-17.   Network configuration and protocols for packet switching using B channel with circuit-switched access.

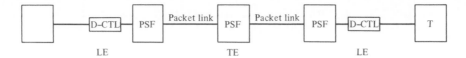

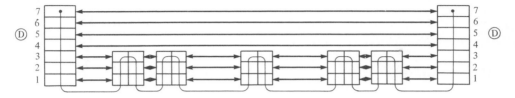

Note: There is another possibility: that LE is transparent to layer 3.

FIGURE 18-18. Network configuration and protocols for packet switching for D channel.

only perform physical layer functions to maintain a transparent connection between the user and the packet-switching node. The latter two entities communicate using X.25 layers 1-3.

There are two sets of variations to consider, one set concerned with the nature of the connection from the user to the packet-switched node, and the other concerned with the nature of the packet-switched service. The connection between the user (via a B channel) and the packet-switch node to which it attaches may be either semipermanent or circuit-switched. In the former case, the connection is always there and the user may freely invoke X.25 to set up a virtual circuit to another user. In the latter case, the D channel is involved, and the following sequence of steps occurs:

- The user requests, via the D-channel protocol, a circuit-switched connection to a packet-switched node.
- The connection is set up using SS7 and the user is notified via the D channel.
- The user sets up a virtual circuit to another user via the X.25 call establishment procedure on the B channel.
- The user terminates the virtual circuit using X.25 on the B channel.
- After one or more virtual calls on the B channel, the user is done, and signals via the D channel to terminate the circuit-switched connection to the packet-switched node.
- The connection is terminated via SS7.

Another source of variability is whether the packet-switched service is provided directly by the ISDN provider or is provided by a separate packet-switched network. In either case, a semipermanent or switched connection is possible. One observable difference is that ISDN-provided packet-switching via the B channel allows the establishment of virtual circuits to users employing the D channel.

For D-channel access, the ISDN provides a packet-switching capability as part of the network. The D-channel provides a semipermanent connection to a packet-handling node within the ISDN. The user employs the X.25 level 3 protocol as is done in the case of a B-channel virtual call. Since the D channel is also used for control signalling, some means is needed to distinguish between X.25 packet traffic and ISDN control traffic. This is accomplished by means of the link layer addressing scheme, as explained below.

LAP-D

All traffic over the D channel employs a link-layer protocol known as LAP-D (Link Access Protocol–D Channel).

LAP-D Services.   The LAP-D standard provides two forms of service to LAP-D users: the unacknowledged information transfer service and the acknowledged information transfer service. The **unacknowledged information transfer service** simply provides for the transfer of frames containing user data with no acknowledgement. The service does not guarantee that data presented by one user will be delivered to another user, nor does it inform the sender if the delivery attempt fails. The service does not provide any flow control or error control mechanism. This service supports both point-to-point (deliver to one user) or broadcast (deliver to a number of users). This service allows for fast data transfer and is useful for management procedures such as alarm messages and messages that need to be broadcast to multiple users.

The **acknowledged information transfer service** is the more common one, and is similar to the service offered by LAP-B and HDLC. With this service, a logical connection is established between two LAP-D users prior to the exchange of data.

LAP-D Protocol.   The LAP-D protocol is based on HDLC. Both user information and protocol control information and parameters are transmitted in frames. Corresponding to the two types of service offered by LAP-D, there are two types of operation:

- *Unacknowledged operation:* Layer 3 information is transferred in unnumbered frames. Error detection is used to discard damaged frames, but there is no error control or flow control.
- *Acknowledged operation:* Layer 3 information is transferred in frames that include sequence numbers that are acknowledged. Error control and flow control procedures are included in the protocol. This type is also referred to in the standard as multiple-frame operation.

These two types of operation may coexist on a single D channel.

Both types of operation make use of the frame format illustrated in Figure 18-19. This format is identical to that of HDLC (Figure 5-16) with the exception of the address field.

To explain the address field, we need to consider that LAP-D has to deal with two levels of multiplexing. First, at the subscriber site, there may be multiple user devices sharing the same physical interface. Second, within each user device, there may be multiple types of traffic: specifically, packet-switched data and control signaling. To accommodate these levels of multiplexing, LAP-D employs a two-part address, consisting of a terminal endpoint identifier (TEI) and a service access point identifier (SAPI).

Typically, each user device is given a unique **terminal endpoint identifier (TEI).** It is also possible for a single device to be assigned more than one TEI.

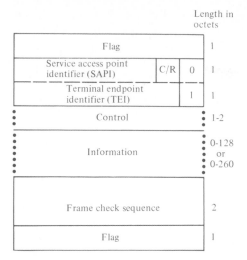

FIGURE 18-19. LAP-D format.

This might be the case for a terminal concentrator. TEI assignment occurs either automatically when the equipment first connects to the interface, or manually by the user. In the latter case, care must be taken that multiple equipment attached to the same interface do not have the same TEI. The advantage of the automatic procedure is that it allows the user to change, add, or delete equipment at will without prior notification to the network administration. Without this feature, the network would be obliged to manage a data base for each subscriber that would need to be updated manually. Table 18-10a shows the assignment of TEI numbers.

TABLE 18-10 SAPI and TEI Assignments

(a) TEI Assignments

TEI Value	User Type
0–63	Nonautomatic TEI assignment user equipment
64–126	Automatic TEI assignment user equipment
127	Used during automatic TEI assignment

(b) SAPI Assignments

SAPI Value	Related Layer 3 or Management Entity
0	Call control procedures
1	Reserved for packet mode communication using I.451 call control procedures
16	Packet communication conforming to X.25 level 3
63	Layer 2 management procedures
All others	Reserved for future standardization

The **service access point identifier (SAPI)** identifies a layer 3 user of LAP-D, and thus corresponds to a layer 3 protocol entity within a user device. Four values have been assigned, as shown in Table 18-10b. A SAPI of 0 is used for call control procedures for managing B channel circuits; the value 16 is reserved for packet-mode communication on the D channel using X.25 level 3; and a value of 63 is used for the exchange of layer 2 management information. The most recent assignment, made in 1988 is the value of 1 for packet-mode communication using I.451. This could be used for user-user signaling.

For acknowledged operation, LAP-D follows essentially the same procedures described for HDLC in Chapter 5. For unacknowledged operation, the user information (UI) frame is used to transmit user data. When a LAP-D user wishes to send data, it passes the data to its LAP-D entity, which passes the data in the information field of a UI frame. When this frame is received, the information field is passed up to the destination user. There is no acknowledgment returned to the other side. However, error detection is performed and frames in error are discarded.

Frame Relay.   One of the 1988 recommendations, I.122, makes reference to services referred to as frame relaying and frame switching; in the literature, the two concepts are collectively referred to as frame relaying [LAI89, CHER89]. Although only a very general description is provided in the recommendation, much interest has been stirred, and a number of products have already been developed [BUSH89].

The intent of frame relaying is to provide a packet-switching service on the B channel as an alternative to X.25. The key differences from a conventional packet-switching service are these:

- In frame relaying, the signaling for setting up and clearing virtual calls on the B channel is accomplished using the I.451 protocol on the D channel. In contrast, X.25 uses, in effect, inband signaling, since call control packets are carried on the same channel and same logical connection as the data packets.
- Multiplexing of virtual connections on a B channel take place at layer 2 with frame relaying and at layer 3 with X.25.

Thus, frame relaying combines layer 2 and layer 3 functionality. As with circuit-mode service, it provides a separation between signaling and the transfer of user information. In order to provide this separation, I.451 is used. When a user wishes to set up a virtual circuit on a particular B channel, the I.451 SETUP message is sent on the D channel to request the creation of a new virtual call on the B channel. Once the virtual circuit is established, data are transferred on the virtual circuit using LAP-D frames.[1]

Multiple virtual calls can be set up on the same B channel by repeated use of the SETUP message on the D channel. To achieve this multiplexing, each virtual circuit must have a unique identifier. For this purpose, the SAPI and TEI portion of the LAP-D frame are treated as a 13-bit virtual circuit number, referred to as a data link connection identifier.

In I.122, the term *frame relaying* is reserved for an unacknowledged service that provides the following core functions:

---

[1]In this case, LAP-D frames are being transmitted on the B channel. Since the LAP-D format is retained, the protocol is referred to as LAP-D even though it is functioning on a B channel.

- Frame delimiting
- Frame multiplexing/demultiplexing using the LAP-D address field
- Detection of transmission errors

Any frames that are detected in error are discarded. Thus, this is an unacknowledged connection-oriented service, similar to that provided in LLC (Chapter 13).

The frame switching service is an acknowledged connectionless service, which includes flow control and error control, in addition to the functions provided for frame relaying.

Let us consider the advantages and disadvantages of this approach. The principle disadvantage is that we have lost the ability to do link-by-link flow and error control. In X.25, multiple virtual circuits are carried on a single physical link, and LAP-B is available at the link level for providing reliable transmission from the source to the packet-switching network and from the packet switching network to the destination. In addition, at each hop through the network, the link control protocol can be used for reliability. Meanwhile, flow and error control at the virtual circuit level are provided by layer 3 functions of X.25. With the use of frame relaying, LAP-D becomes an end-to-end protocol, and hop-by-hop link control is lost. However, with the increasing reliability of transmission and switching facilities, this is not a major disadvantage.

The advantage of frame relaying is that we have streamlined the communications process. The protocol functionality required at the user-network interface is reduced, as is the internal network processing. As a result, lower delay and higher throughput can be expected. Preliminary results indicate a reduction in frame processing time of an order of magnitude [BUSH89]. Thus, we can expect to see frame relaying supplant X.25 as ISDN matures.

Physical Layer

The ISDN physical layer is presented to the user at either reference point S or T (Figure 18-11). The mechanical interface was described in Chapter 4 (Figures 4-12 and 4-13).

The electrical specification depends on the specific interface. For the basic access interface, pseudoternary coding is used (Figure 3-2). Recall that with pseudoternary, the line signal may take one of three levels. This is not as efficient as a two-level code, but it is reasonably simple and inexpensive. At the relatively modest data rate of the basic access interface, this is a suitable code.

For the higher-speed primary access interface, a more efficient coding scheme is needed. For the 1.544-Mbps data rate, the B8ZS code is used, while for the 2.048-Mbps data rate, the HDB3 code is used (Figure 3-5). There is no particular advantage of one over the other; the specification reflects historical usage.

The functional specification for the physical layer includes the following functions:

- Full-duplex transmission of B-channel data
- Full-duplex transmission of D-channel data
- Full-duplex transmission of timing signals
- Activation and deactivation of physical circuit
- Power feeding from the network termination to the terminal
- Terminal identification

- Faulty terminal isolation
- Rate adaption
- D-channel contention access

The first seven functions are straightforward. Rate adaption was described earlier and is considered a physical layer function. The final function, also considered a physical layer function, is required when multiple TE1 terminals share a single physical interface (i.e., a multipoint line). In that case, no additional functionality is needed to control access in the B channels, since each channel is dedicated to a particular circuit at any given time. However, the D channel is available for use by all the devices for both control signalling and for packet transmission. For incoming data, the LAP-D addressing scheme is sufficient to sort out the proper destination for each data unit. For outgoing data, some sort of contention resolution protocol is needed to assure that only one device at a time attempts to transmit.

The D-channel contention-resolution algorithm has the following elements:

1. When a subscriber device has no LAP-D frames to transmit, it transmits a series of binary ones on the D channel. According to the signal encoding scheme that is used, this corresponds to the absence of line signal.
2. The network, on receipt of a D-channel bit, reflects back the binary value as a *D-echo bit*.
3. When a terminal is ready to transmit a LAP-D frame, it listens to the stream of incoming D-echo bits. If it detects a string of 1-bits of length equal to a threshold value X_i, then it may transmit. Otherwise, the terminal must assume that some other terminal is transmitting and wait.
4. It may happen that several terminals are monitoring the D-echo stream and begin to transmit at the same time, causing a collision. To overcome this condition, a transmitting station monitors the D-echo bits and compares them to its transmitted bits. If a discrepancy is detected, the terminal ceases to transmit and returns to a listen state.

The electrical characteristics of the interface (i.e.,1-bit = absence of signal) are such that any user equipment transmitting a 0-bit will override user equipment transmitting a 1-bit at the same instant. This arrangement ensures that one device will be guaranteed successful completion of its transmission.

The algorithm also includes a primitive priority mechanism based on the threshold value X_i. Signalling information is given priority over packet information. Within each of these two priority classes, a station begins at normal priority and then is reduced to lower priority after a transmission. It remains at the lower priority until all other terminals have had an opportunity to transmit. The values of X_i are 11 and 10 for signal information and 9 and 8 for packet information.

With the above background, we can return to Figure 18-7 and describe the overhead bits in the D channel frame. Recall that pseudoternary coding is used. Each frame begins with a framing bit that is always transmitted as a positive pulse. This is followed by a DC-balancing bit that is set as a negative pulse to balance the voltage. These bits provide a means of synchronizing the frame. The remaining balance bits in the frame follow the rule: The balance bit is set to binary zero if the number of binary zeros following the previous balance bit is odd; otherwise it is set to one. The remaining bits in the frame format are easily explained. The activation bit is used to activate user equipment. The echo bit reflects the most recently transmitted D bit from the terminal.

SIGNALING SYSTEM NUMBER 7

Signaling System Number 7 (SS7) was first issued by CCITT in 1980, with revisions in 1984 and 1988. SS7 is designed to be an open-ended common channel signaling standard that can be used over a variety of digital circuit-switched networks. Furthermore, SS7 is specifically designed to be used in ISDNs. SS7 is the mechanism that provides the internal control and network intelligence essential to an ISDN.

The overall purpose of SS7 is to provide an internationally standardized general-purpose common channeling signaling system. The scope of SS7 is immense, since it must cover all aspects of control signaling for complex digital networks, including the reliable routing and delivery of control messages, and the application-oriented content of those messages. The latest edition of the SS7 Recommendations consists of 38 separate recommendations. In this section, we provide an overview of the structure of SS7.

Architecture

With common channel signaling, control messages are routed through the network to perform call management (setup, maintenance, termination) and network management functions. These messages are short blocks or packets that must be routed through the network. Thus, although the network being controlled is a circuit-switched network, the control signaling is implemented using packet-switching technology. In effect, a packet-switched network is overlaid on a circuit-switched network in order to operate and control the circuit-switched network.

SS7 defines the functions that are performed in the packet-switched network but does not dictate any particular hardware implementation. For example, all of the SS7 functions could be implemented in the circuit-switching nodes as additional functions. Alternatively, separate switching points that carry only the control packets and are not used for carrying circuits can be used. Even in this case, the circuit-switching nodes would need to implement portions of SS7 so that they could receive control signals.

So far, we have been discussing SS7 architecture in terms of the way in which functions are organized to create a packet-switching control network. The term architecture can also be used to refer to the structure of protocols that specify SS7. As with the open systems interconnection (OSI) model, the SS7 standard is a layered architecture. Figure 18-20 shows the current structure of SS7 and relates it to OSI.

The SS7 architecture consists of four levels. The lower three levels, referred to as the **message transfer part** (MTP) provide a reliable but connectionless (datagram style) service for routing messages through the SS7 network. The lowest level, **signaling data link**, corresponds to the physical layer of the OSI model, and is concerned with the physical and electrical characteristics of the signaling links. The **signaling link** level is a data link control protocol that provides for the reliable sequenced delivery of data across a signaling data link; it corresponds to layer 2 of the OSI model. The top level of the MTP, referred to as the **signaling network** level or function, provides for routing data across multiple control points from control source to control destination. These three levels together do not pro-

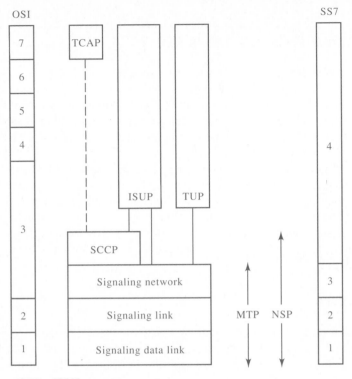

ISUP = ISDN user part
MTP = Messsage transfer part
NSP = Network service part
SCCP = Signaling connection control part
TCAP = Transaction capabilities application part

FIGURE 18-20. **Signaling system number 7 protocol architecture.**

vide the complete set of functions and services specified in the OSI layers 1–3, most notably in the areas of addressing and connection-oriented service. In the 1984 version of SS7, an additional module was added that resides in level 4, known as **signaling connection control part** (SCCP). The SCCP and MTP together are referred to as the **network service part** (NSP). A variety of different network-layer services are defined in SCCP, to meet the needs of various users of NSP. The remainder of the modules of SS7 are at level 4 and comprise the various users of NSP. NSP is simply a message delivery system; the remaining parts deal with the actual contents of the messages. The **telephone user part** (TUP) is invoked in response to actions by a subscriber at a telephone. TUP control signals deal with the establishment, maintenance, and termination of telephone calls. The **ISDN User Part** (ISUP) provides for the control signaling needed in an ISDN to deal with ISDN subscriber calls and related functions. Finally, the **transaction capabilities application part** (TCAP) provides the mechanisms for transaction-oriented (as opposed to connection-oriented) applications and functions.

Signaling Data Link Level

The signaling data link level corresponds to the physical layer of the OSI model. The signaling data link is a full-duplex physical link interconnecting two signaling nodes and dedicated to SS7 traffic. This level specifies the physical, electrical, and functional characteristics of the link.

Signaling Link Level

The signaling link level corresponds to the data link control layer of the OSI model. Thus, its purpose is to turn a potentially unreliable physical link into a reliable data link. The SS7 signaling link level uses the same principles as the better-known data link control protocol, HDLC, and its variants such as LAP-B. However, the formats and some of the procedures are different.

Signaling Network Level

As Figure 18-21 illustrates, the signaling network level includes functions related to message handling and functions related to network management. The **message handling functions** fall into three categories:

- *Discrimination:* Determines if a message is at its destination or is to be relayed to another node. If this is the destination, the data unit is delivered to the distribution function; otherwise, it is delivered to the routing function.
- *Routing:* Determines the signaling link to be used in forwarding a message. The message may have been received from the discrimination function or from a local level 4 entity.
- *Distribution:* Determines the user part to which a message should be delivered. The decision is based on analysis of the service indicator.

For a given source/destination pair, several alternate routes may be possible. These different routes are, in effect, different internal virtual circuits. In general,

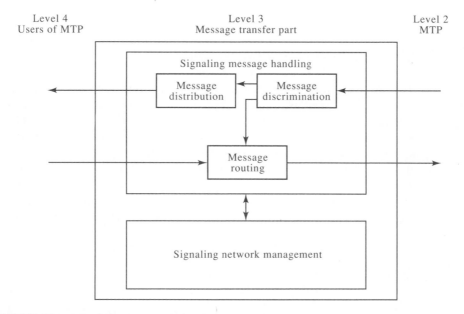

FIGURE 18-21. Message transfer part—level 3.

all of the control signals associated with a single call will follow the same route; this guarantees that they will arrive in sequence. However, the MTP needs to distribute traffic uniformly. This requirement can be satisfied if the user part varies the route selection from one call to the next.

The other function of the signaling network level is the **signaling network management function**. The main objective of this function is to overcome link degradations (failures or congestion). To meet this objective, the signaling management function is concerned with monitoring the status of each link, with dictating alternate routes to overcome link degradation and communicating the alternate routes to the affected nodes, and with recovering from the loss of messages due to link failure. The goal for SS7 is no more than 10 minutes of unavailability per year for any route. This goal is achieved through redundancy of links and dynamic re-routing.

This emphasis on the internal management of the network is rare; virtually all other network protocols make no mention of network management. In most cases, it is preferable to leave network management details to the provider, so that the provider can pursue the most cost-effective approach and be responsive to changes both in customer expectations and advances in technology. However, in the case of SS7, there are strong reasons for the emphasis on network management:

1. The function being specified is critical. The performance of a network's control signaling architecture affects all subscribers to the network.
2. The various networks involved must support international traffic. Degradations in one nation's signaling system will have repercussions beyond that nation's borders. Thus, some international agreement on the degree of reliability of national networks is indicated.
3. Recovery and restoration actions may involve multiple networks (e.g., in the case of international calls). If SS7 did not include failure and congestion recovery procedures, it would be necessary for the administration of each public network to enter into bilateral agreements with a number of other networks.

Signaling Connection Control Part

The signaling network level does not provide all of the routing and addressing capabilities that the OSI model dictates for the network layer. As an example, the message distribution function provides only a limited addressing capability. For newer user part applications, a more complex specification of the user of a message at a node is necessary; this can be provided by the signaling connection control part (SCCP). The SCCP enhances the connectionless sequenced transmission service provided by the MTP, to meet the needs of those user parts requiring enriched connectionless or connection-oriented service to transfer signaling information between nodes. For those user parts for which MTP suffices, the extra overhead of SCCP can be avoided.

Four classes of network service are defined for SCCP:

0—Basic unsequenced connectionless
1—Sequenced (fixed signaling link selection number) connectionless class
2—Basic connection-oriented
3—Flow control connection-oriented

ISDN User Part

The ISDN user part (ISUP) of Signaling System No. 7 defines the functions, procedures, and interexchange signaling information flows required to provide circuit-switched services and associated user facilities for voice and nonvoice calls over ISDN. We can state three requirements for the ISUP:

- It must rely on the message transfer part or network service part of SS7 for the transmission of messages.
- Its design must be flexible to accommodate future enhancements of ISDN capabilities.
- It must interwork with the user-network I.451 call control protocol.

This last point highlights the distinction between the ISUP, which is defined in CCITT Recommendations Q.761–Q.766, and I.451, which is the common-channel signaling control protocol between a subscriber and ISDN. The call control protocol defined in I.451 refers to common channel control signaling facilities open to use by the ISDN subscriber. I.451 is used by the subscriber to set up calls to other subscribers, with associated user facilities. ISUP refers to signaling facilities employed by the network provider on behalf of the ISDN user. Thus, ISDN communicates with the ISDN user (subscriber) via I.451 for the purpose of call control, and uses ISUP internal to the network to implement subscriber call control requests. The term ''user part'' is unfortunate since this does not refer to the ISDN user; rather, it refers to the fact that the ISUP is a user of the lower layers of SS7.

As Figure 18-20 indicates, ISUP has an interface to both the signaling network level and SCCP. The latter is used for end-to-end signaling between the two local exchanges involved in a call. The network procedures for establishing, controlling, and terminating a call occur as a result of ISUP messages exchanged between exchanges and signal transfer points with the network.

The messages can be divided into nine categories. **Forward set-up messages** are used to set up a circuit. In addition to identifying the exchange endpoints, these messages allow for the specification of the desired characteristics of the call. These messages propagate in a forward direction, from the exchange originating the call to the exchange that is the destination point. **General setup messages** are used during the call establishment phase. They provide a means of transferring any additional information required during call setup, plus a means for checking that a circuit which straddles more than one ISDN maintains the desired characteristics across all networks. **Backward set-up messages** support the call setup process and initiate accounting and charging procedures. **Call supervision messages** are additional messages that might be needed in the process of call establishment. This group includes indications of whether the call was answered or not and the capability to support manual intervention between ISDNs that cross national boundaries. **Circuit supervision messages** relate to an already-established circuit. Three key functions are supported. A circuit may be released, which terminates the call. A circuit may be suspended and later resumed. Finally, a circuit may be established which is not currently being used for a call. In this case it is possible to block the circuit so that outgoing calls on the circuit are prevented, saving the circuit for incoming calls. In the case of a group of circuits that are treated as a single unit for control. **Circuit group supervision messages** perform similar functions. **In-call modification messages** are used to alter characteristics or associated network facilities of an active call. Finally, **end-to-end messages** are used between the call originating and terminating exchanges, to request or respond to requests for additional call-related information, to invoke a supplementary service, or to transfer user-to-user information transparently through the network.

Transaction Capabilities Application Part

TCAP is the most recent addition to SS7, being added in the 1988 version of the recommendations. It provides the means to establish communication between two nodes in the signaling network for functions or applications that are not related to a specific circuit or call. This would include functions such as network management and maintenance. In its present form, TCAP is a connectionless service and is suited for request-response type of dialogue. Future enhancements may involve the use of layers 4 through 6 of the OSI model to provide for a richer set of connection-oriented services.

Summary

Signaling System Number 7 is a layered set of protocols that is used for control communication internal to a digital network. It provides a powerful and flexible set of facilities for establishing, maintaining, and terminating connections. SS7 is the "glue" of a digital network and will play a key role in ISDN.

18-7

BROADBAND ISDN

The planning for ISDN began as far back as 1976 and is only in the past few years moving from the planning stage to prototypes and actual implementations. It will be many years before the full spectrum of ISDN services is widely available, and there will continue to be refinements and improvements to ISDN services and network facilities. However, with the ink hardly dry on the first definitive set of ISDN standards (the 1988 recommendations), much of the planning and design effort became directed toward a network concept that will be far more revolutionary than ISDN itself. This new concept is referred to by CCITT as **Broadband Aspects of ISDN** (B-ISDN).

CCITT modestly defines B-ISDN as "a service requiring transmission channels capable of supporting rates greater than the primary rate." Behind this innocuous statement lie plans for a network and set of services that will have far more impact on business and residential customers than ISDN. With B-ISDN, services, especially video services, requiring data rates orders of magnitudes beyond those that can be delivered by ISDN, will become available. To contrast this new network and these new services to the original concept of ISDN, that original concept is now being referred to as **narrowband ISDN**.

In 1988, as part of its I-series of recommendations on ISDN, CCITT issued the first two recommendations relating to B-ISDN: I.113, *Vocabulary of terms for broadband aspects of ISDN*, and I.121, *Broadband aspects of ISDN*. These documents represent the level of consensus reached among the participants concerning

TABLE 18-11 Noteworthy Statements in I.113 and I.121

Broadband: A service or system requiring transmission channels capable of supporting rates greater than the primary rate.

The term B-ISDN is used for convenience in order to refer to and emphasize the broadband aspects of ISDN. The intent, however, is that there be one comprehensive notion of an ISDN which provides broadband and other ISDN services.

Asynchronous transfer mode (ATM) is the target transfer mode solution for implementing a B-ISDN. It will influence the standardization of digital hierarchies and multiplexing structures, switching and interfaces for broadband signals.

B-ISDN will be based on the concepts developed for ISDN and may evolve by progressively incorporating additional functions and services (e.g., high quality video applications).

The reference configuration defined in I.411 is considered sufficiently general to be applicable not only for a basic access and a primary rate access but also to a broadband access. Both reference points S and T are valid for broadband accesses.

the nature of the future B-ISDN, as of late 1988. They provide a
description and a basis for future standardization and development wc
the important notions developed in these documents are presented in

The basic defining document, I.121, covers the following topic
B-ISDN:

- Service aspects
- Architecture models
- Asynchronous transfer mode characteristics
- Broadband channel rates
- User-network interface
- Network aspects

Service Aspects

When the capacity available to the ISDN user is increased substant
range of services that it can support also increases substantially. CCITT classifies
the services that could be provided by a B-ISDN into interactive services and
distribution services. **Interactive services** are those in which there is a two-way
exchange of information (other than control signaling information) between two
subscribers or between a subscriber and a service provider. **Distribution services**
are those in which the information transfer is primarily one way, from service
provider to B-ISDN subscriber. Annex A of I.121 lists a number of examples of
each service, of which some are discussed in what follows.

Conversational services provide the means for bidirectional dialogue communication with bidirectional, real-time (not store-and-forward) end-to-end information transfer between two users or between a user and a service provider host.
These services support the general transfer of data specific to a given user application. That is, the information is generated by and exchanged between users; it
is not "public" information.

This category encompasses a wide range of applications and data types, including
moving pictures (video), data, and document. In the long run, perhaps the most

important category of B-ISDN service is video conversational services, and perhaps the most important of these services is video telephony. Video telephony simply means that the telephone instrument includes a video transmit and receive/display capability so that dial-up calls include both voice and live picture. The first use of this service is likely to be the office environment. It can be used in any situation where the visual component of a call is advantageous, including sales, consulting, instruction, negotiation, and the discussion of visual information, such as reports, charts, advertising layouts, and so on. As the cost of videophone terminals decline, it is likely that this will be a popular residential service as well.

Another video conversational service is videoconference. The simplest form of this service is a point-to-point capability, which can be used to connect conference rooms. This differs from videophone in the nature of the equipment used. Accordingly, the service must specify the interface and protocols to be used to assure compatible equipment between conference rooms. A point-to-point videoconference would specify additional features such as facsimile and document transfer and the use of special equipment such as electronic blackboards. A different sort of videoconference is a multipoint service. This would allow participants to tie together single videophones in a conference connection, without leaving their workplaces, using a video conference server within the network. Such a system would support a small number (e.g., five) of simultaneous users. Either one participant would appear on all screens at a time, as managed by the video conference server, or a split screen technique could be used.

A third variant of video conversational service is video surveillance. This is not a distribution service since the information delivery is limited to a specific, intended subscriber. This form of service can be unidirectional; if the information is simple video images generated by a fixed camera, then the information flow is only from video source to subscriber. A reverse flow would come in to play if the user had control over the camera (change orientation, zoom, etc.). A final example is video/audio information transmission service. This is essentially the same capability as video telephony. The difference is that a higher quality image may be required. For example, computer animation that represents a detailed engineering design may require much higher resolution than ordinary human-to-human conversation.

Audio conversational services could include the transfer of multiple sound streams. For example, a program could be transmitted in multiple languages.

The next type of conversational service listed in Annex A is for data. In this context, the term data means arbitrary information whose structure is not visible to ISDN. Examples of applications that would use this service:

- file transfer in a distributed architecture of computer and storage systems (load sharing, back-up systems, decentralized databases, etc.)
- large-volume or high-speed transmission of measured values or control information
- program downloading
- computer-aided design and manufacturing (CAD/CAM)
- connection of local area networks (LANs) at different locations

Finally, there is the conversational transfer of documents. This could include very high resolution facsimile or the transfer of mixed documents that might include text, facsimile images, voice annotation, and/or a video component. Two types of applications are likely here: a document transfer service for the exchange of documents between users at workstations, and a document storage system, based on the document transfer service, which provides document servers for the filing, update, and access of documents by a community of users.

Messaging services offer user-to-user communication between individual users via storage units with store-and-forward, mailbox and/or message handling (e.g., information editing, processing and conversion) functions. In contrast to conversational services, messaging services are not in real time. Hence, they place lesser demands on the network and do not require that both users be available at the same time. Analogous narrowband services are X.400 and Teletex.

One new form of messaging service that could be supported by ISDN is video mail, analogous to today's electronic mail (text/graphic mail) and voice mail. Just as electronic mail replaces the mailing of a letter, so video mail replaces mailing a video cassette. This may become one of the most powerful and useful forms of message communication. Similarly, a document mail service allows the transmission of mixed documents, containing text, graphics, voice, and/or video components.

Retrieval services provide the user with the capability to retrieve information stored in information centers that is, in general, available for public use. This information is sent to the user on demand only. The information can be retrieved on an individual basis; that is, the time at which an information sequence is to start is under the control of the user.

An analogous narrowband service is Videotex. This is an interactive system designed to service both home and business needs. It is a general-purpose data base retrieval system that can use the public switched telephone network or an interactive metropolitan cable TV system. The Videotex provider maintains a variety of data bases on a central computer. Some of these are public data bases provided by the Videotex system. Others are vendor-supplied services, such as a stock market advisory. Information is provided in the form of pages of text and simple graphics.

Broadband videotex is an enhancement of the existing Videotex system. The user would be able to select sound passages, high-resolution images of TV standard, and short video scenes, in addition to the current text and simplified graphics. This service could be used for remote education and training, and video-based advertising.

Another retrieval service is video retrieval. With this service, a user could order full-length films or videos from a film/video library facility. Since the provider may have to satisfy many requests, bandwidth considerations dictate that only a small number of different video transmissions can be supported at any one time. The user would be informed by the provider at what time the film will be available to be viewed or transmitted to the subscriber's video recorder.

Distribution services without user presentation control are also referred to as broadcast services. They provide a continuous flow of information which is distributed from a central source to an unlimited number of authorized receivers connected to the network. Each user can access this flow of information but has no control over it. In particular the user cannot control the starting time or order of the presentation of the broadcasted information. All users simply tap into the flow of information.

The most common example of this service is broadcast television. Currently, broadcast television is available from network broadcast via radio waves and through cable television distribution systems. With the capacities planned for B-ISDN, this service can be integrated with the other telecommunications services.

In addition, higher resolutions can now be achieved and it is anticipated that these higher-quality services will also be available via B-ISDN.

An example of a nonvideo service is an electronic newspaper broadcast service. This would permit the transmission of facsimile images of newspaper pages to subscribers who had paid for the service.

Distribution services with user presentation control also distribute information from a central source to a large number of users. However, the information is provided as a sequence of information entities (e.g., frames) with cyclical repetition. So, the user has the ability of individual access to the cyclical distributed information and can control start and order of presentation. Due to the cyclical repetition, the information entities, selected by the user, will always be presented from the beginning.

An analogous narrowband service is Teletext. Teletext is a simple one-way system that uses unallocated portions of the bandwidth of a broadcast TV signal. At the transmission end, a fixed set of pages of text is sent repeatedly in round-robin fashion. The receiver consists of a special decoder and storage unit, a keypad for user entry, and an ordinary TV set. The user keys in the number of the page desired. The decoder reads that page from the incoming signal, stores it, and displays it continuously until instructed to do otherwise. Typically, pages of Teletext form a tree pattern with higher-level pages containing menus that guide the selection of lower-level pages. Thus, although the system appears interactive to the user, it is actually a one-way broadcast of information. Since only a small portion of the TV signal bandwidth is used for this purpose, the number of pages is limited by a desire to reduce access time. A typical system will support a few hundred pages with a cycle time of a few tens of seconds. Examples of information presented by such a system are stock market reports, weather report, new, leisure information, and recipes.

With BISDN, an enhancement to Teletext known as cabletext can be provided. Whereas Teletext uses only a small portion of an analog TV channel, cabletext would use a full digital broadband channel for cyclical transmission of pages with text, images, and possible video and audio passages. As an electronic newspaper that uses public networks, or as an in-house information system for trade fairs, hotels, and hospitals, cabletext will provide low-cost access to timely and frequently-requested information.

Architectural Models

The section of I.121 dealing with architecture models discusses both reference configurations and protocol architectures.

Reference configurations were developed for ISDN in 1984 and appeared unchanged in the 1988 edition of the recommendations. It has been concluded that no new reference points are needed for B-ISDN, but that the S and T reference points already defined in ISDN are sufficient.

It is in the area of **protocol architectures** that new elements are introduced, as depicted in Figure 18-22. For B-ISDN, it is assumed that the transfer of information across the user-network interface will use what is referred to as asynchronous transfer mode (ATM). ATM is, in essence, a form of packet transmission across the user-network interface in the same way that X.25 is a form of packet transmission across the user-network interface. One difference between X.25 and ATM

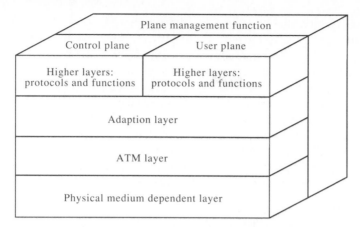

FIGURE 18-22.   B-ISDN protocol model for ATM (CCITT Figure 5/I.121).

is that X.25 includes control signalling on the same channel as data transfer, whereas ATM makes use of common-channel signaling. The decision to use ATM for B-ISDN is a remarkable one, explored briefly in the next subsection.

The use of ATM creates the need for an adaption layer to support information transfer protocols not based on ATM. Two examples listed in I.121 are PCM voice and LAP-D. PCM voice is an application that produces a stream of bits. To employ this application over ATM, it is necessary to assemble PCM bits into packets (called cells in the recommendation) for transmission and to read them out on reception in such a way as to produce a smooth, constant flow of bits to the receiver. For LAP-D, it is necessary to map LAP-D frames into ATM packets; this will probably mean segmenting one LAP-D frame into a number of packets on transmission, and reassembling the frame from packets on reception. By allowing the use of LAP-D over ATM, all of the existing ISDN applications and control signaling protocols can be used on B-ISDN.

Asynchronous Transfer Mode Characteristics

I.121 states the ATM is the target solution for the ISDN user-network interface. This implies that B-ISDN will be a packet-based network, certainly at the interface and almost certainly in terms of its internal switching. Although the recommendation also states that B-ISDN will support circuit-mode applications, this will be done over a packet-based transport mechanism. Thus, ISDN, which began as an evolution from the circuit-switching telephone networks, will transform itself into a packet-switching network as it takes on broadband services.

The current recommendation provides only a sketchy description of the ATM scheme. Information is exchanged between users in the form of packets, referred to as cells. Each cell will consist of a header in the range of 3 to 8 octets in length, and an information field in the range of 32 to 120 octets in length. At a minimum, the header must contain a virtual channel identification and an error-detection code. Whether cells are to be fixed or variable size, how cells are assigned dynamically to user entities, and other design issues are not addressed at this stage. Thus, much work needs to be done in defining ATM at the user interface as well as in defining the network mechanisms that will support ATM.

The obvious alternative to the ATM scheme is some sort of synchronous time-division multiplexing scheme, such as currently employed for both basic and primary rate access to ISDN. It would appear that synchronous TDM is well-suited to applications that involve a continuous flow of information, such as telephony and video, whereas ATM and other packet-mode schemes are well-suited to non-continuous applications such as terminal and computer interaction. However, with the use of appropriate algorithms to compensate for the variable delay of a packet transmission, ATM can support continuous-flow applications.

ATM is a similar concept to frame relay, but intended for BISDN; it takes advantage of reliability and fidelity of modern digital facilities to provide faster packet switching than X.25. Some of the expected characteristics of ATM are:

- No link-by-link error control
- No link-by-link flow control
- End-to-end error control if needed
- Use of internal virtual circuits
- Switching based on table lookup; switch looks at first N bits of incoming frame to make routing decision
- Fixed packet size

These characteristics are intended to allow for streamlined packet-switching at broadband rates. The scheme is sometime referred to as fast packet switching.

Broadband Channel Rates

CCITT has produced a preliminary definition of new broadband channel rates to be added to the existing narrowband channel rates. The new rates are:

- H21: 32.768 Mbps
- H22: 43 to 45 Mbps
- H4: 132 to 138.24 Mbps

The H21 and H22 rates would be appropriate for full-motion video for conferencing, video telephone, and video messaging. The H4 rate is sufficient for bulk data transfer of text, facsimile, and enhanced video information.

The H21 rate is equivalent to 512 64-kbps channels. The recommendation specifies that the H22 and H4 rates must also be multiples of 64 kbps.

User-Network Interface

For the user-network interface, CCITT has proposed two bit rates, one of approximately 150 Mbps and another at approximately 600 Mbps. These rates are based on the following line of reasoning. The local exchange to which subscribers attach must be able to handle both BISDN and ISDN subscribers. ISDN subscribers can be supported with twisted pair at the basic and primary access rates. For BISDN subscribers, optical fiber will be used. The data rate from network to subscriber will need to be on the order of 600 Mbps in order to handle multiple video distributions, such as might be required in an office environment. The data rate from subscriber to network would normally need to be much less, since the typical subscriber does not initiate distribution services. A rate of about 150 Mbps or less is probably adequate, since it will support at least one video channel.

Network Aspects

The section on network aspects briefly touches on a number of topics relating to the characteristics of a B-ISDN, but primarily leaves the details for future work. One noteworthy item is that, using ATM, user information and control signaling are to be carried on separate virtual channels, preserving the common-channel signaling nature of ISDN. Enhance or extended LAP-D and I.451 access protocols are to be used in B-ISDN to accommodate the addition of B-ISDN capabilities.

18-8

RECOMMENDED READING

A detailed technical treatment of ISDN can be found in [STAL89]. Other book-length treatments include [RONA87], [LANE87], and [DICE87]. [STAL88b] contains reprints of a number of the key papers. Two special issues on broadband ISDN are [COUD88] and [LEON89].

18-9

PROBLEMS

18-1   Is an IDN necessary for an ISDN? Sufficient? Explain.

18-2   It was mentioned that user-implemented multidrop lines and multiplexers may disappear. Explain why.

18-3   Does Figure 18-1 suggest why long distance telephone charges are more a function of time than they are of distance?

18-4   Refer to Figure 18-6. Why should not the subscriber pay for the cost of his local loop by the month, just as is currently charged?

18-5   An ISDN customer has offices at a number of sites. A typical office is served by two 1.544-Mbps digital pipes. One provides circuit-switched access to the ISDN; the other is a leased line connecting to another user site. The on-premises equipment consists of a CBX aligned with packet-switching node logic. The user has three requirements:
   - Telephone service.
   - A private packet-switched network for data.
   - Video teleconferencing at 1.544 Mbps.
   How might the user allocate capacity optimally to meet these requirements?

18-6 Figure 18-8 indicates that an ISDN basic access frame has 32 B bits and 4 D bits. Suppose that more bits were used, say 160 B bits and 20 D bits per frame. Would this reduce the percentage overhead and therefore the basic access bit rate? If so, discuss any potential disadvantages.

18-7 In Figure 18-16, under what circumstances would user layer 3 on the B channel not be null?

18-8 Compare the addressing schemes in HDLC, LLC, and LAP-D:
a. Are the SAPI of LAP-D and the SAP of LLC the same thing?
b. Are the TEI of LAP-D and the MAC-level address of IEEE 802 the same thing?
c. Why are two levels of addressing needed for LAP-D and LLC, but only one level for HDLC?
d. Why does LLC need a source address, but LAP-D and HDLC do not?

18-9 What is the percentage overhead on the basic channel structure?

18-10 From Figure 18-15, it would appear that layers 4–7 of the OSI model are little affected by ISDN. Would you expect this? Why or why not?

18-11 Would it be possible to provide a circuit-switched rather than a packet-switched implementation of SS7? What would be the relative merits of such an approach?

18-12 Is something like SS7 needed to provide control signaling in a packet-switched network? If so, why not use SS7?

18-13 In the United States, there has been considerable thought given to the types of telecommunication services that should be subject to government regulation of price and quality, and those that should be offered competitively with little or no regulation. Two important efforts in this regard are the Computer Inquiry II by the Federal Communications Commission (FCC) and the Modification of Final Judgement (MFJ) which resulted in the break-up of AT&T. In Computer Inquiry II, the FCC defined the following terms:

Basic Service   limited to the common carrier offering of transmission capacity for the movement of information

Enhanced Service   any offering over the telecommunications network which is more than a basic transmission service. Such services employ computer processing applications that act on the format, content, code, protocol or similar aspects of the subscriber's transmitted information; provide the subscriber additional, different, or restructured information; or involve subscriber interaction with stored information.

The MFJ produced the following definitions:

Telecommunication   the transmissions, between or among points specified by the user,

Service   of information of the user's choosing, without change in the form or content of the information as seen and received, by means of electromagnetic transmission, with or without benefit of any closed transmission medium, including all instrumentalities, facilities, apparatus, and services (including the collection, storage, forwarding, switching, and delivery of such information) essential to such transmission

Information Service   a capability for generating, acquiring, storing, transforming, processing, retrieving, utilizing, or making available information which may be conveyed via telecommunications, except that such service does not include any use of such capability for the management, control, or operation of a telecommunications system or the management of a telecommunications service.

Compare these two pairs of definitions with these definitions from I.112:

Bearer Service   a type of telecommunication service that provides the capability for the transmission of signals between user-network interfaces.

Teleservice   a type of telecommunication service that provides the complete capability, including terminal equipment functions, for communication between users according to protocols established by agreement between Administrations and/or RPOAs.

Queuing Analysis

In a number of places in this book, reference is made to queuing analysis, and the results based on such an analysis are presented. Indeed, queuing analysis is one of the most important tools for those involved with data and computer communications. It can be used to provide approximate answers to a host of questions, such as:

- What happens to terminal response time on a multidrop line when line utilization goes up?
- Does response time change if both line speed and the number of terminals on a line are doubled?
- How many lines should a time-sharing system have on a dial-in rotary?
- How many terminals are needed in an on-line inquiry center, and how much idle time will the operators have?

The number of questions that can be addressed with a queuing analysis is endless and touches on virtually every area discussed in this book. The ability to make such an analysis is an essential tool for those involved in this field.

Although the theory of queuing is mathematically complex, the application of queuing theory to the analysis of performance is in many cases remarkably straightforward. A knowledge of basic statistical concepts (means and standard deviations) and a basic understanding of the applicability of queuing theory is all that is required. Armed with the above, the analyst can often make a queuing analysis on the back of an envelope using readily-available queuing tables, or with the use of simple computer programs that occupy only a few lines of code.

The purpose of this chapter is to provide a practical guide to queuing analysis. A subset, although a very important subset, of the subject is addressed. In the final section, pointers to additional references are provided. An annex to this appendix reviews some basic concepts in probability and statistics.

A-1

WHY QUEUING ANALYSIS?

There are many cases in the field of data communications and computer networking when it is important to be able to project the effect of some change in a design: either the load on a system is expected to increase or a design change is contemplated. For example, an organization supports a number of terminals, personal computers, and workstations on a 4-Mbps token ring LAN. An additional department in the building is to be cut over onto the network. Can the existing LAN handle the increased workload, or would it be better to provide a second LAN with a bridge between the two? There are other cases in which no facility exists but, on the basis of expected demand, a system design needs to be created. For example, a department intends to equip all of its personnel with a personal computer and to configure these into a LAN with a file server. Based on experience elsewhere in the company, the load generated by each PC can be estimated.

The concern is system performance. In an interactive or real-time application, often the parameter of concern is response time. In other cases, throughput is the principal issue. In any case, projections of performance are to be made on the basis of existing load information or on the basis of estimated load for a new environment. A number of approaches are possible:

1. Do an after-the-fact analysis based on actual values.
2. Make a simple projection by scaling up from existing experience to the expected future environment.
3. Develop an analytic model based on queuing theory.
4. Program and run a simulation model.

Option 1 is no option at all: we will wait and see what happens. This leads to unhappy users and to unwise purchases.

Option 2 sounds more promising. The analyst may take the position that it is impossible to project future demand with any degree of certainty. Therefore, it is pointless to attempt some exact modeling procedure. Rather, a rough-and-ready projection will provide ballpark estimates. The problem with this approach is that the behavior of most communications systems is not what one would intuitively expect. If there is an environment in which there is a shared facility (e.g., a network, a transmission line, a time-sharing system), then the performance of that system typically responds in an exponential way to increases in demand.

Figure A-1 is a typical example. The upper line shows what happens to user response time on a shared facility as the load on that facility increases. The load is expressed as a fraction of capacity. Thus, if we are dealing with a packet-switching node that is capable of processing 1000 packets per second, then a load of 0.5 represents an input of 500 packets per second, and the response time is the

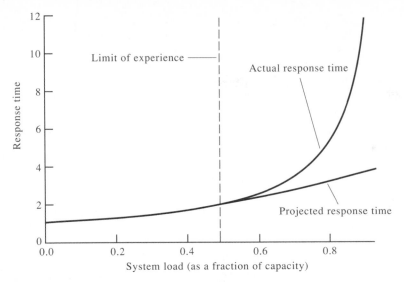

FIGURE A-1. Projected versus actual response time.

amount of time it takes to retransmit any incoming packet. The lower line is a simple projection[1] based on a knowledge of the behavior of the system up to a load of 0.5. Note that while things appear rosy when the simple projection is made, performance on the system will in fact collapse beyond a load of about 0.8 to 0.9.

Thus, a more exact prediction tool is needed. Option 3 is to make use of an analytic model, which is one that can be expressed as a set of equations that can be solved to yield the desired parameters (response time, throughput, etc.). For networking and communications problems, and indeed for many practical real-world problems, analytic models based on queuing theory provide a reasonably good fit to reality. The disadvantage of queuing theory is that a number of simplifying assumptions must be made to derive equations for the parameters of interest.

The final approach is a simulation model. Here, given a sufficiently powerful and flexible simulation programming language, the analyst can model reality in great detail and avoid making the many assumptions required of queuing theory. However, in most cases, a simulation model is not needed or at least is not advisable as a first step in the analysis. For one thing, both existing measurements and projections of future load carry with them a certain margin of error. Thus, no matter how good the simulation model, the value of the results are limited by the quality of the input. For another, despite the many assumptions required of queuing theory, the results that are produced usually come quite close to those that would be produced by a more careful simulation analysis. Furthermore, a queuing analysis can literally be accomplished in a matter of minutes for a well-defined problem, whereas simulation exercises can take days, weeks, or longer to program and run.

Accordingly, it behooves the analyst to master the basics of queuing theory.

---

[1]In fact, the lower line is based on fitting a third-order polynomial to the data available up to a load of 0.5.

QUEUING MODELS

The Single-Server Queue

The most basic queuing system is depicted in Figure A-2. The central element of the system is a server, which provides some service to items. Items from some population of items arrive at the system to be served. If the server is idle, a item is served immediately. Otherwise, an arriving item joins a waiting line.[2] When the server has completed serving a item, the item departs. If there are items waiting in the queue, one is immediately dispatched to the server.

The figure also illustrates the basic parameters associated with a queuing model. Items arrive at the facility at some average arrival rate (items arriving per second) λ. At any given time, a certain number of items will be waiting in the queue (zero or more); the average number waiting is w, and the mean time that an item must wait is t_w. Note that t_w is averaged over all incoming items, including those that do not wait at all. The server handles incoming items with an average service time s; this is the time interval between the dispatching of an item to the server and the departure of that item from the server. Utilization is the fraction of time that the server is busy, measured over some interval of time. Finally, there are two parameters that apply to the system as a whole. The average number of items in the system, including the item being served (if any) and the items waiting (if any), is q; and the average time that an item spends in the system, waiting and being served, is t_q.

If we assume that the capacity of the waiting line is infinite, then no items are ever lost from the system; they are just delayed until they can be served. Under these circumstances, the departure rate equals the arrival rate. As the arrival rate, which is the rate of traffic passing through the system, increases, the utilization increases and with it, congestion. The waiting line becomes longer, increasing waiting time. At $\rho = 1$, the server becomes saturated, working 100% of the time.

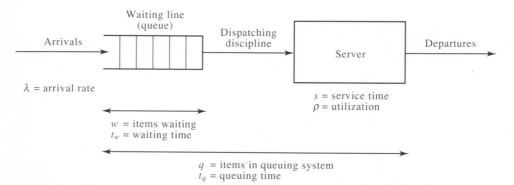

FIGURE A-2.   Queuing system structure and parameters for single-server queue.

---

[2]The waiting line is referred to as a queue in some treatments in the literature; it is also common to refer to the entire system as a queue.

Thus, the theoretical maximum input rate that can be handled by the system is:

$$\lambda_{max} = \frac{1}{s}$$

However, waiting lines become very large near system saturation, growing without bound when $\rho = 1$. Practical considerations, such as response time requirements or buffer sizes, usually limit the input rate for a single server to 70 to 90% of the theoretical maximum.

To proceed, we need to make some assumption about this model:

- *Item population:* Typically, we assume an infinite population. This means that the arrival rate is not altered by the loss of population. If the population is finite, then the population available for arrival is reduced by the number of items currently in the system; this would typically reduce the arrival rate proportionally.
- *Queue size:* Typically, we assume an infinite queue size. Thus, the waiting line can grow without bound. With a finite queue, it is possible for items to be lost from the system. In practice, any queue is finite. In many cases, this will make no substantive difference to the analysis. We address this issue briefly, below.
- *Dispatching discipline:* When the server becomes free, and if there is more than one item waiting, a decision must be made as to which item to dispatch next. The simplest approach is first-in, first-out; this discipline is what is normally implied when the term queue is used. Another possibility is last-in, first-out. One that you might encounter in practice is a dispatching discipline based on service time. For example, a packet-switching node may choose to dispatch packets on the basis of shortest first (to generate the most outgoing packets) or longest first (to minimize processing time relative to transmission time). Unfortunately, a discipline based on service time is very difficult to model analytically.

Table A-1 summarizes the notation that is used in Figure A-2, and introduces some other parameters that are useful. In particular, we are often interested

TABLE A-1 Notation Used in this Appendix

λ = mean number of arrivals per second
s = mean service time for each arrival
σ_s = standard deviation of service time
ρ = utilization; fraction of time facility is busy
q = mean number of items in system (waiting and being served)
t_q = mean time an item spends in system
σ_q = standard deviation of q
σ_{tq} = standard deviation of t_q
w = mean number of items waiting to be served
t_w = mean time an item spends waiting for service
t_d = mean waiting time for items that have to wait (not including items with waiting time = 0)
σ_w = standard deviation of w
M = number of servers
$m_x(r)$ = the rth percentile; that value of r below which x occurs r percent of the time

in the variability of various parameters, and this is neatly captured in the standard deviation.

The Multiserver Queue

Figure A-3 shows a generalization of the simple model we have been discussing. In this case, there are multiple servers, all sharing a common waiting line. If an item arrives and at least one server is available, then the item is immediately dispatched to that server. It is assumed that all servers are identical; thus if more than one server is available, it makes no difference which server is chosen for the item. If all servers are busy, a waiting line begins to form. As soon as one server becomes free, an item is dispatched from the waiting line using the dispatching discipline in force.

With the exception of utilization, all of the parameters illustrated in Figure A-2 carry over to the multiserver case with the same interpretation. If we have M identical servers, then ρ is the utilization of each server, and we can consider $M\rho$ to be the utilization of the entire system. Thus the theoretical maximum utilization is $M \times 100\%$, and the theoretical maximum input rate is:

$$\lambda_{max} = \frac{M}{s}$$

Basic Queuing Relationships

To proceed much further, we are going to have to make some simplifying assumptions. Unfortunately, these assumptions have the effect of making the models less valid for various real-world situations. Fortunately, in many cases, the results will be sufficiently accurate for planning and design purposes.

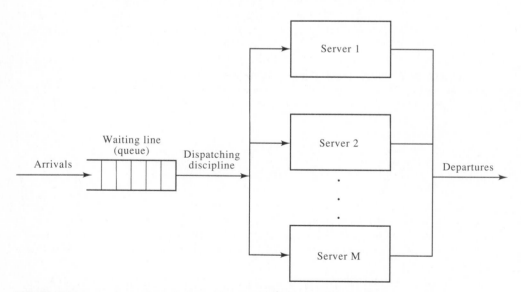

FIGURE A-3.   Queuing system structure for multiserver queue.

TABLE A-2   Some Basic Queuing Relationships

$\rho = \lambda s$	for a single server
$\rho = \dfrac{\lambda s}{M}$	for multiple servers
$q = \lambda t_q$	Little's formula
$w = \lambda t_w$	
$t_q = t_w + s$	
$q = w + \rho$	for a single server
$q = w + M\rho$	for multiple servers

There are, however, some relationships that are true in the general case, and these are illustrated in Table A-2. By themselves, these relationships are not particularly helpful.

Assumptions

The basic task of a queuing analysis is as follows: Given the following information as input:

- Arrival rate
- Service time

Provide as output information concerning:

- Items waiting
- Waiting time
- Items queued
- Queuing time.

What specifically would we like to know about these outputs? Certainly we would like to know their average values (w, t_w, q, t_q). In addition, it would be useful to know something about their variability. Thus, the standard deviation of each would be useful (σ_q, σ_{tq}, σ_w, σ_{tw}). Other measures may also be useful. For example, to design a buffer associated with a multiplexer, it might be useful to know what is that buffer size such that the probability of overflow is less than 0.001? That is, what is the value of N such that $Pr[q < N] = 0.999$?

To answer such questions in general requires complete knowledge of the probability distribution of the arrival rate and service time. Furthermore, even with that knowledge, the resulting formulas are exceedingly complex. Thus, to make the problem tractable, we need to make some simplifying assumptions.

The most important of these assumptions is that the arrival rate obeys the Poisson distribution, which is equivalent to saying that the interarrival times are exponential. This assumption is almost invariably made. Without it, practical queuing analysis is impractical. With this assumption, it turns out that many useful results can be obtained if only the mean and standard deviation of the arrival rate and service time are known.

Matters can be made even simpler and more detailed results can be obtained if it is assumed that the service time is exponential or constant.

A convenient notation has been developed for summarizing the principal assumptions that are made in developing a queuing model. The notation is X/Y/N, where X refers to the distribution of the inter-arrival times, Y refers to the distribution of service times, and N refers to the number of servers. The most common distributions are denoted as follows:

G = general independent arrivals or service times
M = negative exponential distribution
D = deterministic arrivals or fixed length service.

Thus, M/M/1 refers to a single-server queuing model with Poisson arrivals and exponential service times.

A-3

SINGLE-SERVER QUEUES

Table A-3a provides some equations for single server queues that follow the M/G/1 model. That is, the arrival rate is Poisson. Making use of a scaling factor, A, the equations for some of the key output variables are straightforward. Note that the key factor in the scaling parameter is the ratio of the standard deviation of service time to the mean. No other information about the service time is needed. Two special cases are of some interest. When the standard deviation is equal to the mean, the service time distribution is exponential. This is the simplest case, and the easiest one for calculating results. Table A-3b shows the simplified versions of equations for σ_q, σ_{tq}, σ_w, and σ_{tw}, plus some other parameters of interest. The other interesting case is a standard deviation of service time equal to zero, that is, a constant service time. The corresponding equations are shown in Table A-3c.

Figures A-4 and A-5 plot values of average queue size and queuing time versus utilization for three values of σ_s/s. Note that the poorest performance is exhibited

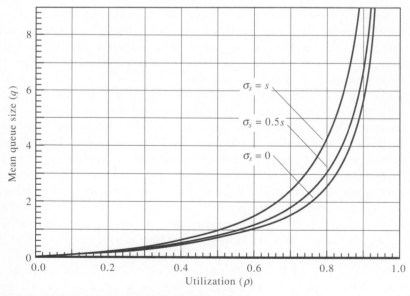

FIGURE A-4.   Mean queue sizes for M/G/1 model.

TABLE A-3 Formulas for Single-Server Queues

Assumptions:
1. Poisson arrival rate.
2. Dispatching discipline does not give preference to items based on service times.
3. Formulas for standard deviation assume first-in, first-out dispatching.
4. No items leave the queue (lost calls delayed).

(a) General Service Times (M/G/1)

$$A = \frac{1}{2}\left[1 + \left(\frac{\sigma_s}{s}\right)^2\right]$$ useful parameter

$$q = \rho + \frac{\rho^2 A}{1 - \rho}$$

$$w = \frac{\rho^2 A}{1 - \rho}$$

$$t_q = s + \frac{\rho s A}{1 - \rho}$$

$$t_w = \frac{\rho s A}{1 - \rho}$$

(b) Exponential Service Times (M/M/1)

$$q = \frac{\rho}{1 - \rho}$$

$$w = \frac{\rho^2}{1 - \rho}$$

$$t_q = \frac{s}{1 - \rho}$$

$$t_w = \frac{\rho s}{1 - \rho}$$

$$\sigma_q = \frac{\sqrt{\rho}}{1 - \rho}$$

$$\sigma_{tq} = \frac{s}{1 - \rho}$$

$$Pr[q = N] = (1 - \rho)\rho^N$$

$$Pr[q \leq N] = \sum_{i=0}^{N} (1 - \rho)\rho^i$$

$$Pr[t_q \leq t] = 1 - e^{-(1 - \rho)t/s}$$

$$m_{tq}(r) = t_q \times \log_e\left(\frac{100}{100 - r}\right)$$

$$m_{tw}(r) = \frac{t_w}{\rho} \times \log_e\left(\frac{100\rho}{100 - r}\right)$$

(c) Constant Service Times (M/D/1)

$$q = \frac{\rho^2}{2(1 - \rho)} + \rho$$

$$w = \frac{\rho^2}{2(1 - \rho)}$$

$$t_q = \frac{s(2 - \rho)}{2(1 - \rho)}$$

$$t_w = \frac{\rho s}{2(1 - \rho)}$$

$$\sigma_q = \frac{1}{1 - \rho}R$$

$$R = \sqrt{\rho - \frac{3\rho^2}{2} - \frac{5\rho^3}{6} - \frac{\rho^4}{12}}$$

$$\sigma_{tq} = \frac{s}{1 - \rho}\sqrt{\frac{\rho}{3} - \frac{\rho^2}{12}}$$

by the exponential service time, and the best by a constant service time. Usually, one can consider the exponential service time to be a worst case. An analysis based on this assumption will give conservative results. This is nice, since tables are available for the M/M/1 case and values can be looked up quickly.

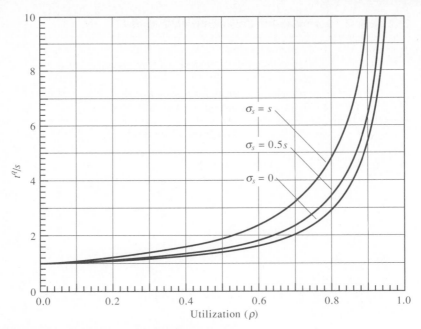

FIGURE A-5.   Mean queuing time for M/G/1 model.

What value of σ_s/s is one likely to encounter? We can consider four regions:

- *Zero:* This is the rare case of constant service time. If all transmitted messages are of the same length, they would fit this category.
- *Ratio less than 1:* Since this ratio is better than the exponential case, using M/M/1 tables will give queue sizes and times that are slightly larger than they should be. Using the M/M/1 model would give answers on the safe side. An example of this category might be a data entry application from a particular form.
- *Ratio close to 1:* This is the most common occurrence, and corresponds to exponential service time. That is, service times are essentially random. Consider message lengths to a computer terminal: a full screen might be 1920 characters, with message sizes varying over the full range. Airline reservations, file look-ups on inquiries, shared LAN and packet-switching networks are examples of systems that often fit this category.
- *Ratio greater than 1:* If you observe this, you need to use the M/G/1 model and not rely on the M/M/1 model. The most common occurrence of this in a communications system is a bimodal distribution, with a wide spread between the peaks. An example is a system that experiences many short messages, many long messages, and few in between.

Incidentally, the same consideration applies to the arrival rate. For a Poisson arrival rate, the inter-arrival times are exponential, and the ratio of standard deviation to mean is 1. If the observed ratio is much less than one, then arrivals tend to be evenly spaced (not much variability), and the Poisson assumption will overestimate queue sizes and delays. On the other hand, if the ratio is greater than 1, then arrivals tend to cluster and congestion becomes more acute.

TABLE A-4   Formulas for Multiserver Queues (M/M/N)

Assumptions: 1. Poisson arrival rate.
2. Exponential service times
3. All servers equally loaded
4. All servers have same mean service time
5. First-in, first-out dispatching
6. No items leave the queue

$$K = \frac{\displaystyle\sum_{N=0}^{M-1} \frac{(M\rho)^N}{N!}}{\displaystyle\sum_{N=0}^{M} \frac{(M\rho)^N}{N!}} \qquad \text{useful parameter}$$

Probability that all servers are busy =

$$B = \frac{1 - K}{1 - \rho K}$$

$$q = B \frac{\rho}{1 - \rho} + M\rho$$

$$w = B \frac{\rho}{1 - \rho}$$

$$t_q = \frac{B}{M} \frac{s}{1 - \rho} + s$$

$$t_w = \frac{B}{M} \frac{s}{1 - \rho}$$

$$\sigma_{tq} = \frac{s}{M(1 - \rho)} \sqrt{B(2 - B) + M^2(1 - \rho)^2}$$

$$\sigma_w = \frac{1}{1 - \rho} \sqrt{B\rho(1 + \rho - B\rho)}$$

$$Pr[t_w > t] = B e^{-M(1 - \rho)t/s}$$

$$t_d = \frac{s}{M(1 - \rho)}$$

A-4

MULTISERVER QUEUES

Table A-4 lists formulas for some key parameters for the multiserver case. Note the restrictiveness of the assumptions. Useful congestion statistics for this model have been obtained only for the case of M/M/N, where the exponential service times are identical for the N servers.

A-5

NETWORKS OF QUEUES

In a communications environment, isolated queues are fortunately not the only problem presented to the analyst. Often, the problem to be analyzed consists of

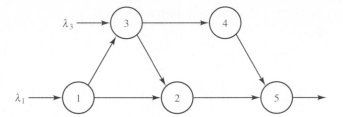

FIGURE A-6.   Example network of queues.

several interconnected queues. Figure A-6 illustrates this situation, using nodes to represent queues, and the interconnecting lines to represent traffic flow.

Two elements of such a network complicate the methods shown so far:

- The partitioning and merging of traffic, as illustrated by nodes 1 and 5 respectively in the figure.
- The existence of queues in tandem, or series, as illustrated by nodes 3 and 4.

No exact method has been developed for analyzing general queuing problems that have the above elements. However, if the traffic flow is Poisson and the service times are exponential, an exact and simple solution exists. In this section, we first examine the two elements listed above, and then present the approach to queuing analysis.

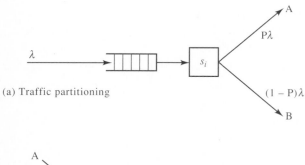

(a) Traffic partitioning

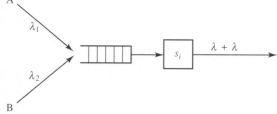

(b) Traffic merging

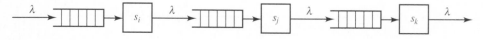

(c) Simple tandem queue

FIGURE A-7.   Elements of queuing networks.

Partitioning and Merging of Traffic Streams

Suppose that traffic arrives at a queue with a mean arrival rate of λ, and that there are two paths, A and B, by which an item may depart (Figure A-7a). When an item is serviced and departs the queue, it does so via path A with probability P and via path B with probability $(1 - P)$. In general, the traffic distribution of streams A and B will differ from the incoming distribution. However, if the incoming distribution is Poisson, then the two departing traffic flows also have Poisson distributions, with mean rates of $P\lambda$ and $(1 - P)\lambda$.

A similar situation exists for traffic merging. If two Poisson streams with mean rate of λ_1 and λ_2 are merged, the resulting stream is Poisson with a mean rate of $\lambda_1 + \lambda_2$.

Both of these results generalize to more than two departing streams for partitioning and more than two arriving streams for merging.

Queues in Tandem

Figure A-7c is an example of a set of single-server queues in tandem: The input for each queue except the first is the output of the previous queue. Assume that the input to the first queue is Poisson. Then, if the service time of each queue is exponential and the waiting lines are infinite, the output of each queue is a Poisson stream statistically identical to the input. When this stream is fed into the next queue, the delays at the second queue are the same as if the original traffic had bypassed the first queue and fed directly into the second queue. Thus the queues are independent, and may be analyzed one at a time. Therefore, the mean total delay for the tandem system is equal to the sum of the mean delays at each stage.

This result can be extended to the case where some or all of the nodes in tandem are multiserver queues.

Jackson's Theorem

Jackson's theorem can be used to analyze a network of queues. The theorem is based on three assumptions:

1. The queuing network consists of m nodes, each of which provides an independent exponential service.
2. Items arriving from outside the system to any one of the nodes arrive with a Poisson rate.
3. Once served at a node, an item goes (immediately) to one of the other nodes with a fixed probability, or out of the system.

Jackson's theorem states that in such a network of queues, each node is an independent queuing system, with a Poisson input determined by the principles of partitioning, merging, and tandem queuing. Thus each node may be analyzed separately from the others using the M/M/1 or M/M/N model, and the results may be combined by ordinary statistical methods. Mean delays at each node may be added to derive system delays, but nothing can be said about the higher moments of system delays (e.g., standard deviation).

Jackson's theorem appears attractive for application to packet-switching networks. One can model the packet-switching network as a network of queues. Each packet represents an individual item. We assume that each packet is transmitted separately and, at each packet-switching node in the path from source to destination, the packet is queued for transmission on the next length. The service at a queue is the actual transmission of the packet and is proportional to the length of the packet.

The flaw in this approach is that a condition of the theorem is violated: namely, it is not the case that the service distributions are independent. Since the length of a packet is the same at each transmission link, the arrival process to each queue is correlated to the service process. However, Kleinrock [KLEI76] has demonstrated that, because of the averaging effect of merging and partitioning, assuming independent service times provides a good approximation.

Application to a Packet-Switching Network[3]

Consider a packet-switching network, consisting of nodes interconnected by transmission links, with each node acting as the interface for zero or more attached systems, each of which functions as a source and destination of traffic. The external workload that is offered to the network can be characterized as:

$$\gamma = \sum_{j=1}^{N} \sum_{k=1}^{n} \gamma_{jk}$$

where

γ = total workload in packets per second
γ_{jk} = workload between source j and destination k

Since a packet may traverse more than one link between source and destination, the total internal workload will be higher than the offered load:

$$\lambda = \sum_{i=1}^{L} \lambda_i$$

where

λ = total load on all of the links in the network
λ_i = load on link i

The internal load will depend on the actual path taken by packets through the network. We will assume a routing algorithm is given such that the load on the individual links, λ_i, can be determined from the offered load, γ_{jk}. For any particular routing assignment, we can determine the average number of links that a packet will traverse from these workload parameters. Some thought should convice you that the average length for all paths is given by:

$$E[\text{number of links in a path}] = \frac{\lambda}{\gamma}$$

Now, our objective is to determine the average delay, T, experienced by a packet through the network. For this purpose, it is useful to apply Little's formula (Table

---

[3]This discussion is based on the development in [MOLL89].

A-2). For each link in the network, the average number of items in the queue for that link is given by:

$$q_i = \lambda_i t_i$$

Where t_i is the yet-to-be-determined queuing delay at each queue. Suppose that we sum these quantities. That would give us the average total number of packets waiting in all of the queues of the network. Now, it turns out that Little's formula works in the aggregate as well.[4] Thus, the number of packets waiting in the network can be expressed as γT. Combining the two:

$$T = \frac{1}{\gamma} \sum_{i=1}^{L} \lambda_i t_i$$

To determine the value of T, we need to determine the values of the individual delays, t_i. Since we are assuming that each queue can be treated as an independent M/M/1 model, this is easily determined:

$$t_i = \frac{s_i}{1 - \rho_i} = \frac{s_i}{1 - \lambda_i s_i}$$

The service time s_i for link i is just the product of the data rate on the link in bits per second and the average packet length in bits. To be consistent with commonly used notation we will denote these values as C_i and $1/\mu$ respectively. Then:

$$t_i = \frac{\dfrac{1}{\mu C_i}}{1 - \dfrac{\lambda_i}{\mu C_i}} = \frac{1}{\mu C_i - \lambda_i}$$

Putting all of the elements together, we can calculate the average delay of packets sent through the network:

$$T = \frac{1}{\gamma} \sum_{i=1}^{L} \frac{\lambda_i}{\mu C_i - \lambda_i}$$

A-6

EXAMPLES

Let us look at a few examples to get some feel for the use of these equations.

Terminal Queuing

Consider a computer that has a leased telephone line with 10 remote terminals on the line. The average transmission time of messages on the line is 6 seconds, and the standard deviation is estimated to equal the mean. At peak times, the message rate over the line reaches 2 per minute. We would like to find:

- The average response time ignoring line overhead.

---

[4] In essence, this statement is based on the fact that the sum of the averages is the average of the sums.

- If a 15-second response time is considered the maximum acceptable, what percent growth in message load can occur before the maximum is reached?
- If 20% more utilization is experienced, will response time increase more or less than 20%?

We will assume an M/M/1 model, with the transmission line being the server. Facility utilization is calculated as:

$$\rho = \lambda s$$
$$= (2 \text{ arrivals per minute})(6 \text{ seconds per transmission})/(60 \text{ sec/min})$$
$$= 0.2$$

The first value, average response time, is easily calculated:

$$t_q = s/(1 - \rho)$$
$$= (6/(1 - 0.2) = 7.5 \text{ seconds}$$

The second value is more difficult to obtain. Indeed, as worded, there is no answer since there is a nonzero probability that some instances of response time will exceed 15 seconds for any value of utilization. Instead, let us say that we would like 90% of all reponses to be less than 15 seconds. Then, we can use the equation from Table A-3b:

$$m_{tq}(r) = t_q \times \log_e (100/(100 - r))$$
$$m_{tq}(90) = t_q(\log_e (10)) = \frac{s}{1 - \rho} \times 2.3 = 15 \text{ sec}$$

We have $s = 6$. Solving for ρ yields $\rho = 0.08$. In fact, utilization would have to decline from 20% to 8% to put 15 seconds at the 90th percentile.

The third part of the question is to find the relationship between increases in load versus response time. Since a facility utilization of 0.2 is down in the flat part of the curve, response time will increase more slowly than utilization. In this case, if facility utilization increases from 20% to 40%, which is a 100% increase, the value of t_q goes from 7.5 seconds to 10 seconds, which is an increase of only 33%.

Multilink Protocol

In Chapter 13, we referred to the multilink protocol (MLP) that is part of X.25. A similar facility is available in SNA in the transmission group sublayer of the path control layer (see Chapter 12). With MLP, a set of links exists between two nodes, and it used as a pooled resource for transmitting packets, regardless of virtual circuit number. When a packet is presented to MLP for transmission, any available link may be chosen.

This approach requires extra processing and frame overhead compared to a simple link protocol. As Figure 13-4 illustrates, a special MLP header is needed for the procedure. The alternative would be to assign each newly created virtual circuit to a particular link, and to try to balance the number of virtual circuits assigned to each link. This would simplify processing. The question is: what effect would this have on performance?

Let us consider a concrete example. Suppose that there are five 9600-bps links connecting two nodes, and that the average packet size is 100 octets. Thus the average service time is (100 octets × 8)/(9600 bps) = 0.0833 sec. Assume that the standard deviation of service time is observed to be 0.079 sec. Note that this is about 95% of the mean; thus we will assume exponential service time. During peak load time, packets arrive at the rate of 48 packets/sec.

Single-Server Approach. If virtual circuits are evenly distributed among the links, then the load for each link is 48/5 = 9.6 packets per second. Thus,

$$\rho = \lambda s$$
$$= 9.6 \times 0.0833 = 0.8$$

The queuing time is then easily calculated:

$$t_q = \frac{s}{1 - \rho} = \frac{0.0833}{0.2} = 0.42 \text{ sec}$$

Multiserver Approach. Using the multilink protocol, we now have an aggregate arrival rate of 48 packets per second. However, the facility utilization is still 0.8 ($\lambda s/M$). To calculate the queuing time from the formula in Table A-4, we need to first calculate B. If you have not programmed the parameter, it can be looked up in a table under a facility utilization of 0.8 for 5 servers to yield B = 0.554. Substituting,

$$t_q = (0.0833) + \frac{(0.544)(0.0833)}{5(1 - 0.8)} = 0.13$$

So the use of MLP has reduced average queuing time from 0.42 sec down to 0.13 sec, which is greater than a factor of 3! If we look at just the waiting time, the difference is 0.047 seconds compared to 0.34 seconds, which is a factor of 7.

Although you may not be an expert in queuing theory, you now know enough to be annoyed when you have to wait in a line at a multiple single-server queue facility.

Calculating Percentiles[5]

Messages arrive at a switching center for a particular outgoing communication line with a mean arrival rate of 5 per second. The average message length is 144 characters, and it is assumed that message length is exponentially distributed. Line speed is 9600 bps. The following questions are asked:

1. What is the mean queuing time in the switching center?
2. How many messages are in the switching center, including those waiting for transmission and the one currently being transmitted (if any), on the average?
3. Same question as (2), for the 90th percentile.
4. Same question as (2), for the 95th percentile.

$\lambda = 5$ msgs/sec
(144 characters $\times$ 8 bits/char)/s = 9600 bps = 0.12 sec
$\rho = \lambda s = 5 \times 0.12 = 0.6$

Mean queuing time:

$$t_q = s/(1 - \rho) = 0.3 \text{ sec}$$

[5]Based on example in [IBM71].

Mean queue length:

$$q = \rho/(1 - \rho) = 1.5 \text{ messages}$$

To obtain the percentiles, we use the equation from Table A-3b:

$$Pr[q = N] = (1 - \rho)\rho^N$$

To calculate the rth percentile of queue size, we write the above equation in cumulative form:

$$\frac{r}{100} = \sum_{k=0}^{m(r)} (1 - \rho)\rho^k = 1 - \rho^{1+m(r)}$$

Here $m(r)$ represents the maximum number of messages in the queue expected r percent of the time. In the form given, we can determine the percentile for any queue size. We wish to do the reverse: given r, find $m(r)$. So, taking the logarithm to the base 10 of both sides:

$$m(r) = \frac{\log\left(1 - \frac{r}{100}\right)}{\log \rho} - 1$$

If $m(r)$ is fractional, take the next higher integer; if it is negative, set it to zero. For our example, $\rho = 0.6$ and we wish to find $m(90)$ and $m(95)$:

$$m(90) = \frac{\log(1 - 0.90)}{\log(0.6)} - 1 = 3.5$$

$$m(95) = \frac{\log(1 - 0.95)}{\log(0.6)} - 1 = 4.8$$

Thus, 90% of the time there are fewer than 4 messages in the queue, and 95% of the time there are fewer than 5 messages. If we were designing to a 95th percentile criterion, a buffer would have to be provided to store at least 5 messages.

A-7

OTHER QUEUING MODELS

In this appendix, we have concentrated on one type of queuing model. There are in fact a number of models, based on two key factors:

- The manner in which blocked items are handled
- The number of traffic sources

When an item arrives at a server and finds that server busy, or arrives at a multiple-server facility and finds all servers busy, that item is said to be blocked. Blocked items can be handled in a number of ways. First, the item can be placed in a queue awaiting a free server. This is referred to in the telephone traffic literature as *lost calls delayed*, although in fact the call is not lost. Alternatively, no waiting line is provided. This in turn leads to two assumptions about the action of the item. The item may wait some random amount of time and then try again; this is known as *lost calls cleared*. If the item repeatedly attempts to gain service, with no pause, it is referred to as *lost calls held*. The lost calls delayed model is the most appropriate for most computer and data communications problems. Lost calls cleared is usually the most appropriate in a telephone switching environment.

The second key element of a traffic model is whether the number of sources is assumed infinite or finite. For an infinite source model, there is assumed to be a fixed arrival rate. For the finite source case, the arrival rate will depend on the number of sources already engaged. Thus, if each of L sources generates arrivals at a rate λ/L, then when the queuing facility is unoccupied, the arrival rate is λ. However, if K sources are in the queuing facility at a particular time, then the instantaneous arrival rate at that time is $\lambda(L - K)/L$. Infinite source models are easier to deal with. The infinite source assumption is reasonable when the number of sources is at least 5 to 10 times the capacity of the system.

A-8

RECOMMENDED READING

Perhaps the most useful reference that you could acquire is [MART72]. Despite the age of this book, it is a valuable practical source. The book provides a number of graphs and tables that can be used to perform quick queuing analyses. It also provides detailed guidance for the application of queuing analysis plus a number of worked-out examples.

In addition to Martin's book, there are several obscure but readily available publications that are of great practical assistance. [IBM71] is an excellent concise treatment of queuing analysis applied to computer and communications problems, with many examples, plus graphs and tables. [FRAN76] is a good collection of tables for various queuing models. An excellent guide to the practical application of statistics is [NBS63]; the book contains tables, formulas, and examples that aid in determining the proper procedure for estimating values from samples and in evaluating the results.

The above references are sufficient for those who wish to apply queuing analysis. For those who wish to delve more deeply into the subject, a host of books is available. Some of the more worthwhile ones are the following. Good texts that provide a treatment of queuing theory and its application to computers and communications are [MOLL89] and [KOBA78]. [STUC85] is an excellent treatment that focuses on data communications and networking. [COOP81] covers the subject with an emphasis on concepts of telephone traffic analysis. The classic treatment of queuing theory for computer applications, with a detailed discussion of computer networks, is found in [KLEI75] and [KLEI76]. [CONW89] provides a good summary of queuing results including more recent results; the mathematical treatment, however, makes for rather stiff reading.

ANNEX A

BASIC CONCEPTS

Measures of Probability

A continuous random variable X can be described by either its distribution or density function:

$$F(x) = Pr[X \leq x] \qquad \text{distribution function}$$

$$f(x) = \frac{d}{dx} F(x) \qquad \text{density function}$$

For a discrete random variable, its probability distribution is characterized by

$$P_X(k) = Pr[X = k]$$

We are often concerned with some characteristic of a random variable, rather than the entire distribution. For example, the mean value:

$$E[X] = \int_{-\infty}^{\infty} x f(x) \, dx \qquad \text{continuous case}$$

$$E[X] = \sum_{\text{all } k} k \, Pr[x = k] \qquad \text{discrete case}$$

Other useful measures:

Second moment: $\quad E[X^2] = \int_{-\infty}^{\infty} x^2 \, f(x) \, dx \qquad \qquad$ continuous case

Second moment: $\quad E[X^2] = \sum_{\text{all } k} k^2 \, Pr[x = k] \qquad \qquad$ discrete case

Variance: $\qquad \text{Var} [X] = E[(X - E[X])^2] = E[X^2] - E^2[X]$

Standard deviation $\quad \sigma_X = \sqrt{\text{Var}[X]}$

The variance and standard deviation are measures of the dispersion of values around the mean.

The Exponential and Poisson Distributions

The exponential distribution (Figure A-8a and A-8b) is given by:

$$F(x) = 1 - e^{-\mu x} \qquad \text{distribution}$$
$$f(x) = \mu e^{-\mu x} \qquad \text{density}$$

The exponential distribution has the interesting property that its mean is equal to its standard deviation:

$$E[X] = \sigma_X = \frac{1}{\mu}$$

When used to refer to a time interval, such as a service time, this distribution is sometimes referred to as a random distribution. This is because, for a time interval that has already begun, each time at which the interval may finish is equally likely.

This distribution is important in queuing theory because we often assume that the service time of a server in a queuing system is exponential. In the case of telephone traffic, the service time is the time for which a subscriber engages the equipment of interest. In a packet-switching network, the service time is the transmission time and is therefore proportional to the packet length. It is difficult to give a sound theoretical reason why service times should be exponential, but the fact is that in most cases they are very nearly exponential. This is good news because it simplifies the queuing analysis immensely.

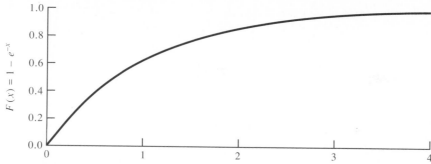

(a) Exponential probability distribution function

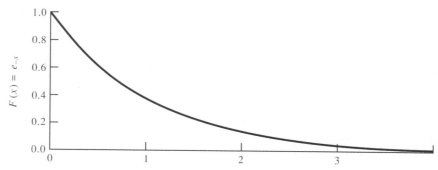

(b) Exponential probability density function

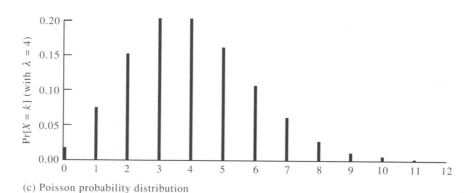

(c) Poisson probability distribution

FIGURE A-8. Some probability functions.

Another important distribution is the Poisson distribution:

$$Pr[X = k] = \frac{\lambda^k}{k!} e^{-\lambda}$$

$$E[X] = \sigma_X = \lambda$$

The Poisson distribution is also important in queuing analysis because we must assume a Poisson arrival pattern in order to be able to develop the queuing equations. Fortunately, the assumption of Poisson arrivals is usually valid.

The way in which the Poisson distribution can be applied to arrival rate is as follows. If items are arriving at a queue according to a Poisson process, this may be expressed as:

$$Pr[k \text{ items arrive in a time interval } T] = \frac{(\lambda T)^k}{k!} e^{-\lambda T}$$

$$\text{Expected number of items to arrive in time interval } T = \lambda T$$

$$\text{Mean arrival rate, in items per second} = \lambda$$

Arrivals occurring according to a Poisson process are often said to be random. This is because the probability of arrival of an item in a small interval is proportional to the length of the interval, and is independent of the amount of elapsed time since the arrival of the last item. That is, when items are arriving according to a Poisson process, an item is as likely to arrive at one instant as any other, regardless of the instants at which the other customers arrive.

Another interesting property of the Poisson process is its relationship to the exponential distribution. If we look at the times between arrivals of items Ta (called the inter-arrival times), then we find that this quantity obeys the exponential distribution:

$$Pr[Ta \leq t] = 1 - e^{-\lambda t}$$

$$E[Ta] = \frac{1}{\lambda}$$

Thus the mean interarrival time is the reciprocal of the arrival rate, as one would expect.

Sampling

To perform a queuing analysis, we need to estimate the values of the input parameters, specifically the mean and standard deviation of the arrival rate and service time. If we are contemplating a new system, these estimates may have to be based on judgment and an assessment of the equipment and work patterns likely to prevail. However, it will often be the case that an existing system is available for examination. For example, a collection of terminals, personal computers, and host computers are interconnected in a building by direct connection and multiplexers, and it is desired to replace the interconnection facility with a local area network. To be able to size the network, it is possible to measure the load currently generated by each device.

The measurements that are taken are in the form of samples. A particular parameter, for example, the rate of packets generated by a terminal or the size of packets, is estimated by observing the number of packets generated during a period of time.

To estimate a quantity, such as the length of a packet, the following equations can be used:

sample mean:
$$\overline{X} = \frac{1}{n} \sum_{i=1}^{n} X_i$$

sample variance:
$$S^2 = \frac{\sum_{i=1}^{n} (X_i - \overline{X})^2}{n - 1}$$

$$= \frac{n \sum_{i=1}^{n} X_i^2 - \left(\sum_{i=1}^{n} X_i \right)^2}{n(n-1)}$$

sample standard deviation: $S = \sqrt{S^2}$

where

n = sample size
X_i = ith sample

To estimate the arrival rate from a sample, we can use the following:

$$\bar{\lambda} = \frac{n}{T}$$

where n is the number of items observed in a period of time of duration T. Another approach is to consider each arrival time as a sample and calculate the sample mean and sample standard deviation as above.

When we estimate values such as the mean and standard deviation on the basis of a sample, we leave the realm of probability and enter that of statistics. This is a complex topic which will not be explored here, except to provide a few comments.

It is important to note that the sample mean and sample standard deviation are themselves random variables. For example, if you take a sample from some population and calculate the sample mean, and do this a number of times, the calculated values will differ. Thus, we can talk of the mean and standard deviation of the sample mean, or even of the entire probability distribution of the sample mean.

It follows that the probabilistic nature of our estimated values is a source of error, known as sampling error. In general, the greater the size of the sample taken, the smaller the standard deviation of the sample mean, and therefore the closer that our estimate is likely to be to the actual mean. By making certain reasonable assumptions about the nature of the random variable being tested and the randomness of the sampling procedure, one can in fact determine the probability that a sample mean or sample standard deviation is within a certain distance from the actual mean or standard deviation. This concept is often reported with the results of a sample. For example, it is common for the result of an opinion poll to include a comment such as: "The result is within 5% of the true value with a confidence (probability) of 99%."

There is, however, another source of error, which is less widely appreciated among non-statisticians, namely bias. For example, if an opinion poll is conducted, and only members of a certain socio-economic group are interviewed, the results are not necessarily representative of the entire population. In a communications context, sampling done during one time of day may not reflect the activity at another time of day. If we are concerned to design a system that will handle the peak load that is likely to be experienced, then we should observe the traffic during the time of day that is most likely to produce the greatest load.

GLOSSARY

Some of the terms in this glossary are from the *Glossary of Telecommunication Terms*, FED-STD-1037A, National Communications Systems, 1986. These are indicated in the text by an asterisk.

Aloha. A medium access control technique for multiple access transmission media. A station transmits whenever it has data to send. Unacknowledged transmissions are repeated.

Amplitude. The size or magnitude of a voltage or current waveform.

Amplitude modulation.* A form of modulation in which the amplitude of a carrier wave is varied in accordance with some characteristic of the modulating signal.

Amplitude-shift keying. Modulation in which the two binary values are represented by two different amplitudes of the carrier frequency.

Analog data.* Data represented by a physical quantity that is considered to be continuously variable and whose magnitude is made directly proportional to the data or to a suitable function of the data.

Analog signal. A continuously varying electromagnetic wave that may be propagated over a variety of media.

Analog transmission. The transmission of analog signals without regard to content. The signal may be amplified, but there is no intermediate attempt to recover the data from the signal.

Angle modulation.* Modulation in which the angle of a sine wave carrier is varied. Phase and frequency modulation are particular forms of angle modulation.

Application layer. Layer 7 of the OSI model. This layer determines the interface of the system with the user.

Asynchronous transmission. Transmission in which each information character is individually synchronized (usually by the use of start elements and stop elements).

Attenuation. A decrease in magnitude of current, voltage, or power of a signal in transmission between points.

Automatic repeat request. A feature that automatically initiates a request for retransmission when an error in transmission is detected.

Balanced transmission. A transmission mode in which signals are transmitted as a current that travels down one conductor and returns on the other. For digital signals, this technique is known as differential signaling, with the binary value depending on the voltage difference.

Bandlimited signal. A signal all of whose energy is contained within a finite frequency range.

Bandwidth.* The difference between the limiting frequencies of a continuous frequency spectrum.

Baseband. Transmission of signals without modulation. In a baseband local network, digital signals (1's and 0's) are inserted directly onto the cable as voltage pulses. The entire spectrum of the cable is consumed by the signal. This scheme does not allow frequency-division multiplexing.

Bell operating companies. Before divestiture, the 22 Bell operating companies (BOCs) were AT&T subsidiaries that built, operated, and maintained the local and intrastate networks and provided most of the day-to-day service for customers. After divestiture, the BOCs retain their identity within seven regional companies and are responsible for local service as defined by local access and transport areas (LATAs).

Bit stuffing. The insertion of extra bits into a data stream to avoid the appearance of unintended control sequences.

Bridge. A device that links two homogeneous packet-broadcast local networks. It accepts all packets from each network addressed to devices on the other, buffers them, and retransmits them to the other network.

Broadband. The use of coaxial cable for providing data transfer by means of analog (radio-frequency) signals. Digital signals are passed through a modem and transmitted over one of the frequency bands of the cable.

Broadcast. The simultaneous transmission of data to a number of stations.

Broadcast address. An address that designates all entities within a domain (e.g., network, internet).

Broadcast communication network. A communication network in which a transmission from one station is broadcast to and received by all other stations.

Bus.* One or more conductors that serve as a common connection for a related group of devices.

Carrier. A continuous frequency capable of being modulated or impressed with a second (information carrying) signal.

CATV. Community Antenna Television. CATV cable is used for broadband local networks, and broadcast TV distribution.

Cellular radio. The use of low-power radio transmitters arranged in a honeycomb pattern, to permit reuse of a frequency multiple times in a small area.

Checksum. An error-detecting code based on a summation operation performed on the bits to be checked.

Circuit switching. A method of communicating in which a dedicated communications path is established between two devices through one or more intermediate switching nodes. Unlike packet switching, digital data are sent as a continuous stream of bits. Bandwidth is guaranteed, and delay is essentially limited to propagation time. The telephone system uses circuit switching.

Coaxial cable. A cable consisting of one conductor, usually a small copper tube or wire, within and insulated from another conductor of larger diameter, usually copper tubing or copper braid.

Codec. Coder-decoder. Transforms analog data into a digital bit stream (coder), and digital signals into analog data (decoder).

Collision. A condition in which two packets are being transmitted over a medium at the same time. Their interference makes both unintelligible.

Common carrier. In the United States, companies that furnish communication services to the public. The usual connotation is for long-distance telecommunications services. Common carriers are subject to regulation by federal and state regulatory commissions.

Common channel signaling. Technique in which network control signals (e.g., call request) are separated from the associated voice or data path by placing the signaling from a group of voice or data paths on a separate channel dedicated to signaling only.

Communications architecture. The hardware and software structure that implements the communications function.

Communication network. A collection of interconnected functional units that provides a data communications service among stations attached to the network.

Connectionless data transfer. A protocol for exchanging data in an unplanned fashion and without prior coordination (e.g., datagram).

Connection-oriented data transfer. A protocol for exchanging data in which a logical connection is established between the endpoints (e.g., virtual circuit).

Contention. The condition when two or more stations attempt to use the same channel at the same time.

Crosstalk.* The phenomenon in which a signal transmitted on one circuit or channel of a transmission system creates an undesired effect in another circuit or channel.

CSMA. Carrier Sense Multiple Access. A medium access control technique for multiple-access transmission media. A station wishing to transmit first senses the medium and transmits only if the medium is idle.

CSMA/CD. Carrier Sense Multiple Access with Collision Detection. A refinement of CSMA in which a station ceases transmission if it detects a collision.

Current-mode transmission. A transmission mode in which the transmitter alternately applies current to each of two conductors in a twisted pair to represent logic 1 or 0. The total current is constant and always in the same direction.

Cyclic redundancy check. An error detecting code in which the code is the remainder resulting from dividing the bits to be checked by a predetermined binary number.

Data circuit-terminating equipment. In a data station, the equipment that provides the signal conversion and coding between the data terminal equipment (DTE) and the line. The DCE may be separate equipment or an integral part of the DTE or of intermediate equipment. The DCE may perform other functions that are normally performed at the network end of the line.

Datagram. In packet switching, a self-contained packet, independent of other packets, that does not require acknowledgment, and that carries information sufficient for routing from the originating data terminal equipment (DTE), without relying on earlier exchanges between the DTEs and the network.

Data link layer. Layer 2 of the OSI model. Converts unreliable transmission channel into reliable one.

Data terminal equipment (DTE).* Equipment consisting of digital end instruments that convert the user information into data signals for transmission, or reconvert the received data signals into user information.

Decibel. A measure of the relative strength of two signals. The number of decibels is 10 times the log of the ratio of the power of two signals, or 20 times the log of the ratio of the voltage of two signals.

Delay distortion. Distortion of a signal occurring when the propagation delay for the transmission medium is not constant over the frequency range of the signal.

Demand-assignment multiple access. A technique for allocating satellite capacity, based on either FDM or TDM, in which capacity is granted on demand.

Differential encoding. A means of encoding digital data on a digital signal such that the binary value is determined by a signal change rather than a signal level.

Digital data. Data consisting of a sequence of discrete elements.

Digital private branch exchange. A local network based on the private branch exchange (PBX) architecture. Provides an integrated voice/data switching service.

Digital signal. A discrete or discontinuous signal, such as voltage pulses.

Digital switch. A star topology local network. Usually refers to a system that handles only data but not voice.

Digital transmission. The transmission of digital data, using either an analog or digital signal, in which the digital data is recovered and repeated at intermediate points to reduce the effects of noise.

Digitize.* To convert an analog signal to a digital signal.

DOD Protocol architecture. A communications architecture that has evolved from the ARPANET project and DOD standardization activities.

Encapsulation. The addition of control information by a protocol entity to data obtained from a protocol user.

Error detecting code.* A code in which each expression conforms to specific rules of construction, so that if certain errors occur in an expression, the resulting expression will not conform to the rules of construction and thus the presence of the errors is detected.

Error rate.* The ratio of the number of data units in error to the total number of data units.

Fast select.   An option of the X.25 virtual call that allows the inclusion of data in the call setup and call clearing packets.

Flow control.   The function performed by a receiving entity to limit the amount or rate of data that is sent by a transmitting entity.

Frame check sequence.   An error-detecting code inserted as a field in a block of data to be transmitted. The code serves to check for errors upon reception of the data.

Frequency.   Rate of signal oscillation in hertz.

Frequency-division multiple access.   A technique for allocating capacity on a satellite channel using fixed-assignment FDM.

Frequency-division multiplexing.   The division of a transmission facility into two or more channels by splitting the frequency band transmitted by the facility into narrower bands, each of which is used to constitute a distinct channel.

Frequency modulation.   Modulation in which the frequency of an alternating current is the characteristic varied.

Frequency-shift keying.   Modulation in which the two binary values are represented by two different frequencies near the carrier frequency.

Full-duplex transmission.   Data transmission in both directions at the same time.

Gateway.   A device that connects two systems, especially if the systems use different protocols. For example, a gateway is needed to connect two independent local networks, or to connect a local network to a long-haul network.

Half-duplex transmission.   Data transmission in either direction, one direction at a time.

HDLC (high-level data link control).   A very common bit-oriented data link protocol (OSI layer 2) issued by ISO. Similar protocols are ADCCP, LAP-B, and SDLC.

Header.   System-defined control information that precedes user data.

High-speed local network (HSLN).   A local network designed to provide high throughput between expensive, high-speed devices, such as mainframes and mass storage devices.

Impulse noise.   A high-amplitude, short-duration noise pulse.

Integrated services digital network.   A planned worldwide telecommunication service that will use digital transmission and switching technology to support voice and digital data communication.

Intermodulation noise.   Noise due to the nonlinear combination of signals of different frequencies.

Internet.   A collection of packet-switched and broadcast networks that are connected together via gateways.

Internet protocol.   An internetworking protocol that provides connectionless service across multiple packet-switched networks.

Internetworking.   Communication among devices across multiple networks.

Local area network (LAN).   A general-purpose local network that can serve a variety of devices. Typically used for terminals, microcomputers, and minicomputers.

Local loop.   Transmission path, generally twisted pair, between the individual subscriber and the nearest switching center of the public telecommunications network.

Local network.   A communication network that provides interconnection of a variety of data communicating devices within a small area.

Longitudinal redundancy check.   The use of a set of parity bits for a block of characters such that there is a parity bit for each bit position in the characters.

Manchester encoding.   A digital signaling technique in which there is a transition in the middle of each bit time. A 1 is encoded with a high level during the first half of the bit time; a 0 is encoded with a low level during the first half of the bit time.

Medium access control (MAC).   For broadcast networks, the method of determining which device has access to the transmission medium at any time. CSMA/CD and token are common access methods.

Message switching.   A switching technique using a message store-and-forward system. No dedicated path is established. Rather, each message contains a destination address and is passed from source to destination through intermediate nodes. At each node, the entire message is received, stored briefly, and then passed on to the next node.

Microwave.   Electromagnetic waves in the frequency range of about 2 to 40 GHz.

Modem. Modulator/Demodulator.   Transforms a digital bit stream into an analog signal (modulator), and vice versa (demodulator).

Modulation.*   The process, or result of the process, of varying certain characteristics of a signal, called a carrier, in accordance with a message signal.

Multicast address.   An address that designates a group of entities within a domain (e.g., network, internet).

Multiplexing.   In data transmission, a function that permits two or more data sources to share a common transmission medium such that each data source has its own channel.

Multipoint.   A configuration in which more than two stations share a transmission path.

Network layer.   Layer 3 of the OSI model. Responsible for routing data through a communication network.

Network terminating equipment.   Grouping of ISDN functions at the boundary between the ISDN and the subscriber.

Noise.   Unwanted signals that combine with and hence distort the signal intended for transmission and reception.

Nonreturn to zero.   A digital signaling technique in which the signal is at a constant level for the duration of a bit time.

Optical fiber.   A thin filament of glass or other transparent material through which a signal-encoded light beam may be transmitted by means of total internal reflection.

Packet assembler/disassembler. A device used with an X.25 network to provide service to asynchronous terminals.

Packet switching. A method of transmitting messages through a communication network, in which long messages are subdivided into short packets. The packets are then transmitted as in message switching. Usually, packet switching is more efficient and rapid than message switching.

Parity bit.* A check bit appended to an array of binary digits to make the sum of all the binary digits, including the check bit, always odd or always even.

PBX. Private branch exchange. A telephone exchange on the user's premises. Provides a switching facility for telephones on extension lines within the building and access to the public telephone network. May be manual (PMBX) or automatic (PABX). A digital PBX that also handles data devices without modems is called a CBX.

Phase. The relative position in time within a single period of a signal.

Phase modulation. Modulation in which the phase angle of a carrier is the characteristic varied.

Phase-shift keying. Modulation in which the phase of the carrier signal is shifted to represent digital data.

Physical layer. Layer 1 of the OSI model. Concerned with the electrical, mechanical, and timing aspects of signal transmission over a medium.

Piggybacking. The inclusion of an acknowledgment to a previously received packet in an outgoing data packet.

Point-to-point. A configuration in which two stations share a transmission path.

Poll and select. The process by which a primary station invites secondary stations, one at a time, to transmit (poll), and by which a primary station requests that a secondary receive data (select).

Presentation layer. Layer 6 of the OSI model. Concerned with data format and display.

Protocol. A set of rules that govern the operation of functional units to achieve communication.

Protocol data unit. A block of data exchanged between two entities via a protocol.

Public data network. A government-controlled or national monopoly packet-switched network. This service is publicly available to data processing users.

Pulse code modulation. A process in which a signal is sampled, and the magnitude of each sample with respect to a fixed reference is quantized and converted by coding to a digital signal.

Residual error rate. The error rate remaining after attempts at correction are made.

Ring. A local network topology in which stations are attached to repeaters connected in a closed loop. Data are transmitted in one direction around the ring, and can be read by all attached stations.

RS-232-C. A physical layer interface standard for the interconnection of equipment, established by EIA.

RS-449/422-A/423-A. A set of physical layer standards developed by EIA and intended to replace RS-232-C. RS-422-A and RS-423-A specify electrical characteristics; RS-449 specifies mechanical, functional, and procedural characteristics.

Satellite-switched time-division multiple access (SS/TDMA). A form of TDMA in which circuit switching is used to dynamically change the channel assignments.

Service access point. A means of identifying a user of the services of a protocol entity. A protocol entity provides one or more SAPs for use by higher-level entities.

Session layer. Layer 5 of the OSI model. Manages a logical connection (session) between two communicating processes or applications.

Simplex transmission. Data transmission in one preassigned direction only.

Single channel per carrier. A technique for allocating satellite capacity in which the bandwidth is divided into a number of individual voice-frequency channels.

Sliding-window technique. A method of flow control in which a transmitting station may send numbered packets within a window of numbers. The window changes dynamically to allow additional packets to be sent.

Space-division switching. A circuit-switching technique in which each connection through the switch take a physically separate and dedicated path.

Spectrum. Refers to an absolute range of frequencies. For example, the spectrum of CATV cable is now about 5 to 400 MHz.

Star. A topology in which all stations are connected to a central switch. Two stations communicate via circuit switching.

Statistical time-division multiplexing. A method of TDM in which time slots on a shared transmission line are allocated to I/O channels on demand.

Stop and wait. A flow control protocol in which the sender transmits a block of data and then awaits an acknowledgment before transmitting the next block.

Switched communication network. A communication network consisting of a network of nodes connected by point-to-point links. Data are transmitted from source to destination through intermediate nodes.

Synchronous time-division multiplexing. A method of TDM in which time slots on a shared transmission line are assigned to I/O channels on a fixed, predetermined basis.

Synchronous transmission. Data transmission in which the time of occurrence of each signal representing a bit is related to a fixed time frame.

TDM bus switching. A form of time-division switching in which time slots are used to transfer data over a shared bus between transmitter and receiver.

Telematics. User-oriented information transmission services. Includes Teletex, Videotex, and facsimile.

Teletex. A text communications service that provides message preparation and transmission facilities.

Teletext. A one-way information retrieval services. A fixed number of information pages are repetitively broadcast on unused portions of a TV channel bandwidth. A decoder at the TV set is used to select and display pages.

Thermal noise. Statistically uniform noise due to the temperature of the transmission medium.

Time-division multiple access. A synchronous TDM scheme for satellite capacity allocation.

Time-division multiplexing. The division of a transmission facility into two or more channels by allotting the facility to several different information channels, one at a time.

Time-division switching. A circuit-switching technique in which time slots in a time-multiplexed stream of data are manipulated to pass data from an input to an output.

Time-multiplexed switching (TMS). A form of space-division switching in which each input line is a TDM stream. The switching configuration may change for each time slot.

Time-slot interchange (TSI). The interchange of time slots within a time-division multiplexed frame.

Token bus. A medium access control technique for bus/tree. Stations form a logical ring, around which a token is passed. A station receiving the token may transmit data, and then must pass the token on to the next station in the ring.

Token ring. A medium access control technique for rings. A token circulates around the ring. A station may transmit by seizing the token, inserting a packet onto the ring, and then retransmitting the token.

Topology. The structure, consisting of paths and switches, that provides the communications interconnection among nodes of a network.

Transmission medium. The physical path between transmitters and receivers in a communications system.

Transport layer. Layer 4 of the OSI model. Provides reliable, transparent transfer of data between endpoints.

Tree. A local network topology in which stations are attached to a shared transmission medium. The transmission medium is a branching cable emanating from a headend, with no closed circuits. Transmissions propagate throughout all branches of the tree, and are received by all stations.

Twisted pair. A transmission medium consisting of two insulated wires arranged in a regular spiral pattern.

Unbalanced transmission. A transmission mode in which signals are transmitted on a single conductor. Transmitter and receiver share a common ground.

Value-added network. A privately owned packet-switched network whose services are sold to the public.

Videotex. A two-way information retrieval service accessible to terminals and TV sets equipped with a special decoder. Pages of information at a central resource are retrieved interactively over a switched telephone line connection.

Virtual circuit. A packet-switching service in which a connection (virtual circuit) is established between two stations at the start of transmission. All packets follow the same route, need not carry a complete address, and arrive in sequence.

X.21. A network access standard for connecting stations to a circuit-switched network. Includes OSI layers 1-3 functionality.

X.25. A network access standard for connecting stations to a packet-switched network. Includes OSI layers 1-3 functionality.

X.75. An internetworking protocol that provides virtual circuit service across multiple X.25 networks.

REFERENCES

ABBO84   Abbott, G. F. "Digital Space Division: A Technique for Switching High-Speed Data Signals." *IEEE Communications Magazine*, April 1984.

ABRA70   Abramson, N. "The ALOHA System—Another Alternative for Computer Communications." *Proceedings, Fall Joint Computer Conference*, 1970.

AHUJ82   Ahuja, V. *Design and Analysis of Computer Communication Networks*. New York: McGraw-Hill, 1982.

AMAN86   Amand, J. *A Guide to Packet-Switched, Value-Added Networks*. New York: Macmillan, 1986.

AMOR80   Amoroso, F. "The Bandwidth of Digital Data Signals." *IEEE Communications Magazine*, November 1980.

ANON88   Anonymous. "SEL Claims Mark for Optical Transmission." *Electronics*, March 3, 1988.

ANSC82   American National Standards Committee. *American National Dictionary for Information Processing Systems*. X3/TR-1-82, 1982.

AOYA88   Aoyama, T.; Daumer, W.; and Modena, G., eds. *Voice Coding for Communications*. Special issue of the IEEE Journal on Selected Areas in Communications, February 1988.

ARRL84   American Radio Relay League. *AX.25 Amateur Packet-Radio Link-Layer Protocol, Version 2.0*. Newington, CT. 1984.

ATKI80   Atkins, J. "Path Control: The Transport Network of SNA." *IEEE Transactions on Communications*, April 1980.

ATT61   American Telephone and Telegraph Co. *Principles of Electricity Applied to Telephone and Telegraph Work*, 1961.

BACH79   Bachman, C., and Canepa, M. *The Session Control Layer of an Open System Interconnection*. International Organization for Standardization OSIC/TG 6/79-10, 1979.

BACH83   Bachmann, L. "Statistical Multiplexers Gain Sophistication and Status." *Mini-Micro Systems,* March 1983.

BACK88   Backes, F. "Transparent Bridges for Interconnection of IEEE 802 LANs." *IEEE Network,* January 1988.

BARC81   Barcomb, D. *Office Automation.* Bedford, MA: Digital Press, 1981.

BART86   Bartee, T. *Digital Communications,* Indianapolis, IN: Howard W. Sams & Co., 1986.

BASC87   Basch, E., editor. *Optical-Fiber Transmission.* Indianapolis, IN: Howard W. Sams, 1987.

BBN81   Bolt, Beranek, and Newman Inc. *Specifications for the Interconnection of a Host and an IMP.* Report 1822, December 1981.

BBN83   BBN Communications Corp. *Defense Data Network X.25 Host Interface Specification.* December, 1983, reprinted in [DCA85].

BEDE86   Bederman, S. "Source Routing." *Data Communications,* February 1986.

BELL82a   Bell Telephone Laboratories. *Transmission Systems for Communications,* 1982.

BELL82b   Bellamy, J. *Digital Telephony.* New York: Wiley, 1982.

BELL86   Bell, P., and Jabbour, K. "Review of Point-to-Point Network Routing Algorithms." *IEEE Communications Magazine,* January, 1986.

BERT80   Bertine, H. U. "Physical Level Protocols." *IEEE Transactions on Communications,* April 1980.

BERT87   Bertsekas, D., and Gallager, R. *Data Networks.* Englewood Cliffs, NJ: Prentice-Hall, 1987.

BHAR83   Bhargava, V. "Forward Error Correction Schemes for Digital Communications." *IEEE Communications Magazine,* January 1983.

BHUS85   Bhushan, B., and Opderbeck, H. "The Evolution of Data Switching for PBX's." *IEEE Journal on Selected Areas in Communications,* July 1985.

BIND75a   Binder, R.; Abramson, N.; Kuo, F.; Okinaka, A.; and Wax, D. "ALOHA Packet Broadcasting—A Retrospect." *Proceedings, National Computer Conference,* 1975.

BIND75b   Binder, R. "A Dynamic Packet Switching System for Satellite Broadcast Channels." *Proceedings of the ICC,* 1975.

BIND81   Binder, R. "Packet Protocols for Broadcast Satellites." In [KUO81].

BLAC82   Black, U. "Data Link Controls: The Great Variety Calls for Wise and Careful Choices." *Data Communications,* June 1982.

BOGGS80   Boggs, D.; Shoch, J.; Taft, E.; and Metcalfe, R. "Pup: An Internetwork Architecture." *IEEE Transactions on Communications,* April 1980.

BOSI82   Bosik, B., and Kartalopoulos, S. "A Time Compression Multiplexing System for a Circuit Switched Digital Capability." *IEEE Transactions on Communications,* September 1982.

BOUL89   Boule, R., and Moy, J. "Inside Routers: a Technology Guide for Network Builders." *Data Communications,* 21 September 1989.

BROD83a   Brodd, W. "HDLC, ADCCP, and SDLC: What's the Difference?" *Data Communications,* August 1983.

BROD83b   Brodd, W., and Boudreau, P. "Operational Characteristics: BSC Versus SDLC." *Data Communications,* October 1983.

BROO83   Broomell, G., and Heath, J. "Classification Categories and Historical Development of Circuit Switching Topologies." *ACM Computing Surveys,* June 1983.

BRUN84   Bruninga, R. "Linking Personal Computers by Packet Radio." *Proceedings, COMPCON 84 Fall,* September 1984.

BURG83   Burg, F. "Design Considerations for Using the X.25 Packet Layer on Data Terminal Equipment." *Proceedings, IEEE INFOCOM 83,* 1983.

BURG89   Burg, F., and Iorio, N. "Networking of Networks: Interworking According to OSI." *IEEE Journal on Selected Areas in Communications.* September 1989.

BURR83   Burr, W. "An Overview of the Proposed American National Standard for Local Distributed Data Interfaces." *Communications of the ACM,* August 1983.

BUSH89 Bush, J. "Frame-Relay Services Promise WAN Bandwidth on Demand." *Data Communications,* July 1989.

BUX83 Bux, W.; Closs, F.; Kummerle, H.; and Mueller, H. "Architecture and Design of a Reliable Token-Ring Network." *IEEE Journal on Selected Areas in Communications,* November 1983.

BUX87 Bux, W.; Grillo, D.; and Maxemchuk, N. editors. Interconnection of Local Area Networks. Special issue of *IEEE Journal on Selected Areas in Communications,* December 1987.

BYTE85 Bytex Corporation. *Autoswitch Technical Manual,* 1985.

CANE86 Caneschi, F. "Hints for the Interpretation of the ISO Session Layer." *Computer Communication Review.* July/August 1986.

CARG89 Cargill, C. *Information Technology Standardization: Theory, Process, and Organizations.* Bedford, MA: Digital Press, 1989.

CARL80 Carlson, D. E. "Bit-Oriented Data Link Control Procedures." *IEEE Transactions on Communications,* April 1980.

CARP81 Carpenter, R. *A Survey of Routing Algorithms for Distributed Digital Radio Networks.* MITRE Technical Report MTR-81W00074, March 1981.

CAST88 Castiel, D. "Satellite Links for the Masses: The Final Frontier." *Data Communication,* November 1988.

CERF78 Cerf, V., and Kristein, P. T. "Issues in Packet-Network Interconnection." *Proceedings of the IEEE,* November 1978.

CERF83 Cerf, V., and Lyons, R. "Military Requirements for Packet-Switched Networks and Their Implications for Protocol Standardization." *Computer Networks,* October 1983.

CERN84 Cerni, D. *Standards in Process: Foundations and Profiles of ISDN and OSI Studies.* National Telecommunications and Information Administration, Report 84-170, December 1984.

CHAN72 Chandy, K., and Ramamoorthy, C. "Rollback and Recovery Strategies for Computer Programs." *IEEE Transactions on Computers,* June 1972.

CHAN76 Chang, K. Y. "Transmission of Analog, Video, and Digital Signals Over Analog-Repeated Coaxial Lines." *IEEE Transactions on Communications,* September 1976.

CHAN88 Chanson, S.; Ravindran, K.; and Robinson, J. "The Design and Tuning of a Transport Protocol for Local Area Networks." *Proceedings, IEEE INFOCOM '88,* March 1988.

CHAP82 Chapin, A. "Connectionless Data Transmission." *Computer Communication Review,* April 1982.

CHAP83 Chapin, A. "Connections and Connectionless Data Transmission." *Proceedings of the IEEE,* December 1983.

CHAR79 Charransol, P.; Hauri, J.; Athenes, C.; and Hardy, D. "Development of a Time Division Switching Network Usable in a Very Large Range of Capacities." *IEEE Transactions on Communications,* July 1979.

CHER89a Cheriton, D., and Williamson, C. "VMTP as the Transport Layer for High-Performance Distributed Systems." *IEEE Communications Magazine, June 1989.*

CHER89b Cherukuri, R., and Derby, J. "Frame Relay: Protocols and Private Network Applications." *Proceedings, IEEE INFOCOM '89,* April 1989.

CHES88 Chesson, G. "XTP/PE Overview." *Proceedings, 13 Conference on Local Computer Networks,* October 1988.

CHIL90 Chilton, P. *X.400: The Messaging and Interconnection Medium for the Future.* Oxford, England: NCC Publications, 1990.

CHOU83 Chou, W., ed. *Computer Communications, Vol. I: Principles.* Englewood Cliffs, NJ: Prentice-Hall, 1983.

CHOU85 Chou, W., ed. *Computer Communications, Vol. II: System and Applications.* Englewood Cliffs, NJ: Prentice-Hall, 1985.

CHU73 Chu, W. "Asynchronous Time-Division Multiplexing Systems," In *Computer Communication Networks* (ed. Abramson and Kuo). Englewood Cliffs, NJ, 1973.

CLAI88   Clair, M., and Orlov, M. "Is It Wise for Users to Run Ethernet Over Existing Nonshielded Twisted Pair?" *Network World*, January 11, 1988.

CLAR88   Clark, D. "The Design Philosophy of the DARPA Internet Protocols." *Proceedings, SIGCOMM 88 Symposium*, August 1988.

CLAR89   Clark, D.: Jacobson, V.; Romkey, J.; and Salwen, H. "An Analysis of TCP Processing Overhead." *IEEE Communications Magazine*, June 1989.

COCH88   Cochrane, P., and Brain, M. "Future Optical Fiber Transmission Technology and Networks." *IEEE Communications Magazine*, November 1988.

COCK87   Cockburn, A. "Efficient Implementation of the OSI Transport-Protocol Checksum Algorithm Using 8/16-Bit Arithmetic." *Computer Communications Review*, July/August 1987.

COHN88   Cohn, M. "A Lightweight Transfer Protocol for the U.S. Navy Safenet Local Area Network Standard." *Proceedings, 13th Conference on Local Computer Networks*, October 1988.

COHN89   Cohn, M. "A Case for XTP." *Data Communications*, July 1989.

COME88   Comer, D. *Internetworking with TCP/IP: Principles, Protocols, and Architecture.* Englewood Cliffs, NJ: Prentice-Hall, 1988.

CONA80   Conard, J. "Character-Oriented Data Link Control Protocols." *IEEE Transactions on Communications*, April 1980.

CONA83   Conard, J. "Services and Protocols of the Data Link Layer." *Proceedings of the IEEE*, December 1983.

CONW89   Conway, A., and Georganas, N. *Queueing Networks—Exact Computational Algorithms: A Unified Theory Based on Decomposition and Aggregation.* Cembridge, MA: MIT Press, 1989.

COOK84   Cooke, R. "Intercity Limits: Looking Ahead to All-Digital Networks and No Bottlenecks." *Data Communications*, March 1984.

COOP81   Cooper, R. *Introduction to Queuing Theory, Second Edition.* New York: North Holland, 1981.

COOP84   Cooper, E. *Broadband Network Techynology.* Mountain View, CA: Sytek Press, 1984.

COOV85   Coover, E. "Notes from Mid-revolution: Searching for the Perfect PBX." *Data Communications*, August 1985.

COTT81   Cotton, J.; Giesken, K.; Lawrence, A.; and Upp, D. "ITT 1240 Digital Exchange: Digital Switching Network." *Electrical Communication*, No. 2/3, 1981.

COUC87   Couch, L. *Digital and Analog Communication Systems, Second Edition.* New York: Macmillan, 1987.

COUD88   Coudreuse, J.; Sincoskie, W.; and Turner, J., editors. Special Issue on Broadband Packet Communications. *IEEE Journal on Selected Areas in Communications*, December 1988.

CROC83   Crochiere, R. E., and Flanagan, J. L. "Current Perspectives in Digital Speech." *IEEE Communications Magazine*, January 1983.

CROC89   Crockett, B. "The Changing Role of Satellite in Telecommunications." *Telecommunications*, June 1989.

CROW73   Crowther, W.; Rettberg, R.; Walden, D.; Orenstein, S.; and Heart, F. "A System for Broadcast Communication: Reservation ALOHA." *Proceedings, Sixth Hawaii International System Science Conference*, 1973.

CUMM85   Cummins, E.; Pavey, C.; and Rice, R. "Packet-Demand Assignment Multiple Access." Proceedings, IEEE MILCOM, July 1985.

CUNN80   Cunningham, J. E. *Cable Television.* Indianapolis: Howard W. Sams, 1980.

DARP81   Defense Advanced Research Projects Agency. *Internet Control Message Protocol.* RFC: 792, September 1981.

DAVI73   Davies, D. W., and Barber, D. L. *Communication Networks for Computers.* New York: Wiley, 1973.

DAVI77   Davidson, J.; Hathaway, W.; Postel, J.; Mimno, N.; Thomas, R.; and Walden,

D. "The ARPANET Telnet Protocol: Its Purpose, Principles, Implementation, and Impact on Host Operating System Design." *Proceedings, Fifth Data Communications Symposium,* 1977.

DAVI88 Davidson, J. *An Introduction to TCP/IP.* New York: Springer-Verlag, 1988.

DAVI79 Davies, D.; Barber, D.; Price, W.; and Solomonides, C. *Computer Networks and Their Protocols.* New York: Wiley, 1979.

DAY81 Day, J. "Terminal, File Transfer, and Remote Job Protocols for Heterogeneous Computer Networks." In *Protocols and Techniques for Data Communication Networks* (ed. F. F. Kuo). Englewood Cliffs, NJ: Prentice-Hall, 1981.

DCA85 Defense Communications Agency. *DDN Protocol Handbook.* December 1985.

DEAT79 Deaton, G. "Flow Control in Packet-Switched Networks with Explicit Path Routing." *Proceedings, Conference on Flow Control in Computer Networks,* Paris, 1979.

DECI82a Decina, M. "Managing ISDN Through International Standards Activities." *IEEE Communications Magazine,* September 1982.

DECI82b Decina, M. "Progress Towards User Access Arrangements in Integrated Services Digital Networks." *IEEE Transactions on Communications,* September 1982.

DERF83 Derfler, F., and Stallings, W. *A Manager's Guide to Local Networks.* Englewood Cliffs, NJ: Prentice-Hall/Spectrum, 1983.

DHAS86 Dhas, C., and Konangi, U. "X.25: An Interface to Public Packet Networks." *IEEE Communications Magazine,* September 1986.

DICE87 Dicenet, G. *Design and Prospects for the ISDN.* Boston: Artech House, 1987.

DIGI82 Digital Equipment Corp.; Intel Corp.; and Xerox Corp. *The Ethernet: A Local Area Network Data Link Layer and Physical Layer Specifications, Version 2.0,* November, 1982.

DIJK59 Dijkstra, E. "A Note on Two Problems in Connection with Graphs." *Numerical Mathematics,* October 1959.

DINE80 Dineson, M. A., and Picazo, J. J. "Broadband Technology Magnifies Local Network Capability." *Data Communications,* February 1980.

DIXO83 Dixon, R.; Strole, N.; and Markov, J. "A Token-ring Network for Local Data Communications." *IBM Systems Journal.* Nos. 1/2, 1983.

DIXO88 Dixon, R., and Pitt, D. "Addressing, Bridging, and Source Routing." *IEEE Network,* January 1988.

DOD83a Department of Defense. *Military Standard Internet Protocol,* MIL-STD-1777, August 12, 1983.

DOD83b Department of Defense. *Military Standard Transmission Control Protocol,* MIL-STD-1778, August 12, 1983.

DOLA84 Dolan, M. "A Minimal Duplex Connection Capability in the Top Three Layers of the OSI Reference Model." *Proceedings, SIGCOMM '84,* June 1984.

DOLL78 Doll, D. R. *Data Communications: Facilities, Networks, and System Design.* New York: Wiley, 1980.

DONN74 Donnan, R., and Kersey, J. "Synchronous Data Link Control: A Perspective." *IBM Systems Journal,* May 1974.

DORR83 Dorros, I. "Telephone Nets Go Digital." *IEEE Spectrum,* April 1983.

DUC85 Duc, N., and Chew, E. "ISDN Protocol Architecture." *IEEE Communications Magazine,* March 1985.

EDEL72 Edelson, B., and Werth, A. "SPADE System Progress and Application." *COMSAT Technical Review,* Spring 1972.

EDEL82 Edelson, B.; Marsten, R.; and Morgan, W. "Greater Message Capacity for Satellites." *IEEE Spectrum,* March 1982.

EIA69 Electronic Industries Association. *EIA Standard RS-232-C Interface Between Data Terminal Equipment and Data Communication Equipment Employing Serial Binary Data Interchange,* October, 1969.

EIA71 Electronic Industries Association. *Application Notes for EIA Standard RS-232-C,* May 1971.

ELSA86   Elsam, E. "The Defense Data Network Hits Its Stride." *Telecommunications,* May 1986.

EMMO83   Emmons, W., and Chandler, H. "OSI Session Layer Services and Protocols." *Proceedings of the IEEE,* December 1983.

ENNI82   Ennis, G.; Kaufman, D.; and Biba, K. *DoD Protocol Reference Model,* Sytek, TR-82026, September 1982.

ENNI83   Ennis, G. "Development of the DoD Protocol Reference Model." *Proceedings, SIGCOMM '83 Symposium,* 1983.

ENOM85   Enomoto, O.; Kohashi, T.; Aomori, T.; Kadota, S.; Oka, S.; and Fujita, K. "Distributed Microprocessors Control Architecture for Versatile Business Communications." *IEEE Journal on Selected Areas in Communications,* July 1985.

ERIK86   Eriksen, S. "The How and Where of Switched 56-kbit/s Service." *Data Communications,* August 1986.

FALK83   Falk, G. "The Structure and Function of Network Protocols." In [CHOU83].

FARM69   Farmer, W. D., and Newhall, E. E. "An Experimental Distributed Switching System to Handle Bursty Computer Traffic." *Proceedings, ACM Symposium on Problems in the Optimization of Data Communications,* 1969.

FEHE83   Feher, K. "SCPC Satcom Systems for Voice and Data Services." *Telecommunications,* June 1983.

FIEL86   Field, J. "Logical Link Control." *IEEE Infocom 86,* April 1986.

FINN89a   Finnie, G. "VSATs: A Technical Update." *Telecommunications,* February 1989.

FINN89b   Finnie, G. "Lighting up the Local Loop." *Telecommunications,* January 1989.

FLET82   Fletcher, J. "An Arithmetic Checksum for Serial Transmissions." *IEEE Transactions on Communications,* January 1982.

FOLT81   Folts, H. "Coming of Age: A Long-Awaited Standard for Heterogeneous Nets." *Data Communications,* January 1981.

FOLT83   Folts, H. *OSI Workbook.* Vienna, VA: OMNICOM, Inc., 1983.

FORB81   Forbes, V. "RF Prescribed for Many Local Links." *Data Communications,* September 1981.

FORD62   Ford, L., and Fulkerson, D. *Flows in Networks.* Princeton, NJ: Princeton University Press, 1962.

FORR86   Forrest, S. "Optical Detectors: Three Contenders." *IEEE Spectrum,* May 1986.

FRAN76   Frankel, T. *Tables for Traffic Management and Design.* abc Teletraining (P.O. Box 537, Geneva, IL 60134), 1976.

FRAN81   Franta, W., and Chlamtec, I. *Local Networks.* Lexington, MA: Lexington Books, 1981.

FRAN84   Frank, C. "Legal and Policy Ramifications of the Emerging Integrated Services Digital Network." *Journal of Telecommunication Networks,* Spring 1984.

FREE89   Freeman, R. *Telecommunication System Engineering, Second Edition.* New York: Wiley, 1989.

FREE85   Freeman, R. *Reference Manual for Telecommunications Engineering.* New York: Wiley, 1985.

GALL68   Gallager, R. *Information Theory and Reliable Communication.* New York: Wiley, 1968.

GARL77   Garlick, L.; Rom, R.; and Postel, J. "Reliable Host-to-Host Protocols: Problems and Techniques." *Proceedings, Fifth Data Communications Symposium,* 1977.

GEOR82   George, F. and Young, G. "SNA Flow Control: Architecture and Implementation." *IBM Systems Journal,* Number 2, 1982.

GERL80   Gerla, M., and Kleinrock, L. "Flow Control: A Comparative Survey." *IEEE Transactions on Communications,* April 1980.

GERL81   Gerla, M. "Routing and Flow Control." In [KUO81].

GERL84   Gerla, M. and Pazos-Rangel, A. "Bandwidth Allocation and Routing in ISDN's." *IEEE Communications Magazine,* February 1984.

GERL88   Gerla, M.; Green, L.; and Rutledge, R. editors. Special issue of *IEEE Network,* January 1988.

GERW84   Gerwin, P.; Verhoeckx, N.; and Claasen, T. "Design Considerations for a 144 kbit/s Digital Transmission Unit for the Local Telephone Network." *IEEE Journal on Selected Areas in Communications,* March 1984.

GIFF86   Gifford. W. "ISDN User-Network Interfaces." *IEEE Journal on Selected Areas in Communications,* May 1986.

GITM76   Gitman, I.; Van Slyke, R.; and Frank, H. "Routing in Packet-Switching Broadcast Radio Networks." *IEEE Transactions on Communications,* August 1976.

GLEN86   Glen, D. *Networks, Signaling, and Switching for Post-Divestiture and the ISDN.* National Telecommunications and Information Administration, Report 86-191, February 1986.

GOPA85   Gopal, I. "Prevention of Store-and-Forward Deadlock in Computer Networks." *IEEE Transactions on Communications,* December 1985.

GOUL84   Gould, R. "Transmission Standards for Direct Broadcast Satellites." *IEEE Communications Magazine,* March 1984.

GOUL85   Gould, R., and Reinhart, E., eds. *Special Issue on Broadcasting Satellites, IEEE Journal on Selected Areas in Communications,* January 1985.

GRAY72   Gray, J. "Line Control Procedures." *Proceedings of the IEEE,* November 1972.

GREE77   Greene, W., and Pooch, U. "A Review of Classification Schemes for Computer Communication Networks." *Computer,* November 1977.

GREE80   Green, P. "An Introduction to Network Architectures and Protocols." *IEEE Transactions on Communications,* April 1980.

GREE90   Green, P.; Naemura, K.; and Williamson, R. editors. Heterogeneous Computer Networks Interconnection. Special issue of *IEEE Journal on Selected Areas in Communications,* January 1990.

GROE86   Groenbaek, I. "Conversion Between the TCP and ISO Transport Protocols as a Method of Achieving Interoperability Between Data Communication Systems." *IEEE Journal on Selected Areas in Communications,* March 1986.

GURU87   Guruge, A. *SNA: Theory and Practice.* Elmsford, NY: Pergamon Press, 1987.

HA86   Ha, T. *Digital Satellite Communications.* New York: Macmillan, 1986.

HALS88   Halsall, F. *Data Communications, Computer Networks and OSI, Second Edition.* Reading, MA: Addison-Wesley, 1988.

HAMM86   Hammond, J., and O'Reilly, R. *Performance Analysis of Local Computer Networks.* Reading, MA: Addison-Wesley, 1986.

HAMN88   Hamner, M., and Samsen, G. "Source Routing Bridge Implementation." *IEEE Network,* January 1988.

HARR86   Harrington, E.; Cipriano, G.; and Micheroni, V. "Public Switched 56-kbps Networks." *Telecommunications,* March 1986.

HART88   Hart, J. "Extending the IEEE 802.1 MAC Bridge Standard to Remote Bridges." *IEEE Network,* January 1988.

HASK87   Haskell, B.; Pearson, D.; and Yamamoto, H., eds. *Low Bit-Rate Coding of Moving Images.* Special issue of the IEEE Journal on Selected Areas in Communications, August 1987.

HEAT89   Heatley, S., and Stokesberry, D. "Analysis of Transport Measurements Over a Local Area Network." *IEEE Communications Magazine,* June 1989.

HECH86   Hecht, J. "Bell Labs Transmits 8 Gbit/s Over 68.3 km." *Lasers and Applications,* May 1986.

HEGG84   Heggestad, H. "An Overview of Packet-Switching Communications." *IEEE Communications Magazine,* April 1984.

HELD83   Held, G. "Strategies and Concepts for Linking Today's Personal Computers." *Data Communications,* May 1983.

HELD86   Held, G. *Data Communications Networking Devices.* New York: Wiley, 1986.

Hens88   Henshall, J., and Shaw, S. *OSI Explained: End-to-End Computer Communication Standards*. New York: Wiley, 1988.

Hind83   Hinden, R.; Haverty, J.; and Sheltzer, A. "The DARPA Internet: Interconnecting Heterogeneous Computer Networks with Gateways." *Computer*, September 1983.

Hind89   Hindin, E. "XTP: A New LAN Protocol Promises Multi-Megabit/s Throughput." *Data Communications*, March 1989.

Hirs85   Hirschheim, R. *Office Automation*. Reading, MA: Addison-Wesley, 1986.

Hobe80   Hoberecht, V. "SNA Function Management." *IEEE Transactions on Communications*, April 1980.

Hohn80   Hohn, W. C. "The Control Data Loosely Coupled Network Lower Level Protocols." *Proceedings, National Computer Conference*, 1980.

Holm83   Holmes, E. "A Closer Look at AT&T's New High-Speed Digital Services." *Data Communications*, July 1983.

Hone82   Honeywell Information Systems, Inc. *Distributed Systems Architecture*, CT37-01, 1982.

Hong86   Hong, J. "Timing Jitter." *Data Communications*, February 1986.

Hope73   Hopewell, L.; Chou, W.; and Frank, H. "Analysis of Architectural Strategies for a Large Message-Switching Network: A Case Study." *Computer*, April 1973.

Hopk80   Hopkins. G. T., and Wagner, P. E. *Multiple Access Digital Communications System*. U.S. Patent 4,210,780, July 1, 1980.

Hopk82   Hopkins, G. T., and Meisner, N. B. "Choosing Between Broadband and Baseband Local Networks." *Mini-Micro Systems*, June 1982.

Hsie84a   Hsieh, W., and Gitman, I. "How Good Is Your Network Routing Protocol?" *Data Communications*, May 1984.

Hsie84b   Hsieh, W., and Gitman, I. "Routing Strategies in Computer Networks." *Computer*, June 1984.

Hsie84c   Hsieh, W., and Gitman, I. "How to Prevent Congestion in Computer Networks." *Data Communications*, June 1984.

Hurl87   Hurley, B.; Seidl, C.; and Sewell, W. "A Survey of Dynamic Routing Methods for Circuit-Switched Traffic." *IEEE Communications Magazine*, September 1987.

Ibm71   IBM Corp. *Analysis of Some Queuing Models in Real-Time Systems*. IBM Document GF20-0007, 1971. Available from IBM document distribution centers.

Ibm85a   IBM Corp. *Systems Network Architecture: Concepts and Products*, GC30-3072, 1985.

Ibm85b   IBM Corp. *Systems Network Architecture: Technical Overview*. GC30-3073, 1985.

Ieee85a   The Institute of Electrical and Electronics Engineers. *Logical Link Control*. American National Standard ANSI/IEEE Std. 802.2-1985.

Ieee85b   The Institute of Electrical and Electronics Engineers. *Carrier Sense Multiple Access with Collision Detection (CSMA/CD) Access Method and Physical Layer Specifications*. American National Standard ANSI/IEEE Std. 802.3-1985.

Ieee85c   The Institute of Electrical and Electronics Engineers. *Token-Passing Bus Access Method and Physical Layer Specifications*. American National Standard ANSI/IEEE Std. 802.4-1985.

Ieee85d   The Institute of Electrical and Electronics Engineers. *Token Ring Access Method and Physical Layer Specifications*. American National Standard ANSI/IEEE Std. 802.5-1985.

Ieee85e   IEEE Computer Society. *Draft IEEE Standard 802.1 (Part A): Overview and Architecture*, October 1985.

Ieee88a   The Institute of Electrical and Electronics Engineers. *IEEE Standard 802.1: Overview and Architecture*. July 1988.

Ieee88b   The Institute of Electrical and Electronics Engineers. *IEEE Standard 802.1: MAC Bridges*. September 1988.

Ieee88c   The Institute of Electrical and Electronics Engineers. *IEEE 802.5, Appendix D: Multi-ring Networks (Source Routing)*. November 1988.

Ingr88   Ingram, D. *Mastering Packet Radio*. Indianapolis, IN: Howard W Sams, 1988.

IRLA78   Irland, M. "Buffer Management in a Packet Switch." *IEEE Transactions on Communications*, March 1978.

ISO84   International Organization for Standardization. *Basic Reference Model for Open Systems Interconnection*, ISO 7498, 1984.

ISO86a   International Organization for Standardization. *Connection Oriented Transport Protocol Specification*, ISO 8072, 1986.

ISO86b   International Organization for Standardization. *Transport Service Definition*. ISO 8072, 1986.

ISO86c   International Organization for Standardization. *Basic Connection Oriented Session Service Definition*. ISO 8329, 1986.

ISO86d   International Organization for Standardization. *Basic Connection Oriented Session Protocol Specification*, ISO 8327, 1986.

ISO86e   International Organization for Standardization. *Protocol for Providing the Connectionless-Mode Network Service*. DIS 8473, 1986.

ISO87a   International Organization for Standardization. *File Transfer, Access and Management*. DIS 8571, 1987.

ISO87b   International Oreganization for Standardization. *Interface Connector and Contact Assignments for ISDN Basic Access Interface Located at Reference Points S and T*. ISO 8877, 1987.

ISO87c   International Organization for Standardization. *Network Service Definition, Addendum 1: Connectionless-mode Transmission*. ISO 8348/Add. 1, 1987.

ISO88   International Organization for Standardization. *Protocol for Providing the Connectionless-mode Network Service (Internetwork Protocol)*. ISO 8473, 1988.

ISRA87   Israel, J., and Weissberger, A. "Communicating Between Heterogeneous Networks."' *Data Communications*, March 1987.

JAIN88   Jain, R., and Ramakrishnan, K. "Congestion Avoidance in Computer Networks with a Connectionless Network Layer: Concepts, Goals, and Methodology." *Proceedings, Computer Networking Symposium*, April 1988.

JAYA84   Jayant, N., and Noll, P. *Digital Coding of Waveforms*. Englewood Cliffs, NJ: Prentice-Hall, 1984.

JAYA86   Jayant, N. "Coding Speech at Low Bit Rates." *IEEE Spectrum*, August 1986.

JAYA87   Jayasumana, A. "Performance Analysis of Token Bus Priority Schemes: *Proceedings, INFOCOM '87*, 1987.

JAYA90   Jayant, N. "High-Quality Coding of Telephone Speech and Wideband Audio." *IEEE Communications Magazine*, January 1990.

JEWE85   Jewett, R. "The Fourth-Generation PBX: Beyond the Integration of Voice and Data." *Telecommunications*, February 1985.

JOEL77   Joel, A. E. "What Is Telecommunications Circuit Switching?" *Proceedings of the IEEE*, September 1977.

JOEL79a   Joel, A. E. "Circuit Switching: Unique Architecture and Applications." *Computer*, June 1979.

JOEL79b   Joel, A. E. "Digital Switching—How it Has Developed." *IEEE Transactions on Communications*, July 1979.

JOEL85   Joel, A., ed. *Special Issue on Serving the Business Customer Using Advances in Switching Technology*. IEEE Journal on Selected Areas in Communications, July 1985.

JOHN87   Johnson, M. "Proof that Timing Requirements of the FDDI Token Ring Protocol are Satisfied." *IEEE Transactions on Communications*, June 1987.

JORD85   Jordan, E., ed. *Reference Data for Engineers: Radio, Electronics, Computer, and Communications*. Indianapolis, IN: Howard Sams & Co., 1985.

JUNK83   Junker, S., and Noller, W. "Digital Private Branch Exchanges." *IEEE Communications Magazine*, May 1983.

KADE81   Kaderali, F., and Weston, J. "Digital Subscriber Loops." *Electrical Communication*, Vol. 56, No. 1, 1981.

KAHN77   Kahn, R. "The Organization of Computer Resources into a Packet Radio Network." *IEEE Transactions on Communications*, January 1977.

KAHN78   Kahn, R.; Gronemeyer, S.; Burchfiel, J.; and Kunzelman, C. "Advances in Packet Radio Technology." *Proceedings of the IEEE,* November 1978.

KAJI83   Kajiwara, M. "Trends in Digital Switching System Architectures." *IEEE Communications Magazine,* May 1983.

KAMI86   Kamali, B., and Davis, G. "Modulation Codes in Digital Magnetic Recording Systems." *Proceedings, Fifth Annual International Phoenix Conference on Computers and Communications*, March 1986.

KANE80   Kane, D. A. "Data Communications Network Switching Methods," *Computer Design,* April 1980.

KANO86   Kano, S. "Layers 2 and 3 ISDN Recommendations." *IEEE Journal on Selected Areas in Communications,* May 1986.

KARN85   Karn, P.; Price, H.; and Diersing, R. "Packet Radio in the Amateur Service." *IEEE Journal on Selected Areas in Communications,* May 1985.

KASA83   Kasac, H.; Ohue, K.; Hoshino, T.; and Tsuyuki, S. "800 Mbit/s Digital Transmission System Over Coaxial Cable." *IEEE Transactions on Communications,* February 1983.

KASS79   Kasson, J. M. "Survey of Digital PBX Design." *IEEE Transactions on Communications,* July 1979.

KEIS85   Keiser, B., and Strange, E. *Digital Telephony and Network Integration.* New York: Van Nostrand Reinhold, 1985.

KELC83   Kelcourse, F., and Siegel, E. "Switched Digital Capability: An Overview." *IEEE Communications Magazine,* January 1983.

KELL84   Kelley, R.; Jones, J.; Bhatt, V.; and Pate, P. "Transceiver Design and Implementation Experience in an Ethernet-Compatible Fiber Optic Local Area Network." *Proceedings, INFOCOM 84,* 1984.

KESS89   Kessler, G. "Splitting Hairs and Bits." *Data Communications,* February 1989.

KHAN89   Khanna, A., and Zinky, J. "The Revised ARPANET Routing Metric." *Proceedings, SIGCOMM '89 Symposium,* 1989.

KIMB75   Kimbleton, S., and Schneider, G. "Computer Communication Networks: Approaches, Objectives, and Performance Considerations." *ACM Computing Surveys,* September 1975.

KLEI75   Kleinrock, L. *Queueing Systems, Volume I: Theory.* New York: Wiley, 1975.

KLEI76   Kleinrock, L. *Queueing Systems, Vol. II: Computer Applications.* New York: Wiley, 1976.

KLEI78   Kleinrock, L. "Principles and Lessons in Packet Communications." *Proceedings of the IEEE,* November 1978.

KLEI86   Klein, M., and Balph, T. "Carrierband is Low-Cost, Single-Channel Solution for MAP." *Computer Design,* February 1, 1986.

KNOW87   Knowles, T., Larmouth, J.; and Knightson, K. *Standards for Open Systems Interconnection.* Boston, MA: BSP Professional Books, 1987.

KOBA78   Kobayashi, H. *Modeling and Analysis: An Introduction to System Performance Evaluation Methodology.* Reading, MA: Addision-Wesley, 1978.

KOPF77   Kopf, J. "TYMNET as a Multiplexed Packet Network." *Proceedings, National Computer Conference,* 1977.

KOST84   Kostas, D. "Transition to ISDN—An Overview." *IEEE Communications Magazine,* January 1984.

KRUT81   Krutsch, T. E. "A User Speaks Out: Broadband or Baseband for Local Nets?" *Data Communications,* December 1981.

KUMM80   Kummede, K., and Rudin, H. "Packet and Circuit Switching: Cost/Performance Boundaries." *Computer Networks,* No. 2, 1980.

KUMM87   Kummerle, K.; Limb, J.; and Tobagi, F. *Advanced in Local Area Networks.* New York: IEEE Press, 1987.

KUO81   Kuo, F. *Protocols and Techniques for Data Communication Networks.* Englewood Cliffs, NJ: Prentice-Hall, 1981.

LAI89   Lai, W. ''Frame Relaying Service: An Overview.'' *Proceedings, IEEE INFOCOM '89,* April 1989.

LAM80   Lam, S. ''Packet Broadcast Networks—A Performance Analysis of the R-ALOHA Protocol.'' *IEEE Transactions on Computers,* July 1980.

LAM83   Lam, S. ''Data Link Control Procedures.'' In [CHOU83].

LANE87   Land, J. *The Integrated Services Digital Network (ISDN).* Manchester, England: The National Computing Centre, 1987.

LECH86   Lechleider, J. ''Loop Transmission Aspects of ISDN Basic Access.'' *IEEE Journal on Selected Areas in Communications,* November, 1986.

LEIN87   Leiner, B.; Nielson, D.; and Tobagi, F., editors, Special Issue on Packet Radio Networks. *Proceedings of the IEEE,* January 1987.

LEON89   Leon-Garcia, A., editor. Special Issue on Broadband Networks. *IEEE Network,* January 1989.

LEWA83   Lewan, D., and Long, H. ''The OSI File Service.'' *Proceedings of the IEEE,* December 1983.

LIN90   Lin, D. ''Minimum Mean-Squared Error Echo Cancellation and Equalization for Digital Subscriber Line Transmission.'' *IEEE Transactions on Communications,* January 1990.

LINI89   Linington, P. ''File Transfer Protocols.'' *IEEE Journal on Selected Areas in Communications,* September 1989.

LIU78   Liu, M. T. ''Distributed Loop Computer Networks.'' In *Advances in Computers, Vol. 17* (ed. M. C. Yovits). New York: Academic Press, 1978.

LIU80   Liu, J. ''Distributed Routing and Relay Management in Mobile Packet Radio Networks.'' *Proceedings, COMPCON FALL 80,* 1980.

LUCZ78   Luczak, E. C. ''Global Bus Computer Communication Techniques.'' *Proceedings, Computer Network Symposium,* 1978.

MALO81   Malone, J. ''The Microcomputer Connection to Local Networks.'' *Data Communications,* December 1981.

MANR89   Manros, C. *The X.400 Blue Book Companion.* Twickenham, England: Technology Appraisals, 1989.

MARI79   Marill, T. ''Why the Telephone Is on Its Way out and Electronic Mail Is on Its Way In.'' *Datamation,* August 1979.

MART70   Martin, J. *Teleprocessing Network Organization.* Englewood Cliffs, NJ: Prentice-Hall, 1970.

MART72   Martin, J. *Systems Analysis for Data Transmission.* Englewood Cliffs, NJ: Prentice-Hall, 1972.

MART 76   Martin, J. *Telecommunications and the Computer, 2nd Ed.* Englewood Cliffs, NJ: Prentice-Hall, 1976.

MART 78   Martin, J. *Communications Satellite Systems.* Englewood Cliffs, NJ: Prentice-Hall, 1978.

MART87   Martin, J., and Chapman, K. *SNA: IBM's Networking Solution.* Englewood Cliffs, NJ: Prentice-Hall, 1987.

MART88   Martin, J., and Leban, J. *Data Communication Technology.* Englewood Cliffs, NJ: Prentice-Hall, 1988.

MARU83   Maruyama, K., and Shorter, D. ''Dynamic Route Selection Algorithms for Session-Based Communication Networks.'' *Computer Communication Review,* April 1983.

MCCL83   McClelland, F. ''Services and Protocols of the Physical Layer.'' *Proceedings of the IEEE,* December 1983.

MCCO88   McConnell, J. *Internetworking Computer Systems: Interconnecting Networks and Systems.* Englewood Cliffs, NJ: Prentice-Hall, 1988.

MCFA79   McFarland, R. ''Protocols in a Computer Internetworking Environment.'' *Proceedings, EASCON 79,* 1979.

MCNA88   McNamara, J. E. *Technical Aspects of Data Communication, Third Edition.* Bedford, MA: Digital Press, 1988.

McQu78 McQuillan, J., and Cerf, V. *Tutorial: A Practical View of Computer Communications Protocols*. Silver Spring, MD: IEEE Computer Society Press, 1978.

McQu80 McQuillan, J.; Richer, I.; and Rosen, E. "The New Routing Algorithm for the ARPANET." *IEEE Transactions on Communications*. May 1980.

Meij82 Meijer, A., and Peeters, P. *Computer Network Architectures*, Rockville, MD: Computer Science Press, 1982.

Meij87 Meijer, A. *Systems Network Architecture: A Tutorial*. London: Pitman, 1987.

Mess84 Messerschmitt, D. "Echo Cancellation in Speech and Data Transmission." *IEEE Journal on Selected Areas in Communications*, March, 1984.

Mess86 Messerschmitt, D. "Design Issues in the ISDN U-Interface Transceiver." *IEEE Journal on Selected Areas in Communications*, November, 1986.

Metc76 Metcalfe, R. M., and Boggs, D. R. "Ethernet: Distributed Packet Switching for Local Computer Networks." *Communications of the ACM*, July 1976.

Metc77 Metcalfe, R. M.; Boggs, D. R.; Thacker, C. P.; and Lampson, B. W. *Multipoint Data Communication System with Collision Detection*. U.S. Patent 4,063,220, 1977.

Metz83 Metz, S. "The Different Flavors of SNA Compatibility." *Data Communications*, April 1983.

Mier84 Mier, E. "The ABCs of FEC." *Data Communications*, May 1984.

Mier86 Mier, E. "Light Sources and Wavelengths." *Data Communications*, February 1986.

Mier89 Mier, E. "Coming Soon to an Outlet Near You: Premises Fiber." *Data Communications*, February 1989.

Mill81 Miller, L. "An Analysis of Link Level Protocols for Error Prone Links." *Proceedings, Seventh Data Communications Symposium*, 1981.

Mill82 Miller, C. K., and Thompson, D. M. "Making a Case for Token Passing in Local Networks." *Data Communications*, March 1982.

Mill84 Mills, D. *Exterior Gateway Protocol Formal Specification*. RFC 904, April 1984. Reprinted in [DCA85].

Mine89 Minet, P. "Performance Evaluation of GAM-T-103 Real-Time Transfer Protocols." *Proceedings, IEEE INFOCOM '89*, April, 1989.

Miya75 Miyahura, H.; Hasegawa, T.; and Teshigawara, Y. "A Comparative Evaluation of Switching Methods in Computer Communication Networks." *Proceedings, International Communications Conference*, 1975.

Moen84 Moeneclaey, M. "Synchronizability of a General Class of PCM Formats, Including NRZ, Manchester, and Miller Coding." *IEEE Transactions on Communications*, September 1984.

Moll89 Molloy, M. *Fundamentals of Performance Modeling*. New York: Macmillan, 1989.

Moy89a Moy, J., and Chiappa, N. "OSPF: A New Dynamic Routing Standard." *Network World*, 7 August 1989.

Moy89b Moy, J. *The OSPF Specification*. RFC 1131, October 1989. Available from the DDN Network Information Center, SRI International, Menlo Park, CA.

Mura87 Murakami, H.; Matsumoto, S.; Hatori, Y.; and Yamamoto, H. "15/30 Mbit/s Universal Digital TV Codec Using a Median Adaptive Predictive Coding Method." *IEEE Transactions on Communications*, June 1987.

Mura88 Murakami, H.; Hashimoto, H.; and Hatori, Y. "Quality of Band-Compressed TV Services." *IEEE Communications Magazine*, October 1988.

Mura90 Murano, K.; Unagami, S.; and Amano, F. "Echo Cancellation and Applications." *IEEE Communications Magazine*, January 1990.

Naka88 Nakassis, A. "Fletcher's Error Detection Algorithm: How To Implement It Efficiently and How to Avoid the Most Common Pitfalls." *Computer Communications Review*, October 1988.

Nbs63 National Bureau of Standards. *Experimental Statistics*. NBS Handbook 91 (Available from Government Printing Office, GPO Stock No. 003-003-00135-0), 1963.

N<small>BS</small>80a   National Bureau of Standards. *Features of the Transport and Session Protocols,* ICST/HLNP-80-1, March 1980.

N<small>BS</small>80b   National Bureau of Standards. *Features of the File Transfer Protocol (FTP) and the Data Presentation Protocol (DPP).* ICST/HLNP-80-6, 1980.

N<small>BS</small>81   National Bureau of Standards. *Specification of the Session Protocol,* ICST/HLNP-81-2, March 1981.

N<small>BS</small>83   National Bureau of Standards. *Specification of a Transport Protocol for Computer Communications.* ICST/HLNP-83-1 to ICST/HLNP-83-5, January 1983.

N<small>BS</small>85   National Bureau of Standards. *Local Area Networks: Baseband Carrier Sense Multiple Access with Collision Detection (CSMA/CD) Access Method and Physical Layer Specifications and Link Layer Protocol.* FIPS 107, 1984.

N<small>ETR</small>88   Netravali, A. *Digital Pictures: Representation and Compression.* New York: Plenum Press, 1988.

N<small>EUM</small>83   Neumann, J. "OSI Transport and Session Layers: Services and Protocol." *Proceedings, INFOCOM 83,* 1983.

N<small>G</small>77   Ng, S., and Mark, J. "A Multiaccess Model for Packet Switching With a Satellite Having Some Processing Capability." *IEEE Transactions on Communications,* January 1977.

N<small>IEL</small>85   Nielson, D. "Packet Radio: An Area-Coverage Digital Radio Network." In [C<small>HOU</small>85].

O<small>ETT</small>79   Oetting, J. "A Comparison of Modulation Techniques for Digital Radio." *IEEE Transactions on Communications,* December 1979.

O<small>NEA</small>80   O'Neal, J. "Waveform Encoding of Voiceband Data Signals." *Proceedings of the IEEE,* February 1980.

O<small>RLO</small>88   Orlov, M. "Another Twist: Twisted-Pair Ethernet May Not Be All It's Cracked Up to Be." *LAN Magazine,* August 1988.

P<small>AOL</small>75   Paolette, L. "AUTODIN." In *Computer Communication Networks* (ed. R. L. Grimsdale and F. F. Kuo). Leyden, The Netherlands: Noordhoff International, 1975.

P<small>ARU</small>90   Parulkar, G. "The Next Generation of Internetworking." Computer Communications Review, January 1990.

P<small>AVE</small>86   Pavey, C.; Rice, R.; and Cummins, E. "A Performance Evaluation of the PDAMA Satellite Access Protocol." *Proceedings, INFOCOM '86,* April 1986.

P<small>E</small>89   Protocols Engines, Inc. *XTP Protocol Definition, Revision 3.4.* Santa Barbara, CA, 17 July 1989.

P<small>EEB</small>87   Peebles, P. *Digital Communication Systems.* Englewood Cliffs, NJ: Prentice-Hall, 1987.

P<small>ENN</small>79   Penny, B. K., and Baghdadi, A. A. "Survey of Computer Communications Loop Networks." *Computer Communications,* August and October 1979.

P<small>ERL</small>84   Perlman, R. "An Algorithm for Distributed Computation of a Spanning Tree." Proceedings, Ninth Data Communications Symposium, 1984.

P<small>ETE</small>61   Peterson, W., and Brown, D. "Cyclic Codes for Error Detection." *Proceedings of the IRE,* January 1961.

P<small>HEL</small>86   Phelan, J. "Signaling System 7." *Telecommunications,* September, 1986.

P<small>ICK</small>83a   Pickens, R. "Wideband Transmission Media I: Radio Communication." In [C<small>HOU</small>83].

P<small>ICK</small>83b   Pickens, R. "Wideband Transmission Media II: Satellite Communication." In [C<small>HOU</small>83].

P<small>ICK</small>83c   Pickens, R. "Wideband Transmission Media III: Guided Transmission: Wireline, Coaxial Cable, and Fiber Optics." In [C<small>HOU</small>83].

P<small>ICK</small>86   Pickholtz, R. *Local Area Networks.* Rockville, MD: Computer Science Press, 1986.

P<small>ISC</small>84   Piscitello, D., and Chapin, L. "An International Internetwork Protocol Standard." *Journal of Telecommunication Networks,* Fall 1983.

PISC86   Piscitello, D.; Weissberger, A.; Stein, S.; and Chapin, A. "Internetworking in an OSI Environment." *Data Communications*, May 1986.

PITT85   Pitt, D.; Sy, K.; and Donnan, R. "Source Routing for Bridged Local Area Networks." *Proceedings, Globecom '85*, December 1985. Reprinted in [KUMM87].

PITT87   Pitt, D., and Winkler, J. "Table-Free Bridging." *IEEE Journal on Selected Areas in Communications*, December 1987.

PONT83   Pontano, B.; Dicks, J.; Colby, R.; Forcina, G.; and Phiel, J. "The INTELSAT TDMA/DSI System." *IEEE Journal on Selected Areas in Communications*, January 1983.

POST81   Postel, J. B.; Sunshine, C. A.; and Cihen, D. "The ARPA Internet Protocol." *Computer Networks*, 1981.

POTT77   Potter, R. "Electronic Mail." *Science*, March 19, 1977.

POUZ78   Pouzin, L., and Zimmermann, H. "A Tutorial on Protocols." *Proceedings of the IEEE*, November 1978.

POUZ81   Pouzin, L. "Methods, Tools, and Observations on Flow Control in Packet-Switched Data Networks." *IEEE Transactions on Communications*, April 1981.

PRIT84   Pritchard, W. "The History and Future of Commercial Satellite Communications." *IEEE Communications Magazine, May 1984*.

QUAR86   Quarterman, J., and Hoskins, J. "Notable Computer Networks." *Communications of the ACM*, October 1986.

RAJA78   Rajaraman, A. "Routing in TYMNET." *Proceedings, European Computing Conference*, 1978.

RAMA88   Ramabadroan, T., and Gaitonde, S. "A Tutorial on CRC Computations." IEEE Micro, August 1988.

RAWS78   Rawson, E. G., and Metcalfe, R. M. "Fibernet: Multimode Optical Fibers for Local Computer Networks." *IEEE Transactions on Communications*, July 1978.

RELC87   Relcom, Inc. *Carrier-Band Network Handbook, Second Edition*. Forest Grove, OR, 1987.

REY83   Rey, R., editor, *Engineering and Operations in the Bell System, Second Edition*. Murray Hill, NJ: AT&T Bell Laboratories, 1983.

RIND77   Rinde, J. "Routing and Control in a Centrally Directed Network." *Proceedings, National Computer Conference*, 1977.

RIND79a   Rinde, J. "Virtual Circuits in TYMNET II." *Proceedings, National Electronics Conference*, 1979.

RIND79b   Rinde, J., and Caisse, A. "Passive Flow Control Techniques for Distributed Networks." *Proceedings, IRIA Flow Control and Computer Networks Conference*, 1979.

ROBE70   Roberts, L., and Wessler, B. "Computer Network Development to Achieve Resource Sharing." Proceedings, Spring Joint Computer Conference, 1970.

ROBE73   Roberts, L. "Dynamic Allocation of Satellite Capacity Through Packet Reservation." *Proceedings, National Computer Conference*, 1973.

ROBE74   Roberts, L. "Data by the Packet." *IEEE Spectrum*, February 1974.

ROBE75   Roberts, L. "ALOHA Packet System With and Without Slots and Capture." *Computer Communications Review*, April 1975.

ROBE78   Roberts, L. "The Evolution of Packet Switching." *Proceedings of the IEEE*, November 1978.

ROBI86   Robinson, R. "Digital Voice Compression." *Telecommunications*, February 1986.

ROBI90   Robinson, J.; Friedman, D.; and Steenstrup, M. "Congestion Control in BBN Packet-Switched Networks." *Computer Communication Review*, January 1990.

ROCH79   Rocher, E. "Taking a Fresh Look at Local Data Distribution." *Data Communications*, May 1979.

ROEH85   Roehr, W. "Inside SS No. 7: A Detailed Look at ISDN's Signalling System Plan." *Data Communications*, October, 1985.

RONA87   Ronayne, J. *The Integrated Services Digital Network: from Concept to Application*. London: Pitman, 1987.

Rosn82 Rosner, R. *Packet Switching: Tomorrow's Communications Today.* Belmont, CA: Lifetime Learning, 1982.

Ross89 Ross, F. "An Overview of FDDI: The Fiber Distributed Data Interface." *IEEE Journal on Selected Areas in Communications.* September 1989.

Roul81 Rouleau, R., and Hodgson, I. *Packet Radio.* Blue Ridge Summit, PA: TAB Books, 1981.

Rudi76 Rudin, H. "On Routing and Delta Routing: A Taxonomy and Performance Comparison of Techniques for Packet-Switched Networks." *IEEE Transactions on Communications,* January 1976.

Rush82 Rush, J. R. "Microwave Links Add Flexibility to Local Networks." *Electronics,* January 13, 1982.

Rybc80 Rybczynski, A. "X.25 Interface and End-to-End Virtual Circuit Service Characteristics." *IEEE Transactions on Communications,* April 1980.

Sabn89 Sabnani, K. and Netravali, A. "A High-Speed Transport Protocol for Datagram/Virtual Circuits." *Proceedings, SIGCOMM '89 Symposium,* 1989.

Salt79 Saltzer, J. H., and Pogran, K. T. "A Star-Shaped Ring Network with High Maintainability." *Proceedings, Local Area Communications Network Symposium,* 1979.

Salt83 Saltzer, J.; Pogran, K.; and Clark, D. "Why a Ring?" *Computer Networks,* August 1983.

Salw83 Salwen, H. "In Praise of Ring Architecture for Local Area Networks." *Computer Design,* March 1983.

Sand80 Sanders, R. "Effects of Switching Technologies on Network Delay." *Data Communications,* April 1980.

Scac86 Scace, E. "Integrated Services Digital Networks." In [Bart86].

Scar83 Scarcella, T., and Abbott, R. "Orbital Efficiency Through Satellite Digital Switching." *IEEE Communications Magazine,* May 1983.

Schl86 Schlanger, G. "An Overview of Signalling System No. 7." *IEEE Journal on Selected Areas in Communications,* May 1986.

Scho81 Scholl, T. H. "The New Breed—Switching Muxes." *Data Communications,* June 1981.

Schw77 Schwartz, M. *Computer-Communication Network Design and Analysis.* Englewood Cliffs, N.J.: Prentice-Hall, 1977.

Schw80 Schwartz, M., and Stern, T. E. "Routing Techniques Used in Computer Communication Networks." *IEEE Transactions on Communications,* April 1980.

Seid78 Seider, R. "How Statistical TDMs Let Network Lines Support More Terminals." *Data Communications,* September 1978.

Selv82 Selvaggi, P. "The Department of Defense Data Protocol Standardization Program." *Proceedings, EASCON 82,* 1982.

Sevc87 Sevcik, K., and Johnson, M. "Cycle Time Properties of the FDDI Token Ring Protocol." *IEEE Transactions on Software Engineering,* March 1987.

Seye84 Seyer, M. *RS-232 Made Easy.* Englewood Cliffs, NJ: Prentice-Hall, 1984.

Shac86 Shacham, N., and Tornow, J. "Packet Radio Networking." *Telecommunications,* September 1986.

Shar89 Sharma, R. "Satellite Network Design Parameters and Trade-Off Analysis." *Telecommunications,* June 1987.

Shar89 Sharma, R. "VSAT Network Economics: A Comparative Analysis." *IEEE Communications Magazine,* February 1989.

Shel82 Sheltzer, A.; Hinden, R.; and Brescia, M. "Connecting Different Types of Networks with Gateways." *Data Communications,* August 1982.

Shim85 Shimayama, H.; Kato, K.; Oshima, G.; and Yano, K. "State-of-the-Art SCPC Satellite Communications Systems." *Signal,* February 1985.

Shoc78 Shoch, J. F. "Internetwork Naming, Addressing, and Routing." *Proceedings, COMPCON 78,* 1978.

SHOC82   Shoch, J. F.; Dala, Y. K.; and Redell, D. D. "Evolution of the Ethernet Local Computer Network." *Computer,* August 1982.

SHUF84   Shuford, R. "An Introduction to Fiber Optics." *Byte,* December 1984.

SHUM89   Shumate, P. "Optical Fibers Reach Into Homes." *IEEE Spectrum,* February 1989.

SIRB85   Sirbu, M., and Zwimpfer, L. "Standards Setting for Computer Communication: The Case of X.25." *IEEE Communications Magazine,* March 1985.

SKAP79   Skaperda, N. J."Some Architectural Alternatives in the Design of a Digital Switch." *IEEE Transactions on Communications,* July 1979.

SKLA88   Sklar, B. *Digital Communications: Fundamentals and Applications.* Englewood Cliffs, NJ Prentice-Hall, 1988.

SKLO89   Sklower, K. "Improving the Efficiency of the OSI Checksum Calculation." *Computer Communication Review,* October 1989.

SKOV89   Skov, M. "Implementation of Physical and Media Access Protocols for High-Speed Networks." *IEEE Communications Magazine,* June 1989.

SLON87   Slonim, J.; Schonbach, A.; Bauer, M.; MacRae, L.; and Thomas, K. *Building an Open System.* New York: Van Nostrand Reinhold, 1987.

SPIL77   Spilker, J. *Digital Communications by Satellite.* Englewood Cliffs, NJ: Prentice-Hall, 1977.

STAH82   Stahlman, M. "Inside Wang's Local Net Architecture." *Data Communications,* January 1982.

STAL87   Stallings, W. *Computer Communications: Architecture, Protocols, and Standards, Second Edition.* Washington, DC: IEEE Computer Society Press, 1987.

STAL88a   Stallings, W. *Local Network Technology, Third Edition.* Washington, DC: IEEE Computer Society Press, 1988.

STAL88b   Stallings, W. *Integrated Services Digital Networks (ISDN), Second Edition.* Washington, DC: IEEE Computer Society Press, 1988.

STAL89   Stallings, W. *ISDN: An Introduction.* New York: Macmillan, 1989.

STAL90a   Stallings, W. *Local Networks, Third Edition.* New York: Macmillan, 1990.

STAL90b   Stallings, W. *Computer Organization and Architecture, Second Edition.* New York: Macmillan, 1990.

STAL90c   Stallings, W. *Handbook of Computer-Communications Standards, Volume 1: The Open Systems Interconnection (OSI) Model and OSI-Related Standards, Second Edition.* Carmel, IN: Howard W. Sams, 1990.

STAL90d   Stallings, W. *Handbook of Computer-Communications Standards, Volume 2: Local Area Network Standards.* Carmel, IN: Howard W. Sams, 1990.

STAL90e   Stallings, W. *Handbook of Computer-Communications Standards, Volume 3: The TCP/IP Protocol Suite, Second Edition.* Carmel, IN: Howard W. Sams, 1990.

STAL90f   Stallings, W. *The Business Guide to Local Area Networks.* Carmel, IN: Howard W. Sams, 1990.

STAL92   Stallings, W. *Operating Systems.* New York: Macmillan, 1992 (forthcoming).

STIE81   Stieglitz, M. "Local Network Access Tradeoffs." *Computer Design,* October 1981.

STIF83   Stifle, J. "The Interactive Difference in Multiplexing." *Data Communications,* October 1983.

STRA89   Strauss, P. "Header Prediction Will Boost Packet Throughput." *Data Communications,* August 1989.

STRO83   Strole, N. "A Local Communication Network Based on Interconnected Token-Access Rings: A Tutorial." *IBM Journal of Research and Development,* September 1983.

STRO86   Strole, N. "How IBM Addresses LAN Requirements with the Token Ring." *Data Communications,* February 1986.

STUC85   Stuck, B., and Arthurs, E. *A Computer Communications Network Performance Analysis Primer.* Englewood Cliffs, NJ: Prentice-Hall, 1985.

STUT72 Stutzman, B. "Data Communication Control Procedures." *ACM Computing Surveys,* December 1972.

SUDA83 Suda, T.; Miyahara, H.; and Hasegawa, T. "Performance Evaluation of an Integrated Access Scheme in a Satellite Communication Channel." *IEEE Journal on Selected Areas in Communications,* January 1983.

SUNS81 Sunshine, C. "Transport Protocols for Computer Networks." In [KUO81].

TANE88 Tanenbaum, A. *Computer Networks, Second Edition.* Englewood Cliffs, NJ: Prentice-Hall, 1988.

THAK86 Thaker, G., and Cain, J. "Interactions Between Routing and Flow Control Algorithms. *IEEE Transactions on Communications,* March 1986.

THUR85 Thurber, K., ed. *The LOCALNetter Designer's Handbook.* Minneapolis, MN: Architecture Technology Corporation, November 1985.

TILL90 Tillman, M., and Yen, D. "SNA and OSI: Three Strategies for Interconnection." *Communications of the ACM,* February 1990.

TOBA80 Tobagi, F. A. "Multiaccess Protocols in Packet Communication Systems." *IEEE Transactions on Communications,* April 1980.

TOML75 Tomlinson, R. "Selecting Sequence Numbers." *Proceedings ACM SIGCOMM/ SIGOPS Interprocess Communication Workshop,* 1975.

TYME81 Tymes, L. "Routing and Flow Control in TYMNET." *IEEE Transactions on Communications,* April 1981.

VAN84 van Gerwen, P.; Verhoeckx, N.; and Claasen, T. "Design Considerations for a 144 kbit/s Digital Transmission Unit for the Local Telephone Network." *IEEE Journal on Selected Areas in Communications,* March, 1984.

VAUG59 Vaughan, H. "Research Model for Time Separation Integrated Communication." *Bell System Technical Journal,* July 1959.

VAZQ88 Vazquez, et al. "Performance of OSI Transport Over Accunet and Iberpac." *Proceedings, INFOCOM '88,* March 1988.

VONA80 Vonarx, M. "Controlling the Mushrooming Communications Net." *Data Communications,* June 1980.

WALK82 Walker, S. "Department of Defense Data Network." *Signal,* October 1982.

WARE83 Ware, C. "The OSI Network Layer: Standards to Cope with the Real World." *Proceedings of the IEEE,* December 1983.

WATE84 Waters, A., and Adams, C. "The Satellite Transmission Protocol of the Universe Project." *Proceedings, SIGCOMM Symposium on Communication Architectures and Protocols,* June 1984.

WATS89 Watson, R. "The Delta-T Transport Protocol." *Proceedings, 14th Conference on Local Computer Networks,* October 1989.

WECK80 Wecker, S. "DNA: The Digital Network Architecture." *IEEE Transactions on Communications*, April 1980.

WEIS78 Weissler, R.; Binder, R.; Bressler, R.; Rettberg, R.; and Walden, D. "Synchronization and Multiple Access Protocols in the Initial Satellite IMP." *Proceedings, COMPCON FALL 78,* 1978.

WEIS83 Weissberger, A. "Bit Oriented Data Link Controls." *Computer Design,* March 1983.

WEIS87 Weissberger, A., and Israel, J. "What the New Internetworking Standards Provide." *Data Communications,* February 1987.

WERN86 Wernli, M. "The Choices in Designing a Fiber-Optic Network." *Data Communications,* June 1986.

WHAL89 Whaley, A. "The X-Press Transfer Protocol." *Proceedings, 14th Conference on Local Computer Networks,* October 1989.

WILL87 Williams, R. *Communication Systems Analysis and Design.* Englewood Cliffs, NJ: Prentice-Hall, 1987.

WILL89 Williamson, C., and Cheriton, D. "An Overview of the VMTP Transport Protocol." *Proceedings, 14th Conference on Local Computer Networks,* October 1989.

WOOD85   Wood, D. "Computer Networks: A Survey." In [CHOU85].

YEN83   Yen, C., and Crawford, R. "Distribution and Equalization of Signal on Coaxial Cables Used in 10 Mbps/s Baseband Local Area Networks." *IEEE Transactions on Communications,* October 1983.

YUM87   Yum, T., and Schwartz, M. "Comparison of Routing Procedures for Circuit-Switched Traffic in Nonhierarchical Networks." *IEEE Transactions on Communications,* May 1987.

ZHAN86   Zhang, L. "Why TCP Timers Don't Work Well." *Proceedings, SIGCOMM '86 Symposium,* August 1986.

ZIEM83   Ziemer, R.; Tranter, W.; and Fannin, D. *Signals and Systems: Continuous and Discrete.* New York: Macmillan, 1983.

INDEX

ACRONYMS

ADCCP	Advanced Data Communication Control Procedures
AM	Amplitude Modulation
ANSI	American National Standards Institute
ARQ	Automatic Repeat Request
ASCII	American Standard Code for Information Interchange
ASK	Amplitude-Shift Keying
CATV	Community Antenna Television
CBX	Computerized Branch Exchange
CCITT	International Consultative Committee on Telegraphy and Telephony
CRC	Cyclic Redundancy Check
CSMA	Carrier-Sense Multiple Access
CSMA/CD	Carrier-Sense Multiple Access with Collision Detection
DAMA	Demand-Assignment Multiple Access
DARPA	Defense Advanced Research Projects Agency
DCE	Data Circuit-Terminating Equipment
DM	Delta Modulation
DTE	Data Terminal Equipment
EIA	Electronic Industries Association
FCS	Frame Check Sequence
FDM	Frequency-Division Multiplexing
FDMA	Frequency-Division Multiple Access
FM	Frequency Modulation
FSK	Frequency-Shift Keying
FTAM	File Transfer, Access, and Management
HDLC	High-Level Data Link Control
ICMP	Internet Control Message Protocol
IEEE	Institute of Electrical and Electronics Engineers
IP	Internet Protocol
ISDN	Integrated Services Digital Network
ISO	International Organization for Standardization
IWU	Interworking Unit
LAP-B	Link Access Protocol—Balanced